THE SYNGE LETTERS

Bishop Edward Synge to His Daughter Alicia
Roscommon to Dublin

1746-1752

THE SYNGE LETTERS

Bishop Edward Synge to His Daughter Alicia
Roscommon to Dublin

1746-1752

Edited by Marie-Louise Legg

THE LILLIPUT PRESS
in association with the Irish Manuscripts Commission
Dublin
MCMXCVI

First published 1996 by
THE LILLIPUT PRESS LTD
4 Rosemount Terrace, Arbour Hill,
Dublin 7, Ireland.

A CIP record for this
title is available from
The British Library.

ISBN 1874675 49 X

Set in 10 on 12.5 New Baskerville
by Verbatim Typesetting & Design Ltd
Printed in England
by Hartnolls Ltd of Bodmin, Cornwall

Contents

ILLUSTRATIONS

Introduction

'It would not be amiss if you now and then employ'd a leisure hour in reading over my letters. ... I design'd them to be instructions for life.' [1]

The difficulties posed to historians of Ireland by the partial survival of its archives has been compared to peering through a keyhole at a ballroom and watching a group of dancers. Occasionally a couple moves into focus. But for all one knew, just out of sight, there could be a group of naked men and women, dancing the Lancers.[2] The gaps in our knowledge and our understanding of how society worked – the loss of assize records, visitations, the records of the operation of local justice – are enormous. Their loss is why the two hundred letters written by Edward Synge to his daughter Alicia are so valuable. Covering five years from 1747 to 1752 and written in the summer months when Synge was in his diocese, they are the letters of a rich man, a widower, to his only surviving child. Like Jonathan Swift's letters to Stella, they are one-sided; like Swift to Stella, they are critical, humorous and lively. We know something of one segment of Synge's society from the letters of Emily, duchess of Leinster[3] and the ubiquitous Mary Delany,[4] and from travellers like chief baron Edward Willes.[5] But Synge's preoccupations were not those of Emily Fitzgerald, and his social round was more varied than that of Mrs Delany. Emily Kildare's circle was grand; Mary Delany was childless. Both women were English by birth and their letters from Ireland were, in the main, from Dublin to England. Synge's world is centred on Ireland.

Written from Elphin, Co. Roscommon, to Kevin Street, Dublin, Edward Synge enlarges our knowledge of day to day life in the capital and the provinces. By 1747, Synge had been a bishop for nearly twenty years. He moved easily in high politics, but politics do not occupy him here. He lived with his daughter, his niece Jane and their French governess. Many years later, he referred to the hazards of living in a house with 'a parcel of romping girls'.[6] He writes of gardening and the servant problem, of visits to tailors and dressmakers, manners and books, of ironmongers and wine merchants, of transactions with his banker and lawyer, of formal calls and sending gifts of melons and grapes to prominent acquaintances. His Roscommon news is of the building and furnishing of his new Palace, of visitors, harvests and the weather, of food and drink. Synge's account of

vii

his new house in Roscommon illustrates how dependent the provinces were on Dublin trades and Dublin taste. He writes spontaneously, and he encourages his daughter to write freely in return: '*Sauve votre modestie* I must see you naked', he urges; 'Give your thoughts free Scope, and Scrawl away.'[7] Synge's vivid prose, his lack of formality, his intimate portraits of his neighbours, his clergy and his servants open up a view of Irish society that we have only glimpsed elsewhere. When he writes about his servants, their voices too are heard. The words of Jennet, the still-room maid, recounting her problems making barm for bread come straight from Maria Edgeworth:

Indeed, My Lord, says she, I get Barm sometimes as red as a Fox, sometimes black, full of Hop-leaves, Bog-bane, Wormwood, Artichoak leaves ... By straining I get rid of all these; and the first Sheering, so she calls pouring, after the liquor has stood about quarter of an hour, frees it from the great dross, which remains in the bottom, red like brick-dust, or darker; the Second, after standing a night, gives me barm as white and as tough as Starch. With this, My Lord, I make all your bread, and Many a hard shift I make to get it.[8]

But Edward Synge is more than this. His expression of his love and concern for his adolescent daughter, by turns stern, relaxed and teasing, augments our understanding of the relations between parents and children and between men and women. His concern for Alicia's education and, as she matures, his insistence on her independence give us new insight into women's place in Irish society.

Edward Synge was a member of a great dynasty of Irish clerics. He was the son of an archbishop, the grandson and great nephew of bishops; the brother of a bishop, the nephew of a dean and the uncle of an archdeacon. (His brother, Nicholas Synge bishop of Killaloe, was the direct ancestor of the playwright J.M. Synge.) The Synge[9] family first arrived in Ireland when George Synge, from Bridgnorth, Shropshire, the son of Richard Synge a bailiff, went to Armagh in 1621. George Synge became bishop of Cloyne in 1638, but lost all in the rebellion of 1641.[10] By 1652 he had returned to Bridgnorth to die. George Synge's younger brother, Edward (Edward Synge's grandfather) was born in Bridgnorth in 1614, but he was educated at Drogheda and entered the ministry of the Church of Ireland. In 1661 he became bishop of Ardfert, and in 1663 was translated to Cork, Cloyne and Ross. He had two sons, Samuel and Edward, and five daughters. Samuel Synge became dean of Kildare, married the daughter of Michael Boyle, archbishop of Armagh and had two children, Michael and Mary. Samuel Synge was wealthy, and his will had important consequences for his nephew, Edward, since the estate of the former eventually passed to the latter.[11] Michael Synge did not marry and died young. Edward Synge senior inherited the income from his brother's estate during his life and this then passed to his elder son. Samuel Synge's estate helped to make the younger Edward Synge rich, and its existence made Alicia, his only surviving child, a considerable heiress.

Edward Synge the elder, Samuel Synge's brother, was born at Inishannon, Co. Cork, in 1659. He was a commoner at Christ Church, Oxford, and completed his education at Trinity College, Dublin. He married Jane Proud, the daughter of a Cork clergyman, Nicholas Proud, and was vicar of Christ Church, Cork, when his eldest son, Edward was born on 18 October 1691.

George Synge was the last member of this branch of the family to be born and educated wholly in England and, by the middle of the eighteenth century, the Synge family appears to have lost close touch with England. There is no record in Edward Synge's father's will, his own marriage settlement or his own will that he had property in England. He seems not to have visited England, and there are only half a dozen isolated references to English place-names in his letters. On T.C. Barnard's analysis of Irish Protestant identity, Edward Synge should be classified, not as an Anglo-Irishman, but as an Irish Protestant.[12] Educated in Cork by a Mr Mulloy, Synge entered Trinity College, Dublin, in 1706 and took his BA in 1709. In 1710 he became a Fellow of the College and Junior Dean in 1715.[13]

Successful careers are owed in part to chance. In 1714 the younger Synge was twenty-three and on the threshold of his career. Queen Anne died and the Whigs came in: he was in the right place at the right time. Synge's father was the first in the family to benefit from the change of government. The writer of numerous popular religious tracts, Edward Synge senior was regarded as 'learned, prudent, pious and active'. Although 'it was owned that none was better fitted for a bishop',[14] his politics until now had been a fatal obstacle to his promotion. (His personal wishes too, played a part in the long wait for preferment: he had refused the deanery of Derry in 1699 because his elderly mother did not wish to leave Cork.)[15] In 1705, he became Chancellor of St Patrick's; in November 1714 he was consecrated bishop of Raphoe and in June 1716 translated to the archbishopric of Tuam. This elevation, and his close relationship with William King, archbishop of Dublin, now made the advancement of his son's interest possible. The new Lord Lieutenant, the duke of Bolton, made the younger Synge his chaplain. It was noted that Bolton was anxious to assist the younger Synge as his father's son, 'they seem inclined to oblige a man that is a son to a person they think very rising'.[16] In 1719 he obtained the living of St Audoen's, Dublin, and a prebendal stall in St Patrick's cathedral. St Audoen's church was used by the lord mayor and corporation of the city; as incumbent Edward Synge was well placed to be noticed by the city, and he was made a Freeman in 1722. It was not a rich living, however, and in 1720 Synge had married. His father, now aged sixty-one, was anxious that his son should be preferred and that he himself should receive help in Tuam.

Preferment was an elaborate dance, involving many partners. When Archbishop Synge wrote to the archbishop of Canterbury, to suggest that his son should be appointed provost of Tuam, he phrased it in terms of several removals: 'His present preferment (for which he quitted his Fellowship of the College) is the Parish of *St Audoens* in this City, worth at utmost, as I compute, 170 pounds per annum, over and above the maintaining Two to assist him in the discharge of the Cure ... the Deanery of Lismore, worth near 400l a year, being now vacant. If my Lord Lieutenant would be pleas'd to remove the Dean of *Tuam* thither, and give that Deanery (worth between 200 and 300) to my son, both he and I should take it as a very great Favour ... it will be a great comfort to me, in my old Age, sometimes to have my son's company there.'[17] But temporarily, the archbishop had fallen out of favour. With King he had spoken strongly against the Toleration Act of 1719 on the ground that it would endanger the state by allowing dangerous sects to flourish,[18] and his suggestion was disregarded. Synge acknowledged the possible consequences of his actions on his son, hoping that 'the suppos'd Mistakes of the Father, will not fall heavy upon the Son, who had no hand in them'.[19] The younger Synge had to wait until 1726 for his provostship.[20] In 1727 he was appointed to be Chancellor of St Patrick's, like his father before him.[21] At the beginning of 1729, his name was mentioned for the diocese of Clonfert,[22] and on 7 June 1730 Edward Synge was consecrated by his father in St Werburgh's, Dublin, his brother Nicholas preaching the sermon.[23] A year later, he was translated from Clonfert to Cloyne. This was partly because no-one else on the bishop's bench wanted the diocese, but partly because it would be agreeable 'as he has some estate in the neighbourhood of Cloyn, [he] will be obliged by being sent thither ...'.[24] Synge no longer suffered from any taint of disloyalty; he was described as one of a number 'zealously affected to his Majesty and family'.[25] Two years later, in February 1733, he was sent to Ferns and Leighlin where he stayed for six years. In May 1740 he was translated to the diocese of Elphin and he remained there until his death in 1762.

Synge's personal characteristics were marked. Physically large, a doggerel poem described him as 'a priest of six foot and more'. Mrs Delany told her sister, 'On Saturday I was reading in the portico at the farthest end of our garden ... I saw stalking up the walk a huge man. Upon nearer approach I saw it was the bishop of Elphin.'[26] Like his father he had an independent mind which he asserted when, as a young College Fellow, he declined to conform to the orders of the Vice-Provost and be dragooned into assembling with other College office holders to go to the Tholsel and vote for the Recorder and Alderman Burton, the Whig candidates in the parliamentary election of 1713. He voted for them the following day.[27] Despite their different politics, Synge partly owed his promotion to Jonathan Swift, who recommended him as one of a number of Dublin clergymen 'the most distinguished for their learning and piety', adding that this recommendation was made 'without any regard for friendship'. Letitia Pilkington reported that Swift told her he had recommended Synge because he wanted a living for Dr Patrick Delany, 'and Pox take me if I ever thought him worth my Contempt, till I had made a Bishop of him'.[28] Chesterfield, Lord Lieutenant from 1745 to 1746, said that the younger Synge was 'without dispute equal, if not superior, in abilities to any on the Bench; and who is also the Speaker and the efficient man in the House of Lords'.[29] Although known in Dublin as 'Proud Ned',[30] he disliked honours. Mrs Pilkington, who claimed kinship with the Synge family, said that Synge told her that 'his Honours did not sit easy on him, and that he would willingly dispence with his Friends not saluting him with his Title of Lord, as it always made him uneasy'.[31] He disliked promotion just for the sake of honour, and claimed to have retracted a request he had made to the Lords Justices, saying 'He who has views of ambition, can never act freely, seldom virtuously.'[32] In his will, he asked that his sermons be burnt and his body put in a plain oak or deal coffin with a black cloth covering it and no ornament except his name and age.[33]

Wealth made pious and disinterested actions possible; both Synges used their income to improve the ministry. Archbishop Synge had gained great respect in Tuam for giving a quarter of his tithes, the *quarta pars episcopalis*, to his clergy to make up the incumbent's stipend in return for resignations from plural livings.[34] His son confronted the resistant owners of land increasingly set to grazing, and tackled the problem of tithe agistment (the collection of tithes on dry and barren cattle) by taking them to court.[35] He pointed out that his insistence on its collection was not for personal gain but rather to improve the ministry in his diocese of Ferns. 'I freely own, that my Revenues in the Church are very considerable; and I hope I know how to make a proper, and a Christian use of them.'[36]

Church of Ireland preachers during the years after 1661 annually emphasized the horrors faced by the country during and after the Rebellion, and on the need for vigilance against the possibility that these dangers should recur.[37] Edward Synge the younger is best known for a sermon which, as the Lord Lieutenant's chaplain, he preached to members of the House of Commons on 23 October 1725 to commemorate the 1641 rebellion.[38] Using a text from Luke's Gospel, 'Compel them to come in',[39] Synge was critical of those parts of the penal laws which had been passed to preserve the security of the state, but whose effect had been to invade Roman Catholics' liberty of conscience. Referring to the 'late times of confusion', he believed that the present cause of 'the enmity' between Protestants and Roman Catholics had 'always been due to a furious and blind zeal for Religion'. However expedient these laws might have been, they were unjust and should not be continued.[40] Making a clear distinction between legislation to ensure public order, and the regulation of private affairs, he pointed out the uncomfortable fact that, by enforcing obedience in religious worship, Protestants had themselves fallen into 'Romish practices'.[41] Conversion through education was, he believed, the best way and he pressed for the education of Roman Catholic children in Protestant charity schools.[42]

He shared his abhorrence of religious persecution with his father. In 1721 the elder Synge had told his congregation that men who were told they were eternally damned for practising their beliefs would 'run hazard to do it; [if you] drive them from cities and places of resort, they'll meet in fields or in the desert'.[43] They both concluded that those who live peaceably in society had a right to worship God according to their consciences. At the same time, they did not approve limitless toleration. The younger Synge did not advocate the repeal of the penal laws, and nowhere suggests that they should be amended to allow Roman Catholics to own property. Underpinning this stance was the fear that the land that had been so hard won by 1690 might yet be reclaimed. In 1740 Synge was the writer of a report by a Lords Committee set up to examine the state of the public records. Here, he expressed anxiety about the safety of archives in the King's Bench Office. Stored in a building considered insecure, the records contained 'several Outlawries and attainders; those particularly of Papists, on Account of the Rebellions in 1641 and 1688'. Synge feared that, if these were destroyed, Protestants' possession of land would be at risk and they would be open to 'vexatious Lawsuits to Defend and Establish their Titles to many forfeited Estates'.[44]

Synge's interest in toleration was reinforced by his close friendship with Francis Hutcheson, the Presbyterian philosopher, Hutcheson had come from Armagh to Dublin at the invitation of a number of dissenters anxious to start an academy in the city.[45] Hutcheson's arrival in Dublin in about 1720 may have been one of the reasons for Synge's reluctance to leave the city in 1719. No correspondence between Synge and Hutcheson has survived, but Hutcheson acknowledged his debt to Synge, and their friendship, in the Preface to his *Inquiry into Beauty and Virtue*.[46] They were both members of the group which gravitated towards the nominally Anglican Irish peer, Robert Molesworth. George Berkeley, another of Edward

Synge's close friends, was on the edge of this group.[47] Hutcheson shared some of Edward Synge's qualities; he was said to have been 'utterly free of all stateliness or affectation'.[48] Hutcheson's doctrine was far from Presbyterianism's emphasis on sin and reprobation. God was benevolent, and the object of all law was human happiness through virtue. He believed, with Synge, that it was hypocritical to coerce men's religious beliefs, and unjust for them to be punished for doctrines which did not threaten the state. 'Such persecution is the most horrid iniquity and cruelty.'[49] Although Synge's letters never refer directly to Hutcheson's ideas, it is possible, without forcing the text, to perceive points on which both men agreed. Hutcheson stresses the importance of instruction for young minds on the existence and providence of God; and to his daughter Synge reiterates God's providence. Hutcheson and Synge are at one on the duty of children to their parents. Hutcheson says, of parents' duty to their children, 'Generation no more makes them a piece of property to their parents, than Sucking makes them the property of their nurses ... the child is a rational agent, with rights valid against their parents.'[50] Of an arranged marriage, Synge tells Alicia, 'Parents may, they ought indeed to, controule their children's imprudent inclinations. But to abuse or force them to compliance, against so setled an aversion is cruel, is Wicked. ...'[51] Synge's emphasis on the education of children echoes that of Hutcheson who said that married couples should 'consult the prosperity of their family, and chiefly the right education of their common children'.[52] Regretting the marriage of a flighty young woman, Synge reminded his daughter that the girl probably knew no better: 'perhaps she is not so much to blame as her Education. Few young persons have the advantage which you, My dearest, have had of an early opening of their minds. ...'[53] Hutcheson stresses the importance of children 'obtaining their liberty as soon as they can safely enjoy it; since without it they cannot be happy. ...';[54] Synge urges his daughter not to consult him; to be independent and take decisions for herself.[55] Hutcheson left Ireland in 1730 and did not return. His *System of Moral Philosophy* was posthumously published in 1755, and Synge bought ten sets.[56]

When both Synges defended the right to liberty of conscience, they were undoubtedly influenced by their close relationship with members of the Huguenot refugee community. In 1692, after the Revocation of the Edict of Nantes, an act of parliament provided for a charter of refuge to encourage foreign Protestants to settle in Ireland. Uniquely, this guaranteed their freedom of worship,[57] and in the last decade of the seventeenth century, a large group of Protestant refugees arrived in Dublin.[58] Many French families settled in the parishes of St Peter's and St Kevin's, on the Synges' doorstop.[59] The Synges' reiteration of the horrors of religious persecution and its consequences should be read in the light of their own family association with the Huguenot community in Dublin. The word 'desert' used by Archbishop Synge in his sermon of 1721 has Huguenot resonances. '*Le désert*' can mean a refuge, and '*La periode du Désert*' was the time spent by Huguenots in hiding after the Revocation of the Edict of Nantes.[60] The Synges knew Elie Bouhéreau, the first Keeper of Marsh's Library, and their close neighbour in Kevin Street. Bouhéreau's daughter married a fellow Huguenot, Jean Jourdan, who subsequently became the Church of Ireland rector of Dunshaughlin, Co. Meath. Their daughter Blandine was Alicia Synge's governess and companion Mrs Jourdan.[61] French influence in the Synge household is apparent. French was used in day-to-day correspondence,[62] French books were read,[63] and French food was eaten.[64]

Synge was a member of the political circle[65] around the Speaker, Henry Boyle, which included the earl of Kildare, the Gores and Thomas Pakenham, who figure on the margins of the letters.[66] These men were in opposition to the group around Primate Stone, the Lord Lieutenant, the Duke of Bedford, and his son and private secretary, Lord George Sackville. Synge was active during the dispute on the Money Bill, which legislated to apply the surplus Irish revenue to reduce the national debt, and was defeated by the Irish House of Commons in December 1753. He reacted sharply to the measures taken after the rejection of the bill by Holderness, the southern secretary, who on behalf of the king prorogued the Irish parliament and removed a number of advisors. The tone of Holderness's letter written after the vote, shocked Synge. 'I own the style choked me. Except for four years, it has not been much in use since the Revolution.'[67] To Lord Limerick he tellingly quoted 'a French Apothegm', *Il faut se defendre du prejugé de confonder l'esclavage avec la fidelité* – One must guard against confusing slavery with loyalty.[68] But Synge sat easy under Ireland's constitutional arrangements, and wrote of the mob celebrating the defeat of the bill that 'Angry Patriotism was not for the Meridian of Ireland'. The best policy was to 'leave to time and future dutifull and loyal Conduct to shew that the discipline was undeservedly apply'd'.[69] He was no radical, and was himself adept in using the system to his own advantage.[70]

Edward Synge married Jane Curtis, daughter of Robert and Sarah Curtis of Roscrea, Co. Tipperary, in 1720. Robert Curtis, MP for Duleek, Co. Meath, was a rich man who had bought leases from the Ormonde estate. In 1703 he bought 2867 acres in Roscrea for £3399, which he sold in 1722 for £22,000.[71] Synge's marriage settlement was advantageous,[72] and from it he could now expect an annual income of about £800. When his father died in 1741, he inherited the income from Samuel Synge's estate, the product of a hundred years of investment in good quality land in Cork, improved by the judicious setting of leases. Fate played its part. His mother was dead,[73] and with the death of his wife and all his children save Alicia, he had no need to provide jointures for a widow, pin money or to provide and supplement marriage settlements for numerous children.[74] With his personal income and his episcopal income from successive dioceses over thirty years, Edward Synge became rich. He was said to have recommended his daughter Alicia and her husband, Joshua Cooper, to follow his own policy and 'buy up always all the land that they could'.[75] In 1762 Edward Willes said that the net episcopal income of Elphin was £3500 a year and that Synge was worth £100,000, this was 'all of the acquisition of the church'.[76]

Edward's and Jane Synge's married life was visited by repeated sorrows. Often, in his early letters, Edward Synge refers to them. Reflecting on his parting with Alicia in 1747, he thought back to an earlier parting: 'You were then an infant, and could give me pleasure only by looking at you. ... But I had then other objects of my tenderest affection. You only now remain.'[77] The Synges had six children; Edward was born in 1722 and died in 1739. Sarah was born in 1722/23 and died two years later. Jane also died in 1724. It is not known when Catherine and Mary were born; they both died in 1733/34. Robert was born in about 1725; he was admitted to TCD in 1742/3, but was dying when the letters open in July 1746. Alicia was born on 12 December 1733 and she alone survived. When her mother died in December 1737, Alicia was just four years old.[78]

All but a handful of Edward Synge's letters were written from Elphin to Dublin. Despite that, his house in Dublin is almost as vivid as that in Elphin. The Kevin Street house and land had been bought by Archbishop Edward Synge, his son and Michael Synge from the Rev. Philip Ferneley in 1726. In 1667 lieutenant colonel Philip Ferneley had leased land from the dean and chapter of St Patrick's for sixty-one years. Part of this land, later known as 'the Cabbage Garden', was appropriated by the dean and chapter to create a new burying ground for the parishioners of St Patrick's. The remainder was divided between Swift, who there created his 'Naboth's Vineyard', and the Synge family. The house was of rendered brick and built around a courtyard,[79] with large doors facing on to the south side of Kevin Street.[80] There were stables, a coach house, brew house and wash house, and it was later described as 'a very airy, large handsome and spacious house'.[81] Edward Synge writes of a great parlour, a blue parlour, an outer study and his inner study. In 1812 there was a large dining parlour and two other parlours on the ground floor. Panelled and papered, and decorated by the master carver, John Houghton,[82] the interior was clearly well-appointed. The rooms on the ground and the upper floors had views of the Dublin mountains.[83] Two Irish acres of grounds were bounded by a high wall running along Liberty Lane and St Kevin's churchyard on the east, Long Lane on the south and land belonging to St Anne's Guild on the west.[84] A door in the garden wall led on to Long Lane at the rear. At the end of the gardens, fields stretched away towards the mountains.[85] The plot was divided into two gardens,[86] with flower borders, a vegetable garden and an orchard. It is clear from Synge's frequent references to melons and grapes that he must have had hot beds and a glass house. In the 1720s society had moved away from the old city, crowded around the castle and the two cathedrals. Fashionable Dublin was now centred on St Stephen's Green and the surrounding streets to the north developed by Joshua Dawson and by Edward Synge's friend, Edward Nicholson.[87] On the edge of the Liberties, the Synges and their neighbours, the archbishop of Dublin at the Palace of St Sepulchre and the Deanery of St Patrick's, were surrounded by the weavers, dyers, clothiers, and brewers on the Meath estate.[88] Sectarian and recreational faction fighting frequently broke out on their doorstep.[89] To his daughter, Synge referred to local inhabitants as 'your low neighbours ... the rabble among whom you do, and I must live'.[90]

When Edward Synge's letters open in 1747, he is building a new house at Elphin. The cult of improvement which informed eighteenth-century Ireland – the building and decoration of houses, the purchase of furniture, china and garden plants, the acquisition of paintings – has been extensively explored through letters, inventories, account books, diaries and travel writing.[91] Clergymen responded to the impulse to build because of the pressure on them to live in their parishes; bishops had to make a substantial presence in the diocese.[92] If bishops were the active part of the House of Lords, they were also the active men in the country.[93] An observer wrote that the 'the Diminution of the Power of the Nobility has made the Lay-Lords here careless of Improvement, and of preparing themselves to support with Dignity that which remains to them'.[94] Primate Boulter said that the prevalence of absentee landlords meant that 'in many places one fourth or one fifth of the resident justices are clergymen for want of resident gentlemen'.[95] A bishop, residing in his diocese during the summer months, in a substantial house with a good table, entertaining visiting clergy, officers, judges on assize and carrying out his annual Visitation, made up for deficiencies in the local gentry. In the first half of the century see houses were non-existent or grossly inadequate. Archbishop Synge lamented the absence of a proper house at Tuam: 'If I had but any Sort of Habitation at Tuam, it would not only be great Satisfaction to me, but enable me with much less trouble than now to discharge my Duty; but until I build a House for the Archbishop (which I resolve as soon as may be to do) I must be forc'd to take up with a Lodging in a thatch'd cabin. ...'[96] Of Elphin, the archbishop told Wake that Bishop Hodson had begun to build a 'very good Episcopal house' in Elphin in the 1680s, but by the 1720s it had become derelict.[97] Robert Howard, Edward Synge's predecessor, who had succeeded to Elphin in 1730, told his brother that he had found there 'a very bad, ill-contrived house, for some of my predecessors were very indifferent architects'.[98] Edward Synge himself wrote of floods and damp in the old house; by 1747 he had started to build.[99]

There are no contemporary pictures of Edward Synge's new Palace. The house itself has gone and only the ruined offices remain. Described by Edward Willes as 'an extreme[ly] good gentlemen's house of six rooms on a floor',[100] it was built on high ground on the road to Boyle near the cathedral, now in ruins.[101] It had a three-storey central block linked by sweeps to two-storey offices on either side, making a hollow square. Its design was similar to many other eighteenth-century Irish houses, such as Sherwood Park, Ballon, Co. Carlow, and grander examples at neighbouring Strokestown Park and Frenchpark.[102] Its exterior was faced with plaster, with a round-headed door with side-lights at the top of a shallow flight of steps and with a 'Venetian window' above.

The name of the architect is not definitely known, but there is a strong case for believing that it was Michael Wills, and that he is the Dublin 'Mr Wills' to whom Synge frequently refers in his letters of 1747. Michael Wills was a son of Isaac Wills, a carpenter who had worked on the building of St Werburgh's church, Dublin.[103] The younger Wills was clerk of works during the building of Dr Steevens' Hospital between 1721 and 1723 and he competed unsuccessfully for St Patrick's Hospital in 1749. In 1754 he was employed by the Committee for repairing St Werburgh's after a disastrous fire, and he supervised the rebuilding of St Peter's between 1750 and 1752.[104] Michael Wills carried out a survey of the Palace for probate after Edward Synge's death in 1762.[105] There are two reasons for assigning the design to Michael Wills. In 1745 he submitted an album of 'Designs for Private Buildings of Two, three, four, five and six Rooms on a Floor And one of Eight rooms. Dublin 9th May 1745' to a competition, describing them as 'Vitruvian Designs in the Oeconomique Style'.[106] A set of plans made in 1873 show the ground plans of the Palace and proposals for their alteration.[107] Here, the ground plans of the house follow the ground plans of 'House No.2' in the drawings of 1745. The elevation of the house is, with one exception, very close to the elevation of the Palace as shown in a drawing of the exterior, dated about 1813.[108] The exception to Michael Wills's 1745 drawings is the insertion of a rather awkward third storey. This may be the 'attic storey' to which Synge refers in 1747.[109]

The western dioceses of the Church of Ireland were unpopular with the clergy. The distance from Dublin and the small numbers of Protestant gentry meant few congenial neighbours, and non-residence was frequent.[110] Even the eastern half of Roscommon was two days or more travel from the capital, and temporal pleasures foregone were compounded by pastoral difficulties. An absence of bookshops and printers meant a lack of bibles and prayer books, and the lack of tailors led to shabby dress.[111] The diocese of Elphin exhibited the want of Protestants and want of churches which were one of the many problems faced by the Church.[112] The diocese covered most of Co. Roscommon, a large part of Sligo and Galway and a small part of Co. Mayo. There were seventy-five parishes of which the bishop presented to seventy-two; the parishes were large, and the churches were often absent or ruinous.[113] The population was overwhelmingly Roman Catholic; in 1732 in Co. Roscommon alone there were 790 Protestant families to 7312 Catholic families.[114] Synge used a Catholic apothecary, and refers to a few Catholic doctors, but Alicia had to remain in Dublin during the summer in order to be close to a Protestant physician. There was a sprinkling of Catholic gentry, like the antiquarian Charles O'Conor of Belanagare, who had managed to hang on after the confiscations of the seventeenth century. But even poor Protestants were still economically and socially the superiors of the growing Catholic tenant-farmer class.[115] In 1720 Synge's father said that it needed 'an active Bishop' and required 'some time to bring it into that tolerable order of which it is capable'.[116]

Elphin[117] may have been a rich bishopric, but the town itself was poor. Synge's predecessor, Robert Howard, wrote that it was in 'a very rich deep country, the roads bad, the country pleasant enough, a good demesne, but a bad dirty Irish town'.[118] Away from the Palace, the schoolhouse and the deanery, the poor of Elphin lived in cabins, 'built of sods and covered with rushes, flax-shoves, or the like, not sufficient to keep out a shower of rain ... inhabited by eight or ten men, women and children half-naked'.[119] The land surrounding Elphin was of rich, loamy soil overlying a stratum of limestone which was dug out and laid as a top dressing to counteract the soil's peaty acidity. In the 1740s it let for about 25 shillings an Irish acre.[120]

Synge's life in Elphin was not just devoted to pastoral duties and hospitality. In 1731 Robert Howard had an income of £1433.13s.3d from leases and rentals on the demesne land.[121] Synge was an improving farmer and would have considerably increased his income with monies from the sale of stock, crops and linen. He was influenced by the agricultural reformer, Charles Varley, whom he had met about 1746. Varley (c.1725-96) had come to Ireland from Yorkshire to seek his fortune. Edward Synge introduced him to 'the heads of the Kingdom' and was instrumental in arranging for him to lease land in Co. Leitrim and receive premiums from the Linen Board. Varley wrote of Synge that he was his 'benefactor, tutor and father ... his house and stables were open to me ... his library for my education and his advice for my guide'. Varley's description of a day spent with Synge riding around his demesne echoes closely a similar description recounted by Synge to Alicia in 1747.[122] For a brief while, Varley took the place of Synge's lost sons.[123]

Varley thought that the quality of the land in Ireland made the landlords idle; with a few exceptions, they were 'great slovens in husbandry ... turn it up in any fashion, and corn must grow'.[124] Roscommon's economy was held back by the domination of the graziers over tillage and in the production of linen by the large numbers of spinners and the small number of weavers. Varley shared Synge's concern about the imbalance between grazing and tillage, and he attributed Ireland's prevalent evils of poverty and begging to the 'great graziers ... the chief and real bars to the riches, prosperity, improvement, industry, good morals, regularity, cloathing and feeding of the poor in Ireland'.[125]

When Varley arrived in Ireland, Edward Synge was a Trustee of the Linen Board. Varley, who came from Rotherham where flax was grown widely, noticed that the combination of the land and the climate in Ireland, together with the premiums offered by the Board, made the growing of flax potentially lucrative. Irish flax was thought to be far superior to foreign flax and, unlike imports from Germany and the Low Countries, imports of linen into England were free of duty.[126] The Roscommon soil was particularly good for flax growing, and the Board made grants to local contractors to buy looms. Synge makes clear his dependence on Varley's advice when it comes to growing flax,[127] and his letters have many orders for hatchels, scutching boards and parts of looms to be sent from Dublin. However, reports to the Linen Board on the state of the industry in the late 1750s, said that in Roscommon particularly, the easy production of flax was countered by difficulties in its processing into cloth. In Roscommon the poor were thought to benefit little from the high quality of the yarn produced by local spinners. There were too many spinners, an unskilled trade generally carried out by women, and not enough weavers, a skilled job carried out by men. This imbalance impoverished whole families.[129]

Our knowledge of the social structure of the diocese of Elphin owes much to Edward Synge himself.[129] In 1749 he ordered a census of the diocese which greatly extended the counts of papists and mass houses made by earlier incumbents of Elphin.[130] Each of Synge's clergy was commissioned to list everyone in their parish including not just Roman Catholics but also Protestants, Presbyterians and Quakers. The survey listed by parish, place of abode, head of household, religion, their profession or trade, children over or under fourteen, and servants, male or female, Catholic or Protestant. The extent and completeness of Synge's census may have been the result of discussions with Charles Varley, who later wrote a pamphlet recommending a census with similar headings.[131]

The 1749 census says that Synge had seventeen servants in his household, twelve men and five women. They were all, at least nominally, Protestant.[132] He can be irritated by their performance: he curses Tom for shaving him badly, Shannon for breaking all his water glasses 'at one slap' and the grooms for taking out his horses and getting fuddled in his neighbours' kitchens, but still to him they are 'My Family'. He chooses his upper servants with care – the interviewing of a potential steward and his wife takes up a dozen letters – but once hired, they are cared for, educated and sent to the Mercer's Hospital in Dublin for treatment. Many of his comments on his servants' performance and about household disasters, such as lost keys, broken bottles and 'the new House all going to Ruin before it is finished', are identical to those of Swift.[133] In 1750 Synge says he is determined to get rid of his house steward Shannon, but despite his determined resolution Shannon is still there in 1752. Some of his comments on his servants and the peasantry are brutal. He himself recognizes this when he says to Alicia, 'You know me to be strict and severe with regard to the conduct of servants. This is not the effect of temper but prudence. Harshness, irksome to myself, I find necessary to keep them in order.'[134] He may be harsh too when he says of their grief at a death that the peasantry are 'not agitated with so strong passions as We are' but, he continues compassionately, 'it is owing to their Condition, in which their is no variety, little highly pleasing, and of consequence less distress. ... All is soon over, and they return to their usual Employment. Their necessitys oblige them to it; and as they have not leisure to grieve, the impression soon goes off.'[135] Persuading Alicia not to criticise the appearance and manners of her new maid, sent from Elphin to Dublin, he writes, 'Reflect, My Dear as often as you see her, that had you been neglected as she has been, you might have been as she is: Bless God for the advantages you have had and have, and make a right use and improvement of them.'[136] Irish, to Synge, denotes a lack of manners or ignorance; Dr Dignan, a local man without the qualifications of a Dublin doctor, is characterized as 'Irish' for presuming on hospitality, and Alicia's errors in spelling are sharply corrected with the words "Tis brogue'.[137]

Synge took book catalogues and read booksellers' advertisements in the Dublin papers. Synge was sarcastic about the books in his predecessor's library. He marked Robert Howard's inventory, commenting on copies of Euripedes *Tragedies*, 'mighty bad', Straboni's *Geographica* '1 vol.

a very old Bad edition' and Pearson's *Exposition of the Creed* 'miserably abused'.[138] His English books, although naturally dominated by theology, included Aubrey, Berkeley, Milton, Prior, Shakespeare, Swift and Wycherley. He was fascinated by Roman Catholic doctrine and the Catholic apologetics. Using the Catholic apothecary as an intermediary, he borrowed books critical of Protestant historians of the rebellion of 1641 from his neighbour Charles O'Conor.[139]

Synge played the harpsichord and took a close interest in the music in his church.[140] As Chancellor of St Patrick's, he was 'minister in musicis' at the cathedral, where he was a good judge of singing. At the same time, as rector of St Werburgh's, he suspended the organist 'for many irregularities and for prevaricating with the Minister'.[141] Synge's musical ability made a strong impression on Handel when the composer was in Dublin. To his librettist Charles Jennens, Handel wrote of Synge as 'a Nobleman very learned in Musick'.[142] With his letter, Handel enclosed Synge's impressions of the first performance of *The Messiah* in the New Musick-Hall in Fishamble Street on 13 April 1742. Synge wrote that it was 'A Species of Musick different from any other – the composer is very Masterly and artificial, yet the Harmony is So great and open, as to please all who have Ears and will hear, learned and unlearn'd.' He was impressed by the attention of the audience, and remarked that 'to their great honour, tho' the young and gay of both Sexes were present in great numbers their behaviour was uniformly grave and decent'.[143] The moral dimension of Handel's music and the object of its performance would have appealed to Synge. Unlike London, where music was performed commercially, Dublin had a tradition of performances for charity, and proceeds from *The Messiah* were to be shared 'by the Society of relieving Prisoners, the Charitable Infirmary and Mercer's Hospital'.[144] Synge suggested that Handel might write a sequel, called 'The Penitent', but Handel never took up his proposal.

Synge can unquestionably be tiresome and pedantic in his letters to Alicia, returning frequently to her writing, her grammar, her spelling and her pen nibs. After the first few references, our eyes may glaze over his comments, but his purpose was clear. She had to take her place in society as his daughter, and he confesses, 'I love to teach you in trifles with Exactness which may be of real use in affairs of more importance.'[145] He despises children who care only for dress and diversions, and blames their parents, 'If their chief point all their lives has been to please, no wonder ... they resolve at once to make the most of it.'[146]

Alicia remains a shadowy figure, and no known portrait of her survives. We know that like her father she was tall,[147] but of her character and temperament we know nothing. She was certainly encouraged to be independent. After a mob attempted to storm Kevin Street and a man was shot dead, Edward Synge told of a girl, 'One of the finest young Women of her time ... when about your Age, a Maiden, defended her Father's Castel ... against robberys, and not only plaid the Gentleman well, but her self fir'd the great Guns and beat them off. I would have you like her in Courage, tho' I don't wish it may ever be so try'd.'[148]

Mrs Delany met Alicia at a dinner given by her father in Dublin in early 1752, and wrote that she 'will be a vast fortune and is brought up like a princess; she is a fine young woman about nineteen, all the young men have already proposed'.[149] There is no evidence in her father's letters of Alicia's many suitors, but Synge is clearly careful (which he could well afford to be) that she should not marry for the sake of money. Of a young woman whose parents forced her to marry, he said, 'I can't find terms strong enough to express my detestation of the behaviour of the parents to sacrifice a Child to Convenience and County interests.'[150] He said that he would not listen to any proposal of marriage until Alicia was twenty-one years old, and she was twenty-five when she married Joshua Cooper of Mercury (now Markree Castle) Co. Sligo in June 1758.[151]

With one exception, a single stray letter from 1746, Edward Synge's letters to Alicia run from May to October for each year from 1747 to 1752. Those written in 1748 are missing, although we know that he was in Roscommon that summer.[152] The remains of stitching on the fold of the paper is evidence that they were bound by an amateur at some time in their early life. The letters have been in the Cooper family since 1758, and form part of a corpus of papers which included deeds and leases for Synge lands in Tipperary and which were inherited by Alicia's great grandson, Richard Cooper. In 1866 he married his first cousin, Alicia's great grand-daughter, Cicely Cooper, and they lived in England. The letters have been in England since then and are now in Trinity College, Dublin.

Edward Synge died on 27 January 1762, aged seventy-one, and was buried in the Synge vault in the old churchyard of St Patrick's, just under the wall of Marsh's Library.[153] Alicia and Joshua Cooper's marriage lasted for over forty years, but it was accompanied by sorrow. They had three sons and a daughter, but two of their children died in infancy. Joshua Cooper died in 1800, and in 1804 his heir, Joshua Edward, was declared mentally deranged and the Cooper estates put into the hands of the Masters in Lunacy. As her father told her, 'The happiest marriage brings cares &c. It was a saying of your Grandmother's when a young Damsel was gay and cheerfull. The Black Ox has not yet trod on her foot. An homely image of Matrimony, but too too often a just one.'[154] Alicia died at Kevin Street in 1807, it was said of a broken heart.[155] She was buried near her father.[156]

NOTES

1. Edward Synge to his daughter, Alicia. Letter 136.

2. David Hayton, Irish history seminar Hertford College, Oxford May 1993.

3. Brian Fitzgerald (ed.), *Correspondence of Emily, duchess of Leinster 1731-1814* 3 vols (Dublin 1948-57).

4. Lady Llanover (ed.), *The Autobiography and Correspondence of Mary Granville, Mrs Delany* 6 vols (London 1861).

5. James Kelly (ed.), *The Letters of Lord Chief Baron Edward Willes to the Earl of Warwick 1757-1762* (Aberystwyth 1990).

6. Edward Synge to the Duke of Bedford, Elphin [undated] 1758 PRONI, T. 2915/6/7.

7. Letter 3 and 68.

8. Letter 152.

9. The family name was originally Millington. Henry VIII (or Queen Elizabeth) was supposed to have heard one of the family as a choir boy in Rochester cathedral and to have said that his name should not be Millington, it should be Sing. There are variants of this account. K. Synge, *The Family of Synge or Sing* (privately printed 1937) p.v.

10. Synge, pp.xi-xii.

11. He left land in Limerick and a house at Finglas to his wife Margaret for life, and after her death to his son, Michael, for life and to his heirs male. Failing these, the lands were to pass to his nephew, Edward Synge, for life and to his heirs male, and failing these to his nephew Nicholas and his heirs male. Will of Samuel Synge, dean of Kildare, 29 August 1706. Copies of Synge Wills made by R.A. Synge from Four Courts Records in 1902. TCD ms 6199.

12. T.C. Barnard, 'Crises of identity among Irish protestants 1641-1685' *Past and Present* 127 (1990) pp.39-83.

13. G.D. Burtchaell and T.U. Sadleir, *Alumni Dubliniensis* (Dublin 1935), pp.797-8.

14. King to Wake 30 September 1714. C.S. King (ed.), *A Great Archbishop of Dublin: William King DD; 1650-1729* (London 1906), p.172.

15. Entry for Archbishop Edward Synge. *Dictionary of National Biography* (Oxford 1975).

16. T.W. Moody, F.X. Martin and F.J. Byrne (eds), *New History of Ireland* Vol. 9, *Maps, Genealogies, Lists: A Companion to Irish History* (Oxford 1984) p.492; Robert Howard to Archbishop William King 4 July 1717, Archbishop King Papers, TCD Mss 1995-2008.

17. Synge to Wake 12 April 1720 TCD Stephens/Synge Papers ms 6201.

18. R. Mant, *History of the Church of Ireland* 2 vols (London 1849) Vol. 2, pp.334-43, 341.

19. Synge to Wake Dublin 12 April 1720 TCD ms 6201.

20. Hugh Boulter, archbishop of Armagh to the Lord Lieutenant, Lord Carteret 20 August 1726, *Letters written by His Excellency Hugh Boulter DD Lord Primate of all Ireland* 2 vols (1770) Vol.1, p.80.

21. Boulter to Carteret 18 September 1727, *Letters* Vol.1, p.161. Synge the younger was instituted as Chancellor on 28 March 1727. H.J. Lawlor, *The Fasti of St Patrick's* (Dublin 1930), p.65.

22. Boulter to the duke of Newcastle 10 January 1728/9 *Letters*, p.278.

23. Synge's former patron the duke of Bolton pressed Carteret's nomination on Newcastle. Henry Maule, bishop of Clonfert, to Edward Synge 29 May 1730, loose in a volume

of the personal and household accounts of Edward Synge, archbishop of Tuam 1717-22 NLI ms 2173.

24. Duke of Dorset to the duke of Newcastle 9 February 1731/2 PRONI T.722/1 pp.30-31.

25. *Ibid.*

26. The inscription on the grave of George Synge, bishop of Cloyne, Edward Synge's great-uncle recorded that he too was a tall man. *An Excellent New Song, To a good Old Tune* (Dublin 1726); Mrs Delany to Mrs Dewes 8 June 1753 Delany, Vol.1, pp.233-4; Synge, p.xii.

27. E.H. Alton, 'Fragments of College History' I, *Hermathena* 57-8 (1941), pp.25-58, 121-65.

28. Swift to Lord Carteret 3 July 1725 H. Williams, (ed.), *The Correspondence of Jonathan Swift* 5 vols (Oxford 1965) Vol.5 p.124; Vol.3 p.71.

29. Chesterfield to the duke of Newcastle 20 November 1745 B.L. Add.Mss 32,705 f.393.

30. J.T. Gilbert, 'The Streets of Dublin – III' *Irish Quarterly Review* 2 March 1852, p.55.

31. She was related to the Synges through her mother's cousin Dean William Meade of Cork who married Helena Townshend, a relation of the Synge family through Archbishop Synge's sister Mary, who married Bryan Townshend of Castletownsend, Co. Cork. Text from the original edition Vol.3 (Dublin 1754) pp.61-2. A.C. Elias, Jr., *Memoirs of Laetitia Pilkington* (pending University of Georgia Press). I am most grateful to Mr Elias for information on the Pilkington/Synge connection.

32. Letter 208.

33. Will of Edward Synge, bishop of Elphin, 31 July 1761. PRO PROB11/894/563.

34. Mant, Vol.2, p.314.

35. He successfully filed eight cases against landowners in the court of Exchequer in 1735. For an account of the tithe agistment controversy, see L. Landa, *Swift and the Church of Ireland* (Oxford 1954) pp.135-50; and on the system of tithes, M.J. Bric, 'The Tithe System in Eighteenth-Century Ireland', *Proceedings of the Royal Irish Academy* Vol. 86, Sect.C. (1986) pp.271-88.

36. Mant, Vol.2, p.555; Edward Synge, lord bishop of Ferns and Leighlin, *Two Affidavits in Relation to the Demands of Tythe Agistment in the Dioces of Leighlin; with an introduction* (Dublin 1736), p.6.

37. For an analysis of the sermons preached on the anniversary of the 1641 rebellion, see T.C. Barnard, 'The uses of 23 October 1641 and Irish protestant celebrations', *English Historical Review* Vol.106 (October 1991) 421, pp.889-920.

38. Edward Synge, *The Case of Toleration considered with Respect both to Religion and Civil Government in a Sermon ... preach'd on Saturday 23rd October 1725* (Second edition 1726). Two recent historians have, understandably, wrongly attributed this sermon to Archbishop Synge. F.G. James 'The Church of Ireland in the early eighteenth century', *Historical Magazine of the Protestant Episcopal Church* Vol.48 (1979), p.450; Thomas Bartlett, *The Fall and Rise of the Irish Nation* (Dublin 1992), p.26.

39. 'And the Lord said unto the servant, Go out into the high ways and hedges, and compel them to come in, that my house may be filled.' Luke 14:23.

40. *The Case of Toleration ...* p.2.

41. *The Case of Toleration ...* p.12.

42. Synge's sermon led to an attack by the Rev. Stephen Radcliffe, in *A Letter to the Rev. Mr. Edward Synge ... occasion'd by a Late Sermon* (1725). Radcliffe vehemently attacked

Synge for being ingenuous about the nature of Catholics and Catholicism. Synge replied in *A Vindication of a Sermon ... in Answer to the Rev. Mr Radcliffe's Letter* (1726), saying that as Radcliffe's diatribe was so confused it was impossible for him to reply. The efforts of Archbishop Synge and his son to find oaths of allegiance suitable for Catholics to take and of the younger Synge in sermon and pamphlet controversy is examined in Patrick Fagan, *Cornelius Nary: Dublin's Turbulent Priest* (Dublin 1991), pp.122-5 and 166-74.

43. Edward Synge senior, *Sermon against Persecution on account of Religion, Preached ... October the 23. 1721* (Dublin 1721).

44. Although he could be pugnacious on this subject in public, in private Synge was lenient. He continued to lease a house in Dublin to a man whom he believed to be a Roman Catholic, saying that although he could have consulted a lawyer to see whether the lease was valid, and 'the Popery Acts might give an open for doing it', he would not attempt to overturn it and eject his tenant. [Edward Synge, bishop of Ferns] *A Report from the Lords Committees Appointed to Inspect into the State of the Publick Offices of Record in this Kingdom and in what Manner and Place the Same are now kept* (1740); Edward Synge's title to different lands and tenements in the counties of Cork, Tipperary and Dublin NLI ms 2101.

45. Ian McBride, 'The School of Virtue: Francis Hutcheson, Irish Presbyterians and the Scottish Enlightenment' in D.George Boyce, Robert Eccleshall and Vincent Geoghegan (eds), *Political Thought in Ireland since the Seventeenth Century* (London 1993), pp.79-80.

46. Hutcheson spoke of his 'Obligations to the Reverend Mr. EDWARD SYNG; not only for revising these Papers, when they stood in great need of an accurate Review; but for suggesting several just Amendments in the general Scheme of Morality. The Author was much confirm'd in his Opinion of the Justness of these Thoughts, upon finding, that this Gentleman had fallen into the same way of thinking before him; and will ever look upon his Friendship as one of the greatest Advantages and Pleasures of his Life.' Preface to the second edition of Francis Hutcheson, *An Inquiry into the Original of our Ideas of Beauty and Virtue* (London 1726), p.xx-xxi.

47. Synge wrote to Berkeley's son after the bishop of Cloyne's death in 1753, 'It will always give me pleasure to be consider'd as your good Fathers friend. I have been so these 43 years, with exquisite pleasure and great advantage to my self, while we were together, but with much regret and uneasiness, since the distance of our situations and his constant residence interrupted all intercourse except now and then by letter.' David Berman has pointed out that Synge was probably the link between Hutcheson and Berkeley, who were both teaching in Dublin in the 1720s. Synge, as well as Berkeley, would probably be one of the 'few speculative friends in Dublin' mentioned by Berkeley in 1727. Edward Synge to George Berkeley, 26 January 1753, BL Add.Mss. 39,311, f.70; David Berman, 'Dr Berkly's books', Francis Hutcheson Supplement to *Fortnight* July/August 1992, p.23.

48. William Leechman, introduction to Francis Hutcheson, *A System of Moral Philosophy* (London 1755), pp.xxviii-xxix.

49. Hutcheson, *A System of Moral Philosophy* Vol.1, p.315. See also the passage on the 'Useful Refugee' *An Inquiry ...*, p.117.

50. Hutcheson, *A System of Moral Philosophy* Vol.1, p.192.

51. Letters 152 and 189.

52. Francis Hutcheson, *A Short Introduction to Moral Philosophy* (Glasgow 1753) p.248.

53. 12 June 1752.

54. *A Short Introduction ...*, p.254.

55. Letters 133 and 136.

56. The list of subscribers contains clues as to which of Synge's friends mentioned in the letters were part of Hutcheson's circle: Thomas Adderley, Brabazon Disney, Henry Hamilton, Lord Chancellor Newport, John Lawson, the Rev. Arthur Mahon archdeacon of Elphin, Dr Ezekial Nesbitt, the Rev. John Owen dean of Clonmacnoise, and Synge's close friend, Godfrey Wills, were all subscribers.

57. J.-P. Pittion, 'Religious Conformity and Non-Conformity' in C.E.J. Caldicott, H. Gough and J.-P. Pittion (eds), *The Huguenots and Ireland* (Dublin 1987), p.289.

58. Around 1800 people – 452 families – arrived between 1692 and 1701. Raymond Hylton, 'The Huguenot Communities in Dublin 1662-1745' (Ph.D National University of Ireland 1985), p.85.

59. Hylton, p.144.

60. *Le désert: en tant que lieu de refuge.* Paul Imbs (ed.), *Trésor de la Langue française* (Paris) 1978; entry for Ferrières, Michelin Guide *Gorges du Tarn* (Paris 1989), p.81.

61. Jourdan, 'the old man of Dunshaughlin' who figures in Synge's letters, had been chaplain to Henri de Ruvigny, the first Lord Galway, on his mission to Portugal in 1703. Edward Synge's first important patron, Charles Paulet, later duke of Bolton, had accompanied de Ruvigny when he came to Ireland as a Lord Justice in 1697. See Biographical Register. Patrick Kelly 'Lord Galway and the Penal Laws', in Caldicott, Gough and Pittion, p.244.

62. Synge frequently uses phrases in French and occasionally refers to the different spelling of the same words in French and English. In particular, he refers to bodily functions in French. Alicia wrote to her cousin, Molly Curtis, in French. Letter 197.

63. Synge's library was rich in French literature. He owned the 1718 Rouen edition of Gui Joly's *Mémoires* (1718), the Rouen edition of Joachim du Bellay, *Oeuvres françoises* (1592), Louis de Maimbourg, *Histoire du Calvinism* (1682), all probably bought from the sale of Swift's books in 1745. He owned a number of histories of France in the original and read Racine, Corneille, Molière, Montaigne, Bussy Rabutin and Descartes. Patrick King, Catalogue 13 (Stony Stratford, Bucks 1987), item 45.

64. See his concern about the problem of making a French dessert, *les cremets*, in Elphin. Letter 103.

65. For this section, I have drawn heavily on Declan O'Donovan, 'The Money Bill Dispute of 1753' in Thomas Bartlett and D.W. Hayton (eds), *Penal Era and Golden Age: Essays in Irish History 1690-1800* (Belfast 1979).

66. O'Donovan, p.55.

67. 'Except for four years'. Declan O'Donovan says that the Tory years up to 1714 included the last four years of Shrewsbury as Lord Lieutenant, when Whigs like the elder Edward Synge were kept out. Synge to Limerick 24 January 1754 PRONI Mic. 147/9 ff.114-15; O'Donovan p.66.

68. Synge to Limerick 24 January 1754.

69. Synge to Limerick 20 and 25 December 1753.

70. When personally threatened by a bill containing a clause critical of his actions in the administration of a charity, he lobbied hard in his own interest, first in Dublin and then in London. Edward Synge to Godfrey Wills 10 January-12 April 1760. Representative Church Body archives ms 426/ff.1-11.

71. Thomas P. Power, *Land, Politics and Society in Eighteenth-century Tipperary* (Oxford 1993), pp.81, 121-3.

72. Robert Curtis pledged himself to pay £2000 as his daughter's marriage portion,

and in turn, Archbishop Edward Synge agreed to pay over £3000 to trustees in order that land should be bought to provide his son with an income for life. This income was to be used should his wife survive him, and if she did not, then for his sons' maintenance or his daughters' maintenance and their marriage portions. Additionally, Archbishop Synge covenanted to convey lands in the city and county of Cork to the trustees of the settlement. The settlement also provided that during Archbishop Synge's lifetime he would pay his son £168 a year. Jane Curtis stood to inherit monies on her mother's death; in consideration of this, Robert Curtis agreed to pay Edward Synge £50 a year while he and his wife were living. NLI Synge Papers PC 344 (7).

73. Jane Synge, the Archbishop's wife, had died in 1723, 'after a very long and heavy sickness', Synge to Wake 21 October 1723 TCD ms 6201.

74. For the variable effect of chance on the size of estates, see Anthony Malcolmson, *The Pursuit of the Heiress: Aristocratic Marriage in Ireland 1750-1820* (Belfast 1982).

75. T.O'Rorke, *The History of the Antiquities and Present State of the Parishes of Ballysadare and Kilvarnet* (Dublin 1878), p.163.

76. Willes, p.94.

77. Letter 3.

78. Jane Synge was buried on 1 January 1737/8 in the Synge vault. 'On Sat last Died after two days illness, the Lady of the Rt Revd. the Lord Bishop of Ferns and Laughlin, at his House in Kevan's Street. She was a Lady of great Charity, Piety and Humanity which makes her death greatly lamented.' *Pue's Occurrences* 2 January 1737/8.

79. Edward Synge refers to annual whitewashing of the exterior of the building. Letter 30; Letter 70.

80. See map p.392. The College of Technology now covers the site of the house and grounds. Abstract of an indenture, 8 August 1877 TCD ms 5823; Roger Kendrick, 'A map of a piece of ground near New Street Called Naboth's Vineyard, & another piece adjoining thereto belonging to the Rev. the Dean & Chapter of St. Patrick's Dublin', Maps and Plans of St. Patrick's 1741-1825 Marsh's Library Z.2.1.14 f.v-viii.

81. Brief of affidavits before the Master in Lunacy Sir Samuel Romilly which deal with the case of Joshua Edward Cooper 1812 NLI ms 10,306.

82. Letter 12 and 16.

83. 20 January 1815. Abstract of the title of the Incorporated Society to premises in Kevin Street, Dublin TCD ms 5823; Brief of affidavits.

84. See map p.392. John Rocque's 1756 map of Dublin shows the house and grounds clearly. J.H. Andrews points out that although Rocque claimed to show 'every dwelling-house, ware-houses, stable, yards, back-houses and gardens', the backs of houses were more exacting to measure; Rocque's surveyors would have found it difficult to be accurate in plotting irregular groups of buildings like those at Kevin Street. The south-west corner of 'Bp. Synge's Garden' appears on the edge of Roger Kendrick's 1749 map of Swift's Naboth's Vineyard. Abstract of title of 1845, 1868 and 1877 TCD ms 5823; J.H. Andrews, *Two Maps of 18th Century Dublin and its Surroundings*, (Lympne 1977) n.p.; Kendrick, loc.cit.

85. Brief of affidavits.

86. Advertisement to let Kevin Street. *Faulkner's Dublin Journal* 5-9 March 1765.

87. Robert Clayton, bishop of Clogher, and Richard Robinson, bishop of Killala, lived in St Stephen's Green, as did Synge's father in old age and Synge's brother, Nicholas. *The Georgian Society Records of Eighteenth-Century Domestic Architecture and Decoration in Dublin* 5 vols (Dublin 1909-13), Vol.2, pp.81-2, 63, 47 and 98-9.

88. David Dickson has pointed out that, as in many contemporary French cities, the eighteenth-century Liberties were artisanal in character, and south-west Dublin remained the main industrial neighbourhood for generations, aided partly by the water supplied by the river Poddle. 'Large-scale developers and the growth of eighteenth-century Irish cities', in P. Butel and L.M. Cullen (eds), *Cities and Merchants* (Dublin 1986), p.113.

89. Riots took place between the 'Ormond boys' who were mainly Catholic butchers, and the 'Liberty Boys' who were Protestant weavers from the Coombe, joined occasionally by students from Trinity College. A truce was supposed by have been struck in July 1748 but it was unstable. Rioters protesting against the import of cotton fabric continued into the 1760s. Maurice Craig, *Dublin 1660-1860: A Social and Architectural History* (Dublin 1980), p.89; Benjamin Houghton, *Considerations humbly addressed to the magistrates of the city and county of Dublin: and more particularly to the housekeepers and master-manufacturers thereof* (Dublin 1764).

90. Letter 138.

91. In particular, see T.C. Barnard 'Improving clergymen', in Alan Ford, James McGuire and Kenneth Milne (eds), *As by Law Established: the Church of Ireland since the Reformation* (Dublin 1995); 'The world of a Galway squire: Robert French of Monivae' in R. Gillespie (ed.), *Galway: History and Society* (forthcoming); 'Domestic Servants' paper read at a conference of the Irish Economic and Social History Society September 1993; 'Gardening, diet and improvement in later seventeenth century Ireland', *Journal of Garden History* 10/8 (1990) Vol. 10, pp.71-86.

92. As Barnard has noted, Robert Howard, bishop of Elphin from 1730 to 1740, fused the spiritual and material spheres in his role as connoisseur, agricultural improver, preacher, landlord and politician. 'Improving Clergymen'.

93. Lord Chesterfield believed that the Irish House of Lords 'in truth consists only of bishops'. Chesterfield to the duke of Newcastle 20 November 1745 BL Add.Mss. 32,705 f.393.

94. [Edmund Sexton Pery], *Letters from an Armenian in Ireland to his Friends in Trebisond* Translated in the year 1756 (London 1757), p.16.

95. Boulter to Carteret, n.d. Quoted in *A Great Archbishop*, p.171 fn.1.

96. Archbishop Synge to Wake Dublin 15 January 1716/17 TCD ms 6201.

97. Synge to Wake Dublin 12 April 1720 TCD ms 6201.

98. Robert Howard to Hugh Howard 18 July 1730 TCD mss 1995-2008.

99. Nicholas Synge, when translated to Killaloe, faced problems with his Palace. Letter 65.

100. Willes, p.94.

101. The first cathedral at Elphin was built in *c.* 1240 and was partly destroyed in 1641 during the rebellion. It was rebuilt by Bishop John Parker and in 1685 Bishop John Hodson established a trust to found a grammar school in the town and to support and repair the cathedral. By 1757 the cathedral was again in a ruinous state; the seventeenth-century cathedral was demolished and was rebuilt with a grant by the board of First-Fruits. Edward Synge was very much involved in the design and construction of the new building. This building was destroyed in a storm in 1957. Peter Galloway, *The Cathedrals of Ireland* (Belfast 1992) p.95-7; Edward Synge to Godfrey Wills, 5 September 1760, 24 March, 5 May, 14 July 1761. RCB ms 426/f.10,13,14,16.

102. Maurice Craig, *Classic Irish Houses of the Middle Size* (London 1976), pp.22, 24-5,

and fig.46-7, p.123.

103. Maurice Craig, *Dublin* pp.113, 171.

104. Kenneth Severens, 'A new perspective on Georgian building practice; the rebuilding of St Werburgh's church, Dublin (1754-59)', *Bulletin of the Irish Georgian Society* (1992-3), 35, pp.3-11.

105. Michael Wills was paid £28 by Edward Curtis, 'for his attendance, travelling charges &c. at the Commission held at Elphin in August last.' 15 November 1763. [Joshua Cooper] Notes of financial transactions arising out of the administration of the estates of Edward Synge, bishop of Elphin, deceased 1762-5. NLI ms 2102.

106. Maurice Craig describes them as 'pretentious'. Michael Wills, 'Album of 16 designs ...'. Drawings Collection Royal Institute of British Architects Shelf D.3 f.2 and 3; Craig, *Classic Irish Houses* p.48.

107. Proposed alterations to the Palace, Elphin 1873. McCurdy and Mitchell Drawings collection, Irish Architectural Archive, Bin VII, roll 15.

108. See the drawing from William Hampton's road survey book, and the photograph 'Elphin, Bishop's Palace' *c.* 1860. NLI ms 3242; Irish Architectural Archive, ref. 51/82. Reproduced in the Knight of Glin, David J. Griffin and Nicholas K. Robinson, *Vanishing Country Houses of Ireland* (Dublin 1988), p.125.

109. Letter 29.

110. In Tuam in 1717, Archbishop Synge found fourteen resident clergymen out of a total of eighteen. Sean Connolly, *Religion, Law and Power: the Making of Protestant Ireland 1660-1760* (Oxford 1992), p.182.

111. Archbishop Synge subscribed 200 Bibles printed in Dublin in 1719. In 1750 Edward Synge ordered copies of the Book of Common Prayer for two boys he was teaching. When Synge lent his gown to the bishop of Killala to enable him to preach at Elphin, he found himself without another and had to stay at home. Receipt of Elihal Dobson 26 May 1719 NLI Synge Papers PC 344 (1); Letter 219.

112. Problems identified by Bishop Dopping in 1697. Connolly, p.178.

113. Synge built and consecrated two churches in 1747. Edward to Alicia Synge 13 July 1750. Connolly, p.178; D.A. Beaufort, *Memoir of a Map of Ireland* (London 1792), p.135.

114. *An Abstract of the Number of Protestant and Popish Families in the Several Counties and Provinces in Ireland* (Dublin 1732), p.6; Connolly, p.149; map fig. 5.1 p.146.

115. Connolly, p.146.

116. Synge to Wake 12 April 1720 TCD ms 6201.

117. The name Elphin, *Ail Fionn,* means the rock of the clear spring. 'The foolish Common People are silly enough to dream, that the Name of this Place was taken from a huge Stone, there to be seen called the Stone of the Giant Fin-Mac-Cool. Others with more Probability interpret the Name to signifie, a Stone of a clear, transparent Fountain...' *The Works of Sir James Ware, concerning Ireland revised and improved* (Dublin 1764), p.627.

118. Robert Howard to Hugh Howard 18 July 1730 Wicklow Papers NLI PC 227.

119. Charles Varley, *A New System of Husbandry* 3 vols (York 1770) Vol.III, p.78-9.

120. *A New System of Husbandry* Vol.3, p.31-2.

121. Wicklow Papers NLI PC 223 (6).

122. Letter 4.

123. Varley's close friendship proved transient, and he is quite candid about his relationship with Synge. After describing Synge's kindness to him and how dependent Synge

was on his advice Varley states brutally that 'now trade and farming began to gain much upon me (for I had taken much land in farming) that I dropped my bishop and my salary'. He returned to England in 1760. In later life, Varley went to America, where he made an abortive claim to land in New Jersey. He died in England. [Charles Varley], *The Modern Farmer's Guide by a Real Farmer* (Glasgow 1768), pp.xliii-xlv; DNB.

124. Varley, *A New System* ... Vol. 2, p.33.

125. Varley, *The Modern Farmer's Guide*, Vol. 3, pp.210-12.

126. Varley, *A New System of Husbandry* Vol. 3, p.223; [Robert Stephenson], *Considerations ... on the Present State of the Linen Manufacture* (Dublin 1754), pp.28, 30.

127. '... Flax in a very bad condition. I know not how to manage it and Varley is ill.' Letter 105.

128. 'By the want of the work for the men, the Expence of the Family falls on the Spinners.' Robert Stephenson, *Reports and Observations* (Dublin 1762), pp.59-61.

129. Census of the diocese of Elphin. National Archives of Ireland M.2466.

130. Synge's predecessor at Elphin, Bishop Robert Howard, had a list of the inhabitants of Elphin. He also made a list of Protestants who sent their children as charity boys to the school in Elphin and a partial list of the mass houses in the diocese and a report on the state of the popery. A list of papers delivered to the Rt Rev. Dr Edward Synge Bp of Elphin by Mr Robert Houlding found among Papers belong to the Rt Rev Dr Howard late Bp of Elphin. Wicklow Papers NLI PC 223 (6).

131. His purpose was to argue for imposing a dog-tax. Charles Varlo, *Schemes offered for the perusal and Consideration of the Legislature* (London 1775), pp.175-7.

132. Census, f.1.

133. 'The Blunders, Deficiencies, Distresses, and Misfortunes of Quilca' in H. Davis (ed.), Jonathan Swift, *Miscellaneous and Autobiographical Pieces, Fragments and Marginalia* (Oxford 1969), pp.219-21.

134. Letter 175.

135. Letter 200.

136. Letter 186.

137. Letter 53; Letter 121.

138. List of Robert Howard's books, Wicklow Papers NLI PC 223 (6). I am grateful to Patrick King for discussing Synge's library with me and for letting me see notes that he made on the manuscript catalogue of 1763. I am also grateful to A.C. Elias Jnr for information on Synge's purchases from the library of Jonathan Swift.

139. John Curry, *Historical Memoirs* and Nicholas French, *The Bleeding Iphigenia* (1675).

140. His interest in music is another link with Michael Wills, who wrote approvingly of the acoustics of Smock Alley Theatre and the concert rooms at Crow Street, 'where musick was heard in perfect harmony'. Christine Casey, '"De Architectura": an Irish eighteenth-century gloss', *Architectural History* Vol. 37 (1994), p.88. I am grateful to David Griffin for drawing my attention to this article.

141. Synge to Swift 18 September 1738, *Correspondence*, Vol. 5, pp.124-5; minutes of vestry meeting, 20 February 1727/8 St Werburgh's Vestry Book f.90, Representative Church Body archives.

142. Richard Luckett, *Handel's Messiah: A Celebration* (London 1992), p.132.

143. Luckett, p.129

144. Harry White, 'Handel in Dublin', *Eighteenth Century Ireland* 2 (1986), p.182, 184.

145. Letter 185.

146. Letter 187.

147. *Ibid.*

148. Letter 134.

149. On her marriage to Joshua Cooper in 1758, Alicia Synge was said to be worth £50,000. Mrs Delany to Mrs Dewes, 15 February 1752. Delany Vol.3, p.87; *Universal Advertiser* 10 June 1758.

150. Letter 171. Here is another link with Francis Hutcheson, who said of marriage settlements that he had 'an abhorrence of that spirit of traffick which often mingles so deeply in forming this alliance'. William Leechman, Preface to Hutcheson, *System of Moral Philosophy*, pp.xlii-xliii.

151. They were married in the cathedral at Elphin. *Faulkner's Dublin Journal* 3-6 June 1758.

152. Letter 48.

153. W. Monck Mason, *The History of St. Patrick's* (Dublin 1820); Parish Register Society of Dublin, *The Register of St. Patrick's*, (Dublin 1907), p.71.

154. Letter 168.

155. Evidence of Ann Mulholland, housekeeper. Brief of affidavits.

156. *St Patrick's*, p.81; Monck Mason, p.99.

Synge Pedigree

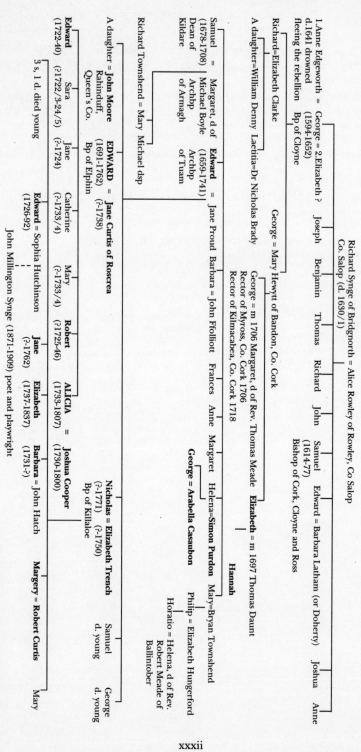

Richard Synge of Bridgnorth = Alice Rowley of Rowley, Co Salop
Co. Salop (d. 1630/1)

1. Anne Edgeworth = George = 2. Elizabeth ?   Joseph   Benjamin   Thomas   Richard   John   Samuel   Edward = Barbara Latham (or Doherty)   Joshua   Anne
d.1641 drowned   (1594-1652)   (1614-77)
fleeing the rebellion   Bp of Cloyne   Bishop of Cork, Cloyne and Ross

Richard = Elizabeth Clarke

A daughter = William Denny   Laetitia = Dr Nicholas Brady   George = Mary Hewyt of Bandon, Co. Cork

Samuel = Margaret, d of   Edward = Jane Proud   Barbara = John Ffolliot   Frances   Anne   Margaret   Helena = Simon Purdon   Elizabeth = m 1697 Thomas Daunt
(1678-1708)   Michael Boyle   (1659-1741)   George = Arabella Casaubon
Dean of   Archbp   Hannah
Kildare   of Armagh   Archbp   George = m 1706 Margaret, d of Rev. Thomas Meade
                              of Tuam   Rector of Myross, Co. Cork 1706
Richard Townshend = Mary Michael dsp   Rector of Kilmacabea, Co. Cork 1718

A daughter = John Moore   EDWARD = Jane Curtis of Roscrea   Mary = Bryan Townshend
              Rahinduff,   (1691-1762)   (?-1738)   Philip = Elizabeth Hungerford
              Queen's Co.   Bp of Elphin   Horatio = Helena, d of Rev.
                                                                                      Robert Meade of
                                                                                      Ballintober
Edward   Jane   EDWARD = Sophia Hutchinson   Catherine   Mary   Robert   ALICIA = Joshua Cooper   Nicholas = Elizabeth Trench   Samuel   George
(1722-40)   (?-1724)   (1726-92)   (?-1733/4) (?-1733/4) (?1725-46) (1733-67) (1730-1800) (?-1771) (?-1750)   d. young d. young
                                                                                              Bp of Killaloe
3 s, 1 d. died young   Edward = Sophia Hutchinson   Jane   Elizabeth   Barbara = John Hatch   Margery = Robert Curtis
                                                                                                             (?-1762)   (1737-1837) (1731-?)
                                                                           John Millington Synge (1871-1909) poet and playwright   Mary   Mary

Bold = mentioned in Edward Synge's letters

Source: K. Synge, The Family of Synge or Sing (privately printed 1937)

xxxii

Editorial Principles

The main object in editing this text has been to ensure that Edward Synge's letters are easy to read. In preparing the text for publication, the conventional abbreviations yt, yr, dr, & have been silently expanded. Because of Synge's continual emphasis on Alicia's spelling, punctuation and grammar, his own spelling and punctuation and his somewhat erratic use of capital letters have all been left as they appear in the manuscript. The use of [*sic*] has been kept to a minimum. Synge's handwriting is clear, but if the text is obscure it is where sentences have been left incomplete or where the manuscript has been damaged, either where the wax seal has torn the paper or over time.

The footnotes attempt to provide information about the people to whom Synge refers, the authors and full titles of books, the location of places and details of houses. Passages in French and Latin have been translated. An attempt has been made to amplify references to food and drink, medicine, plants and agriculture. The Dublin press supplied full details of events of the period.

The identification of the people mentioned in the letters has been the most time-consuming task. They come from five distinct groups. First, the aristocracy and gentry; second, Synge's circle of fellow clerics; third, professional and mercantile groups: lawyers, academics, doctors, surgeons and the tradesmen of Dublin; fourth, Synge's households and last, the peasantry of Elphin. The identification of people within the first three groups has been relatively simple. The pedigrees of the aristocracy and gentry are available in editions of Burke's *Peerage* and *Landed Gentry* and in privately printed pedigrees, although their emphasis tends to be on the male line. Published abstracts of Irish wills have identified the many missing women. Genealogical reference books are only as good as the information provided by the families they contain, and members of different generations can be difficult to disentangle. Wherever possible, each person has been verified from different sources. The published admission books of the King's Inns, the English Inns of Court and the alumni of Trinity College, Dublin, together with the archives of the Royal College of Physicians of Ireland (formerly the King's and Queen's Colleges), all provided the professional classes. Canon Leslie's lists of the clergy of the Church of Ireland, published and unpublished, provided the careers of the clergy. Watson's Dublin directories provided the names and addresses of the official classes and Dublin traders. The Synge pedigree and Synge's own letters both here and elsewhere give the members of his family and the names and status of servants in his households.

What is unusual in a correspondence of this kind is that we can identify the peasantry of Elphin. Synge's 1749 census in the National Archives of Ireland provides information about many men and women and their families who would otherwise just be names.

Edward Synge's letters are written in the main on double-foolscap paper, folded lengthwise. The paper is then folded across twice for postage and the address written across the centre. The name of the post town is embossed near the address. When privileged post was allowed, Synge wrote 'Free Edw:Elphin' below the address, and the word FREE stamped and embossed. These 'Free' letters have been identified between square brackets [], together with any marginalia not part of the text. The date of each letter, provided in the manuscript at the end near his signature, is here printed at the beginning. Most of the letters were written from Elphin and any exceptions are printed with the date. Most of the letters were written 'To Miss Synge/at the Bishop of Elphin's/Kevin-street/ Dublin'. Again, any exceptions are printed within square brackets at the end of the letter.

In order to help the reader, the names and biographies of the people most frequently referred to by Edward Synge are printed in a Biographical Register.

Acknowledgments

I am grateful, above all, to Toby Barnard. Roy Foster suggested in 1990 that Toby Barnard should read Edward Synge's letters because of his particular knowledge both of Synge's period and his world. I am indebted to him for his assessment of Edward Synge's letters as a major source for the social history of eighteenth-century Ireland; for his continued belief in and pressure for their publication; and for ensuring that I met historians of the period, both in Ireland and Oxford, whose contribution is noted elsewhere. Last, I am grateful to him for allowing me to tap his unrivalled knowledge and understanding of Irish seventeenth- and eighteenth-century life, from the taste and substance of Kinnegad cheese to the architecture, decoration and furnishing of the houses of the gentry.

The British Academy gave me a small research grant which made early research on Synge's 1749 census possible. I am indebted to David Dickson, for initial guidance on research into eighteenth-century Dublin and Roscommon, and for successive discussions and encouragement. Allen Synge, a descendant of Edward Synge's brother Nicholas, gave me particular help in lending me his copy of the Synge pedigree and allowing me to read letters from Edward Synge to his niece, Jane.

There are over 650 people mentioned in Synge's letters, and their identification has been my first task. I am particularly grateful to Paul Pollard, for information on Irish eighteenth-century books, booksellers and bookbinders; to David Griffin of the Irish Architectural Archive for his help in research on Edward Synge's Palace at Elphin; to Muriel McCarthy at Marsh's Library for assistance with maps and archives of the Kevin Street area. Ray Refaussé, librarian and archivist of the Representative Church Body of the Church of Ireland drew my attention to Edward Synge's papers in the archive, and Canon Leslie's records there made possible the identification of the Elphin clergy. Robert Mills, librarian of the Royal College of Physicians of Ireland was extremely kind in making the Kirkpatrick archive of Irish physicians available. Richard Luckett, Pepys Librarian at Magdalene College, Cambridge, discussed Handel in Dublin. Susan Hood's work on the development of Strokestown widened my understanding of the economy of Roscommon and I am indebted to her for providing the map of Co. Roscommon and its parishes. Arch J. Elias Jnr was generous with his information on the Synge family and on Synge's library, and with information from his forthcoming edition of the *Memoirs of Letitia Pilkington*. Patrick Kelly, for unravelling members of the Donnellan family. Sir Derek Oulton, for help with the Oulton family. Dr Rachel Bromwich, Sean Connolly, Gerard McCoy, Ian McBride, Edward McParland,

Patrick Fagan, Andrew Forrest, Ray Gillespie, the Knight of Glin, the Rev. Geoffrey Lang and David Hayton have drawn my attention to particular sources and have discussed the period with me. I am also indebted to Michael Hunter, Emma Dench, and Dorothy Porter at Birkbeck College for their help with specific points. Robin Hillyard at the Ceramics Department of the Victoria and Albert Museum, London, discussed references to china. To the staff of the Oxford English Dictionary in helping define obscure words, and to Juliet Field, who talked to me about the early use of the phrase 'spend a penny'. Tom Jago helped me with the history of wine, bottles, barrels, corks and casks, and Penelope Jago with recipes and the identification of quotations.

Dr Catherine Fahy and the staff of the National Library of Ireland have been unfailingly patient and helpful. I am also most grateful to Bernard Meehan, Keeper of Manuscripts, and his staff in the Manuscripts Department of Trinity College, Dublin; to the staff of the National Archives of Ireland, the Public Record Office of Northern Ireland, and the Royal College of Surgeons in Ireland. I am grateful to Alan Tadiello and the Master and Fellows of Balliol College, Oxford, for assistance with the Conroy Papers; the staff of the London Library; the Library of the University of London at Senate House; the Society of Genealogists, London; the Drawings Collection of the Royal Institute of British Architects. Library staff at Birkbeck College, the Wellcome Institute for the History of Medicine, the Lindley Library of the Royal Horticultural Society, the Library of the Herbarium at the Royal Botanic Gardens, Kew, and the library of the London Borough of Richmond-upon-Thames have been unfailingly helpful. I owe special thanks to Edward McParland, Antony Farrell, Vivienne Guinness, Paul Pollard and John and Ann Boland for their hospitality in Dublin, and Roy Foster and Toby Barnard in Oxford.

Roy Foster argued for the publication of the letters over many months, and Antony Farrell and David Dickson recognized their importance and have made their publication possible. Judy Collingwood, Fiona MacDonald and Alison Slienger typed the text, and Judy Collingwood's assistance was invaluable in checking Edward Synge's manuscript against the typescript and in preparing the final text for publication. Martin Rowson generously offered to draw the maps.

I look back with pleasure to a journey around Co. Roscommon with Toby Barnard and Anthony O'Connor which made me begin to understand Synge's world. Last, I thank my husband, Tom Legg, for talking about Synge over the past five years, for his help too in checking the manuscript, and for his calm support in the face of a singular obsession.

MARIE-LOUISE LEGG
Birkbeck College, London, November 1995

Biographical Register

NATHANIEL BARTON (*c.*1710-71) was born in Co. Meath, son of John Barton, dean of Ardaugh. He was admitted to TCD in 1726/7; was Scholar in 1729. Prebendary of Ballintubber, diocese of Elphin, 1741-61 and Tibohine 1761-70. He witnessed Edward Synge's will in 1761.[1]

JAMES BLAIR (1706-77) was born in Sligo and educated by his father. He was admitted to TCD in 1723 and took BA in 1727. He became vicar of Abbytown and prebendary of Kilgoghlin 1752-77 and vicar of Roscommon, Kilbride and Kilteevan 1742-77. James Blair was one of the witnesses of Edward Synge's will in 1761. The census has a Hatton Blair, who may be his mother, as a member of his household. His household had two Protestant servants and three Catholic servants.[2]

OLIVER CARY (1705-*c.*77), son of Charles Cary, was born in Carrick on Shannon. Admitted to TCD in 1720, he took BA in 1724. He was prebendary of Kilcoole, diocese of Elphin 1743-67. In 1759 he was presented to Enniscorthy, and in 1767 he resigned Kilcoole and was made precentor of Ferns. The name of Oliver Cary's first wife is not known, but in 1749 he had two children over fourteen, and four Protestant and two Catholic servants. In February 1749 he married Frances Southwell. His will was proved in 1777.[3]

LUCY CAULFIELD (?-1752) was a daughter of Frederick Trench I of Garbally, Ballinasloe and Elizabeth Warburton and sister of Frederick Trench II. In 1720 she married Tobias Caulfield of Clone, Co. Kilkenny, second son of the 1st Viscount Charlemont, and they had three daughters. She died in June 1752 (see Letter 192); he died in February 1758.[4]

CHARLES COBBE (1686-1765), archbishop of Dublin. Charles Cobbe was instituted to Killala on 20 May 1720; translated to Dromore 16 February 1727; translated to Kildare 16 March 1732 and translated to Dublin 4 March 1743, where he remained until his death on 14 April 1765.[5]

JOHN CONROY (1704-69), collector of Cork. Sole legitimate son of Farfeasa Conry, he married Elizabeth Fowke, daughter and heiress of Robert Fowke of Mallow, Co. Cork. Edward Synge took pity on the Conroys and through him Josiah Hort, archbishop of Tuam, granted John Conroy a 'bishop's lease' (a lease renewable on a fine for ever) to build a house. Their grandson John Conroy was equerry to the duke of Kent and head of the household of the duchess of Kent, Queen Victoria's mother. In 1749, John and Elizabeth Conroy's household had two Catholic and four Protestant servants.[6]

JOSHUA COOPER (1730-1800) was the eldest son of Joshua Cooper and Mary Bingham of Mercury (now Markree Castle), Co. Sligo. He was admitted to TCD in 1748 and took BA in 1752. He married Alicia Synge in May 1758. He was MP for Castlebar 1761 and Co. Sligo 1769. He became a Privy Councillor. Joshua Cooper was one of the members of the Irish Parliament who voted against Union.[7]

EDWARD CURTIS (1705-c.76) was almost certainly a relation of Edward Synge through Jane Curtis, his wife. He was a Dublin apothecary, and Synge used him to deal with his affairs in Dublin. In his will, Synge called him 'my old and useful friend', and left him £50. Curtis's own will was proved in 1776.[8]

GEORGE DAUNT (1712-86) was the second son of Henry Daunt of Knocknamana, Co. Cork. Surgeon to the Mercer's Hospital. He married his cousin Hannah Daunt. His portrait is in the Royal College of Physicians of Ireland.[9]

RICHARD DOHERTY (c.1710-60), son of captain Latham Dogherty of Co. Cork and Jane Richardson. He was distantly related to Edward Synge through his grandfather, John O'Doherty (d. 1679) who married Bridget, daughter of William Lathum and sister-in-law of Edward Synge, bishop of Cork, Cloyne and Ross. His uncle, the Rev. John Doherty, left Edward Synge senior a mourning ring in his will. Richard Doherty was admitted to TCD in 1724 aged fourteen and took BA in 1729. He was collated prebendary of Kilmacullen and vicar of Drumcliffe in 1755.[10]

CATHERINE DONNELLAN (?-1756) was a daughter of Sir John Meade who married, first Thomas Jones of Osbertstown, and second Nehemiah Donnellan II.

NEHEMIAH DONNELLAN II (c.1695-c.1771) of Artane Castle, Co. Kildare. Son of chief baron Nehemiah Donnellan I by his second wife, Martha Ussher. (She later married Philip Percival and died in August 1751, see Letter 157.) Nehemiah Donnellan II was admitted to TCD and took BA in 1718. He married Catherine Jones. They had three children: Nehemiah III, who married Catherine Nixon of Ravensdale, Co. Kildare; Catherine, 'Kitty', who married Lewis Ormsby; and Elizabeth. Nehemiah Donnellan II's will was proved in 1772. The executors of Edward Synge's will paid £20.0s.0d to Nehemiah Donnelan III.[11]

JEFFRY FRENCH (?-1754) was a son of Arthur French of Cloonyquin, Co. Roscommon and Sarah Farrell. He married Catherine Lloyd of Cloghan, Co. Roscommon. He was a barrister and member of the Middle Temple and was called to the Irish Bar in 1731. He became MP for Milborne Port 1741-47 and Tavistock 1754. Resident in England, he owned an estate in Roscommon.[12]

ROBERT FRENCH (1692-1772) was born in Liverpool, a brother of Arthur and William French. He matriculated at TCD in 1708 and took BA in 1715. He was called to Irish Bar in 1717, and became Justice of the Common Pleas in 1745. Robert French married Frances Hull of Leimcon, Co. Cork. He lived in Smithfield, Dublin and was buried in St Michans.[13]

WILLIAM FRENCH (1704-?) was born at Frenchpark in 1704. He was pre-bendary of Kilgoghlin, diocese of Elphin from 1731 to 1752, and precen-tor of Elphin 1752. He married Arabella Frances Marsh. He was one of the witnesses of Edward Synge's will in 1761.[14]

ALEXANDER GUNNING was born in Dublin and admitted to TCD in 1729 where he gained BA in 1734, MA 1739. He was collated vicar of Kilgeffin 1740. In 1749 Mr and Mrs Gunning had one child under fourteen and four Catholic servants.[15]

MRS HAMILTON Anne Hamilton (?-1770) was a sister of Arthur Dawson, baron of the Exchequer. She married the Hon. Henry Hamilton, brother of Lord Boyne. She lived in Anne Street and was a close friend of Mrs Delany.

BLANCHE OR BLANDINE JOURDAN (1705-*c.*80), French governess and com-panion to Alicia in Dublin. 'Mrs' is a courtesy title. She was a daughter of the Rev. John Jourdan of Dunshaughlin and Blandine daughter of Elie Bouhéreau, the first librarian of Archbishop Marsh's Library. Elie Bouhéreau wrote that she was baptized Blanche, '*le même nom que Blandine, celuy de la mère*'.[16]

CHARLOTTE JOURDAN (1707-?) was a daughter of John and Blandine Jour-dan and was born 14 August 1707. It is not clear whether she was mar-ried.[17]

JOHN JOURDAN (?-1758). The Rev. John Jourdan, was rector of Dun-shaughlin, Co. Meath from 1699 to his death, and prebendary and vicar of Castleknock, Co. Dublin 1751-8. Jean Jourdan had been chaplain to Lord Galway on his mission to Portugal in 1704. In 1699 he married Blan-dine, daughter of Elie Bouhéreau, the first librarian of Marsh's Library.

They had a large family, and five of his children are mentioned in Edward Synge's letters. The most important is Blandine Jourdan, Alicia Synge's governess. Jourdan's parish at Dunshaughlin adjoined Rathbeggan, one of Swift's parishes, and he made a claim on Swift for tithes. Swift also employed Jourdan as a curate in May 1734, paying him £8.[18]

JOHN LAWSON (1712-59), Alicia Synge's tutor, was born in Magherafelt, Co. Derry. He was admitted to TCD in 1720 and became a Fellow in 1735. He was Archbishop King's Lecturer in 1746 and Professor of Divinity in 1753. He was said to have had a wide acquaintance with European languages and excelled as a preacher. Author of *Lectures concerning Oratory* (1758) and *Occasional Sermons ∴* (1764).[19]

WILLIAM LENNOX of Lennox and French, bankers, Lower Ormond Street. He was married to Godfrey Wills's sister, Sarah. Lennox and French's Bank collapsed in March 1755, leaving Edward and Nicholas Synge considerably embarrassed.[20]

JANE LUSHINGTON was a sister of Frances Cary and Rachel Sandford.

WILLIAM LUSHINGTON married Jane Southwell in June 1748. He was a witness of Edward Nicholson's will. His own will was proved in 1786.[21]

JANE MAHON (?-1783), daughter of Sir Maurice Crosbie of Ardfert, Co. Kerry, married Thomas Mahon in 1735.[22]

THOMAS MAHON (1701-82) of Strokestown Park, Co. Roscommon. The eldest son of John Mahon and Eleanor Butler. He was MP for Roscommon Borough 1739-63, for Roscommon County, 1763-82. In 1749 they had five children under fourteen. They lived at Strokestown with ten Protestant and ten Catholic servants.[23]

JOHN MILLER was the steward at Kevin Street. It is likely that he was a long-standing servant in the Synge family; in 1710 Margaret, widow of Samuel Synge, dean of Kildare, left a John Miller £20. He may also have been the John Miller, a liveried servant in the household of Archbishop Edward Synge, to whom he left £10.[24]

ROBERT JOCELYN, LORD NEWPORT (1688-1756), Lord Chancellor of Ireland. He was born in Hertfordshire and became MP for Granard in 1725. He was appointed Attorney General of Ireland in 1730 and Lord Chancellor in 1739. He was one of the Lords Justice in 1746 and Speaker of the House of Lords in 1747-8. Created Viscount Jocelyn in December 1755. Newport encouraged the study of Irish history and antiquities.[25]

EDWARD NICHOLSON and HARRIET NICHOLSON of Primrose Grange, Co. Sligo, and Leinster Street. Edward Nicholson had a company office on Ormond Quay. His wife was Harriet, a daughter of Robert Sandford of Castlerea, Co. Roscommon, whose aunt was the dowager Lady Kildare. He wrote a large number of pamphlets attacking the belief in salvation through works and refuting the arguments of the Roman Catholic Church. He ran a charity school on his estate, and wrote *A method of charity-schools recommended, for giving both a religious education, and a way of livelihood to the poor children in Ireland* (Dublin 1712).[26]

LEWIS ORMSBY (1716-?) of Tubbervaddy, parish of Fuerty was a son of George Ormsby and Jane Wynne. He was admitted to TCD in 1733.[27]

THOMAS PALMER (1706-74) was born in Killcommock, Co. Longford, the son of Col Patrick Palmer. He was admitted to TCD in 1724/5 and took BA in 1729, MA 1732. He became prebendary of Termonbarry, diocese of Elphin, in 1743. A trustee of Edward Synge's estate.[28]

RICHARD ROBINSON, bishop of Killala. He was nominated bishop of Killala on 31 October 1751 and translated to Ferns on 19 April 1759; translated from Ferns to Kildare 26 March 1761. He was translated from Kildare to Armagh on 8 February 1765 and was archbishop of Armagh until his death on 10 October 1794. He was created Baron Rokeby on 26 February 1777.[29]

MRS SILVER of Dublin figures frequently in Edward Synge's letters as an adviser and model for Alicia. Unfortunately, she is not in any of the usual reference books. The will of a Joan Silver of Dublin was proved in 1760.[30]

HENRY SINGLETON (1682-1759), the Lord Chief Justice of Common Pleas. He was educated in Drogheda and matriculated from TCE in 1698. He was called to Irish Bar in 1707 and served as Chief Justice of Common Pleas 1740-53. He became Master of the Rolls in 1754. He lived in Jervis Street and at Drumcondra.[31]

HUGH STAFFORD, an apothecary. A Catholic, he lived in Elphin with his brother and mother and four Catholic servants. He was a friend of both Edward Synge and the Catholic antiquary, Charles O'Conor of Belanagare. He frequently acted as a go-between the two neighbours.[32]

ALICIA SYNGE (1733-1807), the recipient of the letters. Alicia was born on 12 December 1733. In 1758 she married Joshua Cooper of Markree, Co. Sligo, in Elphin. She died in Kevin Street, and was buried in the Vicar's Bawn, St Patrick's Cathedral, on 16 October 1807. Alicia Synge and

Joshua Cooper had at least four sons and one daughter. The eldest was Joshua Edward (1762-1837) TCD BA 1782. He married Elizabeth Lindesay and was MP for Co. Sligo from 1790 to 1806, but was certified a lunatic and dsp. Richard was born in 1763 and took BA at TCD in 1784, but died without issue. (He may be 'Squire Cooper's son' who was buried 12 August 1787 in the Synge vault in the Vicar's Bawn.) Edward (1763-1830), who may have been Richard's twin brother, took BA at TCD in 1783 and married Ann, daughter of Harry Verelst, governor of Bengal. Jane Mary died a spinster. A Robert Cooper was interred in 'the Rt. Rev. Dr Edward Synge's vault in the old churchyard, 8 March 1769'.[33]

EDWARD SYNGE (1659-1741), 'your grandfather'. Edward Synge was nominated bishop of Raphoe on 7 October 1714, translated to Tuam on 8 June 1716 and was archbishop of Tuam from 19 May 1716 until his death on 23 July 1741. He married Jane, daughter of Rev. Nicholas Proud of Cork and they had nine children. She died in 1723, and was buried in the Synge vault in the Vicar's Bawn on 24 August 1723. After her death he lived in St Stephen's Green, on the corner of Dawson Street. He died on 23 July 1741 and was buried in Tuam.[34]

EDWARD SYNGE (1691-1762), bishop of Elphin. The eldest son of Edward Synge, archbishop of Tuam, and Jane Proud. He was born in Cork and educated there by Mr Mulloy, a Scot. He entered TCD in 1706 and took BA in 1709. He became Fellow in 1710 and Junior Dean 1715 and became DD in March 1727. He married Jane Curtis of Roscrea in 1720. Edward Synge was minister of St Audeons, Dublin, and prebendary of St Patrick's and in 1727 he was minister at St Werburgh's, Dublin. Freeman of City of Dublin 1722. Provost of Tuam 1726-30; chancellor of St Patrick's 1726-30. His first promotion was when he was nominated bishop of Clonfert on 14 May 1730. He was translated to Cloyne on 22 March 1732 where he was instituted by his father, the archbishop of Tuam, on 18 February 1732. He moved to Ferns in February 1734 where he was bishop until his translation to Elphin in 1740. He was bishop of Elphin from 30 April 1740 until his death on 27 January 1762. He served on numerous Dublin bodies: as commissioner of the Tillage Act or Inland Navigation; governor of the Workhouse; governor of Dr Steevens Hospital; governor of the Blue Coat Hospital and treasurer of Erasmus Smith's Schools. He was a trustee of the Linen Manufacture. Synge was buried on 1 February 1762 in the Synge vault in the old churchyard, St Patrick's Cathedral.[35]

EDWARD SYNGE (*c.*1725-92), Edward Synge's nephew, was the only son of Nicholas Synge. He was christened on 13 September 1725 at St Kevin's Church, Dublin. Admitted to TCD 1742. He later became archdeacon of

Killala. Bishop Edward Synge officiated at his marriage to Sophia Hutchinson on 15 February 1752. He was a major beneficiary of Edward Synge's estate, inheriting all the land entailed on the male line under the will of Samuel Synge, dean of Kildare.[36]

ELIZABETH SYNGE (?-1750), 'your aunt', wife of Nicholas Synge, bishop of Killaloe and daughter of Frederick Trench II of Garbally, Ballinasloe, Co. Galway. She married Nicholas Synge on 27 October 1724. She died in November 1750 and was buried 9 November 1750 in the archbishop of Tuam's vault in the churchyard of St Patrick's Cathedral.[37]

JANE SYNGE (?-1737), 'your mother'. Edward Synge's wife was a daughter of Sarah and Robert Curtis of Roscrea, Co. Tipperary. She married Edward Synge in 1720 and they had six children. She died in 1737, and was buried on 1 January 1738 in the Synge vault in the old churchyard, St Patrick's Cathedral. 'On Sat last Died after two days illness, the Lady of the Rt. Revd the Lord Bishop of Ferns and Laughlin at his House in Kevan's Street. She was a Lady of great Charity, Piety and Humanity which makes her death greatly lamented.'[38]

JANE SYNGE (*c.*1730-63), 'your cousin'. A daughter of Nicholas and Elizabeth Synge, she lived with Alicia at Kevin Street. She died in November 1763 and was buried in the archbishop of Tuam's vault, St Patrick's Cathedral. Edward Synge left her £1000 in his will, but she only survived him by nine months.[39]

NICHOLAS SYNGE (1693-1771), 'your uncle'. Bishop of Killaloe, Edward Synge's younger brother. Born in Cork, he was admitted to TCD in 1708; gained BA in 1712; MA 1715; DD 1734. His brother installed him as precentor of Elphin in 1742 and he became archdeacon of Dublin in 1743. He was instituted as bishop of Killaloe on 23 December 1745 and remained there until his death on 19 January 1771.[40]

FREDERICK TRENCH II (1688-1752) was the son of Frederick Trench I (1633-1704) and Elizabeth Warburton. He was MP for Co. Galway and colonel commanding the County Militia. He married Elizabeth Eyre of Eyrecourt, Co. Galway. Their children appearing in the letters were Richard, Eyre, Elizabeth, who married Nicholas Synge, and Emily, who married Richard Eyre in 1752.[41]

LUKE VIPOND, son and heir of William Vipond of Dublin, gentleman. He was admitted to the Middle Temple in 1715 and to the King's Inns *c.*1734 and became attorney in the Court of Exchequer, practising in Montrath

Street. He wrote an introduction to Edward Synge, *Two Affadavits in Relation to the Demands of Tythe Agistment in the Dioces of Leighlin with an Introduction* (Dublin 1736). His will was proved in 1775.[42]

JOHN WHITCOMBE (1694-1753), bishop of Clonfert. He was born in Cork and, like Edward Synge, was educated by Mr Mulloy. He took BA at TCD in 1716, became a Fellow in 1720 and DD in 1731. He was nominated bishop of Clonfert in November 1735 and was translated to Down in March 1752. He became bishop of Down in December 1752; and was translated to Cashel in September 1752. He was bishop of Cashel until his death on 22 September 1753. In 1735 Whitcombe attracted adverse comment when he asked for a dispensation to hold a fellowship at the same time as holding a living in Co. Louth. He was thought to have used his position as tutor to the Lord Lieutenant's son to his own advantage, and was criticised for becoming a non-resident cleric in a parish which, according to Swift, 'abounds with Papists'.[43]

GODFREY WILLS (d. 1778) of Willsgrove, Ballintubber, Co. Roscommon, was a son of James Wills (d. 1731) and Martha Curtis. He was admitted to the Middle Temple in 1715. He was lieutenant colonel of the Roscommon Militia and high sheriff of Roscommon in 1755. Godfrey Wills married Sarah Montgomery; they had two sons and two daughters. Their household had four Protestant and six Catholic servants. Godfrey Wills's relationship with Edward Synge was not just as a Roscommon neighbour; he advised Synge in 1760 on the repair of the cathedral at Elphin, and was executor and trustee of Edward Synge's will.[44]

MICHAEL WILLS (*fl.* 1721-52), architect. Michael Wills is almost certainly the 'Mr Wills' referred to in Edward Synge's letters during 1747, when the new Palace was under construction. He was a son of Isaac Wills a carpenter who worked on the building of St Werburgh's church, Dublin, completed in 1719. Michael Wills was clerk of works during the building of Steeven's Hospital 1721-23 and competed unsuccessfully for St Patrick's Hospital in 1749. He was employed by the Committee for repairing St Werburgh's in 1754 after a disastrous fire and supervised the rebuilding of St Peter's (1750-52). In 1762 he was paid 'for his attendance and travelling charges &c. at the Commission held at Elphin. Paid in August last £28. 8s. 9d'. He submitted an album of 'Designs for Private Buildings of Two, three, four, five and six Rooms on a Floor And one of Eight rooms Dublin 9th May 1745' to a competition, describing them as 'Vitruvian Designs in the oeconomique Style'. Wills also wrote *A scheme for enlarging Essex-Bridge: whereby, not only three-fourths of the expence of a new bridge will be saved: but the publick shall enjoy the benefit in six months.* (Dublin 1752).[45]

NOTES

1. *Alumni*, p. 45; J.B. Leslie, 'Biographical succession list of clergy for the diocese of Elphin (1934)' RCB 61.2.5p. 66; Will of Edward Synge f. 255.

2. *Alumni*, p. 71; Leslie, Elphin pp.45-6, 143; will f.255; census, f.111.

3. *Alumni*, p.140; J.B. Leslie, *Ferns Clergy and Parishes* (Dublin 1936); Leslie, Elphin p.153; census f.2; *The Registers of St Peter and St Kevin* (Dublin 1911), p.327; Arthur Vicars, *Index to the Prerogative Wills of Ireland* (1897), p.80.

4. T. Cooke-Trench, *Memoir of the Trench Family* (Dublin 1897) Table 11, p.26.

5. *NHI* Vol. 9, pp.437, 424, 404.

6. Draft of a Conroy family history by Edward Conroy (*c.*1840-45), Conroy Papers Item 13d. Balliol College, Oxford; Katherine Hudson, *A Royal Conflict* (London 1993) 26-7; census f.45.

7. *Alumni*, p.175; Burke *Irish Family Records* (1979), p.273; *Faulkner's Dublin Journal* 3-6 June 1758; 'The Original Red List ... or the Members who voted against the Union in 1799 and 1800', Sir Jonah Barrington, *The Rise and Fall of the Irish Nation* (Dublin 1868), pp.289-90.

8. P.J. and R.V. Wallis, *Eighteenth Century Medics* (Newcastle upon Tyne 1985), p.64; will f. 254; Vicars, p.118.

9. Kirkpatrick Archive, Royal College of Physicians of Ireland.

10. J. Burke, *Landed Gentry of Ireland* (1912), p. 185; W.H. Welply, 'Irish Wills: extracted from wills deposited at the Public Record Office, Dublin' 21 vols (1938), ts in Society of Genealogists, London Vol. 7, p. 146; *Alumni*, p.235; Leslie, Elphin pp.50, 131.

11. Will f.255; Vicars, p.138.

12. Burke (1979), p.449.

13. *Alumni*, p. 309; J. Burke, *Dictionary of the Peerage and Baronetage of the British Empire* (1916), p.610; Ball Vol. ii, p.208.

14. Leslie, Elphin 26; Burke (1916), p.610; Will f.255.

15. *Alumni*, p.352; Leslie, Elphin p.154; census f.3.

16. The Diary of Dr Elie Bouhéreau of La Rochelle 1689-1719, Marsh's Library, Dublin Z2.2.2. 29 April 1705, 11 May 1705; Vicars, p.285.

17. Bouhéreau, 14 August 1707.

18. Bouhéreau 31 August 1704; J.B. Leslie, 'Biographical succession list of the clergy of the diocese of Meath', RCB ms 61.2.14.1 p.272; J.J. Digges la Touche, *The Registers of the French Conformed Churches ...* (Dublin 1893), pp.vii, 68, 97; E. Johnston, 'The diary of Elie Bouhéreau' *Huguenot Society Publications* Vol. 15 (1933-4), p.65; P.V. and D.J. Thompson, *The Account Books of Jonathan Swift* (1984), pp.xcv, 267. Swift to Knightly Chetwode, 27 September 1714. H. Williams (ed.), *The Correspondence of Jonathan Swift* (Oxford 1965) Vol. 2, p.134.

19. *Alumni*, p.486; *Dictionary of National Biography* (compact edition Oxford 1975).

20. John Watson, *The Dublin Directory for the Year 1752* (bound in with *The Gentleman's and Citizen's Almanack*), p.13; Thomas Waite to Lord Sackville, 4 March 1755. Hist. Mss. Commission Stopford Sackville Mss. Vol.1 (1904), p.238; *The Case of Edward, Lord Bishop of Elphin in Relation to Money, part of the Rents of the Ranelagh Charity, lodged in a public Bank in Dublin* (Dublin 1760), p.5; probate of Nicholas Synge's will 22 April 1768. NLI Synge Papers PC 344 (9).

21. Parish Record Society of Dublin, *The Registers of St Peter and St Kevin* (Dublin 1911), p.326; P.B Eustace, *Registry of Deeds Dublin. Abstracts of Wills* (Dublin 1954), Vol. 2, pp.612, 301; Vicars, p.294.

22. Burke (1979), p.774.

23. Burke (1979), p.774; census f.84.

24. Welply Vol.7, p.10; will of Edward Synge, archbishop of Tuam 27 March 1740 (in private possession).

25. *DNB*; Burke (1916), p.1726; F. Elrington Ball, *The Judges of Ireland 1221-1921* 2 vols (Oxford 1926) Vol.2, pp.203-04.

26. Eustace, Vol. 2, pp.612, 301; NLI ms 2102; *Directory* p.15; J. Burke, *Landed Gentry of Ireland* (1912) p.1040.

27. *Alumni*, p.642; Burke (1912), p.542.

28. Leslie, Elphin p.63; *Alumni*, p.652; will, f.255.

29. *NHI* Vol. 9, pp.437, 428, 394.

30. Vicars, p.426.

31. Ball Vol. 2, p.205.

32. Census f.1; R.E. Ward, J.F. Wrynn and C.C. Ward, *Letters of Charles O'Conor of Belanagare* (1988).

33. Burke (1979), p.273; *Faulkner's Dublin Journal* 3-6 June 1758; *Register of St Patrick's*, pp.76, 81.

34. *NHI* Vol. 9, pp.410, 432; Synge, p.xiv.

35. *NHI* Vol. 9, pp.414, 426; *St Patrick's*, p 71; *Alumni*, pp.797-8.

36. *St Peter and S. Kevin*, p.242; *Alumni*, p.798; Parish Record Society of Dublin *Marriage Entries from the Registers of the Parishes of St Andrew, St Anne, St Audoen and St Bride* (Dublin 1913), p.52; Synge, p.7; will f.254.

37. Cooke-Trench, Table 11, p.26; *St Patrick's*, p.57.

38. *Pue's Occurrences* 2 January 1738-9.

39. Synge, p.7; *St Peter and St Kevin*, p.249; *Register of St Patrick's*, p.72; will, f.254.

40. Leslie, Elphin p.26; *NHI* Vol. 9, p.418.

41. Cooke-Trench, Table 11, p.26.

42. Henry F. MacGeagh, Register of Admissions to the Honourable Society of the Middle Temple (London 1949) 3 vols. Vol.1, p.276; *King's Inns*, p.491; [John Watson], Supplement to *The Gentleman's and Citizen's Almanack* (Dublin 1760), p.58; Vicars, p.468.

43. *Alumni*, p.872; *NHI* Vol. 9, pp.434, 401, 411; Swift to the Duke of Dorset 14 January 1734/5, *Correspondence* Vol.4, pp.284-7.

44. Burke (1912), p.624; MacGeagh, Vol.1 p.294; census f.271; Edward Synge to Godfrey Wills 5 May 1761 RCB ms 426 f.14; will f.255.

45. Maurice Craig, *Dublin 1660-1800* (Dublin 1968), pp.113, 171; Kenneth Severens, 'A new perspective on Georgian building practice; the rebuilding of St. Werburgh's church, Dublin (1754-59)', *Bulletin of the Irish Georgian Society* 1992-3, 35, pp.3-11; Michael Wills, 'Album of 16 designs ...'. Drawings Collection Royal Institute of British Architects Shelf D.3 f.2 and 3.; NLI ms 2102; Christine Casey, '"De architectura": an Irish eighteenth-century gloss', *Architectural History* Vol. 37 (1994), pp.80-95.

THE SYNGE LETTERS

Bishop Edward Synge to His Daughter Alicia
Roscommon to Dublin

1746-1752

Hurry'd agen, My D.r Girl. you must be content w.th a short
letter; & Mrs Jourdan must wait, till privilege comes in. But tell
her in the mean time, That Her acc.t of N— made me laugh—
yet I fear it is more than naiveté. J'ai peur qu'elle est sotte. You'll
soon find whether she be or not; & if, you must say so, & not attempt
impossibilitys.—If you could mould her, & yo.r little pupil together, Two
better than either might come out—

I see some marks of carelessness in yo.r Madam, tho' well written.—Did you
read it over, before you seal'd it? I always do, & thus correct many mistakes.
one of yo.rs, is an omission of a Word.—None of letters, my or your, wanting.
Either will do—The next is an odd Spelling. a compound of French & English.
but, like L.d Paoli's language, neither correct. estomach. The e. French.
The h. English. One should be away. Rather the e. To write English
a la françoise; looks like affectation, tho' I charge you not w.th it—another
false Spelling. w.ch I don't charge as a fault. Lodanum.—It should be Laudanum.
But in the next line, vomitting you are to answer for. There should be but one t
I am griev'd at the unlucky accident, y.t has happen'd to the a.s.t. It must
hasten him. Mr W— was more to blame than Button, tho' He is not to be
excus'd.—Thanks to the D.r for his Ticket.—I's best have the Man on the
Spot. I'll send him off in a day or two. Let the D.r see him, a soon as He gets
to you, & support him, till a Bed is empty. John may make him ready—

A Word now for John. He knows already that his Mule waits for
Mathew. I suppose therefore y.t He'll hasta the Bellows. When they are ready.
Let him send them, & the Crockery Ware, & not wait for Sledge & Hammers.
but I did or ought to have mention'd an anvill. He must send one—Let
him choose two doz. Iron hoops for Barrels; The rest for Ridges. & so My
D.r D.r Girl for this time Adieu.   y.re Edw: Elphin

Elphin. July. 12. 1751.
Our Weather from Sunday has been fine—
To day very wet. I am in pain for my fine
wheat. Bid John not mow, till All is settled—
I fancy his grass is in a growing state—
The Pamphlet is a very bad one—

1746–7

The Bishop's Palace, Elphin, in 1813 and c.1870, after alteration (sketch from William Hampton's Road Survey Book of Co. Roscommon, courtesy the National Library of Ireland; photograph courtesy the Irish Architectural Archive).

1

My Dear Girl.

I send Billy¹ agen with your and Mrs Jourdan's² letters. Your's I see is from Miss Corbet.³ I hope there may be something in it to amuse you. I did not open Mrs Jourdan's. It came as you see it.

Before this you have seen Mr Mahon,⁴ who to be sure told you that your Brother⁵ after his very bad night was better. So indeed He was, and, for any thing I know to the contrary since, is. For I will not suffer one of them to speak a word to me about him. On Friday night I gave him up; and the first and only question I ask'd about him on Saturday morning, was whether He was alive. Some time after there were appearances of a change for the better, and they rather improv'd than otherwise, till Evening. This set me up. I gave a loose to pleasing thoughts, and was by this means so unhinged, that when towards night, I saw cause to be alarm'd; being off my guard, I was more distress'd, than I had been since his ilness. But I bless God, I in some time recover'd my self, and was tolerably well compos'd before bed time. This day I am perfectly so. Ask Mr Mahon. And upon my word, Ally, I had as good a night as I told you. And now I'll tell you what I am fix'd in on this trying occasion. In the first place I have resign'd my Boy absolutely, and quitted all thoughts of his recovery; whatever hopes there may be of it. In the next place, As even in case He should recover, there must from the nature of his distemper and the delicacy of his constitution be perhaps twenty of these turns before such an happy event; I am resolv'd not to ask a single question about him, but, whether alive; nor to suffer any person to tell me even what they think good news about him. Were I to be toss'd to and fro between hopes and fears as I was yesterday and the day before, for a Week to come, I might be destroy'd, tho' your Brother should be well at the conclusion. The most prudent way is, while doubt remains, to suppose the worst. Thus only I can be prepar'd for it, if it comes. You may depend upon it, that I do and will take all possible care of my self as to diet, sleep and exercise; and I have no doubt but that, by the blessing of God I shall get the better of this severe affliction, in case it does come, with infinitely more ease, than I did of the death of your Brother Ned.⁶ Always provided my Dear Ally helps me. If you suffer your self to be toss'd by hopes and fears, and by indulging your great tenderness for your Brother and me, alarm me about your health, I should then be sunk indeed. To prevent this, I have given you this particular account of mine own purposes and resolutions, and recommend it to you most strongly to copy them. Be no longer eager or inquisitive, impatient for the morning to have tidings, and, for the Evening, to have fresh ones. From me you shall henceforth have none, except of my self, unless it pleases God sometime hence, to put it in my power to send you certain or very probable good ones of your Brother. Compose your self, My Dear, and learn thus early that Resignation to the Will of God, which is the best, indeed only support and stay of the mind and body under afflictions. Turn your thoughts upon me, and Remember that upon your welfare, mine depends. Don't however constrain your self. Nor do I forbid crying. I rather recommend it. I believe you've already found that it gives ease, and It will always do so. But divert grief, rather than indulge it. Amuse your self with your good friends, who have taken you under their care, and I am sure will do every thing to please and serve you. I here do the same. I was yesterday at Church morning and afternoon. I dine and sup as usual. Lord Strangford[7] is still here, and so far from being a Constraint, that He really is of use to me. I use him with little form. But that little amuses. Poor Lawson,[8] however inwardly struck is, as always proper. Cary[9] takes care of every thing. His wife too does well.[10] Poor Bob King[11] is the only stupid one amongst us. Depend upon it, My Dear Ally, Fall what can fall, I shall be well if you be.

This, Hussy, is a very odd letter for me to write to a Girl of thirteen. But I flatter my self that you are your good Mother's daughter in understanding, as well as in feature. I pray God you may be like her in every thing, but her bad health. I can't wish you any thing more for your advantage. I am My dearest Dear child

> your most affectionate Father
> Edw: Elphin

Be under no concern about the visitation. Will: French[12] can do the business at Church if I don't chuse to go; and the Clergy will dine at Cary's, where I will not go. I shall be quite out of the hurry –

[To Miss Synge at Stroaks-town[13]]

1. Billy Smith or Billy Beaty: a servant.
2. Blanche or Blandine Jourdan (1705-*c*.80; see Biographical Register): French governess and companion to Alicia in Dublin.
3. The sister of the Rev. Francis Corbet, dean of St Patrick's.
4. Thomas Mahon (1701-82; see Biographical Register) of Strokestown Park, Co. Roscommon. Alicia was staying with the Mahon family.
5. Robert Synge (1725-46) was born in Dublin, the youngest son of Edward Synge and Jane Curtis. He was admitted to Trinity College Dublin on 21 January 1742/3. He died in 1746, and was buried on 7 November 1746 in the Synge vault in St Patrick's

churchyard. *Alumni*, p.798; *St Patrick's*, p.49.

6. Edward Synge (1722-40). The eldest son of Edward Synge and Jane Curtis, he was born in Dublin. He was admitted to TCD on 8 May 1739 and died later that year. He was buried on 27 December 1739/40 in the Synge vault in St Patrick's churchyard. *Alumni*, p.798; *St Patrick's*, p.41.

7. Philip Smythe, 4th viscount Strangford (1715-75). He was admitted to TCD in 1733 and took LLD in 1731. He was installed as precentor of Elphin on 26 July 1746, which dates this letter more exactly. He was dean of Derry 1752-69, rector of Maghera 1769-87, archdeacon of Derry 1769-74 and rector of Langfield in 1775. In 1741 he married Mary Jephson, a daughter of Anthony Jephson of Mallow, Co. Cork, and a cousin of Edward Synge. *Alumni*, p.767; J.B. Leslie, 'Biographical succession list of clergy for the diocese of Elphin' (1934), Representative Church Body, RCB 61.2.5, p.26; Burke, *Peerage and Baronetage of Great Britain and Ireland* (1871), p.1076; will of Margaret Synge, 1710, Welply, Vol. 7, p.10.

8. The Rev. John Lawson (1712-59; see Biographical Register): Alicia Synge's tutor.

9. The Rev. Oliver Cary (1705-*c.*77; see Biographical Register): Edward Synge's land agent. He would have been responsible for setting the tithes annually and for paying ecclesiastical charges. After the tithes were set, farmers lodged bonds with the landlord or his receiver, and the agent collected the tithes when they were due, both in cash and in kind. For this work he was paid a fee; Jonathan Swift paid his land agent 12d in the £. On Edward Synge's estate, Oliver Cary would have contracted labour and, in Edward Synge's absence, would have supervised work on the church, the house and the garden. Thompson, *Account Books*, p.cxv.

10. The maiden name of Lucy, Oliver Cary's first wife, is not known.

11. Bob King: not known.

12. The Rev. William French (1704-?; see Biographical Register).

13. Strokestown Park, Co. Roscommon. The original seventeenth-century house was altered and refaced in the nineteenth century. It has a central block which is joined by sweeps to two wings, thought to have been added in the 1730s. Until recently, these alterations were thought to have been designed by Richard Castle, but they are now believed to have been carried out by a local architect, perhaps Michael Wills. Bence-Jones p.267; Giles Worsley, 'Strokestown Park', *Country Life*, 1 April 1993.

2

Glanmore[1], May 6, 1747

It will please you, my Dear Girl, to know, that I am thus far safe and well on my journey; and have had no accident on the road. The Days were hot, and part of the road a little dusty. But neither heat nor dust incommoded me in the Chariot. I had company both at dinner, and at night, and, by good luck, agreable; Dr Disney,[2] and Eyre Trench[3] at Kilcock,[4] and young Mr Echlin[5] at Kinnegad.[6] But you know this already, if they took care to do what I desir'd. To morrow early, God willing, I propose to go off to Elphin;

but hope, before I set out, to have the letter you promis'd, and an account that you are quite well. Nothing now can be so great a Cordial to your most affectionate Father.

[To Miss Synge/at the Lord Bp of Elphin's/in Kevin-Street/Dublin. Stamped `Ballymahon']

1. Glanmore, between Ballymahon and Keenagh, Co. Longford, was about fifty-five miles from Dublin. The home of Thomas Palmer and his family.
2. Dr Brabazon Disney. DD. (1711-90) became professor of laws at Trinity College, Dublin in 1747 and Archbishop King's lecturer in 1754. He was professor of divinity in 1759 and chancellor of Armagh. *Alumni*, p.231.
3. Eyre Trench (?-*c*.1776; see Biographical Register).
4. Kilcock, Co. Kildare, sixteen miles from Dublin.
5. Mr Echlin: not known.
6. Kinnegad, Co. Westmeath, thirty-nine miles from Dublin.

3

Elphin May 9, 1747

Here I am, My Dear, very well, I bless God, tho' somewhat solitary: so I must ever be when you are not with me. But I can bear that, or any thing else, for your good.

Our parting brought to my mind a former one, when I left your good Mother[1] and my Family to go to Cloyn.[2] You were then an infant, and could give me pleasure only by looking at you – yet I was sorry to part with you. But I had then other objects of my tenderest affection. You only now remain.[3] God of his mercy spare you to me, to be the comfort and support of my decline.

Next to the discharge of my Duty, Nothing in this World is of so much consequence to me as your Welfare, not meerly because you are my Child, mine only Child; but because I hope and believe you'll be worthy of your Mother. May you be like her in everything, but her ill health. The Establishment of yours is my most important concern. Right sorry I am that it is so delicate – But I have good hope it will improve, and in time be confirm'd. In this hope, I denied my self the pleasure of bringing you down. My business call'd me hither, and I judg'd it too early to venture my whole treasure with me. I did not indeed expect so very warm Weather. But that brought to my mind your first journey to Elphin, and the effects of it. The night you came here, I would have given half I was worth, that I had not brought you from town. I should now on a like occasion give all – But I thought it best not to run the risque. In a little time Riding and the

German Spa[4] will, by God's blessing make you stout, and fit for any under-taking. In the use of these Dr Anderson[5] and your trusty old Adviser Ned Curtis[6] will direct you. Amusements too will be of use. In these Let Mrs Jourdan be your guide. She knows that I desire you should take all that are innocent and prudent. But don't mind Lawson nor any such idle fellows who never allow an objection to what they have a mind to. Tell Mrs Jour-dan she must not mind them either. Once at Strokes'town she own'd her self, tho' by another hand, to be ore-perswaded. Assoon as your Doctors agree to it, I would have you wait on Mrs Palliser.[7] You may introduce your selves, or take Ned, if in town, to do it. Excuse my not seeing her. You know the hurry I was in. But I had another reason for declining the inter-view – you'll too easily guess it. A visit to Artaign[8] on a fine day, will be pleasant. Nor am I against your taking a Walk or two in the Green[9] on a very fine Evening. Let it not be too late. You'll probably have many invita-tions abroad. Do not decline any, which are proper – In this point Mrs Jourdan's prudence will aid yours – But I shall go on pratling and advis-ing, till I have room for nothing else.

Cary met me at Glanmore, and brought rather a Command than an invitation from our friends at Strokes'town, to dine with them next day – I comply'd, but with reluctance. I was impatient to be at home. I found no one there, but the good Woman, her husband, the Children, the Major[10] and Garret.[11] The Solitude appear'd very strange.

Cary heard there, that Mrs Mahon[12] was to go to Dublin, for a very short time, next Monday. Learn from the Ladys, when she gets thither. I believe I need not prompt you to pay her all the civilitys you can.

As soon as I got hither, I run to my building, and had the pleasure to find every thing very well.[13] But I came just time enough to prevent mis-chief. The Plaisterer was doing things in a way I did not like. He is himself honest, and I believe, skilfull. But His Workmen are Rogues and idlers; and He has the Spirit of Government no more than poor Shannon,[14] or Mrs Hunter.[15] But All will now be right. The Scaffolding is all down, and the House almost pointed, and It's figure is vastly more beautifull than I expected it would be. Conceited people may censure it's plainess. But I don't wish it any further ornament than it has. As far as I can yet judge, the inside will be very commodious, and comfortable. Were it finish'd and season'd, I could wish you here this minute. But I hope we may yet pass some pleasant days together in it.

I have seen your Peacocks.[16] They are very well. You have now three hens and two cocks. I hope this Season will produce many more. Mrs Cary has promis'd to take great care of them. Your Stock too is well, all but the Mother Cow, who, I fear is declining, and your little Garden is prettily adorn'd. But not quite so prettily as the flower garden in Kevin-Street.

Young Nicholson is here. He came to see me with his Nurse Mrs Cary, who has indeed been an excellent one. He is as stout a fine boy as I ever saw. He was very angry that Miss Synge was not come with her Babies.[17] I saw little Jeny[18] at Strokes'town; She is a very fine Girl, but has been out of order with teeth. Your little Girl,[19] and all the rest at Glanmore are very well. But I believe you have before this seen Mrs Palmer.[20]

Between Shannon and me, some Maps were forgot. They lye in the lower drawer of the old Scriptoire in the Study. Roll or fold up all the Parchment ones, and get Palmer,[21] when he returns with his Wife, to put them up in his Cloak-bag. He can easily send them from Glanmore hither. Or perhaps you may get Mrs Mahon to bring them down. You may just hint it. But take care of incommoding her; and Try, if you can, to send them by him or her who leaves town first. You may in the same way send down the *History of Patriotism*,[22] the *Case of the Genoese*,[23] which lyes with it on my Table, and any other Pamphlets which come out, and Lawson tells you are worth reading. I see one Advertis'd of the Adventures of the Young Pretender.[24] But possibly it is Grub street. He'll tell you.

I am glad your Mare is so well. In a little time I hope to hear that you've agen rode her. My little horse fell lame much in the same way on the road. But He is almost well. I ride the chesnut, who goes [as – *damaged ms*] quietly as I could wish. I was on his back yesterday at six, and view'd every inch of the Demesne. All things are in a fine way. But my wheat the most surprizing sight of the kind I ever saw. A fine season will make the Crop glorious. A Wet one ruins it.

I must now conclude, my Dear, for the same reason that you do, because I have no more room. But I don't fear your being displeas'd at my very long letter: Nor need you have made any Apology for yours. Your prattle either with tongue or pen, will always be pleasing to me. But I would not have you distress your Self for my entertainment. Write just as time, and other Engagements allow. But whatever you write, let it be all your own. Your letters to others, you are very right to submit to Mrs Jourdan's corrections, or to form from her hints. But, *Sauve vôtre modestie*, I must see you naked. Don't be quite careless, nor labour too much about your writing. Time and practice, with a little care, will bring you to write well and quick. It pleases me much, that tho' part of your letter was wrote in a hurry, yet there is not a word mispelt but Dada, and Jeny. Thus they ought to be. My proper Compliments at Stephen's-green[25] and York-street,[26] and to Madam Flirt[27] and Mrs Jourdan. I long for Monday as much as you do; and hope for as comfortable tidings as I send. I am My Dear Girl

Your most affect Edw. Elphin

Since I wrote this I have learn'd that Mrs Mahon leaves home to morrow. She'll be in town on Monday night.

Tell Mrs Jourdan that between her and Wilkinson,[28] I have the poorest pimping Soop-dish, that I ever saw. It is less than the one I complain'd of. Will French is here. He gives his service to you all.

Carlboe[29] has measur'd the new Soup dish, and the old one of which I complain'd last year, which, it seems, is still here – I have order'd him therefore to lay the new one by, in order to return it. Once using I suppose will not hinder Wilkinson from taking it. Desire Mrs Jourdan to send for him immediatly, and order him to make one out of hand, that will hold a Pottle more. He must not make it broader, but deeper, and the Rim broader. He'll say perhaps He has no mold. But He must find one or Some one else must be apply'd to. I must have this as I direct, if Dublin will give it me

1. Jane Synge (d.1738) Edward Synge's late wife.

2. Cloyne, Co. Cork. Seat of the bishops of Cloyne (see Biographical Register).

3. Edward Synge was instituted as bishop of Cloyne on 18 February 1732 and remained there until February 1734. At the time he went to Cloyne he had five children living: Edward, Catherine and Mary who died in 1733/4, Robert and Alicia, who was born on 12 December 1733. *NHI*, Vol. 9, p.414.

4. Spa water was imported to Dublin from England and the continent. 'German Spa Water Ware-House in Dame Street. German Spa Water, in Whole and Half flasks and other Mineral Water sold by Wholesale and Retail by Edward Sankey.' *Faulkner's Dublin Journal*, 27-30 June 1747.

5. John Anderson (*c.*1708-62), physician, was born in Dublin. He took BA at TCD in 1732; MB 1738, and was admitted to the King's and Queen's College of Physicians of Ireland in 1740. He became fellow in 1742/3 and president in 1751. He was Physician to the Mercer's Hospital. Kirkpatrick Archive. Royal College of Physicians of Ireland.

6. Edward Curtis (1705-*c.*76; see Biographical Register): apothecary.

7. Possibly Mary, daughter of Matthew Pennefather of Cashel, who married William Palliser (1698-1768), a son of William Palliser, archbishop of Cashel (d.1727). Burke (1912), p.548.

8. Artane Castle, Co. Dublin, was the seat of the Donnellan family. 'The hamlet of Artane has a pleasant appearance, and occupies an agreeable site, near the northern shore of Dublin bay, about two miles from Dublin Castle. A castle which stood at the hamlet about 17 years ago [1827] and was then in habitable repair, was long the seat of the Doxellans [*sic*] of Ravensdale.' *Parliamentary Gazetteer of Ireland 1842-44* (Dublin 1844), p.87.

9. St Stephen's Green, Dublin, five minutes walk from the Synge house in Kevin Street. Stephen's Green was first developed by the City Council in the 1660s.

10. Possibly William Mahon, who was a 2nd lieutenant in Colonel Richbell's Regiment of Foot, 29 October 1745. PRO WO64/9, f.197.

11. The Rev. Richard Garrett (?-1769) was admitted to TCD in 1727 and took BA in 1731. He was vicar of Bumlin, Kiltrustan and Lisonuffy, diocese of Elphin. Possibly the Richard Garrett who witnessed Edward Synge senior's will in 1740. *Alumni*, p.318; Leslie, Elphin, p.111-12; Welply, Vol. 12, p.6.

12. Jane Mahon: wife of Thomas Mahon (?-1783; see Biographical Register).

13. In 1747, Edward Synge was still living in the old Palace at Elphin. Of the old Palace, in 1720 Synge's father, Archbishop Edward Synge of Tuam, reported to Archbishop Wake that bishop Hodson, who had died in 1685, had 'left the shell of a very good Episcopal house at Elphin, of which no care has since been taken. And tho' it look'd pretty to the Eye, when I was there near two years agoe, yet I was told that the Roof was very decay'd and all the Timber within it very much injur'd by the weather.' Ten years later, Robert Howard, Edward Synge's immediate predecessor as bishop of Elphin, described the old Palace as 'very bad, ill-contrived, for some of my predecessors were extreme bad architects. We should have drowned in the ground room if I had not immediately made a great drain.' Synge to Wake, 12 April 1720. TCD ms 6201; Robert Howard to Hugh Howard, 29 July 1730. NLI, Wicklow papers, PC 327. I am indebted to Dr T.C. Barnard for drawing my attention to this reference.

14. Shannon was Edward Synge's steward at Elphin. In 1750 Synge himself defined the duties of his steward, 'the Orderly Government of my Servants, the buying in all provisions for my house and Stables, and inspecting the consumption of the latter, and the keeping of accounts.' Letter 106. *Alumni*, p.204; Leslie, Elphin, p.60; will, f.254; Vicars, p.188.

15. Mrs Hunter: a housekeeper.

16. Peacocks were not just ornamental. Lord Orrery ate a pea-chick for dinner in 1743. Lord Orrery to Lady Orrery 18 February 1743/4. Countess of Orrery (ed.), Earl of Orrery, *The Orrery Papers* 2 vols (1903) Vol.2, p.185.

17. The Nicholsons and the Carys were related through Harriet Nicholson, who was a Miss Sandford of Castlerea, Co. Roscommon. Young Nicholson is not known. Burke, *LGI*, p.1040.

18. Jane, daughter of Thomas and Jane Mahon. She married George Knox. Burke, *IFR*, p.774.

19. Anne Palmer, for whom Alicia was to stand as godmother. See Letter 46.

20. Formerly Mary Cope of Shrule, Co. Longford. Died 1774. Leslie, Elphin p.63.

21. The Rev. Thomas Palmer (1706-74; see Biographical Register).

22. *The history of the rise, progress and tendency of patriotism drawn from a close observation of the conduct of many of our late illustrious patriots. With a curious dissertation on the diseases and cures of patriots. Necessary to be read by all freeholders and voting families of all kinds.* Dedicated to the Right Hon the Earl of Chesterfield. By a freeholder. The third edition. (London: printed. Dublin: re-printed by George Faulkner, 1747.) Advertised *Faulkner's Dublin Journal*, 9 May 1747.

23. [G. Gastaldi?] *The case of the Genoese impartially stated; wherein the conduct of that people, the Austrians and the Piedmontese, during the late convulsions is candidly examined. ... In a letter to a Member of Parliament* (London: printed for L. Gilliver [1747]).

24. [Ralph Griffiths] *Ascanius or, the young Adventurer. A true history. Translated from a manuscript privately handed about at the Court at Versailles. Containing a particular account of all that happened to a certain Person during his wandering in the North, from his first Arrival there in August 1745, to his final Escape on September 19 in the following year. The whole introduced with a more critical and candid History of the Rise, Progress and Extinction of the late Rebellion than any yet published and interspersed with Remarks on the Characters of the principal Persons who appeared in the interest of Ascanius particularly the Celebrated Miss C , Miss MacDonald, the Duke of Perth, the Earl of Kilmarnock, Messrs Sheridan and Sullivan &c &c.* This day published by the Printer hereof. Price 6d. Advertised *Faulkner's Dublin Journal*, 2-5 May 1747.

25. Edward Synge's brother Nicholas, bishop of Killaloe, and his family lived at St

Stephen's Green.

26. Lord Newport, the Lord Chancellor of Ireland, lived on the west side of St Stephen's Green. The house was referred to as being in York Street as it was entered from that side. *Georgian Society Records* Vol.2, p.99.

27. Jane Synge (*c.*1730-63; see Biographical Register). She lived with Alicia at Kevin Street.

28. Possibly John Wilkinson of Golden Lane or Abraham Wilkinson of Park Street, merchants. Watson (1752), p.21.

29. Laurence Carleboe was Edward Synge's cook. Synge left him £10 in his will. His own will was proved in 1774. Will of Edward Synge, 31 July 1761, PRO, PROB 11/894/563, f.254; Vicars, p.76.

4

Elphin. May 13, 1747

My Dear Girl's long letters are very pleasing; and if you manage so as not to distress or embarrass your self with writing them, I care not how long they are – you may do as I do, Take a whole sheet, and fill it with Girl's prattle as I do mine with Old Dad's. I am pleas'd to see, that your last is much better wrote, than the former, and in the whole, I see but two false spellings; *siting.* It should be *sitting. droped.* It should be *dropped.* But you quite neglect stopping your letters. This, My Dear, you must take care of.

I did believe your hoarseness would end in a Cough. I had a letter from the Doctor which gave me great comfort about it. I hope by this time it is gone – I bless God I am very well; and if I have the joyfull tidings that you are so, I shall be easy and happy, even at this distance from you – You must be so too, Huzzy – I would not for the World, but you lov'd me. But you must love with discretion, and suffer not your fondness to be, or grow such as to make you uneasy, for what can't be avoided. After a short absence We shall see each other with more pleasure.

I am glad the Post-chaise is come. As you had the notice of it, from Mr Letablaire,[1] I suppose Lady Kildare[2] is arriv'd, and Mr and Mrs Nicholson[3] with her. Pray send to him, if you have not your heels at liberty to go to her, and tell him, with my service, that I beg the favour of him to see it put together and to order Jones[4] to make proper harness for it, and a Box for the Seat, which is not yet made. Desire him in short to order every thing that may put it into complete traveling order. Mrs Mahon is in town. So you must get the Dimensions of the Plate-basket from her there.

Bid John Miller[5] pay Mr Ross.[6] What I objected to was the Price of your Saddle. But I must yield, since he will not, and if the Saddle be good in proportion, shall not grudge the Expense. I shall think nothing too dear, that is of use to you. I am rejoic'd that your Mare is well – Sympson[7] advises right, that one of the Girls should ride her, before you do. But don't let that be, till you are ready, to ride her your Self. The longer time She is allow'd, to recover perfectly of her strain, the greater security against a return. My black horse is quite well. But I don't yet ride him. The Chesnut is very quiet. Send to Jac. Curtiss[8] for the Bill of your Gold lace, and let it be paid.

I thank you for *Ascanius.* You have spelt that wrong, putting an o before the u. But that I don't charge to your Account. 'Tis a Latin-word.[9] However if you observe a little, you'll learn how to Spell such words when they come in your Way. By dipping a little into it, I fancy, it is a Romance. But it will divert in a rainy day. The Advertisement[10] I had seen before. But I am mighty glad you sent it. It will afford some diversion with Mrs Cary. Since you make so good use of your franks as to save me a great deal of postage, Send Will[11] to Mr Wild, Lord C[hancello]r's Gent,[12] with your Service, and desire him to get you some more. Lord C[hancello]r[13] told me, He would give them from time to time. They serve for any weight.[14]

I am sorry, Charlotte[15] did not come to town, with Miss Vignoles,[16] but more for the reason of her not coming. It will please me much to know that Mr Jourdan[17] is recover'd. I wish him very well for his own, and his family's sake; but particularly for Mrs Jourdan's whose affection to him, I cannot but approve of, at the same time, that I wish it were, as I wish yours to me, less passionate. 'Tis quite disinterested. For she, I hope, believes that I think her, more my charge than his. So must you. Between us She must be made easy for life. I hope it will fall to your share to make her so, as a friend and companion, when her Care of you, as a Governess, is no longer necessary.[18]

I don't know, whether Mr Palmer entertain'd you, with the Adventure of Cary's, or rather my Bullock, which Cary very cunningly sent to Dublin, by a fellow who lam'd him on the road. It paid me in laughing, what I've lost in his price – and I shall besides win half a Crown from Sage Nol.

I am glad Bob Curtis[19] got a Praemium. His Father[20] gave me an account of it, and at the same time an indifferent one of his own health. I am in pain for him, and his family. For I really have no great opinion of his long life.

By the time you get this, Lyons the Carr-man will be in town. We are in great want of an Iron-Coal-Box. That We had, has holes, and they use a wooden one, which may be dangerous. Desire Mrs Jourdan, to send John Miller if in town, or Will Conry, to Turner's[21] for a good one, not quite so clumsy as the last, and let Lyons bring it down. Mr Cary desires that He may also bring down some bundle, I know not what, that is left for him in Kevin-street.

You must also order Jac. Davies[22] to send down by him six of the Watering Bridles, carefully made up so as not to be injur'd by the Carriage. Let him count them before Lyons and then make them up. I am in very great distress for want of them, and must therefore have them be my stay here ever so short. They ride the Horses to air and to water in their Collars, and on Sunday evening I saw three of them galloping about the fields. They had broke from their leaders. I believe this has happen'd oft'ner, but then it could not be conceal'd. This is a piece of poor John's[23] Wisdom. He told me He wanted bridles to carry down, hoping, I suppose, to have a new set. I bid him take down those He had. He said He would, but did not. His pretence is He had not room.

It just comes into my mind to give you a little bit of advice about your Diet. I have hinted it formerly, but think it of use to speak more plainly. You appear fonder of broil'd meats, and meats roasted high and brown, than of any other. I apprehend that both are bad for your little scurvy,[24] which may grow worse, and invade your face. Think of that and Guard in time against what you'll be sorry for, if it comes. But consult the Doctor and Ned Curtis, and follow their Advice.

Direct John Miller to go to Mr Nelson,[25] and give him my Service, and desire him to chuse for him any where, that He pleases 8. Beams. each 16f:6 inches long and a foot Square; and as soon as He can get Carriage convenient, let him send them down. If Mr Nelson be not well, let him get Mr Eaton[26] to assist him. Direct him also to wait on Mr Wills[27] on Saturday morning, to whom I write about some things, which are to be order'd, or not, as He approves, or disapproves. John must follow his directions, taking Nelson, or Eaton to his assistance. Get a note of £10 from Ned Curtis or Mr Lennox,[28] and give it to Sympson, when your Mare is quite well, not before. But let him know that you have such a note for him. This may make him more carefull and exact, about what is of the greatest importance to me, because it affects you. I hope by the time you are remounted, 'Spark', and 'Cream' will be ready to receive their riders. I long to have an Account of all my Damsels being on horse-back. Direct John Miller to have 'Nancy' shoed up, and trial made whether she goes firm. If she won't do for either Jeny, or Mrs Jourdan, or they do not want her, I'll order her down here.

And now that I have wrote every thing like business, that has come to my mind, I'll tell you my way of life, which I believe you'll be pleas'd to know. I rise early and get upon my Horse, and visit every Corner of my Land, where any thing is doing, or is done so as to please. Cary has done a great deal; but He is not so pushing, as I wish he were. I have set many hands to work, where He had few or none, so as to push with great vigour, what He was loitering about. Among other things I have set fifty fellows and some horses and Tumbrils about levelling and dressing a field which is much more crooked than that I was managing last year, which is now so pretty that it encourages me to go on with the other. This is at present my Hobby-horse. I visit it three or four times before I return, giving orders which do, at least I fancy they do, help the Work. I carry out bread in my pocket. About 10 – I return and with the remainder of my bread, take a Draught of Sweet-Whey, which pleases me much. They make it very good. Soon after this, when Shannon has brought me the Bill of Fare, and Carleboe is chid or commended, I walk out to my building where I have employment for an hour. Everything there is very well. But As I told you in my last, I came just in time to prevent mischief. The Plaisterer was going on in a way not to be approv'd. But luckily His fine Work was but a very little way advanced. I have turn'd off one of his Botches. I hope never a one remains; and He has [sent *damaged ms*] for two good hands from Dublin. Till they come, His fine work must stop. My Masons give me no trouble. There are but three at work, and they go on very well, tho' Byrne[29] was drunk yesterday, and as great as a Prince. They have almost finish'd the pointing the house, which indeed makes a beautifull figure. As soon as that is done, I must set about digging the Area round it. This will be a new Work, and a troublesome one. Having view'd and directed every thing, I return between eleven and twelve and till I am quite cool or longer amuse my Self with a Book. Then dress, and perhaps walk out agen before dinner. At dinner I have not yet wanted Company: Nor am I likely to want, and then only I much like it, such at least as is at present in my power. Meat and Wine being over, I pack them off, and retire to a Walk or a Book, or thinking of you, and so pass my time very agreably till the day closes. At supper Cary and I, except one night that Will. French made a third, sit down to some little thing, and one bottle, of which Cary takes his share more kindly than Mrs Jourdan does hers – and so to bed, where I have slept very well every night since I came hither. This is my Course; and if I have the comfort of knowing twice a Week that you, My Dear, are well, I shall pass my time as agreably as I can without you; and, by God's blessing, return to you in better health, and more cheerfull than I left you. But how goes the family? I know but little of it. At my first coming I spoke to Mrs Heap[30] in general, and she engag'd for every thing, even Washing, which was what I fear'd most being at a loss about. Jennet[31] drudges and scolds as usual. They have got a red-hair'd Wench, and Paddy Lough[32] in the Kitchen and Carlboe makes no complaints; and there is a little Stump of a Chamber-maid, who with Jennet's or Mrs Heap's help, Shannon standing by, makes my Bed very well, and keeps the rooms as they should be. Thus you've a full and true account of my living at Elphin. In return, you may, when you've nothing else to write, tell me of yours in Dublin, particularly how Mr Robinson,[33] the old Scotch-man and the rest of the men behave themselves. The Women I don't doubt about, nor have I any thing to say to them.

Gunning[34] went off yesterday morning to conclude his match. I know not but He may be marry'd before his return. I try'd once or twice, with Mrs Cary's assistance too, to get a little mirth out of him upon the occasion. But He is so completely insipid, that It was to no purpose. Temper in him supplies the place of skill. He feels nothing, and will I believe meet his Bride with as solemn an Air, as He may have, if he burys her. Perhaps more so. By all I can learn He marrys very prudently. The young Woman by his own account is 25. or 26. neither ugly nor handsome, tall, nor low, fair rather than brown and has £300. They who know her and her family speak very well of them, and say she'll make a very fit Wife, for him and his school.[35]

And now, My Dear, I must stop. My paper is more than full. But writing to you is as agreable an amusement at least, as any I have. God of his mercy bless you and preserve you to –

your most affectionate Father
Edw: Elphin

My service and blessing at the Green. You do not mention them. They tell me this minute that they want in the Kitchen 3 Hair Sieves for Carleboe, and a Jack-line.[36] The Sieves Mrs Jourdan will order. I wish they could be got to come down by Lyons. Bid John Miller get the Jack-line, of the strongest kind. The last was bad. Let him tell Bagshaw[37] this, and order him to make one on purpose. We can wait a while for a good one. Desire Ned Curtis to send me down, some powder and shot, the usual quantity, and tell him I expect now and then a letter from him.

Never send me two covers of the Chancellor by the same post.[38]

The Weather has been various since I came here. Have a care of cold which quickly succeeds to heat, and in Cold or doubtfull days chuse the four Wheel'd Chair rather than riding. Be bold, but not too bold.

Cary is come in with his Commission. John Miller must get half a dozen Collars and Haims[40] of the best kind to be sent down by Lyons, who I now find does not go to town quite so soon as I thought, so that Every thing else I have wrote for as well as these Collars may be got ready for him to bring down. Tell John We want no straddles.

1. The Rev. Daniel Letablère (1709-75) was a son of René de la Douespe Letablère, an ensign in du Cambon's regiment which fought at the battle of the Boyne. Admitted to TCD 1725, he took BA 1731; MA 1734, DD 1748. He became vicar of Larabryan 1742, rector of Rathangan; prebendary of St Patrick's and dean of Tuam 1750; prebendary of Yagoe 1759; prebendary of Maynooth 1763. Lord Kildare was Daniel

Letablère's patron; he presented him to the benefices of Larabryan and Rathnagan, and to Yagoe. Letablère married first in 1749, Madeleine Vareilles and second in 1760 Blandine Jourdan. He is buried in St Patrick's Cathedral. T.P.Le Fanu, 'The Huguenot Churches of Dublin and their Ministers', *Proceedings of the Huguenot Society of London*, Vol. 8 (1905-8) p.133; *Alumni*, p.498; Lawlor, *Fasti*, pp.186, 131; *Correspondence of Emily Duchess of Leinster*, Vol. 1, pp.83, 91, 98, 129, 149; *Gentleman's Magazine* (1775), p.454.

2. Mary, dowager Lady Kildare (1692-1780). She was born Mary O'Brien, daughter of the 3rd earl of Inchiquin and married the 19th earl of Kildare in 1708-9. Burke, (1916), p.1242.

3. Edward and Harriet Nicholson (see Biographical Register).

4. Jones: coachbuilder.

5. John Miller: the steward at Kevin Street (see Biographical Register).

6. Andrew Ross: saddler, Dame Street. Watson (1760), p.37.

7. Sympson: a horse-dealer.

8. John Curtis, laceman, Fishamble Street. Watson (1752), p.9.

9. The title of the book parallels Charles Edward Stuart's journey to Italy with that of Ascanius, the son of Aeneas, whose travels with his father are narrated in Virgil's *Aeneid*.

10. The Advertisement: not known.

11. William Conry: Alicia Synge's manservant. A William Conry, servant, witnessed a lease for Edward Synge, bishop of Elphin to John Egan, 12 May 1749, Registry of Deeds, 135 232 91190.

12. Lord Chancellor's Gentlemen were members of his official household.

13. Robert Jocelyn, Lord Newport (1688-1756; see Biographical Register): Lord Chancellor of Ireland.

14. Members of Parliament could frank letters for friends to allow them free postage. A stamp marking letters 'Free' had been introduced in 1706. Mairead Reynolds, *A History of the Irish Post Office* (Dublin 1983), p.39.

15. Charlotte Jourdan (1707-?; see Biographical Register).

16. Miss Vignoles may be Isabel Vignoles of Dunshauglin, Co. Meath, whose will was proved in 1758. It was a common name in the Dublin Huguenot community; Elie Bouhéreau, who paid monies on Lord Galway's account to French people living in Dublin, made quarterly payments to a Made. de Vignoles. A Mr Vignolles was a cleric at St Anne's Dublin in 1749. Vicars, 468; Bouhéreau, accounts 11 December 1706; 30 January 1708/9; *St Andrew, St Anne, St Audoen and St Bride*, p.15.

17. The Rev. John Jourdan (?-1758; see Biographical Register).

18. Blandine Jourdan married Daniel Letablère at St Kevin's Church on 9 April 1760, and the ceremony was performed by Edward Synge. A week before, Edward and Alicia Synge settled an annuity on her for £100 a year. *St Peter and St Kevin*, p.334; Synge to Jourdan, 1 April 1760, RD 204 252 135223.

19. Robert Curtis was a son of Rev. Robert Curtis, Edward Synge's brother-in-law. He was born in Co. Tipperary. Admitted to TCD in 1746 aged seventeen, he gained BA 1750; MA 1753. He became prebendary of Tomgraney. Edward Synge left him some books in his will. He is probably the Rev. Robert Curtis who married Nicholas Synge's daughter, Margery, and whose own will was proved in 1799. *Alumni*, p.204; Leslie, Elphin, p.69; will, f.2545; Vicars, p.188.

20. Robert Curtis (?-1765): Alicia's uncle. Born in Dublin, he was a son of Robert Curtis MP for Duleek. He was educated at Eton and entered TCD in 1709, aged seventeen and took BA 1714; MA 1719. *Alumni*, p.204; J.B. Leslie, *Biographical succession list of*

clergy for the diocese of Killaloe (1946) p.67; Eustace, Vol. 2, pp.182-3.

21. Timothy Turner, ironmonger, College Green, or Richard Turner, ironmonger, Dame Street. Watson (1752), p.25.

22. John Davies: a groom at Kevin Street.

23. John Aske: groom at Elphin.

24. Scurvy is caused by a lack of vitamin C in the diet. The symptoms are swollen and bleeding gums and lethargy. In the eighteenth century scurvy was attributed to an excess of undesirable elements in the diet, rather than a lack of nutrition. Roger K. French, 'Scurvy' Kenneth Kiple (ed.), *Cambridge World History of Human Disease* (Cambridge 1993), pp.1000-1, 1004.

25. Mr Nelson: not known.

26. Richard Eaton: glazier, York Street. Watson p.15.

27. Michael Wills (*fl.* 1721-1752), architect (see Biographical Register).

28. William Lennox: Edward Synge's banker (see Biographical Register).

29. Byrne: a workman.

30. Mrs Heap: the housekeeper at Elphin.

31. Jennet: the still-room maid at Elphin.

32. Paddy Lough: kitchen hand.

33. Mr Robinson: in 1747 an apprentice cook at Kevin Street.

34. The Rev. Alexander Gunning (see Biographical Register).

35. Alexander Gunning was the master of Bishop Hodson's Grammar School, Elphin, founded in 1685. Michael Quane, 'Bishop Hodson's Grammar School, Elphin', *Journal of the Royal Society of Antiquaries of Ireland,* 96 (1966), pp.157-77.

36. Jack-line: part of the mechanism of a spit to turn and roast meat.

37. Bagshaw: not known.

38. The franking system was much abused; in 1764 an act of parliament was passed to prevent fraud. Reynolds, p.39.

40. Haims: curved pieces of wood forming the collar for a draught horse.

5

Elphin May 16, 1747

Last post I wrote you a very long letter, Huzzy. You must not expect the same always. I shall not have leisure or materials for them. I have not very much to say, this time – yet I take a sheet – Possibly something may start up, that I don't now think of, to fill it.

I bless God I am very well, and much rejoic'd at the good account you give of your Self, and the Doctor of you. Pray give him my service, and Tell him I hope he'll favour me often with letters. But he will, I also hope, excuse me from returns when I have nothing to say, but what He knows already, That I wish you confirm'd health, and hope by God's blessing on his and trusty Ned's endeavours you'll soon have it.

Even this slight disorder occasions me to reflect on the greater anxiety

I should have, if you were here, where you could not have either of their advice, nor more than a chance for Dr Mulloy's.[1] I have not seen him, but hear He is much impair'd in his health. His old fate attends him. He is now engag'd in a quarrel with his Father and Mother in Law, the beginnings of which set them at variance for a time with each other. The story is on his side ridiculous enough – I can't write the particulars. What pity it is, that A Man so valuable as a Physician, should be of so perverse and crooked a temper, as every where to give offence, or to take it. Your friend Diganan[2] was here on Thursday. He is much mended in his looks, and the same Man in every thing else. Barton[3] was with me when He came hither. He found us at breakfast; and gave us a very good laugh. Little Hugh[4] is very well. So is his old Mother. There's an account full and true of your Medical people at once.

Every thing in relation to you has been order'd, just as I wish'd. I thought the Weather too cold for you to go out with the remains of your little cough on you. It is yet unsetled. But I hope it will soon be such as will encourage the Doctor and Ned to give you full liberty of ranging, with discretion. That I am sure you'll always do, while Mrs Jourdan has the credit with you that I hope she will always have. Give her my service, and Tell her I have no doubt of her Exact and tender care of you, and am very easy, tho' absent from you, when I reflect that you are in her hands. In my last I express'd the gratefull sense I have of her whole Conduct. I trust in God you will, I hope too that I shall live, to shew it by effects.

I am pleas'd that you've so much company, if they be agreable. Encourage those that are so, to go frequently to you, and make them as welcome, as you please. Tell Miss Vignoles she may have as much Vin Episcopal[5] (you spell it *Episcopale*. Let Mrs Jourdan or Her say, which is right) as she pleases, provided she do not get drunk. Mr Wills, I find, has been very good. I am sure He is always agreable.

I have a letter from him, by which I have reason to fear that our intended Expedition to Killaloe[6] will be somewhat embarrass'd. He can't go early, and I can't with convenience go late. I have indeed a great mind to go, and see your Uncle's[7] situation there, and I know he reckons upon it. Mr Wills proposes to me, to go at mine own time, that He'll meet me there, if He can: If He cannot, He says he'll take a trip by himself, to see and advise my Brother as to his building. How this may be I can't tell. But upon the whole It will be much more convenient to me, to make this Excursion soon now, tho' alone; than to wait, till the latter end of Summer to do it, even in his Company. I think it too, much better to do it, while you are in Dublin, than to leave you here. I should be as much absent, and at as great a distance from you as now, and We could not hear from each other, in less than a fortnight, which I know would be very disagreable and painfull to both. I should also be cramp'd as to the time of my visitation, and perhaps cramp your Uncle, in his Excursions to several parts of his Dioces, or keep him there longer than He chuses. For these reasons I resolve, God willing, if your Uncle leaves town as He propos'd, to set out towards him the Monday before Whitsun-tide. One day will carry me to Garbally,[8] and one I'll stay there, so as to be at Killaloe the latter end of the Week. Perhaps Ned[9] may go with me from thence, if your Aunt,[10] He &c. leave town as they intend. Or if He does not, Traveling alone is not a jot disagreable. Pray tell your Uncle, that I resolve thus. This will just come time enough to you, to do it. I don't write to him, partly out of laziness, and partly because I pacqueted him last post.

It pleases me much, My Dear, to see your letters so writ. I see they are not writ with the exactness of a Copy, and yet they are well. In time you may come to write as well and quick as I do. This will be one advantage of your writing so much to me, tho' I would not, either for that, or the great pleasure your prattle gives me, have you distress your Self, or be over eager in writing. Eagerness, my Dear, is one of your little failings. It is a Constitutional one, and therefore more to be excus'd. But guard against it, now you are young. It will be for your health, as well as advantageous in every other respect. Be eager in nothing, but doing good. Even in that you may avoid it, and the more calm, a good temper, or Action are, the more Virtuous. I have examin'd your long letter with great exactness to find out false spellings, and have the satisfaction to find them very few. One I've mention'd, if it be one. There are but four more. *imediatly,* there ought to be two m's. *seting,* there should be two t's. *ofered* should be with two f's and 'Tis not *infermary* but *infirmary.* But these are very few trips, in so long an Epistle, and you'll soon come to Spell, as well as any one. As a means to this, when your letters are wrote, Go them over with Mrs Jourdan, and get her to point out to you, any Corrections of this sort, that may be wanting. That I allow. But if I catch her tripping, Let her look to it. She'll deserve no quarter.

One of your little trips, brings your Nurse[11] to my mind. Write to Dr Lehunt[12] about her. He promis'd me, He would keep her in the Hospital[13] the 6 Months, which are not yet near Expir'd, and I am sure He will overrule the Chirurgeon (I see with pleasure that you have spelt that Word the right way, tho' Custom has almost establish'd a wrong one). If you don't chuse to write to the Doctor, Get Ned Curtis, who is Hack-General, to go to him, and Let him also endeavour, to get the poor Woman into the Incurables.[14] Till that can be done, Do you support her as you please. All things consider'd, this should be your Act not mine; and if your Privy-purse[15] wants supplys, Take any you've a mind to. I care not what expenses you make, that are charitable and prudent, nor would I have you balk your inclination in innocent trifles.

My little black horse is, as Daniel[16] tells me, quite well; tho' I have not yet rode him. I have besides, two young ones, one of Mr Palmer's, the other of Mr Cary's providing, which promise very well; So that I have a prospect of being completely mounted I'll get you a second pad, if it be to be had above ground. I am very glad, that the only one, on which I care at present to venture you, is well. I long till you are on her back agen. But such Weather as we now have, will not allow this.

It would have made you laugh heartily to see poor Cary's long face, and hear his groans, when I told him the fate of his Bullock. He is more griev'd much than I, who am a great looser, by his greediness. For that Bullock, and another that was left lame on the road, and probably did not sell for a Moydore, He refus'd £14 at my Door. Such is often the Fate of those who grasp at too much.

Ascanius diverted me much. 'Tis, as I said, a Romance, form'd out of News-papers and rumours. But many of the Facts We know to be true.[17] Perhaps the rest are in substance so. But the writer is conceited. I see another Pamph[l]et advertised, called *the Wanderer*,[18] which promises a better account and a critick on this. Lawson will tell you whether it be good for anything, and if it be, send it down by Mrs Mahon. It was very kind and good natur'd in her and her Sister[19] to make you so early a visit. But It is like their whole Conduct. Their husbands were here on Tuesday, but went off in the Evening, tho' I desir'd them to relieve their own and my solitude by giving me, as much of their Company, as they could, in the absence of their Wives. Assoon as I received yours, I sent a letter to Mr Mahon, challenging your performance, of what it gave me reason to expect. He has excus'd himself till Monday. Then I expect him. His company is agreable. But I am in no distress. On Thursday Blair[20] came. He and Barton go off to day. Will French was here yesterday; and some others. But I won't waste paper with names, any more than you do.

I am glad Mrs Silver[21] was to see you. She has a multitude of good Qualities with all her Wildness; and you may profit much by conversing with her. She may probably introduce you to some new acquaintance, who may help to supply the place of those you are near loosing for a time. I am sure she'll introduce you to none but good ones. As you grow up, an acquaintance a little more general will be right for you. You may treat them with different degrees of confidence. Of those now going to the Country, I regret Miss Corbet most. But I believe her stay will not be long.

I don't remember, that I mention'd Billy Smith to you, tho' I intended it. He is grown [fatter ? *damaged ms*], and more unlucky. On Wedensday I confin'd him three hours to the remains of the Iron Coal Box. It was a Mansion for him two years ago; but now will scarce [hold? *damaged ms*] him. His crime was misbehaviour at Church.[22] But He repeated it yesterday, and has been [*damaged ms*] whipp'd. He is a fine boy, but I fear he'll be spoil'd.

Carleboe confesses what Mrs Jourdan lays to his charge, looks silly and says He thought &c. Assoon as the new Dish is made, Let it be sent down the first opportunity. The other is laid up after being once us'd. I suppose Wilkinson will take it agen.

I write this day to Mr Sullivane[23] my Wine merchant to send me down two hogsheads of wine. It will travel better now, than in hotter Weather; and tho' I am in no hazard of wanting, my stock is lower than I computed it. If Lyons be in town when you get this, Let John Miller, or Will. get him to bring them down. If He can, let Will. go to Sullivane, and tell him that a carrier is ready and the time. He will be punctual. He lives in Michael's lane. His name is Tim.

I think, considering how I set out, that I have fill'd my paper pretty well. But you must not expect this always. 'Tis a wrong thing to give a good Child a bad Custom. Sometimes you must take up with three lines, so will I; and sometimes you must go without a letter at all. I am determin'd to serve you thus, lest a letter should miscarry, as mine from hence sometimes do, and then you'll be frighten'd. But I won't give you the same liberty. You, Mrs Jourdan, or Some one must write every post; if it be only to say, that, Thank God, you are well. God send those joyfull tidings always to

your most affectionate Father
Edw: Elphin

Depend on it, My Dear, I take all possible care of my self, and am as well as you've seen me this twelve-month; and Pitts[24] lyes every night where you desir'd he should, and meerly because you desir'd it.

I intend, God willing, to consecrate the Church of French park on Ascension Day.[25]

Barton does not own the charge of being a good nurse. But His looks confess it.

Shannon has brought me down a parcel of Handkerchiefs which are Raggs; and has lock'd up most of my new ones. He says that five are out – I suppose they were in the Wash. You may get Mrs Mahon to bring them down to me. I must not appear ragged in a strange Country. Killaloe is so.

1. Dr Edward Molloy TCD MA; member of the Dublin Society, *Alumni*, p.772.
2. David Digenan of Cloghr Begg, parish of Elphin: a doctor. He was Catholic with four Catholic servants. Census f.8.
3. The Rev. Nathaniel Barton (*c*.1710-71; see Biographical Register).
4. Dr Hugh Stafford (see Biographical Register): an apothecary.
5. Vin episcopal: probably a play upon words, but the drink may have been Bishop, port heated with an orange stuck with cloves and roasted and spiced with cinnamon,

cloves, mace, allspice and nutmeg. Dorothy Hartley, *Food in England* (London 1954), p.556.

6. Killaloe, Co. Clare. Michael Wills was probably planning to visit Nicholas Synge to advise on the building of a new Palace. Like Edward Synge at Elphin, Nicholas Synge had problems with his house at Killaloe on his institution in 1745. In his will he said that he had found the See house at Killaloe 'in a ruinous condition', and had proposed to spent £250 on it. He lodged this money in Lennox's bank, but the repair was 'by all Persons deemed impracticable', and his £250 was later lost by the 'shutting up' of the bank. The present house, Clarisford, was built by Robert Fowler, bishop of Killaloe in 1774-8. Probate of Nicholas Synge's will, 22 April 1768. NLI, Synge Papers PC 344 (8); Bence-Jones p.84.

7. Nicholas Synge (1693-1771; see Biographical Register): Edward Synge's younger brother.

8. Garbally, Ballinasloe, Co. Galway.

9. Edward Synge (c.1725-92; see Biographical Register): Edward Synge's nephew, the only son of Nicholas Synge.

10. Elizabeth Synge (?-1750; see Biographical Register): wife of Nicholas Synge.

11. Alicia's nurse: not known.

12. Francis Le Hunte (?-1750) of Brenanstown, Co. Dublin. Son of George and Alice Le Hunte. He took BA at TCD in 1708, MB and MD 1719. He became a fellow of King's and Queen's College of Physicians in 1726, was president in 1729 and 1741. Elected governor of Dr Steevens' Hospital in 1738. Physician to the hospital 1741/2. Kirkpatrick.

13. Dr Steevens' Hospital, founded 1733. Edward Synge was a trustee.

14. The Hospital for Incurables was founded by members of the Charitable Music Society who gave concerts in Crow Steet for the relief of poor insolvent debtors held in various Dublin prisons. The committee became concerned about the welfare of patients suffering from incurable diseases and resolved to spend their surplus funds on founding a hospital. The first hospital was opened on Blind Quay (now Lower Exchange Street) in 1744 and it was moved to Lazar's Hill (now Townsend Street) in 1753. *Irish Builder,* 39 (1897), p.29.

15. Under her parents' marriage settlement, Alicia received £100 a year until she either married or reached the age of twenty-one. Marriage articles of the Rev. Edward Synge, son and heir of Edward Synge, archbishop of Tuam, and Jane, daughter of Robert Curtis of Roscrea, Co. Tipperary. Articles of agreement between Edward Synge, archbishop of Tuam and Robert Curtis of Roscrea 26 November 1720. Synge Papers NLI PCC 344, folder 7.

16. Daniel: a groom at Elphin.

17. The author of *Ascanius* may have been Dr John Burton, portrayed by Laurence Sterne as Dr Slop in *Tristram Shandy.* The writer protests that he is not writing fiction and uses what appears to be original material in what is essentially an historical romance. The book plays upon the reader's anti-Jacobite prejudices, portraying Charles Edward Stuart as an 'archetypal villain of almost mythical proportions'. Jerry C. Beasley, *Novels of the 1740s* (Athens, Georgia 1982), p.71.

18. [R. Savage] *The wanderer or surprising escape. A narrative founded on true facts. Containing a series of remarkable events, during a late very extraordinary adventure, from the first projection, to its appearance in the north, and total defeat. ... with some remarks on a romance called Ascanius, shewing the author thereof very defective in his materials and candour in the relation.* Dublin: printed for William Brien and Richard James, 1747. Advertised in

Faulkner's Dublin Journal, 9-12 May 1747.

19. Jane Mahon was one of four daughters of Sir Maurice Crosbie of Ardfert. Anne married Bartholomew Mahon, Elizabeth married Lancelot Crosbie of Tubrid, Co. Kerry, and Dorothea married Richard Pigott of Cork. *Irish Builder,* 38 (1895), p.40.

20. The Rev. James Blair (1706-77; see Biographical Register).

21. Mrs Silver (see Biographical Register).

22. Edward Synge had twelve male and five female servants; they were all Protestant. Census, f.1.

23. Daniel Sullivan: wine merchant, Michael's Lane. Watson, p.41.

24. Pitts: a servant.

25. Ascension Day was on 28 May in 1747.

6

Elphin May 19, 1747

My Dear Girl's Post-script I transcribe for the beginning of my letter. The greatest pleasure I have, is to hear that you are well, and enjoy your self. No sooner I have read one of your letters, than I long for another. And yet, Huzzy, there is more eagerness in this, than I'll allow you to indulge. Be sedate in every thing, even in your affection to me. I can give you few more usefull lessons.

I am much pleas'd with your having invited Mrs and Miss Mahons.[1] I hope you had Meg and Kitty[2] as well as the rest. It was right also to ask your Uncle &c – You may give as many instances of your boldness this way as you please. I was much pleas'd with Molly's[3] Epistle. It brought to my mind some of yours about the same age which your good Mother us'd to write from your prattle.

I am glad the Servants behave themselves so well; and particularly that Robinson does his part right. But Take care of letting him know your opinions. It will spoil him.

I am glad some of the things I wrote for are come off; the rest, I hope, will be ready to be sent by Lyons. I have no new Commission now, But to desire that a Tin-pint, and half-pint may be sent down. If I want a little Warm Water to wash my mouth, Tom[4] with his important face brings up the Tea-Kettle, or one of the Cook's Sawce-pans.

My new Tooth does very well. But you were unlucky in asking about it, when you wrote in so much hurry. How do you think you spelt it? Do so no more. However I have very few faults of this sort to charge you with. I have not time now to examine your letter exactly for them. I have observ'd but one, and that twice repeated – *Spaking* It should be *speaking*. But this I don't impute to want of Care. I see how you have been led into it. Spake in the Preter tense is right. *Speak, Speaking,* in the present. Tell Oracle Ned, that I take not above a pint of Whey, and that with bread, which I don't apprehend can hurt my gout more than 2 or 3 dishes of Tea, for which I sometimes change it. But if He forbids, I'll refrain it.

I would fain contribute any thing in my power to poor Keegan's[5] recovery. On the days that you don't ride out, I see no objection to his riding Lawson's horse, or John Miller's Mare. I am sure the Masters will make none. Therefore so let it be.

I have no reason to doubt your ready compliance with my advice. I hope I shall have as few occasions, as I have had, to command. But I care not to lay you under any restraints, but for your good; and where I am not a Competent judge my self, I would have the matter determined by those who are. Ask the Doctor therefore or Ned about brown and broil'd meat.

Your *Wanderer* is a very Simple paper. I blame not you for sending it. But if Lawson encourag'd you to do it, He deserves to be abus'd.

Tell Mrs Jourdan with my service, that I had the same scheme in my head that she had, but knew not how conveniently to execute it. It happens that there is no occasion. For the little Stump does well enough.

I am glad your Garden furnishes you so plentifully. Pray did you ever send Mrs Hamilton[6] a dish of Asparagus as I desir'd? I fancy it went out of your head. It is no great matter. I believe it is now too late. If you do send any, let it be very fine. She likes the white. You may cut the Beds in the Upper Garden to the End of this month, no longer: Those in the lower garden, you may continue to cut, as long as you please.

Tell John Miller that if little 'Nancy' be not fit now to be shoed up, she never will. I would have him turn her immediatly to breed. I spoke to him on that subject before I left town. Let him do, as I then bid him without delay.

You say nothing of Palmer or his Wife; nor have I any tidings of my Maps. I suppose they did not leave town at the time they propos'd.

Gunning is return'd un-married. But Every thing is setled; and He is to be finish'd in the Holy-days. I had a little diversion with him last night. He seems to be as indifferent about it, as you've seen him about trivial things. He provides neither new Coat, nor Gown, nor Shirt, not even a night-gown. He says He has an old one, which is somewhat thread-bare. It will do. He owns fairly that He should not have thought of a ring, but that His friend who made the Match put him in mind of it, and then He was horribly puzzled how to get the measure of her finger. A Widow sister in the house help'd him at this dead lift. Upon sifting him throughly, I can't discover any thing of inclination. He considers it as a matter of meer Convenience. When I ask'd him, why He left his Mistress on Saturday, as his Church was provided for, His answer was, It was to no purpose to stay; For the papers were gone to Dublin. A Marriage setlement It seems there must be. But for all this He may be very happy, and, I believe will be so. I have not the same opinion of the other odd Man's adventure, and therefore did not mention it. I pity him. He has not been here since I came.[7]

The Weather has not been on the whole very pleasant since I got hither. But As it is very good for the Country, and I matter it not, because it does not keep me within, I feel it only on your account. Yesterday was fine. I hope you had an airing. This day is very boist'rous; and there has been a showr or two. I hope you keep close in your nest. Depend upon it, My Dear, that I take as much care of my Self as you can wish, and will do so. I have not, since the day after I came hither, rode without my Surtout Coat, nor walk'd so as to wet or even to dirty my Shoes. Wet them I could not, unless I endeavour'd it, or were out when a showr is actually falling. For what falls, soon drys, and the face of the Country is very dry. In all other respects I am, I bless God, full as well as when I left you; I really think, I am better. Nor do I fear any thing hurting me, while I know that you are well. Those tidings will always cheer

your most affectionate Father
Edw: Elphin

Desire Ned Curtis to tell Nat Smith[8] that I shall at the latter end of the season want a Purple Bath rug Sur-tout[9] very fine and very light. Let him get a choice one ready or make it as he did before.

Send Will to Waters[10] from whom I buy Corks, for two Groce of the twenty-penny Corks, which have, ready to send down, by the next Opportunity.

Let me know, if the Coach-Gelding, whom We call 'Nip', be well of his sore neck, and gone to Work. If He be not, Sympson must be spoken to to attend him carefully.

I have sent you the new pityfull Soup-dish by a Carr-man who call'd here just now. His name is *Noon*.[11] You may send any thing by him.

Send me down the *Suspicious Husband*.[12] Mrs Cary has not seen it. Ned. Curtis will get his friend to free it. It is too large for Lord C[hancellor]'s frank.

Direct John Miller to learn from Mr Nelson, or some one where the best Glue is to be got, and to buy 3. Stone, and send it down by *Noon*, who carrys up the Dish. The Corks may come by him too.

Barton is just come in. He did receive Mrs Jourdan's letter, but would not answer it, privilege being cut.

Wednesday 20.
The morning is wet. Your Uncle is not lucky in his Weather. But I hope this rain will setle it; and that your Aunt &c. will have a fine day to morrow.

Adieu, My Dear. The post waits.

Bid John Miller, as soon as Eaton returns to Town, to desire his Assistance in providing Sash-line of the very best kind that is to be had, and enough to hang all the Sashes here. Let it be got ready assoon as conveniently it can. For it will not be long before I want it.

1. Miss Mahon may have been Eleanor Mahon, daughter of Nicholas Mahon and Magdalen French, and aunt of Thomas Mahon. In 1749 'Elen Mahon' of Strokestown had one female Protestant servant. Burke, *IFR*, p.773; Census, f.84.

2. Meg is not known. 'Kitty', Katherine Mahon, was a daughter of Peter Mahon, dean of Elphin, and Katherine Gore. She married Gilbert Ormsby of Grange, Co. Roscommon, in 1751. Burke, *LGI*, p.542.

3. Mary Synge (*c.*1742-1808), daughter of Nicholas and Elizabeth Synge, who would have been aged four at beginning of the letters. She married William Peisley Vaughan. Edward Synge left her £500 in his will. Synge, p.7; will, f.254.

4. Tom: a servant who acted as Edward Synge's valet.

5. Keegan: not known.

6. Mrs Hamilton (?-1770; see Biographical Register).

7. Obscure.

8. Nat. Smith: not known.

9. A surtout was a large, loose overcoat which came below the knees. The skirt was flared and it had a back vent to enable it to be worn while riding. It had a broad flat collar and a small collar which could be turned up in cold weather. It was buttoned from neck to hem. 'Bath' was a thick, doubled raised baize and 'rug' a coarse kind of frieze. C. Willett Cunnington and Phillis Cunnington, *Handbook of English Costume of the Eighteenth Century* (Buxton 1972), pp.76-8, 416, 420.

10. Waters: a cork merchant. Wine was generally sent from Dublin to the country in hogsheads, together with corks and bottles. In 1758 eight gross of best long corks cost Thomas Mahon £1.1.8d. Bill of Christopher Harrison, 27 September 1758. Pakenham Mahon Papers NLI ms 10,081(2).

11. Hugh Noon, a car man, lived at Lissonuffy, near Elphin. He was Catholic, married with four children under fourteen. Census, f.67.

12. [Benjamin Hoadly] *The Suspicious Husband.* A comedy. As it is acted at the Theatre Royal in Covent-Garden. By Dr Hoadly. With an epilogue. The second edition (Dublin: printed by S. Powell, for G. and A. Ewing. 1747).

7

Elphin. May 23, 1747

You beg so hard, Huzzy, for a letter, that I yield to write to you this post. But the next I believe it will not be in my power. I shall be at French-park,[1] which lies very remote from all Posts, and the Conveyance is not certain.

Your account of your self gave me great joy; and the Doctor confirms it. I hope you will continue your liberty, and enlarge your bounds. I long to have you on Horse-back. But the Weather does not yet favour you. When I go from home, It will be better. Mrs Jourdan's little accident was very unlucky. But I hope it is over. Pray Give my service to her, and tell her that one of her Corrections twice repeated was unnecessary. Tooth-ack is right, more so than *Ake*, tho' that is often us'd. This in return for her *Agen.* I think it is spelt both ways, and as there is a little variety in the use of it, so in some Senses, one Way of spelling is rather more proper than the other. But I can't enter into the criticism in a letter; and perhaps I am mistaken. Now I am ent'red on spelling, It is as good go through with it. *Thiner* – Thinner. *Spaking*, speaking. *Write*, Wrote, in the perfect Tense, So you use it. This is a defect in Grammar. In Miss Vignoles' words, you have put *qui*, for *qu'il.* I suppose she did not see, tho' she dictated them. *Dined* is right. The n you have interlin'd, superfluous. In the date of your letter you write *Saturday* for *Tuesday.* This is not false spelling, but a little bit of giddiness, my Dear Girl. Or rather you wrote the latter part of your letter in hast and made it up in haste; and this I take to be the reason, why any thing escap'd Mrs Jourdan's Correction. But look to it between you for the future. I'll examine with Eagle's Eyes to catch her tripping.

I have wrote to Mr Clements[2] to send you my Watch. You may wear it if you please, tho' I fear it will be too large for so little a Girl's side. You shall have mine at my return. But before you can wear either, you must get a proper chain. That you have, I believe will not do. I would have one of the best kind for you. What that is I don't know.[3] You must consult the learned. I believe Mrs Silver will be as proper a person as any. You have said nothing to me about your little Boy *Hall.*[4] I fear you have not got him yet into the Hospital. Whose fault is it? Mrs Hunt[5] told me there was a Vacancy. Send to him agen and agen, till you get the matter fix'd; and if you want your Boy up, Dean Owen[6] will put you in the Way.

Bid John Miller send me off by the first Carrs He can get a full load, or two, if he pleases, of strong good Slating-Laths. Eaton, if return'd to Town will get them for him, or He may get them himself from the Man in Bull alley.[7] Let him send by the Carr-man a letter with an account of the Number. If Lyons does not go to you, these or any thing else may be sent by *Noon* who carry'd up the Dish. The Wine too may be sent by him.

If George Stephens[8] has prepar'd every thing for shutting up the little Closet, you had as good take down your China for a while, and order him to do it.

Shannon says He left the 5 Handkerchiefs with Molly Fagan.[9] If she has them, I know who deserves something for not making full enquiry. If she has not, They are gone. If you have not yet sent your own, Do not. I can make shift; and they are too little. But I thank you for your readiness to supply my Wants.

Bid John Miller wait on Mr Wills. He'll receive orders from him about more Plaister of Paris.

Pray tell Miss Vignoles, that I much applaud her sober resolution. It will save my Vin Episcopal. The odd letter you enclos'd was indeed an odd one. As it is very short and will give you a laugh, Here it is. Who the person is I know not.

My Lord

As I always eat the Calf in the Cow's belly, when a neighbour of your Lordship's; & am indebted to old Esquire Davis the Usurer, paid him exorbitant use, will repay him & all my Creditors with Honour. My duty to your tender flock & am

your Lordship's most dutifull
Kevin-bail Dragoon
S. Aubery
14 May 1747.

No place and the post mark is defac'd.

Mrs Mahons were expected home last night. I intend to dine at Stroke's-town to morrow, in hopes of seeing them.

Tho' I go to French-park next Week I sha'n't consecrate the Church. The Church-yard is not completely enclos'd, and some things in the Church are not quite finish'd. My deferring this solemnity will be a Spur to them.

My blessing to Jane. I always intend to send it, but sometimes forget. God be thanked I am very well, and very happy because you are so. I am

My Dear Girl
your very affectionate
Edw:Elphin

The letter which you write in answer to this Direct hither. That the following Saturday, direct to Roscommon. I shall catch it on my way. The following post direct to me at Nenagh.[10] Afterwards to me at Killaloe near Limerick. The night you direct to Nenagh, Desire Jeny to write to her Mama, that if I should stay there a day longer, I may have an account of you.[11]

Bid John Miller bespeak six Spades of the same kind which those He sent me down hither last year; and as soon as they are ready, to send them by the first Opportunity that offers. Long and small is the kind. But they must be very strong. The Man who made those last year did not do me justice.

1. Frenchpark, Co. Roscommon. The house was built for John French the barrister in the 1730s, probably to the designs of Richard Castle. Like Strokestown, it had a central block joined by curved sweeps to flanking two-storey pavilions. The interior was dismantled in the 1950s and the remains of the house demolished in the 1970s. The entrance gates are now at Leixlip House, Co. Kildare. Glin, Griffin and Robinson, p.125.

2. Mr Clements: not known.

3. In his will, Edward Synge left Alicia her mother's gold watch. Will, f.254.

4. Hall: not known.

5. Mrs Hunt: the wife of Dr Francis Le Hunte, physician to Dr Steevens' Hospital.

6. The Rev. John Owen (1690-1760). Admitted to TCD in 1706, he took BA 1707; MA 1710; DD 1730. He became dean of Clonmacnoise in 1742. He was prebendary of St Michael's, Dublin, 1736-46; precentor of Kildare 1737; prebendary of Swords 1744 and of St John's in Christ Church 1746-60; *Alumni*, pp.647-8; Lawlor, p.161.

7. The man in Bull Alley. Not known.

8. George Stephens: a carpenter.

9. Molly Fagan: a servant.

10. Nenagh, Co. Tipperary.

11. Edward Synge was to stay at Garbally, Ballinasloe, which was the family home of Elizabeth, his brother's wife and Jane Synge's mother.

8

Elphin. May 29, 1747.

I am just return'd from French-park, where I got my Dear Ally's letter. But I am sorry to find by it that you are chang'd from Daughter to Niece. So you subscribe your Self. I hope this was owing to your gaiety on your return from Mrs Wills's.[1] The thought of your being well and happy will keep me so. Business multiplys upon me so, that I know not which way to turn my self. I wish I were off my Killaloe jaunt. But your Uncle would feel my not going there so much, that I will go, tho' my stay will be short, at most but ten days. It is almost necessary for me to be back here in a very short time. I have great reason to think my worthy Register[2] a great R – and must therefore proceed against him in my Court, which I am unwilling to do unless personally present. But my Suspicions are so strong, and the Case so urgent that I intend to have all the Books and papers of his Office remov'd to Bob. King's room next Week, that they may be less in his power. This is a Secret yet. Say nothing of it but to Mrs Jourdan. I had fix'd my Visitation for July 8 before this came out, and I must begin with the Gent before that; so that I have no time to spare. I say nothing of my house, tho' that requires my presence every minute. But this unlook'd-for affair engrosses me more at present, even than that does. However I have a prospect of much good from it. You see I must return hither from Kil-laloe.

I am greatly pleas'd, my Dear, with your answer about the Watch. Such an indifference about a thing that Girls are apt to be fond of confirms me in the hope I have that you'll act with superior understanding in every thing; and value those things only, which are truly valuable.

I am sorry to tell you that Dr Mulloy's story of himself has not one word of truth in it. He was not engag'd here, and the occasion of his going to town He long foresaw. It was an unnatural Law-suit between him and his Brother, in which both are much to blame, but the Brother more than He. Depend on it – He had no thoughts of seeing me. But He has a mind to preserve appearances with you. I am sorry that a Man whose skill in his profession might entitle him to the regards of every one sick or well, should make himself so odious and contemptible. Take you however no notice of this, but carry your self with Civility to him if He goes agen to you.

Tell John He may sheer my sheep whenever He pleases and if no Carrs offer themselves before you get this, Let him look out for Mr Dominick French Merchant in Abbey-street,[3] and tell him, with my Service, that I desire He would recommend some Carr-men to him, on whose honesty and care He can depend. I am however in no hurry for any thing but the Timber. I long till that comes down. Just as I was writing this, a Carr-man came hither to offer his Service. He is an old acquaintance of John's. His name Gregory Dunne. If the timber be not sent off before you get this, Let John send it by him. He'll be in town Whitsun-Eve.[4] I have agreed with him for eighteen shill. the Tun. He may send the Wine and everything else by him if He has Carrs enough. But the timber must have the preference.

Ned Curtis's expedient about sending your letters to me at Killaloe is a very good one. Since He has a friend in the post-office, I may have news from him for the future as well as my Brother, and indeed Mr Buchanan[5] or his Clerks neglect me. Desire Ned therefore to go immediately to Mr Buchanan at the post-office, and order him not to send me any more. He must pay him £4 for two years and take his receit. The 2d year is just now at an end. I use to pay him £2 a year for two Dublin-papers[6] when here, and one English one, The *General Evening-post*,[7] while in town. I'll pay the same to Ned's friend, or whatever more He thinks I should. But let Mr Buchanan be put off. If a reason be necessary, The neglect of his Clerks is sufficient. They oft'ner send me wrong papers than right ones, so they did last and every former year. I am weary of it.

Desire Ned to go to Lennox, and enquire after a draft I have sent to him this post of Luke Dowel's[8] on Patrick McCabe[9] for £60. It won't be amiss to give Lennox notice of this, lest it should miscarry. If it does not, Let him get Lennox's receit for it.

By the directions I have given, your letters will come safe to me, and in due time, till I leave Killaloe. Before that you shall have new ones. I'll write to you as often as I can. But if a letter should miscarry among the cross posts you must not be surpris'd. I pray God preserve and bless you My Dearest. Blessing and love to Jane and Mrs Jourdan. I am

> your most affectionate
> Edw: Elphin

Let Dr Anderson know that I rejoice at his Son's recovery. I long with great impatience for the coming in of the German Spa, that you may begin with it. Whenever my letters are overcharg'd to you besure you make the post-office do you justice. 'Tis not my folding but their sharping that occasions it.

You should sometimes tell me [how] little Shannon[10] does a [*sic*] you did once. It will be a comfort to the poor Father to know that He is well.

1. Sarah Wills, wife of Godfrey Wills, was born a Miss Montgomery. The will of Sarah Wills, widow of Dublin was proved in 1792. Burke, (1912) p.624; Vicars, p.493.

2. The Rev. John Hickes (*c.*1700-80) of Castlestrange, parish of Fuerty. Admitted to TCD in 1718, he took BA in 1726. He was collated vicar of Dunamon in 1741 and became vicar of Athleague 1734-80; prebendary of Oran 1758. He had six children and two Protestant and three Catholic servants. *Alumni*, p.396; Leslie, Elphin, pp.26, 136; Census, f.208.

3. Dominick French, grocer, Abbey Street. Watson (1752), p.12.

4. Saturday, 6 June 1747.

5. George Buchanan: an official at the Post Office. George Buchanan to the earl of Limerick. Roden Papers PRONI Mic.147/9 f27.

6. Edward Synge took *Pue's Occurrences* and the *Dublin Courant* regularly and refers to *Faulkner's Dublin Journal.* He refers frequently to news and advertisements, mainly from the *Dublin Courant.*

7. *The General-Evening Post* was founded in London in 1733 and ran until 1800.

8. Luke Dowell (*c.*1721-*c.*55) was born in Elphin and lived at Mantua, Co. Roscommon. He took BA at TCD in 1742. He was a tenant of the bishop of Elphin, paying £3.00 a year rent; he had eleven Catholic servants. His will was proved in 1755. *Alumni*, 241; Papers of Robert Howard, bishop of Elphin, Wicklow Papers NLI PC 223 (6); Census, f.19; Vicars, p.142.

9. Patrick McCabe: not known.

10. Son of Shannon, the butler at Elphin and probably a servant in the Kevin Street household.

9

Garbally.[1] June 3, 1747.

I rec'd my Dear Girl's and the Doctor's at Roscommon. It gives me great joy that you are so well, and agen on Horse-back. The Doctor's method of seeing you early to direct the Exercise of the day, is very right and kind. If your Weather be like ours, You've been oblig'd of late to intermitt that agreable Exercise. Pray How do 'Spark' and 'Cream' perform? I am glad your Mare improves. Ride cautiously not cowardly. After a few more trials in the Park,[2] I fancy you may sometimes vary, and ride to Mil-town,[3] or Stilorgan.[4] But this as Mrs Jourdan advises.

I came hither yesterday, very well, I bless God; and I had company from Roscommon. Mr Lewis Ormsby[5] part of the Way; and Lancaster,[6] who came to meet me, the rest. I found all here very well. Molly shews to great advantage. Her two little Cosens Netterville and Shaw are excellent foils, if she wanted any.[7] To morrow I go off to Killaloe. Ned[8] goes with me, and Coll. Trench.[9] I am in some pain about the latter, lest any disorder should come on him. I'll take the best care I can. But go He will. I can't say No! -

Mrs Silver was kind in her Cards &c. – You say they tir'd you, and I am not sorry for it. But I would have you command your self so as to comply on such occasions without being tir'd or uneasy, tho' I never wish you to be in that point a fashionable Lady.

Tell John Miller that All the things by Lyons came safe on Sunday to Elphin. He must let Mr Sullivan know that the Wine came. Bid him send me down five thousand more Laths as soon as He can.

Desire Ned Curtis to pay Dr Bland[10] ten English half Crowns for the Bale of Coffee. I would have Mrs Jourdan try it, and if she finds it Excellent, she may get a Mill and roaster that you may have it to treat Mr Wills or your other friends. I have time for no more. God bless you, My Dearest, and Jane and Mrs Jourdan.

I am yours &c.
Edw: Elphin

We have yet no sign of Straw-berrys. But yesterday there was at dinner a pretty large parcel of Cherrys, half ripe.

Tell John Miller I think He had best turn 'Dunn' to grass, and He must feed him very well with oats so as to have him in Excellent traveling order. He must reduce 'Nip', who He says is too fat, to the same. I design these Horses to bring down my Chaise, about which I have wrote fully to Mr Wills.

1. Garbally Court, Ballinasloe, Co. Galway. The present house was built in 1819 to replace an earlier house, which was burnt down in 1798. Bence-Jones, p.131.

2. Phoenix Park, Dublin.

3. Milltown, Uppercross, Co. Dublin.

4. Stillorgan House, Stillorgan, Co. Dublin, the seat of Lord Allen. The house begun in 1695 by the Allen family was demolished in 1860. Bence-Jones, p.265.

5. Lewis Ormsby (1716-?; see Biographical Register) of Tubbervaddy, Co. Roscommon.

6. Lancaster: not known.

7. The children of Mabel Trench, younger sister of Elizabeth Synge, who married Frederick Netterville and of another sister, Mary who married Thomas Shaw. Cooke-Trench, Table 11, p.26; Burke (1876), p.860.

8. Edward Synge: Nicholas Synge's son.

9. Frederick Trench II (1688-1752; see Biographical Register).

10. Nathaniel Bland (1696-1760) was a son of the Rev. James Bland of Killarney, Co. Kerry. He was admitted to TCD in 1712 and became DD and LLD in 1727. A judge of the Prerogative Court of Dublin, he was vicar general of the diocese of Ardfert. Dr Bland was a grandfather of Dorothy Jordan, the actress and mistress of the future William IV. Burke, (1979) p.129; *Alumni*, p.73; *Gentleman's Magazine* (1760), p.542; Claire Tomalin, *Mrs Jordan's Profession* (London 1994), pp.10-11.

10

Nenagh. June 5, 1747

I came hither about half an hour ago, and after a short dinner shall set out for Killaloe, which is but eight miles. But As I sha'n't get thither time enough to overtake the post, I write this to let you know that I am so near my journey's end, very well, I bless God, both in health and spirits. You must not be sawcy, if I tell you that your letter which I just now received and Mrs Jourdan's account of you to your Aunt which I got just before setting out from Garbally have contributed a great deal to this. My fellow travelers too are well. Our journey has been very pleasant. We have certainly had less rain than you. Tuesday morning the Coll. and I rode about his Land for 3 hours. There was now and then a little show'r, but not enough to drive us in or Wet us. Yesterday, there was some rain, but not such as to wet. In the afternoon I took a long Walk. Some rain towards night. This morning lowr'd. But the day has improv'd, and is now very fine, and likely to continue so. The Coolness of the day has been very convenient for traveling.

I am sorry for Jemy's fall. You don't tell me how He got it. If either of the Servants' riding horses fail, John Miller must get another. He may buy a right good Servant's horse whenever He can get him. I would not have any of you debarr'd of the pleasure and advantage of riding. Agen I say, ride prudently not cowardly.

Desire Ned Curtis to let Mr Lennox know, that I have sent him by this post two Drafts one of Jona. Tanner, Bandon,[1] on Mr William Skeys Dublin[2] for £91.–.– payable to me at 15 days sight, the other at like sight draft of Andw Dom and Jno. Lynch[3] on Messrs Gleadon and Company[4] for £80 and accepted 15 May payable to Coll. Trench. 'Tis right to give this notice for fear of accidents by the post. One of the drafts came in the letter you enclos'd.

I'll write to you from Killaloe. But as the post from thence is a by-one, Don't be uneasy if you don't get a letter from me this day-senight. Direct your answer to this to Killaloe near Limerick. But your letter on Saturday following must be directed to me at Birr.[5] I propose to be there on Monday se'night. Your Tuesday's epistle Direct to me at Coll. Trench's. You know how. God bless you My Dearest, and Jane and Mrs Jourdan.

I am your &c
Edw: Elphin
[Stamped NENEAGH]

1. Probably a tenant on land at Bandon, Co. Cork, inherited by Edward Synge under the will of Samuel Synge, dean of Kildare in 1708. NLI. Synge Papers, PC 344 (20).

2. William Skeys, merchant, Batchelor's Walk. Watson (1752), p.23.

3. Andrew Dom and Jonathan Lynch: not known.

4. Gleadowe's Bank was founded by Thomas Gleadowe in a house opposite Castle Gate. J.T. Gilbert, *A History of the City of Dublin* 3 vols (facsimile edition Shannon 1972), Vol.1, p.26.

5. Birr, King's County.

11

Killaloe.[1] June 8, 1747

I wrote to my Dear Girl from Nenagh. That afternoon I got hither very well, and, Blessed be God, I continue so. My traveling has done, and I am sure will do, me a great deal of good.

Saturday We had some rain, and yesterday a vast deal. But this day is fair; and I have made use of the morning to take a full view of your Uncle's situation; which has enough of natural beauty, but will require some Expense and skill as well as time to put into order. I am afraid your Uncle has not quite enough of activity for what He has to do. But He promises fairly.

The Beautys of this place are very different from those of Elphin.

Instead of fine plains, lofty venerable Mountains, much too near, which interrupt every prospect but that of a most noble river. This is fine at Killaloe; But two or three miles distant from hence, The river forms a very large lake, which from the road is one of the most beautifull views I ever beheld. On this lake stands Tinneranna.[2] I saw it as I pass'd on the other side, and I believe it is all I shall see of it. Dr Purdon[3] and his son[4] were here on Saturday, and press'd me much to go thither. But George's wife[5] was just brought to bed, which furnish'd me with a most reasonable excuse for declining an Expedition I was not over fond of.

Your Uncle is very well, and sends you his best wishes. He desires you would tell Jeny that He received hers, and will write to her when he has more time than at present. His being here is much more comfortable than I expected. His Landlord and Land-lady are very orderly people; and We are all very well lodg'd and fed. I brought Carleboe with me for fear of wanting him. But He has had no employment. Only that I think they have this day desir'd him to dress some tench.

I hold my purpose of leaving Killaloe this day senight. If you get this letter at all, you'll get it on Friday. Direct the letter you write on Saturday to Birr as I bid you before – and so My Dearest Adieu.

yours &c.
Edw: Elphin

[Stamped LIMERICK]

1. Killaloe, Co. Clare.
2. Tinerana, Co. Clare, on the river Shannon.
3. Simon Purdon (1691-?): son of Simon Purdon and Helena Synge, daughter of Edward Synge (1614-77), bishop of Cork, Cloyne and Ross. Edward Synge's first cousin and exact contemporary, he was admitted to TCD in 1708 and took BA in 1712. He married a cousin, Elizabeth Purdon. Synge, p.7.
4. George Purdon: eldest son of Simon Purdon. Synge, p.7.
5. Arabella Casaubon of Mallow, Co. Cork. Synge, p.7.

12

Killaloe. June 11, 1747

My Dear Girl must be content with a very short letter this bout, just to tell you, that, Blessed be God, I am very well, and much rejoic'd that you are so. The Weather has not been pleasant since I came hither. Yet I have made a shift to ride every day, but one, and have view'd the Demesne &c. as much as I desire – and, as some good arises from whatever happens, so this broken wet weather has furnish'd me with a pretence of declining some visits which I had no mind to make. I propose leaving this on Monday. Let your next be directed to Garbally.

As to painting your dressing room, Do as Mr Wills advises. But Ask him whether it won't be better to paint the new pannels now, and deferr painting the whole, till Houghton[1] puts up his new Carvings? Prevail on Mr Wills to enquire how near they are being finish'd.

Tell Simpson I care not whether He goes to Mullingar fair[2] or not. He does or may know every Coach-Horse which the Jockeys bring to Dublin, and may get right good ones for me as well as He did for the Archbishop of Tuam.[3] He has time enough before him. If He will not do this for me, as He ought, He may let it alone. I have long thought him more careless and indifferent about doing any thing for me than He should be.

Your Uncle is very well. He sends you all his blessing. So does

your most affectionate &c.
Edw: Elphin

[Stamped LIMERICK]

1. John Houghton: carver and gilder, Duke Street, Dublin. There were at least three generations of Houghtons with the same Christian name. The Knight of Glin, *A Directory of the Dublin Furniture Trade 1752-1800* (Dublin 1992), p.9.
2. In 1747 the fair at Mullingar, Co. Westmeath, was held on Tuesday 23 June. Watson (1747), p.84.
3. Josiah Hort (1674?-1751), archbishop of Tuam. He was educated in London at a dissenting academy and although he was admitted to Clare Hall, Cambridge, he did not take a degree. In 1709 he went to Ireland as chaplain to the Lord Lieutenant. In 1722 he became bishop of Ferns and was translated to Kilmore in 1727 and to Tuam in 1742, where he remained until his death in December 1751. He married Elizabeth Fitzmaurice, a cousin of Lord Kerry. *DNB*; *NHI*, Vol. 9, pp.426, 405, 432; Burke (1916), p.1078.

13

Garbally. June 17, 1747

My Dear Girl will, I am sure, be pleas'd to know, that I am thus far safe and well on my return to Elphin. The journey was pleasant, the Weather being fine. And thro' the whole We had no accident, only that one of the yerks[1] in the rough road near Killaloe, snapp'd a trace, which was immediatly supply'd by a Spare one. If John had been as improvident, as once when the same accident happen'd near Glanmore, We had been in a bad way. I propose to go from this on Friday to Mr Waller's[2] and thence on Monday home. But direct yours to Roscommon: For there I shall get it earlier. I hope Ned Curtis has setled about the News. If He has, Let his friend begin to send it on Saturday night directed to Elphin. The *Dublin Courant*[3] and Pue's paper[4] are those I desire.

I got all your letters, but have time now to say very little in answer. Your account of your Self and Companions pleases me much. I hope you'll all continue as well as you are.

Next time you see Mrs Silver, Desire her to carry you to wait on Lady Maude.[5] I have seen her some few times many years ago, when it was hard to say, whether she was most beautifull or genteel. But, which is better than both, She is said to be a very good Woman. I am glad you have it in your power to be known to her.

If 'Spark' be not return'd, Send John Miller to Mr Vipond,[6] and Let him not rest, till He gets him back. You should not have let him go.

My only plague at present is Tom. He grows more absurd and wrong-headed every day, and I have lately found out, that He is near sighted, which occasions his shaving me, for the most part but half. I must part with him; and if among you, you would look out for a right good one again I go to town; You'd do me a great piece of service. It may be one chance, if you speak of this, as by accident, when Mrs Silver is with you. Between you and Mrs Jourdan you may describe my Wants, and Expectations reasonable and unreasonable. Could I get one to answer them, I should scruple no terms. She knows every body. If she takes it in her head, she'll get me one, if above ground. But one I must have.

I am call'd away. The Bishop of Clonfert, Lady &c.[7] are just come in. They and every one here send you all their best wishes. Your Aunt desires you would tell Jeny, that she got her letter – and will write to her soon. Adieu My Dearest.

yours &c.
Edw: Elphin

I suppose your pocket money is all gone; Get more from Ned Curtis, whenever you please.

1. Yerks: bumps, jerks.
2. At Kilmore, Co. Roscommon.
3. The *Dublin Courant*, run in 1747 by Oliver Nelson, was much used by booksellers to place advertisements. Edward Synge refers frequently to books whose advertisements have previously appeared in the *Courant*. R.J. Munter, *The History of the Irish Newspaper 1685-1760* (Cambridge 1967), p.179.
4. *Pue's Occurrences*, founded by Richard Pue in 1703 and run subsequently by his relatives. Pue's position as bookseller, coffee house proprietor and auctioneer made his

newspaper particularly valuable to readers of estate and property advertisements. Munter, p.159.

5. Elizabeth Cornwallis, wife of Sir Robert Maude, 1st bart. He died in 1750. Burke, (1916), p.1014.

6. Luke Vipond: Edward Synge's lawyer (see Biographical Register).

7. John Whitcombe (1694-1753), bishop of Clonfert (see Biographical Register). His wife's name is not known.

14

Kilmore.[1] June 20, 1747

My Dear Girl

Yesterday morning I left Garbally, at six, without taking leave of any one but your Aunt, whom I let into my design the night before. I was forc'd to this; For otherwise I must either have disturb'd the whole Family, or been late here. But with this management I made my journey very cleverly, and was at the end of it by eleven. I left them all very well.

This place is as beautifull as a Vast open of a noble river, and fine trees can make it. But these are beautys which do not strike me as strong as they do most others. The House is not good. The people I need not describe. You've heard me speak of them. They are as agreable as any can be. Monday I'll however run away from them. For I long to be at Elphin.

Your account of 'Nip' would vex me, if I had not resolv'd against being vex'd at things of that kind. But I desire that you or John Miller would tell Sympson, that I think this his fault, not only as He bled the Horse carelesly, but as he obstinately refus'd to open his neck, tho' I press'd him twenty times to do it. Tell him, that if the Horse miscarrys, I'll use him as Mr Davis did. He'll richly deserve it.

I am pleas'd that you have been at Rathfarnam.[2] You would do well to go there again, as you promis'd. The Lady[3] is very genteel and agreable; and if you choose a fine day, a ramble thro' those fine Gardens, will please you much. I shall expect your opinion of them.

Pray Ask John what condition my orchard at Finglas[4] is in. Those in the neighbourhood of Killaloe have got a severe blast.

I have time for no more. God bless and preserve you & your Companions. I am

your most affectionate
Edw: Elphin

Direct your next to Elphin.

Tell John that He should look out now for 2 or 3 Pigs to be fed with offal of Garden and Kitchen for Winter. I take it for granted that now Fruits are coming in, you'll provide largely for Pyramids[5] to be look'd at. I'll allow you as much sugar as you please.

When you see Mr Wills, Tell him with my service that I got his letter and will write fully to him assoon as I get to Elphin, unless he be set out before that for Killaloe. If He be, I hope He proposes coming from thence to this Country and if he does, He must make Coll. Trench's his way. 'Tis by much the best, and the Coll. desir'd me to let him know that He hopes he will do him the favour.

Tell John that the Fair of Mullingar will make carriage very cheap. If the Chimney pieces be ready, then will be the time for sending them down. He must take his directions about Deal &c. for packing from Mr Wills. Ask if He has got my Barrel of beans from Mr Donnelan.[6] If not, He must get them.

[Stamped ATHLONE]

1. The home of Robert Waller. Married with six children under fourteen, he had eleven Protestant and eleven Catholic servants. Census f.150. The Shannon makes a long sweep round the north of Kilmore parish, so as to peninsulate about one-third of the landed area. *Gazetteer.*

2. Rathfarnham Castle, Rathfarnham, Co. Dublin. Home of the Loftus family. The sixteenth-century castle was altered and refaced in the eighteenth century. Bence-Jones, p.239.

3. Henry Loftus, 4th viscount Ely (1708-83), married Frances Munroe of Roe's Hall, Co. Down. Burke (1916), p.759.

4. Edward Synge farmed sixty-seven acres near Finglas, three miles north of Dublin. It was managed for him by John Miller, his steward in Dublin. 'Part of the Lands in my possession I hold by lease from the See of Dublin, Part under a Guild of St Scythe. I am not Master of the Title. But my Uncle who purchased and those deriving under him have been in quiet possession every since I can remember, and as I believe ever since the Revolution and were before. No demand whatsoever of rent. Nor, as far as I apprehend can any be made. Rent to the See £15.15.0d. ... I have the greater part of this in mine own hands, about 45 acres including house-plots, yards and gardens. The value of this is at least £100.0s.0d p.a. Rent deducted £84.0s.0d. ... part under the See of Dublin 40 Acres; under Guild of St Scythe 26 acres.' The land was thought to be 'of sumptuous fertility and ornateness ...'. Advertisement *Faulkner's Dublin Journal* 4-8 January 1763; Edward Synge's title to different lands and tenements in the county of Cork, Tipperary and Dublin 1813. NLI ms 2102; F. Elrington Ball, *South of Fingall ... a History of the County of Dublin* (Dublin 1920), p.112.

5. Possibly table decorations.

6. Nehemiah Donnellan II (*c.*1695-1771; see Biographical Register).

15

Tubbervaddy.[1] June 24, 1747

I told my Dear Girl in my last that I propos'd being at Elphin on Monday. But I could not keep my resolution. The obliging importunity of Mr and Mrs Waller detain'd me at Kilmore with great satisfaction to my self till this day; and here I am in for a day beside this; so that I shall not be at home till Thursday. I bless God I am very well and have no doubt of continuing so, as long as I have the satisfaction to know that you are so.

I can't write you long letters as formerly, till I return. Nor take notice of particulars in yours. But tho' I am call'd on while writing, I won't stir till I desire you to call Mrs Jourdan Lady Squeamish for her nicety about Miss Vignoles. And so my Dear Adieu

yours &c.
Edw: Elphin

1. Tubbervaddy, Lewis Ormsby's house near Athleague, Co. Roscommon. Census, f.208.

16

Elphin. June 27, 1747

My Dear Girl,

Yesterday about 3 I got home, very well, I bless God, and your letter would have given me spirits, if I had wanted them. Your being well and easy is the important point. But your account of Mrs Silver made me laugh heartily.

I have not time this post to write much to you. You must therefore be content with meer business. [In another hand: Chair ready to be sent for.]

Assoon as you get this, Send for Jones the Coach-maker; and know from him whether harness and every thing about my Post-chaise be ready. Ask particularly about the Box under the Seat, which, I find, is the only convenience it has for carrying any thing. Enquire the same things from Mr Wills; and learn from him by the by whether He has any thought of going in it to Killaloe. If He has, Say not a tittle against it, tho' I fear it may interfare a little with my intended Expedition to the C. of Sligo. But As his journey thither is a great instance of good nature, and will be of vast use to your Uncle, So I would contribute any thing in my power to make it easy and agreable. If He does not intend to use it, and it be throughly equipp'd, I'll immediatly send Peter[1] to town to bring it down. He is the person I have pitch'd on to lead it, and He may acquaint himself with it on the road. I'll send up one horse by him; and you may tell John Miller that 'Dunne' must be the other. I won't have 'Snead' come down, lest any thing should be amiss with either of yours, and so you be kept from your rambles. I am glad 'Nip' is in a way of mending. Tell Sympson that the only amends he can make me for his carlesness and obstinacy in relation to that Horse is, to provide me a clever match for him.

Bid John Miller go to Mr Nelson, and tell him with my Service, that I am much at a loss for two good hands, Carpenters. If He could provide me two, who are not above taking directions, and are capable of following them He would do me a very important piece of service; and the Sooner the better. If the Chaise comes down, they may come in it. If not, They shall be allow'd traveling charges, and have ten shill. a week here, if they deserve it. There will be work for them for three months at least, I believe indeed for double the time. John must get Mr Nelson to do his utmost. For I am much delay'd in my work for want of a sufficient number of clever hands. Inside house-Carpenters are the men I want. Floors, Window Sheets and doors their business. If that Scoundrel George Stephens were not so drunken a rogue, It might be for his advantage to come down. I am almost inclin'd to venture on him, if it might be of service to his poor Family. But two good ones must be got for me, if to be had.

Give my Service to Mr Wills, and tell him that I choose to wait a post before I write to him, that I may recollect every thing I have to say. He knows already that I have stopp'd quarrying for Hearth Stones. Desire him to order Darling[2] to provide them of Palmers-town stone 2 feet and ½ for every room on the two floors, but the Big-parlour, and that 3 feet. He has undertaken that they shall be thick and good. They may be got ready to be sent down with the Chimney-pieces; and I fancy that All except that of the Big-parlour, which is to be a piece of Mr Wills's vanity, may come down together. I am not in a hurry for them. The Plaisterers will be some time, before they'll want them. They go on with the cielings first, &, as far as I can judge, very well. But the want of Carpenters delays them. I shall be undone if this want be not speedily reliev'd. Tell Mr Wills also, that I fancy, a Lanthorn or Lustre or some such fine thing might hang prettily from the Center of the cieling of the great Stairs. If He thinks so, Let him send me down a proper Hook and pully to be fix'd in the joice before the Cieling there is done. If He agrees to this, I'll hold a wager He orders a rose or Some such foolish thing to be put round it. But I must set my face against his foppery as much as I can.

Give my Service to Mrs Jourdan, and tell her, That The Grocerys she sent down being design'd only for a short stay here, will in some Articles fall short, if not supply'd. The demand at present is for some Powder Sugar,[3] half a stone of Currans, half a stone of Raisins, a pound of Stone blue,[4] two bottles of Oyl, and a small cask of vinegar. Desire her to provide them, so as to be ready for the next Carrs. I know not what quantity of Tea she sent. I have not us'd much yet. But I believe a supply of a Couple of pound will not be amiss. I shall have a great demand for it next Week. For Mr Waller, and, I believe, his Lady, and a good many more will spend it with me. You see I am not likely to be much alone. Shannon says Powder is wanting for my Wigs. You may send down this, and the Tea in the Chaise-Box. The Tea must be good *Coute que coute.*[5] And so My Dearest Adieu

yours &c.
Edw: Elphin

I sent Lennox up three Bills one for £60 another for £91. The third for £80, and directed him to give receits to Ned Curtis. Ask Ned if He has got them. Tell Lawson He is very good. I have not yet time to say more to him.

Ask Ned Curtis if He has fix'd my news as I desir'd it. By the Mark on the outside, I can't tell from whom I have it. But I think it is still Mr Buchanan. If it be I am much disappointed. One reason of my thinking it comes from him is that the Papers are not those I desir'd. He has sent *Faulkner*[6] instead of the *Dublin Courant.*

Tell John Miller that I believe It is time for him to discharge the Mullingar Horse from Work, that He may be full fat and sleek for Palmer's-town fair which is early in August.[7] He must sell him there or some where. For I don't intend to keep him, if I can make him off. He knows that He cost £15:-:-. I shall be content not to loose by him.

Desire Ned Curtis to get a Rheam of the good Writing paper, Pro patria they call it, cut ready to be sent down in the Chaise-Box. Half of it in quarto. I hope care has been or will be taken to have a good lock to that Box.

Tell Mr Wills, that I earnestly entreat him to see Houghton before he leaves town, and fix with him about the Carving &c. I violently suspect that He intends to play you a trick and shall be uneasy till I know what you have to depend on [*damaged ms*]. Whoever suffer'd him to take down the Work, while you were abroad deserves a Sound Chiding.

You may order Woodward[8] to make frocks[9] for Jac. and Will whenever you please. But I think they may wait till I return to town. Those Gentlemen are upon some occasions more Exact than they ought to be.

I am absolutely determin'd in relation to Tom. I doubt much whether I shall hold out till I get to town. So that a Servant must be got for me, or I must be without one.

Commissions multiply. If the post waited a few hours more, I should have twenty more. Tell Mr Wills, that Crawford desires a Set of Screws for pressing Floors. He is to be at the Expense of them. If Mr Wills thinks them to be of use towards making the floors more perfect, I beg He would immediatly order them to be provided and ready to be sent down the first opportunity. Crawford approves of the pattern hinges. I beg Mr Wills would order them to be made. He knows the number of each kind wanting.

Desire Lawson to send me Littleton's Pamphlet[10] assoon as it comes out.

A Roll of Tobacco[11] for Snuff will not be amiss.

1. Peter Healy: Edward Synge's coachman, to whom he left £5 in his will. Will, f.254.

2. William Darling, stone-cutter, was used by Michael Wills on the building of Steevens' Hospital. Michael Wills cash book (1731-7), Irish Architectural Archive 81/88, f.11.

3. Powder sugar. Four types of sugar are mentioned by Edward Synge: powder, brown, coarse and loaf. Powder sugar was white refined sugar ground in a mortar for use on the table in bowls and sugar casters. Brown and coarse sugars were unrefined and imported from the West Indies, often via Lisbon. Large households, as in Kevin Street and at Elphin, bought loaf sugar: white refined sugar formed into conical loaves where unrefined sugar was boiled in water, skimmed and poured into cone-shaped moulds. Elizabeth David, *English Bread and Yeast Cookery* (London 1977), pp.139-41.

4. A compound of indigo with whiting starch, used by laundresses.

5. At all costs.

6. *Faulkner's Dublin Journal.*

7. Palmerstown Fair was held on Monday 10 August 1747. Watson (1747).

8. A Hezekiah Woodworth was a tailor in Baldwin's Court. Watson (1760), p.47.

9. Frock-coats.

10. George, 1st Baron Lyttelton (1709-73), *Observations on Conversion and Apostleship of St Paul. In a letter to Gilbert West Esq* (Dublin 1747). 'O Strange World! For some time past, it was the Fashion to be Atheists and Deists! People who proffessed Religion were reckoned ill bred & vulgar! Of a sudden the scene is quite changed! Religion and Virtue are now more predominent Fashions than ever appeared in England! The Nobility and gentry, and what is more surprising, all the Ladies of Quality in Country, City and Court, now read and talk of nothing but the Authority and Proofs in the Scripture for the Foundation of Christianity! Why, it is the ingenious Mr Lyttleton, a Lord of the Treasury, who hath lately written Observations on the conversion and Apostleship of St. Paul which has made more converts to Christianity in a few Days, than all the controversial Books than were ever published.' Advertisement, *Faulkner's Dublin Journal,* 27-30 June 1747.

11. The cultivation of tobacco in eighteenth-century Ireland was widely promoted by the landed gentry as a means of improving their estates. I am grateful for this information to Dr Susan Hood.

17

Elphin. July 1, 1747

My Dear Girl,

The Company I told you I expected came to me on Monday. Mr and Mrs Waller, Miss Ormsby, Her Brother, Mr Waller's son, and Nephew,[1] Blair and one or two more. You'll easily believe that with so many about me, I have not much leisure. I have stolen from them for a quarter of an hour to let you know that I am very well, and happy because you are so. My Company too are very agreable, cheerfull, and easy and pleas'd with what they can get. But, all things consider'd We do pretty well hitherto. I hope We shall hold it to the End of the Week. For so long they'll stay.

I am vex'd that any thing interrupts all your riding. If Lawson's horse does not recover, Make John Miller buy a good one fit for a servant: Or for a while Let him send 'Dunne' to Cool blue.[2] He'll serve Jemy to ride till I send for him with the Chaise. You may then get 'Snead' for the same purpose. Jac. Davies and Jemy between them must take care of him. I hope he is in Stable. Let me know whether He be or not. My little black Horse is very well of his Lameness. His broken Wind is incurable. But I ride him constantly.

I am much surpriz'd that you have no account of Noon, or the Soop-dish. For He has been here, and told Mr Cary that He had deliver'd it. I suppose He has mistaken the place. Enquire at the Arch-Bishop of Dublin's.[3] The dish you sent me down is perfectly right.

I would have you by all means go to see Mrs Crofton of Grange.[4] If her daughter answers her appearance on further acquaintance, she'll add to the number of your agreable acquaintance. But It is right to be Civil to any of your Country friends who are in town.

It would be right in you to take some opportunity of waiting on Lady Newport[5] who is, I suppose, at Merion.[6] You should make a handsome speech to my Lord C[hancello]r, if you meet him, for troubling him for so many franks.

I am sorry your Garden affords you so little fruit. I expected there would be straw-berrys and Goosberrys enough. Pray what prospect of Apricots, Peaches, or Nectarins? Tell old Smith[7] He must provide better against another year.

Tho' the weather be broken and unpleasant, I have not yet suffer'd by it. My hay, as much as is cut, is very near all safe and my Wheat is not *lodgeded.*[8] So you spell it. Your hurry made you write more than you ought. Mine makes me break off. I am My Dear Girl's

most affectionate
Edw: Elphin

1. Not known.
2. Coolblue or Coolblow: the name of a place or a field.
3. Charles Cobbe (1686-1765, see Biographical Register): archbishop of Dublin. He lived in St Sepulchre's Palace, Kevin Street. The Garda barracks was built on the site of the Palace, but the original stone gate pillars remain. *NHI*, Vol. 9, pp.437, 424, 404.
4. Probably Susanna Crofton of Grange, parish of Aughrim, the widow of captain Henry Crofton who died in 1741. In 1749 she had one child over fourteen and lived with two Catholic and three Protestant servants. H. Crofton, *Memoirs of the Crofton Family* (Dublin 1910), p.204; Census, f.32.
5. Charlotte Anderson: wife of Lord Chancellor Newport. Burke, (1916), p.1726.
6. Merrion, Co. Dublin. On the south side of Dublin Bay, three miles from the city.
7. Old Smith: a gardener at Kevin Street.
8. Lodged: beaten down by wind or rain.

18

Elphin. July 4, 1747

I am much pleas'd with my Dear Girl's observation on her own letters. Two or three times I was upon the point of making it to you. But I thought it better to leave you to find it out your Self. There is no occasion for telling me, every minute thing, that happens, and the time when. Your own observations on material occurrences, and as much *plaisanterie* as you can, will be more improving to you, as well as entertaining to me.

My Company are still with me. I would not suffer them to go off till Monday. I pass my time very agreably, but have not so much to give to you as I would chuse. However I'll try to answer all your Questions.

My visitation I hold the 8th. The day following I'll send Peter up for my Chaise. I can't well spare him till that hurry is over. One of my Coach-horses which I intended he should ride up, 'Button', is sick. They are doc-toring him. But I think he'll dye. I'll send up another, and with him a young Horse, who, I hope, will be fit for mine own riding. I commit him to Jemy's care. Give him a great charge of him. As soon as He is rested from his journey, John Miller must put him into Doyle's hand to be well [*damaged ms*]. He is already broke, and rides well in a Snaffle. He is as gentle as a Dog – Jemy must keep him so. Tell John that I shall not care to sell the Mullingar-horse for less than He cost. Ask him how He rides: If well, or can be easily made to do so, He'll carry a Servant well, and then I sha'n't care whether I sell him or no.

I am almost sure that I told you in one of my letters, that Mrs Cary intended writing to Mrs Jourdan immediatly after I set out for Killaloe. She owns she did not do it, and begs pardon. She says she'll write by Peter. I think she is some what broke since you last saw her. She has had two ugly brushes, since I first came hither. She is just out of the second, and as merry and cheerfull as usual.

Gunning is marry'd, but his Wife not come home. It was well you did not ask Old Goldsmith[1] about him. He made some advances towards Jeny. It was a great baulk there that He did not proceed. But He was not to blame, tho' they are much offended.

The Mahon familys set out for Kerry, the Monday before I return'd home. We have accounts of the Sandfords from Munster. Harry[2] was here the other day.

Carleboe says He can't account for the Hams failing, unless they were suffer'd to hang in the Kitchen. He desires that those which are safe may be put into the Box with seeds. But if they be doubtfull, use them. I need give no directions about those that are gone, and going.

Mrs Silver's present made me laugh as well as you. She is indeed a strange Woman, but has many good Qualitys worthy your imitation. I doubt not but that you have sense enough, to discover them.

In return for this laugh I'll try to give you one. I don't know whether you were return'd from Strokes-town, when one Mr Hughes[3] a Nephew of Dr Blackford's[4] din'd here last Summer. I found him at Kilmore, and He came thence to Tubbervaddy. He was married to Mrs Ormsby's sister.[5] I invited him with the rest, and as He is one of a particular Cast, and I knew that my Gent, tho' sober, lik'd a bottle more than I do; so for a little mirth, and that I might be at liberty to go off when I pleas'd without stinting them; I committed the care of the Wine after dinner to him. One day I observ'd him going off before I did, or intended it; and ask'd him with some surprize Mr Hughes where are you going? My Lord, says he, I am going to p-ss. The Women present. Such a stun, follow'd by such a shout, I have seldom seen. Do you find out how this happen'd? He wanted wine, and meant to say, I am going to Pitts. But he dropp'd the tt's. He was, alone, not conscious of his blunder, and his Astonishment, first at our laugh, and afterwards when He knew the Cause of it, added greatly to our Mirth. I have been so long telling my merry story, that I have time only to add, that

I am My Dear Girl's most affectionate
Edw: Elphin

The Weather very uncomfortable – Thursday excessively wet – Yesterday broken with showers. Much rain last night, and lowrs greatly this morning. But yesterday Evening I had rec'd no damage.

In one of your letters before I went abroad you told me that Mrs Jourdan had read to Jeny and you your Grandfather's little tract in relation to the Sacrament,[6] and very much approv'd of it. She certainly judges right. I thought she had been long since acquainted with it. I would have you and Jeny read it agen, and agen carefully, and consider it. There is nothing in it, but what you may fully understand; and if you do, you may and I hope will put your Selves into a right frame of mind to receive the H. Communion. I would have you, in the name of God, do it the next Sacrament Sunday at St Peter's.[7] Or if the Weather settes dry, Go with Miss Corbet to the Cathedral of St Patricks any Sunday that is convenient. The Closet there is warm and Commodious – But remember this both of you: That to lead a truly Christian virtuous life is the thing well-pleasing to God. Without this neither prayers, nor receiving the Communion at certain times signifys any thing.

The next time you see Miss Corbet or the Dean,[8] Ask what becomes of the Law-suit, and give me an account of it.[9]

1. Old Goldsmith is not known, but 'Jeny' may be Jane, a sister of Oliver Goldsmith. There is a story, possibly apocryphal, that Edward Synge refused to ordain Goldsmith because he appeared before him in red breeches. John Ginger, *The Notable Man* (1977), p.54, 61.

2. Henry Sandford of Castlerea, Co. Roscommon. Admitted to TCD in 1736/7, he was MP for Co. Roscommon 1745, Kildare 1761 and Carrick 1768. *Alumni*, p.732.

3. Mr Hughes: not known.

4. Dr Blackford: not known.

5. Susan Ormsby was a Miss Lloyd, daughter of Owen Lloyd of Rockville, Co. Roscommon (?-1660). This may have been her sister Isabella. E.S. Gray, 'The Ormsbys of Tobbervaddy', *Irish Genealogist*, 1 (1941), 284.

6. A divine of the church of England [Edward Synge], *An answer to all the Excuses and pretences which men ordinarily make for their not coming to the Holy Communion. To which is added, a brief account of the end and design of the Holy Communion* (seventh edition London 1703). This was an extraordinarily popular tract; it was translated into Welsh soon after publication *(Attebbion i'r hôll wâg escusion a wnae llawer o bobl. yn erbyn dyfod i dderbyn y cymmun bendigedig* [by Edward Synge] *a gyfieithwyd gan M. Jones* [Shrewsbury] 1698) and was read in 1829 by W.E. Gladstone. Entry for 25 December 1829. M.R.D. Foot and H.C.G. Matthew (eds), *The Gladstone Diaries* 14 vols (1968-94) (1968), Vol. 1 p.275.

7. St Peter's, Aungier Street, Dublin. Holy Communion was celebrated every Sunday in Dublin churches. Watson (1747) p.62.

8. Francis Corbet (*c.*1683-1775): dean of St Patrick's. He was admitted to TCD in 1701, scholar 1704 and took BA in 1705; MA 1708; DD 1735. He became dean of St Patrick's in 1746. *Alumni*, p.178; Lawlor, p.50; *Gentleman's Magazine* (1775), p.454.

9. Reference obscure.

19

Elphin. July 8, 1747

My Dear Girl.

As I am now in the hurry of my visitation, you must be content with a short Epistle.

I am glad you were so well diverted at the College.[1] But you have full entertainment for a Morning behind, when Lawson will allow you to go there. When next you see him, Give him my thanks for his letter. But the next He sends to you to enclose to me, Examine, before you send it. This brought me a very Galant Billet design'd for you. Desire him to write it over for you; For, to send it, would cost you a groat.[2] 'Tis directed as to a Princess.

The Weather is now good. I hope it will continue. Hitherto I have suffer'd, nothing by the bad. We had a good deal of rain, but not continu'd, except on Thursday last, and then it clear'd up before evening.

Your Complaints of the Garden are I believe just. But consider that your stay in town was unexpected – Cherry-trees there are very few. They don't thrive. Do as well as you can this Season – I hope old Smith will order things better for the next.

If the Tea Mrs Jourdan got Mrs Silver to buy, be of a fine kind, keep it for your fine people, or to treat me at my return. I'll have none of it. Good plain green Tea was what I desir'd, and is what I would have. You may send me a Supply by Peter. I believe I shan't send him off to you till Saturday. I should have been glad of fine for my Company, who left me yesterday; But I shall not now have occasion for any, while I stay here.

John Miller was lucky in discharging his Work-men. But I hope he'll now push the Hay as fast as possible.

I thank you for your present. But the Secret is still impenetrable to me. I have not had time to study it by your Key.

Your Card from Miss Corbet was very acceptable. Let her or the Dean, or which-ever of the Family you see first know how much I am pleas'd with the issue of the Cause. I think there's an end of it.

Give my Service to Mrs Jourdan, and desire her to look among your Mama's receits for that for the King's Evil,[3] and to copy it for me. I want it for a poor Boy, whom I intend to make Hugh Stafford try it upon. If I remember right the whole receit consists of a Diet-drink, and a Plaister. I have time for no more. God bless you, My Dearest, and your Companions. I am

your most affectionate
Edw: Elphin

Turn

Direct Will to bespeak immediately three Groce of the best kind of Corks from Waters, that they may be ready for Peter to bring down.

1. Trinity College, Dublin.

2. A groat was fourpennies.

3. Scrofula, 'the King's Evil', was popularly believed to be curable by the sovereign's touch alone; this ceremony formed part of the quasi-sacerdotal nature of kingship. After the death of Queen Anne, the last sovereign to touch sufferers from scrofula, Hanoverian kings made no attempt to continue the practice. The tradition divided Whigs and Jacobites; Whigs were repelled by what they thought to be a superstitious ritual but Jacobites held that the sovereign's touch was confirmation of their legitimacy. Scrofula was diagnosed by the presence of an itch and tumours in the glands, joints and tissues. Sometimes patients were treated in a hot room with mercury sweats to unblock their glands. Figwort was prescribed as a treatment under the doctrine of signatures, its root resembling scrofulous tumours. Kiple, p.999; J. Barrow, *Dictionarium Medicum Universale* (1749).

20

Elphin. July 11, 1747

I rec'd my Dear Girl's by the Archdeacon[1] on Wedensday morning, and that by post on Thursday. It delights me to find by both and by the Archdeacon's account, that you, and your Companions are well. God keep you so.

I got thro' my Visitation very well. Dinner was the most troublesome part. But my Company broke up early. Carleboe perform'd very well. Mr French, Barton, Blair, Palmer and Tisdal[2] staid here on Thursday. Yesterday morning they all took their flight. After so much hurry of Company to be alone is by no means disagreable.

Your Impenetrable secret afforded a good deal of Sport on Wedensday Evening. All I have nam'd above, were and are much amus'd at it, and try'd in vain to discover it. When I have made Gunning stare, I intend to make a present of it, and the Key to Billy Cary.[3] It will afford him much diversion. The Archdeacon returned yesterday morning towards Dublin. A Grave letter from me brought him down. I wish I knew the reason of his long stay in town, and quick return to it. They say here, He is going to be marry'd. Learn the truth, if you can, without appearing too inquisitive.[4]

I spoke to Nat. Smith before I left town, to provide a proper piece of

Blue Cloath for the lining of the New-Coach. I desir'd that it might be a fuller Blue than the Servants Big-Coats. Get Ned Curtis to ask, if it be provided; and if it be, Desire Mrs Jourdan to send for and examine it. Let her keep it a day or more, till she shews it to Jones; and learns from him, if He has any objection. If He has, Let her make it as from her Self, and tell him that she will do so. Trades-men are shy of finding faults one with the other. As I am not in haste, so if the Cloth be not perfectly right, It is best to wait till another piece be provided. All the directions I have to give to Jones, are, That He put it in, in the neatest manner, particularly, that He nail the lining close and tight to the head, and not leave it swaying, as I think it is in my present coach: That He put in an hook for a Net, so as that it may be put in, when I travel, and taken out when in town, and that He provide a right good net for it. He must also get a very decent handsome fringe for the Hammer-Cloth,[5] and a Leather one for journeys. I care not a half-penny for Brass Mitres. Tell him I would also have good clever large pockets at the Doors, very well bound and Secur'd against tearing. They'll not look ugly in town, and will be very convenient on a road. These are all the particular directions I have to give. In general I hope he'll take care to have every thing neat, strong, and perfect. Let him give the Carriage as much paint, and the Leather as much oyl and black as they will take. There will be time for this. For I won't have the coach us'd, till I go to town.

Peter goes off instantly to bring down the Chaise. He'll be in town on Monday evening. I have order'd him to stay some days, that He may go out with the Chaise, and acquaint himself perfectly with the manner of leading it. When He has done this, Let him return, and Let 3 Crowns be given him for his Charges. I have given him money to bear them to town. He carrys up the young Horse. I hope he'll do for me, but am not certain. John must give Doyle[6] a very great charge of him.

Desire John to speak to Smith to send me down an hundred wheels as expeditiously as He can. Carly[7] and Lyons will be in town, by the time you get this. If all, or any part be ready, they may bring them down. I want no reels. Don't forget to send me a Roll of Tobacco by Peter. I expect some other things by him formerly wrote for. Forget none of them if you can.

Bid John Miller send a quarter of an Ounce of Collyflower seeds,[8] and the same quantity of Cabbage Lettuce seed by him.

You wrote twice to me about the Watch. The second time I intended to have answer'd you, but forgot it. In the way, that Watch hangs, It will be hard to bring it to time. If you can get Ned Curtis to carry it in his Fob, He'll soon set it to rights, by raising the Spring a little. If He won't take charge of it, let it hang as it does. Only keep it going. When you come to have a Watch of your own, You'll find the same inconvenience, and hard to remedy it. But Ladys watches are chiefly for shew.

I am much pleas'd that you and Jeny have been twice at the Holy Communion. Remember both of you, that this is not a Service to be performed now and then, but as often as occasion offers in the Church you frequent; and that It is your duty to form your whole Conduct so as never to be taken unprepar'd. I pray God bless you both, and keep you innocent and virtuous as long as you live. There is no solid comfort and satisfaction from any thing, or all this World affords, without this.

I thank you for sending me the Tea with so much Expedition. It shews how intent you are upon furnishing me with any thing I want. But I believe I shall keep this, and return it, to you fine people, as I rec'd it.

My Service to Mrs Jourdan, and tell her I now and then find a false spelling in your letters, which shews me that she does not look over them exactly. My Dear Girl, Watch your Self, and Let her watch you in this Article. To spell well is a great accomplishment, in a Female particularly – Now or never is the time to obtain it – I would have you all perfection, because I am

> your most affectionate Father
> Edw: Elphin

Bid John Miller the minute you see him to go to Mr Wills. He has some orders for him, about Carpenters, who, if to be had, are to come down in the Chaise; and then any thing that will not go conveniently with them, must be reserv'd for Carriers. If they do not come in it, you may send any thing which will not injure it. There is no danger of loading it. But I think you have not any thing to send but what will go in the Box. Be sure, send the Key. Tell Lawson that I am almost sure my Sligo expedition will not be made this Season, and that I shall be at home the remainder of the time I stay here so that He may come whenever He is dispos'd. He gave me leave to flatter my self with the hopes of seeing him here. Read these polite Words to him. He'll know what they point at. Our Weather is very fine, and the Hay consequently in fine order. I hope John makes use of it at Finglas. The wheat Flax &c. promise greatly.

Tell Ned Curtis that I desire he would pay Mr Sullivane the Wine Merchant £40 for the two hogsheads of Wine which He sent me down since I came hither. He may order Will to go to him and desire him to call on him at his shop, at any hour, or day that He pleases to appoint.

I am much vex'd that there is no news yet of right German Spa. I long till you and Mrs Jourdan try it, I believe it will be very good for you both. Honest Jane wants none.

1. The Rev. Arthur Mahon (*c.*1715-88): archdeacon of Elphin. Collated archdeacon

of Elphin, rector of Killucan, vicar of Kilcola, Eastersnow, Creeva and Toomna 1743. Prebendary of Howth 1750; precentor of Connor 1752. Leslie, Elphin, pp.32, 216.

2. The Rev. William Tisdall DD: rector and vicar of Castleblaney 1743/4-54. Leslie, Elphin, p.119.

3. Son of Oliver Cary by his first wife.

4. Arthur Mahon married Henrietta, daughter of Robert Downes, bishop of Ferns, in 1748. Burke (1979), p.773.

5. Hammercloth: a cloth covering the driver's seat or box in a coach.

6. Doyle: not known. There is a reference to 'Doyle the horse rider' being Jane Synge's cousin in Letter 34.

7. Carly: not known.

8. In 1685 Nicholas Shepherd supplied Trinity College, Dublin, with seeds for cauliflowers and turnips. E.C. Nelson, '"This Garden to adorne with all Varietie": the Garden Plants of Ireland in the Centuries before 1700', *Moorea* Vol. 9 (1990), p.45.

21

Elphin. July 14, 1747

My Dear Ally.

I should be very glad, that you spent not Wedensday only, but every day pleasantly. I hope you do. The thought of this makes my days more pleasant. Monday was by no means so. After one of the finest evenings I ever saw on Sunday, and a fair night; the morning set in for rain, which continu'd almost the whole day. This day, Tuesday, is fair, but doubtfull. If the Weather continues thus, the Harvest will suffer. I have yet rec'd no damage. Wheat, Flax &c. stood Monday's rain very well. The greater part of my Hay is quite sav'd. I wish it were so at Finglas. Now privilege[1] is come in, Tell John He must sometimes give me an account, how all matters go under his charge. Pray order him immediatly to give me an account how many Beams He sent down the last turn by the Queen's-County-men.[2] I wrote for 17 and have, that I can find but 9. They came when both I and my Carpenter who receives those things were abroad. If He sent but 9 desire him to send off the remainder, the first convenient Carriage He can get, of the dimensions formerly mention'd.

I am much pleas'd with your Weekly engagement at Artaign. You must prevail with Mrs Donnelan to let the Girls spend a day now and then with you.[3] It may perhaps be too sawcy to expect it from her. But try. The next time you go thither, Tell Mr Donnelan that I am seriously apprehensive He is angry with me for something I know not what, because I have not had a line from him, since I left town.

In one of your late letters you told me that your young Ladys from

Rathfarnam[4] were with you to fix a day for your dining there. As you have not told me that you had din'd there, I suppose your Engagement went off some way. Pray How? I would not have you slight any Overtures made to you from thence.

Your account of Adlock[5] surprizes me. You certainly did right to discharge him. But I am very sorry that the poor Man, whose bread depends on scholars should have such a misfortune. Could you, among you, judge, whether it was in any degree the effect of dirtiness? If it be, an hint to his Wife would not be amiss, in order to remedy it. I hope you'll take care not to loose what you have got. If so this interruption will be insignificant. Does Mr Delamain[6] attend you? You have not nam'd him in any of your letters. Perhaps the Weather is too Warm for dancing: Or It interfares with your riding or other Engagements. If so, It is equal to me, whether you continue it or not. One thing only I am concern'd about, your Carriage. I should be pleas'd with a full certificate from Mrs Jourdan in your favour. Now privilege is in, Tell her I shall expect a letter from her now and then. Say the same to Jane; and that she must write to me with as much freedom as she does to others. I saw at Garbally a letter of hers to Bab[7] which pleas'd me much, all but the writing, which was too careless. I would have her improve in that, and in every thing. I think your constant writing to me has improv'd you. But, Huzzy, you are still careless in Spelling, and in ten lines, I don't see a Stop. A little care will mend this. Pray, My Dear, take it. I'll note the false spellings in your last. For bear, you write, bare. For *shopping* you write *shoping*. For *patient*, you write, *petient*. These are but three: but they are three too many.

I am sorry you can't hear of a Servant. But you've time before you. I must get one, or go without. Tom's heighth and conceit grow every day less tolerable. Besides his near-sightedness disqualifys him for shaving me right. I always complain'd of this, but did not till lately know the cause.

Lawson's billet was put within his letter, just as you put his last within yours. Next post when privilege will be undoubted, I'll send it to you. I frank this at a venture. Let me know, if you get it free.

You say your Aunt Heaton[8] goes out of town. Pray whither, and for how long? You have had bad luck in your Coffee. Mrs Cary has some out of the same ship, as good as ever was drank. If yours when carefully roasted be not so, Desire Mrs Jourdan to sell it, and buy good with some of the Money. There's a black guard speech for you. But seriously, Let her dispose of it in the best way she can, I care not whether at loss or not. For I will not have you, and your friends drudge thro' such a quantity of sow'r stuff.

If Mrs Jourdan or you write to Mrs Cary Do not take any notice of what I said about her health. I hope I am mistaken. She is hearty and cheerfull as ever. She as well as her husband and Willy have been beating their brains about your Secret. To no purpose. In a few days I intend to give Willy the Key. And now I have said Everything I can think of. Adieu. My Dearest

yours &c.
Edw: Elphin

If you can easily find my black Octavo Common-prayer Book in the study, send it by Peter.

Tell Lawson that I'll write to him next post, if I can find time. But Let him tell me by the return of this, whether what is said in the Papers of the Arrest of Admiral Medley[9] be true.

Whose hand is the Evil-receipt in?

Bid John go to Nelson and tell him with my service that I would not have him give himself much trouble or comply with any unreasonable Conditions, to prevail on the two hands which I wrote for last post to come down. If they'll come I shall be glad of them, and they shall have work while there is any, which, as I said in my last to Mr Wills, I believe there will be the whole Winter and longer. But I can't engage positively: and I am the more indifferent because since I wrote last Saturday, I have got one very good hand, and expect two more.

Upon questioning my Carpenter closely, He can't tell what number of Beams I wrote for, or He then wanted. Nine only are come. If that was the Number John was order'd to send, Let him send no more till further orders. The Boards and Grocerys are just come.

[Free Edw: Elphin]

1. 'Privilege of Parliament comes in next Friday.' *Dublin Courant*, 11-13 July 1747.

2. Queen's-County-men: probably car men.

3. Catherine Donnellan (see Biographical Register). Nehemiah and Catherine Donnellan had two daughters, Catherine and Elizabeth.

4. 'The young ladys from Rathfarnham' are unknown; Henry and Frances Loftus had no children. Burke, (1916), p.759.

5. Adlock: not known. From the context, perhaps a tutor.

6. Henry Delamain: dancing teacher. Brian Boydell quotes the *Dublin News-Letter* for 22 June 1742 that he was 'from the opera in Paris ... Lately arrived'. Brian Boydell, *A Dublin Musical Calendar* (Dublin 1988), p.277.

7. Barbara Synge (1731-?) daughter of Nicholas and Elizabeth Synge. She married John Hatch of Swords, Co. Dublin. Synge, p.7.

8. Elizabeth Curtis: daughter of Robert Curtis of Inane, Co. Tipperary. Alicia Synge's aunt on her mother's side. She married Francis Heaton of Mount Heaton, King's County, in 1731. Elizabeth Heaton and Frances Curtis witnessed the marriage settlement between Edward Synge and Jane Curtis of Roscrea in 1720. Burke, (1912), p.12; Articles of Agreement ... Synge Papers NLI PCC 344/(7).

9. Henry Medley (d. 1747): vice admiral of the Red. 'They write from Turin by letters of 3rd June that vice-Admiral Medley would certainly be very soon before Bisogno with 8 men of war, and that he would answer for it that no more succours should get into Genoa.' *Dublin Courant*, 23 June 1747. Information that Admiral Medley had been arrested was without foundation. *Dublin Courant*, 11-14 July 1747; *DNB*.

22

Elphin. July 17, 1747

I send you, My Dear Girl, Lawson's Billet Galant, as I promis'd. He writes thus to you, that you may be accustom'd to the Flattery, which Girls meet with from fine people, and learn early to laugh at, and despise it.

I am glad Peter and his Horses got safe to you. You say He is fat. I believe his head is so too. My directions to him were, That He should go out with the Chaise two or three times, so as to understand the manner of leading it; and when He had learn'd this, to come off unless Mr Wills detain'd him. This was with a view to Carpenters about whom I wrote to him. I think I mention'd them in my Postcript to you, the same post.

You are a little Buzz, and Lawson a great one. The pamphlet you sent from him, you had sent me before, soon after I came here. I had it six Weeks before I left town, and wrote to you for it, for the entertainment of my friends here.

Willy Cary is still in the dark. I have not seen him for some days. The next time He comes here, I'll put him into possession of the Secret.

I shall always be pleas'd at any thing fortunate that happens to good Mrs Carleton or her sons.[1] The match you give me an account of seems to be so. I guess the young Lady to be Lady Mary Colley's daughter.[2] If she be, I believe her fortune is greater than you mention. Assoon as Mrs Carleton arrives, Go to see her.

Will. French brought here the other day a little Pad which he hop'd might fit you, or Jeny. I see no objection to it, but it's size which is not higher than 'Nancy'. For that reason I did not lay my hands on her.

As I was writing, in came Cary, and Crawford the Carpenter, and they have kept me so long setling the Dimensions of a Church to be set about immediatly, that I have time only to tell you, that I am very well and

your most affectionate Father
Edw:Elphin

[Free Edw:Elphin]

1. Mrs Carleton: not known.

2. Lady Mary Colley was a daughter of James, 7th earl of Abercorn. She married Henry Colley, MP for Strabane, in 1719. They had two daughters. Mary married Arthur Pomeroy on 20 October 1747. The other daughter, who may have married Mr Carleton, is not mentioned in Burke's *Peerage*. Burke, (1916), p.55.

23

Elphin. July 21, 1747

I got my Dear giddy Brat's two Epistles. Your long one I open'd first, and, when I found not the pattern, had resolv'd to rally you heartily on your omission. But you've escap'd this bout. Take care of the next.

Pray make my Compliments to Mrs Silver, and tell her I have so high an opinion of her judgment in every thing, that I readily submit to it in the Choice of a lining for my Coach. Send to Mr Smith, and see if He has any right good Cloth of the Same Colour. If He has not, He may perhaps get from the Draper, who sold Lord Grandison's as much of the same piece as will do. Some way it must be provided. I leave it to you. But be sure that Mrs Silver sees and approves of the Cloth, before it be put in. Assoon as the pattern is fix'd, Let Jones see it, that He may provide Fringe for the Hammer Cloth. Clothes of those colours ought to be rather finer than Blue. When you see Mr Smith, Pray Ask him whether I spoke to him about Clothes for liverys. I intended to speak for them and the Coach-lining at the same time, and thought I had done it.

It just now comes into my head, that I have you on the trip, Madam, for a piece of giddiness. Pray what is become of Peter and my Chaise? By a letter from Mr Nicholson, It should seem that He left town on Saturday. But I have yet heard nothing of him. I hope Lawson has kept him. But should not you have told me something of his Motions?

I am glad you are so pleas'd at Artaign. I think you very right in liking the Company more than the place. For that is by no means pretty. Pray did you deliver my Message to Mr Donnelan? If you did not, score that too. If you did, score, for not telling me his answer.

As I am writing, Peter is come into the yard with the Chaise. I was as eager, as you would have been, to see it. I like it much on the view, and sitting in it. To morrow or next day, I'll try how it moves.

I was this morning at Stroke's-town. As it was very hot I chose to go thither in the Chariot. The House and all about it, looks desolate. After much knocking, The door open'd; and in some minutes the Major appear'd with a frighten'd countenance. He look'd too as if just awake but ask'd me civilly, if I would go in and drink tea. I refus'd, and having enquir'd about our Kerry friends, who, He told me, are all well, return'd.

I did not doubt but you would be pleas'd with your reception and entertainment at Rathfarnam. I think you would do well some fine afternoon to go and make a visit there. If you are encourag'd to go again to dinner, Do – I hope you know the proper Medium between too great reserve and forwardness – Or if you do not, you have one with you who does. The Lady there is a very good Woman. She is also genteel and well bred. Some intercourse with such persons will be of use to you. But my favorite in these, and indeed in every other respect, is Mrs Nicholson. I would have you see her, as often as without impertinence you can, and observe her well, you'll find in her every thing worthy your imitation. I believe Mrs Jourdan thinks of her as I do.

You tell me you ate some of a pine-apple.[1] I am pleas'd you did, but sorry you do not at this time of day know how to spell *apple*. You write it with a single p. But this is the only false spelling I can discover in your letter. There is indeed another which to me is so. But use is of your side. *Prentice.* The true spelling is Apprentice – Your French, if attended to, had taught you this, – and when you loose your giddiness, you'll spell as well as I do.

I am glad your second Visit to the College was so diverting. But I perceive you have left something for a third. This however must be deferr'd; Or you must get a new Entertainer.

My prayer-book is found. I thought I had left it here, but not finding it in the Study concluded that I had carry'd it up. It seems Mrs Heap took it out in my absence, and did not think fit to restore it, till after I rec'd yours yesterday, upon enquiring from Shannon about it, It came out, that she had it. It was a better print than her own.

This very fine Weather makes us all very happy. I presume it has the same good effect on you. But it obliges you to be out very early when you ride. So much the better. You'll have more time for your other Amusements; and now and then an hour for reading, not trifles, but somewhat that may improve. Now is your time, my Dear Girl, for improving mind, body, and behaviour. I hope you are as desirous of making use of opportunitys, as I am of giving you all in my power. To see you a Valuable Accomplish'd Woman, will be the greatest joy and Comfort to

My Dear Dear Girl
your most affectionate Father
Edw: Elphin

For a day or two lately I had a little pain in my Ear and Jaw, such as I am accustom'd to have. A little carelesness in going out one of our uncertain days, I believe, occasioned it. But it is quite gone; and, I bless God, I

am as well as usual, better much than when I left you. – Order John Miller
to send down another hundred weight of Plaister of Paris just such as He
sent me before.

[Free: Edw:Elphin]

1. Pineapples were first grown in Ireland by Bullen, a nursery gardener who cultivated a four-acre garden and nursery in New Street, Dublin. John Phelan 'at the Sign
of the Pineapple' in Christchurch Lane, grew pineapples there in 1750. He charged a
guinea for plants nine to ten tiers high. E. Charles Nelson, 'Some Records (*c.*1690-
1830) of greenhouses in Irish Gardens', *Moorea* Vol.2 (1983), p.23; Eileen McCracken,
'Irish Nurserymen and Seedsmen 1740-1800', *Quarterly Journal of Forestry* Vol. 59 (1965),
2, p.135.

24

Elphin. July 24, 1747

My Dear Giddy Brat.

You see I begin this, as you taught me to begin my last, and with some
reason. For you tell me you got a letter which you enclose, – and yet none
was enclos'd in yours but Mrs Jourdan's. Indeed I rec'd a letter, on which
I see, *Dublin* blotted out and Elphin wrote, but not in your hand. If this be
it, you should have told me so in a Postcript; and Pray tell me now, How
you come to think it like a Petition? 'Twas a letter from your Cos. Sam.
Townsend.[1]

Give my Service to Mrs Jourdan. Tell her I thank her heartily for her
letter, but not at all for saying at the end of it that her next shall be
shorter. I have not time now to write to her, nor must she mind whether
I write or no but give me the satisfaction now and then of hearing from
her. The Enclos'd is an answer to the only part of it, that requires haste.

Pray Tell Madam Jane, that I will not accept her duty, nor any thing else
from her, till she sends it her Self. I insist on her writing to me, and when
she does, that she does not write a starch'd formal short letter, but in the
same free easy way that she writes in, to her own Father or Mother. If she
does not, We shall positively quarrel. She can speak briskly enough to me
sometimes, and I am much pleas'd when she does. Am I more awfull at a
distance? I would have your Ladyship and her afraid of doing bad things,
and of nothing else. As long as you avoid these, you need not be afraid of
me.

I had got thus far on Thursday evening, when in came Dr Lawson,
sooner somewhat than I expected. He rode the journey, it seems in two

days. You tell me, He has made you a present of Books. I think He might as well have let it alone. There is however no occasion for sending them back. I have some curiosity to see his letter, which neither Mrs Jourdan nor you knew how to answer. Send it me – I'll return it to you.

Your Cosen Molly Curtis's[2] account of her Father does indeed trouble me. But by Dr Lawson's, of his health, when He left town, I hope his low Spirits are only the effect of his journey, or a change of scene, and that He'll agen be well. His life is of great consequence to his Family.

You saw Lord Grandison[3] at Mrs Silver's. By your account I fear you wanted at that interview a little of that presence of mind, which is necessary on many occasions. When Mrs Silver said she intended to bring the Ladys to walk in the Garden, It had been polite in you, to have desir'd her to carry you to wait on them. Take the first opportunity of making this request. 'Tis now several years since I saw either of them. But when I knew them they appear'd to me, such as I would wish you to know, Women of sense, and of exceeding good behaviour.

I am pleas'd that you have been at Christ-Church.[4] What surpriz'd you there, was right. If the Primate[5] were at Church here, I ought to give the blessing, as Bishop of the Dioces.

The Church I am going to build is that near Mr Hawkes's.[6] I wish it were done. He is so odd a Man, that I shall have some trouble with it.

As your letter has under-gone no correction, I am pleas'd to see so few false spellings. There are but two, and both of a kind you are subject to. You often leave out one of two letters, l's, p's &c. that ought to be put together. Chancellor. two l's. You have put one. Stopp'd. two p's. You have but one. Observe this, and you'll avoid many mistakes.

By yours and Dr Lawson's account I find you usually ride in the Park. In this dusty season, I believe it to be the pleasantest place. But a ride sometimes about Merion, and Stillorgan will I fancy be not less agreable. I doubt not but you may have leave from Baron Dawson,[7] or Lady Allen's[8] Servant, to ride in the park[9] there, if you apply for it. You may desire Mrs Hamilton to get it for you from her Brother?[10] I hope that by this you are a Stout Horse-Woman.

I am just come from Charles-town,[11] where very kind enquirys were made after you. I have time for no more – I am

My Dearest
your most affectionate Edw: Elphin

[Free Edw: Elphin]

1. Samuel Townsend: son of Samuel Townsend, entered TCD in 1747 and graduated BA in 1751. He was Alicia's cousin through the marriage of his grandfather,

Richard Townsend (1684-1742) of Castletownsend, Co. Cork, to Mary, daughter of Samuel Synge, dean of Kildare. *Alumni*, p.819; Burke (1912), p.699.

2. Mary Curtis: Alicia's cousin. Probably a daughter of the Rev. Robert Curtis, Edward Synge's brother-in-law.

3. John, 5th viscount Grandison (d. 1766). Burke (1916), p.1129.

4. Christ Church Cathedral, Dublin.

5. George Stone (1708?-64): archbishop of Armagh. The Primate of Ireland. He was nominated bishop of Ferns in May 1740 and translated to Kildare in May 1743. He was translated to Derry in May 1745 and to Armagh on 28 February 1747. He was archbishop of Armagh until his death on 19 December 1764. He lived at 5 Henrietta Street, which was known as Primate's Hill. *NHI*, Vol. 9, pp.426, 428, 399, 394; *Georgian Society Records*, Vol.2, pp.11, 13.

6. The Rev. Lewis Hawkes: vicar of Kilglass. Born at Roscommon, the son of John Hawkes. Educated by Mr Contarine. Admitted TCD in 1723, he took BA in 1728. Leslie, Elphin, p.156.

7. Arthur Dawson (1698-1775): son of Joshua Dawson of Castle Dawson, Co. Londonderry. Baron of the Exchequer 1741. He lived in St Stephen's Green. Ball, Vol.2, pp.206-7; *Georgian Society Records* Vol.2, p.90.

8. Margaret Allen (d. 1758): daughter of Samuel du Pass and widow of John, 2nd viscount Allen (1685-1742). Lord Allen refused to acknowledge her as his wife, so she tricked him by advertising that she had inherited a fortune and he immediately sought to prove that he was her husband. They 'ever afterwards lived in great harmony' even after the deceit was unmasked. B. Burke, *Dormant, Abeyant, Forfeited and Extinct Peerages* (1883), p.5; *Gentleman's Magazine* (1758), p.146; Gilbert, Vol. 1, p.352.

9. Stillorgan Park.

10. Mrs Hamilton was Arthur Dawson's sister.

11. Charlestown, Clogher, Co. Roscommon, situated on the right bank of the Shannon near Drumsna. Seat of Gilbert King. The present two-storey house is late Georgian. Bence-Jones, p.81.

25

Elphin. July 28, 1747

After dispatching a multitude of other letters, I come to my Dear Girl. Like Children with their goodys, I keep the best for last. I have more pleasure in writing to you, than to any one else, yet not so much, as in reading yours, especially as they have hitherto brought me the pleasing tidings, that you are well. I pray God to keep you so.

I am glad that you and Mrs Jourdan are to begin with Spaa Water.[1] I hope it will agree with you. You may, manage so as that it may not interfare with your Exercise or Amusement. Should it so happen, you may spend your penny[2] near town, as you us'd to do on the road. But in this and every thing else that regards your health, you'll be guided by the

Doctor and honest Ned, to whom my Service.

I know that riding, Company &c. employ you, and 'Tis my intention they should. It will contribute both to your health and improvement; and I am particularly desirous that you should spend your time as agreably during my absence from you as possible. But I hope and believe it will be always agreable to you to spend some time in improving your mind. A little well employ'd will do, and It will not interfare with any thing else. As your relish for usefull Books improves, you'll be fonder of them. Two or three pages now and then of your new present. You'll hardly meet with one that will not please or instruct, or both.

You've justify'd your Self fully from my Charge about Mr Donnelan. But I have yet had no effect from your speaking. Next day at Artaign, ask him in a pleasant way, if He has wrote to me. The Gent. is indolent, and wants a Spur. But I am more surpriz'd at his not having done what He said He would, than at his Son's not delivering your Message. That Gentleman's giddiness is great, and likely to continue. For his Father's sake I wish He were cur'd of that, and of other things. But I have long since despair'd.

I am glad you've walk'd in the green. To be sometimes there, is pleasant enough. I wonder at their taste, who are fond of it often. I was not, when young and sprightly as the best of them.

I don't doubt but that your two false spellings were owing to giddiness. I am also sure that one I have found in yours now before me is owing to the same Cause. But Tell me, Mrs Bold-face, Is this an excuse? What says the Proverb? A Bird that can sing &c.[3] with a little little care, you may avoid this and some slighter imperfections, which I now and then observe in your letters. But these notwithstanding, I have the pleasure to see that you improve greatly both in the matter of your letters, and, when you please, in your writing; tho' I think it may be time now for you to give your hand a little more of a Female turn. Ask Mrs Jourdan. You tell me that I am to expect but a short letter from you next post; and I hope it will be so. Nor will I expect other than short ones, while you drink the Water. I always found it inconvenient either to write or read when I drank it, especially in the morning. Avoid both. I believe the Doctor will in this join me. A line from you, or Mrs Jourdan, or from Madam Jane who wants no Water, to let me know that you are well, will content me. I have wrote to that Lady this post. If she drops the correspondence, I shall not be pleas'd.

I see your friend Mrs Silver is kind in every way that she can be. You did very right to invite her to her own Venison. Mrs Donnelan's answer to you was very polite and kind. I am pleas'd that you've observ'd it. Mrs Jourdan did miscall the Carr-man. But I knew whom she meant. I am glad you got Betty Donnelan's[4] ears bor'd. Pray tell her I ask'd whether she roar'd like a Bull? Give her and Kitty[5] my service. You tell me that Ned Curtis has my

Watch, but don't say whether it goes better in his pocket, than it did on your Nail. I wish I had it in the place of the one I have. It has got such a trick of galloping of late, that it is become useless. It is now very fit for a young Damsel's side. The Society pacquet[6] I have no business with here, nor much any where else. Put it into the Study.

Dr Lawson is well. I leave him to pursue his own inventions, while I pursue mine. At breakfast, dinner, and in the Evenings We meet. But I foresee He'll ruin me in Tea. Your late Supply will not last him long. Last Sunday I broke in upon the Canister you sent of Fine, and indeed It is very fine. I have seldom tasted so good. But this Extravagance was not for him. Mr King of Charles-town[7] was here. But now the Gent. has got a taste of it, I reckon it will all go. For some days He has been employ'd in doing the honours of the Town to Mrs Gunning.[8] She came hither last Friday, and with her A Brother's Wife and a Maiden sister. Two Brothers also attended her. On Saturday morning I sent for Gunning and bid him bring them all to dine here; and at Church He told me they would come. But about an hour after He came with a sneaking embarrass'd Countenance to make an Apology. The Brother's Wife had got the Tooth-ach, and they could not leave her. I said it was very well, and so none of them came. By her appearance, and what Lawson and Mrs Cary told me, this Brother's Wife is a sort of Lady Squeamish. But their account of Gunning's Wife is very different. I have yet only seen her at Church; Her person is agreable rather than otherwise. But they speak very favorably of her sense, and behaviour. If she answers upon further Trial, Insipid Gunning has had very good luck. They are now in a round of invitations, with which I have nothing to do. I would not dine with them yesterday at Cary's. When that is over, I'll ask them agen and treat her for the future as I find she deserves. Her fine Sister-in-law is gone off, much to poor Gunning's joy.

Yesterday about Noon, It began to rain, not heavily. But the Evening was dropping and there fell a good deal last night. There have been some showers to day, but no mischief is yet done. If fair Weather does not return, Corn and Flax must suffer. The [*damaged ms*] almost all up. Tell John that I have got a very complete [*damaged ms*] for 'Nip'. I hope He is growing well. I have neither time nor room for more. So My Dear Dear Girl Adieu

yours &c. Edw: Elphin

I had almost forgot to point out your false Spelling. You write *spaking*. In one of my letters sometime ago, I ask'd you whether you could get a Certificate of your holding up your head. Am I to take your Silence for a confession, that you are not entitled to one?

I have had some sport between Mrs Cary, and Dr Lawson. He with a face three quarters grave had told her twenty storys of Mrs Nicholson, and she has wrote her an account of most of them. My hope is, that she'll complain at Kevin-street. You are to report. Something perhaps may arise, that will heighten our mirth. It has done, what we have had, very well, to sweeten an unpleasant Evening.

Willy Cary by a little hint I gave him, and the strength of his Memory has form'd to himself a method of discovering your Impenetrable Secret as quick and sure as if He had the Key, which I have not yet told him.

[Free Edw:Elphin]

1. Spa waters were believed to cleanse the body of excesses and impurities. From the eighteenth century on, drinking mineral water to cleanse the body supported the popular cultivation of greater hygiene. Spas were scattered throughout Britain and Ireland and used by large numbers of both sick and healthy people. Waters bottled at source and exported, such as those from Germany drunk by Alicia, were not held to have the value of a visit to the spa itself; gases in the water went flat and, more seriously, the patient was not felt to have the advantage of the regimen prescribed by the spa's attendant physicians. Mme de Maintenon is thought to have been one of the first to drink bottled spa water: in 1681, Fagon, the king's physician, arranged for her to drink the waters of Sainte-Reine. Illness and health were jointly matters of mind and body and had to be treated by the spas's amenities of scenery, food, peace and amusement to be most effective. Roy Porter (ed.), *The Medical History of Waters and Spas* (London 1990), p.viii; David Harley, 'A sword in a madman's hand: professional opposition to popular consumption in the waters literature of Southern England and the Midlands 1570-1870', op.cit., p.48; L.W.B. Brockliss, 'The development of the spa in seventeenth century France', op.cit., p.40; Christopher Hamlin, 'Chemistry, medicine and the legitimization of English spas 1740-1840', op.cit., pp.70-71.

2. This early reference to the phrase 'spend a penny' contradicts the usual link with the installation of public lavatories in mid-ninteenth century London. Paul Beale (ed.), *A Concise Dictionary of Slang and Unconventional English* (London 1989).

3. 'A Bird that can sing and won't sing, must be made to sing.' William Robertson, *Phraseologia Generalis* (1693), p.1133.

4. Elizabeth: daughter of Nehemiah and Catherine Donnellan. She died unmarried.

5. Catherine Donnellan: daughter of Nehemiah and Catherine Donnellan, married Lewis Ormsby in 1749.

6. Society pacquet. Not known.

7. Gilbert King of Charlestown, Boyle, parish of Kilmore. MP for Jamestown, co Roscommon. Magistrate. His wife was called Ann. He had three children, and a household of nine Protestant and five Catholic servants. Census, f.36.

8. Mrs Gunning: her maiden name and the names of her relations are not known.

26

Elphin. July 31, 1747

My Dear Girl

I return you your letter. It is wrote in the same flattering Stile, in which I have seen many of his. It is one way He has of diverting himself. I have formerly given you the Key to such things written or spoken. Consider them as matter of advice; and Endeavour to be, what you are told you are. No answer was best. But I am sure Mrs Jourdan could not have been at a loss for a proper one.

You were not to blame about the letter. But Lawson was; and He confesses it. But you have misspelt *bloted*. It should be *blotted*, the same kind of mistake, that I observ'd to you before.

I am glad your Salts[1] agreed so well with you. I wish Mrs Jourdan's had done the same. But perhaps tho' they us'd her a little roughly, they may have thereby prepar'd the way the better for the Water.[2] I shall long to know how it agrees with you both. I hope it will make you spend your penny bravely.

I am sorry there were so few Apricots. That is the true spelling. But I don't charge your Spelling it wrong as a fault now. I shall, if you do it agen. If they be cheap, Let some be bought. If not, We can do without them. While you drink the Spaa, you must neither eat fruit nor Garden things. So that, to you, cheap or dear, they are now of no consequence. Before, you might have eaten as many as were good for you, with all my heart. I believe I know the pear Tree you speak of. It is a Bergamet.[3] About Micmas the fruit will be good, tho' small. It is a very old Tree. If the goodness of the fruit does not on trial make amends for the size, It shall come down. Let John Miller mark it. For on second thoughts I believe I guess wrong, or you have describ'd wrong. The Tree I mean is not in the quarter with the Mulberrys but on the other side of the Alley.

My Jaw and Ear-Ach are gone; I have had no return since I gave you an account of them.

Gunning, his Wife, and her Sister dined with me yesterday. I like his Wife very well. She appears to be meek, well-humour'd, not unbred, nor deficient in sense. But she is not as brisk and lively as some I know. Her person is well. You'll think so, when I tell you, that I think the Air of her face like Mrs Hunter's, and Dr Lawson agrees. *Mais elle n'est pas si belle.*[4] She is about Mrs Jourdan's heighth. Gunning is Ditto, and will be so while He lives.

I thank you for your news. It was very well worth sending. As it came while We were at Table, It cost me the other bottle.

You are very right in returning Dr and Mrs King's[5] Civilitys. I would have you do so to all from whom you receive any, in a proper manner.

You have not told me whether you desir'd Mrs Silver to carry you to wait on Lady Grandison.[6] I should be glad you knew them. You say she was to be with you at Mrs Nicholson's. I fancy those two Ladys whose manner is so perfectly opposite, make a pretty kind of Contrast. With what rapidity one talks and sometimes swears! How gracefully and calmly the other! I don't know whether you've observ'd Mrs Nicholson's manner of speaking. 'Tis the most distinct without formality, or Slowness, that ever I heard. In this, as in every thing else, she is worthy your imitation.

I was going on with my prattle, when word was brought me, that there was a house full below. Counc[illo]r Trench, his Wife, and Daughter,[7] and Coll. Folliot[8] and Major Wynne.[9] So I must bid you for this time Adieu.

yours &c. Edw: Elphin
To morrow morning I go off to lay the first stone of my Church.

[Free Edw:Elphin]

1. Possibly Epsom salts, hydrated magnesium sulphate, a crystalline salt used as a laxative.

2. There are frequent references in Edward Synge's letters to the use of purges, laxatives, bleeding and of spa waters. According to Hippocrates, Aristotle and Galen, the belief in humoural physiology, still current in the eighteenth century, dictated that there were four humours: blood, phlegm, yellow bile and black bile; the four elements: earth, air, fire and water interacted with them. These humours had to be in balance, and illness occurred when one humour became out of balance with the others. This could be caused by excess which might be due to constitutional strain or through diet or external events. Balance was restored by ridding the body of excess by purges, vomiting, bloodletting and blistering and the use of laxatives. The physician approached the disease by examining the patient's symptoms, rather than by examining the disease itself. The analysis of urine and vomit formed part of this approach. E. Lomax, 'Disease of infancy and early childhood', in Kiple, p.147-8; Keith Thomas, *Religion and the Decline of Magic* (London 1973), p.10.

3. Bergamot: a variety of pear. In 1653, John Percival imported fruit trees to Ireland from Arnold Banbury of London including '3 Summer burgamottes [and] 3 winter burgamottes.' E.C. Nelson, *Moorea* Vol. 9 (1990), p.45.

4. But she is not so pretty.

5. Dr James King (?-1759) was the eldest son of the Rev. Thomas King, prebendary of Swords who was a relative of Archbishop King. In his will, Thomas King asked the archbishop to oversee the education of his three sons. In 1725 James King was appointed assistant librarian of Marsh's Library. He was made prebendary of Tipper in 1726, of Donoughmore and Timothan in 1730 and of Tipper again in 1737. He became incumbent of St Bride's in 1730 and curate assistant of St Peter's. He was twice

married; in both cases to cousins. Swift was fond of him and left him a medal of King Charles I. W.G. Carroll, *Succession of Clergy in the parishes of S. Bride, S. Michael le Pole, and S. Stephen, Dublin* (Dublin 1884), pp.21-2.

6. Elizabeth Villiers: created countess Grandison in her own right in 1746. Married Alan John Mason in 1739. Burke, (1916), p.1129.

7. Eyre Trench's wife and family are not known.

8. Probably John Ffolliott of Hollybrook, parish of Aughana, Co. Sligo. John Folliot enlisted as a lieutenant in major general Bowles's Regiment of Horse 1709. He became captain in 1714; major in Lord Cathcart's Regiment of Foot in October 1729; lieutenant colonel July 1737. He was made colonel in the 18th Regiment or Royal Irish Col Folliots' on 22 June 1743 and took command 23 December 1747. His household had four Protestant and three Catholic servants. PRO WO64/10 f.15; WO64/9, f.172; Census, f.359.

9. Possibly John Wynne who served in the 12th regiment of Dragoons in 1748. *A List of the Colonels, Lieutenant Colonels, Majors, Captains, Lieutenants and Ensigns of His Majesty's Forces on the Irish Establishment* (London 1740).

27

Elphin, Aug. 9, 1747

My Dear Girl

For once I take small paper as well as you, and for the same reason. I have not much to say, nor much time to say any thing in.

But I must once more call you my Dear giddy Brat. If you had thought ever so little, I flatter my Self that you would not have sent me that paltry Chronicle. This hint is sufficient. I won't call in question your Sense, or regard for things sacred, by pointing out the reasons, why you ought to dislike it.

In my last I gave you an account of Gunning's Wife. I have not seen her since. I don't know how He lodg'd his Company. But He was in a great fuzz about them, as you'll easily believe.

I hope you've before this made the proper return to Lady Grandison's condescension. You call it so, very properly, but mispell the word. That and two or three more I have mark'd in a Scrap of paper by themselves. One of them is not so properly a false Spelling, as incorrect, tho' Common, English. Always in the Preter-tense, and Sometimes in the Present, *wrote* is more proper than *writ*; tho' as you use it, *written*, would be better than either. I observe that you have us'd that word once in this letter very rightly. You say very true, my Dear, that your letter is, I won't say, badly but, indifferently written. I hope you'll keep your promise, that the next shall be better; and that you may write completely well. Let me recommend it to you to mind your Stops, and to avoid running two words into one, and dividing one into two, of both which you are pretty often guilty. Perhaps you'll think me too Exact. But Consider, My Dear, I would have you all perfection.

I like the lining for the Coach mighty well. Let it be got immediatly; and order Jones to get a handsome fringe for the Hammer Cloth. Tell him I'll consider him for it. What He says I believe is true. But I have alter'd my mind, imagining that you will like fringe better. If you do not, or if it be not the mode, Let it alone. The Coach is more yours than mine, so order it as you please, provided that you don't let Madam Jane put any of her Vagarys into your head. Give my blessing to that Lady, and tell her I will not let her know whether I like her letter or no. So she must try agen as she promises.

I don't know any thing of poor Heney.[1] I fear he has suffer'd. Saturday was a bad day. But the Flax has suffer'd none, and the wheat very little. I passed the Evening as you guess. For Mr French was here. You pass'd yours very well.

My service to Mrs Jourdan, and tell her that since my coming hither I have had two or three quarrels with Mrs Heap, who really does just nothing at all, but keep the Linnen and Grocerys, how well, I know not, nor do I enquire. Since my return from Killaloe, I enquir'd about my consumption of wheat, and found it within a trifle as great as last year, when my constant Family was 17 more than now, and I had much more occasional Company.[2] She made some idle pretences, but could give no good account, and now, since I made a bustle, about half the quantity serves. Upon examining further I found that the whole affair of the Dairy, and poultry was left to Jennet. She order'd Milk, and butter and bought in Meal and dispens'd it as she pleas'd. Mrs Heap gave her Self no trouble. She lyes a bed till eight or nine, and then saunters about as she pleases. She spends most of her time in the Servants Hall, or in her own room, they with her; and as far as I can observe Darning, or pretending to darn is her chief employment. While I am away she has nothing to do, and therefore does nothing while I am here. She vex'd me greatly last Sunday. On Friday, when the Company came on me unexpectedly, a veal was kill'd, in the afternoon. It was natural to expect Jelly on Sunday, especially for Ladys. But none appear'd. When I ask'd her in the Evening, how that came, she said that Carleboe had not boil'd the Feet.[3] She never thought of doing it her Self, or relieving him so far, who had business more than enough on his hands. In short she seems to me ten times more insignificant, than ever. I won't trouble Mrs Jourdan to write to her. But perhaps it may not be amiss, if you or she, or Both, tell Mrs Hunter that I have complain'd and with particulars. You may add, that if she does not mend her manners, I see not of what use it is to keep her; as indeed I do not.

Tho' my paper was small, and time short I have made a shift to write a great deal. But I have time for no more and so My Dearest Adieu –

yours &c. Edw: Elphin

I am very glad the Spaa agrees with you.

1. Heney: not known.
2. Edward Synge often used the word 'family' to describe his servants as well as his own relations.
3. Hannah Glasse made a jelly from boiling calves' feet in water with 'a Pint of mountain wine, half a Pound of Loaf Sugar, the Juice of four large Lemons', and clarified it with whites of eggs. It was served in glasses. A Lady [Hannah Glasse], *The Art of Cookery made Plain and Easy* (first published 1747, reprinted London 1983), p.145.

28

Elphin. Aug. 7, 1747

My Dear Girl.

To explain what I mean by giving your hand a female turn, I write this letter in the way I wish you to write. It will be a very short one, for I am just setting out for French-park to consecrate the Church, and have time only to tell you, that I am well, and rejoice that you are so.

As the Evenings are now growing shorter, I think you had better make your Visit to Rathfarnam some morning.

You rec'd L[or]d Chancellor's Card on Monday. This gave you time to send to Artaign to excuse your selves for one Wedensday; and you might have done it without offending. But it is no great matter. I believe you spent your day there full as pleasantly, as you would have done at the Hill.[1]

Tell Mrs Jourdan I thank her for her letter. In it she speaks of an old Acquaintance whom she met at St Bridget's[2] Church. I knew her well many years ago and if Mrs Scott[3] be as good a Woman, as Hannah Gladstanes was a Girl, I shall be much pleas'd, that it has thus fallen in your way to know her. Adieu

yours &c. Edw: Elphin

Excuse me to the Doctor for not writing.
Desire Ned Curtis to get his Watch-maker to bring the Watch to time. Raising the spring will do it.

[Free Edw:Elphin]

1. The Hill: possibly Henrietta Street. See Letter 24 fn.5.

2. St Bridget's, Bride Street. Rebuilt in 1684 by Nathaniel Foy, later bishop of Waterford. Demolished in 1898. Craig (1980), pp.40-1.

3. Hannah Scott (?-1776): daughter of Thomas Gledstanes, she married William Scott of Willsborough, Co. Londonderry, who became a baron of the exchequer. Burke (1912), p.210.

29

Elphin. Aug. 11, 1747.

My Dear Girl

Yesterday Evening I return'd from French-park, very well, I bless God. I left the poor Coll. in but an indifferent way. All the rest were well. You were there remembred constantly in the kindest manner.

You were in the right not to answer for the writing of your letter, till it was finish'd. There is a great difference between the beginning and the End. However tho' it be one of the longest I have had from you, I like it the best both as to writing and contents. I hope you'll improve daily in this, and in every thing else that is good. But I am sorry to find that All the practice which your constant correspondence with me has given you, has not yet brought you to write with more ease and quickness. I have often told you that the posture of your hand on your writing-table is the great impediment to this. Let me advise you agen, to change it. It may perhaps be a little awkard to you at first. But if instead of laying your wrist on the Edge of the Table, just under your chin, you would lay your Elbow fairly on it as I do, I am confident you'd quickly find that your pen would move with more glibness, and answer the rapidity of your thoughts, or your little tongue, which when set agoing moves sometimes as nimbly as the best.

You are disappointed in your intended triumph over Cary. My wheat is almost reap'd. I began on Friday; and We are to have a loaf of new to morrow. Shall I send it to you? If this fine Weather continues a Week longer, The harvest will come in so fast, that We shall not know what to do with it. But this is not a thing to be complain'd of.

Every thing at the house goes on very well. The Attick story is, to a trifle, finish'd; and now All hands are at work at that, which I intend for your Apartment. It will be a very fine one. But I sha'n't think it too good for you, if, as I hope, you continue good your Self.

I had a letter last Thursday from Godfrey Wills[1] dated Wills-grove.[2] In it He tells me that his Uncle[3] was alive, but a miserable spectacle. I have since heard nothing. If the Old Gent. lingers, I hope Mr Wills will step over to me for a day some time this Week. You shall then have a more distinct account.

Your Uncle gave me an account of his gout.[4] I hope it is gone off. I fancy'd this morning, that I had a little touch of it. But I believe now 'twas a false alarm. I walk'd a good deal on Sunday evening at French-park. But A short smart Visit would not displease me. I shall make it welcome by eating and drinking as usual. So Dr Curtis advises; and while the Weather continues thus hot, there is no stirring out to walk or ride: So that it is as good be confin'd as not. However I am to dine to morrow at Carrigins[5] with old Daniel.[6] His letter of invitation is as Extraordinary in it's kind as his nephew's, which once gave us a laugh. Here it is for you, spelling and all

My Lord
I promised to doe my Self the Honr to have the Feavr of yr Ldship &c.
to dine with me at Cargins to morrow being a Wednsday & am
yr Ldship's
Most obedient Hble Servt
D.K.

I thank you for wishing you could supply me with new Pamphlets. But there is no occasion. Lawson, Cary and his Wife, besides chance comers, fill up my leisure time agreably enough. But you would not be pleas'd if you thought that I did not feel some want of you. I do indeed, My Dear, and yet I have not once wish'd you here, since We parted. For I am satisfy'd that It is much better for you on all accounts to be where you are; and I can cheerfully give up mine own greater satisfaction to my Dear Girl's good.

The letters you sent came safe. That from Galway was from Governour Eyre.[7]

I am glad your Coach-horses hold out so well. Should either of them fail, John Miller has recruits for you. I would have your staying at home always the effect of choice, not of Compulsion of any kind.

You did very well to send a Melon to Mrs Hamilton. If they come in plenty, dispose of such as you don't use at home, where you think they'll be acceptable. One or two at different times to the Arch-Bishop would not be amiss. But send none that are not very good.

I don't wonder that you were much delighted at Merion. It is one of the prettiest places I ever saw. The particular spot that you describe I don't remember. But I am pleas'd with your lively natural description of it. One word you have mispelt in it. I believe 'tis one you are not acquainted with. You write *deal*. It should be *dale*. You did well not to take the Bird. To be sure It was offer'd to please Miss, who probably has not yet learn'd the Art of disguising a little, the surprize and pleasure with which she sees a new thing, and thus appears fonder of it than she is; at least than she would be in half an hour.

I am much troubled at what you tell me of Mrs Nicholson. Pray in your next, let me have a particular account of her. Let me also know what is become of poor Palmer.[8] I am under great concern for him. When He was here at the Visitation, I thought him in a bad way.

I am oblig'd to Mrs Silver for contributing to feed my family. She is indeed an odd Woman. But with all her oddness, she has many qualitys very worthy of imitation. I hope you'll profit by the one, without being infected by the other. Make my Compliments to her as often as you think it convenient. I give you a general Commission.

I was not at all surpriz'd with the news of Dr Gratan's[9] death. I have long expected it. It is wonderfull that He liv'd so long. I am afraid poor Jac. will soon follow. See, my Dear, what a silly thing this world is. Young as you are, It is not amiss sometimes to make this reflection.

I am sorry for Miss Mahon's ill health. Take this occasion of returning to her the great kindness she shew'd to you in your distress at Strokestown.[10] See her as often as is convenient to her and you. Our Kerry[11] friends are not expected home this month. I believe Mr Mahon will return assoon as he possibly can. For his Water improvement,[12] begun in his absence, goes on heavily, and under such a Management, as makes me fear it will be much more expensive than He imagin'd.

Your bit of a Postcript in which you beg quarter which you do not much want for blots and mistakes, is wrote in a hand, which would please me well for your constant one.

Desire Ned Curtis to get a ferkin of Gun-powder, such as he us'd formerly to send me for blasting rocks. Let it be ready to come down by the next opportunity. All I had, has been employ'd in blowing up the rocks in the Well in the Kitchen-yard. I think I may now say that I have a certainty of good Water there. This has been one great work of the Summer. The Canal has been another, which I have enlarg'd and dug to a proper depth. I hope to have it a fine Tench pond.[13]

Give the enclos'd to Ned Curtis. Desire him to give it to Mr Lennox and get his receit in the usual Way. And So My Dear Girl Adieu

yours &c.
Edw: Elphin

How are the Grapes?[14]

[Free Edw:Elphin]

1. Godfrey Wills (d. 1778; see Biographical Register): a close neighbour of Edward Synge in Roscommon. Confusingly Godfrey Wills also advised him on building affairs.

2. Wills Grove, Castlerea, Co. Roscommon. Birthplace of William Wilde, Oscar Wilde's father. *Irish Booklover*, 6 (1914) 1. Now demolished.

3. Caspar Wills: an army captain who with Godfrey Wills's father purchased the Willsgrove estates, part of the forfeited possessions of James II. He married Sarah Cole of Enniskillen. High sheriff of Roscommon 1708. His will was proved in 1749. Burke (1912), p.624; Vicars, p.493.

4. Gout is a chronic disease which flares up intermittently. The symptoms are swollen joints. It is caused by a high level of uric acid in the blood. Gout can be caused by lead poisoning, where the kidneys are poisoned by a high concentrate of lead (from food containers; badly glazed china and lead water pipes) and the kidneys are unable to excrete uric acid efficiently. In the eighteenth century it was thought to be caused by the excessive consumption of food and drink, and moderation in all things was counselled. The importing of port from Portugal after the Treaty of Methuen in 1703, led to an enormous increase in its consumption. The brandy used to fortify wine in making port was distilled in stills which contained lead parts. T.G. Benedex, 'Gout' Kiple, p.763, 821; Arthur C. Aufderheide, 'Lead poisoning', Kiple, p.824.

5. Cargins Park, near Tulsk, Co. Roscommon. The eighteenth-century house has gone, to be replaced by a two-storey Victorian house. Bence-Jones, p.56.

6. Daniel Kelly of Cargins Park.

7. Stratford Eyre of Eyrecourt, Co. Galway (1700-*c*.68), was a son of Samuel Eyre and Anne Stratford. He was high sheriff of Co. Galway in 1731; governor of Galway and vice admiral of Munster. His will was proved in 1768. An extreme Protestant, his violent correspondence with Dublin Castle was lost in the fire in the Four Courts in 1922. *Alumni*, p.270; Vicars, p.160.

8. Thomas Palmer.

9. Dr James Grattan (*c*.1673-1747): Fellow King's and Queen's College of Physicians of Ireland. King's Professor of the Practice of Medicine. He was a governor of Steevens' Hospital. Kirkpatrick; Watson (1746), p.65.

10. Eleanor Mahon's kindness to Alicia was on the occasion of Robert Synge's illness and death in 1746. See Letter 1.

11. Thomas Mahon and his wife.

12. The works no longer survive at Strokestown. The present lake was made later in the century.

13. Archbishop Synge made a fish-pond at his Palace at Tuam in 1719. 'Paid or Expended in taking 251 trouts and carrying them Alive by two men from Ballygaddy river to the Fish-pond at Severall times £1.8s.0d.' NLI ms 2173.

14. The marquis de Ruvigny's Huguenot colony in Portarlington grew grapes and trained their apples and pears on espaliers. Sheila Pim, 'The history of gardening in Ireland' in E.C. Nelson and A. Brady, *Irish Gardening and Horticulture* (Dublin 1979), p.48.

30

Elphin. Aug. 14, 1747.

Very well, Miss Sly-boots! You ask a question in your postcript, that you might give me a Bob[1] for writing two hands in the same letter. I confess the charge. But you knew well enough, Huzzy, which was to be your pattern. If you can't follow it, It is no great matter. What I see you can do, will satisfye me. Only write always, as you've wrote the Superscription, and the middle part of your letter; and you need not envy either Molly Curtis or me.

I told you in my last that I was to dine on Wedensday at Daniel Kelly's. But I did not then recollect that It was Court-day. This oblig'd me to put off my Expedition to yesterday. Will French and I went thither in the Chariot, and Lawson and Barton in the Post-chaise, which pleases us all hugely. We met several there, and were very well entertain'd. Mrs Kelly enquir'd for you all with great kindness.

At my Court on Wedensday I broke Mr Hickes.[2] He appear'd guilty of many bad practices. If He submits, and confesses what I am sure He is guilty of, I may possibly restore him. If He continues to behave himself in the same silly absurd manner, that He has done in the Course of my Enquiry, I resolve to appoint another Register.

I am glad Sympson has bought me horses. Desire Ned Curtis to pay for them if it be not done already; and Let the enclos'd be given to Simpson assoon as you can.

And now I must say as you do, My pipe is out. And so My Dearest Adieu

yours &c. Edw:Elphin

Lawson with his Tea morning and evening consumes so much Sugar, that I must have a supply. Desire Mrs Jourdan to get three Loaves to be sent off by the next Carrs. If they don't offer soon, I shall be out. According to laudable custom no notice given, till the Stock is just gone.

Bid John Miller go to Mr Eaton, and tell him I desire that He would examine the Windows, and Pallisades of the house, and if they want painting, order it to be done as usual. I should have wrote about this Earlier. But it is not yet too late. Let no time be lost, if painting be necessary.

What says Houghton about your Carving? Send to him. For his time is now come.

Ladys Grandison[3] have been very kind. You should in a short time wait upon them, and when you do, beg leave to see them sometimes, without putting them to the trouble of returns, to which you are not entitled. Mrs Jourdan will instruct you in what terms to make your compliment. Probably she has given you the Advice.

I hope you don't neglect to enquire about a Servant. Tom must go at all Events. His pride and oddnesses are not to be born. I wrote to Mr Nicholson about one. When it comes conveniently in your way, Ask him whether He has any hopes.

[Free Edw:Elphin]

1. A blow.

2. His Registrar. See Letter 8.

3. The Dowager Lady Grandison was Frances Carey, widow of John, Earl Grandison of Limerick. Burke, (1916), p.1129.

31

Elphin. Aug. 19, 1747

I am sorry my Dear Girl has had any ruffle. But the Doctor's account and your own, give me the Comfort of thinking, that It was a very little one. I hope to morrow's post will confirm it. I fancy something that you ate, disagreed with you. If this were the Case, Be more cautious for the future; tho' to do you justice, you are usually cautious enough.

I am much pleas'd with the writing of your letter. You are now in a very right way. Persist in it, and you'll soon be as perfect as I desire. But you must learn quickness of writing from Madam Jane, as I would have her learn fairness from you. In this and every thing else, Correct each other's faults, and learn each other's perfections. You'll thus be both more perfect than you are. Tell your Cosen what I say; and at the same time, that her last letter is much better wrote than her former ones. I have not time to write to her this post, but hope to do it, the next. She must not mind whether I do or not, but continue to write to me, whatever comes into her Coltish head.

Mrs Nicholson's paper I have been long acquainted with. I am pleas'd that you found it. I am very glad she is so well. I hope she'll abuse Dr Lawson plentifully. For indeed He deserves it. He has the confidence to say that He's sure she will not, because He wrote some flattering verses, which will disarm her rage, if Mrs Jourdan has not spitefully suppress'd them.

It was a little unlucky that you were depriv'd of your Walk at Merion. But you had some amends made you by seeing that surprizing Worm,[1] which you so well describe.

When next you go to Artaign, Tell the Squire there, that I deferr writing, to punish him for his silence; and Tell the good Lady, that I am more oblig'd to her, than I can well express.

My gout is absolutely gone. Melons I care not whether you have or no. But if your grapes fill well, and do not shrivel, you may depend on it they'll ripen. The leaves do not contribute to the ripening, but to the filling.

On Saturday night We had here a terrible storm. But it has done no damage, or next to none. The rain of the day secur'd the Corn. All my wheat was in Stack. My Oats are all reap'd. They have begun upon my Barley. The Flax is in stack, and my hay at home; so that As to Harvest I am in a prosperous way. If next post brings me an account that my Dear brat is quite well; I shall be as happy as I expect or desire to be, till I see her. I am My Dearest

your most affectionate Edw: Elphin

[Free Edw:Elphin]

1. 'Surprizing Worm': reference obscure.

32

Elphin. Aug. 22, 1747

I had just finish'd a pretty long letter of raillery to Jeny, and was going to write to my Dear Girl when Coll. Wynne[1] came in, and stopp'd me. You'll easily believe that I have since had no time. You must therefore be content with a line or two.

Tho' I thought your disorder slight, and was not therefore alarm'd, yet your own and the Doctor's account of your being perfectly well rejoic'd me much. Excuse to him my not writing. I really have not time.

I see I accus'd you without reason. You ask'd about e and I thought you meant, hand.[2] I did not observe the e in your former letter till I read your last. You may use which you please, or both. A set hand is not the best. But if you continue to write as you've done of late, I desire no better. Between Mrs Jourdan and you make the Filly do so.[3]

I am glad Mrs Jourdan has got Mrs Hamilton's butter Woman even for 8d. I wish it were more. If you've paid Pasmore[4] 6d all the Summer, you've been giddy managers.

My gout stay'd but a day. I bless God I am quite well.

yours &c. Edw: Elphin

We were alarm'd on Thursday for a quarter of an hour. The Chimney of the Landry-room took fire, and being very dirty, the burning soot fell upon the Shingles and had almost set them on fire. But It was perceiv'd in time, and immediatly extinguish'd.

[Free Edw:Elphin]

1. A Major John Wynne was called to the King's Inns in 1721. The Wynne's Dublin

house was at 3 Henrietta Street. *King's Inns*, p.522; *Georgian Society Records*, Vol.2, p.19.

2. Reference obscure.

3. Edward Synge compared Jane Synge's writing style to that of a 'young well-bred Filly', and told her that 'One of the most celebrated Toasts in Town, about fifteen years ago, was known by the name of The Galway Filly. Why then should not I call you The Kevin Street Filly?' Edward Synge to Jane Synge 11 and 22 August 1747. I am most grateful to Allen Synge for allowing me to transcribe this correspondence.

4. Pasmore: a butter-maker.

33

Elphin. Aug. 26, 1747.

My Dear Girl cannot have more pleasure in writing than I have in reading her letters, especially when they bring an account of your being very well. Tho' your letter is well wrote, yet It is not quite so well as your two or three former ones. You say, Mrs Jourdan thinks one you wrote after, better. Tell me, pray, Did you write it with the same pen? If you did, I can easily account for it's being better written, tho' you took less care. For the pen more us'd, mov'd more freely, and gave it's ink better. Your pens are generally too fine nibb'd. They draw hair strokes. But 'tis impossible to cut letters with them as well as with those not so fine, but a little softer. I would have you use your Self to this sort. You'll quickly find the ease, and advantage of it.

I am sorry Jac. Davies has been ill. I hope He is by this time recover'd. I am much more uneasy at your wanting the Convenience of my Coach, than at the Expense of Coach, and Chair-hire. While the Weather continues thus fine, you may use Hackneys[1] without inconvenience. Make Will or Jac take care to choose those that are Warm and good. As for pocket Money, or other Expenses, I shall never blame you for extravagance, unless you trifle money away; and I don't think all girlish expense trifling neither. It is suited to your Age. When you commence Woman, you'll disdain it.

You were a little mistaken as to Mrs French of Porte.[2] You ought to have attempted to see her before you invited her to dinner. This was the polite return to her kind visit. I was indeed to blame, that I did not give you an account of her Expedition to town. I intended to do, but forgot, it. She went up to the Doctors. I hear she has receiv'd benefit by them. Assoon as Jac. Davies is able to drive, I desire you would go all of you to see her. Go in the morning, and call first at Smithfield.[3] If they tell you there, that she is at John's-town, Go thither. Jac. Davies knows the way. It is a little beyond Glasnevin.[4] And desire her to introduce you to the Judge's Lady. She is an exceeding good Woman whom I have known since We were Boy and Girl. I am sure, she'll receive you with great kindness.[5] I am pleas'd with your inviting the Miss Mahons and Mrs Nicholson. Her you can't see too often. But proper Civilitys to your friends and acquaintance you do well to pay. You'd make a great figure with your Haunch, if you get it well dress'd.[6]

I deliver'd your Message to Dr Lawson, and was much pleas'd with it. I would have you always proof against flattery from every one. He indulges himself in that foolish way more than He ought. You were much in the right not to shew his verses. Observe the same conduct always.

Next time that Will. goes that way, order him to call at Kenny's the Wig-maker,[7] and to ask him whether He has the Wig ready which I bespoke. I shall want it, when I go to town. When that will be I can't yet say. My house requires constant attendance, much more than even last year. Many things are doing, which would go wrong, if I were not at the beginning and end of them. I can't trust Cary himself. You've heard me sometimes complain of his want of Exactness. I have had more reason this year than ever. Besides this, I must get money, Huzzy, to support your Extravagance; and that I can't hope for till our great Fairs. You are therefore in the right not to expect me soon; and yet I believe you wish for me soon. I am sure I wish eagerly to see you. God send us a happy meeting. I am My Dearest

your most affectionate Edw: Elphin

I observe one, and but one, false spelling which I place to the account of giddiness. You saw Mrs N. – pass buy. I need not tell you how it should be. But you are not yet carefull about your stops.

Fail not to pay all the regards to Ladys Grandison, which their very kind notice of you deserves. As for Mrs Silver, you know among you, how to deal with her. Have you had any good, at least any number of good, Peaches?[8] I have had some here, much better than I ever saw here before.

It may not be amiss to speak to Eaton the Glazier about a servant for me. I spoke to him last year, but was fool enough to try whether Tom could be reform'd. It is impossible.

[Free Edw:Elphin]

1. Hackneys: sedan chairs.

2. Possibly Catherine, daughter of Robert Lloyd of Cloghan, Co. Roscommon. She married Jeffry French MP for Milborne Port, which may account for her title here. Burke, *IFR* (1979), p.449.

3. Smithfield: north of the river Liffey. This area was first developed in the late seventeenth century. Maurice Craig says that a number of noblemen's houses remained in this area until the late eighteenth century. Lord Justice Robert French lived in Smithfield; possibly his brother's wife was staying there. Craig, (1980) p.85; Ball, Vol. 2, p.208.

4. Johnstown: near Glasnevin, two miles north of Dublin.

5. Lord Justice Robert French married Frances Hull of Leimcon, Co. Cork. Ball, Vol. 2, p.208.

6. Haunch of venison.

7. Kenny, wig-maker. Not known.

8. William King, while archbishop of Dublin, grew melons, peaches, apricots and almonds at Mount Merrion. In 1755 John Phelan sold imported peach, nectarine and apricot trees. W. O'Sullivan, 'Mount Merrion in 1714 – was there a stove-house?', *Moorea* Vol. 3 (1984), p.22; E. McCracken, 'Irish Nurserymen and Seedmen 1740-1800', *Quarterly Journal of Forestry* Vol. 59 (1965), 2, p.135.

34

Elphin. Aug. 29, 1747

To know that my Dear Girl is well, will always give me the greatest pleasure. But indeed, Ally, I was more disappointed at your last, than I have been at any letter I have rec'd from you since I left you. Don't be in a flutter now. It is no great matter. But I expected an account from you of Madam Jane's reception of my letter; and as I hop'd it would give you a laugh, pleas'd my Self with having from you a merry account of it. I was baulk'd at your taking no sort of notice of it, tho' you complain'd of want of news. But perhaps it was dull, tho' I strove to write as pleasantly as I could. Jane her self has answer'd it very properly. Tell her I say so; and that she must write to me agen, tho' I have not time to write to her. For the Explication of the Terms, broken neck'd, and Cavison,[1] I must referr her to Jac. Davies, or Doyle her Cousen the Horse-rider.[2] He breaks horses.

Mr Wills came hither on Thursday, and I had scarce sugar for him yesterday. But Mrs Cary has supply'd me. Did no Carrs leave town, Mistress mine, since I wrote for three Loaves? If any did, whom am I to blame, your Ladyship or Mrs Jourdan that they were not sent?

I don't know how Lawson look'd while He apprehend'd danger. For We were looking one way. But He has since confess'd that He was frighten'd, and wonder'd at me for joking. I saw there was no danger. Shannon with his usual gravity and phlegm, said that a Goose was the best thing to let down a Chimney on fire. I bid him go and let himself down. He gap'd, and recovering himself, said half aside Humh! That's good. Are not you a sawcy Madam for thinking that your being here would have added to my distress? And yet it is very true. On twenty other occasions this Summer I have made the same reflexion, and rejoic'd that you were safe in Kevin-street. And yet the most pleasing thought I have in fitting up my house, is that I may be so happy as to have you with me in it. God send I may; and continue you well and good. I have no more to ask in this world.

Tell Eaton that He may take his own time for the painting. The sheets are at present too dusty for it. In this part of your letter you've contriv'd to make two false spellings in one Word. You write *deffer*. It ought to be *deferr*. I have observ'd but one more, which I take to be a little bit of giddiness. juant for jaunt. Your writing is very well. Let it never be worse. It will soon be much better. I have time for no more. I am My Dearest's

most affect.
Edw: Elphin

The days do shorten sensibly. But As the Weather continues fine, this is easily born. At night We play Whist according to Custom. My harvest is almost at home.

[Free Edw:Elphin]

1. Cavison: a type of nose-band used to discipline difficult horses.
2. Doyle: not known.

35

Elphin. Sep. 1, 1747

My Dear Girl,

Give the enclos'd to Mrs Jourdan. The same reason that made me break off pratling to her, hinders me from writing more than three words to you.

I rejoice that you are well. I bless God I am so. I hope you'll be no longer depriv'd of the pleasure of going to Artaign. Let Mrs Donnelan know that I am greatly concern'd at her indisposition, and Tell him, that if He has a mind I should write to him, He must beg it in a second letter. I am spitefully inclin'd to make him feel the pangs of seeming neglect.

Shannon tells me that some part of the Door Case in Kevin-street is rotten. Get Eaton to look at it before it be painted; and if there be any thing quite rotten, Let him order George Stephens to repair it. I would have nothing done that is not absolutely necessary. For I intend a new one some time or other.

My Dearest Adieu
yours &c. Edw:Elphin

36

Elphin. Sep. 4, 1747

My Dear Girl

Whenever I observe you guilty of any fault or omission, I think it right to admonish you, in order to your avoiding the like for the future. To my great comfort I have not frequent or great occasion. I hope it will always be so.

Your want of something to write, is not owing to a poorness of imagination, but rather to this that you don't accustom your Self enough to think and observe. But As you grow up, you'll find this will mend, and you'll be able to write a long letter about nothing, as well as the best of them. This sort of writing is only talking on paper. Do you find your self at a loss for prattle? I think not. What hinders you then from writing as you prate?

The Sugar is not come. But that's neither John's fault nor yours. I am in some pain, not about them, but about my Timber. John writes that three Load were dropp'd at Chappel-izod. I fear He has got careless men.

Give my service to Mrs Jourdan, and tell her that Dr Lawson will, I am sure, wait her leisure for an answer. He is still employ'd, as I told her in my last. On Wedensday after Church He squired his Ladys, and two or three more who came to see them, to the new house, and spent two hours in shewing them every thing. Assoon as We rose from Table, away to them agen, and when Mr Wills and I return'd from our Walk, and wanted Tea, He had left they [*sic*] key with Shannon, to avoid being call'd upon. He did not return till We had almost play'd our first Rubber.[1]

Yesterday Evening and to day, We have had a little sprinkling of rain, but the Air is so mild, that I hope We shall still have good Weather. When will the Doctor think it cool enough for you to resume your riding? I hope your Mare is quite well. All my searches for another have been hitherto in vain. Will. French had one which I intended to pillage, but unluckily it dy'd.

I heard the other day, that Mr Palmer was a good deal better; Ask the Doctor about him; Or Learn from Mrs Cope in what way He is.[2]

The day after you get this, you'll, I suppose, see your Uncle &c. I long to know that they are safe in their winter Quarters. I shall wish my Self in mine, before I shall get there. Indeed I do it already. But I can't with any convenience stir yet a while. God send us an happy meeting. I am My Dearest

your most affectionate
Edw: Elphin

1. Of a game of cards.
2. Mrs Cope was Mrs Palmer's mother.

37

Elphin. September 9, 1747

My Dear Girl

I am much rejoic'd, that Jeny is recover'd, and that you continue so well. God keep you all long so.

Tell Mrs Jourdan that Dr Lawson got her letter. But it may be He'll tell her so himself. He is now at full leisure. For his new passion is gone. I don't mean Miss Betty – For she is still here.[1] But the true Coquet Spirit hind'red his fixing long there, when any thing new offer'd. About ten days ago, Two young Gentlewomen came to visit there, and staid till Monday last. After a visit or two, poor Miss Betty was forsaken for these; and of them the younger prevail'd; so that the Superscription ought to have been in *Rachel's* bow'r – That's her name.[2] The Doctor says she has wit. She may for ought I know having seen her only at Church. But sure I am, that neither Rachel nor her Sister have beauty. They are both very Brune, indeed downright yellow, worse than the Kite's foot, and have something particular about their Eyes. The Sister appears at least to Squint, and is of Grenadier size. Rachel is tall, but short neck'd and pokes worse than you or Jeny ever did. B[ut] they were new, and the Gent. idle and Coquet. He was very assiduous, missed [*damaged ms*] but one day of visiting, and on Sunday, which was to be the last, mu[ch – *damaged ms*] ado He stay'd to drink Tea, then run off, and left them not till near nine. All Monday He was sighing that poor Miss Rachel had so bad a day. But now she's gone, I suppose Miss Betty will be in fashion agen, till a new one comes, or He goes off – Monday was indeed a very bad day, which I was very sorry for, tho' not for the same reason [*damaged ms*] Dr. – Your Uncle, Aunt &c. were on their journey.[3] I long to have an account of their being safe and well at the End of it.

As it will not be long now before I hope, God willing, to be with you, so I must think of things that will be wanted on my return. Send Will or some one for Woodward and order him to take measure of all the Livery people for frocks and Waist-coats, so as to have them made throu[*damaged ms*] well by the end of the month. Then send for Mr Smith and desire him to pitch upon good Cloaths, for these frocks and Waist-coats; and he must take care to c[ut *damaged ms*] pieces, which will afford enough to make the same for my servants here, which including Billy, you know are five.[4] I count one in Tom's place. But He must go off. Tell Mr Smith I depend on him to choose good Cloathes and that I would have that for the Frocks a little darker than the last. Charge Woodward to be punctual, and do his best. My servants are grown so shabby, that they will not be fit to appear in town. I believe those with you are not much better. Take care now, My Dear Girl to acquit your Self well of this Commission.

I am glad that the roads on which you use to take the Air, are mended. They will, as you say, be agreable in Winter. I would have every thing so to you, My Dear, as long as you continue good, which I hope will be always.

I am surpriz'd at what you tell me of Mr Mahon's return. The last time I saw Luke, He did not expect him till Micmas.[5] He has begun a piece of work here, which I fear will be very expensive. I wish He were well at the end of it. I believe that hastens him home. It will please me to see him, and his good Wife, before I leave the Country. Pray do you know any thing of the Archdeacon?[6] The next time you see his Sisters or Cosens, enquire carelessly for him. I am much dissatisfy'd at his staying so long in town.

The Old Gent who was in such haste to be marry'd, was one Mr Burke Uncle to Lord Clanrickard. I'll tell you the Lady too. One Miss Eustace.[7] And now, Curious Ladys, you are as wise as ever you were.

Eaton has done right. I think it is best be clean. You know I always recommend it to you. Now the Carving is up, you would do well to have the whole dressing room painted. Get Eaton to you, and engage him to pawn his word, that it shall be done with Nut-oyl,[8] and then the smell will not [offend *damaged ms*]. You don't say whether the Carving be well done. I hope it is. I [am *damaged ms*] much at a loss whether I should desire that to be painted or not. [As *damaged ms*] Mr Wills is not in Town, I think your best way will be to consult [Mr *damaged ms*] Nicholson, and follow his judgment. You see Mrs Nicholson off 'ner than you do him. Get her to tell him that you want to see him, and the occasion. I am sure, He'll go to you.

If the grapes you sent Lady Grandisons were fine, you did well [to *damaged ms*] send them. I am glad you have any ripe so early, but hope they [will *damaged ms*] not all be so, till I get share. It will be news to you, that my [Garden*damaged ms*] here has furnish'd me with about an hundred very fine peaches.

If Saturday were no better a day with you than it was here, you [and*damaged ms*] Mrs Jourdan were very stout to ride in it. But since you came off well, [I *damaged ms*] am glad you did. It would give me great joy, that you were under no [necessity *damaged ms*] of minding weather. Ours has been for some days bad. Monday [ver *damaged ms*]y bad. I allow them fires which

Lawson wonders at, and is pleased with. But [they *damaged ms*] are neither more agreable nor more necessary to me, than formerly. [I *damaged ms*] bless God I am as well this cold wet Weather as I was in the fine [tho' *damaged ms*] not quite so happy, as I can't travel as much about. But I make shift to get my rides. I have miss'd only Monday. I have time for [no *damaged ms*] more, nor more to say now but that I am My Dearest

your &tc
Edw:Elphin

I have not caught you of late at false-spellings. But there is one in this letter *efect.* there should be two f's. Tell Mrs Jourdan that Many of my shirts here [are *damaged ms*] grown ragged. I believe I shall want a Supply.

1. Miss Betty: not known.
2. Rachel: not known.
3. From Killaloe, Co.Clare.
4. The annual provision of livery for servants was quite an expense. Archbishop Synge paid £5.10s.0d 'for cloath, serge, and drugget for the Men's Cloaths and Frocks' in December 1725. NLI ms 2174.
5. Luke Mahon was Thomas Mahon's uncle. He was unmarried and lived at Strokestown with one male Catholic servant. Michaelmas is on 29 September. Burke, *IFR* (1979), p.774; Census, f.84.
6. Dr Arthur Mahon. See Letter 20.
7. Mary: daughter of Alexander Eustace, married Thomas Burke of Lackan, Co. Roscommon, younger brother of the 10th earl of Clanricarde. He died in 1765. Burke, (1916), p.463.
8. Oil from nut-kernels, especially hazelnuts and walnuts, used to manufacture paints and varnishes.

38

Elphin. September 12, 1747

My Dear Girl

I am greatly griev'd, but very little surpriz'd at your news about Miss Sandford.[1] See what comes of levity of behaviour – I hope I never shall have reason to accuse you or your Cosen of it. It is very probable that her poor Father in the bitterness of his soul has aggravated matters. But I believe they are bad enough. I know the Family. It is of good account. But the fortune small and encumb'red; and It may be the person is not the Eldest son. But whether He be or no, or the fortune good or bad, The Girl is undone. In my whole Experience, I never knew one of these marriages tolerably happy. I pity the poor Father, and Mrs Nicholson. Tell her with my service, that I'll be sure to observe her Commands, both for her Father's sake and hers. I should be sorry to have her suffer by her piety to him, which yet I cannot but highly commend.

I am mighty glad that your Uncle &c. are safe in town. The badness of Monday gave me great pain on their account.

I am sorry you miss'd Mrs French. She is now in town at Alderman King's² in Abby-street. Go to see her there, and get her to carry you to the Judge's Lady, if it be convenient. Shew her all the Civility you can.

Your account of poor Palmer makes me very uneasy. But As He is in town, I suppose you'll see him, and then give me a more particular one. You may learn by the by, when He intends to return. But say nothing to him of the time of my going up; only in general that it will be late – Indeed that is all you can say. I would rather not call on him, for fear of incommoding him; and yet I am afraid of grieving him, if I do not. I should think it lucky that He staid in town till I went up, unless ill-health occasion'd it.

My blessing to Jane, and thanks for her letter. Tell Mrs Jourdan that I'll endeavour to remember Kinegad Cheeses.³ But the way to make sure of them is, to put me in mind, just before I set out.

I believe I have seen the Jewel you mention.⁴ I think, as you do, that it is Artificial – and It is pretty, rather than fine.

One false spelling, no more. I have us'd the word on the other side and spelt it right – See if you can find it out. I am

My Dearest yours &c.
Edw:Elphin

A letter came to Lawson last post under cover to me, which I since find was Bob. King's. The Superscription disgusted me. It is a paltry imitation of Mrs Jourdan's; and what is very proper *plaisanterie* in her, from him deserves another name. I desire He may be told that I don't like to be the conveyance of his Wit. I wish indeed that my ludicrous account of the Doctor had been communicated to those only for whom it was design'd.

[Free Edw:Elphin]

1. Miss Sandford, has married imprudently.
2. Robert King, alderman and merchant, Bolton Street. Watson (1752), p.16.
3. Kinnegad cheese was similar to Gloucester cheese. *Notes for the Physico-Historical Society History of Co. Westmeath*, Armagh Public Library, 9.11.23. I am indebted to Dr T.C. Barnard for this reference.
4. Jewel: reference obscure.

39

Elphin. September 15, 1747

I hope soon now to have the pleasure of seeing my Dear Girl. God send I may see you in good health, and that you may continue so. Nothing in this world can now give me so much joy. The first of October is the day I have fix'd for setting out from hence. I shall thus be with you the third. I care not how few know it. For I had rather not be embarrass'd with people at my first arrival. Your Uncle knows what I intend. I need not I am sure desire Mrs Jourdan to give proper orders: and It is rather soon to tell you that I expect my dinner from you on Sunday. But I say it now to have so much off my hands, when my hurry increases. With the same view I tell you now, that you had best order John Miller to bring home the Plate-trunk from Lennox's[1] on Saturday morning. I suppose you'll be afraid to have [it earlier*damaged ms*]. But that will be time enough. I would have Shannon who put it up, to open it. Ned Curtis will find the receit for the Trunk in my Scriptoire.

Our weather has been bad since Saturday, and continues so. This has mortify'd me the more, as I expected Mr and Mrs Wills and Betty on Monday.[2] I hope they will come, assoon as it clears up.

When next you see Mrs Nicholson, Give her my Service, and Tell her I obey'd her Commands. The Coll.'s answer is doubtfull. But I advise her by all means not to think of coming to the Country. If she does not, I am almost sure he'll go to Town. I have wrote to him agen, and challeng'd him to come hither. If He does, I think I shall fix him.

I have heard nothing yet of my Archdeacon. But pray Mrs Giddy-boots, as you very properly call your Self, How come you to mention Palmer so carelessly, when you had before told me that your Uncle said He look'd dreadfully at Kilcock? But I suppose I shall in your next have a particular account of him, because I desir'd it. You tell me, you were to go to see Mercier's pictures.[3] I was at first at a loss whom you meant; and thought it was the Gent. whom you once describ'd as looking no bigger than your Fan. But Dr Lawson explain'd the matter. You forgot at that instant that I had left Town, before that Painter arriv'd. I hope his pictures pleas'd you.

Tell Mrs Jourdan, with my service, that It is indifferent to me where She buys the Linnen. I would encourage Tom King yet not desert Mr Meade.[4] I think too that she ought now and then to buy at Mr Donavane's.[5] A single visit to that shop was too slight a return for the Civility shewn us.

Poor Mrs Cary has been confin'd since Saturday. She then got a surfeit of oysters.[6] She had been out of order some days before, and in some fright about Willy, who I fear'd had got a fever. But He is now well. The want of Mrs Cary now the Evenings are long is considerable. But the Doctor, Cary and I make a good Shift to divert our Selves. I bless God I am very well. And so My Dearest Adieu

yours &c. Edw: Elphin

My blessing to my Filly. Has she told your Uncle and Aunt that I have given her that name?

[Free Edw:Elphin]

1. Lennox and French's bank on Lower Ormond Quay.
2. Godfrey Wills and his wife had two sons and two daughters. Elizabeth (Betty) married Thomas Mitchell of Castle Strange, Co. Roscommon, in 1753. Burke (1912), p.624.
3. Philippe Mercier (1689-1760): portrait painter. A Huguenot, he was born in Berlin, studied under Antoine Pesne and toured Europe, eventually settling in London in 1716, where he became principal painter to the Prince and Princess of Wales. When he fell out of favour with the royal household, he continued to paint and live in London successfully. He exhibited in York, Ireland, Spain and Portugal. At the end of his career, he returned to London where he died. E. Benezie, *Dictionnaire des Peintres, Sculpteurs, Dessinateurs et Graveurs* (1966), p.67.
4. Thomas King, linen draper, Bride Street Watson (1752), p.16; Thomas Mead, alderman and linen draper, Bride Street. Watson (1752), p.18.
5. Robert Donovan, alderman and linen draper, Bride Street, Dublin. Watson (1752), p.10.
6. These would probably have come from Co. Sligo. In 1739 the Rev. W. Henry said that the oysters from the oyster beds at Sligo and Drumcliff were to be 'reckoned for firmness, fatness and delicious taste to excel all others'. J.G. Simms, 'County Sligo in the eighteenth century', *Journal of the Royal Society of Antiquaries of Ireland* Vol. 91 (1961), p.156.

40

Elphin. September 19, 1747

In my last I told my Dear Girl, that the Bad Weather was more grievous as it kept Mr and Mrs Wills from me. But they were so good as not to mind it, and, to my great surprize came hither, and Betty with them on Wedensday before dinner. Just at the same time came Mr Waller and Blair, and a little before, Barton, so that I have had agreable Company enough. But some I must loose this morning. Mr Wills &c. will continue. They have very much lighten'd the Weather. But they allow me no time to write. So that you must be content with knowing that I am well, and long now to be with you.

You say very right that one ought not to promise any thing they don't know they can do. But on the other hand, One ought always to endeavour to their utmost to do what they promise; and I am almost sure, Mrs Giddyboots that you might have given me a proper account of Mercier's pictures, if you had set about it. But probably you had not leisure, and It is no great matter. I'll wait to have it from you when We meet.

But what excuse, Huzzy, will you make for your two last being not so well written, as all your late letters have been? These shew what you can do. It is bad to go back.

I send you with this a receit for Saffron Cakes,[1] which I am told is the right one; and I believe it, because Mr Phibbs from whose Wife[2] it comes sent with it some Cakes, which Mrs Wills and all my Company agree to be for Colour, Taste, every thing as good as the best of Old Gafney.[3] Let me see now how good house Wifes you'll approve your Selves by making some to perfection.

I got the letter you describe. I have time for no more. God send us a happy meeting – and Take notice I won't have you in a flutter. I am My Dearest

yours &c.
Edw: Elphin

My Love to your Uncle &c. I have not time to write to him, nor much to say.

[To Bold Ally]

1. Saffron was grown in Ireland in the eighteenth century. Saffron 'cake' bread was made with warm water in which saffron stamens were steeped and this was used to mix yeast and flour into dough. The cakes were sometimes sweetened with honey or sugar. Elizabeth David has a recipe for saffron cake from *The Closet of the Eminently Learned Sir Kenelm Digby Opened* (1669). David (1977), p.446.
2. Mr and Mrs Phibbs: not known.
3. Old Gafney: not known.

41

Elphin. September 22, 1747.

I am as well pleas'd with the beginning of My Dear Girl's letter, as with any thing she has wrote to me this Summer, Except her telling me that She was well, and my affectionate daughter. I see you'll make good what I told you, that in a little time you'll write about nothing as well as the best of them. But I have not now leisure for that. Therefore to business.

If Mr Smith be not return'd before you get this, Send for Woodward immediatly, and order him to go thither, and chuse Cloaths himself. He knows what Sort I like. He must answer for getting good ones. I will not find fault for 6d a yard more. You may, if you please, desire Ned Curtis's assistance. But I believe the crackbrain'd Tailor will do.

I wish Jac. Davies had spoke earlier of the pavement. If He had, I presume you would have mention'd it. But this is very like himself. I intended to have had the whole street pav'd this Summer, when I left you. But other things drove it out of mine head. It is now too late in the Season to do more than get the Holes mended after a fashion. I write to John Miller about it.

But As bread &c. is in your province, Do you order him to get a Bagg of right good Flower, again I get to you. I thank you for promising me my Dinner. You need not make great preparations. For I don't intend to dine in publick the first day, as L[or]d H— did. I am sorry He is out of order. That and his having no Lady, will make the winter less gay for the fine folks, than usual.[1]

I observe by your manner of mentioning your two friends at Artaign that Kitty is the favorite. I have no objection. But Have a care that this preference is not owing to the Out-side. If it be 'Tis a foible, which you must learn to guard against. In sense and good humour the other is at least Equal. I am sorry the good Mother is not better. I depend on your account of her looks more than on the Doctor. I know his manner.

Mr and Mrs Wills are still here. I'll keep them, if possible to the end of the Week. Mrs Cary has been here every day since they came, till Monday, that her head-Ach return'd. I believe too that She has had some of Jeny's disorder.

I told you that Barton was here, and He is here still. On Saturday We encourag'd him to rebell against his Sovereign Lady, and Cary went to Castlerea to preach. By his account Mr Sandford appears very easy. He says he'll go to town in November, but is positive against Mrs Nicholson's coming down. Something was said of Bob's[2] being brought there. I have no right to advise. But if Mrs Nicholson sends him, I shall change my opinion, and think her capable of doing a Wrong thing. You may tell her so if you please.

All last week the Weather was very bad. I did not ride from Sunday to Saturday. Then I did. But It was cold and unpleasant. Sunday was a most delicious day, and I enjoy'd it. I hop'd too that We should have more. But yesterday was excessive Wet and windy. To day the wind continues but not much rain. I have had a pleasant ride, which would have been longer, but that I came in to Scribble thus to you. I am

My Dearest
your most affectionate
Edw: Elphin

You have mis-spelt one of your French Words. *apetit* – there should 2 p. The Enquirys for a Servant must be continued. I must get, or go without, one. Speak to Mr Nicholson, and to Eaton.

Mrs Heap has sent you 51 doz. of Candles in 2 Boxes – and I have sent Mrs Jourdan two doz. Bottles of Ale in the hogshead with Hams &c. Unfortunately I did not find the goodness of the Ale, till it was almost out.

[Free Edw:Elphin]

1. William Stanhope, 1st earl of Harrington (?-1756), was appointed Lord Lieutenant in November 1746, and sworn in on 13 September 1747. He was a widower, his wife having died in 1719. *NHI*, Vol. 9, p.493; Burke (1916), p.1000.
2. Bob: not known.

42

Elphin. September 25, 1747

You have convicted your Self, My Dear Girl. This letter is so well written, that it proves my accusation. Make it a rule to your Self always to do every thing as well as you can. This is the way to excell.

Mr Wills &c. are still here. They don't move till Monday. Bess has often wish'd for you. But my heart is much the lighter for your being where you are.

I hold my resolution of setting out next Thursday; Unless the weather should prove bad. If it be, you must not expect me. Better wait two or three days, than run hazards. On second thoughts It will be best to make your Uncle give us a dinner on Sunday. The Servants will be in a hurry at their first going to Town. Write no more to me, unless you've a mind to scribble a line or two directed to Glanmore near Balymahon to let me know how you all are. I am not sure that I shall go there. It will depend on the account I have of him by Mark[1] whom I send off to morrow morning for that purpose.

I have got the letter you describe. It came from the same person, who formerly, as you thought, sent a begging one.

Once more, My Dear, take care not to be in a flutter, while you expect, or when you see me. God send us an happy meeting. I am

your most affectionate Father
Edw: Elphin

When next you are at a loss for something to write, Look over the letter you are to answer, and see if there be nothing there, which will furnish you. I ask'd you lately about my Filly, whether she had told your Uncle and Aunt, that I had given her that name. Not a word in return! This might have furnish'd matter for a Page.

[Free Edw:Elphin]

1. Mark: a servant.

43

Elphin. September 30, 1747

I write this just to tell, My Dear Girl, that I hold my resolution of setting out from hence to morrow, if bad Weather, of which We have of late had a great deal does not detain me. Every thing else I referr to our meeting. God send us an happy one. Dr Lawson is very well. He must as to your charge answer for himself.

Take notice now; Mistress mine, that I wo'n't have you run into the street, Or Court,[1] like a mad thing to meet me. Have a good fire in the great parlour, and there receive me. I shall run to you as fast as I can, for now the time is so near, I confess my impatience to see you. I am

My Dearest
your most affectionate Father
Edw: Elphin

[Free Edw: Elphin]

1. Edward Synge's house in Kevin Street was built around a large court, with gates that fronted on the street.

1749

'Great care must be taken of your Grandfather's picture' (Letter 49): Edward
Synge DD, archbishop of Tuam 1738 (by 'A. De L.', in private possession).

44

Kinnegad. Wedensday Evening.

I am sure it will please my Dear Dear Girl to know that my fellow-traveller
and I are thus far safe and well on our journey. We din'd very comfortably
on your provisions. Mr D[1] would have hot meat, but he soon quitted it,
and ate with me very heartily of the cold Mutton. Your Asparagus too were
very pleasing. But I was much mortify'd at seeing some in the house twice
as large as the largest among them, much larger than that which astonish'd Mrs Jourdan. They were sent a present to Mr Daly[2] whom I met
there. He would have given me some. But I chose to eat mine own. He
promis'd, He would let you know that He saw me so far well. I suppose He
has done it. We are just going to sit down to the remainder of your treat,
then to bed, that We may be early at Palmer's to morrow.

Mr D told me on the road what He knew last night; and therefore
ought to have told me. That It was current in town, that Dic. Hamilton[3]
Lord Boyne's Brother was dead. If so, a fine fortune comes to Gusty.[4] I
should be glad to know the certainty of this. Don't send but go to Mrs
Hamilton's, before you write that you may give me an account of it. My
blessing to Jeny and Mrs J – I am

My Dear Girl's
most affectionate &c. Edw: Elphin

[Free Edw: Elphin Stamped BALLYMAHON]

1. Richard Doherty (*c.*1710-60; see Biographical Register).
2. Not known. The Daly family owned an estate in the Kinnegad district.
3. Dic. Hamilton: not known.
4. The Rev. Gustavus Hamilton: vicar of Raddinstown, Co. Meath. He was a nephew
of Frederick Hamilton, Lord Boyne. Burke (1916), p.1293.

45

Glanmore. May 31, 1749

My Dear Dear Girl,

I am got thus far safe, and twenty per cent better than when I left you.
I mean, in my body. For the state of my mind is the same, and will be so,
unless I hear of some considerable amendment in your poor Aunt.[1] God

send I may, for her own sake, as well as my Brother's whose distress I feel, more, I believe, than He wishes.

I find Mr Palmer very well. Mrs Palmer just as I left her; in looks at least. But she speaks comfortably of her Self. Your present has made the little thing extremely happy. Father and Mother seem pleas'd too, but they do not shew it with the same naiveté. All the Children are well.

Mr Wills has not, I believe, given his Wife the same bad Custom that I have given you. I don't see that He troubles himself to write. But I fancy he'll not be displeas'd if you send to let her know that He is very well. I am sure she wo'n't. As much indifference as He shew'd to my carrying Eatables and drinkeables for the road. He enjoy'd them at least as much as I did. My Dear Girl Adieu. Blessing to Jane and service to Mrs Jourdan.

> I am yours &c.
> Edw:Elphin
> [Stamped BALLYMAHON]

1. Elizabeth Synge.

46

Elphin. June 2, 1749

My Dear Girl.

I got very safe and well hither yesterday about two. We had not the least accident of any kind on the road. I found things here in the disorder I expected. But a little time will bring me into as much order, as I am capable of, till the new Offices are built, which are going on briskly.[1] The Material thing is, That The House is as dry as you could wish. I lay last night as well and as Warm as ever I did in my life, and quite free from the only nuisance I fear'd, the smell of paint, and am, I bless God, as well to day, as I was, when I wrote from Palmer's.

You see, huzzy, that I did not forget to write to you from thence tho' I did not desire you to write to me there. I can't say I forgot to do this, or was indifferent about it. But I was sure you needed no bidding to write to me somewhere; and I was not sure how the post would answer from Balymahon. But as it happen'd, I got yours before I set out, some hours before I should have got it if you had directed hither. It would have given me more complete pleasure, if it had brought a better account of your poor Aunt. I need not repeat, that I am in great pain about her.

Mrs Nicholson's message was owing to a chance Word of mine to her husband on Sunday Evening. As the Dowager Kildare is a Lady of whom I have a very high opinion, and one by whose acquaintance I thought you might profit, I express'd to him an inclination, that his Wife should introduce you to her. As I was not sure, whether she would do it, I said nothing to you. You need not be in a hurry about going there. When you do, I am sure you'll behave your Self properly, and for this I have better security than your own, tho' I begin to have a tolerable opinion of that, because I with pleasure observe you still dispos'd to follow the good advice you have always at hand. I hope you'll ever be so.

The Weather is extremely sharp.[2] Fear not that I'll venture on Linnen-night-Caps, or do any thing else that is giddy to hurt my Self. Be you cautious, My Dearest, how go out, [*sic*] till Summer comes. Mrs Jourdan, I am sure, will for you. Tell her I sent her letter to Lisdurn;[3] but there's no one at home. Blessing to Jane, and service to Mrs J. Most affectionate love at the green – This is all I have time for now but that I am

My Dear Girl's
most affectionate
Edw:Elphin

Tell Jeny that Her Spark Dr Diganan is married.

Write under Cover, tho' you have nothing to send but your letter. You have a good many Franks, and may have more when you please. But mine own privilege will be in before those are spent.

Send Will sometime next Week to enquire about my Watch, and when it is brought to time, deliver it to Dr Lawson, unless you chuse to send your own to Mr Holmes[4] to be set right and then you may use mine till the Doctor comes to the Country.

When you are call'd on to stand to Ned Curtis's Child,[5] Give three Guineas. I'll pay you, tho' this sort of Tax you ought to bear your Self, as it is a personal one.

My affairs here are ten times more embarrass'd, than ever they were. I wish I be able to set them right by Micmas. Cary has been less attentive, and Crawford[6] extremely negligent. Hitherto I have no complaint of Byrne.[7] But I think I sha'n't be long so. I fear Mrs Heap's softliness has hurt me in the removal of my things.[8] But I can't yet tell how much.

1. The offices were being built at the end of curved walls leading from the main block of the house. The house itself, still under construction in 1747, was now complete.

2. The first half of June 1749 was 'cold and winter-like' after a very cold spring and it snowed on 5 May. John Rutty, *A Chronological History of the Weather and Seasons And of the Prevailing Diseases in Dublin* (1770), pp.147-9.

3. Lissadoorn, Co. Roscommon on the road to Carrick on Shannon. The home of John Crofton and his family.

4. Robert Holmes: watchmaker, Castle Street. Watson (1760), p.22.

5. As godmother.

6. James Crawford: the carpenter. See Letter 22.

7. Carbry Byrne of Cloghermore, parish of Elphin: a constable, he was Catholic and married, with one child under fourteen. Census, f.8.

8. From the old Palace.

47

Elphin. June 6, 1749

My Dear Girl's gave me great joy, as it brought an account of your being very well. It would have been complete, could you have said the same, or any thing like it of your poor Aunt.

You know before this, that your giddiness, as you call it, had no bad consequence. But don't you, Huzzy, in your Apology betray some Vanity? How come you to imagine that my not hearing from you the Evening of the day on which I left you, would make me uneasy? Especially as you observ'd, I did not bid you write. But thus young Damsels are wont to set a high Value on themselves and thence to fancy that others do. After all I was rather pleas'd at your letter. See that you keep your promise, and avoid giddiness and hurry the remaining part of the summer.

I have done what your Uncle and you desire, ever since I came hither, and shall continue to do so, while the Weather continues Cold. But with respect to damp, be assur'd, there is no more occasion for fires here, than in your apartment. The whole House is completely dry, and comfortable within. Without all is disorder, and must for some time be so. I do all I can to remedy, but will not fret at it.

I rejoice much at the happy Escape from 'Rover's' Madness. Since He did no mischief, I am not sorry for his fate. It will cure you of your liking of such animals about the House.

I am glad Miss Cooper[1] is in so good a way. It was lucky that you learn'd she was ill. Otherwise your not sending might have been thought neglect. Be sure you send often, and go, when it is proper, to wait on Mrs Cooper.[2]

If Beef &c. be dear, Manage accordingly. I have often told you, that I value you not Expense, but carefull Management I very much approve of. It is necessary in any fortune, and you can't yet tell what your future one may be. Learn therefore early every thing that may enable you to become a high one, and be easy with a moderate one.

Send Sam. Cow's[3] letters in one of your Covers, or two, if one won't hold them. Or if you can get John to return it to the post-office, with the direction chang'd thus *At Strokes-town near Elphin,* that will be best of all. For thus the Man will get them without any trouble to me. For I have no dealings with him. Do which-ever is easiest to your Self. Only take care that no pacquet you send to me, be awkardly made up. And now for a multitude of Commissions.

To lead the Van, Foxal[4] must be sent to instantly, to provide three *celles percées,* such as He made last for me, with all Expedition. Two pans must be got. They say there is a third here.[5] Those utensils have been much abus'd in the remove. I wish I don't find others of more consequence treated in the same Way. Mrs Heap is too softly, as I have always complain'd. But she has good qualitys to ballance this, more than her Sister.[6]

I find my rooms here require more Chairs than I computed. In the little parlour, which I never do nor shall use, there are a dozen black Leather Chairs, which there do no good, but here will be extremely usefull. Make Foxal, clean, oyl, and put them in order, and pack them up carefully in Mats to be sent off hither when Carriage offers.

In the same parlour stands a little yew Table quite useless there. It would be usefull here. If you or Jeny can find any use for it, keep it. If not Let that come down.

There stands there also a Marble Cistern, which I want much here. That must be sent. But I wish it were first a little better polish'd. On Second thoughts I believe, if that can be done at all, I may get it done here. Consult Eaton the Glazier about it. He'll come to you, if you send to him, and tell you whether it can be mended, and at what Expense. If it can be done for a trifle, Desire him to get it done. I am very indifferent about it. Only in one Shape or other it must come, and soon.

Carleboe is short in China Dishes. It seems We borrow'd last Summer, which I knew not. Those he wants, He says are about the size of the Small ones of the Burnt-China.[7] It matters not, if they be a little larger. Four will do; and there must be a dozen China Plates got, as like the few old ones blew and white which you have, as you can get them. Desire Mrs. Jourdan to have no palpitations about these, but chuse as she likes. I promise before hand that I will like them.

Desire Ned Curtis to send me down a parcel of choice powder and shot as usual. I thought there had been some here but it is all gone.

I shall want another Bed of the pencil'd Cotton, and, of the same kind, enough to make two pair of Window Curtains for rooms eleven feet high. Send to Mr Moore[8] to know what number of yards will do, and then go your Self to Grant's at Ball's bridge, and bespeak them to be done this summer. The Choice of the pattern I'll leave to himself. I would have it rich and bold. That which I got from him before is by much the handsomest here.

Something like that will do very well. But I had rather have it a little vary'd than directly the same. You know the Bed must have a lining.

Desire John Miller to speak to Sympson to bespeak immediatly a Bit fit for the Chesnut Horse. He knows the kind. Two came down, but one broke on the road. Tell John that every Saddle Horse shod by the new Smith suffer'd on the journey and are now lame, my little black in the Number. Don't be uneasy at this, For the Chesnut carrys me completely well, and as quietly as is possible. 'The Major' alone escap'd who was shod at Finglas. Not my servants only, but Mr Cary, and the Smith here impute this to the shoeing, and I believe justly. I am not inclin'd to use the fellow any more. Let John inform himself quietly about the Smith in Bride-street.[9] He knows whom I mean. If He be sober and a good Shoer, He is much more conveniently situated for me, and I can't well suffer more by any one, than I have done by the present.

Send John to Turner's to tell him that the Jack Chains He sent down last year are very bad, and too short. He must immediatly send down better and longer. Carleboe complains that these are soder'd, so as that if there be any breach, He can't mend them and desires that the New ones may not be so. If Turner does not send those that are excellent John may tell him, I shall quarrel with him downright. He must desire him to add two to the four Latches with Brass-Nobs, which I wrote for by Mathew,[10] i.e. He must send six in all. He must also send Scrapers for shoes to be fix'd at the Entrance of our Doors, plain, strong and decent. We must be very cleanly in our new house. I'll consent to a Couple of a better kind for the Great door. They must be let in to the Hewn-stone. If Turner be at a loss to chuse these, Let him go to Mr Nicholson, who will direct him.

Bid John send me down two Gross of Bottles. Let him apply for these to Mr Sullivane, and tell him that I expect He'll get them for me at the same rate with the last. But the Bottles must come.

I would have every thing I have wrote for got ready as fast as possible, and sent off as soon as Carrs can be got. John may get Carrs for these, which will not carry Timber. After Mullingar fair there will be a multitude of them.

Send Will to Woodward the Taylor, and bid him, as soon as Mr Minchin[11] has got the Cloth, to make up my Coat – I shall soon want it.

I have now given my Dear Girl a multitude of Commissions. See that you do not neglect or over-look any. The way to guard against this is, as soon as you've read my letter, to sit down, and make an Index of them all exactly and pin it up as Mrs Jourdan does her Memorandum papers. If you do not one way or other take care that Every thing I write for be done speedily and effectually you'll not escape the charge of giddiness – and so with love to Jeny and service to Mrs J – My Dear Girl

Adieu

yours &c. Edw: Elphin

Shannon begs a couple of little penny white or Brown Stone Mugs with covers to [*damaged ms*] in for the Table. M [*damaged ms*] has made a large parcel of very good carpeting, which will be of great use to keep us clean.

Coll. Sandford, his son,[12] and Barton din'd here to day. The first is gone off. But the young Man and Barton stay. The latter looks very well and seems very proud of his Second Son.

Since I wrote about the Cistern, I have talk'd to my Stone-Cutter Mulvihil,[13] who says that it is by much the best way to have it polish'd in Dublin. Talk therefore to Eaton about it, and if it is capable of being made handsomer, and can be made so at a Small Expense, Let him get it done with what expedition He can. If, as I rather think, it be difficult or expensive, Let it be sent off as it is. It must either way be put up in a good strong case.

Was my letter sent to Dr Barry?[14] If you owe a Visit there, pay it, and if you find the Lady[15] at home, Ask her about the Wine. You may say that I am in pain about it. So indeed I am.

1. Possibly an aunt of Joshua Cooper of Markree, Co. Sligo, Alicia Synge's future husband. He had five, of whom one, Elizabeth, died unmarried. Burke (1979), p.273.

2. Mary Cooper, Joshua Cooper's mother and Alicia Synge's future mother-in-law, was a daughter of Lord Justice Henry Bingham. Her will was proved in 1763. Burke (1976), p.273; Vicars, p.103.

3. Samuel Cow: possibly a tenant or employee of Thomas Mahon at Strokestown.

4. Thomas Foxhall: joiner, Nicholas Street or William Foxhall, joiner, Inns Quay. Watson (1760), p.18.

5. From the reference in Letter 50, Edward Synge is referring to *chaises percées*, commodes.

6. Mrs Heap's sister: not known.

7. Burnt china may have been Chinese export porcelain which had a toast brown underside, or it may have been a tin-glazed earthenware – delftware – which had a decoration fired on with the glaze.

8. George Moore: linen draper, Bride Street. Watson (1760), p.31.

9. Smith in Bride Street: not known.

10. Matthew Smith: a servant.

11. Francis Minchin, woollen draper, Castle Street. Watson (1752), p.19.

12. Edward Sandford enlisted as a cornet in the 1st regiment of Foot Guards on 5 January 1727, became a lieutenant on 8 November 1737 and captain 6 May 1740. By 1749 he could well have become colonel. His son is not known. PRO WO64/11, f.83.

13. Mulvihil: stone-cutter in Elphin. Not known.

14. Dr Edward Barry (1698-1776): physician, born in Cork. He took BA at TCD in 1717 and gained MD at Leyden in 1719. He returned to Ireland to take MB and MD in 1740. He gained an MD Oxon 1759 and FRCP in London in 1761. He was a Fellow of the King's and Queen's College of Physicians of Ireland 1740; Fellow of the Royal Society 1733. MP for Charleville 1743-4. Physician General of the Forces in Ireland 1745.

He was created baronet 1776. He died in Bath. He wrote *A treatise on a consumption of the lungs* (Dublin 1726). Kirkpatrick.

15. Mrs Barry: not known.

48

Elphin. June 9, 1749

Be assur'd, My Dear Girl, that the House is as completely dry as you could wish it, and so comfortable, that having an account of your being well, I should be as happy as I can be without you, were it not for the very bad account you give of your poor good Aunt. This grieves but does not surprize me, tho' it be worse than my hopes. If I have not a better by next post, I shall think her fate nearer than lately I thought it. It is very grievous. But God's will be done in all things. Take you care, not to hurt your Self by unavailing tenderness. Whatever happens, you cannot be surpriz'd. Poor Jane! She has always appear'd to me the most affected; and yet she'll feel the loss the least.

I don't recollect any thing in mine that should have made you doubt about a Visit to either Lady Kildare. I indeed mention'd only the Dowager to Mr Nicholson; and she is the person to whom I think it might be for your advantage to be known.[1] But there was no reason for declining the other, when Mrs Nicholson offer'd it, and it would be odd to do the one & decline the other. There is however no harm done; and As they are gone to Car-town,[2] and probably will pass the whole summer there, It will be as well that your acquaintance begin next Winter. Act as Occasions offer, or as Mrs Nicholson would have you.

Mrs Hunter's mistake shews how carefull you ought to be about every thing. If I don't mistake, you are not quite clear, Mistress. Don't you remember that I ask'd about this and you all said 6sh[illings] – you in effect own this in your letter. Let this be a warning to you to enter Memorandums and lay by such contracts, where you may have immediate recourse to them.

I had yesterday a house full of Company, Lord Kings-borough,[3] Gilbert King and a long &c. [*sic*] But Carleboe was well prepar'd, tho' they were not expected, and the House shew'd for the first time. Kitchen, Ovens, and every thing else about it, answer mighty well. Now for Commissions, of which I have not yet as many as went in my last. Perhaps they may multiply, before I end my letter.

Desire John to tell Eaton that I must deferr painting any more, till I return to town, on account of the Smell, and am therefore in some pain about keeping my Oyl in Casks.[4] They stand in a very cool Vault, and the Painter says, that the Oyl will keep there extremely well. If Eaton thinks it will not, He must get me two or three Oyl jarrs, which may be sent down safely, if carefully pack'd.

Bid him also go to John Smith the Wheelwright and desire him to make me up a Diaper-Loom[5] with as much Expedition as He can. He must give him a great charge to make it perfectly good. When it is ready, John will send it down. Let him know from Smith what it is to cost.

He must go to Turner, and tell him that one of my Doors here claps on the opening of the great door, so as to make a very great and disagreable noise, and that I want a remedy. Will French tells me that there is a kind of Spring which properly put on is a complete one, and that His brother the Judge[6] has one of them to his street Door. Probably Turner is well acquainted with this kind of Spring. If He be not, He must go to the Judge's and view his, and get me such a one, only less, as it is design'd for an inside door, which tho' strong, and pretty large is not near so heavy as a Street-Door. His Man Jac. knows all the Doors here, as well as I do. If He has any doubt about this remedy and can propose a better, Let him consult Mr Nicholson, and do whatever He orders. He must send down half a Tun of Iron, of which I stand in great need.

Order him also to get a dozen good Shovels, and half a dozen right good Spades such as He got me before, but He must take great care, that there be no flaws or defects in the latter. He must let me know the price of these, because the persons for whom they are design'd must pay for them here.

This is all I have yet. I am My Dear Girl's

most affectionate &c.
Edw: Elphin

One of the Letters you enclos'd brought me an account of old Mr Moore's death. His Wife is my Cousen Germain so there's another slight mourning for you.[7]

My most affectionate love &c. at the Green, and to your Uncle and Aunt Curtis.[8] You seem, Mistress, to have forgot the pretty hand in which many of your letters last Summer were wrote. I wish you would return to it; and whether you do or not, Pray don't in your first writing omit so many words, as to oblige you to so frequent interlineations. One of them is no less than six Words, the chief part of two sentences. This, Huzzy, is giddiness.

Assoon as Kitty Donnelan is marry'd, Be sure you pay your visit in form.[9]

Mr Lennox will send you by my order a letter containing 6 Promissory notes for £20 each, which I desire you would send to Mr Palmer. His name is Thomas. Write a few lines to him in which say what Civil things you please, but desire him to own the receit of the Bills. They are to pay for Horses, if Sympson buys any. Bid John take care that He be in time at the Fair.

Tell John that of the half Tunn of Iron, wrote for above, eight hundred must be half flat, one hundred broad Bar, and one hundred Square Bar.

Let him desire Mr Turner also to make me an Iron-lock for an Outdoor with a Brass Nob, just such a one, as the one I brought down with me, only that it should be of smaller dimensions. Eight or nine inches by six, I think will be enough. It must be a Left hand-lock. The Door is two inches thick. Turner must send me half a dozen cranks. They are little Springs on which the Bell-Wires turn. Those he sent hither break every day.

1. Mary Fitzgerald, dowager Lady Kildare, was Mrs Nicholson's aunt. Mrs Nicholson was therefore well placed to introduce Alicia to the Kildares.
2. Carton, Maynooth, Co. Kildare. Enlarged by the earl of Kildare to the designs of Richard Castle from a house first built in the seventeenth century. Altered again in the nineteenth century, it was sold by the Leinsters in the 1940s. Bence-Jones, p.60.
3. Sir Robert King was created baron Kingsborough in 1748. He died in 1755.
4. Linseed or possibly walnut oil, used for mixing paint.
5. Diaper looms were used to weave a linen fabric with patterns using opposite reflections on its surface, and consisting of diamonds, with the spaces filled up by parallel lines, leaves and dots.
6. Lord Justice Robert French (1692-1772; see Biographical Register).
7. Edward Synge's elder sister married John Moore of Rahinduff, Queen's County. She or their son's wife may be the 'cousin-germane' mentioned here. She may be the Catherine Moore, widow of Raheenduff whose will was proved in 1755. Synge, p.7; Vicars, p.333.
8. The Rev. Robert Curtis. His wife's name is not known.
9. Lewis Ormsby married Catherine Donnelan in June 1749. They lived in Digge Street, Dublin. Burke (1912), p.542; Gray, 285.

49

Elphin. June 13, 1749

You must learn, My Dear Girl, to distinguish between the Serious, and jocose tho' in grave Words – what I wrote about your betraying vanity, was of the latter kind, and you have taken it in the former. I would indeed have you clear of that and every other imperfection. Decent pride is not one But vanity is a very great one, tho' every one of us have a spice of it. If you have no more than what I charg'd you with, i.e. to think that your

Welfare is of some importance to me, I shall not think you very guilty. I have caught you here, Huzzy, at a false spelling, and I see what betray'd you into it. *Aimable* is right in French. The English Word is Amiable. You have jumbled both, and wrote Aimiable. I don't blame you for this. If, now you are inform'd, you do it agen, I shall.

Your Uncle has wrote me a particular account of your poor Aunt from which however I cannot judge whether she be better or Worse. I perceive He rather hopes the former. God grant it may be so, and that if there be any Amendment, It may daily encrease. Pray give both of them my most affectionate love, and tell your Uncle, I don't write to him, because I can only repeat what I have said already. When He does not, Be sure you give me a particular account of her.

I am glad you went to see the Bride, tho' you got no admittance. By a letter yesterday from Mr Donnelan, I find they'll all be in this Country, the latter end of the Week.

I hope you have taken notice of Mrs Nicholson's message. If you have not, Pray fix a day assoon as you can, for waiting on that good Lady with her. Deferring it now will shew an indifference; which will not suit well with my request.

I thank Mrs Jourdan for the *Censors*.[1] Pray continue to send them. I think as you do of poor Jane's absence one day in near a fortnight. But you are right in leaving her to her Self. She seems to me sufficiently inclin'd to do every thing in her power to assist, or comfort her good Mother in her great distress.

Till privilege comes in I must convey by you answers to John's and Mr Nelson's letters.

Bid the former take care, that Sympson leaves town so as to be at Mullingar early the Thursday before the Fair,[2] if possible in the morning; and Let him order him to buy two, three, or four the best Geldings He can find, and not baulk price if He can find any perfectly to his mind, but not, for his life, to meddle, with any which are not very light and nimble in their going, as well as comely in their shapes and marks, well neck'd, and crested particularly. Whatever He gets, Let him convey them safe to town, where John must take care of them. In this Mr Palmer can assist him better than any one.

John has done right about the Coals. I think they will certainly be cheaper; and besides I would have my Coal-hole for once quite emptied – whenever He puts in a stock, Let what remains in the Coal-hole, if any, be throughly mix'd with them. Coals, by lying long, decay.

His great work will be the providing Carrs for Timber &c. Mr Nelson writes that the Timber I have wrote for will take a great number. But He may send them by degrees, a parcel now, and a parcel then, as He can find

Carrs. Mr Nelson will take care to send off first what will be first wanted.
If the Beams and joyce be here by this day month, It will do tolerably well.
For the Boards I can wait longer, and if 500 come this Summer, it will do.
The rest are rather for stores so we may wait till the market falls. I want
these boards chiefly for floors of Hay-lofts, and other offices – about which
there will be no great niceity. Which ever will answer best for these purposes, and come cheapest, Mr Nelson will chuse, either those He calls
Wrecks or others. He knows better what is fit for me, than I do my Self;
and He has always consulted my interest. Bid John to give him my affectionate service, and tell him I leave every thing to him.

For fear of mistakes, Do you, or rather Desire Mrs Jourdan who has a
quicker pen to, transcribe the above paragraph, and Let John carry it to
Mr Nelson.

Mr Mahon is much out of order. By a letter I had from him yesterday
I fear a fever. I am going to see him, and shall be able at my return to give
you a fuller account.

I am in great haste for the several necessarys which I wrote for. John
may certainly pick up Carrs for them when ready, which may not be fit for
timber.

We are undone for want of rain; and yet if the Winds were not so
excessively cold, the pleasantness of dry Weather, and the ease that it gives
in many of my Works would make me less regret that want. But the Cold
is sometimes as great as at Christmas. If you have the same, I hope you
take care of your Self. Be assur'd I do, and never sup or go to bed without
fire, tho' really the House is so comfortably Warm, that, within Doors, I
feel the Cold little. I bless God I am very well, and rejoice much that you
are so. As for Jane, and Madam Jourdan, I send them now blessing and
service for the whole season. They may suppose it repeated in every letter,
tho' I omit to write it, and so My Dearest Adieu

yours &c. Edw:Elphin

If you can put up Mr Orr's sermons[3] safe in any Box that comes down,
send them. Be sure Take care they be not injur'd. I hope John obliges the
Scavanger to keep the street clean.[4] Let the Marble Cistern come down as
it is.

Next time you see Mr Nicholson speak to him about your intended
dressing room. When you go about it, the Bed there must be taken down,
and put in the room over it.

Jeny will have no objection to lying in the room where Shannon lay for
the present, as it is. In time We'll put it in better order for her: George
Stephens must doctor the Windows as was propos'd, and must reform the
Wains-coat over, and about the Chimney, and take away those little dirt

holes, which are on each side. Great care must be taken of your Grandfather's picture,[5] when taken down. The securest place, I think to lay it in, will be in the Room over the state-dressing room. When All is made ready for Paper; chuse the sort and colour that you like. Mr Nicholson's opinion will not be amiss. But please your own fancy. He told me, it would cost a groat a yard – As the great Walnut press is to stand where it does, there will be no occasion for paper behind it; and as your present Book-case is to be mov'd thither, and I intend to make you a present of another to stand by it on the side opposite the Windows, there will be as little occasion for Paper behind them. Send for Mr Eaton, Shew him your Book-Case, and desire him to bespeak one of the same dimensions, same stuff, and in all points directly like it. He may bespeak it from whom He pleases. For I have no particular person to name. He'll say that Irish Oak is not to be had. I believe it will be dear. But I hope it will be found, and I am content to pay for it, for you.

I am just come from Mr Mahon's. I found him much better than I expected. My fears for him are at present over. I saw all the Children, but your Godson, who, they said, was broken out. Mrs Mahon looks very well. Nelly as usual. They all send their compliments.

A new Commission and a very disagreable one to me. Half my brass Locks on the first and middle story are without particular Keys; There are Master Keys to each set – But many of the Keys which belong to each Seperate Lock are missing. Order John to go to Turner and desire him to search his Books, and give him the Number of Brass Locks, Keys, and Master Keys which He sent down here for the two storys and which Jac. put on when here. Let him be very exact as to the number of Keys.

Desire John to tell Sympson that Pat.[6] complains very much of 'Dainty's' feet. He did so, before I left town. He says his hoofs are fleshy. I mention this now, that Sympson may be caution'd particularly to examine the hoofs of any He buys. Every one of the Coach-horses have suffer'd more or less by their shoeing, and were not able to do anything till shod agen – 'Dainty' is still lame. How long He'll be so, I can't tell. The rest are now well.

1. *The Censor, or Citizen's Journal*: a series of pamphlets published between 1748 and 1749 by Charles Lucas (1713-71), a Dublin apothecary, to advance his candidature to represent the city in parliament. Lucas supported William Molyneux's policy of parliamentary independence for Ireland. He was twice threatened with imprisonment and had to leave the country. Sean Murphy, 'Charles Lucas: a forgotten patriot?', *History Ireland* (Autumn 1994), pp.26-9.

2. Mullingar Fair was on Saturday, 24 June 1749.

3. John Orr, *Sermons upon the following subjects. The natural difference between moral good and evil. ... The love of our country, explained, illustrated, and inforced* (London 1749).

4. Under an act of parliament, scavengers were required two days a week to remove 'Dirt, Soil and Filth' from the streets and lanes. Dublin householders were required before nine in the morning to sweep the rubbish and dirt outside their houses, buildings and walls to the end of the street, to be ready 'for the Scavengers to carry away'. Dublin householders paid to keep the street outside their property clean. Under the heading 'Taxes and Cesses', Jonathan Swift paid a scavanger 5d in May 1735. 'Agreement of the Church-Wardens of sev. Parishes' Dublin 19 November 1725 Marsh's Library Z.2.17 (42); *Accounts*, p.269.

5. Edward Synge, archbishop of Tuam (1659-1741; see Biographical Register). The painting of Edward Synge, archbishop of Tuam, by an unknown artist is in private possession. See p.94.

6. Pat: a coachman or groom.

50

Elphin. June 15, 1749

My Dear Girl.

I believe every alteration for the better in your poor Aunt, affects you as it does me. How would it delight us, if there were a fair prospect of the Dear little Woman's recovery. I rather ascribe the Change for the better, to the Strong infusion of mint, than to the Broom.[1] You don't say that Her bulk is less'ned and the Amendment in her stomach is more probably the Effect of the mint. I wish it may continue and increase. There may then be some hope of her bearing up under disorders, which perhaps cannot be entirely cur'd. If Mrs Jourdan thinks the use of the Broom will be of service to her, I desire she would speak her thoughts freely to her, or my Brother.

It is no great matter whether the Plates you have bought, be like the old ones you have, or not. You know I have two or three kinds here. What signifys it, if there be a new one added; provided they be pretty and strong. If Mr S[?] can get four dishes such as I want, it will be clever. But I am afraid of presents. Avoid taking them in that way, if possibly you can, without offending.

You had e'en as good take another airing to Grant's, and bespeak as many more yards, as will make eight Cushions. Ask him too about Handkerchiefs. If He has, or is like to have, any remarkably good, I may probably want a few more.

I believe Foxal is right as to the Number of Chairs. Let him clean and fit them up well, and particularly, supply any nails that are wanting, and pack them up and with them the Table since you have no use for it. If Foxal keeps his word about the *Chaises percées*, they'll be ready before John can get Carrs. See how I have wrote that Dainty Term. You write it thus. *Chaise Percés*. Ask Mrs Jourdan which is right. She'll not be so much offended at this, as if I enquir'd about a LOUSE.

I am sorry you miss'd the new-marry'd friend and her Mother.² You have here been guilty of a little inaccuracy in writing. We sha'n't see them, you say, before they *Go* out of Town. with a big G. I take the more notice of this, as you appear to have wrote it right at first and to have corrected it into wrong. But However that may be, Take this general Rule. That Big letters are seldom necessary, generally improper, except in the beginning of a Sentence, or the name of a person, in which last case, they must always be us'd; In the middle of a Sentence, they may be us'd in Noun-Substantives, but never in Verbs; and they are better avoided even in the former, except in Words of Dignity – God, Lord, &c. I too must be always a big letter. I mean, when it denotes the first person. If you'll cast your Eye on some of the Books lately and accurately printed, they'll instruct you in this little niceity, better than I can at this distance. Dr Swift's works I think are the most exact, in this, as well as in pointing. I am not sure whether I put you in possession of them. If not, they are in the Study on the Shelf at the back of my writing-Table. Take them when you please.

I am glad your Neck-lace and Earings please, or can easily be made to do so Pay for them immediatly, if you have not done it already. I hope I need not put you in mind that you ought to wait on Lady Tullamoure.³ And yet perhaps there may be occasion to do it, and that you may hesitate upon it, as you did about waiting on the Dowager Kildare, after having rec'd my letter, in which you found something, what I can't imagine, that made it appear doubtfull to you whether you should or not. This and some other things of a like kind, which I have from time to time observ'd, make me think it right to put you in mind, of the Wide difference there is, between prudent Caution, and Scrupulousness. The former is a great perfection, and will I hope be the Rule of your whole Conduct. But the latter is a Weakness, which often betrays persons into doing wrong, lest they should do wrong. Its distinguishing property, is a bastard kind of sagacity, in finding out doubts and difficultys, where really there are none. Ask Dr Lawson, what *Nodum in Scirpo*,⁴ is. This, if He be in a talking mood, will give him occasion to explain to you more fully what I mean, tho' I'll do it my Self by an instance or two –

I see, My Dear Child, and I see with the utmost joy, how desirous you are, in all points, to conform your Self to my Will, and inclinations. Now when you know, or may reasonably presume you know, my inclinations, why should you doubt about acting conformably to them and at the same time to Common Sense and reason, from some careless expression, which you, ingeniously, construe to something I never meant? It happen'd that

I mention'd only Lady Dowager, who was indeed alone my object. But could you imagine, My Dearest, that after having desir'd Mr Nicholson to speak to his Wife to carry you to her, and that she had agreed to do it, I would have you decline it meerly because you must also wait on the young one,[5] against whom there lay no objection? Could you think I would involve you and my Self too, in the guilt of rudeness, meerly to avoid what might be done or not done. This, Huzzy, was scrupulousness.

Another instance of a like kind, tho' in a lower affair, your letter affords. I did not it seems in so many Words desire you to enclose the Notes and letter to Mr Palmer in one of your Franks, and therefore you doubt whether you had done right, and hope you have done as I wish'd. You have indeed, and I should have been apt to call you Silly, if you had done otherwise. For how could you once make a doubt about it? Could you imagine that I would direct Lennox to send the Notes to you, and you to write your self and enclose them, meerly to multiply postage upon Mr P. Was it not plain and natural, almost necessary to think, that, As I knew you had franks, so I had a mind you should use one of them to free a Gentleman from expense about my business? Indeed, Ally, it was very ingenious in you to find a doubt in so plain a case. But your ingenuity here is of a bad kind, a kind for which I know no one so remarkable as poor Shannon. The difference between you is, That you, after doubting, acted right. But He, poor fellow, always acts wrong. So far you have the better of him. But your doubting at all, is an instance of that imperfection, from which as from every other, I would have my Dear Girl's conduct perfectly free. I have dwelt thus long upon this, because I have upon many occasions observ'd something of the same Leaven in you. Nor is your Wiser friend perfectly free. In what a puzzle were you, both I suppose, about going to see Kitty, on her marriage, when, considering your intimacy, It was impossible to offend, but by not going? Tell me honestly now, Has not going to visit Lady T[ullamore] – been the subject of some consultation? The thing it self is as plain, as that two and two make four; and yet perhaps you wait for orders, tho' you have not ask'd for any. Nor do I expect or wish you should ask for any in such cases. In matters of importance or niceity, I would have you always consult me. But in the Common innocent occurrences, Let your own, or your friend's prudence, not scrupulousness, be your guide. Ten to one But you'll do as I wish. If not, there's no great harm, nor shall I ever take notice of it, except it be to convey to you my Sentiments, when I think they may be of use on future occasions.

Your letter, tho' not quite to my mind any more than to yours, is much better, than any which this bout I have had from you. If the latter part were as well as the beginning I should find no fault. A little care, and practice will bring you to what I wish.

Billy Smith is fat and well. So are your Pea-birds, all but one Cock, which was kill'd, no one knows how. The Hens are, they tell me, breeding. But I expect no good from them in their present situation.

To your Question about the China. My answer is this. That, if you intend to be good Managers, you ought to keep the accounts of your Expenses seperate. If otherwise, The skill is, to blend all together, that when I find fault with the Sum Total, you may plead the multitude of Articles, that you have nothing to say to, and make more of them than they are. Seriously, your best way will be not to plague Ned Curtis with these kind of things, but to pay for, and enter them in a seperate account.

The two *Hatchils*,[6] (you write *Heckles*, I don't blame you now, but do so no more) must be sent down hither.

Mrs Silver's news is in one of the publick papers, and is contradicted in another. I am very indifferent which is true.

Tell Mrs Jourdan, with my service, That what she call'd Two pair of fine English Blankets is but one pair, at least for my large Beds, and that I desire she would immediatly get me, not what she calls two, but in reality two, pair more. I mean four Blankets such as the two she sent down. All the Blankets I have here are too little for the large Beds. The six other pair she sent down are not of the same size. I don't know whether she was aware of this. If not, The Seller cheated her. I must also desire her to buy another pair of sheets of the same kind with the finest pair she bought this year. They and the Blankets may be sent safely in a Box, which John will order George Stephens to knock together for them. The Sooner they come the better. The reason of my desiring them is, that when Mrs Donnelan &c. are so near me, I must ask them all here, and with them Mrs Waller. So there will be three Ladys with their Husbands, who must be accommodated alike. The rest must take their Chance with what the House affords.

Desire John to tell Smith the Wheel-wright, that the Diaper-Loom I want is not a Broad one. I think £4:5:- too high a price for it. He must let me have it as cheap as He can, as it is not a Grant from the Board.[7]

Bid him to provide the Spades and Shovels immediatly, and weigh the latter [*damaged ms*] together, and Let me know what the whole amounts to. I'll divide it equally upon the twelve.

You were very right in having fires and not going out on Tuesday Evening. I hope you observ'd the same caution, some following days which have been here excessively cold, tho' no little cold oblig'd you to it, which yet I shall not wonder at your having got, nor think it a Mark of tenderness. Few are able perfectly to stand such Unnatural Weather. I have been so carefull of my self as to stay within mostly, tho' I bless God, I have not got the least cold. We have had fine rain this morning, which We wanted very much. But I think the cold continues. I long for some Summer. My love at the Green &c. I am

> My Dear Girl's
> most affectionate Edw:Elphin

One of the letters you enclos'd to me was from Mr Daunt.[8] He gives a most melancholy account of his Wife. In the Small-pox, with Spots – I fear the next post will bring an account of her death.[9] I am sorry for Molly Fagan's (you spell her name wrong) ilness. If the Doctor patches her up agen, I see no objection to the sending her to Finglas.

Still fine rain this Evening, but still cold.

Half a dozen white Chamber Pots. As many Basins must be got, and four Pewter Chamber Pots for the Servants' rooms. Mrs Jourdan fancy'd there were enough of these kind of things – But it seems, there are not. They must come down with the first.

1. Broom, *cytisus scoparius*, was used as a diuretic; mint was probably prescribed as an infusion of peppermint, *mentha palustris*, used for soothing the stomach and for diarrhoea. E.G. Wheelwright, *The Physick Garden* (London 1934), p.168.
2. 'Last Thursday Lewis Ormsby of Tubbervaddy in the Co. of Rosscommon Esq, was Married to Miss Donnellan, Daughter of Nehemiah Donnellan Esq Knight of the Shire for the County of Tipperary, an accomplished young lady with a very large fortune.' *Dublin Courant*, 3-10 June 1749.
3. Hester Coghill, daughter of James Coghill, LLD, married Charles 2nd baron Tullamore in 1737. They had no children. After his death in 1764, she married Major John Mayne, who took the name Coghill. Burke (1871), p.211.
4. *Nodium in scirpo quaeris*. You seek a knot in a bulrush: you find difficulties where none exist. Terence *Andria* v.5, 38.
5. Emily Lennox, daughter of the duke of Richmond and aunt of Charles James Fox, married James Fitzgerald, 20th earl of Kildare, in February 1746. Burke (1916), p.1242.
6. Hatchel. An instrument for combing flax.
7. The Trustees of the Linen Board in Dublin, of whom Edward Synge was one, were empowered to enforce the Board's regulations, carry out educational work and to give grants for new projects and for work of high quality. In the first half of the eighteenth century the Linen Board concentrated on making capital grants to a small number of contractors in the southern provinces. This policy was beset with difficulties and in 1727 it was resolved that no more than six looms be granted to any one contractor. Conrad Gill, *The Rise of the Irish Linen Industry* (Oxford 1925), pp.72, 76-8.
8. George Daunt (1712-86: physician, see Biographical Register).
9. Hannah: daughter of Thomas Daunt of Owlpen, Gloucestershire, and Elizabeth, daughter of the Rev. George Synge, prebendary of Kilbrogan, Bandon, Co. Cork. Kirkpatrick; Synge, p.3.

51

Elphin. June 21, 1749

My Dear Girl –

I am much pleas'd with your objection and your Manner of making it. This is genteel and proper to me. That shews your regards to your Cosen, and such a desire to have her pleas'd as very much becomes you. I see that She expects and you wish for great matters on her remove, and tho' I think, that more indifference about a place meerly to sleep, dress and be private in, would shew more wisdom, I yet am dispos'd as always, rather to gratify than to baulk her. But I can't do it at present. My necessary expenses are so great, as to oblige me for the present to avoid multiplying those which are not so. Some time hence perhaps I may indulge my friend Jane in fitting up an Apartment. And if, till I can do this, she likes her present situation best, and preferrs a passage room, with bare Walls, a great press and three or four Scriptoires and Chests of Drawers, to two rooms above, which tho' meanly or not at all furnish'd, may be clean and warm, and will be private, I shall be very well pleas'd that she continue as she is. For this I assure you, and you may her, that the uneasiness I have been under at seeing her so ill accommodated, had much more share in my little Scheme, than a desire to add to the Grandeur of your Apartment. This last is to me a trifle, and I hope is so to you. The other was with me the point of importance, so that what you've said to her is strictly true, that Her being mov'd was design'd entirely for her Conveniency. But if she thinks otherwise of this Conveniency than I do, she has my full consent to remain as she is, till I can do, what will please and give her content. In short, Please your Selves, and Do that which may make you most happy, and best satisfy'd within your Selves, and with each other, and I shall be pleas'd; and so Go on, with my Scheme, or post-pone it as you like. But pray, Let them rooms Above be clean'd, and the Chairs, which were in your Bed Chamber be placed there. I hope they are not destroy'd as useless lumber.

I am glad the Wine is come. When Sullivan has examin'd and setled it, Let John desire him to write me his thoughts of it, and give his letter to him, that you may enclose it. You did right not to pay the Porters. John may learn from Sullivan what ought to be paid, and pay it.

I made a mistake in my last. The Second fine pair of sheets came last Summer. I would have a third now of the same kind.

You told me, you had bespoke 68 yards of pencil'd Cotton for the outside of a Bed, and two pair of Window Curtains. By accident I found an old Memorandum of Mr Moore's in which He directs 49 yards & ½ for the out-side of a Bed and one pair in a room 13 feet high. Will one pair of Window Curtains take 18 & ½ yards? Let Mr Moore be ask'd about this. But do you bespeak, what will answer the purposes intended.

Desire Ned Curtis to send down three pounds of flower of Brim-stone.[1] He must send very good, not sow'r. It is for men, as well as Horses, I have prescrib'd some to Jemy for the Piles. Ask the Doctor whether this be right, or what else is – they are inward, and don't bleed. I must take care of Jemy, for He alone takes right care of my Horse.

Bid John tell Turner, that the Latches with brass nobs will not answer my purpose. Let him send but one, and instead of the rest, five of the same sort with the Iron ones, which He sent down, but of a much smaller size, fit for light Closet doors. John has sent off a parcel of Timber which I am very glad of because I could not do without it. But He has given a most excessive rate for Carriage. The fellows certainly exacted upon him, on account of his Eagerness, which yet I cannot blame him for. But He must be more cunning for the future. I shan't care to have him exceed twenty shill. the Tun. For all other things, and perhaps for Boards He'll get Carrs enough after Mullingar fair, at a much cheaper rate. Tell him that one Casey a Carr-Man will call about that time at Kevin-street. I desire He may have loading. He is one whom I intend to encourage.

Let Will learn from Ross[2] what the Books cost. Send the money and take his receit. Bid him ask Ross about Shewen's *Parliament Cases*.[3] This was the book I most desir'd. He has done very ill in letting it go.

How go Straw-berrys with you? We have had abundance here, but bad. Scarce any Wall-fruit or Apples. How are these last with you or at Finglas? I fear We shall have no Cyder.[4] That will be bad for Mrs Jourdan.

I have time for no more. The post waits. God bless and preserve you all. I am

yours &c. Edw:Elphin

1. Charles Varley recommended 'Bracken's Cordial Ball to keep a horse temperate in his body and give him free respiration.' This was a mixture of aniseed, caraway, car-damons, flower of brimstone, turmeric, saffron, liquorice powder, and wheat flour beaten together and made into a ball 'about the size of a pigeon's egg'. *A New System of Husbandry* Vol.2, pp.291-2.

2. William Ross: bookseller, Grafton Street. Watson (1760), p.37.

3. Possibly William Shewen, *A Brief Testimony for Religion ... Presented to the considera-tion of all, but more especially those that may be chosen Members of Parliament, that they may see cause to concur with the King's Gracious Declaration for Liberty of Conscience* (London 1688).

4. Cider apples were widely grown in Ireland; by the mid-eighteenth century cider was a popular drink as an alternative to beer. T.C. Barnard, 'Gardening, diet and "Improve-ment" in later seventeenth century Ireland', *Journal of Garden History* Vol. 10 (1990), pp.73-4.

52

As I wrote last post in an hurry, I forgot somethings, which I dispatch now, to avoid hurry after the next comes in.

Tell John, that We are in great distress for Plough-Shares, otherwise call'd Socs. We us'd to be furnish'd from some Iron-Works near us;[1] but none are to be had there now. He must provide half a dozen. Turner can, I believe, direct him where the best are to be had, or perhaps furnish them. I care not where He gets, so He gets them, and good. He must send them rough. For We fit them our Selves. He must bespeak two more Pick-axes, and two small Sledges[2] of 6 or 7 pounds, like the last.

Bid him speak to Sullivane about the philtring stones,[3] and never cease speaking to him, till they are got. I want them much here.

I had lately a letter from the Bishop of Clonfert, in which Mrs Whet-combe puts in her claim to White-lilly roots this Season. The time for taking them up is at a great distance. But I mention this now, that All We can spare may be secur'd for her.

I hope Gannon has before this taken up the Hyacinths. Let him in the proper Season take up the Tulips, Ranunculuss, and Anemonys, and keep the good ones seperate. You may superintend and direct this, and every thing else in the Garden as you please. But I don't desire that you or Gannon should trouble your Selves with Mr Hawker.[4] I am not much sat-isfy'd, with the behaviour of that Spark. Get Eaton to order the Frame of the Tulip-beds to be painted. It must be done, when perfectly dry. Ask him, if He has sold my rope. I shall be sadly baulk'd if He has not. I see by the news that the Spire of St Patrick's is begun.[5] He propos'd to sell it to the Undertakers of the Work.

Shannon does better in his double capacity than I expected. But I shall be lame without a Butler, unless Jac. advances into one, of which indeed I have not much hope. I should be glad of a right good one, gen-teel, honest, and clever, tho' no fine Gent, and one that can write and understands figures. Enquire at your leisure, and mention my Want occa-sionally to Madam Silver. By chance you may hear of one. You've time before you. I shall not greatly want, till I go to town.

I see advertis'd in the News-paper a little book call'd *the Governess* &c.[6] Do you know it? And Is it good for any thing? If from thence, I should some times give Mrs Jourdan a new name, I hope she'll not take it too gravely.[7]

Yours and Mrs Jourdan's are now come in with the truly pleasing tidings of your being very well, and your Aunt better. May you continue well, She improve.

I am not sure but that my last may stop the intended alterations. If it does, I sha'n't be displeas'd, but then there will be no present occasion for the Book-case. If it goes on, you may order it to be made of Dantzick Oak, since Irish is so hard to be got.[8] The Difference will be only in Colour. Yet I would rather have Irish, if it can be got even on tolerable Terms.

I am in great pain about Mrs Daunt. Pray send to the Townsends[9] at the College to know what is become of her.[10]

I am glad to know that the Notes are safe with Mr Palmer – I am afraid that Sympson came a day after the Fair. But that was neither his fault, nor mine, but Palmer's and others who misled me, if I have been misled. But 'tis no great matter. If I don't get Horses, I keep my money.

You need never trouble your Self with writing particular Compliments. I suppose people to say and do with affection, or Civility or both prompt them to.

Now for Mrs Jourdan (Dare I say Mrs Teachum) to whom I won't write seperate letters, at least till privilege comes in.

She must excuse me. I did not say she was Wise, but Wiser; nor do I remember I charg'd Scrupulousness on her, tho' I own honestly, I think she has her share of it. Let her get rid of it her Self, and so reform it in you. For that's the likeliest way.

What she thought of buying, I can't tell. But this I am sure of, that in the Memorandum I have here there is 2 pair of Fine English Blankets. I thought it was in her hand but find it in the Upholsterer's. This occasions these Rasures. [*two lines deleted*]

Sullivane is the formal Man she describes. But she must bear with him as I do, as long as He supplys her with *Vin Episcopal*, as Miss Vignoles calls it. His and his Cooper's folly about the hogshead of Cyder is most egregious. Scrupulousness is too mild a name for it. Pray let it be hoop'd immediatly. It is not my fault that it was not done before. Tyghe[11] assur'd me, it did not, nor would, want it this Season. Let him be tax'd with this. I had rather loose the best hogshead of Wine in my Cellar, than that which I have been nursing these dozen years. Strange it is, that Among you, you have not said, whether the Wine newly arriv'd, be good, bad or indifferent. Pray let Sullivane be desir'd to write to me his thoughts of it.

It is no great matter that the Basons and Chamber-pots are a little delay'd. There are enough for present occasions. A crowd of Company would require more. But that I sha'n't have till my Visitation. Never be in pain any of you, about my wanting Company. I can dispense with that want much better here than in the Old house, having all my Amusements at my door, without even taking a Walk for them. Between them and my study, which is very pleasant as well as Commodious, I am as happy alone, as with Company, nay! more so, than with some. An empty Table is the only thing I dislike. But that I seldom have at dinner, and at Supper I can very well dispense with it.

I won't disgust Mrs J's niceity by insisting on Pewter-Chamber pots. I think of them as she does. But Shannon was for them and I yielded, because I would not dispute. In lieu of them a parcel of Brown earthern ones must be provided.

I wonder I forgot to speak to you of the four-Wheel Chair. I intended you should air in it as usual, and resolv'd to leave Lister[12] in town, on purpose that Will might ride out with you. I won't say you were scrupulous in not doing this, as usual, but if I had not been ask'd about it, I should have charg'd you home, with this simple behaviour. I take airings in that to be healthier, as well as more pleasant, than in the Coach. But I fear you are now too big to pack three into it. You may chuse occasions, when Jeny is with her Mother. I am sure, she wo'n't take it amiss, if you desire her sometimes to go there, on purpose to favour such an Expedition.

Mrs J's account of my Sister gives me pleasure mix'd with pain. Could I, with the other hopefull symptoms, find that Her bulk lessen'd, I should be more set up. Her talking of Roscrea[13] was a piece of her little pleasantry. I seriously fear she will not be able to do it, and that she thinks so her Self. Assure her always of my most hearty good Wishes.

Tell John that His first Cargo of timber is come, and that the Fellows on my talking to them did not deny their Exaction. I call'd them Rascals, and paid them. I hope He'll be able to send off the rest at a cheaper rate next Week. The price of other goods by the hundred is much higher, than usual at this time a year. The Carr-men have found him out: Or He has lost his knack of making good bargains. By Mr Turner's list, I see the Spring-latches, which I would have stopp'd, are come down. I must return, what I have not occasion for.

I would not have John too hasty in his mowing. Grass now will grow a great deal, and Hay is like to be so scarce in many places, that We ought to make the most of ours. I leave him to his own discretion.

He must be sure to find loading of some kind or other for Casey. He may send the Chairs by him, and if He has nothing else ready, He may send two Gross more of Bottles, which I shall soon Want, tho' I do not this instant, and with them a couple of Gross of Corks. He may send the Diaper Loom too, if ready. But load him He must For I promis'd He should.

Let John tell Mr Nelson, that one Taafe of Strokes-town[14] near me has got down some Swedish Timber lately, for which He says He paid but forty shill. the Tunn – I don't believe him, and yet I believe Timber is falling.

I wish Mrs Jourdan would find, or seek an occasion of talking to formal Sullivane about his French Tobacco, and tell him the mighty difference between that and what Mr Wills gets from Crommie his Wine-merchant.[15] If this Gent's wine were as much better than Sullivane's as his Tobacco is, The Formal Gent would be in great danger of loosing my Custom. By doing this cleverly, she may have a good chance for a *Régale*[16] for her nose, the next importation.

Gannon's story about Cucumber is a poor pretence. The storm here was as violent as it could be; and yet We have plenty of them. How go Melons? Among the great heap of Flower-roots sent down last year, there were but few Tulips, and a multitude of Fox-gloves, not worth Carriage, nor planting.

Mrs Jourdan delighted me with the account of your health. Oh! May I always have this delight. One day, she said, she fancy'd you look'd a little pale – I'll tell you the day. It was Tuesday se'night. If you be as sharp as I am, you perceiv'd in mine of this day se'night that I fancy'd you had got a little cold. The truth is, I wonder you escap'd – May you grow in health and every thing that is good – So prays

yours &c. Edw:Elphin

I was at Boyle last Tuesday to return Lord K's visit. Among other prattles, His account of one of his Sisters made me smile.[17] He says that she grew very long legg'd till sixteen and from that time grew a good deal above the Waist, so as to suit her long leggs. Do you know why I tell you this? The same thing may happen to you; tho' it is not two pence matter, whether it does or no. Speak again to Eaton about the Lantherns. If I have them not soon, I shall be baulk'd. Ask if there be no contrivance to save the Cieling from being discolour'd by the smoke. They talk here of a Bell like your glass one, of thin lead. Without some such thing the Lanthern for the Hall will not do. The other is at such a distance from the Cieling that it will not hurt it.

1. Charles O'Conor of Belanagare wrote a pamphlet in 1753 on the development of coal and iron deposits in the Roscommon Triangle (Sligo, Roscommon and Leitrim). Charles O'Conor to Joseph C. Walker, 15 August 1786. O'Conor, pp.470-1.

2. Sledgehammers.

3. Philtering stones: porous stones used to filter water.

4. Mr Hawker: a gardener at Kevin Street.

5. 'Last Monday the Foundation stone was laid for building a Spire on top of St. Patrick's steeple, for the erecting of which the late bishop of Clogher left a considerable sum of money.' *Faulkner's Dublin Journal,* 13-17 June 1749.

6. [Sarah Fielding], *The Governess; or, little female academy. Being the history of Mrs Teachum, and her nine girls. With their nine days amusement. Calculated for the entertainment and instruction of young ladies in their education* By the author of *David Simple* (Dublin 1749). Sarah Fielding (1710-68) was Henry Fielding's sister. It is now thought to be the

first narrative giving an authentic account of the daily life of children and adolescents. Mary Cadogan (ed.), *The Governess* (1987), Introduction p.vii.

7. Mrs Teachum.

8. 'Dantzig oak' came from the substantial forests on the southern coasts of the Baltic between Danzig and Riga. Sven-Erik Aström, 'English Timber Imports from Northern Europe in the eighteenth century', *Scandinavian Economic History Review* Vol. 18 (1970), pp.12-70.

9. There were two Townsend boys at Trinity College in 1749: Richard, son of John Townsend (see next letter) and Samuel, see letter 24. *Alumni*, p.819; Burke (1912), p.699.

10. Mrs Daunt was related through her mother Elizabeth, aunt of Mary Synge who married Bryan Townsend of Castletownsend, Co. Cork. *Alumni*, p.819; Burke (1912), p.699.

11. Tighe: a cooper.

12. Lister: a groom.

13. Roscrea, Co. Tipperary.

14. George Taafe: merchant, Strokestown. Had seven children under fourteen and five Catholic servants. Census, f.84.

15. Either Michael Crommie, merchant of Lower Ormond Quay, or John, merchant, Ann Street, near the Linen Hall. Watson (1752), p.9.

16. *Un régal*: a treat.

17. Lord Kingsborough had four sisters. Burke (1916), p.1168.

53

Elphin. June 28, 1749.

My Dear Girl.

I write this, on Saturday evening, to desire you to tell John that His last cargo came to day. All things safe. But bid him tell Mr Nelson, that two of the Beams No. 26 and No. 28 are half of them rotten, so as that I must loose a length of joice on each. Such vile Stuff I never beheld; and, which cuts of all Excuse, the Rotteness is to be seen and felt on the outside. The twelve short pieces are as bad, just good for nothing – I positively will not pay a half penny for this decay'd stuff, and insist that it be not charge'd, nay! I'll be allow'd for the Carriage. It is hard to pay at the rate of £1: 3: 3 the Tunn for stuff which is scarce fit to burn. I am sure Mr Nelson did not see them. But this shews Mr Bonvillete[1] not to be depended on. My Carpenter complains that the Beams are not saw'd far enough; and I know He says true. For I view'd them my self. He must cut a foot of Each with his hand-saw. It is hard that I should pay twice for sawing. I am much disgusted at this usage, being accustom'd to better. Write out this, and let John carry it to Nelson. I know it will make him dance. But 'tis fit He should know it. He has not been as carefull as formerly; and as for John,

Tell him I say, He hurrys and swears and swaggers himself out of his Wits. With half an Eye He might have seen these defects.

I like the China-dishes, and plates greatly. You said there was a third of one kind of Dish. Secure it. It may come down on some other occasion, and probably will be wanted.

Fine rooms increase Wants. There must, it seems be dressing Tables and Toilettes.[2] Such things as you have in your dressing room. Tables We have scrub enough. You fine people, would say they wanted something to hide them. Mrs Heap has one of this kind, which us'd to be in the Blew-room, you know. But she much wants three more. If you can provide such as are plain and decent very cheap, Do. If not, Let them alone.

Let John ask Turner whether Mr Nicholson order'd them Scrapers,[3] of which too He has sent more than I wrote for, six instead of four. They look to me like Old-Shop-keepers of which He had a mind to be rid. He should take care of sending me any thing not good in it's kind. One, at least of the four Brass-Locks, two of which are now come down is bad. It's own key over-shoots the Bolt, and will not open it agen. Unfortunately It is on my study; and I was lock'd out, and just going to use Violence this afternoon, when the Master key arriv'd with the two last to my relief. I am very angry at this. A few more such things will make us quarrel. This to be wrote out for Turner's perusal.

Send for Woodward and order him to get as much Green Cloth of five or at most six shill. the yard as will make a Frock-Coat for my fowler.[4] He is taller than Philip,[5] and not so tall as John. Lining, and Every thing fit for making it up must also be provided, and Metal-Buttons, such as are to the livery-frocks. He must also get strip'd flannel such as is in Robinson's Waistcoats, enough for two, with what may be wanting to make them up.[6] All must be made up safe in a bundle to be sent down here next Carrs.

Yours came in, My Dearest, with the most pleasing tidings I can have in this World. May I always have them.

Pray tell Ned Curtis, that I am now more interested than I was in the Welfare of his daughter. I believe that your good Mother's in some measure determin'd his choice of a name.[7]

I am always pleas'd when you spend time with Mrs Nicholson. I have no objection to your dining with Dr Lawson, and think you've chosen your Company so far very well. Should not you add Bab. and Madge?[8] Tell the Doctor I begin to long for his coming down. Before He leaves town, I must desire him to see L[or]d Ch[ief] Justice Singleton,[9] and ask him for a small bundle of Papers, which I have desir'd He may give him to bring down to me. Desire him also to give the Elder Townsend twenty-pounds to pay fees and other Expenses of his Master's degree.[10] Ned Curtis must furnish him with the Money. I had rather the young Man had it thro' his hand than my own? [*damaged ms*].

I wish you had accept'd Mrs Fitzmaurice's invitation.[11] I have as little inclination as you to your having acquaintance there. But you must avoid giving offence if you can, and you might have come off at a small party, better than at a large one. But it is no great matter.

I have heard of *The Encampment*.[12] You may easily guess my thoughts of it – I don't remember that I order Ross to buy *The General Abridgment of Cases in Equity*.[13] Unless He says I did, Let it be return'd.

I doubted not Mrs J's cunning. But I had a mind to retrieve mine own mistake, that I might not hereafter be twitted with it.

My service to the Doctor and tell him Mine own prescription has had so good Effects, that I do not intend to change it, and so give him the Credit of the Cure.

I am vex'd at what you write about Strawberrys. Tell Gannon so, and that I insist on his making a new and handsome plantation of every kind white, [*damaged ms*] Almond next August. He may let the best of the Old stand, but must [provide? damaged ms] so as that they may be mov'd the following year. He may edge all his [borders? *damaged ms*] with them. I can't bear to have the Garden thus bare of what would be agreable to you and your friends. As for Apples, &c. We must take what We can get. We cannot command the Seasons.

Sullivane's Letter is not so formal as his appearance. He gives me a tolerable good account of my Wine. The next time He or his Cooper come, I wish Mrs Jourdan would taste it. I shall be glad of her opinion.

Last year I forgot to order a Bottle Drainer to be made up while I [was here? *damaged ms*] I will not forget it now. Order George Stephens to make a plain roomy one of the same kind Let there be three Divisions in it as in the Old One. If any of the Old stuff will do, Let him use it, and the rest I would have of the best kind of Firr. Let the Shelf-Rails for the Bottles be at eighteen inches distance from each other. Shannon says the present are too close. I intend a slated roof to it. So the posts and Top-rail must be fram'd accordingly. It is best consult Mr Nelson, or Eaton about this, lest George should blunder. Eaton is nearest and I believe, best. Consult him, and Be sure it be painted assoon as made. Mr Turner must provide three small Locks for the three doors, which will answer one key, and have two keys made.

Some of the Flags in the Kitchen are Sunk. Bid John speak to Burnet[14] about them and by him or some one else, get those in one place which are sunk very much taken up and laid strait and level. The other little Inequalitys I do not mind. I have time for no more.

yours &c. Edw: Elphin

By mistake I have turn'd my paper upside down – you'll however be able to read what I've written.

Hurry'd as I am, I must note some of your false spellings. I fear that upon a more exact view I should find more – Some of these are very blameable, and shew your want of care. Indeed, My Dear Girl, your writing is on the whole much worse this year than the last, and in stopping you have gone from one extreme to the other. Many more in this last letter, than there ought to be, and you make them such scrawls, as that your writing appears worse than it would do. Unless you amend very quickly I shall despair of your ever writing as I wish'd and formerly hop'd. flower-di-luce. I think it ought to be de

 aprouve – Shamefull

 triffles – an f too many

 Tursday – Brogue -

1. Maximilien Bonvillete, timber merchant, Upper Arran Quay. Watson (1752), p.5. 'Maximilien Bonvillete, who served apprenticeship to the late Mr Anthony Vareilles, merchant, and Matthew Brittain, has opened a timber-yard on the upper end of Arran Quay.' *Dublin Courant*, 7 May 1747.

2. Toilette. A cloth cover for a dressing-table.

3. Footscrapers. See Letter 47.

4. Andrew Young of Elphin. The Elphin census says he was a Protestant. Census, f.2.

5. Philip: a groom.

6. Swift spent £2s.16.2d on his servants' livery in October 1732. *Accounts*, p.227.

7. Jane.

8. Two daughters of Nicholas and Elizabeth Synge. For Barbara Synge see Letter 21. Margery Synge married the Rev. Robert Curtis. Synge, p.7.

9. Henry Singleton (1682-1759; see Biographical Register).

10. Richard Townsend was born in 1725, the son of John Townshend, a barrister. He was Edward Synge's first cousin through the marriage of Bryan Townshend of Castle Townshend, Co. Cork, who married Mary Synge, daughter of Edward Synge's grandfather, Edward Synge bishop of Cork, Cloyne and Ross. Richard Townsend was admitted to TCD in 1742 and took BA in 1746. He became MA in 1749. He married Elizabeth Fitzgerald, a daughter of Viscount Doneraile, in October 1750. He became MP and high sheriff of Co. Cork. *Alumni*, p.819; Burke (1912), p.699.

11. Mrs Fitzmaurice was possibly Mary, daughter of the Hon. William Fitzmaurice and wife of her first cousin, the Hon. John Fitzmaurice who became Lord Dunkerron and viscount Fitzmaurice in 1751 and earl of Shelburne in 1753. Burke (1916), p.1206.

12. *The Encampment:* not known.

13. Charles Viner, *A general abridgment of law and equity alphabetically digested under proper titles with notes and references to the whole* (London 1746).

14. Burnet: not known.

54

Elphin. June 30, 1749

My Dear Girl.

I write in some hurry to day. So that you must probably be content just with knowing that I am well. If I have time for more you shall have it. But I must first dispatch business.

Desire Ned Curtis to give John Miller money £15:10 to pay for a Coach Horse which Sympson has bought. As He may probably buy more at other fairs, Desire him to furnish money for them in the same manner. Tell John that I think it will be right to use the one He has got, and others which I hope He will get, gently to the Carr, not to draw to or from Dublin, but to draw home his Hay, when made, or collect, and lay out his Dung. Desire him to let me know how 'Dragon' does. If He be quite well of his lameness, He may move him to Finglas, and use him the same way. But Let him consult Sympson.

I am much pleas'd with the Change in the rate of Carriage of Timber. John sees now that He was before impos'd on. If He can continue to send at, or near, that price, Let him send off all I wrote for as fast as He pleases. Boards I am in least haste for. Desire him to get from Mr Nelson a copy of the Bill of Scantling,[1] I sent him, and enclose it to me in his next. I have not one, and much want it. As I know not the Man, who bought the Timber, I sha'n't probably be able to learn the yard – but the Fact is, as I told it.

I hope all the things I have from time to time wrote for are now ready and will come off by Casey, or the first opportunity. Let not the Cleanly things be forgotten. Pray was it for them or the LOUSE, that I deserv'd to be call'd Dirty? – Send me down also the two New Card Tables which stood in the Dining room. They are rather an Incumbrance there, and I have very fit places for them here. Perhaps I may want them, when I have mine house full – Let them be made up carefully in a Box, and Let Foxal pack them in it. He understands it better than any one else. Tell Eaton I hope the Lantherns will answer the Expectations He has rais'd. Let him pack them up in the safest manner He can; and send with them Cord proper to hang them, and enough of it. One of them hangs from a great heighth, not less than 25 Feet. After all, I wish We be able to hang them properly. For We, Country folks, are not much us'd to such things. Desire him also to send 6 Panes 13½ ins by 10½ ins and 8 at 12½ ins by 12½ ins. Better exceed the dimensions a little than fall short. Bristol-Crown is the kind.² No great niceity about them.

Tho' I left my friend Jane as absolutely to her choice, as I said I did, yet I am pleas'd that she has made the most sensible one. Tell her this, with my blessing; and that I hope, before Christmas to do what will please her as well as a well fitted up apartment. She may trust me.

I care not how fast your Tongue runs to me, My Dearest, But I wish your pen mov'd slower, till you can come to write quick without so many mistakes and interlineations. One thing I must caution you of among twenty others – you do not leave space enough between your Words, which is a great blemish and imperfection. Upon my Word, Ally, if you don't care Billy Smith will out-write you. By the by I have order'd him a noble whipping to day for an Egregious lye.

Gannon makes very lame excuses for what is really the effect of his own conceited adherence to his own Measures. I left his Melon Beds in so flourishing a way, that Nothing but down-right mismanagement could have hurt them – and as for Cucumbers, tho' the Weather was to the full as bad here, as in Dublin, We have a multitude of them. If your one Melon prove as fine as you hope, Send it to the L[ord] C[hancello]r. But send it not unless it be very perfect. If moderatly good, send it to the Arch-Bishop of Dublin. Ask him if this be all I am to hope for. 'Tis a shame that He should grow worse than He was, by being in a Garden, where He has all Conveniences. Yet this is really the case. I am much out of humour with him, and desire He may know it.

You write *Explaination*. It should be *Explanation*. I am glad the hogsheads of Cyder have escap'd. The loss would have been felt more, as there is so very bad a prospect of Apples.

Tho' you had so little Wine in one Binn; I hope the other will hold you back. I expect you'll have some for me at my return.

Mrs Heap desires a little Saffron to make Cakes upon Occasion. If Ned Curtis makes it up so as to fit one of your Covers, you may send it that way as well as any.

Is my Watch come home? Take care that Lawson does not forget it. I have wrote more than I thought I should get time for. Adieu.

yours &c. Edw:Elphin

1. Scantling: a measure of timber.
2. Bristol crown glass was composed of silica, potash and lime (without lead or iron), made in circular sheets by blowing and whirling.

55

My Dear Girl –

Yours now before me is better wrote than your former ones. But still I want, what, I begin to fear, I shall never get, that you write like one, who had a Command of your pen. I won't bid you observe my Writing, because in your desponding Way, you have an Answer ready. Oh! I am sure I never shall write like my Dada. It may be not. But try. Or, if you think this too much, Try to write like Mrs Jourdan or Jeny. I have a letter of the former now before me, which shews that it was wrote in the hurry, she says it was, and yet one may see in it a form'd hand, and that she can write much better, with a little more care. Whereas, to say the truth, My Dearest Dear, the best of your writing is like a midling Copy of a learner; and whatever pains you may take, you certainly do not advance. I appeal to Mrs J. I would give a good deal of money, that you wrote as she does.

But your writing is not the only thing I have reason to find fault with in your letters. You make a thousand mistakes in stopping; sometimes omitting, where you ought to put stops and often putting them where you ought not. You frequently too put one stop for another, and are very apt to finish a Sentence with a , . This is mighty wrong, and must be corrected. Otherwise those who do not know you, will fancy you do not understand what you write. You give further causes of suspicion of this kind I observ'd one very remarkable one in yours before this last. These are your Words. 'I forgot to tell you that there were but seven bottles.' Tell me now where a stop ought to be, and then I'll tell you where you put one. But Do not, I charge you ask Mrs Jourdan, or any one else. The true reason of all these mistakes, and of all your interlineations, and wedging in of letters, and syllables, is that you do not set down to write with sufficient calmness, and resolution to attend. You hurry your Self, My Dear, and perhaps write under some awe. If you do, you never will write as I wish. In this same letter, that I may once for all tell you all your faults of this kind, I find a false spelling which could proceed from nothing but giddiness. You write spaking, for speaking. You'll say of this, as you do of others, that It was a mistake, and I know it was. But this is no Excuse. Why do you make such mistakes? You may avoid them, if you please; and I had rather have from you six lines, which shew'd that you thought before hand of what you were to write, and took care to form your expressions in your mind first, and then to write them properly, than the longest letter I receive, tho' the prattle of your pen is as agreable as that of your tongue. Don't fret at this now, Ally, but mend. Be assur'd, 'tis of great importance to you to do so; and I am sure Mrs J thinks so as well as I.

Your account of your Aunt, delights me greatly. As much as the Country wanted rain, I am sorry that the Weather is chang'd, lest Wet and Wind incommode her. But who knows? To morrow may be a fine day for her, tho' this be a fine one for the Country. I wish it for mine own sake, as well as hers. For if it be, I propose to make an Excursion to Tubber-vaddy. My scheme is, to dine there from hence, lye at Blair's,[1] and return hither next day. But if the Wet continues, I'll stay where I am. I forgot to tell you in my last that Mr Donnelan was here. He came on Wedensday, and left me on Saturday. He seems very well, and much pleas'd with his daughter's marriage, as indeed He has reason. They, and the Kilmore folks,[2] are all to come here Monday fortnight. If the Toilettes are to be got, I wish they may be here before that time. But this is a matter of small importance. I well remember the sprigg'd Muslin, you mention. It will do very well here. But I fancy you had better keep it for your new dressing-room. If it be a pretty thing in it's kind, of which I am no judge, I had rather you had it for your Apartment, than that it should be sent here. If it be not handsome enough for you, It will do very well here. So Dispose of it, as you please. Pray when do you set about your dressing room?

I am glad the hogshead of Cyder is come, and is likely to be good. As I take it to have come by Sea, I am surpriz'd at the Carr-man's demand for Hoops. But his not coming agen, makes me Suspect an intended imposition. And now, To perplex Mrs Jourdan. As my provision of Cyder here is Scanty, and the demands for it are likely to be great, I should be glad to have either this new-come hogshead, or the one in Shannon's Cellar sent down here, and I must desire her to determine which. The Best, and that which will keep longest in the Vessel, I would have kept, and that sent, which is not the best, but fittest for drinking this Season; and thus far she'll agree with me, because then she'll get share of the best. But if the new-come hogshead be the one which she chuses on these Accounts to keep, what will she do? As John Miller would never rack[3] his, So I fear it won't be good, unless it be rack'd before it travels; and if it be rack'd, the filling it up, will be a new Draft on her poor little Store, which has already had more upon it, than I wish, so many that I wonder it is not exhausted – But now I think of it, I have been writing a good deal to no purpose, For that same Hogshead must have been heartily jumbled in hooping. Traveling will occasion but one jumble more, and it may pitch here, as well as there. So she is reliev'd, and the remains of her Store safe. If she thinks this, on other accounts, fittest to be sent, Let it be sent as it is: only she must get her friend Sullivane, or his Cooper Tighe to bung it up, and case it, lest Carr-men make bold with it on the road. I expected with the Cyder only one cheese. But since two are come, and both excellent, We must be satisfy'd, especially as I believe they cost nothing. I don't think I shall want either here. Let them be carefully preserv'd for Winter. I cut that in the house to try whether it was fit for use, and found it was not. I hope it may be preserv'd as it is. If Mrs J finds it cannot, she may order it to be us'd, as she pleases. You know it came from poor Molly Daunt. As to the Ale, I don't pity you. I desir'd Mrs Jourdan to do what she pleas'd with it. If she chose not to have it drank, she should have order'd it to be bottled in time, What she'll do with it now, I know not. The best would be to get the Brewers to change it. But that perhaps may be unreasonable to ask. If it be, Dispose of it among you as you can. Honest John may perhaps be glad of some of it at Finglas, and the rest you may find customers for. I think it not worth while to put any of it in bottles. The hogshead of Beer, of which I us'd to speak, is very fine. I intend to send it up all. So there will be no want of strong beer for her or my poor Sister, if as I wish, she returns to town, in a Condition to drink it. I am much pleas'd with her account of my Wine, as I have great dependance on her taste. The reason of Sr Formal's importunity with her to taste the Wine us'd in filling was that He might have a Witness that He put none but good into it. He and his Cooper are very reserv'd about this Wine. The opinion they sent me was really no opinion at all. But hers gives me great satisfaction; and I am sure she is right.

I have the same account from Dr Barry.[4] I have desir'd him to go, and taste mine in the Cellar. If you be at home, Pray see him, if He asks for you. You have an unreasonable Shyness towards that Gent, which I wish you had not. Be not afraid He will not prescribe to you, nor, I believe, feel your pulse. If He did, perhaps they would flutter, as they did under Diganan's hand. I believe I have affronted that Gent. At my first coming hither He came to dine as usual, and I bid him welcome. Harry Sandford and Barton were here, and staid as I desir'd they would. *Monsieur le Docteur* unask'd, return'd in the Evening with an intention to stay too. He told Shannon he was to lye here. But I was determin'd He should not, and made Cary carry him away. I suppose He is huff'd at this, and am not sorry if He be. His Irish impudence deserv'd to be so mortify'd. If I had not check'd it then, I had been teas'd with him more than I could bear. A fair riddance, if He comes no more.

I should have told you of Mr Wills's, sore *knee* it is, but that He enjoin'd me silence. In this He has acted as Congreve some where says the Ladys do, who Enjoin Men Secrecy, that they may have the pleasure of telling themselves.[5] By a letter from him the post before this, I find He is now pretty well, and proposes to be here, the latter end of the Week. I am much pleas'd, that you got the good Old Woman to dine with you.

Tell John that I desire He would ask Mr Eaton whether He has any certain near prospect of disposing of the Rope. If He says He has not, Let John speak to Bagshaw or go among the Gabbard men,[6] and sell it to some one or other for what He can get. Better do this, than let it rot. In short it must be dispos'd of one way or other – Mr Eaton has amus'd me about it more than He ought.

[*damaged ms*] Such Straw-berrys as you describe ought immediatly be rooted out. Order Gannon to throw them away. He may as well wait for orders [to root? *damaged ms*] out Dandilion. I fear that fellow is a more obstinate fool than I thought him.

I expect a particular account of Mrs Silver's Raree-shew.[7] By yours and Mrs Jourdan's hints, I believe it was simple enough.

I thank you for Lucas's Book. Tell the Doctor that I took notice of the Words in the Frontispiece. *Tam Marti quam Mercurio*,[8] but am so dull as not to find out the Wit of them. Are they, ask him, to be taken in a Chymical sense? I really am at a loss about them and should be glad to have them Explain'd. The Dedication is really an Extraordinary performance.[9] But How comes it, I have not another *Censor*? Has He dropp'd it already?

Tell John that the last Cargo of Timber is come safe. But there is one piece No. 35 so miserably full of Shakes[10] as to be good for little. Another instance of Mr Bonvillete's honesty and care. He must apprize Mr Nelson of this. I have no letter from him. He must also desire him to add to what Timber remains to be sent, 3 Beams 15 f. long by 12 ins square, saw'd into threes and fours. These are wanting, to supply the defects of the rotten pieces, and remedy some confusion occasion'd by them. The Carr-men said, that John promis'd them grass. I desire, whenever He makes such a promise, that He would tell me so, and I would not have him make any such, if He can help it. Grass is at present a scarce thing; and Hay I fear I shall have next to none. He must desire Eaton to send me a pound of choice sash line. I am sorry Sympson found no Horses to his mind at Dunboyn.[11] But better none, than those which are not right good. He must be on the Watch for such, and go to the later Fairs, particularly to Palmers-town.

Turner must be told, that I did not take notice of the Door-Spring, till yesterday, and now I have it, I know not how to put it on. He must send instructions. He has blunder'd agen. I wrote for a Brass-plate for the Great door and describ'd it exactly, four or five inches long, and one inch broad. Instead of this, He has sent an Entire striking plate which will by no means answer, and as I propose to send it back He must not charge it in his account. There is already a Brass staple for the Bolt to shoot in, which is ten times better than this new one, and fit for the purpose, which the new one is not. This little plate is all I want. It ought not have been omitted, when He sent down the lock. I desire He may send one.

My paper will hold no more. My Dear Dear Girl, Adieu for this time.

yours &c. Edw:Elphin

Desire John to send down a dozen and half of cruppers[12] for Straddles,[13] half a dozen smaller for Mules, and a doz for horses. Both have suffer'd greatly for want of them.

Turner must send down four Iron Latches of the same large size He sent down at first. They are for Doors about the Kitchen.

1. James Blair was the vicar of Roscommon.
2. Robert Waller and his wife.
3. Racking. To draw off wine or cider from the lees in the barrel.
4. Edward Barry wrote *Observations Historical, Critical and Medical on the Wines of the Ancients, and the Analogy between them and Modern Wines. With General observations on the Principles and Qualities of water, and in particular on those of Bath* (London 1775).
5. Congreve play: reference not found.
6. Gabbard men: lightermen on the river Liffey.
7. Raree-shew: Savoyard showmen's pronounciation of 'rare show'. A spectacle.
8. *Tam Marti quam Mercurio.* As well qualified for fighting as for success in the ordinary business of life. Proverb.
9. Obscure.
10. Shakes: pieces of split timber.
11. The fair at Dunboyne, Co. Meath, was on Wednesday 28 June and at Palmerstown, Co. Dublin, on Thursday 10 August. Watson (1749), p.87.
12. Cruppers: leathern straps which are buckled to the back of the saddle and pass under the tail of the horse.
13. Straddles: saddles.

56

Elphin. July 7, 1749

My Dear Girl.

Last night I return'd from my little excursion, which was a very pleasant one. I was at Roscommon by half an hour after nine where I breakfasted and dress'd, got to Tobbervaddy by twelve, staid till seven, and return'd to Blair, where I slept quiet and well. I intended being home in the morning, but an invitation from Mr Gunning to dine oblig'd me to change my purpose. You have seen his Wife with Mrs Carleton.[1] There I din'd very agreably, and came home in good time, without the least accident, but that John Aske got immoderatly fudled at Mr Gunning's. But He made a shift to rock on his horse, without tumbling, and I had no want of him. Philip and Peter were quite sober. So that this Booby has hurt no body but himself. He has destroy'd the only merit He had with me. I would have turn'd him off this morning, if I could have got his place supply'd: But if He does any thing of this kind agen, He walks, whether I can get his place supply'd or not. I think him now not worth keeping, and wish you could get me one who is.

Fret not at your writing, My Dear, but mend – you can if you will. I never shall desire any thing from you, that is impossible, nor repine at what you can't help For instance, your Larks-leggs as you call them. I care not two pence whether they mend or not, provided they serve you to walk firmly; and yet if you could as easily mend them as you can all the defects in your Writing, I should abuse you for having them. Yours now before me, tho' not quite right, is much better wrote than any I have had this season, and almost as well, as some of the best I had last. There is particularly less stifness in the hand, a thing which you ought to endeavour at. As for pens, While you are so extremely delicate about them, you'll never write easily nor well. You see Mrs Jourdan can write with any that comes to hand. But if you will still be delicate, provide for that delicacy, by learning to make them cleverly your Self. How long will you cobble?

You say, your Watch goes at [*sic*] it did. Pray Has Mr Holmes had it? If not, you should put it into his hands, as I bid you; and get Mr Nicholson to give him a particular charge of it.

Your Uncle and Aunt have fine Weather for their journey. I am much delighted with her challenge, and will, if I can, accept it. But As this is very uncertain, Drop no hint of it, even to Jane.

You need not trouble your Self with messages to Ross. If you have not paid him, Do not pay for the Book, till He clears up my doubt. If you have, it is no great matter. I shall have more dealings with him.

I am sorry so simple an Entertainment, as your shew, was so expensive. But since you escap'd without other damage, It's no bad affair. By seeing things of this kind, you'll see the nothingness of, and despise them. I am glad you were pleas'd, and tir'd at Mrs Fitzmaurice's.

The Over-charge of your letters, is perhaps owing to careless folding. You took the right method. But privilege will soon be in now, and free you from further trouble of this kind.

Tell John, that All the things by Casey came safe yesterday. But I was much disappointed at not finding the Lanterns among them. By your account they were ready time enough to have come; and being thus delay'd, they may not arrive, till my expected Company are gone. They come hither Monday fortnight. I wish John could send them and the two

Card Tables, so as to be here before that time.

I had almost forgot to tell you, that Kitty becomes her new situation extremely well. Mr and Mrs Mahon, and Nelly came there about two hours after me, and I believe, staid. There was other company, and she behav'd her Self to them all with great ease, and grace. Bess[2] is just the same. Mr Donnelan very well but Mrs rather low-spirited. They all sent compliments, and the Women regretted much their having miss'd you on leaving town.

Tell John, that since Sympson will not agree to the new Horse being put into a Carr, It must not be done. I'll furnish no pretence for his saying He was spoil'd. For the same reason, I desire that 'Dragon' may not be put into a Carr, even tho' Sympson should consent, unless He speaks out, and says that His lameness will make him ever unfit for any thing else, which by the long continuance of it, I fear will be the Case. If so, the sooner I know it, the better. My chief reason for desiring the new one to be put into a Carr, is that being thus train'd, He may hereafter upon occasion be put to draw my Chaise. I would fain have all my horses train'd so, if I could. Let Sympson be told this, and let him also be ask'd, whether the Horse he bought last, be four past, or, what they call, rising four?

Desire John to give my service to Mr Nelson, and tell him that his having been ill gives me vastly more concern, than ever so great a loss or disappointment in timber could have given me. Assoon as privilege comes in, I'll write particularly to him. In the mean time I desire that the rest of the Timber may come, as Carrs offer; and I beg that an hundred or two of Boards may be sent, with the soonest. For I am in great want of some. If Mr Nelson pleases, He may send some of the Worst kind, in case He thinks they'll answer the purpose, which I mention'd in a former letter, Floors of offices.

John must get from Turner half a dozen pair of Dove-tail hinges. I just now find that they are much wanted.

Palmer and Barton came hither on Wednesday some hours after I set out. They are here still. The former's Eldest Son is just recover'd from a Spotted Fever.[3] He seems well himself, and says his Wife is much better, than when I saw her. Barton is well. He says his Wife and children are so. But she has been oblig'd to give up her nursing.

Last Sunday I appear'd at Church in my Black-cap.[4] I went thro' the Country in the same manner. So that the Wig is now quite laid aside, and, God be thanked, no cold. My oil'd hood[5] is mighty clever in my rides. The Leather one too heavy, as is the Velvet Cap. It is paper'd up safe. I hope our odd Woman will, at my return, change it for a lighter. I have time for no more. Adieu

yours &tc. Edw: Elphin

1. Mrs Carleton: not known.

2. Elizabeth Donnellan.

3. Spotted fever may have been a form of meningitis, characterized by raised blotches (ecchymoses) on the skin. David Patterson, 'Meningitis', Kiple, p.876.

4. This might have been a square cap, as ordered by the injunctions of Elizabeth I in 1559, though they began to disappear when wigs came into fashion for clergymen. (Archbishop Tillotson was one of the first clerics to wear a wig.) The 1738 portrait of Edward Synge's father as archbishop of Tuam shows him in a plain close-fitting round cap, and a portrait of Archbishop Hoadly in 1743 has him in a wig and elaborate dress which is far removed from the plain black of the seventeenth century. Janet Mayo, *A History of Ecclesiastical Dress* (London 1984), pp.71, 80-1.

5. Oiled hood: probably a waterproofed hood, made of oiled cloth.

57

Elphin. July 11, 1749

My Dear Girl.

As my Visitation is to morrow, and some of my Clergy already here, I shall not, I believe, have time to write much.

I have wrote so fully to you about your writing, that there is not occasion for my saying more. I know what you can do, better than you do your Self; and if you'll pursue the way in which you are, in the two last letters, Experience will convince you, before my return, that your disabling speeches have not as much in them as at present you think they have. The two pages of your last are very well. The Scrap of the third was wrote in hurry.

Your account of your Aunt delighted me greatly. I am impatient to have news of her from Roscrea, and have comfortable hopes.

I am not sorry that you were *bien ennuiée*¹ at Mrs Nicholson's. I hope you'll always have sense enough to be so at those kind of entertainments. But, as the World goes, it is necessary to submit sometimes to them; especially at the request of one, with whom you may spend time more agreably and usefully, on other occasions.

It is not two pence matter whether the Toillettes come by the time the Tubbervaddy folks come hither or not. Or whether they come at all. I should be glad to have the Lantherns, and Card-tables. Sure John may contrive to send them.

Poor Wise Shannon has left me very bare of Water-glasses; and what think you was his reason? Why; Because He search'd the Town, and could find none which match'd those I had. By a misfortune on Sunday He at one slap broke four of those I had. So that I am now greatly reduc'd.

Desire Mrs Jourdan to provide a doz. plain ones, broad and squat, like as she can get to what are here. I hope she remembers them. But no great matter if she does not. I shall really want them. But if they do not come in time, I must laugh it off, and make folks shift as well as they can.

I met Mrs Butler[2] passing by my Wall early on Sunday morning, and spoke to her. She told me the melancholy occasion of her journey. She must send that graceless son of hers to Sea. That unruly Element may tame him.

Send my Coat with the green Cloth &c.

I am vex'd at Mrs Silver's most ridiculous shew. Her asking you to it, shews her to be more simple her Self, than I thought her, or to think you all more so, than I hop'd she did. It will please me, if you have found occasion to intimate a little gently to her your great contempt of so childish an Entertainment. But for the future, If she proposes any thing out of the Way, Draw up, and Be not so absolutely at her beck. Do this however without offending, if you can. But Do it, should there be occasion. I am sure Mrs Jourdan thinks as I do.

If John confirms what Gannon says about mildew, I shall believe it. At present I think it an Excuse. We have had no such thing here.

Councillor Costillo's[3] invitation was indeed somewhat extraordinary. You did very well to decline it.

I am glad you saw the New-gardens.[4] But your telling me this has brought you under a Criticism, Huzzy, for bad expression. You should, you say, have had a fine view of them, had they been *light*, you should have wrote, *lighted*.

Entre nous,[5] The Dr's Paper made me smile. What He has found out, was so obvious, that it could not escape any one's observation. I thought there was some conceal'd point, of a higher nature; and puzzled my Self to no purpose about it.

Tell Ned Curtis, That the Farm of Athnid[6] will not be out of Lease these four years. I hope We shall before that have leisure to talk about John Butler.[7] Who He is I know not.

I hope you make the town as agreable as you can to poor Charlotte.[8] Have you her with you, as much as her other Engagements will admit? It will please me that you have.

The other day I made Shannon examine my Ale Cellar; and had the mortification to find that there is a multitude of drink, but not one drop good; and upon making further inquiry I found that Mrs Heap had almost totally neglected that affair, and left it to the Underlings call'd Brewers. She has not even kept an account of what Malt was deliver'd to her, nor of the times of Brewing, and quantitys of Each. This only I can learn from her, that she put 5 Barrels of Malt to two hogsheads of Drink, which Drink is small, and even now so hard as to be scarce drinkable, and at the same time bitter beyond sufferance. But the ground Malt was in the Custody of her Brewers; and I think it impossible but some of it must have been convey'd away. She owns she was seldom present at the Meshing.[9] Instead of that She was asleep and left them to do as they pleas'd. To add to the bad doings, Not one drop of the drink is clear. She endeavours to throw the blame of all on the Malt, and there was one parcel, about ten Barrels which was full of Oats. She either did not discover, or if she did, did not speak of it, till two thirds were us'd. Mr Cary then immediatly return'd the rest. But this happen'd last March, and yet upon this she charges the badness of drink brew'd before Christmas. The Malt was from mine own Barley, the Crack of the whole Country, and the Malster the same who serves Will French, who has this day the finest drink, they say, that ever was seen. All I have to comfort me in this distress, is, that Mine own small Beer,[10] which I have made them Brew, answers mighty well, and gives great content.

This Article of brewing is not the only one, in which I have reason to complain of Mrs Heap. Her carelesness appears in every thing else; she is really as insignificant as her Sister. But I feel it more here, for very good reasons – and when I speak to her, she answers with Sulleness, That She does all she can, and this with an Air of turning me off – I should be glad to know whether She points [?] that way. But indeed unless she mends her hand, she shall point that way, whether she be inclin'd to it or not. She has her niece here with her, by my indulgence, whom she might make helpfull to her, if she pleas'd. But I never see her do a hand's turn. Nor indeed do I trouble my head about her. But by all I can observe, Mrs Heap troubles her self no more about Dairy, brewing, or baking, than if she were not my Servant, and between her and Carleboe, I have not had three times a good Chicken at my table, seldom a good Duck – But she does, all she can. I know nothing she does, but keep Linnen, Grocerys &c., which I believe she does faithfully. But I scarce ever see her in the rooms. Indeed she is not wanted there. For Molly Byrne[11] does every thing to my satisfaction, and I am this day, as clean in my House, as Mrs Fitzmaurice. I feel all this perhaps more than I ought. If a right good House-keeper were to be got, I would have her at any rate. But where shall I find her? I can't tell. This only I know, that Mrs Heap must change, or I must.

Desire John Miller to go to Barrack-street, and enquire there for one John Perry. He is a fellow, who like Davis, in our street, pays out-pensioners of the Hospital. But He deals with those of Chelsea.[12] My Flax-dresser at Strokes-town Samuel Coe[13] is one of these, and this fellow has money for him, which He refuses to pay unless the Man travels to town, which must put him to great expense, and at the same time stop Mr Mahon's work.

What I desire is, That John would, when He finds this man out, tell him that He comes from me, and that I desire to know from him whether He be at all concern'd for Samuel Coe a Chelsea Pensioner? If He says He is, Whether He has any money to pay him on his sending proper powers? If He says yes to this too, Let John desire him to give in writing what powers He wants, and assure him that I'll take care to have them sent up. But that I beg He would not put the poor Man under unnecessary difficultys, nor bring upon himself mine and Mr Mahon's resentment by doing what He ought not to do, by him. In short Let him tell him in plain words, That If He'll quietly and without more ado pay the poor Man his pension, I shall be oblig'd to him. If He will not, He may assure him in as strong, but let them be very quiet, terms, as He can make use of, that I'll find means to have full justice done him, without his going to town. I have time for no more

yours &c. Edw: Elphin

1. *Bien ennuiée*: thoroughly bored.

2. Mrs Butler: not known.

3. Edmond Costello (?-1769): son of Charles Costello of Tullaghane, Co. Mayo. *King's Inns*, p.103.

4. The New Gardens in Great Britain Street were laid out in 1749 by Dr Mosse to imitate Vauxhall Gardens, London and were used for charity concerts in the summer season from 1749 to the 1790s. 'Tomorrow being Wednesday the 16th inst. the NEW GARDEN in Great Britain Street will be illuminated, for the benefit of the Lying-In Hospital.' Boydell, p.266. *Dublin Courant*, 12-15 August 1749.

5. *Entre nous*: between ourselves.

6. Athnid: Edward Synge's land near Thurles, Co. Tipperary, formerly belonged to the Grace family. Between 1750 and 1751 Edward Synge leased land at Athnid Mor and Athnidbeg to George Lloyd for ninety-nine years. Lease of lands at Athnidbegg and Athnidmore 6 March 1750, Cooper Papers in private possession; Edward Synge's title to different lands ... NLI ms 2102.

7. John Butler: not known.

8. Mrs Jourdan's sister.

9. Meshing. To mash is to mix malt with hot water in the first stage of brewing.

10. Small beer: very weak beer.

11. Molly Byrne: a servant.

12. John Perry is not known. Davis would be the paymaster of the out-pensioners of the Royal Hospital, Kilmainham, which was completed in 1684 as a home for old soldiers, and as a copy of Les Invalides in Paris.

13. Possibly James Cow, heckler, of Church Street, Strokestown. Census, f.86.

58

Elphin. July 14, 1749

My Dear Girl.

The Hurry of Visitation is over. No ruffle, nor Embarrasment, at Church; and at home Carleboe and the big room did very well. But I must, I find, get proper Tables for it. Unluckily I had a thiner appearance than usual. Poor Will French had been very ill some days before. I would not suffer him to come. By the last account He was well. Poor Blackburn[1] too was absent, who never us'd to be. He has had a most unlucky accident. Some Company Men and Women din'd with him. The latter, as usual, retir'd, but not to the room He thought. He popp'd upon them, and retreating on the Sudden, slipp'd, so as that his shoulder came against the Banister of the Stairs, and was put out of joint. It was reduc'd by Jac. Crofton's Brother,[2] and He is in a very fair Way. I wanted Barton also. His Excuse was a Purging. I hope it is no great matter. I have heard nothing of him since.

I need not tell you, how much I was delighted with your Uncle's letter. Such tidings from them, and you, My Dearest, well, I shall be happy either alone or in Company. Hitherto I have had less than usual. But I am far from being uneasy at it. Soon I shall have enough, perhaps more than enough. But I can accommodate them all. I hope the Lantherns and Card Tables will come in time. If they do not, I'll not break my heart. I'll have none of your Hoysom Tea.[3] Mine own green is good enough for any one. It would pass upon all here, for the finest. But I think I do it more honour by telling the truth.

I have two pieces of news for you. One will please, the other, not. The latter is, That Billy Smith is turn'd off, as a bad boy, not to be reclaim'd. All join in the opinion, and I think with too much reason. Mrs Heap told me many storys of his pilfering, of which, severe repeated Correction has not cur'd him, and I have found him the coolest and most hardened Liar I ever met with. One morning I order'd him to be severely corrected for this, and a paper to be pinn'd on his back, with LIAR in Capitals. Immediatly He put the paper in his pocket, which I could have forgiven. But it provok'd me highly to see him that very afternoon riding one of the Coach-horses as gay and unconcern'd as if nothing had happen'd. With these dispositions so early shewn I dare not bring him into my Family. Shannon says, and I believe, truly, that He is come of a bad Breed. The Tweeds, My Lord, are the worst people in Elphin. This is not his sillyest Speech.[4]

The pleasing news is, That you have no less than thirteen Pea-chicks the youngest three Weeks old, all healthy and in a fair Way of being rear'd. Shannon is principal Nurse – Jenet under him. The little Garden is their Place, where each Hen has her Seperate Creel,[5] which confines her but leaves free passage in and out for the Chicks. But they break me in Eggs and White-bread. This it seems is their food, the Eggs being boil'd hard. If this adventure succeeds, the Merit is mine. I got from Mr Whetcombe[6] particular instructions, by following which exactly, they have thus far thriven.

I heard long since of what you write about Lords Kildare[7] and Hillsborough.[8] I am sorry for it. But £20000 is a strong temptation, to try the fate of a Law-suit. At present I think the issue uncertain. I pity the Dowager as you do. If Mrs Nicholson can give you an Opportunity of waiting on her, Do not, be sure, miss it.[9]

Pay Ross for the Books, & keep that about which I doubted. I don't remember I gave him any directions to buy it. But give him his money, which He may want. He'll get the other book when He can.

I wrote to Dr Lawson this day se'night, but have no answer. I suppose He intends to surprize me. I hope, tho' you miss'd him, you took care to send him my Watch.

What you write of Madam Forrester[10] is ridiculous indeed. But Consider, My Dear Girl, We all see our Selves with partial Eyes.

I am glad you were at Mrs Oliver's,[11] for the reason you give. But these disagreable things need not be repeated.

Tell John, that if He does not find means to send down the remainder of the Timber, the Masons will soon be at a Stand. He must also speak to Smith to provide forty wheels & Reels in proportion, which He must send hither assoon as He can, without interfareing with timber. I am call'd away.

Adieu yours &c.
Edw: Elphin

1. The Rev. George Blackburn: prebendary of Termonbarry in 1731, was collated vicar of Aughrim in July 1743 and lived at Rushill in Aughrim parish. He had four Protestant servants. Leslie, Elphin, pp.63, 99; Census, f.34.

2. Dr Edward Crofton: physician, educated in Leyden in 1737. He married Elizabeth Jones. Crofton, pp.195-6; Vicars, p.112.

3. Hoysom tea: Hyson is a green tea imported from China.

4. There were four Tweed families in Elphin in 1749: one a weaver, one a widow with a son, one a blacksmith and one a brogue-maker. They were all Protestant. Their relationship to Billy Smith is unclear. Census, f.1-3.

5. Creels. In spinning, a creel was a frame for holding bobbins in the process of spinning yarn.

6. John Whitcombe: bishop of Clonfert.

7. James Fitzgerald, twentieth earl of Kildare (1722-73) and first duke of Leinster. He improved Carton, Co. Kildare, and built Leinster House, Dublin. Kildare was regarded as unsteady; Synge described his mission to London after the Money Bill crisis in December 1753, 'It is not a measure either concerted or approved of. But if Wilful will do it, he cannot be controlled.' Burke (1916) p.1242; Synge to Lord Limerick 25 December 1753 PRONI Mic 147/9.

8. Wills, 2nd Viscount Hillsborough (?-1793), was James Kildare's brother-in-law, Hillsborough having married Margaretta Fitzgerald in 1747. Burke (1916), p.1242.

9. Mary Fitzgerald, dowager Lady Kildare had a long running case in Chancery which arose from the will of her late husband, the 19th earl of Kildare who had died in 1740. It was still being heard by the House of Lords in 1757. Lord Kildare and Lord Hillsborough would have been parties to the cause. *The Right Honourable Mary, Countess of Kildare, and Robert Downes, Esq; executors of Robert late Earl of Kildare, deceased ... To be heard at the bar of the House of Lords on Wednesday, the 5th day of April, 1749* (London 1749); *First appeal. The Right Honourable Mary, Countess of Kildare, and others, on behalf of themselves, and the several creditors of the several banks lately kept by Samuel Burton and Daniel Falkiner ... appellants ... To be heard at the bar of the House of Lords, on Wednesday the 16th day of February 1757* (London 1757).

10. Madam Forrester: not known.

11. Mrs Oliver: not known.

59

Elphin. July 18, 1749

My Dear Girl.

You need not have told me where you had your agreable Entertainment. The description was enough. It is very true. I have din'd at that little Table, and, Were I an Epicure Prince, the Mistress of it, should direct mine.

I am very sorry for poor Mrs Nicholson's malady. I sent her some advice lately in a letter to him. As she is in so good hands, It was unnecessary. You may tell her, that I heartily wish, she may soon be reliev'd.

You did very well to put off going in that Manner to see the Illumination.[1] I wish your curiosity could be gratify'd, in a more proper one.

I have indeed great reason to complain of Mrs Heap; & what makes every thing worse, she does not shew the least sense of having done any thing wrong. Would you believe it? I have not one of the new beds to lye on; nor can I afford my self one, without leaving some one of my best rooms bare. In short the new Ticks are not all stuff'd; and why? She had not Feathers – How came she to want, when Mr Cary had 20-stone more at Command?[2] Indeed, she thought she had enough – Thus carelesly did she manage in a matter about which I gave her the strictest charge, when last I left Elphin, and wrote ten times in the Winter; and instead of taking out the season'd Feathers to fill the new Beds, she fill'd them all with the fresh ones, to avoid double trouble; so that I was in great pain about my best Beds, till I had them lain in by her and Molly Byrne. – The only thing which I see she has done this Winter, except removing things from the Old house, is, That she has made me some good Carpeting, which helps to keep the Rooms clean. I shall be glad if Mrs Jourdan writes to her. But I fear it will signify little. I must bear as well as I can, unless I can find some way to help my Self. Whenever I speak of any thing, she has some paltry excuse to throw the thing off her Self, and troubles her head no further.

Dr Lawson came hither on Saturday morning. He is very well. I saw an account of poor Mrs Marcelles's death in the news,³ long before you wrote it. I was once going to reproach you with your not writing it. What will become of her numerous Family? He seems not well turn'd to take care of them.

I am much concern'd at poor Jane's disorder. But I hope it is of the same kind with others she has had, which, tho' they plague her a little, do her no other damage. I wish they would teach her to be a little more care-full of what she eats. Fruit probably has had some share in this flurry. Do you, My Dearest, take care in this and every other particular, that I may have constantly the pleasing account which yours now gives me, that you are very well. Tell Jane I thank her for her letter, and will write to her as soon as I can get time. But 'tis impossible this post. I am tir'd with letters of business and have scarce time or Eyes to scribble this to you.

We had your storm, and broken Weather ever since, till now that there is hard and seemingly setled rain. I wish We have not too much of it. It is unpleasant, and will be mischievous – and yet the Country certainly wanted some.

Tell John that He must send down the remainder of the Timber, at such rate as He can get Carriage. Otherwise my Masons must stand still. A few Boards will do for the present – Bid him also to bespeak from Wilkinson six more Collars, Haims, and Straddles with Cruppers, for Mules, such as the last.

In a few days, you may expect to see your Mare. I hope she is in foal. She'll be more secure at Cool-blew than here. She is to go up to you, by one of Palmer's drivers. Bid John send 'Hector' the Grey-hound by him, if he'll take charge of him.

As you mend in your writing, huzzy, you grow careless in spelling. No less than three trips have I remark'd in yours without prying for them. Terible for Terrible. Patern, for Pattern, afords, for affords. Faults all of one kind. The double letter omitted. I have found a fourth, in which there is a letter redundant. winddy – There ought to be but one d. I have a little bit of bad English to charge you with too – 'The Miss Holts,[4] who We think to be sweet agreable girls' It ought to be whom. I have light for no more. My Dearest Adieu.

yours &c.
Edw: Elphin

Give Palmer's man who delivers the Mare half a Crown. I suppose you'll pay that your Self Madam.

Tell John that I desire He would order every thing to be done in the Garden that can be to repair the ravages of the Mildew. Amongst the rest I think He should order a good deal of carrot-seed to be sown immediately. Better have small carrots than none.

[Free Edw:Elphin]

1. Illuminations to celebrate the victory at the battle of the Boyne. 'Saturday being the Anniversary commemorating the Victory at the Boyne, obtained by our late Glorious Deliverer King William, it was celebrated with the Ringing of Bells, Bonefires, Illuminations and all possible Demonstrations of Joy.' *Dublin Courant*, 1-4 July 1749.

2. There are a number of feathermongers in Edward Synge's census of Elphin.

3. The death of Mrs Marcelles was reported in the newspaper. 'Friday died greatly lamented Mrs Marcell, wife of Major Lewis Marcell, third Engineer to the train of Artillery.' *Dublin Courant*, 8-11 July 1749.

4. Miss Holts: not known.

60

Elphin. July 21, 1749

My Dear Girl.

I take a quarto to day, because I shall have little time to write, and, now privilege is in, shall not encumber you with John's Commissions &c.

Enclos'd is your Uncle's letter. I need not say that it gave me great pleasure. Tell my friend Jane that I intended to have enclos'd it in one to her Self, but cannot, this post, find time to do it. I rejoice that she is well. Good keep you all so. One of your Pea-chicks only has disappear'd. Shannon fancys a Cat ate it. But We have guarded now against those Creatures. I hope they'll be rear'd, tho' I shan't be so soon for figuring with any. Two of the Old Cocks are dead.

The Carriage, Tables, Lantherns &c. are come safe. We are yet at a loss how to hang the Lantherns. I like the Water-glasses much. So I do the

Toillettes. They'll be up, before my Company comes. I don't remember you told me which hogshead of Cyder you sent.

You may send to John Smith for a Wheel and Reel for Miss Farran[1] if you've a mind to it. But indeed I see no reason why things design'd for those who can't buy, should be given to such as can.

You probably have heard before this that Captain Wills[2] is at last dead. Your Mare will be with you soon after you get this, perhaps before. Send immediatly to John to have the Grey-hound ready to send off. He must get a Collar and Chain, if there be not one already.

Poor Shannon complains of a giddiness in his head. It is most griev-ous when He rises in the Morning. He is neither hot, nor costive, nor any other way, that I can find, out of order. He says that on any sudden noise, even the ringing of the Bell, He finds a pain at the Pit of his Stomach, which pain, on his describing it more Exactly, I think to be rather a kind of nervous affection, such as I have felt when I have been low, and you, I believe, on a Sudden fright. About a Month ago, He had a pretty smart purging, for which I order'd a Puke which cur'd him. Upon this Com-plaint I order'd a Second two days ago, and Camomile Tea[3] with which He begun this morning. He is not reliev'd. Desire the Doctor to give me some directions about him. He is necessary to me here, and indeed behaves himself better than my hopes.

What would you give, you say, to be able to write agreably &c. I'll tell you what you shall give. Give your mind to it, My Dearest. My life for yours it will do. But you must first set your Self steadily to overcome the difficulty of meer writing, which it is certain you do not do. This last, tho' not ill wrote, is more indifferent than your late ones. I am sure you wrote it with less care and in more hurry. I have observ'd one false spelling, of the same kind with those remark'd in my last. *Supose.* The p should be doubled. You've a marvelous propension to dropping a letter. In the same para-graph I observe false English, a thing I must never pass by. I'll give it you at length, and leave you to correct it, which pray do in your next. 'It is a most mortifying thing to have a monkey taken such strict care of five years, should turn out so incorrigibly wicked.' I am call'd away. Adieu.

Yours &c.
Edw: Elphin

[Free Edw:Elphin]

1. Miss Farran: not known.
2. Caspar Wills: Godfrey Wills's uncle. See Letter 29.
3. This was probably an infusion of *anthemis nobilis*, syn. *chamaemelum nobile*, which was used for colic and stone, strains and swellings of sinews and for treating the ague by creating sweats. F. Le Strange, *A History of Herbal Plants* (London 1977) p.26.

61

Elphin. July 25, 1749

My Dear Girl.

All the Tobbervaddy, and Kilmore folks came hither yesterday. They are all very well, only that Mrs Donnelan appears mighty low spirited. Perhaps in a day or two she'll be better. For the journey hither was rather fatiguing. You'll easily believe that with so much Company, I have not much leisure and must for this time be contented with knowing, that I am, I bless God, very well, tho' the Bad Weather frets me, both on account of the Harvest and my Works. God bless you all. I am

> My Dearest girl's
> most affectionate &c.
> Edw:Elphin

I find a false spelling, which you are not as much accountable for as for some others, because it is in a term of Art. You ought to write Guild of Merchants or any other Guild. That is a Common Appellation to all the Corporations. You write *yield.*

A short Commission for John to save another letter. Tell him that the Collars I wrote for, for six Mules must be two sizes less than the former ones, and the Back-bands[1] somewhat shorter. Let him have Cruppers to the Straddles. Bid him give me an account of his Turnip-seed.[2] Again my Timber.

Turn

All your Artane friends desire their compliments in a very affectionate manner.

The Letter you sent me enclos'd was dated July 1. – Strange that it lay so long in the Post-Office. But As it happens, It was no great matter.

Use as much of the Meth,[3] as you please. Some good some not so, shews it is decaying. Is any of poor Mrs King's left?

Before I seal this, I must tho' it be late, divert you with a passage of the day. Our friends at Strokes-town din'd with us. Little Nancy[4] was with them. Lord Kingsborough, also was here. After dinner He attempted to play with the little Girl. But she was extremely shy and would not suffer him to be free with her. As He continu'd his assiduity, and press'd her much to be free with him – No, says she, you'll carry me to Kilcock. Luckily for me I was not by. Her father was and run for it. His Lordship, they say, was abash'd.[5]

[Free Edw:Elphin}

1. Backband: a broad leather strap which passes over a cart-saddle and supports the shafts.

2. There were various types of turnip; Charles Varley discusses the merits of Norfolk sheep turnips, early red-tops and yellow turnip seed, and recommends feeding bullocks on turnips. Charles Varley, *The Floating Ideas of Nature* 2 vols (London 1769), pp.184-5; 186-8.

3. Metheglin: spiced or medicated mead.

4. Anne: daughter of Thomas and Jane Mahon, married David Ross of Beaufort. Burke (1979), p.774.

5. Robert King, now Lord Kingsborough, was a well-known rake. Mrs Delany wrote of his running away with a Miss Johnston in 1747: 'a very pretty girl just sixteen, who ran away on Friday night with Sir Robert King, a vile young rake of a considerable fortune in this country ... the father pursued and overtook them on Saturday morning, held a pistol at the knight's head, swore he would shoot him through the head if he did not instantly marry his daughter, which rather than die he consented to do. A parson was ready and called in, but Sir R.K.'s servants rushed in at the same time, gave him a pistol, and an opportunity of escaping, which he did and left the forlorn damsel to return with her father.' Mrs Delany to Mrs Dewes, Delville 22 December 1747. Delany, Vol. 2, p.482.

62

Elphin. July 28, 1749

The same cause, My Dear Girl, that made me very brief last post, will have the same Effect, this. I bless God I am very well, and my Company, all but Mrs Donnelan, are so too. They are as regular as I could wish, and march off quietly to bed at Eleven. I made that Law the day they came, and they obey cheerfully. All of them as well those who do not, as those who do know you, express great pleasure in your being so well. God keep you so.

You have corrected your bad English right. This proves, what I always say, that hurry and giddiness occasion the faults you commit both in matter and writing. If I pass by any, It is because they are of the same kind with those which I have often noted; and what need is there of multiplying instances, when I have already given you enough? But you have now put the matter upon a footing which will save me future trouble. I appeal to Mrs Jourdan. When she says very well, I shall.

Get the Wheel whenever you please.

Our Weather of late has been very wet. Yesterday it rain'd incessantly. This day is yet fair. But I think it will not continue so. We are just setting out to dine at Strokes-town. So Adieu.

yours &c.
Edw: Elphin

Return'd very well and the day pleasant.

[Free Edw:Elphin]

63

Elphin. Aug. 1, 1749

Our friends still here, My Dearest. You know the Consequence. I have not time to write much. They were for going off yesterday. But I insisted on their keeping this day with me, the day of the late K's accesion, and of the beginning the House.[1] I believe they'll leave me to morrow.

Mrs Jourdan is right. You can't avoid waiting on Mrs Costello.[2] Do it, as soon as you can. I hope you'll be pleas'd with your shew. York-street is a much better place for seeing it, than Jervais-street.[3] For they go through that in the morning, sober, and in order.

Send the Melons as you please. You know my friends, whom I wish to oblige. If you have as many as Gannon promises, your favours may be Extensive. I believe I need not desire you to remember Mrs Silver. Be sure always to make her my Compliments.

Shannon has not time now either to be sick, or to take the Doctor's prescription. As soon as the House is clear He shall begin with it. He says that the two kinds of Meth are in the same Bin. But that there is a kind of division between them. Perhaps this may account for the great difference you found between those you try'd – Try more. The whole is at your Service. Our Stroke's-town friends are come in. So Adieu.

yours &c.
Edw: Elphin

[Free Edw:Elphin]

1. The anniversary of the accession of the house of Hanover. Queen Anne died on 1 August 1714, and George I was proclaimed king in London the same day.
2. Mrs Costello: not known.
3. This may be a reference to the parades held in Dublin on days of celebration.

64

My Dear Girl.

On Wedensday my Company left me. They were very agreable, and I would fain have had them stay a day or two longer. Yet the quiet, succeeding to so much hurry, is very agreable too.

But even this does not allow me time to write much to you this post. I have many letters on my hands, which must not be delay'd.

Your Sentiments on the *Princess of Clèves*,[1] are very natural; much more so than her Character, as drawn in that admir'd book. The Lady who wrote it, had a mind to draw a picture of great Virtue and Excellence, in great distress, and in order to this, has painted higher than the life. This is the fault of all Novels. It is indeed more artfully shaded in this, than in most others. But still it appears to an attentive Reader. I do not think that such a case ever really happen'd, nor can happen, without some degree of weakness or Vanity in the person, which disposes her to indulge a pleasing inclination, in expectation of having it always in her power to master it. If she cannot do this, she is wretched, and many, I believe, have made themselves so. But the fault always has been and always will be their own. The beginnings of such inclinations are easily check'd. This is the prudent Conduct. But it will not furnish matter for so many groupes of Adventures as the other; and therefore the Dealers in fiction chuse not to ascribe it even to their Heroines. If they did, their productions would probably please less, but would convey much more instruction than commonly they do.

But, since We are upon Novels, what think you of *Clarissa?*[2] I have read it through, because you press'd me to do it, and shall be glad to know your thoughts of it, before I tell you mine. I wish to have Jeny's too, and Mrs Jourdan's, if she'll give her Self the trouble of writing them; but each of you upon honour, *vos propres Sentiments.*[3] I have some Curiosity to know how each of you are affected, by a story, which has affected numbers in so very different a manner. Do not do this hastily. For I design it as a trial of the judgment of two of you. Nor will I take it as an Excuse, that you say you've forgot it. If so, borrow it from some one, and read it agen.

You know our Artane friends as well as I do, and therefore I say nothing particular of them, only this, that Kitty behaves her self extremely well in her new Scene, both at home, and abroad. Mrs Waller you have heard me speak of. She is a great favorite. Beside these, I had two young females, of very different Characters, both agreable in their way, but one vastly superior in my opinion to the other. One was a Sister of Mr Ormsby's, the other a niece of Mr Waller's. The former is a cheerfull, laughing girl, well enough behav'd, but fond, as Kitty or Betty, of a fiddle, and not ill pleas'd with application from the Men. Dr Lawson pleas'd her hugely, tho' they quarrell'd two or three times a day, about something, or nothing, generally a kiss. But He made her, I believe, very happy at parting, by some Verses inscribed to her, at which she frown'd, tho' she put them carefully into her pocket. By this account you'll judge that I was neither much pleas'd, nor at all offended with this Damsel. The other indeed pleas'd me. Her whole behaviour was easy and natural, grave without shyness, but as cheerfull and merry, upon proper occasions, as the best of them. She seem'd to have great sprightliness, but to have it perfectly under Command, so that it never once betray'd her into the least levity; and appear'd quite indifferent whether she was particularly taken notice of or not. In short, tho' very young, she behav'd her Self with as much unaffected ease, decency, and good sense as any young Creature I ever saw. There is nothing shining in her person. It is rather agreable. Her deportment sets it off.

The day they came here, some of the young Fellows propos'd her to Cary as a Mistress.[4] This furnish'd great mirth, and cost her some blushes, but without discomposing her, or making the least alteration in her Carriage, which to him was as Easy as to every one else. His to her it is impossible to describe. I must leave you to imagine it. It sometimes look'd so like being in earnest, that I was, and am at a loss to know, whether it was or not. Lawson teazes him still about her. Mrs Jourdan, I believe, knows her Family. Her name is Coddington.[5]

I am glad your shew pleas'd you. At your age I thought it a very fine one. I have time for no more. I am My Dear Girl's

most affectionate
Edw: Elphin

Shannon begun to take the Doctor's prescription this day. Give my service to him, and tell him, I desire to know how long He is to continue. His complaints are much as they were. One of them I forgot to mention before, a pain under the short ribs on the left side inclining towards the Back.

[Free Edw:Elphin]

1. Mme M-M. de la Fayette, *La Princesse de Clèves,* first published in 1678.
2. Samuel Richardson, *Clarissa: or The History of a Young Lady: comprehending the most important concerns of private life.* Published by the editor of Pamela ... (Dublin 1748-9). *Clarissa* was an instant success in Ireland. It kept Lord and Lady Orrery up until two in the morning, and Mrs Delany analysed Clarissa's character and actions in detail in let-

ters to her sister, writing of 'the catastrophe of Clarissa ... nothing can ever equal that work'. Lord Orrery to Thomas Carew, 12 March 1747. *The Orrery Papers* Vol. 2, p.23; Mrs Delany to Mrs Dewes 2 June, 10 and 30 November 1750, Delany, Vol. 2, pp.550, 561, 622-3.

3. *Vos propres Sentiments*: your own feelings.

4. Oliver Cary's first wife died some time after October 1747.

5. Dixie Coddington of Athlumney Castle, Co. Meath, married his second cousin Hannah, eldest daughter of Robert Waller of Kilmainham Castle, Kells, Co. Meath, and Mr Waller's niece. Kells is about twenty miles from Dunshaughlin, Mrs Jourdan's family home. Burke (1979), p.252.

65

Elphin. Aug. 8, 1749

My Dear Girl,

I intended writing you a long letter to day, about something or nothing, but have not time for it. So you must be content with a short one. I bless God I am very well. But our Weather is uncomfortable. Unless it takes up soon, The Country will be in a bad Condition. And yet I think We have less rain than you have. If I understand yours right, Friday was a very wet day with you. We had here only one or two showers. Saturday was a very fine day – so was Sunday till about five. The little Doctor and I got about that time into the Chariot, for an Evening's airing. But violent rain soon drove us home. It continu'd all night, and return'd agen yesterday afternoon with great Violence. To day the ground is so wet, that Nothing can be done, and I fear We shall still have more rain. But that is a much less evil within doors here; than in the other house. Poor Cary was flouded, as We us'd to be. But Here all Staunch and Warm, and Comfortable, and not the least damp upon Walls or any where else.

How came it to pass that you so long deferr'd your visit to Mrs Palliser, since you intended one? Would it not have been better, when the days were longer? I really think they are now too short for such an afternoon Expedition.

I believe my Company lik'd the House. I troubled not my self much to enquire their thoughts of it. You'll know Mrs Donnelan's from her Self.

I can't do much in the New-Garden unless dry Weather returns. I have a great deal of levelling work there, and till that is finish'd, can go upon nothing else. I hope to have part of it ready for planting, before the Season is over. I am glad your Myrtle is so finely increas'd. I hope you've transplanted them so, as that they may be cover'd, when winter comes on. Without that, your stock will quickly be reduc'd. You may plant what you please in the Borders of the green Court. I believe Holyhawks, and Lillies will do very well there.

Your Visit to Mrs Costello is over before this. If you were in any distress It was your own fault. How easy to send in your Names by the Footman?

Those never ending storys are sometimes tiresome. You must in this, as in every thing else, take the bad and the good together.

I am in some pain about Shannon. His looks are alter'd for the Worse, and his Complaints continue. Last Sunday afternoon He rode out. To that He ascrib'd his Vomiting in the night after. Whether truly or not, I can't tell. But He told me in the morning what had happen'd to him, and said that what He threw up was sow'r as Vinegar. I take the more notice of this, as I gave him another Vomit before He begun the Doctor's prescription. Pray tell the Doctor this, and desire him to give me further directions, how to manage him.

Poor Carleboe met with an Accident on Sunday too, but came off very well. He rode out on 'Johnson', who fell with him just by Stafford's. Very luckily He escap'd with no other hurt than a bruise on the Elbow; But the Horse came to the ground with such Violence, as tore off all his flesh from his Flank. He is in a piteous Condition. Had the poor fellow been under him, His fat guts had been squelch'd. He could not indeed have escap'd. I leave it to your discretion whether you'll let his Wife[1] know this. If you do, you may assure her from me, that He is very well, all but a slight bruise on the Elbow which signifys nothing. I have wrote more than I thought I should have time for.

Adieu My Dearest
yours &c. Edw: Elphin

I observe, my Dearest, that you are under frequent anxiety about the Contents of your letters. Believe me, this anxiety makes them worse than otherwise they would be. The way to come to write well, is to write freely whatever comes upper-most. But while you strive to excell, and weigh every word and sentiment, you loose some of the best. You can talk freely enough. Why don't you write the same way? I shall be as well pleas'd with your prattle on paper, as by the fire side, and make all the allowances, for what you call trifling, which you can desire. But while you write in trammels, you never will have a good gait. You write to me always under some awe. This hurts you, and makes you write sometimes, as awkardly, as you would danse before a room full of strange folks. In such Circumstances you would hobble much more than if none but your friend and Master were by. Thus your pen and your thoughts hobble in writing to me. Whereas if you wrote with that freedom and ease, which I have always encourag'd and advis'd, you would in a short time come to write as correctly as I wish or desire.

Familiar writing, like speaking in publick, is a Talent in which scarce any have excell'd at once and they who have excell'd in either, have given themselves full liberty at first, and by saying whatever came uppermost, have in time brought themselves to say just what they ought.

[Free Edw:Elphin]

1. Mrs Carleboe: not known.

66

Elphin. Aug. 11, 1749

Well, My Dear Girl! Do you think you shall at last be able to overcome the difficulty of writing familiar letters, without much business, in an Agreable way? Yours rec'd yesterday gives no unpromising Specimen. I am much pleas'd with it, and observe no slips, but a few in pointing.

It is thought wise and edifying, to young persons Especially, to keep company Wiser and Older than themselves. And It is certainly right to converse for the most part with such. But they may not be always the most improving Correspondents, because a Sense of their superiority sometimes restrains that freedom in writing, without which it is impossible to excel in it. I believe this has been a Weight upon you. You have more awe of me, your Chief Correspondent, than in writing I wish you to have; and I believe you are not without some of Molly Curtis, and Miss Corbet, who have been at different times, next to me the persons to whom you've wrote most frequently. As they are both older, and more experienc'd than you, It is not to be wonder'd, that they should write better; and you by endeavouring to imitate them have often wrote worse than other wise you would. To tell you freely my thoughts, I think neither of them a pattern. Nor will you ever do right while you set your self any. Follow nature, Write freely, and avoid all anxiety. In a little time you'll come to write as you wish. If you can't bring your Self to write thus to me, Write to one of your Cosens at Roscrea. As they are more upon the level with you, you'll write to them just with the Same freedom, that you speak; and tho' for a time there may be many silly inaccuracys in your Epistles, you'll by degrees get rid of these, and acquire a habit of writing both easily and correctly.

You fear being brought to shame about *Clarissa*. I don't know but you may. But if you are, It will be of use towards future amendment. Reading is of little use, without making some judgment of what you read. If you have made none on this book, you have been so far to blame, and must grow wiser in time to come.

I am sorry you miss'd waiting on Lady Kildare, but hope Mrs N[icholson] will give you another opportunity of doing it. I know where your other Visit was made, but am at a loss for what you mean by *Visage de bois*.[1] So it ought to be. You write *boi*. Pray explain this term of Art.

I knew nothing of Mrs Whetcombe's ilness before I rec'd yours. I am glad she is recover'd. The mention of her brings your Pea-chicks to my mind. They are all very well. I now hope We shall rear them.

The Character I gave of Miss Coddington is such as Every girl of sense and prudence, may, if she pleases, arrive at. Her name is Hannah. Lawson says she has a sister much handsomer, whose name is Fiddy; whether Fidelia, or Fridiswide I know not.[2]

Your dispute about the Bird made me smile. You are a parcel of wise folks indeed, who at the End of three months, can't tell whether a Black bird be a Black-bird, without the Eloquence of a fat-headed Scullion – I beg his pardon.[3] I think He is now out of his time and therefore entitled to be treated with more respect. Pray learn among you which way He points. I think it will be for his interest to stay some time longer where He is, that if He may make himself more perfect in his trade. If He be Enclin'd to this, I'll consent to his staying a year longer, and give him Wages. But if He has a mind to try his pinions, before He be throughly fledg'd, He may for me. It will be right to know in time, which He chuses, that I may either bring his Intended successer up, or leave him here for another Season. Carleboe's bruise has prov'd a more Severe one, than I thought it when I wrote last. But He is now in a fair way of being well of it. He has no other complaint.

Tell Mrs Jourdan, that I think so small a Sum of money safe enough in her hands. I am tir'd with writing, a multitude of letters. This is unluckily my Case almost every post-day, so that I have less time to prattle to you than I wish. Adieu.

yours &c.
Edw: Elphin

[Free Edw:Elphin]

1. Poker-face.
2. Dixie and Hannah Coddington had eight daughters. Hannah married, first Thomas Knox MD and second, Nehemiah Donnellan II. Fidelia or Fridiswide is not known. Burke (1979), p.252.
3. The reference is to Robinson, the apprentice cook at Kevin Street, whose articles were about to be completed.

67

My Dear Girl.

When I was an idle School-boy, My Father one day ask'd my Master[1] how I went on. His answer was, Master Neddy does well, but He might do more. I must apply this to your Cosen and you. You have both done well in your observations on *Clarissa*. But you might do more. 'Tis time now for you both, My Ladys, to read for something more than present Amusement, and the way to do this is to think of what you read, and form some judgment of the design of Every book, whether serious or diverting. All well written books even of the latter kind, are wrote with some regular design, as well as those of the former, tho' this on a hasty reading does not always appear; and you Girls are always apt to read thus hastily, especially where the Story is interesting, and engages your passions. You then hurry on, sometimes happy, sometimes wretched, to know the Event, and when you know it, and the ferment and flutter into which you are put, subside, you are just as wise, as at setting out. I am sure this is the Case of you both, with regard to that book, which took up so much of your time and cost you so many tears. You, Madam, own fairly that you do not know you ever before thought about it, and tho' my friend Jane does not say so, I am sure it is her case as well as yours. Both your observations shew it, which tho' just enough, are yet loose and disjointed, and much fewer than they ought to be. I can't say, than I expected: For I did indeed imagine that you read this, as, I believe, you have done most other diverting books, just in this less profitable manner, and for that reason, when you of your Self gave me your thoughts in much the same way, on the *Princess of Clèves*, I laid hold on the occasion, and resolv'd to put you both to the Trial and now I think it right to go a little further with you, and, by putting you on giving me some farther account of the impressions this Book has made on your minds, lead you into the Way of reading others of a like kind with improvement. Recollect therefore, each of you your Selves as well as you can and tell me.

1. What you take to be the main design of the work – and if this design be complicated, point out the chief particulars.

Tell me. 2. How far this design is to be approv'd of, and give your reasons.

and 3. Give your opinions, as well as you can, on the Manner, in which the design is pursu'd.

To do this last cleverly, will, I am sensible, require more skill, knowlege and Experience, than I can expect such Girls as you to be Mistresses of. But I have a mind to see how far you can go, and what judgment, if any, you have form'd on the great Variety of incidents and characters which appear in that Work. How far they are forc'd, how far natural, and which deserve Censure, which approbation. Do this for me, Girls, cleverly, or rather nakedly just as things come into your heads, and at my return to town, I'll give each of you a — Kiss.

Don't be afraid now you, Miss Anxiety, but write with the same freedom, that you would speak to Mrs Jourdan, and let your pen run as fast as it will, without minding how you cut your letters. By giving you this Exercise, I intend the improvement of your mind rather than of your hand; and if you comply with my Views, you'll find it will be of more use to you, than you are at present aware of. When Mrs Jourdan reads this, She'll see that I expected more from you all, than barely to tell me how you were affected in reading it. That she has done in a very proper Manner; nor Do I doubt but she can do the rest, when she pleases.

Mrs Jourdan was right, you wrong. I wish you had seen the L[or]d Chan[cello]r. I can't see why you should shut your Selves up from those whose Visits do you and me honour. Sure you are not such Slatterns, as not to be fit to be seen. If that be the Case, I shall be very much displeas'd with you. But I hope it is not.

When next you see the Doctor, Give my Service to him, and tell him that Shannon is better. He has had no pain in the side these four days, and very little giddiness in his head. His chief remaining Complaint is the pain in his Stomach, which goes off in some time after breakfast. If He grows worse, I'll make all the Enquirys He has directed. But If He continues to mend, I think the best way is not to tamper, but wait till the Doctor sees him himself. His pain, when He had it, was in his left side. He must excuse my sending to him thus by you. For I have not time to write to him, nor to say more to you. Adieu.

yours &c.
Edw: Elphin

It may perhaps be right to tell the Doctor that Shannon's almost constant Malady, a Cough, has quite left him, since he began to complain of his present disorders.

I did not imagine there would be so much joiner's work in your new room. Pray tell me the particulars. I hope the Drainer is not forgot. Tell Mrs Jourdan she is very right in getting new Nobs for the great press. I forgot this in mine to her.

Tell Mr Eaton that my being in town could be of little Service to him for the purpose mention'd in yours – The Linnen board[2] agreed by you great with Mr Semple[3] for the whole Work.[*sic*] There is therefore no room left for recommending particular Work men. I would serve him if there were.

[Free Edw:Elphin]

1. Mr Mulloy of Cork. *Alumni*, p.797.

2. The Linen Board was founded in 1711, with a Board of eighty Trustees, of which Edward Synge was one. Its purpose was to improve the quality of linen produced in Ireland and to enforce regulations set down by parliament. It distributed praemiums and bounties to encourage production by providing flax-seed, and parts of looms: the wheels, creels and reels that Synge orders from Dublin. The Linen Hall was on a site north-west of Capel Street and Bolton Street. Gill, pp.65-6, 79.

3. George Semple: architect and engineer, added the steeple to St Patrick's in 1748-9 (see Letter 52) and built St Patrick's Hospital. He also worked on the engineering for the rebuilding of Essex Bridge in 1753-5 (see Letters 133 and 189). He wrote *A Treatise on building in water* (1776). The building project for the Linen Board, of which Edward Synge was a Trustee, is not known. Severens, p.4.

68

Elphin. Aug. 18, 1749

My Dear Girl.

Nothing in yours to day obliges me to recant; and if you'll do as I advise, I never shall have occasion to recant. It is certainly right in you to have a Modest opinion of your Self, and your performances. But too great diffidence is an imperfection, and will make them always worse than otherwise they would be. You should always write to me with freedom. Nor should any opinion you have of my judgment make you do otherwise. I sometimes fancy that the frequent rebukes I have given you about the negligence of your writing, embarrasses you as to the Contents. If you find this, Give your thoughts free Scope, and Scrawl away. Better Scrawl good sense, or what may entertain, than write simply in the finest hand, and yet I would have you always remember that writing well is a pretty thing. You have shewn me that you can do this, and write sense too. The first page of your letter is very well written. The rest not bad.

I have no objection to your dining with Mrs Taylor.[1] I hope the day will favour you. If you do not take the opportunity of speaking about the Ale, I shall blame you.

There was no Occasion for troubling me about Molly Fagan's bread. It was very wrong that between her and John, payment for it, was so long neglected. Do you pay for it. I am sure I before directed you to pay all such things as these, and charge them to the Article of Contingencys. It is better not to multiply little Articles in Ned Curtis's accounts. Pray when next you see him, tell that I am greatly disappointed at not hearing from him. He knows that He has not yet given me a satisfactory answer from Mr Dexter.[2]

In your account of M. Fagan's bread, you have wrote bad English, Madam – You write, between John and *She*, It ought to be *her*.

When first I spoke to Mr Nicholson about your dressing room, He told me that papering down to the floor, i.e. to the skirting Board, was the High fashion.[3] For which reason I agreed to it. If He has since chang'd his mind, or you like it in the way, it is now order'd, with all my heart. But pray press Every body concern'd to have the Work done with the utmost Expedition. For if the finishing be long deferr'd, there will be a damp in the plaister, which may make the room useless to you this Winter. I suppose Mr Eaton provides the Plaisterer; and hope that the Work will be better done there than on the Stair. I think that too dark, and It is certainly too Coarse.

Tell Mrs Jourdan that Her sister[4] had granted to her five Wheels and one Reel. Perhaps Sr. Tho.[5] thinks three enough for her. She may let him know what is her right, and then give it up, if she pleases.

Dr Donnelan[6] and the Cornet[7] came hither yesterday. This and a multitude of letters disables me from writing more. I am

My Dear Girl's
most affectionate &c. Edw: Elphin

Which ever of you writes next to Roscrea I desire your Uncle may be told that I thank him for his letter, but have not time to answer it. Monday Tuesday and Wedensday were here very fine. My wheat is cut, and in good order. This morning was wet. But the day has prov'd good.

[Free Edw:Elphin]

1. Mrs Taylor: not known.
2. Mr Dexter: not known.
3. Edward Nicholson was one of the developers of Kildare Street and had an office on Ormond Quay. Watson (1747), p.15.
4. It is not known which of Mrs Jourdan's sisters this is.
5. Sir Tho: possibly a play on words; Thomas Jolly was the Store-keeper to the Linen Board. Watson (1755), p.53.
6. The Rev. Christopher Donnelan (1702-50/1): a son of Nehemiah Donnellan I and Martha Ussher. He was educated by Mr Sheridan in Dublin and took BA at TCD in 1723, MA 1726. Fellow 1728-35, DD 1740. Rector of Ballymaglassen, diocese of Meath 1734; of Inishcarra 1735; prebend of Kilnaglory and Athnowen, diocese of Cork 1737. *Alumni*, p.236.

7. Probably Nehemiah Donnellan IV, son of James Donnellan, the eldest son of Chief Baron Nehemiah Donnellan I by his first marriage. Born 1708, TCD 1723. Nehemiah Donnellan IV enlisted as a cornet in the 1st Regiment of Foot, Col Brown's, on 1 May 1744, promoted to lieutenant on 15 March 1749. He was referred to as Col Nehemiah Donnellan in Anne Donnellan's will of 12 November 1758. *Alumni*, p.237; PRO WO64/11, f.13.

69

Elphin. Aug. 22, 1749

My Dear Girl.

I am much pleas'd with your and your Cosen's letters. As this kind of Exercise may be of great use to you both, I have a mind you should continue it. Let me therefore have in the same way both your observations on *Tom. Jones.*[1] I do not expect them by the return of the Post. Take whatever time you find necessary to make them complete as you can.

There is now in Elphin as strong and pityable an instance of the Misery of a Girl's marrying her Self, as can well be given. You have heard, to be sure of Johny Conroy[2], Farfas's[3] eldest son, and know, perhaps, that He, a few years ago, marry'd a young Lady of Family and fortune in the C. of Cork. The Man was not to blame, further than by making himself agreable. She would have him. At the time of her marriage, Her fortune was moderate, about £1000. But soon after, the death of a Brother left, her an Only Child, and Her father, an Estate of about £800 a year; in his own power; out of which He has left her £300 a year for her life, and to her Children £1000 but the Estate goes by his Will to some more distant relation. This young Woman and her Husband came hither last Week, and their Scheme is to settle on Carrow-more, Farfas's farm, which the son has redeem'd, and live frugally there upon this Annuity, a Small Employment, and the produce of that Farm. As Her Grandfather was a friend of my Father's, and of a Family much Esteem'd in the C. of Cork, I sent to ask her and her Husband to dine on Sunday, before I had seen her; and have since thought of little else, than the distress to which she has reduc'd her Self. You may judge by this that I think her a young Woman of some merit; and so indeed she appears to be. She is handsome, very well behav'd, and, as far as I can judge on one day's conversation, has Sense. Lawson, who has seen her offner, says she has very good, and assures me that Her behaviour has been, except this fatal step, *sans reproche.* Imagine then the Condition of such a young Woman (she seems now not above one and twenty) educated with great care, and suitably to her Father's fortune, traveling, I know not how, from Mallow[4] hither, here lodg'd at Andrew

Cumin's,[5] and environ'd with all the *Canaillé* of Conrys assembled to see
their new Relation; and probably condemn'd to pass her days among
them in a Caban. What a fall is this, from an Estate of £800 a year, which,
without this horrid prank, she had been now in possession of, and which,
with her personal qualifications, would have entitled her to shine in the
first rank! One would think she must be either absolutely giddy, or insen-
sible, to support her Self; and yet without the appearance of either, She
behaves her self with ease and cheerfulness. She has indeed this comfort,
That Her Husband, as I am told, behaves himself very well to her. But It is
not in his power to raise her or himself higher, or to provide better for her
than his narrow fortune will allow. I can't help pitying her, tho' she has
been her own Executioner, and will make her stay here, as agreable to her
as I can. Her distress has indeed made so strong an impression on me, that
I could not help describing it to you.

Whatever fine Melons you destin for great folks, you had better send
to those who may be suppos'd to want them. I fancy the Primate has
enough of his own. But I had rather they went among our private friends.
Send a very fine one now and then to the Chan[cello]r. The others dispose of as you will. Desire the Seed, whenever you send a good one.

Robinson shall stay a year, since you desire it. I would willingly do the
poor fellow good. But I am not sure whether it would not do him more,
to be first at my Brothers or some such House, than to be second at mine.
But do you and Mrs Jourdan setle it as you will. Only setle it in time, and
know the poor grinning Gawky's Expectations. I shall never think you too
bold in saying any thing to me, where your motive is compassion and good
nature.

John has wrote about Oats for the Hogs. Since Mrs Jourdan has been
so good as to take them under her protection, I'll give no orders about
them. Desire her to give what she pleases. I do not desire that any Ham
should be kept for me. Use what you have. I shall send a supply from
hence sufficient to serve till New comes in.

I am afraid I shall soon send you a present from hence which will not
be agreable. Poor Billy Beaty[7] has got a most terrible sore leg; and my
Scheme is to send him up on a Carr to the Doctor and Daunt, and Mercer's
hospital.[8] He presses to stay here. But if He will stay, I shall wash my hands
of him. I am very sorry for this accident on the boy's account. But the inconvenience to me is a trifle. Pat has made Shancen[9] as good a Postilion as He
is – I try'd him the other day to Rathcrohan[10] and He rode notably.

As I have never had a Word from you about a Butler, I am sure you
have not got me one. I shall be much at a loss for want of a right good one,
when I get to you. If no such person can be heard of, the only expedient
I can think of is to get a Boy, of some smartness, who can read write and

understands figures to put into the pantry, under Shannon, or, if you please, Dow-bak'd Jac.[11] Could we light right, Such a one might be brought up to be good for more, than Jac. ever will. If you like this, Speak to Dr King, He may get one, out of his Charity-School.[12] His Clerk your friend Luke,[13] would, I believe, pique himself on getting you a right good one. Speak to him. Not one here can read or write.

Now We are upon Servants, How does Drozel[14] behave her Self? The Girl who came down hither has, as far as I have observ'd, behav'd her Self extremely well. I shall be unwilling to have her turn'd off at my return. More news from Mrs Heap. Yesterday morning We had not a morsel of bread for breakfast.

The Letter you sent was, of business. By good luck there is no great matter in it's being delay'd. But Take care for the future. I am called away – Adieu.

yours &c. Edw: Elphin

1. Henry Fielding, *The History of Tom Jones* (1749). '*Tom Jones, A foundling* published this day' by John Smith on the Blind Quay. *Dublin Courant*, 20-22 June 1749.

2. John Conroy (1704-69; See Biographical Register).

3. Farfeasa Conry (1661-1746) of Carrowmore, near Roscommon, married Elizabeth Aylmer and was the father of John Conroy. Farfeasa was said to have been the first member of the family to convert to Protestantism in order to avoid the penalties on holding land. He was a tenant of Robert Howard, bishop of Elphin, in 1739. Conroy Papers, item 13d; Wicklow Papers, NLI PC 223 (6).

4. Mallow, Co. Cork.

5. Andrew Cumins was a tenant of the bishop of Elphin in 1739. NLI, Wicklow Papers, PC 223 (6).

6. Rabble.

7. Billy Beaty: a servant.

8. The Mercer's Hospital was founded in Dublin in 1724/5 by Mary Mercer, daughter of Dr Richard Mercer, to relieve the sick poor. In Stephen Street, it was funded by monies left by Mary Mercer, by benefactions and by subscriptions to an annual concert of sacred music held in one of the Dublin churches. On 16 February 1740 Handel's 'Te Deum Jubilate' and two anthems were performed at St Andrew's church and Edward Synge, who was then bishop of Ferns, preached a sermon commissioned by the Trustees. *Irish Builder*, xxxix (1897) 15; Royal College of Surgeons in Ireland Mercer's Hospital Governors Minute Book 1 (1736-72), f.85, 89.

9. Shancen: a postillion.

10. Rathcrogan, Co. Roscommon, is a prehistoric burial mound on the road between Mantua and Ballintober. 'This is a round artificial Mount of 400 feet diameter at the top. It is made with sods covered with grass, and in very good preservation. It is situated in a field in the Barony of Ballintubber four miles from Ballinagar [Belanagar]. Here the kings of Connaught were inaugurated and kept their provincial assemblies assembling on the top and encamping roundabout not far from the mount is the burial place. ...' Gabriel Beranger, 'Tour through Connaught in 1779 under the direc-

tion of the Rt. Hon William Burton.' NLI ms 5628.

11. Obscure.

12. Dr James King was named in Mary Mercer's will as one of the trustees of her
female boarding school which on his advice was conducted partly on the principles of
the Red Maids School in Bristol, and partly on the methods of the Charter schools. In
1748 King moved the St Bride's parish school from Golden Lane and Maiden Lane to
Little Ship Street. Dr King lived in Kevin Street. Carroll, pp.21-2.

13. Luke, clerk to Dr King: not known.

14. Drozel: scullery maid.

70

Elphin. Aug. 25, 1749

Your charming hopes, My Dear Girl, will soon be turn'd into certainty.
Continue in the way in which you are, and you'll setle in to a good hand,
and write to please your Self and me. Too much anxiety sometimes, and
a little hurry and giddiness at others, have till lately hind'red your doing
in both respects as well as I wish'd.

Your account of poor Mrs Bland[1] grieves me much. I hope however,
that the Doctor will find some means to relieve her, at least to keep off the
Evil day.

I think the lower part of your Walls done in finishing,will be prettier
than paper, and if it be soon done, the damp will be insignificant. If
George[2] be slow, or can't single make sufficient haste, Let him get another
hand to assist him. For positively the Work must be push'd, as quick as it
can be. Consult Mr Eaton upon this, and if He see there is room for a
Second Work man, Desire him to provide a good one.

I believe it will be both difficult and Expensive to provide proper Balls
for that press. If the present Worm-eaten ones can be made to support it
any how, till I get to you, I had rather nothing were done more, till I see
it.

I thank you for putting me in mind of the White-washing, because that
has made me recollect a thing of more importance, the painting the outside of the House as usual. It ought to be done this year. Send immediatly
to Mr Eaton and desire him to put it in hand, and not to loose this fine
Weather. Besides if it be not enter'd on presently, It will not be finish'd
and dry, by the time I get to you. White-wash too as usual.

I am hurry'd and can only add that I am

My Dear Girl's
most affectionate Edw: Elphin

Billy goes off towards you to morrow. But He rides. Desire the Doctor to provide for him in his Hospital.

[Free Edw:Elphin]

1. Probably Lucy Heaton, who was Dr Nathaniel Bland's second wife. Lucy Heaton would have been a relation of Edward Synge through his wife's family. Burke (1979), p.129.
2. Probably George Stephens, the carpenter.

71

Elphin, August 29, 1749

Don't plume your Selves too much, Mistress, either you or your Cosen, on account of my general Commendation of your performances. It is right to encourage young beginners, when they aim well, to make them exert themselves. How do you know but this may be my skill? But lest this may too much damp your joy, I tell you seriously that I was pleas'd. Take care both of you, that I be more so with you next. You call upon me for the performance of my promise. I must at present answer as the children do. I confess I promis'd to give you my thoughts of C[larissa]. But I did not tell you when; and you must, I believe, indulge me till my return. I'll keep you and your Cosen's letters, and in going over them with you over the fire, I shall have an opportunity of telling you my thoughts with more ease to my Self, perhaps with more advantage to you, than by writing, for which, besides, I have not, nor, while here, can I hope to have time.

Our Artaign friends are at Stroke's-town. Some of them with the Family were here yesterday. But We wanted Kitty and her Husband. He could not, and therefore she would not come. He was in his bed from an Accident, which might have been fatal to him. His Coach man being sick, He drove his own Coach from Tobber-vaddy, and just at Mr Mahon's new Basin, as he was sitting carelesly in the Box, a jolt from a small Stone, which took the Wheel, threw him out of it. When he found himself going, He jump'd, and came to the ground on his feet, but strain'd the Sinews so violently about the Ankles, that, after attempting to conceal and bully his halt all Saturday, on Sunday He was forc'd to submit. His Ankle, Leg, and thigh swell'd greatly, and the Apothecary there said the Sinews were knotting. I can't tell whether He spoke sense or not. But the whole Limb was, as they told me, swoln and enflam'd. By that same Apothecary's advice He was blouded in the foot, and much reliev'd by it. Bandage, and

Spirits of Wine and Camphire[1] are the Applications now. I hope they are right. I don't know yet how he is to day, but shall before I seal this letter. Poor Kitty! This is with her the beginning of Matrimonial Sorrow. Some falls to every one's share. I hope hers will be short, and that He will be soon well; and learn from this, not to play the Coach-Man any more. The Accident is a very Common one. But why should Gent[lemen] turn Coach-men? His excuse is his servant's ilness.

Mr Donnelan too had a very great escape. He drove himself in a Chair, and was within an inch of tumbling down a precipice, by downright carelesness. But He got off safe, and Both He and Wife are vastly better than when they were here before. They and Betty enquir'd for you with great affection. So did your good friend Mrs Mahon, who never fails to do it, tho' I fail to tell you she does. But Strange news! The Major[2] was here, for the first time – I believe He'll come agen, when He can, as He did yesterday, get a place in the Coach. Dr Lawson run away from us to Will French's, from whence He return'd this morning. He is in great disgrace with the Girls for this flight.

Mrs Silver is very kind. I wish she spar'd her presents. Do you take care to make proper returns, in Civility and respect.

Among the persons you visited, you mention Mrs King. I can't now recollect any acquaintance you have of that name.

Mr Wills's stay will not be long in town. *Entre nous* I am not sure that He is to be depended on for a Butler. He is, like some folks I know, a little too confiding. If I could get a right good clever Boy, such as I have already describ'd, I am inclin'd to that scheme; and for this, among other reasons, because Shannon has some advantages now, which if I have a profess'd Butler He cannot have. Here especially. For in town they are trifling. With all his faults or rather imperfections, I have great pity for him, and the more as I have lately discover'd, that his disorders are in part owing to a great anxiety for his Family. All things consider'd, He has no reason. For He is with me in a better way than He ever was, or can hope to be any where else. But whether with or without reason, This is upon his mind and hurts him. I believe it will puzzle the Doctor to cure this disorder. He shall try, when We get to town. But till then I'll do nothing, unless upon this notice He gives fresh orders. Camomile Tea and riding are my present prescriptions.

Billy is before this with you. My positive orders are that He goe to Mercer's Hospital, and there observe the Doctor's directions exactly. Perhaps He'll not like this. But I will hear nothing against it. I design his good, and know better what is for that than He does. If He does as I order, He need not fear but that proper care will be taken of him. As to Robinson, I am full as well satisfy'd that He should stay, as go, and probably it will be more for his advantage. It may, if Carleboe pleases, and I believe He has now no jealousy of him.

What to say about your Maids I know not. The new one here I am at present very well satisfy'd with, and shall be against parting with, and The Character you give of the other is a very good one. Yet Both are too many while We are together. Should We again be divided, Both will be wanting; and this is not impossible. If it please God that I continue well, and you are so, I resolve to return to the Country much earlier next Spring than I could bear to venture you here, whatever I may do in Summer. A multitude of Schemes, which I have in my head, will require my presence. For indeed little is done, while I am away, much less than ought to be. Have this in your view, and plan matters accordingly. The Expense of an additional servant I value not. It is better, than to run the hazard of getting a bad one when you want. As you know 'long and lank's' merits better than I do, you can better determine this arduous point. But pray what condition is Molly Fagan in? I fear she'll be useless as long as she lives. If that be the case, I think it more adviseable to give her a Small Annual allowance, than to continue her in my house; unless she'll come here, when she may be more easily supported, and perhaps have a better chance for something like health. Some thing must be done about her; It shall be what you please; only that She must not stay meerly to be an incumbrance in the house. Resolve what and break it to her by degrees. The Sooner the better. I have wrote more than I intended. Adieu.

yours &c.
Edward Elphin

Mr Ormsby is better. He din'd at Clonfree[3] to day.

I had yesterday a letter from Molly[4] in which she complains of you, and Jeny for not answering hers to you. One or both of you should write to the Brat. It will make her very happy.

1. Spirits of Wine was alcohol. It may have been 'first shot', a harsh spirit from the first distillation of a whiskey still, which was used as a rub for aches and sprains. 'Camphire' was camphor oil from the plant, *camphora officinarum*, used for rubbing on sprains. K.H. Connell, *Irish Peasant Society* (Oxford 1968), p.5 fn.

2. Major Mahon.

3. Clonfree, Co. Roscommon. Near Kilglass, north-east of Strokestown. A Mahon house.

4. Mary Synge, Jane Synge's younger sister.

72

Elphin. September 1, 1749

My Dear Girl

I have little time to write, and as it happens, little to say.

In my last I gave you an account of Lewis Ormsby's accident. I wish it doe not prove a bad one. I saw him on Thursday, not able to stir; and by the account yesterday, the other foot is affected. Prithee ask the Doctor whether this can be the effect of a shock seven days before? I suspect the gout. It is a poor Case, that they have not a person of any skill to ask a question of.

I am glad you saw my L[or]d C[hancello]r, and you see you are gainers by it. Since He has no Melons of his own, you may supply him with what you can spare from other friends. I think you'll do well to send one to Mrs Fitzmaurice.

Your observation on Mrs P – affectionate Compliments is just.[1] But such things you'll find in the Course of your life very Common Civil words, and great professions cost little They are easily made. But without suitable actions, what are they good for? They are not even fit to deceive. For prudent people never mind them. I hope you said enough to Mr. P[2] – just to let him see, that you knew what value to set upon such fine speeches, without resenting the neglect, which, all things consider'd, was a great one. By the by, Madam, I have caught you here at a false spelling, the only one I have observ'd of late. You write *consistant*. It ought to be an e. What you write of Nancy Hamilton surprizes me[3]. The best way is not to seem to observe it. I hope you have given her no offence.

Paint or White wash as you please else-where. But meddle not with my rooms. Let them stand as they do.

The rotting of the Hyacinths vexes me; and the more as I am not certain, but that this may be skill in Gannon, to shew you rotten ones as the best, and so to have them sound to dispose of himself. The loss of my fine Tulip last year rais'd some suspicion of him. This increases it. I wish I could come at the truth. At present It is best to say nothing, further than this. Tell him I say He must have been very careless, or this could not have happen'd.

The Weather continues very fine, and I enjoy it every way as much as I can. My hay is coming home, and, what is quite new to me, I am making great Reeks of Turf.[4] Adieu My Dearest

Yours &tc Edw: Elphin

[Free Edw:Elphin]

1. Mrs P.: not known.
2. Mr P.: Not known.
3. Obscure.
4. Reek: a rick or pile.

73

Elphin. September 5, 1749

My Dear Girl.

I see you and your Cosen are easily mortify'd. But I can't see that you have reason to be so. On the contrary you ought to be much pleas'd that you've succeeded so well in a task difficult enough in it self, and perfectly new to you. I assure you honestly that you've both done much better than I expected; and these first Essays leave me no room to doubt but that in a little time, and with proper care and application, you'll do as well as I wish you to do. Most of your observations are just and sensible enough, consider'd singly. The point in which you have fail'd most is That you have not enter'd enough into the true design of the Works on which you observe; and you have done this less in your present performance, than in the former. I wonder the less at it, because it is more difficult in this than in the other. Jeny has made an offer at this. But Her remark is too general. The design of every work of invention almost, that is worth reading is to recommend virtue in one shape or other. But the manner of doing this is different in different works; and To discover this, is To enter into the true design of the Writer.

As you have employ'd some time and thought upon these two books, Let me recommend it to you to employ a little more – a good deal of usefull instruction may be learn'd from both; and I do not know, but it may be worth your while to give both another and more deliberate reading, when you are not otherwise employ'd in the long evenings that are now coming on. If you'll do this, I shall from time to time give you such assistance, as may make your study more usefull, perhaps more entertaining. All I shall say further to you at present is That The way to enter into the true design of any Works of this sort, is to fix your attention first and principally to the principal Personages, or Characters, and observe minutely their Manners and their Fate. Thus you'll discover the principal Aim and

Design. Every other Character does indeed deserve some notice more or less according to the importance of it, and Each may furnish some usefull instruction. But the main design of the whole appears from the conduct ascrib'd to the principal Persons, to whom all the rest are some way or other subordinate. If you'll be at the pains of considering either of these Works, in this regular Light, I fancy they'll please and instruct more than they have done.

The *Orage*[1] on Saturday griev'd me the more, on account of your intended jaunt. I hop'd you would stay at home, and am very glad you did so, and that the put off was from His Ex[cellen]cy.[2] Sunday was with us an Hurricane. It has done some mischief to the standing Corn, tho', Cary tells me, not so much as We fear'd.

I am glad your dressing room is so near being finish'd. Pray Is your Book-Case ready to put up in it? You have not of late mention'd it.

I am pleas'd you had little Mahon[3] with you at Finglas – our Tobbervaddy friends are still at Stroke's-town. I made them a morning visit yesterday. Mr Ormsby is now in a way of being well. I am still in doubt, whether there has not been a spice of Gout in his disorder, and shall be so till you send the Doctor's answer to my question. And so My Dear Girl for this time Adieu.

yours &c.
Edw: Elphin

[Free Edw:Elphin]

1. Storm. September 1749 saw 'A hasty onset of winter ... a good deal of rain and frequently cold almost to frost ... ', Rutty, p.149.
2. Lord Harrington, the Lord Lieutenant.
3. Possibly Theodosia, youngest daughter of Thomas and Jane Mahon. Burke (1979), p.774.

74

[Elphin] September 8, 1749

My Dear Girl.

I am to spend this day with Nicholson in setling accounts &c. of his school.[1] I lay hold of a minute before he is stirring, to give you this reason for my writing little this post.

I hope and believe that All fears about Mr Ormsby are over; and I am better pleas'd now to think that there was no mixture of gout, tho' in his ilness, I wish'd it. He was much help'd by bleeding; and I doubt not but the gentle Physick, which the Doctor recommended also, would have been of use. But the Stroke's-town Apothecary's skill did not reach so far as to prescribe it.

I am sorry Mrs Silver is out of order. Tell her this when you have a proper occasion. I hope she is not seriously ill, tho' Mrs Jourdan's account of the Cause and beginning of her disorder makes me wish it were over.

In speaking of Mrs Dean[2] whom you met there, you have wrote bad English, which I the rather take notice of, as I can't blame you for it. The mistake is frequent even among those who write with tolerable propriety. *Whom, la Dame du logis*[3] had told us, design'd us a visit. It ought to be *Who* the Nominative, you have put the Accusative. To shew you at once the wrongness of this, I'll put it another way. *La dame du logis* had told us *Her* design'd us a Visit. *Her* answers to *Whom*. I am sure you know it ought to be *She*, which answers to *Who*.

I can't see why you should be at all distress'd on such occasions as this. If the person spoken of be one, whom you wish to be acquainted with, you may express your satisfaction at the prospect of it in civil, yet encouraging terms. If otherwise, and that you know little or are indifferent about them, Is it not easy to say, She'll do me a great deal of honour or some such Word? Think not, My Dearest, that I would have you Civil, at the Expense of Sincerity. But Custom has given such a meaning to this and such like forms, that they do not deceive. They are rather forms, accounted civil and polite, which have no fix'd meaning at all. I never think a Man more my humble servant, for saying He has the honour to be so. As you grow up, you must expect to have some intercourse with many persons, whom perhaps you would not chuse for intimates; and an Exchange of a Visit or two, where there is no blemish, tho' little to approve of, is no great matter. You may proceed, or stop as you find. This I say in general. Of the Lady you mention I know nothing. Her Mother was a great friend of your's. I think you have seen her.

Hurry'd as I am, I must rally you a little, Madam, on what I can't call a false spelling, but, if design'd, shews you a reformer. We common folks write *repair*. You with more exactness and conformity to the Original, write *repare*. Mr Lucas and the *Censor* do the same. I give you joy of being their disciple.

I have no objection to Molly Fagan's staying at Finglas, if John has not. He may, and yet conceal it. Settle the matter among you, and let her allowance commence from Micmas. Fix this before I go to you, and determine about your Supernumery Maid. Adieu.

yours &c.

Edw: Elphin

It will be time enough to plant your flower-roots, when I go to town. Mrs Jourdan us'd to complain of too much drink at night. At my return she'll probably complain of the Contrary extreme. For I have quite left off Wine at night, and find it of great service to me.

[Free Edw:Elphin]

1. Edward Nicholson founded a charity school on his estate at Primrose Grange, Co. Sligo, in 1710. Edward Synge was its treasurer. He built a schoolhouse, and a chapel with a belfry and a bell. Edward Nicholson, *A Method of Charity-Schools, Recommended, for giving, both a Religious Education, and way of livelihood to the Poor of Ireland* (Dublin 1712), p.38; NLI ms 2102.
2. Mrs Dean: not known.
3. *La Dame du logis*: the lady of the house.

75

Elphin. September 12, 1749

After finishing my other dispatches, I come at last to you, My Dearest, and have less time to write, than I should have had, if some interruptions had not stopp'd my Carreer of writing. But, As it happens, I have not a great deal to say.

I am pleas'd you had your jaunt to Merion, and that the day was so favorable. His Excellency was very kind to your Horses.

That Heavy Coach is too great a load for them. I have from the beginning been vex'd that I had it made so, and just before I left town agreed with Jones to exchange it for a Salisbury, not because it is the fashion, but because it is much lighter, and will enable John Davis to obey your and your Cosen's orders for driving fast, without hurting his Horses. It is now ready for lining; and He by my order will go to receive your directions. It is best always to provide lining our Selves; and, since I have no one now to depend on, as I us'd to do on Nat. Smith, I think your best way will be to send for Woodward, the Taylor, and employ him to bring you patterns. Cloth from 8d to 10d the yard is full fine enough. He knows what is good, and will in that assist you in the choice, at the same time that He'll either divert or teaze you with his oddness. As to the Colour, Please your Selves: Or, if you have a mind, Consult Mrs Silver – She'll take it as a high compliment, if you tell her, that Her fancy in the last was, in mine, and all your opinion so good, that We desire it agen. You may do this or not, as you will. I think some such colour as the last will do very well. But if you had rather have blue, With all my heart. You'll please me, by pleasing your

Selves. The Hammer Cloth must be plain. Fringe, it seems, with such Coaches, is out of fashion.

I should be much pleas'd, if you could overcome your aversion to Mice. It is the only one I know you have. Endeavour, My Dear, to get the better of it. I am sure you will.

Tho' I allow you to write as fast as you please, I can't on this account pass over false spellings, which are owing meerly to this cause. You have wrote *to* for *two*, speaking of your games of Cribbage at Mrs Silver's. You do not tell me, whether she be still confin'd.

I am pleas'd with what you write about Mrs Butler. Her journey to Sligo has, I find, been of use.

Pray get the Work-men to finish as fast as you can. If the Parliament sits, assoon as is now said, I shall be with you, God willing, the beginning of next Month. But I care not how few know this.[1]

I am surpriz'd that Mr Holmes has not before this sent home your Watch – Get Mr Nicholson to speak to him about it, and to see that it be put into complete order. You need not pay him. I'll do it assoon as I go to town. I am

My Dear Girl
yours &c. Edw: Elphin

In the last *Censor*, Notice is taken of *The Cork Chirurgeon's Letter*,[2] a Paper I have never seen. Why did you not send it to me? Pray Do it – I am sure Ned Curtis has seen it, because it is wrote against the Man He so much admires.

When you see Woodward about the lining, Tell him I got his, and that I hope, He has provided Cloth for my Frocks, as well as for my Liverys. He mentions only the latter.

Upon considering matters, I resolve to leave Molly Meade[3] here if she'll stay. She'll be wanting to take care of the House &c. – This will make all easy.

[Free Edw:Elphin]

1. Parliament reassembled on 10 October 1749. *NHI*, Vol. 9, p.606.
2. Anthony Litten, *The Cork Surgeon's Antidote gainst the Dublin Apothecary's Poison* (Dublin 1749). An attack on Charles Lucas, variously attributed to Sir Richard Cox and Nathaniel Kane. Sir Richard Cox was MP for Clonakilty, Co. Clare. Charles Lucas attacked him in the June 1749 edition of *The Censor*.
3. Molly Meade: a servant.

76

Elphin. September 15, 1749

My Dear Girl.

When I gave your Grandfather any advice which He did not like, or express'd uneasiness at any little management of himself, His fond rebuke to me always was, Go, you're a fool. You must take the same from me for what you write about my leaving off Wine at night – tho' I find you have Mrs Jourdan, and Ned Curtis of your Side. He wrote, as he promis'd, a very affectionate Expostulatory letter to me upon it, to which I have not time now to write an answer. Pray Excuse me to him, and Tell him I hope soon to give him a satisfactory one in person. In the mean time, Ask whether He thinks, that my usual quantity of Wine at dinner, sometimes a little more, with three or four hours riding every day, will not continue sufficient vigor and motion to my bloud till I get into Winter quarters. When I get there, I may perhaps take new measures, tho' I own it will not be easy to convince me that the Method I now am in is hurtfull, which upon a trial of near three months, I have found so very beneficial. I thank him heartily for his Papers.

A strange discovery since my last! Molly Meade packs off to day. I dare not say for what. It would make Mrs Jourdan spit, as Louse does. The Murder came out yesterday, when I order'd Shannon to bring her to me, that I might tell her my intention of continuing her here. He desir'd me to stop, till I saw Mrs Heap – who gave me such an account as made me resolve at once to dismiss her. When I order'd notice to be given her of this, I desir'd she might be told, that if she insisted on her innocence, I would hear her. I find she does insist, but yet declines the Trial. There is therefore no doubt of her guilt. I ought to have been told of it long ago. But I should have continu'd in ignorance, had it not been that I declar'd my intention of keeping her here. Such stuff are Shannon and Mrs Heap. Thus they consult the honour of their Master.

Mr Wills is with me, and We are very busy about building affairs. I have time therefore now for no more.

yours &c.
Edw:Elphin

You fret at your writing. Why don't you mend? The beginning of every letter is well enough. Sure it is in your power to keep on as you set out.

This will do, till practice makes you do all better. But I hope you are growing more delicate your Self. For this letter, that has made you fret is better wrote from beginning to end, than some that you have not made any apology for.

I had yesterday a letter from Mr Clements, in which He gives me an Account of some Carpets He had bought for me. They are more in Number, and not all of the Dimensions I desir'd. But I must now take them. If they arrive before I get to you, He'll send them to Kevin-street. You have nothing to do but to receive them, and, if you will, to open and air them. I believe that will be best.

Tell John Miller, that Carrs will be in town with Luggage and other things from hence the beginning of next month, by the return of which He may send the Iron I last wrote for time enough. But As to Boards He must provide as He can, tho' I am not for them in Violent haste.

[Free Edw:Elphin]

77

Elphin. September 19, 1749

My Dear Girl.

Coll. Wynne is now here. You guess in what way I am. But I contriv'd to send him to bed presently after eleven, and I sit down now to write, before He is up; just to tell you, that I bless God, I continue well; and hope to shew you, and Dr Curtis, the beginning of next Month, that my leaving off Wine at night has done me no harm.

I have the Surgeon's letters, and think they are wrote with Sense and Spirit superior to the avow'd Author. It is not at all improbable that the Person you name may be the real one. In the Papers many things are well said. But I can't subscribe to every thing. You see I write *Surgeon* now. The other spelling is certainly the proper one. But this so commonly us'd of late, that it has almost beat the other out. You may use either, as it comes into your head.

If you, or your Agent Woodward get Cloth for the Coach-lining as good, and as cheap at Mr Minchin's as any where else, you may buy it there. I am quite indifferent. As you like some such colour as that of the present, you may easily determine Mrs Silver to like it too. I am very sorry she is ill.

I don't understand what you write about the Landry Windows – Is the roof, or Are the Walls defective? Slating is a remedy in the latter case, and an Effectual, but an Ugly, one. However it must be us'd if necessary; and so let your orders be obey'd.

The delay of the Work-men is vexatious. I write to Eaton, to quicken him.

Our Weather has been broken and ugly since Saturday. This morning is foggy. Had it not been so, I should not have wrote so much. It is now clearing up. So Adieu.

yours &c.
Edw: Elphin

[Free Edw:Elphin]

78

Elphin. September 22, 1749

What I said to you, My Dear Girl, in my late letter, I must now say to you, and Dr Curtis. Go You're a couple of fools. I suspect a third deserves the same Speech. For, as she her Self says, You are inseperable. How could it enter into your heads, that I gravely ask'd the Question, to which you send an answer. I expected you would have seen, that I put it, to shew in a strong light, the Ridicule of your all making such a Rout about my not drinking Wine at night. But I no more wanted an Answer to it, than if I had ask'd whether two and two make four. However you may tell Dr Curtis, That I thank him for his gracious indulgence, which He was much in the right to give, because I should have taken it, whether He had or no. But I'll make no Conditions with him. I hope in God, I shall soon shew my self in good Health in Town, and then I'll do, as I find this or that Regimen best answers. At present I think I shall continue as I am; and I am almost sure that Dr Anderson will support me in it. Don't you now, Ladys, biass him against me. You can't. He won't be biass'd. Tell Ned further, that I am not such a Simpleton as to ride in the Afternoon. If I did, I should be more disorder'd by it, than by wine at night. The morning is my time, and This has been the most glorious one of the whole Season. I have been five hours on Horseback.

I return you your Pattern. I believe the Cloth is good, and if I read the price right, cheap. Is it not 7sh: 6d-? If it were, just a Shade darker, It would in my judgment be better. But by pleasing your Selves you'll please me; and since this has Mrs Silver's approbation, een stick to it. Let Jones have it, assoon as you can, that He may not pretend He was delay'd. But first, if you can conveniently, Learn from Mr Nicholson whether He has seen the Coach, and approves of it. He promis'd me, He would see it.

I am very sorry for the unlucky accident at Dunshaghlin. But Charlotte's great Escape must comfort them, and their friends for the rest. It pleases me much that Mrs Wills is safe. You should go there assoon as you can, and Be sure you pay your Compliments properly to her Aunt[1] now with her. She is a very good Woman. Mr Wills left me on Sunday morning.

Coll. Wynne went off at nine to day. Judge French leaves me to morrow. I expect Mr Sandford, and shall have company rather more than Enough while I stay.

By a letter yesterday from your Uncle I judge they are all before this in town. I shall be impatient for an account of them God send a good one, and to us all an happy meeting. I am

My Dear Girl's
most affectionate &tc. Edw: Elphin

Ned Curtis has given you a Nick name, you say – Why did you not tell me the reason? I can't guess.

[Free Edw:Elphin]

1. Mrs Wills's aunt: not known.

79

Elphin. September 26, 1749

My Dear Girl.

Your account of your Aunt pleases me much. Your poor Uncle's is still better. He thinks her bulk greatly fallen, and says that you and Mrs Jourdan seem'd on first sight of her, to think the same. I am afraid He flatters himself. But please God she continues in other respects as you describe her. All things consider'd, We shall have great reason to rejoice. When I took leave of her last May, I thought the odds greatly against my seeing her agen, unless I had gone to town to see her dye. God be thanked, It is otherwise. You observe rightly, That Want of Company will be bad for her. So will want of Exercise. We must try what We can do to guard her against both.

I hold my resolution of leaving this on Thursday se'night. I need not desire you to have Bed air'd and every thing ready for me. But you might not perhaps, unless I bid you, order John Miller to get a sack of Flow'r, and Robinson to bake some bread. Charge him particularly to get Excel-

lent Barm.[1] My bread here has been so constantly good the whole
Summer, that I shall be very nice. Don't order a Mutton to be kill'd. I have
but a few, and am not sure of an immediate supply, so that I must manage
what I have, and not have any kill'd, till hurry is over.

You'll easily believe that I am pretty much hurry'd, and that I shall be
so during my stay here. All prattle therefore I must adjourn to our meeting. God send us an happy one.

I am My Dearest
yours &c. Edw: Elphin

Your return to this will be the last letter I can receive from you here.
But I sha'n't be sorry to have a line from you the following post directed
to Palmer's.

Your twelve Pea-chicks are completely rear'd. I hope no accident will
lessen their Number. On this increase of your Family I have ventur'd to
make a present of one of the Elder Hens to Mrs Mahon. She is much
oblig'd by it – I saw her yesterday, when, as always, she enquir'd for you
&c. with great affection. She looks better than She has done for years past.
She does not propose to go to town.

[Free Edw:Elphin]

1. Barm or ale-yeast: the froth that forms on the top of fermenting ale which is used
to leaven bread.

80

Elphin. September 29, 1749

My Dear Girl –

I hold my resolution of setting out next Thursday, and hope to have
the great pleasure of seeing you on Saturday. God send us an happy meeting. In one respect It would be better for you, that We were longer asunder. For yours now before me is better wrote, taking the whole together,
than any letter I have had from you this Summer. A little more practice
now would make you a great proficient. But when We are together, you'll
not have so frequent occasions to write, and will not probably write with
so much care, and so will fall back agen.

Mr Donnelan is now here. He leaves me to morrow, and sets out for
Dublin on Monday. Betty stays till Mrs Ormsby goes, i.e. as you heard, till
the middle of November. But the Old folks will be at Artaign on Wedensday. If Thursday be a fine day, where would be the hurt if you went thither

to see them – Or perhaps Friday will be better.

As I said in my last, All prattle I adjourn to our meeting.

yours &c.
Edw: Elphin

Turn

Let John go on Saturday morning to Lennox's, and bring home the Plate-chest. The receit for it is in one of the little Drawers in the Scriptoire within what is call'd the Prospect. Ned Curtis will give it him. Or if He can't find it, He must desire Lennox to deliver it. Mrs Jourdan will order Beef &c. to be bought that day. I mention these things now lest I should forget them in more hurry next Week.

Be sure to give Will orders to secure Hamilton the Corn-cutter to be with me on Sunday morning. Both my Toes and Hair will want his hand.

[Free Edw:Elphin]

81

Elphin. October 3, 1749

My Dear impatient Fool.

I won't own to be like you, and yet the time will be rather long, till I have the pleasure of seeing you which I hope to have next Saturday. My scheme is to dine with you about four – some Sole, Whiting, or other good Sea Fish will be a treat. But you must have roasted mutton for Lawson, and a couple of roasted Fowl, not rank; For such We shall not be able to taste. This is all I desire. But you must provide plentifully for the Servants who will be hungry and their inside dry. How it may fare with their outside, I can't yet say. This is a very bad day – I hope however that Thursday will be a good one. As We shall all be in a hurry, it will be best not to say any thing of our intention of dining; and if it should be too long for you to fast to our hour, Get your dinner before. If the day be good, I think We shall be with you by four. If bad, We must go Slower, and you'll do well to order our dinner somewhat later.

I had pack'd up *Clarissa* before I rec'd yours. The *Terence* shall be pack'd up. God send us an happy meeting.

yours &c.
Edw: Elphin

If the Weather should continue as bad, as it has been yesterday and to day, It will not be prudent in me to expose my Self, Servants and Horses to it. I shall therefore chuse to deferr setting out, and in case you do not see me on Saturday, Be satisfy'd That this is the reason.

[Free Edw:Elphin]

1. *Terence.* Not known.

1750

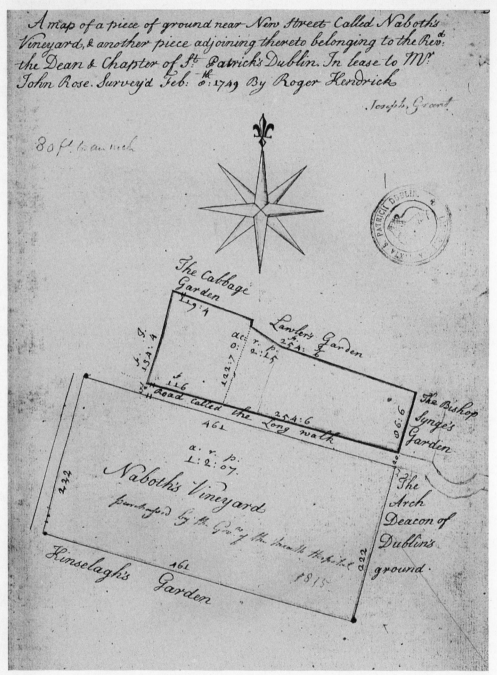

Sketch map of Swift's 'Naboth's Vineyard', 1749, by Roger Kendrick, showing the location of Edward Synge's garden backing onto Long Lane (courtesy Governors and Guardians of Marsh's Library).

82

Glanmore. May 16, 1750

I know, Huzzy, that you'll expect an account of me on the road. I have given you an ill use.

Here I am then; I bless God, very well. So is my fellow traveller.[1] We are thus far without any cross accident, and neither dust, nor Sun incommoded us. The Heat and the great hardness of the roads made Pat drive gently, so that the Horses were as little incommoded as we.

The only thing that has happen'd cross is a trifle. My new boots are too streight. But I hope they may be widen'd. I left them this morning at Kinnegad, with orders to Mr Higgins[2] to send them to you by the stage. When you get them Let Will carry them to the Maker Irwin in Skinner-row[3] with the Ticket on the other side. Jemy may bring them down. Give the Coach-man if He delivers them 6 pence. 2 pence is enough for a Porter.

Palmer appears to me better than when in town. If his Wife be much better, as she says she is, Her looks do not shew it. I remark particularly that she is yellower than usual. The young ones are well, and your adopted, much grown.[4]

Pray make my Compliments particularly to the Doctor. Hurry'd as I was, I could not see him on Monday. But writing will do as well. I'll do it properly. But some time hence will be more convenient than now. Remember Shannon's books you may among you hint this. 'Tis no great matter whether you do or not. I had rather you did; or make Ned Curtis do it. I would not upon any account have him entertain the least suspicion of neglect, to whom I commit what is dearest to me in this World. And So Huzzy Adieu.

yours &c.
Edw: Elphin

Let one of your Men step to poor Cos. Doherty to let her know that Her son is well.[5]
Love and blessing at the Green.

[Free Edw:Elphin BALLYMAHON]

1. Richard Doherty, who travelled with Edward Synge in May 1749.
2. Patrick Higgins, innkeeper at Kinnegad. Christine Casey and Alistair Rowan,

North Leinster (London 1993), p.368.

3. John Irwin: shoe-maker, Skinner's Row. Watson (1760), p.25.

4. This may be Nan Palmer, to whom Edward Synge refers in Letter 178.

5. Jane Richardson, widow of Latham Doherty, Richard Doherty's mother. Burke (1912), p.185.

83

Elphin. May 19, 1750

I wrote to My Dear Girl from Glanmore. God be thanked, the remainder of my journey was as fortunate as it had been to that place, and I am here now very well but too much hurry'd to write. I got here about two yesterday. Hurry'd as I am I can't let a false spelling escape, which from the Word, and the occasion of [*damaged ms*] is remarkable. Unlucky Ally! to stumble just when you express your hopes of not stumbling, and yet I had hopes as well as you, nay! am certain that you will improve because I have the pleasure to see you do. But, Huzzy, you must writ Acquit, not as you have done, aquit. There's another mistake, for which yet you may possibly produce Authoritys. 'Tis Cloak not cloke, as you write it. And So for this time Adieu.

yours &c.
Edw: Elphin

I intend that the Bishop of Clogher's book should come down by Jemy.[1] I begin to find Wants, of which We were not appriz'd. One already. Desire Mrs Jourdan to provide half a dozen Sawce boats, such as were sent down last year. They are all broke. Next post probably may go several Commissions of a like kind.

[Free Edw:Elphin]

1. Robert Clayton (1695-1758): bishop of Clogher. He took BA at TCD in 1714 and became a Fellow. MA 1717; LLD 1722 and DD 1730. He was nominated bishop of Killala in December 1729; translated to Cork and Ross in December 1735 and to Clogher in August 1745, where he remained until his death on 26 February 1758. He built 80 St Stephen's Green, designed by Richard Castle, in 1736. It is now part of Iveagh House. Clayton is best known for his controversial *Essay on Spirit ... with some remarks on the Athanasian and Nicene Creeds* (1751). The book to which Edward Synge refers could have been either *The chronology of the Hebrew bible vindicated ...* (1747) or *A dissertation on prophecy ...* (1749). *NHI*, Vol. 9, pp.437, 415, 396; *Georgian Society Records* Vol.2, pp.81-2.

84

Elphin. May 23, 1750

Tho' I have taken a Folio to write to my Dear Girl on, I am not sure that I shall have time to fill it. Hurry is not yet over.

I bless God I am very well, and much rejoic'd that you are so. Such tidings the whole summer will make me happy. I am sorry for Mrs Jourdan's Cheek. Syrrup of Onions, persisted in, would relieve her.

Your soft rain was, I suppose, on Friday. We had a good deal here; For which reason, and to give my Horses one day's rest, I rode not out that day. But on Saturday I view'd every hole and corner; and was not much pleas'd. But Cary has been wooing, and is marry'd.¹ I hope in a little time to retrieve the wrong steps, and neglects which this has occasion'd.

Ned's horse carrys me so well, as that I less feel the want of my disabled ones. He is not quite strong enough for long rides. But about the Demesne, He carrys me as well as I could wish. Mr Adderley's present will be to me useless.² The Damsel who rode him must have had either a very soft saddle or a very hard B—b. My Chesnut has been so long growing much better, that I begin to fear he never will be well. Mind not Jemy; but enquire from John Miller about him, and charge him, to know certainly from Williams³ what I am to expect, and what is best to be done with him. If Grass be necessary to set him up, Let him be turned out to Cool-blow. Better want him for a summer, than always. and yet I would avoid this, if I could. At all events Let him not stir from town, till I give orders. I know Jemy will be in haste, in Expectation of shill[ings] to be got here in more plenty than I wish. But He must not stir till I am sure my Horse will not suffer by his journey.

I have not yet been long enough here to find out all my Wants. As I find, you shall have notice of, that you may supply them. Those I feel at present are the consequence of mine own folly in heark'ning to Godfrey Wills and Lawson about Tables. A Couple of Vain —— could not be content with good dinners, on plain Old Tables! And I a simple puppy to mind them! At great expense I have forsooth got fine large Tables, and Linnen for them, and must now at more, get a Supply of China-dishes and Plates, which but for them, I should not have wanted. Carleboe and Shannon say, and They say right, that without them the new Tables will be useless. Two of them at least. For the other two, We can make, We have already made shift. As I am at present poorer, than I may perhaps be some time hence, and therefore wish, not to draw much from Lennox, It comes into my head, That it will be best to send me down hither all of the Blew and White kind, Dishes and plates, soup as well as others, which you have. They'll match well with mine and I think will do, and you may use what they call the burnt ones, which are finer than they, but not fine enough to be laid by as a rarity. Towards winter others may be provided, as far as they are wanting. But you know I have little use of China, since Plate came in fashion with me. If among you, you approve of this, Get them pack'd by some skilfull person, that they may not suffer in the Carriage, and send them off. The Sawce-boats may be put up with them for which I think I wrote in my last, half a dozen at least. If you've any objection, make it. I'll rather buy, than rob you.

Saunders has yet neither Colly-flowers nor Straw-berrys. But He gave me on Sunday some fine young Turnips.

I am glad the new bed of Ranunculus are so fine. Magahan[4] rais'd them himself, from seed sav'd in his own garden. You may do the same. The Ranunculus Mr Meade[5] gave you, will afford seed in plenty. Enjoin Gannon strictly to take care to save it. You must attend to this your Self, or it will not be done. So you must to the taking up the Tulips &c. and to every thing else. Ask me as often as you please about such things, which otherwise will go out of my head. I shall be glad to be put in mind of them. I hope you have asparagus now in plenty.

I hope your new Musick-master[6] will continue to please. I believe He is a very good one. It will be your own fault if you do not improve.

Two of Mr Ewing's books I order'd, and am glad of.[7] One is for you. I hope you'll pay for the binding at least. But before you send it to Cudmore[8] Pray shew it to Lawson, unless you can your Self find that it is the fine Novel, which I so much admire, and in which *la Cousine*[9] is. I doubt, because Ewing's note says, *Memoires de Gondez*,[10] which may be some trifling book not worth a button. If so, return it; and return the *Consideration sur la Decadence* &c.[11] I have it already. Lawson I think has it not. Tell him therefore of it. *The Principes du Droit Naturel*, if, *par* Burlomaqui must be bound, – but it need not be sent hither.[12]

As to the Parma-cheese, Eat it, or treat your friends with it. I'll allow no Wine nor butter to it. Nor is it worth while to send it down here. See what a valuable present I make you.

You'll probably expect some account of our new-marry'd neighbour. She appears very properly in her house and every where else, as far as I can yet observe. Coll. Sandford and Rachel[13] were there when I came hither. I din'd with them. They all the next day with me – yesterday I din'd agen there with Strokes-town and Clonfree, who remember you all with great affection. The Ladys are very well.

And now, all things consider'd, I think I have done pretty well; and so My Dear Dear Girl for this time Adieu. Blessing to Jane, and service to Mrs Jourdan but tell her, that if she does not instantly send me down some very good Sallad Oyl, I would not give a Louse for her – Some must be sent, the best that can be got.

yours &c.
Edw:Elphin

In the Study just behind the Door lyes a good deal of Paper in heaps. There are particularly two Parcels of quarto wrote on thus. Rheam of Demi Gilt, or some such Words. Send down one of these parcels just as it is. You may put it in the Case, which must be made for the Table yet to come down. After all, the New Tables are very handsome.

I had a letter yesterday from Godfrey Wills. His second son has the small pox at Athlone, but He tells me it is of a good kind.[14]

Among the papers which I left on my Table were two accounts of Books. See if you can find and send them to me. I don't mean printed Catalogues, but accounts of Books bought by Ross. Most of them were bought for young Hickes here. I want them to account with his Father. If you can't find them Desire Will to go to Ross, and bid him send me a new account as well as He can on his Memory.

If Mr Vipond calls or Sends for the Papers relating to Mr Pearse's affairs, which I shew'd you in the middle drawer of my Table, Let him have them.[15]

Tell John Miller that Casey a Carr-Man whom He knows will be in town almost assoon as this. If the Table be ready, It may come by him. So may the China, and the Oyl and Colours which I wrote to him about last post. Mr Eaton is to get them. Bid him also to send by him, if he has Carrs for it, half a Tunn of Iron of the same kinds and in the same proportion as the last. I wish He would send me 40 or 50 Boards.

Mrs Heap desires a dozen Syllibub[16] Glasses, and a dozen Jelly.

[Free Edw:Elphin]

1. Oliver Cary married Frances, daughter of Col William Southwell and niece of Lord Southwell. They were married by Mr Bradish at St Peter's church, Dublin on 10 February, 1749. She died in 1804. Leslie, *Ferns*, pp.33-4; *St Peter and St Kevin*, p.327.

2. Possibly Thomas Adderly who was Treasurer of the Hospital for Incurables in 1750. *Irish Builder*, xxxviii (1896), p.28.

3. Williams: a Dublin farrier.

4. Magahan: a gardener at Kevin Street.

5. Probably one of the Meade family of Cork. Edward Synge's cousin George Synge married Margaret Meade of Kinsale in 1706. Synge, p.7; Welply, Vol. 18, p.6.

6. George Walsh (d.1765): organist at St Anne's, Dublin, from 1743. Boydell, p.292.

7. George Ewing: bookseller at the Angel and Bible. Gilbert, Vol. 2, p.270.

8. Daniel Cudmore (1714-*c*.87): bookbinder, son of Daniel Cudmore, bookbinder, of Fishamble Street was born in June 1714. On 14 June 1744 he petitioned for admittance to the Guild of St Luke the Evangelist (which contained cutlers, painter-stainers, and stationers) as quarter brother and served apprenticeship to William Smith. Free of City in 1756 by service and sworn free of Guild. Noted as dead in the Guild's annual list in 1787. I am most grateful to Paul Pollard for information about Daniel Cudmore and his wife, Jane.

9. '*La cousine*': a character in a novel. Not identified.

10. [Marguerite de Lussan], *The Life of the Countess of Gondez Written by her own hand in French and dedicated to the Princess de la Roche-sur-Yon And now faithfully translated into English by Mrs P. Aubin* (London 1729).

11. Anon [Henri de Montesquieu], *Considerations sur les causes de Romains et de leur decadence* (Edimbourg 1736).

12. Jean-Jacques Burlomaqui, *[Principes du droit naturel] The principles of natural law. In which the true systems of morality and civil government are established* ... Translated into English by Mr Nugent (London 1748).

13. Rachel Sandford: born a Miss Southwell, a relation of Mrs Cary.

14. See Letter 88 fn. 2. Godfrey and Sarah Wills had two sons. The eldest was Thomas. Burke (1912), p.624.

15. A Daniel Pearce was a tenant of land at Balinresig, Co. Limerick, a property inherited by Edward Synge from Samuel Synge, dean of Kildare. Abstracts of the Bishop of Elphin's Title ... , NLI ms 2102, f.15.

16. Syllabub was a rich dessert, made with cream and served in glasses. Hannah Glasse has a recipe which calls for thick cream, sack, the juice of Seville oranges or lemons and their peel, whisked together with sugar. She suggests that the mixture could be coloured with spinach or cochineal. Glasse, p.144.

85

Dublin [*sic*] May 26, 1750

You must be content this bout, huzzy, with a short letter. I bless God I am very well, but have so many other letters on my hands, that I have no time for you. Besides I have at present little further to say.

Tell your Uncle I thank him for his Letter. In it He mentions a Book sent him by the Author. If it be not the same with that which you told me was left for me, Desire him to send it me by Jemy. He has rais'd in me great Curiosity to see it. Love to your Aunt, and blessing to the Young ones.

I can't say but Boyer[1] may be right. Ask Lawson, if you see him. But I am sure I have caught you, Madam, at a false Spelling, which no Authority can justify. You write *pitence*, it ought to *be pittance*. The Adjective to it is also wrong spelt for company. *Accustomed* is right. You have omitted a c.

Send a Card to Mrs Whetcombe with my Compliments, and Tell her, her Message was unnecessary. For I always think of her, as one who does what she ought.

When next you see Mrs Silver, Pray make my Compliments to her also, and Tell her, Vast hurry prevented my waiting on her before I left town. I must beg she'd excuse this, and further that she'll give her Self the trouble of repeating to you, her method of infusing Hops. I want to have the whole Exact, that Her method may not be discredited by bungling management.

I miss here a Book which ought to have come down. Wilkins's *Sermons.*[2] I sent it to Cudmore's to be bound, and think He sent it home, but am not sure. Some Books are lying on the Floor, or on Chairs in the Outer Study. Look there for it. If you find it not, Ask Cudmore about it.

In my last you had answers to your Questions. So My Dear Dear Girl Adieu.

yours &c.
Edw: Elphin

I am very sorry for the Continuance of poor Louse's jaw-Ach.[3]

[Free Edw:Elphin. In another hand: 'beauty is comely a drole expression']

1. Abel Boyer, *Dictionnaire Royal Française et Anglais, divisé en deux parties* (first edition The Hague 1699), frequently consulted by Edward Synge. Abel Boyer (1667-1729) was a Huguenot who came to England in 1689. He taught French and wrote pamphlets supporting the Whigs. He is best known for his monthly *Political State of Great Britain*, 1711-29. Graham C. Gibbs, 'Abel Boyer: the Making of a British Subject', *Proceedings of the Huguenot Society* Vol. 26 (1994) 1, pp.14-44.

2. Possibly John Wilkins (1614-72), *Sermons preach'd upon several occasions: by ... Dr. John Wilkins, Late Lord Bishop of Chester.* The second edition (London 1701).

3. A reference to Jane Synge at Kevin Street.

86

Elphin. May 30, 1750.

Make up the enclos'd, My Dear Girl, in one of L[or]d Chan[cello]r's Franks, and super-scribe it thus. To Mr Richard Varly at Bohn to be left at Mr. Rowson's at the Blew-bell in Snath Yorkshire Great Britain.[1] Make the pacquet up neatly that L[or]d Chan[cello]r's name be not disgrac'd. You or Mrs Jourdan may write the Superscription in them Words properly dispos'd *a la mode* of Superscriptions.

In No.5 in the Wine Cellar, There's a small parcel of Brandy, mostly pints. But on the Top there are 4 Quarts, three full – One of these full ones, Make up very carefully in something or other and send it off hither. Take care that it doe not break in Carriage as most of my Hungary Water[2] did, by Squire Curtis's carelessness in packing. Ask him who ought to pay for that He or I? You may when you've convenient package send two or three bottles more. When Brandy is wanting on any Occasion, you may use Pints. But Touch not quarts, not even the broken ones.

If Saunders says true, you've a large tuft of some kind of Hellabore in the Garden, in the Herb quarter near the Alley. It's a large Tuft not unlike Angelica. Gannon knew it not. Saunders gives that name to one of the same kind here.

I believe your objections to the sending all the China I wrote for, may be just enough. When I see what you send me, I shall be better able to judge, and to tell what further I want.

Your sentence is awkard, as you say it is. The way to avoid this is to form your whole Sentence in your little pate, before you begin to write. This too will be a cure for that quality of which you so truly, and frankly own that you have a great share. 'Tis indeed a fault that will mend, but not unless Means be us'd. You see the little redness in your leg induces the Doctor to give you a little Physick. I hope it will have the effect.

Poor Jane's adventure made me laugh. I suppose she look'd as sometimes, when I give her a gentle Tap; grave, her colour rais'd, and Eyes cast down – Or did she bounce like a Mad thing and run to the Opposite side of the room? Bid her be comforted, and if Mrs Jourdan insults her on this new Name Let her retort the one I lately gave her; which I expected some sport from. But you only tell me gravely about the Oyl.

I am vex'd at the riots. I wish they do not end in mischief. Agen let me repeat my Caution to you all. Do not appear even at a Window in that kind of dress, till they are over. But let my Window-Curtains stand. I had rather have the Windows broke, than appear to yield to a rabble. But I think they are in no danger.[3]

I give you joy of your Canary bird, and am much pleas'd you refus'd the Nightingale. That Spark is fond of such assiduitys, and presents. He hopes to find his account in them. But He is mistaken – keep him at distance, and leave him as to Garden affairs to Gannon.

I spent Monday at Strokes-town, yesterday at French-park. All at the former place are very well, and Jeny a glorious girl.[4] She is like to be the flower of the Flock. Poor Coll. French is indeed a miserable spectacle. But He is in very good Spirits. Mrs French looks as well, as you ever saw her: so does Matty.[5] Biddy the famous Canary bird is dead. Mrs French imputes her death to her being kept too long in the Breeding Cage, and laying too many eggs. This may be a good Caution to you.

You have probably observ'd little Leather Straps, which they put into the Holes of Sticks or Canes, as Fine Gentlemen do Silken ones. I want a Couple of these. They may be had at Toy-shops, or in Hell – Get them and send them to me.[6] I believe they may come by post, one at a time. Take care that the Weight of all be not two ounces. Adieu. The Post waits.

yours &c.
E. E.

I am glad Bob Curtis is recover'd. News for you. Pat[7] is at last turn'd off – Incorrigibly drunken and boistrous and, as I lately found, makes the Boys so. Monday night He and Billy Beaty were both in an horrible pickle – Don't you be vex'd now at this – Peter shall practice every day, and depend on it, I will not go into the Coach with six, till He is perfect. If I do not find him clever John shall look out for one that is. But Pat is not longer to be born.

You never mention Carbery Berne. Ask the Doctor about him.[8]

[Free Edw:Elphin. In another hand 'I love writing']

1. Richard Varly of Balne, Snaith, Yorkshire, was a relative of Charles Varley the agriculturalist, who was staying with Edward Synge in 1750.

2. Hungary Water: an infusion of rosemary flowers in alcohol.

3. During most of the eighteenth century weavers living in the Liberties frequently rioted in protest against the importation of food and cloth. In May 1734 a mob of weavers had rifled shops in the city which sold English goods and the army had to be called out. Edward Synge was well aware of the risks of living on the borders of the Meath Liberty. The riot in May 1750, when women were assaulted in the streets, was reported as due to 'some wicked and malicious People in Meath Street, the Coombe and Parts adjacent cut the clothes of all women without Distinction who appear in the neighbourhood with Cheque Gowns printed or stained Linen or Cottons ...'. Patrick Fagan, *The Second City: Portrait of Dublin 1700-1760* (Dublin 1986); *Faulkner's Dublin Journal,* 12-15 May 1750.

4. Jane Mahon.

5. Martha French: daughter of William Lennox. In 1751 she married George French, of Innfield, Co. Roscommon, son of Arthur French. Burke (1916), p.610.

6. Hell was a passage leading to the old Four Courts from Christ Church Lane where 'the yard was full of shops where toys, and fireworks and kites ... were exposed for sale.' Gilbert, Vol. 1, pp.142, 144-5.

7. Pat: the coachman.

8. Carbery Byrne had been sent to Mercer's Hospital. Carbry Byrne of Cloghermore, parish of Elphin, was a constable. He was Catholic and married with one child under fourteen. Census, f.8.

87

Elphin. June 1, 1750

A Word or two, My Dear Girl, before the post comes in, to lighten what I may have to write after.

I see in the News an Advertisement of two Humorous little papers, which pray buy and send me. You may divide them into as many Covers as you please. You'll be somewhat entertain'd with them, but not so much as I was and shall, for want of a key. The Titles are

A full and true Account of the dreadfull and Melancholy Earthquake, which happen'd on Thursday &c.[1]

Aminadab one of the people call'd Quakers to the Bishop of L.[2]

Between Shannon and Foxal I am ill serv'd. I order'd two new Coasters, the same with those which Foxal had made for me before. Instead of these, I have two, not so large, nor so deep. They are ugly to the sight, and inconvenient in the Use. Pray order that Gent. to make two right ones, and Let them be sent down the first convenient opportunity. When I chid Shannon for taking such, He gave me according to Custom a Wise answer. Why! He had no others, nor was there then time to get them.

Yours is come with that which always gives the highest pleasure, an account that you are very well. God keep you so. I am sorry your dose of Salts was too small. You must, I suppose, be teaz'd with a *Repetatur cum incremento.*[3] Let the Doctor give you the English. But it is no great matter.

I am glad you've at last got the Boots. It was not Heyney but Higgins that neglected.[4]

I am sorry for the Riots of which you give an account. I hope they will not hurt or frighten you. If you are under any Apprehensions, Get John Miller to sleep in town. Or send to Anthony Robinson.[5] I am sure He'll do every thing He can to keep things quiet about you.

You say I forgot to answer two of your Questions. That in relation to the Butter-Woman I thought I had answer'd before I left town and running mine Eye quick over your letter, I consider'd what you wrote about it, rather as telling me what you had done, than as asking what you should do. You know I told you, you must make as good Terms, as you could. But that I was not fond of putting it to hazard, whether I should have good Butter. Your Question about Mrs Delany[6] went out of mine head. I think you'll do right to go and see her.

Your account of your Aunt[7] pleases. I long to have her safe at Roscrea. By your list of particulars I fear you've done a Simple thing in sending the

China you have sent. It is probable that All the crack'd plates will be broke in the Carriage. I see Mrs Jourdan has wrote in her Memorandum the first letter of her favorite Word, and so has own'd the Name I gave her. Next time I hope she'll be so reconcil'd, as to write it at length.

Lest Mr Vipond should call agen to no purpose, Get the Keys from Ned Curtis, that the Papers may be ready for him.

If one of your last false spellings was inexcusable what will you say for another now before me? You write, Docter. I thought you had known that it ought to be Doctor.

Your sending the Book by Miss Ormsby was lucky enough. By a late letter from Lewis, I find that He and his little Wife intend soon to make me a Visit. It will fall in with one to Mrs Cary, and another at Charles-town. These last din'd here to day.[8] Adieu.

> yours &c.
> Edw: Elphin

[Free Edw:Elphin]

1. [P.D.], *A full and true account of the dreadful and melancholy earthquake which happened between twelve and one o'clock in the morning, on Thursday the fifth instant with an exact list of such persons as have hitherto been found in the rubbish. In a letter from a gentleman to a friend in the country.* The fourth edition (London printed for Tim. Tremor, near the Temple-Gate, Fleet Street. 1750). It is attributed to Richard Bradley or Paul Whitehead.

2, *Aminadab, one of the people called Quakers, to the B——p of L——n; on his Letter to the clergy and inhabitants of London and Westminster, concerning the late earthquakes* (London 1750). B——p of L——n is Thomas Sherlock.

3. Repeat with increasing force.

4. Heyney: not known.

5. Anthony Robinson: not known.

6. Mrs Delany (1700-88): Mary Delany was born Mary Granville. She was brought up in the expectation of being a member of Queen Anne's court, but when the Whigs came to power her family fell out of favour and she married Alexander Pendarves, an elderly widower. On his death she married Dr Patrick Delany in 1743. Her letters to her sister and members of her family are an important source for the social history of Ireland in the mid-eighteenth century. *DNB*.

7. Elizabeth, wife of Nicholas Synge.

8. Gilbert King of Charlestown.

88

Elphin. June 5, 1750

Critical Notes on Miss Synge's last letter, the exact writing of which proves, as much, that she resolves to excell in that accomplishment, as the Correctness of her Expressions shews that she's a Complete Mistress of Stile.

Don't be frighten'd now, Huzzy, as if something terrible was to follow. But being quite alone, and the Afternoon too hot for walking, I can't amuse my self more agreably, than by remarking on some inaccuracys in your writing which ought to be taken notice of some time or other, because indeed they are more or less in every letter. Your general excuse is Giddiness. But it is time now to take away the Cause, at least gradually to lessen it.

The Writing of your first Page is well. That of the second, pretty well. The third betokens hurry, and is like this time two year.

L.2. *receipt* is the Old Spelling. So *temps* in French. But the polite moderns have dropp'd the p in both.

L.3. *I doubt not that half the town.* I can't say I doubt, that this is not correct English. I am sure it is not. Consider it a little and you'll find it out your Self. There ought to be *but*, between not and that, or you might drop *that* to make it run smoother, tho' this is authoriz'd rather by Custom than Grammar.

The same line. *heard yr* speech. It should either be *heard of*, or the word, *repeated*, should be added.

No one hears my speech, who does not hear me speak.

L.6. How come you to write *Kve?* Say honestly, Was it because you did not know how to spell the Word? I apprehend it to be *Keeve*[1] but am not certain.

L.9. *She* goes to Kilkenny. In strict Grammar this should be Mrs Silver – I know you mean Mrs Nicholson.

The Last in the Page. *Saunders is, I believe, right.* This is harsh, as you justly complain'd a Sentence in a late letter was. It should be, *I believe Saunders is right.*

Pag.2. L.4 and 5. I should fear I had a tendency to ingratitude, if I neglected it, so to avoid this Self imputation &c. Lady Arbella's or Molly Curtis's stile! not right, because too swelling. Easy and natural is best.

L.6. and so to avoid Self imputation, you'll teaze me. I thank you. You might have express'd your Self more Civilly, Mistress; as I gave you commission to write about the Garden as much as you pleas'd.

Pag.3.L.3.I COMMITTED a great OMISSION – A bouncer this. A direct Contradiction in Terms. You may as well *be*, and not *be, do* and not *do* at the same time.

And here I'll stop for this time. For this gave occasion to all the rest of my Criticisms. They would not have made a great figure without it.

Now for the Contents. Thank Mrs Silver for her receit, and Tell her I must trouble her with one Question more. It is this. How in nice brewing should the Barm be manag'd? Their Manner here is, To stir it lustily in the Wort once every 24 hours. I have heard this practice much blam'd; and I impute the Constant muddiness of all my drink to it. I can't say 'tis thick – But it has a wheyish look, and wants clearness. In every other respect it is very good. She, who is Exact in Every thing, can probably assign the Cause of this Evil, and put Mrs Heap in a Way of avoiding it for the Future.

The sun is now on the decline. So I'll go Walk. If your Weather be like ours, you'll know that I wrote the above on Monday. For this day is cool, and there has been some rain; nothing equal to our Wants.

I am sorry Ned Curtis plays the fool as you tell me He does. Sure among you all, you may bring him into better order. I know the Hungary Water is paid for. But the bad packing is not. I shall take care not to be in his debt for it. Pray Tell him so. Either I have blunder'd, or you do. The three or four bottles more I desir'd were Hungary Water. Pray Let me know what reason you had for thinking I meant Brandy.

By a letter yesterday from Mr Waller I learn that All the Children are inoculated, and the pock appears on all in the most favorable manner.[2] But Mrs Waller her self has been very ill with a Cold, and Quinancy[3] (That's the true spelling, but I'll allow you to write with the Rabble, Quinzy) which confin'd her to chamber and bed. This, bad at any time, was worse at this. But some good luck with bad. She had the benefit of a good Physician, and is now recovering. Where would be the hurt if you wrote to congratulate her on this recovery, and on her Childrens being all past this ugly disorder? It will be time enough, when you know all is over. Do it then if you like it. But Take care, No Self imputation &c.

You are right about the Tulips. Let the stems of the fine ones be cut with the Sheers about 2 or 3 inches from the Ground. You may serve all in the Beds so. But those in the borders may stand that you may have a Chance for seed.

You did well in sending the Nosegay, and as well in declining the invitation. If your little fond heart be set on shewing your pretty Coat, you may have occasions enough of gratifying it. Tho' I advis'd against galloping as much as usual, I did not mean to have you hermits and recluses – Nor shall I like your being so. See your friends &c. as usual.

Pat. was indeed a nuisance, greater than I apprehended, tho' I saw a good deal of him more than I appear'd to see. But I find since his going, what I did not indeed suspect before, that My Horses waited often at Alehouse-doors, while He was fudling; and to this some of their disorders are certainly to be imputed. The Horse I bought last, has at this time a great cold got, I believe, the day that finish'd the Gent. here. He went to water, and air his horses, his boys with him. The first march was to Mantua,[4] where He visited Mr Dowel's Coach-man; and Beaty was admitted into the

Company. Jac, as He told me himself with great innocence, made a visit at the same time to the Postilion. I believe they had no drink. For Jac was perfectly sober. Beaty was fuddled as well as his Master. But not content with what they got there, They finished them selves with Whisky at Flask.[5] Judge what came of my Horses. I could not after this keep this fellow, tho' ever so destitute of help. I think I am not. For with a little practice Peter will do very well. Poor fellow! Three days ago, I fear'd I should loose him. He was taken excessively ill on Friday. By good luck for him I by accident found it out that Evening, and got Stafford to him, who vomited him. He had been blouded before. All this not withstanding He was so ill Saturday and Sunday, that We thought him in danger. But two bleedings more, one in the foot, and a stout Blister on Sunday night, reliev'd him so that Stafford thinks him in a very good Way. His disorder is a fever. I have not gone near him, nor Will I. So be easy; and He lyes in one of the Offices, so as to be remov'd from the rest of the Servants. Every one else is well. I hope they'll continue so. I chose to depend on Stafford, rather than send for your friend Diganan.

Poor Louse! I am sorry for her painfull adventure, and shall be more so, if she has not lost her pain with the piece of her tooth. She may spit, and say filthy dirty creature as much as she pleases. But she has assum'd the Name by writing the first letter, and so must expect sometimes to have it given her.

What you write of the Calico W—— does not at all prove me mistaken.[6] She went from the Window, that's plain, and I still insist that she look'd as I describ'd her. Her attempt to return to the Window proves it. I think she was right, and you and your Cosen, and Mrs Jourdan wrong in hind'ring her. The Mob would have done her, or the Windows no mischief.

You give a very probable account of your poor Aunt's low spirits. It's a great misfortune to be affected as she is with thunder and light-ning. I think you are yet clear of that folly, tho', if I mistake not, Louse, is not. Keep your Self so, and learn not to be afraid of a Mouse.

The Straps came safe, and are very right. Thank the Apothecary[7] for them. The Carriage is arriv'd, and All safe. This will please you, as I doubt not but you were alarm'd by my last for your crack'd Plates. This supply of Plates will do very well, but for dishes We are still to seek. Upon a general Consultation this morning, It is resolv'd, that if you'll send four dishes of the same size with the one now sent down, We shall be tolerably well equipp'd. Get them therefore and send them, when you can, and with them two Glass-plates, or Salvers, to lay on dishes on which Jellys, or Sill-abubs are to stand. There is one large one here. Two of a midling size, such as would suit not the largest, but the second size of the Burnt China, are wanting. Have a care that there be no cast in them.

Carleboe wants linnen to make cloths in which to boil his Meat. This demand is owing to an hearty chiding He got the other day for sending up a very fine Turky with so very bad a look, that No one car'd to meddle with it.[8] He seems in earnest resolv'd to take more care for the future. But without these same cloths, He cannot do it. Pray Let them be provided, that He may have no excuse.

By a letter from Godfrey Wills yesterday, I find his Son is out of danger. I doubt not but you have all some curiosity to know how I am affected by the Change in Cary's condition. I therefore tell you, that Hitherto matters are extremely different from what they were in old times. But the Change, within doors at least, is so far from giving me uneasiness, that I am rather pleas'd with it. Cary sticks close to home, so as never to have breakfasted, or supp'd here, since I came, only once He took a dish of chocolate because He lik'd it. And He has din'd here but once without his Wife, whom I have ask'd oft'ner than she chose to come. She has now with her, one of the Miss Pocklingtons, who appears to be a grave well behav'd young Woman.[9] They din'd here on Sunday, and probably I may not see them till the next. Mrs C as well as I can yet judge, appears to be of a mild easy temper, well bred, but rather reserv'd. I am far from blaming this on the whole. But I believe it will stand in the way of the same free correspondence, which I had with the good Woman that's gone. Nor can I yet judge whether his sticking so close to home be his own Act, or owing to her. They have indeed been a good deal engag'd in receiving the civilitys of the neighbourhood, and will be in returning them. All this over, things will fall into a setled state. But what that will be, I can't yet judge, nor am I anxious about it. I shall have company enough; and if sometimes I am alone, It will be an agreable variety – What I feel most is, His inattention to matters abroad. But the only notice I take of this is, to attend more to them my Self; and Hitherto I have done very well. There is indeed a great deal to set in order. For there have been great neglects this Winter. But as I expected all this, so I fret not at it, but go on quietly, to bring every thing into a right way. Say nothing of this except to Lawson. When I get him here, I shall be secure from all inconvenience from Solitude. Hitherto I have felt none.

And so My Dear Girl Adieu for this time.

yours &c.
E. E.

I see Captain Clark's *Trial* advertis'd.[10] If it be not a Grub-street paper, send it down. I see in the News that one of the Miss Flack's is dead. Is it my Band-maker?[11]

1. A tub or vat for brewing or bleaching.

2. There was an epidemic of smallpox in 1750. It accounted for some 10 to 15 per cent of all deaths in some European countries in the eighteenth century and 80 per cent of the victims were children under the age of ten. Inoculation was by variolation, the artificial infection with smallpox of healthy people, in the hope of producing a mild case of the disease and subsequent immunity. This was done by taking fluid from active smallpox pustules and scratching the fluid on the skin. If done well, the result was a mild infection; the death rate was around 3 to 4 per cent. Variolation was practised by folk healers, not physicians; it was popular with the upper classes in Britain in the 1720s. A.W. Crosby, 'Smallpox', Kiple pp.1010-11.

3. Quinsy: inflammation of the throat; tonsillitis.

4. Mantua House, Castlerea, Co. Roscommon, was a Palladian house which Bence-Jones says was built in about 1747 for Oliver Grace, who married the daughter of John Dowell. It has been attributed to Richard Castle. However, from Edward Synge's letters it is clear that the house was still lived in by the Dowell family in 1750. It is now derelict. Bence-Jones, pp.200-1; Glin, Griffin and Robinson, p.127.

5. Flask: a village near Elphin.

6. Obscure.

7. Edward Curtis.

8. Hannah Glasse did not like boiling fowls wrapped in a cloth. She believed that by roasting 'They will be both sweeter and whiter than if boil'd in a Cloth.' Glasse, p.7.

9. Miss Pocklington: not known.

10. *The trial of Capt. Edward Clark, commander of His Majesty's ship the Canterbury, for the murder of Capt. Tho. Innes, ... in a duel in Hyde-park, March 12, 1749. At Justice-Hall in the Old Bailey; on Thursday the 26th of April 1750* (London 1750).

11. 'Died Miss Flack, an eminent Milliner, in Werbergh Street.' *Dublin Courant*, 29 May-2 June 1750.

89

Elphin. June 8, 1750

Letters of business have taken me up all day. My Dear Girl must therefore be content with a short one.

I am very glad your riots of all kinds are over. Tho' you are not apt to be frighted except at a Mouse, yet I shall be better pleas'd not to have you put into an Hurry, by any of those Tumults.

You rally Madam Louse on her Aversion. Has she not at least as much reason to laugh at you for yours? I think you had best spend a quarter of an hour Each day in calling each other by the Name of what you detest. It may in time wear off the Aversion. But here you'll have the advantage. Mouse is a fond name. The other not usually so. Yet a fine Horse bore it.

Learn I pray you from Mrs Silver, or in some other way, how a letter may be directed to Arthur Pomeroy,[1] and when you have got his Address, send it in writing to Mr Vipond. That's all. He'll do the rest, I wish to have done.

You may send for little Shannon as often as you please. If you had told me earlier, what his Father said or rather did not say, when by my direction you spoke to him, you had had him before I left you.

Molly Fagan, so you ought to spell the name, is very well. I once or twice intended to have told you so. But a multitude of other things drove this out of my head. When I wrote last I was in great pain for poor Peter. He is now in a fair way of being well.

Desire Mrs Jourdan to get a doz. yards of Canvas bought such as is fit for Safes.[2] Carleboe must it seems have one in his lower Larder. Would you believe it? He and Mrs Heap are fighting in a mild way perpetually for their respective Conveniencys. I told them the other day, that I believ'd I must build an house or two more for them. Thus peoples Wants increase as their Riches do. Few houses in Ireland have as many Conveniencys as this.

Half a hundred of hops must be bought, and sent down to serve us till new ones come in. Mrs Jourdan knows very well how to chuse them.

I shall be uneasy till I have an account of your good Aunt's being at Roscrea. I believe your Uncle said what He did to encourage her. Yet He is apt to entertain sanguine hopes, for which I am too sure there is no foundation. You'll see poor Mrs French of Porte soon in town, if she be able to get thither. By her husband's account to me the other day, I apprehend that she is in somewhat the same condition with your Aunt. This in a Whisper. But she'll have a better chance, as she applys earlier for relief. She'll be under Dr Smith's care.[3]

You may cut Asparagus to the End of the Month, but cut those only which shoot vigorously: and Let a few of the most Vigorous go now for seed. I am glad Finglas Garden makes up for the Deficiencys of Kevin-street. I am here not so well as the Worst of the two. No sign of a Colly-flower yet. A small sprinkling of Pease twice; and as for Cucumbers, Saunders furnish'd one, and when Shannon ask'd for more, He answer'd pompously, that All his first Crop was gone.

I thank you for the Pamphlets. *Aminadab* you could understand. The other is Court History, which I know but imperfectly, you not at all. They are both clever in their kind.

I learn'd the other day that Mrs Wynne[4] remains in town all Summer. I don't know but that the Widow[5] does too. Do not neglect waiting on them.

Let me know if Dr Echlin's family be gone out of town.

Adieu
yours &c. Edw: Elphin

We have had fine rain yesterday and to day.

I am very impatient for some account of my printed Cottons for the Beds. You must spur Grant. If He does not get them ready soon, I must have them provided, if possible, some other Way.

Tell John that He must buy me a barrel of right good Rape seed tho' it were to cost 4d. a quart. I am preparing ground here to sow it. I am tir'd with his account from time to time, that the Chesnut Horse is coming on, and will be very well in a little time. But I know not how to help my Self. He must not be neglected, and yet it is very hard upon me to want him, and Jemy too.

Bid John ask Williams whether He did not send down by Pat some doses of Physick for 'Captain' whose wind was doubtfull. If He did I hope they are here still, but am not sure. Let him however give Jemy, before He comes off, directions about giving it.

A fine soft Brush for brushing my Cloths, with an handle to it. They have one here so hard, that it will wear them out in a Month.

We are in great pother about Pewter. Carleboe says He has not so many plates as last year by two doz. and fewer dishes. As I expect a Service of Rohan Ware,[6] I have no mind to buy more Pewter, if I could help it. Have you any to spare. He must, it seems, have a baking dish or two, such, He says as those in town.

[Free Edw:Elphin]

1. Arthur Pomeroy was a son of the Ven. John Pomeroy, archdeacon of Cork and Elizabeth, daughter of Edmond Donnellan of Cloghan, Co. Roscommon. He married Mary, daughter of Henry and Lady Mary Colley on 20 October 1747. See Letter 22. Burke (1916), p.985.

2. Cupboards to store food.

3. Charles Smith (*c.*1715-62): physician and topographer. Born in Waterford, he became an apothecary in Dungarvan. In 1744 he wrote, with Walter Harris, a history of Co. Down, the first of a proposed series of Irish county histories. In the same year he founded the Physico-Historical Society in Dublin to provide materials for further histories, and went on to write the history of Waterford, Cork and Kerry. In 1758 he was founder with other Dublin doctors, of the Medico-Philosophical Society. He died in Bristol. He practised in Longford Street. Smith is regarded as the pioneer of Irish topography. *DNB*; Watson (1760), p.48.

4. Possibly Anne Butler, wife of Col Owen Wynne. Burke, *LGI* (1912), p.780.

5. Possibly Elizabeth Knott, widow of Lt Col John Wynne and mother of Col Owen Wynne. Burke (1979), p.26.

6. Rohan ware: china made in Rouen (Seine Inferieure), France in the seventeenth and eighteenth century. It was of *pâte dure*, decorated with flowers in bright colours. It appears in mid-eighteenth century Irish inventories as 'Rhoan ware'. M.-A.-A. Mareschal, *Les Faïences anciennes et modernes Leurs Marques et Décors* (Beauvais 1868), pp.48-59.

90

Elphin. June 7, 1750.

My Dear Girl.

The enclos'd is Varly's answer to the letter which came in Mrs Jourdan's. Enclose it in one of the Chan[cello]r's Cover, and direct it, as you did the last. Lest you should have forgot, I send you the direction in Varly's very bad writing. But As you've had it before in better, I suppose you'll make it out. Be sure it goes to the post on Tuesday night.

I still think our Doctor laugh'd with a very grave face. When I get him hither, if it comes into my head, I'll ask him.

The Adventure of the Louse made me laugh heartily. I think you've drawn the Scene very well, tho' probably short of the life. Have a care that Mrs J has not an opportunity of being even with you. The only sure way to guard against this, is to get over your ridiculous antipathy to an Animal even more inoffensive than that which occasions her disgust. She tells me there is some curiosity among you, about my not taking notice of your having din'd at the College. When you do any thing of which I do not approve, you'll certainly hear of it. But I have not always time or room or inclination, to take notice of every thing you do or intend, to which I have no objection. I suppose now you'll think, that the fewer of your adventures I remark on, the better.

I think you judge right between the two Ladys.[1] But As the World goes, She whom you like least, has some merit. Consider, she's a painter, and there is painting in Words, as well as on Canvass – Are you sure, that it was not want of taste in you, that occasion'd your not relishing her descriptions? Be as severe as you please in your Censures on your Self. But with respect to others, Let candor prevail, tho' not to such a degree, as to be blind to real imperfections, or, what is worse, fantastical affectations.

Mr Lloyd[2] has deliver'd his charge. I am much surpriz'd that Wilkins's *Sermons* are not to be found. Did you ask Cudmore about them? I am almost sure I gave them to him to bind, but can't recollect whether He return'd them.

I am glad you like the Stopping exercise. I think I already see you have benefited by it. Perhaps this may be only, because I wish it. But if you have not, you will. Contrary to Custom, your Postcripts are better wrote than your letter, tho' that is not to be complain'd of. But I see one false spelling. It is Chesnut. You have ramm'd in a t.

I believe you've drawn Mrs Hunter's Character very Exactly. She'll hardly shew it.

Pray Ask Mrs Jourdan whether she be acquainted with this phrase, *Dents de Sagesse*.[3] Boyer is not. I know the meaning. But Have you yet any of the kind?

Jane is rearing three Pea-chicks. The Brood was four. But one dy'd the day after it was hatch'd – Another brood is expected. But of the rest, no account. I think you are not very lucky in your pets or Stock. Of all your Cow kind, There remains but one poor yearling Heifer. To comfort you, It is the handsomest you ever had, or this Country affords. It goes by your name, not for that reason, but to fix the property. I hope you'll have better luck with it, than you had with it's Dam or Grandam.

You need not trouble your Self with sending agen to Councellor Trench. When I spoke to Grant and Moore about the Beds, I quite forgot linings. The standing bed must certainly be lin'd. I believe the Field bed would be better so.[4] Determine this among you as you please; and chuse linings as you like. But let the Beds be dispatch'd and sent down. I shall then be furnish'd, as fully as at present I wish to be. Adieu.

yours &c.
Edw:Elphin

Little spotted things are the fittest for linings. If you think otherwise, follow your own fancys.

[Free Edw:Elphin]

1. Obscure.

2. Possibly Christopher Lloyd (1678-1757): dean of Elphin. Admitted to TCD in 1698, he became DD in 1716. He was dean of Elphin 1739-57. *Alumni*, p.505; Leslie, Elphin, p.18.

3. *Dents de Sagesse*: wisdom teeth.

4. Standing beds appear in sixteenth-century inventories. By the eighteenth century they were more usually known as 'stump beds', which had a wooden framework, probably with a sacking bottom, on four short legs with a wooden headboard. Field beds, usually with folding frames, could be easily dismantled. They enabled people to move from one house to another and were also used by travellers in inns, where beds might not be clean. Field beds were not necessarily utilitarian in style; they could be upholstered with velvet or tapestry. Ivan Sparkes, *An Illustrated History of English Domestic Furniture* (Bourne End 1980), pp.40, 41-2.

91

Elphin. June 12, 1750

My Dear Girl.

All this week and the End of the last I have had a Succession of Offi-cers. Some new ones are come to town, whom I expect every minute. This, and long letters of business all this morning disable me from writing much to you.

I see my Critical Notes have for the present some good effects. See that they continue. I find no incorrectnesses in your Stile this bout, nor any more than one false Spelling. You write inflamatery. There ought to be two ms and o instead of e. In strictness these are two. But as they are in one Word, they shall pass for one.

Let Will speak to Ross to send me the Catalogue. Or rather Let him bring it to you, and see that you make it up within weight. *Zayde* is for Lawson. You have it already. Shew it to him. If He does not chuse it want-ing half a leaf, Ross must take it back.

I am sorry poor Louse has seen, or that Will, by her means, has seen, a Ghost. Waters my Cork-cutter has been dead this twelve-month. Sulli-vane provides Corks now from whom I can't tell. If you want any, he'll get them. Get John to call on him, to know when He expects the Rohan-ware. I am distress'd for want of them, or of more pewter. I can't be long with-out one or other. My Visitation is fix'd for the 11th of next month.

I believe Louse is right as to the Etymology of Keeve. But I am not sure whether it ought to be spelt with K or C. Ask Lawson.

Carleboe has his Cloths. I hope He'll take care of them. I have got my book, which Miss Ormsby brought down.

Clark's Tryal is a miserable Sessions paper. Who told you it was well written?

I am pleas'd that your poor Aunt was so far well on her way. I shall be impatient till I have as good an account of her from Roscrea. God bless you all.

yours &c.
Edw:Elphin

Peter's disorder, I hope, is over. I bless God every one else is well.

We want a warming pan. That here is old. Let one be provided to come down the next Carrs. Mrs Jourdan spoke of one some time ago. It seems it was forgot.

What is the English of *Calmar*?[2] I know it is the name of a Fish. But Boyer does not inform me, what fish. This is not the only word about which I have lately consulted him in vain.

You may write to Mrs Waller when you please. She and her Children are all recover'd.

June 13.

Just as I had done writing yesterday, your friend Kitty Ormsby and her husband came to Carys on a Visit. I saw them in the Evening. She look'd not well, but said she was. Soon after I left them, Lewis came to me in a fright, and by his account there was danger of a miscarriage. They who best know those things here, thought the same. I depended on Mrs Heap. By advice of all she was blouded last night about ten. I know nothing of her this morning, but fear she'll do as Madam Avoglio did.[3] I would have a law pass'd that Girls should not be marry'd, till they have more prudence in conducting themselves in the state that marry'd Women usually are in. She ought not to have left home. I hope no ill will betide her. I'll be as carefull of her as I can. Say nothing of this, unless you hear it from others.

[Free Edw:Elphin]

1. [Mme de La Fayette], *Zayde. A Spanish history: compos'd by the inimitable pen of the ingenious Mr. de Segrais* (Dublin 1737).
2. *Calmar*: squid.
3. Christina Maria Avoglio (*fl.* 1729-46): singer. Handel took her to Dublin in 1741 where she was his leading soprano throughout the season. She sang the principal soprano part at the first performance of *The Messiah* on 13 April 1742, remaining in Dublin until June, and returning to London with Handel to sing in operas and in further performances of *The Messiah*. Her last known performance appears to have been in Salisbury on 23 June 1746. It is possible that she died of the miscarriage that is hinted at here. Winton Dean, *The New Grove Dictionary of Music and Musicians*, ed. Stanley Sadie (1980), Vol. 1, p.752.

92

Elphin. June 16, 1750

I must agen bestow a few Criticisms on my Dear Girl's letter. But I hope they'll be the last I shall have occasion for, because you have so often taken Physick. For a Comment on this, if any be wanting, I must referr you to Mr Bays in *The Rehersal*.[1]

The first thing that offers is a fine piece of Brogue-English as ever I met with. You could not have wrote better, had you spent your whole life here 'Have you heard any thing of B.C. since you *are* in the Country' I won't affront you, by telling how it ought to be. To answer your Question. I have not. When next I see Lisdurne folks, I'll enquire.[2]

'The little beast its *self* the s after *it*, is wrong. That immediatly after, *it's name*, is right, only that you have not put the little asterisk between the t and s, as I have done. In several places of this, and your other letters, I observe you, not exact in the use of this Asterisk. You put it sometimes, where it ought not to be, as in *heard, discomposes*; and omit it where it ought to be, as in the instance I have given. The way to avoid this, is To attend constantly to the force of this Asterisk; which is always to mark one or more letters omitted. Thus *it's* name, is an abbreviation for *of it*, or it, *his*, or *her* name. *Daughter's* – of daughter. In all such cases the Asterisk must be. So believ'd, deceiv'd, sav'd. The e being every where omitted. Now, I warrant you'll be ready to say, That *heard* is the same. But it is not. heard is the preter-Tense. But what say you for *discomposes?* There is no omission of a letter there. If you don't see the reason why there ought to be no s added to it, in the sentence which occasions this Criticism; I'll tell it you. The s is the abbreviation of a Genitive case. But it there, is Nominative.

I defended my Self for *taking it*. What think you of this, which is of the same kind? I defended my self *for* an Enemy. You certainly see it ought to be *from*.

These are all the inacuracys in Stile which I have observ'd. But indeed, My Dear Dear Girl, your Errors in stops are without number. Sometimes a Comma, where there ought to be a full stop; and sometimes *au contraire*, a full stop in the middle of a sentence, and a Comma or none at all at the end. If you attended to the sense of what you write ['right' crossed out], these things would not be so frequent. But part of every letter is wrote in an hurry, as appears by these mistakes which are commonly there; as well as by more indifferent writing. No body resolves better than you do. I hope I shall soon find you steady in acting conformably to your resolutions.

Peter is now quite well. He is not yet abroad, but Stafford says He may be in two or three days. I know nothing of Mrs French's intentions in respect to Nancy.[3] It would be well for both that she went to Dublin. But I believe she'll be wanted at home. Mrs French is not now able to travel.

I heartily wish you may get the House-keeper of whom Miss Leigh[4] gives so great a Character. If she be to be had, Let not wages make you decline taking her. If you can't get her, Make all possible enquirys for some other right good one and Be not in too much haste, nor too easy in believing. Mrs Hunter's wages are £10 a year. None are yet due. The 24th or 25th there will be a quarter. You may give her any discharge you please that you think true. I suppose she's now above going to another Service.

As to Pewter, Carleboe says, He has dishes enough, only that He'd be glad of a second soop dish, because sometimes two soops may be wanting. The pack-thread enclos'd will direct the size. The whole length is the Measure of the Hollow for the Soop, and from the Knot to the end not knotted, gives the depth, and the width of the Rim. Let a dish of these dimensions, and two dozen of plates be provided immediatly and sent down hither with the baking dishes. I hope the old and useless pewter you have will provide these. Those very large new dishes which Louse mentions are and will be useless. I hope Mr Wilkinson will allow for them suitably to their goodness. If He does not, I shall have reason to take it ill. By Louse's Memorandum, I see she is no longer offended at the name, since she finds it belong'd once to a *beautifull* Horse. I thank her for her remarks on brewing. I believe she's right in them all. I'll have them put in practice, if I can. You say nothing of Hopps. Are they forgotten? Whether they are or no, How will you escape the Charge of some giddiness?

Strange! Strange! Tho' three Chair-men and a Coach-man came from Roscrea, you did not get one line! It would indeed have been somewhat stranger, if so many had come, without bringing you a Message by Word of Mouth. But your not having a line would have been every whit as strange, if only one had come. Perhaps they were a parcel of ragged Rascals, who had none of them a pocket to put a letter in. This My Dear Girl is an instance of your not thinking, of what you write. Something struck you at once as strange, and down it went without more ado. Unluckily you have wonder'd in the wrong place. This ought to have been among the Criticisms. But till now I overlook'd it.

I rejoice much at your Aunt's safe arrival at Roscrea. I knew it on Tuesday Evening, from two stragling fellows, whom I pick'd up in the Demesne, and intended to have wrote it to you for news last post. But Kitty Ormsby's adventure drove that and every other thing out of my head. A bad affair is well over with her. She is in as good a way, as Her friends can wish or Expect.

To put you and Louse on a level as to your Cures, she must get one of the little beasts for a pet, and at every turn hold it out to you to stroke. If she'll go on this Scheme, I'll provide a Silver Chain, and shall be as well pleas'd with it on the Table after diner, as with Miss Rose's Squirrel.[5] By the by How does poor Lucy?[6] If she be still in town, Let her know that I enquir'd after her.

I wish Cos. Doherty had not made you such a present. But As she urg'd you so, you could not avoid accepting it. I have not heard from Dic, since He went to his living. But by Blair's account who went with him there, He was very kindly rec'd by Mr Mahon, and the living is likely to answer better than I expected.

The oft'ner you see Mrs Hamilton the better. Fail not always to make her my Compliments, and Be ready to do every Thing, that may give her the least joy. You say nothing of Mrs Delany. Now you know you may wait on her, you are easy about doing it.

The Tulips and anemonys are to be taken up, when the Stalks and grass are fairly wither'd, not before; and you must not think of stirring them in broken Weather. It ought to be fair over head, and not only so, but the Earth about them should be tolerably dry when they are taken up. All Ranunculus that offer at seed, must remain, till the seed is ripe. For the rest, the Rule is the same as for anemonys.

Some day next Week a servant of Jac. French's[7] will carry to my house, an Oyl'd hood which I am forc'd to send back, because not rightly done. I have wrote to John about it. But I mention it to you, that if it comes, when He is abroad you may take it in.

Still a Succession of officers; when they will end I know not. Some of them are agreable. Most, tolerable. But the other day I sat down with three the strangest Creatures, I ever saw; and they were all my Company. The novelty diverted me for a while, and I soon got rid of them.

I bless God I am very well. I hope the German Spawe will agree with you. I am sure the Doctor does not forget that the continu'd use of it was once or twice the probable cause of a purging. God bless and preserve you My Dearest. I am

yours &c.
Edw:Elphin

I shall soon want more Sallad Oyl. You must send such as can be got.

As John writes to me every post, It is but fair that He should be furnish'd with paper. If He has not got any, Give him some. You know where to find it: in the lower Drawer of my Scriptoire right hand.

You don't mention Mrs Nicholson. Do you ever see her?

[Free Edw:Elphin]

1. Bayes: 'If I am to write familiar things, as Sonnets to *Armida*, and the like, I make use of Stew'd Prunes only, but when I have a grand design in hand, I ever take Physic, and let blood; for, when you would have pure Swiftness of thought, and fiery flights of fancy, you must have a care of the pensive part. In fine, you must purge the Belly.' George Villiers, duke of Buckingham, *The Rehearsal* (1672) Act II, scene 1.

2. B.C. is not known but was probably a member of the Crofton family of Lissadoorn, Co. Roscommon.

3. Anne French: daughter of William French and Arabella Frances Marsh. Burke (1916), p.610.

4. Miss Leigh: one of the Leigh family of Rosegarland, Co. Wexford. Burke (1912), p.395.

5. Miss Rose: not known.

6. Lucy Caulfield (?-1752; see Biographical Register).

7. John French (?-1754): son of Arthur French of Cloonyquin, Co. Roscommon, and Judith Paine. Barrister Middle Temple. Unmarried. Burke (1979), p.449.

93

Elphin. June 20, 1750

My Dear Girl,

I have scribled so much to poor *Mlle Poux*,[1] that I have little left for you, and as little time to say any thing in.

You fear mistakes in your letter. As it happens there are fewer in this, than in some late ones. But by your writing of the last line of your postcript, I see you finish'd in an hurry, so as not to have time probably to read it over. Why do you wish for what is in your power? For all your purposes, French Grammar will do as well, as that of any other Language. That you may understand if you please: and I think it would be of advantage to you. Two pages of your letter are very well wrote, and I see but one false spelling, you write *invited* with an *e*. Pray how come you to drop the h in Rohan? I us'd it. If wrong, set me right. I understand not modern French spelling.

Poor Kitty is as well as her friends can wish, or Expect. She mentions you all with great affection.

By your account Molly Leight's Children[2] will be but in an indifferent way. I see you have a mind to take the Girl. You may if you please. She'll supply Molly Hunter's place. As for the boy, I know not what to say I hope the Father in Law will do something for him. I had but a lame account of the Lease from the Bishop of Clonfert. When I return to town, I'll enquire more particularly from Mr Maple himself;[3] or if things are likely to come to Extremitys earlier, I'll write. I wish you could get Ned Curtis to speak to Cunningham[4] quietly from you about both Children. It may be of use, and He is seldom backward at doing a good natur'd thing. I am very sorry, He is not well. Tell him agen, that I beg He would take more care of himself. Enclos'd is a Memorandum of the very few Books I wish to have out of the fine Catalogue. I have time for no more. God bless you all

yours &c.
Edw:Elphin

My Compliments to Mr and Mrs Leigh and to honest Grace.[5] Ask him what is come of my Dog. Supple's[6] are not worth two pence.

I had a letter from your Uncle as you suppos'd. He seems by it to be much down.

My little black Horse that your Cosen bought has got a lameness. Be not frighten'd now. He'll be well in three or four days, and Mr Adderly's carrys me very well. I give an account of him to John.

[Free Edw:Elphin In another hand: To you fair Ladys now I write of ?arlington... with pleasure.]

1. Miss Louse.

2. Molly Leight: not known.

3. A William Maple was the mortgagee of a house in Kevin Street, leased by J. Egan. William Maple was also Keeper of the Parliament House. NLI ms 2101, f.27; Watson (1747).

4. Possibly Alexander Cunningham, who was one of the first surgeons at the Meath Hospital in 1753. He practised in Eustace Street. John Fleetwood, *History of Medicine in Ireland* (Dublin 1951), p.250.

5. John Leigh of Rosegarland, Co. Wexford. MP for New Ross. He died in 1758. He was married to Mary Cliffe. Their daughter Grace married the 8th earl of Meath in 1758, and died in 1812. Burke (1912), p.395.

6. Supple: the butler at Elphin.

94

Elphin. June 22, 1750

I have not much to say this bout to my Dear Girl. I bless God I am very well, and rejoice that you are so. As you say nothing of poor *Mlle Poux's* malady, I hope it is quite remov'd.

Our Weather has been as hot as yours and continues so, only that yesterday and to day there has been a refreshing Easterly breeze to temper the heat of the sun.[1] I am sure the Doctor has told you, that in such Weather as this great care is to be taken to guard against colds, which are often got by seeking improper relief from the faintness of heat.

Stopping right is a perfection, but a very rare one. Even printed books are generally deficient in this. Dr Swift's works are the most exactly stopp'd of any I know; and it just comes into my head, that you and Jeny, may learn exactness in this nice affair, thus. Let *Mlle Poux* dictate to each of you a Paragraph now and then, from one or other of these Books, which stop your own way. This done, compare your performances with the Book; and she that makes fewest mistakes, may give the other a gentle Pat: Or if after a few trials, you both make many, Madam must give you both *la fouette.*[2] This is the best Expedient I can think of, and upon my Word, Ladys, It will be very well worth your while to go into this Exercise. In a very little time, you'll observe the reason of each stop, and of the different use of them.

I did not think you a great Grammarian. But I find you are not so good a one as I thought you. Man – Woman are sometimes Nominative, sometimes Accusative. Of Man, of Woman, are Genitive. Instead of these We often write Man's. There the s with the Asterisk, is the same as *of*. Look into your french Grammar. That will shew you the Cases and their Powers. Go a little further, and you'll find the difference of Tenses. It will be necessary that you know a little of these things, in order to write correctly.

I am glad you've wrote to Mrs Waller. If your letter be as well wrote as that now before me, care has not been wanting.

As those big Dishes are quite useless, you must e'en exchange them on such Terms as you can. But I am sure Mr Wilkinson will make much more of them than He offers. If I mistake not, they were bought from him.

Kitty comes on very well – Have the Artane folks told you that the Lieutenant is marry'd?[3] If not, Mum, to them; and to Every one else Mum – whether they have or not. It is a strange affair – The *Eclat* is not to be till July 20.

Peter is mended greatly. Tell the Doctor that my Apothecary gave him some Bark,[4] of which I knew nothing when I wrote. As He is now about the house I have seen him once or twice. There seems to be a little quickness in his pulse, and a great dryness of Skin – But He neither coughs nor Sweats.[5]

Tell John that I can't write to him this post – Bid him know from Smith whether 40 Wheels and some Reels which I order'd be ready. Now will be his time for getting them down. Let him bespeak as many more. Adieu.

yours &c.
Edw: Elphin

I din'd to day at Charles-town. Mrs King is much yours.

[Free Edw:Elphin]

1, The weather in June 1750 was abnormally hot. 'From the 17th to the 21st it was the hottest weather in the memory of man; and Fahrenheit's thermometer rose to seventy six.' Rutty, p.154.

2. *La Fouette, le fouet*: a whipping.

3. The lieutenant: Nehemiah Donnellan IV. See Letter 68.

4. Cinchona bark (quinine) was brought to Europe from Peru in 1632 by a Spanish priest (hence its name 'Jesuits' bark') and found to be useful in treating some types of intermittent fevers. This led to physicians in England and Italy to differentiate malaria, which responded to the bark, from other fevers. Nicholas Synge was prescribed 'Choice Jesuits' Bark' in 1741. It cost him 9d. F.L. Dunn, 'Malaria', Kiple, p.860; Harry Rushe's bill to the Rev. Doctor Nicholas Synge August 13th 1741. NLI Synge Papers PCC 344 (20).

5. From the description of his illness and the prescription of bark, Peter would appear to have had a form of malaria.

95

Elphin. June 27, 1750

My Dear Girl

Such an heap of letters as came yesterday, you have seldom seen even with me. I have been all day drudging at Answers to such as immediatly requir'd them. Some I am oblig'd to post-pone. Madam Jane must forgive me that she is of the number. Tell her I thank her for her letter; and will write as soon as I can. But in my present situation I have less time than usual, and this will continue, till your friend Kitty &c. are gone off. When that will be, I know not. She comes on very well, but Her delicacy is such, as requires a good deal of Caution.

What you write of poor Ned Curtis grieves me to the heart. God send me better tidings of him. His ilness affects me so, that I care not to dwell on the thought of it. Let him or his good Wife know in a proper manner my real great Concern; and if any thing, that I have can be of the least use to him, Let him have it. I can think of nothing at present but Old Canary, of which there is a remain in No. 17.¹ Ask the Doctor, and if He says it will be of use, Let him have it while it lasts – Give the Doctor my thanks for his directions about Peter. He is much better than when I desir'd them. Tell him I should be very glad that He'd give me some account of poor Ned.

If Miss Leigh's House-keeper be to be had, Take her immediatly. As to any one else, use your discretion. As to Fanny,² I have done. I hope the Mistress will be cur'd, before she comes to her age. Otherwise I shall despair. And yet, all things, consider'd I do not think you deeply infected. But it is good to keep up your attention. If the same method were us'd to the Maid, It might yet be of use. I think her forgets &c. are more the Effects of heighth and indifference than of sheer girlish giddiness. As to Ally Leight,³ pursue your inclinations. You saw by my last, and that to Mrs Jourdan, that I had no objections. What need then of reasons?

When next you see the Squire of Artane, Tell him I am very angry at his not writing. He may be as negligent with regard to Kitty, as He pleases: but He ought not to neglect my Questions about grass-Seeds. I expect particular and immediate Answers. Thank him for his Caution about Mr A's horse. But tell, what you will be pleas'd to know, that He carrys me incomparably well; and that his starting signifys not a button. At present He stands fair for being a first favorite, even tho' the chesnut get safe.

You've sav'd your Self luckily about Grant. Two or three times I resolv'd to reproach you with your forget. You were sav'd by one of mine own. But what have you to say about Wilkins's *Sermons?*

Mrs Waller well get your letter, tho' it was not right directed. As to your reading, I must suppose you did not read mine to Mrs Jourdan, if you fear, I would exclude such Books as Cyrus's travels[4] or a good Play. By the by the paper you sent me is a very pretty one, and tho' it comes from a strange kind of Author, there is a great deal of good instruction to be got by carefully reading and considering it.

Dispose of your Melons as you please among mine and your own friends. But trouble not your Self with the great ones. Send some to the Archbishop[5] while He continues in town, and now and then a very fine one to the Chan[cello]r. I have nothing to order as to any one else.

What Gannon[6] tells you about the Tulips got last year from Lord Meath[7] is so far true, That Magahan order'd they should remain in the ground. But since you have taken charge of those things your Self, I desire you would have them taken up in your own presence, and keep them by themselves. There ought to be 28, or 27. I suppose you know, that All these things should be dry'd in the Shade. Some of the upper rooms with the Windows open would be an Excellent place.

You know Rabbits were always scarce here. They are more so now than ever. This has determin'd me to enclose a Small yard for a kind of Warren, in which Rabbits may breed and be fed, as yours were. In one of Bradley's Books, there is, I think, a description of Such a Warren.[8] You have them, if I remember right, among yours. If so, find out the Vol. which contains this and send it to me. My neighbour Mr Owen Lloyd[9] is now in town, by whom you may send it. Will knows him. If He goes to Dr Wynne's,[10] He'll learn there, where He may be found. But you must make haste. For his stay in town will be very short. If you can light on him, He'll be a very proper person by whom to send down Mr Lennox's silver. I am sure He'll bring it if desir'd; and a Note from you or Mrs Jourdan will bring him to you. You might have trusted Jemy.

The next time that any things are sent hither, We should be glad of a supply of half a doz. Milk pans, and a deep large Crock.

I have time for no more. God bless you all.

yours &c.
Edw:Elphin

Get Miller[11] from Gannon, and examine it carefully under the general Article of Grass Seeds, or the particular one of Cinque-foil, or *Cinque feuille,* and transcribe for me what He says of that particular Species. Possibly you may find it also in Chomel. If you do, Let me have what He says.[12]

Mrs Jourdan, I believe, will ease you by writing this her self. Your letter will probably find you employment enough. Your last is well written.

Mr Lloyd, as I have learn'd since I wrote the above, may be found at Mr Thewles's an Attorney in Hoey's Court.[13] But the shortest way to get him to you is to write to him my self, which, tir'd as I am, I'll do this minute. See him, be sure, if He calls.

In the Condition in which poor Ned Curtis is, He must not be troubled with my Affairs. You must contrive, Mrs Jourdan and you, to take care of them your Selves, till He is well. Paying the poor will be the most troublesome. But that and whatever else there is, will exercise you a little, and do you good. If He goes to the Country, Get from him my Keys, because I may want something on short notice. In the desk of my Scriptoire lyes a bulky Setlement of Coll. Trench's. I am not sure but there may be two. Whether one or two Let a Card be wrote immediatly to Councillor Eyre Trench, letting him know what you have, and that you'll deliver it or them, according as you find, to him when He pleases to call. Take his receit for what you deliver.

Your quarter is due. You may have it when you please. During poor Ned's ilness, you must draw on Lennox your Self. He'll answer your Drafts.

John writes about Coals. Let them be paid for, when laid in.

1. Sack, which was the most popular wine in England in the seventeenth century. Canary sack was thought to be the best. André L. Simon, *The History of the Wine Trade in England* 3 vols (London 1964), Vol.3, pp.322-4.

2. Fanny: Alicia's maid.

3. Ally Leight: not known.

4. John Hawkey, *The ascent of Cyrus the Younger and the retreat of the ten thousand Greeks.* Translated from Xenophon (Dublin 1738).

5. Charles Cobbe: archbishop of Dublin.

6. Gannon: head gardener at Kevin Street.

7. Chaworth, 6th earl of Meath (1686-1758). Meath is known to have been a notable cultivator of florists' flowers. He bought in quantities from nurserymen; in 1731 he bought carnations and auriculas, which he propagated and cultivated their mutations. He also bought ranunculus and tulips from Holland and from Lille and Brussels and hyacinths from Haarlem and Leyden. A tulip bulb, even a century after the end of 'tulip-mania', could cost £20. He lived in St Stephen's Green. Meath's land, later occupied by the Meath Hospital, adjoined Edward Synge's property in Kevin Street. Pim, p.49; Burke (1916), p.1115; *Georgian Society Records* Vol.2, p.44.

8. Richard Bradley quotes a Mr Gilbert of Aubourn on how to set up and stock a rabbit warren. 'It is necessary always to keep 8000 rabbits for a Stock, in about 700 Acres of such Ground; and [he] judges, that one year with another, the Increase for such a Stock is about 24,000 Rabbits; but these are subject to many Accidents, by Poachers, by Weezels, Polecats, Foxes, and Distempers, tho' the greatest Care be taken of them by watching, setting of Ginns, or in their food ... by his Method of Management, ... he loses few of them,

and his warren is always in better Case than others, and his Rabbits of a greater Price ...'
Richard Bradley, *A General Treatise of Husbandry and Gardening* (London 1724), pp.34-6.

9. Owen Lloyd of Rockville, Elphin, Co. Roscommon, was a magistrate. He had a wife, Susanna, and seven children under fourteen. He employed five Protestant and five Catholic servants. Census, f.34.

10. John Wynne was a son of John Wynne and the brother of Owen Wynne of Hazlewood, Co. Sligo. He was the curate of St Nicholas Without, Dublin, and Keeper of the Publick Library of Dublin, St Patrick's Close (Marsh's Library). Burke (1912), p.780; Watson (1749), p.53; Watson (1747), p.61.

11. Philip Miller, *The Gardeners Dictionary* (London 1731).

12. Under the heading 'Seed-Time', Chomel deals at length with the different types of grass seeds and the correct season for planting and problems in their cultivation. Miller was less helpful, saying of cinque-foil that 'as they are never propagated either for use or Beauty, so I shall not trouble the Reader with an Enumeration of the several Names.' Noel Chomel, *Dictionnaire oeconomique, contenant divers moyens d'augmenter son bien, et de conserver sa santé* ... Seconde édition, 2 vols (Paris 1718).

13. Probably Wentworth Thewles, an Exchequer attorney. He was admitted to the King's Inns and practised in Ship Street in 1760. His will was proved in 1777. *King's Inns*, p.477; Watson (1760), p.59; Vicars, p.453.

96

Elphin. June 30, 1750

My Dear Girl's letter is so well wrote, that I can easily excuse the mistake, especially as it is slight in it Self, and one which I have been often guilty of my Self.

I am much mistaken if you do not find great benefit by the use of my method, to learn to stop. To help a little to the same end, I transcribe a part of your last, in which you have made a very great mistake, and so palpable a one, that you must have recourse to your hackney Apology, giddiness, to apologize for it. 'We there heard of the card of which I enclose a Copy, by Mrs Jourdan's desire she presents her respects &c' These are your Words, and so you have stopp'd. Not one but the Comma, after Copy, which is right, but there ought to have been one after Card. This however is but a slight Omission. The great one is, That there is no stop at all after *desire*, where there ought to have been a . because it concludes the Sentence. By the by, your Card made me laugh. Godfrey Wills, who is now here, says it is an old one. That does not lessen the joke to me who never heard or saw it before. But since you sent this by Mrs Jourdan's desire, Pray ask her, How she came to entertain such filthy Ideas? Without having them, she could not know that it would please so filthy a creature as she calls me. Does she not for this deserve even the French most hated name?

Dr Lawson has fairly bit you by a piece of grave Ironical humour. Do you think He was in earnest in what he said? I should be very sorry He were, because that would be a proof of his having a worse opinion of you, than I believe He has, and you deserve. I am sure He would laugh heartily, if He knew how grave you have been on this. But Be not afraid, I will not betray you. And To remove your Scruples; I am far from thinking that All grave Books are tiresome and disagreable to you. On the other hand, I neither think nor wish, that such only should be agreable. I allow, and approve of reading for amusement, and entertainment, as well as for instruction, and at your time of life, it would shew too much phlegm in your Constitution, if grave and Sententious Authors only were to your Taste. Nay! I'll go further. I am not against your looking into books, in which may be found a multitude of things, of which I should be sorry you did approve. I consider these as I do some of the simple fashionable diversions, into which I encourage you sometimes to enter, that by knowing what they are, you may like them the less. And this was my view in giving you such a *promiscuous*, you should have wrote, miscellaneous Collection. If there be any downright bad one among them, It is more than I know. There are several, of which, Parts are bad, such for instance are Dryden's Plays, some of which gave Mrs Jourdan disgust; and perhaps there is scarce one of them, in which there are not here and there Exceptionable passages. Yet several of his plays are very good, and such as if not nought fit to be read, The whole species except a few must be proscib'd.

The same thing is true of many other Writers, of the diverting kind – Too much niceness in these things is not to be approv'd or recommended. It is a little like, what is said, and I fear truly, of some Women, That they start and are offended at speeches, out of which they extract an offensive meaning, which they neither bear, nor was intended in them. Such Dames are not usually thought the greatest vestals. It is indeed true, That a Damsel cannot be too guarded against using or suffering any licence of Speech. But sometimes, Too quick an apprehension of this kind, has a quite contrary effect from what it is design'd to have; and gives a bad instead of a good impression – What is in some small degree true, even of conversation, is much more so of reading. I remember once a Lady fell very severely upon me, for having own'd that I had read a collection of Poems, some of which were not over grave, tho' many were. But the Collection was accounted one of the best in the English tongue: and what Effect, think you, had this on a large Company present, who were all grave prudent people, and I believe, had read the Poems as well as I? Not one of them thought the better of her, or worse of me: and she betray'd her self into the bargain. She could not have censur'd so, without having read them her self – In short, My Dear Girl, your general reading ought to be books of instruction, in virtue, Politeness, or something that may improve your mind, or behaviour. With them you may mix all Books of innocent Entertainment. In this description, I do not include Romances, nor more than a few Novels. Too much dwelling on these, is apt to give the mind, a very fantastical, if not, a wrong turn. You may see it in your friend Betty at Artane. She has been a greater dealer in these things. I am not for your dealing in them. They are of a bad kind, even where there is not a single Sentence offensive. But they give the mind a wrong turn, infinitely worse than is to be fear'd from now and then looking into a ludicrous Book, perhaps to throw it aside with disgust. Steady fix'd principles of Religion, Virtue, and Exact Decorum in your whole Conduct are and ever will be, I trust in God, armour against any Soil from a transient on such badinage, which yet the less you like, the better. If you find the least tendency look towards being pleas'd with reading such things, That should be a Caution against reading them any more. You see, huzzy, by my Writing thus on this nice subject, that I have no bad opinion either of your Understanding, or the Moral Cast, and turn of your mind. I hope I shall every day find more in both to approve of.

I think you are very right in your judgment. The Sermons are much better to be lik'd than the Author. It seems they are not tiresome or disagreable. You'll find some in Tillotson on like subjects.[1] Read and compare them. But what said the Dame to you, when she found you out? You only tell me that she did not at first know you.

Tell the Doctor I am highly oblig'd by his account of Ned Curtis. I intended to have wrote him my thanks, but have been so interrupted all day, that it is impossible. He'll excuse it, and accept of them by you. I am somewhat reliev'd, tho' not perfectly so. But I fear'd a Consumption for poor Ned. It would give me the greatest joy to know that He was well.

Jemy came hither on Wedensday evening, with his horse, in as good condition I believe, as He left Dublin in. But 'tis such a one as they ought not to have sent him. I'll send him back. Such folly has been among them as would make a Man angry. For particulars I must referr you to my letter to John. God bless you all. Adieu. yours &c.

Edw:Elphin

Will Carbery Berne never be well? I wish He were and here. But since He is where He is, I hope the Doctor will allow him full time for his cure.

I hear that Lady Bingham the Widow of Sir John is in Dublin.[2] If she be, I should be glad that you all went to make her a Visit. I believe Jeny has seen her, when a small girl. But she was a most intimate friend of your Mother's, and therefore I wish you would shew her this much of respect. Go in the Common way to make an afternoon visit, and carry a Card with you. If she does not take notice of it, *Voila qui est fait.*[3] But I believe she will. She was when I knew her, a very genteel agreable woman. But I have not seen her these many years. Introduce your self by sending up your name; and if you find her, Say I directed you to do so.

[Free Edw:Elphin]

1. John Tillotson (1630-94): archbishop of Canterbury. He was admired for the quality of his sermons, which went into many editions during his life and after his death. He was noted for the sweetness of his disposition and for his belief in the efficacy of the pulpit, saying that 'Good preaching and good living will gain upon people.' *DNB.*
2. Lady Bingham was Frances Shaen, daughter and heiress of Sir Arthur Shaen of Kilmore. She married John Bingham in 1738. Burke (1916) p.460.
3. *Voila qui est fait.* That's done.

97

Elphin. July 1, 1750

Tho' I wrote to my Dear Girl on Saturday; and tho' Jemy will travel so slow as that the day after she gets this, She'll have another Epistle from me, yet I write two lines to let you all know that I bless God I am very well – Let John Miller go with the enclos'd immediatly to Turner, and carry with him a Spindle and Brass Nobbs, which Jemy carrys with him. I have wrote Mr Turner directions about it. John must urge him to loose no time in observing them, that Jemy may bring the thing back as it ought to be. He may wait for it till Monday, but then He must come off: For I want him here more, than I care to let the little Gent. know I do. I suppose he'll travel down faster, than He goes up.

Tell John that one Hanly a Carr-man,[1] not the same that He saw lately, will soon be in town, and call at Kevin-street. If He has not yet had an opportunity of sending down the first forty Wheels I wrote for, He may send them by him – and if the second forty be ready, He may send them too. But He must be sure to send five hundred of choice Iron, which I want chiefly for Shoes. God bless you all.

yours &c.
Edw:Elphin

[To Miss Synge]

1. Hanly: not known.

98

Elphin. July 3, 1750

My Dear Girl.

Your account of poor Ned has reliev'd me a good deal. I have a letter to the same purpose from the Doctor enclos'd in one for him/Ned, which I send open, That you may read it your selves, and shew it to the Doctor. Desire him to deliver it, if you cannot do it, your Self, and tell him next time you see him, that if He be afraid of loosing his business, I'll answer for that; and if the worst comes to the worst, will set him up here in Elphin, where I am sure he'd have all the Protestant business of the Country. But, joking a part, I hope he will not be such a Simpleton as not to preferr the care of his health to all other Considerations; and yet I know him so well, as not to care to leave him to his own discretion in this point. Tell the Doctor, that if He will not otherwise obey his order, I commission him to lock him up. I am sorry I have no Moselle Wine. Let him have as much Bristol Water as He pleases. You may direct John, as He goes by, to speak to Sullivane to import another Cargo for us. As that Water is, I know not, how, scarce, It is not amiss to have a stock.

Tho' your letter be well wrote, both hand, and contents, yet there are more false spellings than usual. Some of them you'll attempt to excuse by pleading your not being acquainted with the Words; But I will not admit this plea, as to any but one.

Ranuncula	Ranunculus
Arbutos	Arbutus
you write	you should write
prentice	Apprentice
Mozel	Moselle – here your plea may be good
Cinque foil	*Cinque feuille*

The Chesnut will be with you, before you get this. Don't be uneasy at my returning him. I gave my reasons to John. But Be assur'd I do not want him. Little Black is almost well. But I believe I shall stick to Mr Adderley's horse.

As Jemy is to return immediatly, you may send the Books by him. I could trust his honesty with money. But I am not secure against his folly. So that if Mr Lloyd does not call, Let Lennox's silver remain where it is, till I have some other Conveyance. I am not in immediate want.

All our Saffron is spent in making Cakes for Mrs Ormsby. Send some down in a post-letter. I need not desire it may be Spanish.

I am sorry your Straw-berrys answer so ill. We have plenty of very good here. As you say they abound at Artane. Pray inform your Self from Mr Donnelan how he manages them, and oblige Gannon to do the same. To take away from him all pretence, Desire Mr Donnelan to furnish you with some plants in the Season. Let me know your Success.

Let the Tulips remain or be taken up, as I setled with Ganon. I chose to vary from those instructions only as to L[or]d Meath's. My room will be a very good place. Only you must not suffer the Sun to come upon them.

By your account my little affairs are no burthen to Ned himself. Let them remain therefore as they are.

Your friend Kitty is very well. The day is a little rough, or I would have transported her hither. But I hope to do it to morrow.

Poor Captain Ormsby has met with a very ugly accident. Going to Mr Waller's on Saturday, His horse fell with him. He broke his Arm, and hurt his knee. This is all the account We have had yet. Lewis is gone to see him. About a fortnight ago He had a very ugly fall coming from Charles-town, by which He broke his face most severely. *A ce tems la il etoit enyoré. Je soupçonne la même chose cet autre fois. Mais Je n'en suis pas certain. Il aime trop boire – ceci á l'oreiller.*[1]

Tell *Mlle Poux*, that I can't make out the Lady's name whose management of Rabbits she thinks will be satisfactory. It is the first Word of her writing that has gravell'd me in reading. I told Carleboe of his Rib. He mutter'd and said I know not what. He had indeed nothing to say. He undertakes stoutly for his Hams. But it won't be amiss to examine them. You may use them, whenever you've occasion or inclination. It pleases me to catch one at a trip, who seldom makes one. The beautifull horse has made a stumble in spelling. *Sais.* We English usually write with a y. But when with an i. an e. always follows. She has omitted it twice. And so for this time Adieu.

yours &c.
Edw:Elphin

1. At the time he was drunk. I suspected the same thing on the other occasion. But I was not certain. He likes drinking too much – this for your ears.

99

Elphin. July 10, 1750

My Dear Girl.

To morrow is my Visitation. That is always a day of hurry. But it will be soon over. My new Tables &c. are to make their appearance. Carleboe will cover them with more dishes than need be. But since He is to have the labour, I leave him to do as He pleases.

Your friend Kitty is very well. My point now is to keep her from venturing, to which she is indeed well inclin'd. Yesterday she took the Air. This day she dines at Strokes-town. I was to have din'd there to. But Palmer, Barton, and Dic Doherty are here. Probably before dinner-time, I may have one or two more. I will not leave them to shift. I have enjoin'd Kitty to be early at home. I hope she'll obey orders. They intend to be at Artane the latter end of next Week.

I am pleas'd that Ned Curtis is so well, but very uneasy at his restifness. He'll repent it when it is too late. He sent the Saffron, but no answer to my letter. I suppose the Gent. was asham'd to promise, what He does not intend to perform. He will not, I see, take my advice with regard to his health, any more than He did in money matters. I wish He do not repent it in the one, as He has done in the other case. But *Quos perdere vult Jupiter, dementat.*[1] Make him construe this to you, – and tell him that I'll trouble my head no more about him, tho' I can't help grieving, that He, who so well knows what is right, should act so very absurdly. But for the future, I'll keep my anger and grief to my Self; and thus, Tell him, I take my leave of him. A little care for the remainder of this Summer, might reestablish his health. As He determines to act, He may not feel much till Winter. Then his disorders will return with greater violence; and so there's an End of him. Ask the Doctor if I am not right.

You did very right in going to Mrs Fitzmaurice's. Your Entertainment there, and Reflexions upon it, give me singular pleasures. I must call you, my little Bee, if you thus collect honey from a Dunghil. A very coarse image this; and yet if the whole collection of Dames were of the same stamp with the one you describe, 'tis a just one. You see however, that such filthy creatures have their use. By the absurd monstrous figure they make, a just abhorrence of their vices, is rais'd in the minds of those who are not infected with them; and the impression is stronger from such examples, than from precepts or advice. The way the Spartans took to make their youth in love with Sobriety, was to expose their slaves drunk before them.

Gaming is in it self a most hatefull vice, and the parent of many others.

Whoever is strongly addicted to it man, or Woman, I pronounce them abandon'd. And they must continue so, till they reform, be their other good Qualitys ever so many.

I never thought you in the least danger of being infected with it. But consider my Dear little Bee, that every Vice, every passion unreasonably indulg'd, nay! Every affectation, and folly, when thus exhibited to your view, may be matter out of which you may extract honey. For your Age, you have very just notions of good and bad. You also have some notion of what is proper, becoming, and decorous, and of their contrarys. When therefore you go into these places, in which as in Noah's ark there is usually a collection of all creatures clean and unclean, you may find much matter for improvement, by observing the behaviour, of those particularly, of your own sex. When any thing pleases, Ask your Self why! If, because it is easy, natural, unaffected, proper, Imitate. If you find no such reason for approving, Blame your Self for having too hastily approv'd, and alter your judgment. If on the other hand, you see any absurd, affected, forward, less decent behaviour, I hope I need not bid you, not approve. But it may be of use to trace these vices or imperfections to their Source, and observe the passion or inclination whatever it be, which gives being to them. All wrong behaviour in those who are not downright fools, proceeds from wrong inclinations. By discovering them in others, from their effects, you may correct them in your Self, and avoid the temptation of doing what you disapprove of. I can't go on to more particulars. But if you learn to give your thoughts the same kind of turn, on less striking occasions, that you have given them on this, you may improve your mind and behaviour more at a Drum than in your Closet, and thus turn this fashionable scene of Folly, and giddiness, into a School of Morality, and politeness.

I have time for no more, God bless and preserve you, My Dear Dear Girl, and make you perfect in every thing that is good. I am

yours &c.
Edw:Elphin

I think you would do well to make an afternoon visit at Finglas.

I return poor Katty's letter.[2] I forget what the part address'd to me referrs to. Her description of Charlotte made me laugh. But I do not understand the rest, as well as I use to do her letters.

The Right Word is Ranunculus – you write Re. Ought I not to blame you for this? Is it not so wrote in my letters.

[Free Edw:Elphin]

1. Those whom Jupiter wishes to destroy, he first makes mad.
2. Catherine Jourdan: born 1 March 1704, the daughter of John and Blandine Jourdan. Bouhéreau, 1 March 1703/4.

100

Elphin. July 13, 1750

My Dear Girl.

If Dr Bland be in town, send the Enclos'd to him immediatly. If He be gone to Kerry, send it to the Post; If to England, Learn how to direct to him; and take off the Cover and enclose it in one of the Speaker's Franks, which you or Mrs Jourdan may direct. Loose no time in doing this. For 'tis a letter of business.

I have not time to say much more to you this post, nor any thing to Jeny. Tell her I thank her for her letter.

I am much pleas'd with the grave part of your letter. The Rules you have form'd for your own Conduct in a point delicate enough, are very just. I hope you'll always follow them. The more sharp-sighted you are in observing defects in others that you may avoid them your Self, the better. You may also speak, or write your thoughts freely to me or Mrs Jourdan. But the less censorious your Conversation with others is, the more you'll deserve esteem.

Ned Curtis's account of himself is very different from yours. I enclose his letter [to] Mrs Jourdan, that you may reproach him with it, if He continues to give you occasion.

As to Ally Leight, do as you please. If any good be got of Cunningham, it must be by Mr Maple's means.[1]

Upon enquiry, I find you have a Cow. But she's under strong suspicion of Big-gall,[2] and never was much Worth. She was the first Calf of the Coll.'s present.[3]

Most of your Pea-chicks of last year are in being. There are now five young ones in an hopefull way. This is better than worse.

Kitty continues well. She leaves me to morrow or next day, to go to Charles-town, and from thence, after a Visit of a few days sets out for Artaine – I have time for no more.

yours &c.
Edw:Elphin

When an opportunity Offers, Send me down two plain small Common-prayer Books for two Boys whom I have taken. One of them I intend as a present for you, if He answers my Expectation.

Bid John buy four Wheel-barrows, and get them well shod, to be ready to be sent down hither when an Opportunity offers. He may send them with the Looms; and forty Wheels more, which He should order Smith to get ready, assoon as He can.

[Free Edw:Elphin]

1. Obscure.
2. Big-gall: a swelling or blister, generally on a horse.
3. See Letters 217 and 221 on Col French's present of a cow.

101

Elphin. July 17, 1750

My Dear little Bee must be content with a very short letter this post, just to tell you that I bless God I am very well, and rejoice that you are so. I intended to have wrote you a long one, and to have rally'd you a little on your fright and your fretting without reason. At more leasure perhaps I may do this. But now I can only add that I am

My dear Girl's
most affec &c.
Edw:Elphin

Give my Service to Madam Louse and tell her I owe her no thanks for saying that she will not trouble me a great while agen.

Bid John to buy me 4 Stout Iron rakes fit to rake rough Gravel or Mould Coarse and Clotty in fields, and send them down assoon as conveniently He can. If He can't get any to his mind ready made, Let him bespeak them Handles. We have enough here.

Let him also send down two Lantherns, to carry Candles to Stables and other Out-offices. I believe Tin ones will be best.

A quarter of an Ounce of Colly-flower seed is wanted. He must send this by the return of the Post.

[Free Edw:Elphin]

102

Elphin. July 20, 1750

My Dear Girl
I threaten'd in my last to rally you on your fright and your fret, you had not much reason for either.

Your not sending Roberts's paper was an Omission indeed, but a very slight one.[1] You knew I could not attend; and if you had computed time, you must have seen that you could not send it time enough for me, to go to town, if I would, unless in a case of Life and death. It was dated July 4. Wedensday. You could not have sent it till Saturday, nor I rec'd it till Monday. And Thursday was the day. Had you been less mov'd you had seen this and been easy. But Fright disables us from using our reason as We ought. Somewhere in Ecclus. Fear is describ'd the Betraying the Succours which reason affords.[2] I think I have said this to you before. But it cannot be too often repeated. Fear upon proper occasions is reasonable. But to be thus mov'd on slight ones, will make you uneasy every day of your life.

These Frights beget fretting, and Fretting heightens fright. Your letter shews you were much mov'd, and I fancy the Emotions continu'd or were reviv'd when you wrote. For your letter is more disjointed and confus'd, than any of your late ones. Fret not now at my saying this. As I commend you when you do well, so I must take notice of every thing amiss. But avoid what betray'd you into writing worse than usual; and Learn to preserve on every, even on great occasions, firmness and composure of mind. This will enable you to make the best of every thing to see clearly whether you have made a wrong step, and, if you have, to retrieve it.

You were very ingenious in connecting Roberts's paper with the Sub-peena. I see no foundation for this, but that the Name Burton was in both. With that composure which I now recommmend, you must have seen there was a Wide difference, between the Trustees of Burton's Bank, and three Burtons, between attending a meeting of these Trustees, and appearing in the Court of Chancery.[3] But this is usually the case with those who are frighten'd, and fret. They find out resemblances, where there are none, to encrease their own torment. Had you been cool, you had consider'd these as things which you did not understand, and sent the paper, conceiv'd in such absolute terms, to Mr Vipond – You did well in this. But you had done better in sending it to Dr Roberts. Or if the day fix'd for my appearance was at such a distance as would have admitted of your sending it to me, that had been the most natural step, tho' what you have done is full as well. But I'll lay a penny, that, mov'd as you were, you did not attend to this. Tell me honestly, Did you or not?

You are pleas'd with your new Name; and you shall have it, while you deserve it. But I must not have you deserve it, as you now do, for imitating the little Animal in it's imperfections.

Bees are easily frighten'd, and when they are so, are very fretfull, and sting any person near them, however innocent. I suffer'd thus by one. Something else had anger'd it, and it wreck'd it's spleen on me, fixing it's sting in my Nose. You have heard me describe my pain.

This is usually the Case with fretfull people especially when the occasions of fretting are none or trifling. They are disturb'd they scarce know why, and all who come near them must feel the Effects. If a fine Lady's hair takes not the right ply; or if her Complexion be more Wan, than usual, Poor Abigail suffers. But hold – These to some are not trifles. As I hope they are to you, they may however serve for an instance of what I would observe, that people in a fret seldom confine themselves to the occasion, but let fly at every person and thing near them. I have heard of a fine Lady, who in an high fret rung off the neck of her Parrot. I hope 'Greeny' is safe – By the by, what is become of your young Canary Bird? Dead, I suppose, because you have been silent about it. If so, I fear there was another fret.

Understand me, My Dear little Bee. I don't include in the notion of fretting, that uneasiness, which they, who desire to do all things right, feel, when they think they have done any thing imprudent or wrong. This may be, often is, Virtuous. When it is frequent, and rais'd on trifling occasions, it becomes a Weakness. When it produces Warmth and passion; and when these are transferr'd to persons, and things, who have had no hand in the real or fancy'd Cause of Uneasiness, it degenerates into Vice: And when this vice becomes habitual, it makes the persons themselves, and all who have intercourse with them, wretched. Avoid therefore all approaches to it, and Be rather unmov'd where there is some cause of Emotion, than too much or too often mov'd where there is none or but a small one. I know I am giving you advice here, which I do not always follow my Self. But, As the Parson once said to his Flock, Mind what I say, not what I do. I would have [you] copy me in nothing, but what is worthy imitation.

I had got thus far before yours arriv'd. I should otherwise have lost my turn upon the Canary bird. I am glad you have two.

Mr and Mrs Wills with the two Girls[4] came hither on Wedensday. I was at Charles-town. They din'd at Cary's, and at my return I found them and Dr Lawson who arriv'd about the same time. Their being here, and a Multitude of other letters to be answer'd disable me from saying much more to you. A few short answers to some of your questions I will not omit or postpone.

No jaunquilles to be taken up this year.

Let Ned Curtis have what Lavender He wants. The rest keep to perfume my linnen. Perhaps you'll not like it in yours because not fashionable.

Get your Boxes. But 'tis not worth while to paint them. They'll rot at the bottom do what you will.

The Boy I intend you promises well. If He does not answer, I'll dismiss him as I intend to do Mr Young.[5]

I knew nothing of Mr Leigh's match, till yours inform'd me. Dr Lawson told me the person.[6]

Tell Mrs Jourdan, that the Milk Vessels are arriv'd, and that there is a great uproar about them. Two are broke in the Carriage. Must not the packer be answerable? But those which are come whole, they tell me are rotten, and full of holes thro' which the light may be seen. Whoever sold them has abus'd you.

Kitty Ormsby and all at Charles-town din'd here from thence to day. They are just gone off. She is much better of her Cold. She proposes to set out for Dublin on Sunday. I have time for no more.

yours &c.
Edw: Elphin

[Free Edw:Elphin]

1. Possibly Dr William Roberts, the son of Lewis Roberts, an attorney. He took BA at TCD in 1729, LLB 1721 and LLD in 1726. *Alumni*, p.707.

2. This may be a reference to Ecclesiasticus 22:16 'As timber girt and bound together in a building, cannot be loosed with shaking: so the heart that is stablished by advised counsel, shall fear at no time.'

3. One of the three Burtons may be John Burton, who was the Public Registrar of Deeds and Conveyances, Lower Castle Yard. Watson (1751), p.57.

4. Godfrey and Sarah Wills had two daughters, Elizabeth (see Letter 39) and Martha who married Charles Wood of Larkfield, Co. Sligo. Burke (1912), p.624.

5. Mr Young: possibly Andrew Young, the fowler.

6. Robert Leigh (1729-1803) of Rosegarland, Co. Wexford, married Arabella Leslie of Glaslough, Co. Monaghan. He was MP for New Ross 1759-1800. His Dublin house was in St Stephen's Green. Burke (1912), p.395; *Georgian Society Records*, Vol.2, p.73.

103

Elphin. July 25, 1750

My Dear Girl at every turn makes use of two pleas by way of excuses which I have often told you, I would not allow as such.

One is *I forgot*. This is so far from being an excuse, that it is an Accusation. I admit it to be a true one. For indeed you are very forgetfull, or as you chuse sometimes to term it, very giddy. But this is a fault which you must set your Self to mend. You may if you please. Set your Self to acquire an Habit of attention. Let what you are order'd, or desir'd to do, make a proper impression on your mind, and then you'll not forget. Your neglect to give my last orders to John Miller, is much heighten'd by your telling me that He would obey them. You were indeed very safe in saying this. For He always obeys my orders, when He knows them. But I wonder much at your delaying to give him those orders, when your writing thus brought them agen to your mind. Indeed, My Dear, you were much to blame here, and ought to be asham'd of your being driven to make such a Confession as you have made. You were however right in making it, that John might not be blam'd when you were in fault.

Your other plea is a meer excuse. *Bad pens.* I have often told you I would not take this as an Excuse for bad writing; nor will I. You may, you ought to learn to write with any pen, as I do, as Mrs Jourdan does. I had rather much see a letter from you wrote freely, and every stroke as black as hers, or Sr Ralph Gore's horse,[1] than observe you, to my no small disappointment, continue in a stiff starch'd hand, which plagues you in writing, tho' every stroke be as fine as an Hair. I have often told you, I now repeat it, such Writing will not do for the business of life.

I see clearly that when you wrote about pens &c. you were in that temper which I censur'd in my last. Fretting. The innocent Pens were blam'd, when I know who was in fault. This was heighten'd too by despondency and Despondency produc'd more fret. 'You cannot write near so well now as two years ago'. If this be so, More shame for you. But it is not. I have had some letters from you this Season better wrote than any I remember before. It is true, I have had some as bad, or Worse; and there has been great difference in the Contents of them. Some sensible, proper, and the Sentences *bien tournées.*[2] They pleas'd me greatly. Others were quite the reverse. The one in which you describ'd your fright and fretting, was remarkably confus'd, and disjointed. Now whence this inequality, My Dearest? It must be from the state in which you sit down to write. What should hinder you from writing as well, and as good sense at one time as at another? It must be because you are hurry'd, or your mind is agitated with somewhat. Here is the true Cause, of what when it happens, distresses you. 'Tis in your own power to remove it. Set your Self to do this, and then you'll not have reason to complain of pens, or writing, nor shall I have any to find fault with your matter or Composition. After all your Care, it is very possible that you may not be quite as well dispos'd to write at one time, as at another. I have been, and am often so my Self. Now when this is your Case, or when you have not time to write as you ought, Write little. I had rather see three lines to tell me you are well, than three pages, carrying evident marks, of hurry, inattention or fretting. To comfort you after this Lecture, these bad things do not often happen, and I have on the whole much more reason to be pleas'd than otherwise. But As I often tell you, I would have you perfect in every thing that is good.

I was particularly pleas'd with your Character of Mrs Hunter. I thought it so well drawn, that I suspected Mrs Jourdan had help'd you. But she assur'd me she did not. Now, Huzzy, what quarter are you, who can write so very well, to expect, when you write otherwise? If you be honest, you'll answer None at all.

I return you Mr Moore's letter. Keep it by you. The Quantity is greater than He at first ask'd. As Mr Grant has been so late in getting the Cotton ready, I am indifferent now, whether the Beds be made this Season or not. I can make shift without them. It will therefore be better to deferr making them up, till Winter or next Spring. But let Mr Grant deliver to you the full Quantity of outside which Mr Moore demands. I believe He had best give you all He has made, if it be not much more, for fear of mistakes. As to Lining, chuse now, or deferr chusing till We meet as you please.

Enclos'd you have a list of Grocerys and some other things wanting here. Let them be provided, so as to be sent the first opportunity. I expect the Bishop of Clonfert, and his Dame here next month, after them L[ord] C[hief] J[ustice] Singleton and his Brother Judge and about the same time, I hope, the Chancellor.

Mr Wills &c. are still here, and I hope will stay some time. She told me yesterday that Cornet Lennox was dead.[3]

One thing I have often thought to mention to you, and as often have forgot. If you have any guts in your brains, you'll see the Chain which has just now brought it into my thoughts. The Match in the Artane family will, I suppose, be soon avow'd, if it be not already.[4] Whenever that happens, Make no visit to the young Dame, and, as much as you can, avoid doing any thing that may look like your or consequently my, countenancing, or approving of what she has done. Ten to one but you meet at Artane, where I would have you go as usual. Be very civil, But neither make, nor encourage, advances to further intercourse. I must greatly blame what she has done, tho' a family I love and honour may possibly be benefited by Her folly, and disobedience. You'll here have a delicate Card to play. Play it as well as you can, and Be cautious, on the one hand not to offend those whom you love and esteem, and have reason to do so, except perhaps for their conduct in this affair, which I can't think blameless; on the other, not to do any thing that may shew the least approbation of what has been done. This advice is of such a Nature, that I believe I need not desire you to keep it Secret from every one but her, to whom I do not wish you should have any reserve. God bless you My Dearest. I am

yours &c.
Edw: Elphin

You may plant Mr Waller's bounty where you please. The place you have chosen I think the right one.

I am plagu'd here about Cream Cheeses. I have not had one good. Mrs Jourdan brought down som Tin Vats in which if I mistake not, she us'd to order them to be made. They are in being. But I can't persuade Mrs Heap or Jennet to use them. They say, they do not know how. I desire Mrs Jourdan would instruct them.[5]

1. Sir Ralph Gore (1725-1802) 6th bart. was the second son of Sir Ralph Gore, Speaker of the Irish House of Commons. He succeeded his elder brother in 1746. His 'black and all Black' horse won His Majesty's Plate at the Curragh in 1750. Edward Synge and Henry Hamilton were executors of his mother's estate. G.E. Cokayne, *The Complete Peerage* (London 1949), pp.164-5; *Dublin Courant*, 11-15 September 1750; Eustace, Vol. 1, p.655.

2. *Bien tounée*: well phrased.

3. Wills Lennox was probably a son of William Lennox and his wife Sarah, *née* Wills. He enlisted as a cornet in Lord Molesworth's Dragoons on 6 June 1747; cornet in same regiment 8 June 1749. PRO WO64/9, f.174; WO64/11, f.51

4. Probably the marriage of Nehemiah Donnellan IV. His bride is not known. See Letter 100.

5. The 'tin vats' would be used to make *les crémets*; whipped cream and egg whites placed to drain in china or metal moulds pierced with holes and lined with muslin. Recipes for *les crémets* do not appear in either Hannah Glasse or Dorothy Hartley. The recipe came from Anjou and Saumur. Mrs Jourdan's family came from Anjou; hence her knowledge of how to make them. Elizabeth David, *French Provincial Cooking* (1960), p.443.

104

Elphin. July 28, 1750

Tho' I can write but little to my Dear Girl this post, yet I can't but take notice of the ingenuous manner in which you own your failings. I hope by this they'll never become faults. As long as my Admonitions are thus rec'd, and likely to produce so good effects, I shall with double pleasure continue them.

One false spelling as I pass. *dispence*. It should be *dispense*.

I suppose your taking salts agen, and repeating the German Spa is owing to those little Eruptions continuing, to which you are subject. I hope that both will be of use to you.

This brings the Doctor to my thoughts. See Ned Curtis assoon as you can, and desire him to get from Mr Lennox a Promissory note payable to bearer for £100 and to give it to the Doctor with my service. It is more convenient to me to make this present now, than it was when I left town. He may say this to the Doctor in as Civil Words as He pleases.

I am sorry for your baulk, but wish you had told me what employment the House keeper's husband is fit for. If a Butler, and as good or near as good for that as she is represented for her business, I'll venture on both, tho' against my principle. For I cannot bear Supple, and resolve to part with him when I go to town, whether this project goes on or not. He is a glum sullen, conceited Fool, and plagues, I won't say frets me every day of my life. So that I must get another or go without. If this husband be not fit for a Butler, Let me know what He is fit for, and his perfections and imperfections; and if the Woman be not hir'd, Keep the matter, if you can, depending till you write me a full and particular account. I am inclin'd to strain a point, to get such an Housekeeper as She is represented to be. John does not, I see, understand Milk-pans. If He has got two in the place of the broken ones, Let him send them. Those will be enough.

This letter is better written than your late ones; and from the hand, I think I can pronounce that you wrote it in less time, and with more ease than you have wrote those which I very justly found fault with. But you were not then in a fret. You see by this, that it will cost you less to do well, than indifferently.

Adieu
yours &c.
Edw: Elphin

I gave John Miller an account of Carleboe's ilness last post. I was then in great pain for him. But He is now much better, and I believe out of danger. Mrs Heap supplys his place most notably. The Strokes-town folks din'd here on Wedensday. Mrs Mahon could not conceal her surprize at Dinner's being so very well dress'd and serv'd.

In a letter from Mr Sullivane, I have a paragraph about the Ale. Tell Mrs Jourdan with my service, that I desire it may lye as it is, till September or October.

[Free Edw:Elphin]

105

Elphin. July 31, 1750

Every letter almost, which I have got from you this Season, My Dear Girl, cost you nearer five than four hours hard Work! This is a sad story, Ally, and it imports you much to consider the Consequences. At present you

1750

have a good deal of leasure. When you come more into the World, Business, and consequently occasions of writing will multiply – What then will you do? You have but this choice. Either to throw off writing entirely, or to learn in time, to write with more ease to your Self. The former I hope you wo'n't chuse – If you do, I shall from that moment pronounce you a fine Lady. The latter I am sure is in your power. You may do it if you please; and every summer you make some advances to it. But by the next all is forgot, and you set out in the old way. What you say now of writing quicker, and with more ease, and yet as well, you said about this time last year, and prov'd too as you do now. How came it to pass then, My Dear, that you did not continue in this way? Will you continue in it for the future? It is the only way of getting rid of a very bad habit. If you will not take it, you'll plague your Self and me too. I cannot think with any pleasure on the labour which your letters cost you – and fond as I am of your prattle, shall be apt to forbid you writing more than three words to tell me you are well, if more continues to be such hard work. Indeed I would forbid you instantly, but that I think it of the last consequence to you to get rid of this folly. Such it certainly is; and I'll tell you the true source of it. It arises from a little bit of pride, My Dear, not blameable in it's kind, but in this instance unlucky in it's effect. You would fain excell in writing. For this I blame you not. But your mistake is, that you persist in a Way, which has not succeeded, never will succeed and will not pursue that which on trial has answer'd better, and if continu'd in, would answer to your Wish. Your letter now before me is as well wrote as any I have had from you this Season, and what I take great notice of, there are fewer rasures or interlineations than usual. If you continue to write worse with great labour, than you can do with great ease, I must give you a new name *Mlle Bizarre* – You won't like this as well as you do the last I gave. But you shall have it, if hereafter you give me any occasion. I hope you won't. I have observ'd one false spelling inconsistant. It ought to be ent.

Your Question about waiting on young Leigh's Bride was quite unnecessary. That Marriage I suppose is with Consent on both sides. There can therefore be no objection to your making proper Compliments to a Lady, who thus marrys your relation, and one with whose Mother, sister, and Aunt you are so well acquainted.[1] Propose it to them, when the time comes, and do as they would have you. I think meanly of Matrimonial Parades. But in this, as in other indifferent matters, It is right to conform to the Custom of the World. I never can think it a matter of indifference, to shew any Countenance or approbation of such Marriages, as that which occasion'd my directions. I wonder it is not yet made publick.

We had no thunder here last week, and not much rain. Sunday about one, it began to rain. Yesterday We had a vast deal, and this day there have been some very heavy Show'rs very like thunder show'rs, but no thunder or lightning that We could hear or See. The Bad Weather kept Mr Wills &c. yesterday. They left me this morning. So Lawson and I are for the first time alone. We sha'n't continue long so. For besides chance Customers, I expect the Bishop of Clonfert and his family in a fortnight. I have time for no more. For I must write three lines to Mrs Jourdan. So My Dear Girl Adieu.

yours &c.
Edw: Elphin

I think it full time that the Hospital were eas'd of Carbery Berne. Pray Ask the Doctor whether a longer stay be to any purpose. If not, Let some sort of cloths be put on him, and Order John to send him down by the next Carrs, which come with any thing hither. Let him not be cloth'd like one that is to come into my family. I shall be afraid to venture on him, without very full assurance of a perfect Cure. But even with this, Good Frize will do for the present.

A very wet afternoon, and now at night heavy rain, and likely to continue. Corn, Hay and Flax in a very bad condition. I am in most pain about the last, as I know least how to manage it; and Varley is ill. I believe He has a fever like Peter's, but milder.

[Free Edw:Elphin. In another hand: Shampane, Shampain]

1. The relationship between Alicia Synge and Robert Leigh is not known.

106

Elphin. Aug 3, 1750

An House-keeper is wanting, My Dear, and this Wilkinson is said to be an excellent one.[1] If you don't get her, What chance have you for another as good or near as good as she is represented?

She wo'n't live any where seperate from her Husband, and this Husband is said to be a good Steward. Now such a Servant you all know I want, tho' I have one with that name Poor Simple Shannon as you very rightly stile him. Indeed He seems to grow more Simple every day. I could tell you several Historys since I came hither, which would at the same time vex and make you laugh. What then is, in these circumstances, most prudent for us to do? Surely in common Sense We ought to enquire into the Qualifications of both, and if they answer, to hire both. I have for a long time been making private enquiry for a good Steward, and would have taken one, could I have found him. If thus, one is, by accident, thrown in my way shall I reject him, especially as I at the same time secure a Servant for another place, as hard to get properly fill'd?

I know your and Mrs Jourdan's tenderness for that Simple Fellow, and I have a good deal my Self. But I must not to that sacrifice mine own Convenience, especially as I see him grow every day more careless in things to which his mean capacity undoubtedly extends.

My scheme however is not to part with him, but to keep him with his present appointments as Butler, with the Style of my Gentleman forsooth to save his credit that He may not appear degraded. If He wo'n't submit to this, I hope your tenderness for him will cease; I am sure it ought to do so.

The great point will be, to see that We are not bit in this adventure, by engaging with persons who will not answer Expectation. My principal objection is their being Man and Wife – But this I am contented to wave. I can't hope to have every Circumstance to my mind; and if they are both well qualify'd, and well dispos'd, this will be no evil. Whether they are or no, you and Mrs Jourdan must enquire with the greatest exactness. You know what sort of people I want. I need not therefore go into every particular. Sobriety, honesty, quietness, activity, Care, will of course occurr to your thoughts. The particulars of the House keeper's province I meddle not with. See to them your Selves. The principal parts of the Steward's, you know are, the Orderly Government of my Servants, the buying in all provisions for my House and Stables, and inspecting the consumption of the latter, and the keeping accounts. These are the great Articles. All the lesser ones will fall under one or other of them. If you treat at all with them, Mention as many as occurr to your thoughts; and among them, do not forget that, of letting us know when they go abroad. Asking leave may choque. But I will have no servant who shall think it their privilege to go out when they will without notice.

One thing you must carefully enquire into, and Be not content with a Superficial Answer. How they came to quit Mr Quin?[2] You gave me a sufficient account of the Cause of their leaving Mr Leesen.[3] But as to Mr Quin, the Appearance is against them. They can't have been long there, for He has not been long marry'd; and Servants such as they are describ'd, A Man very well able to keep them would not methinks lightly part with. It looks as if there were something wrong. If there be, it imports us to find it out. Alderman Dawson Mrs Quin's Father[4] is the likeliest person I can think of to inform us. Were I in town, I could speak to him. At this distance I know not how to get at him. Mrs Jourdan will perhaps think it *une demarche trop hardie*,[5] to go to him her self. If I thought so, I would not even hint it to her. But I fear she'll not be well inform'd by sending any one of the Errand. Miss Leigh[6] may perhaps inform you; and to be sure they'll give some account themselves, if ask'd. But I should be better satisfy'd with one from the Alderman.

If they be still unengag'd, send for the Woman, and talk to her of both. And, if you think them likely to do, know their Terms. They'll probably be high, and I shall be content to sacrifice somewhat to all our Ease, and Convenience. But further than £40 a year to both, I will not go. If they look higher, there's an End on't, and you must look out else where. Indeed I think that, a great deal too much. If you see things like to do with them, you must tell them their Accommodation; and Remember particularly, No allowance of Tea or Claret. If the Woman will have the former, she must get it for her Self. I will not carry my niceity as far as your poor Aunt does. But I never will furnish either to Servants. If Shannon stays He shall as now have the care of the Cellar. The Steward will have nothing to say to it.

I have thus wrote as fully on this Domestick affair, as I think there is Occasion. See now what you can make of it. Thus far I am fix'd, Supple I will not keep. If I hire this Man and Wife, Shannon may stay in the manner I have mention'd. If I do not, I must jog on with that Simple fellow, as I have done, till I can get a better, and look out for another Butler, and this last I must do, in case on my hiring this Steward, Shannon should be fool enough to think himself degraded and leave me.

I have wrote so much about this, that I have time for no more. So My Dearest Adieu.

yours &c.
Edw: Elphin

I am a little at a loss as to what you say about *Disobedient.* Pray what disobedient Friend have you had? I recollect none, unless you call Mrs Twisden so.[7]

Lady Arabella would not I believe have wrote *promisery.* It is promissory.[8]

In talking to these people, Perhaps it may be best not to mention either Tea or Claret unless they do. There's no occasion for Supposing such people entitled to either. You may ask the Man, whether He understands Country business, tho' I don't know that I shall have occasion to employ him in any.

They have broke me several of my glass Salt-Cellers. I must desire Mrs J to recollect as well as she can the kind, and to send down four. They are plain, of middling size, and the Hollow circular.

I forgot in my last to her to give an answer to what she wrote about the lower Servants bedding. Whatever is wanting there, Let it be provided.

Reading an idling French book the other day, I met with a very fine description of a young Dame. One part of it struck me. I can't help giving it you, as it exactly suits my Taste – *Elle etoit mise simplement, mais avec noblesse.* This at the Opera where fine folks usually go *fort parées.*[9]

Tho' I have mention'd £40 a year for the two, Don't offer it, till you find that less wo'n't do, nor then unless your information concerning the persons, be in all points very Satisfactory. It is, too much for midling Servants.

Our Weather has been and continues very bad. Monday was the worst day. I think I forgot to tell you in my last, that you may get as many Boxes for your Seeds &c. as you please.

1. Mr and Mrs Wilkinson: not known.

2, Windham Quin (1717-89) of Adare, Co. Limerick. Burke (1916), p.707.

3. Possibly Joseph Leeson (?-1783), son of Joseph Leeson of Dublin and Margaret Brice. He became baron Russborough in 1756. Burke (1871), p.781.

4. Frances Quin was a daughter of alderman Richard Dawson and Elizabeth Vesey. Burke (1916), p.707.

5. Rather too bold.

6. Judith Leigh: daughter of Francis Leigh and Alice Rawlins of Rathnagan, Co. Kildare. She died unmarried in 1788. Burke (1912), p.395.

7. Mrs Twisden: not known.

8. Probably Lady Arabella Denny, second daughter of Thomas, Lord Kerry. She married Arthur Denny of Tralee, who died in 1742. Her will was proved in 1792. Burke (1916), p.1206; Vicars, p.130.

9. She was dressed simply but elegantly ... in the height of fashion.

107

Elphin. Aug. 7, 1750

If I mistake not, you were here, My Dear Girl, when I got your good Mother's receit for the King's Evil for a poor Lad here.[1] He was in appearance cur'd by it. But either by bad Diet, or the ill tone of his bloud, There is a remain of a Scrophulous disorder which disables him from labour and will, unless remov'd, make his life miserable. I would fain have his Cure completed if I could. He is able to crawl to Dublin, and is strongly possessed with a notion that if He got into the Hospital, He should be cur'd. Ask the Doctor if he'll give me leave to send him up to him. He moves my pity greatly and I know not how to help him.

Your resolutions about writing are very good. But remember you have made the like before. I hope you'll now keep them. One thing I am sure would be of great use. I have recommended it formerly without effect. It is this. Accustom your Self to bear a little more than you do on your paper. Your present manner is as your writing shews, just to touch the Surface of your paper, with the nib of your pen. Hence all hair Strokes, and hence less Steady writing, which is not pretty. Your letters sometimes resemble the writing of an Old Man or Woman with a shaking hand. Hence too those great and constant Complaints of pens. It is difficult to get any fit for these hair strokes, impossible to find such as will make them long. If you write so as to feel your paper, and make somewhat a deeper impression on it, your hand will be more steady, and your pens, once right, will hold out longer; and those with somewhat a broader nib will please most, and last a long time. I don't mean by this, that you should chuse hard nibb'd pens. They are the Worst of all, and it is impossible to write perfectly with them. Pens that yield to the impression made and which without this force will make a hair stroke, are those I would recommend. See here the effect of them. I am now writing with the pen with which I begun. But I just touch the paper as you do. I don't think I write the better for it. If your hand be clear, steady and legible, a certain degree of blackness is rather a beauty; and it has this use, that you can write much faster, that way than the other.

Our Weather has been and continues bad. But by your accounts you have had rather more rain than We. We have indeed had a great deal too much.[2] I am afraid I shall suffer much by it in my Hay. Would it were in as good a Condition as John's. Yesterday was fair, except that We had one showr. This day is Wet and Windy. I am most in pain about the latter. My wheat is so ripe, as to make me apprehend shedding.

Varly's ilness has been very unlucky. It would have been more so, had I not by chance pick'd up a Soldier who seems to understand Flax as well as He does. He tells me that All things are very well; and as far as I can judge they are so. But on Sunday I was in great pain for Varly's life. His fever which We thought going off, rose higher. A Blister was judg'd necessary; and much difficulty I had to make him submit to it. But submit He did and He is now in a good way. Stafford has attended all my sick very well. He is marry'd, and to a Sligo Girl. But during his absence All was well. He has left her behind him. I am sure He'll not go for her, till Varly is well. I fear his absence during the Assizes. But unless something unexpected happens, I think Varly will before then be able to bear it.

When Carbery comes, the Doctor's directions shall be observ'd. But you must explain them a little. What is common Lee? If what I guess, and you chose to avoid writing the Word plain, or with a dash, as Mrs J – copy'd from a letter of Bab's, you might have wrote politely Chamber-lee. As I am not certain this was meant, you must tell me.[3]

I am sorry your Melons have not been as good as usual. This may have been owing in some measure to the Season. But the seed I gave Gannon was of different kinds from last year's. Don't save any, unless you stumble on a few remarkably good. Let the Peach-trees, which have given you bad fruit, be mark'd, that I may pull them up, and plant better in their places.

Johny Conroy and his Wife came hither last Week. I gave you last summer an account of her. They talk of setling here.[4] I am not sorry for it. Their Company sometimes will be agreable. They din'd here yesterday, and with them Mr Dowel, and his daughter.[5] She is an agreable young Woman. But I look at her with some pity. She is yet under twenty, and shews such a disposition to be fat, that I fear before thirty she'll be unwieldy. Mrs Cary was to have din'd here too. But she was and is indispos'd. Miss Pocklington did. I don't remember that I gave you any account of that girl. She is of a grave turn, but to me appears inclin'd to the insipid, But she's easy and good natur'd.

Shannon according to custom, has play'd me a trick. About a month ago I enquir'd of him what Stock of French white wine I had. He answer'd that there was a very good one. Little has been since us'd; and just now He comes to tell me that there is but two doz. pints. I must get a Supply, or want when I would most desire not to want. I have wrote to Sullivane to send some down, a hogshead if He has any of the same sort. If He has not, some must be sent from your Cellar. It is in No. 14. If Sullivane calls for any, Let it be given out.

All I can say with regard to your Ladys of Quality is this. Behave your Self to them all with proper regards. But be sure particularly to treat Lady K[6] with the utmost respect. I am not quite of Mrs Nicholson's mind in that point. To me it should seem that it would be better to make a quicker return, and then at a good interval to go a Second time. But she is better acquainted with her, and with these niceities than I am. Have a care that you have not mistaken hers – and so for this time My Dear Girl Adieu.

yours &c.
Edw: Elphin

Still the same pen. You see I can return with it to the Hair stroke. Don't say now Oh! Dada, you can do this, But I can't. I wish I could. You may if you'll endeavour it. Your fingers are as nimble as mine. Use them, and they'll do their office. By the by, How do you and Mr Walsh agree? You have said nothing of him since you gave me an account of your first Lesson.

1. Donald McCormuck: a labourer in Elphin, was a Roman Catholic. He lived with wife and six children over fourteen. Census, f.1.
2. The weather in August 1750 was cold and wet. 'A winterly month ... scarce a day without rain.' Rutty, p.154.
3. Common lees: urine.

4. John Conroy built Bettifield in Shankhill, a parish just west of Elphin, on land granted to him under the bishop's lease, naming the house after his wife, Elizabeth. Conroy Papers, item 13d.

5. Miss Dowell: not known.

6. Possibly the dowager Lady Kildare.

108

Elphin. Aug. 11, 1750

My Dear Girl.

The account which you give of those peoples leaving Mr Quin is so probable, that I believe it to be true. Had I known it in time, I had sav'd Mrs J the pain of making a Visit to the Alderman. Engage them, if you find them fit for our purpose. If Shannon will not stay on the Terms He may have, I must try to live without him. You'll do well to mention every branch you can think of, of both their business. But do not insist too much on things of less consequence, if you find the main ones likely to answer. The Woman's being old is no objection, since she is *hale*. So you ought to write it. I remark some other mistakes in spelling. *asistance*. It should be *Assistance*. take it *of*. It ought to be *off*. This is all I have now time for. I am

yours &c.
Edw: Elphin

Send for Moore and desire him to explain what He means by the fashion of the Bed being particular. I bespoke two. One a field Bed, the other a standing one, which I particularly directed to be of the Common Size. If He has made it larger, because others here are made so He has not observ'd my Order, and I will not meddle with it. But All this must lye as it is, till We meet.

[Free Edw:Elphin]

109

Elphin. Aug. 14, 1750

Hurry, Hurry, My Dear Girl, so great, that I shall not have time probably to write six lines. I expect the Bishop of Clonfert &c. every minute, and some Gent. about business. Till they come, My time is mine own, and I'll give it to you, having dispatch'd all my other letters; and a multitude of them there was, to give answers to. I was half frighten'd at them yesterday, when Shannon brought them in.

According to Custom, the first I open'd was yours; and I was much surpriz'd to find not a Word in it of the domestick affair. Mrs Jourdan's indeed supply'd the defect fully as to Substance. But in politeness, you ought just to have mention'd the thing and referr'd me to her. I don't write this to check, but to instruct – An unexpected interruption here. But I won't waste the minutes I have a chance for by telling you what it was.

I am much baulk'd at Mrs Jourdan's discovery of gout &c. However it was much better made before than after: and It is lucky now that you did not tell me what Mrs Wilkinson said was the reason of their leaving Mr Quin. You see by my last that with all my caution and diffidence I had been caught by it. But Is it right on this, to give up all thoughts of them, without knowing whether the Man's gout be much or little? I think not – Masters sometimes give partial accounts to the prejudice of Servants, as Servants very often do in their own favour – There will be no hurt in endeavouring to know the exact truth, as you may do by means of Judy – If the gout were but a little, It might be born for the sake of two so promising Servants – I believe you'll have time enough to Enquire. For it will not be easy for those two people to find a place to their liking, especially if this Secret of gout be divulg'd; and perhaps if the Woman finds she can't pursue her Scheme, She may submit to take a good place her Self, which may enable her to support her gouty Husband. I can't tell what to say more. But I am on the whole much disappointed. If on enquiry you find it not prudent to go further with these people, you must look out for a good House-keeper; and I must go on with poor Stupid Shannon, till I can get a better. But Supple I am at all events resolv'd to dismiss.

I can't tell what trouble it cost you to manage your new fashion'd pens. But your writing pleases me better than any I have of late had from you. With a little practice, you'll find it easier and pleasanter to write with such, than with those you are more us'd to.

By your and Mr Donnelan's accounts the Weather with you has been worse than here. We indeed have had rain more or less every day, except one, these three Weeks, but not near so violent or continu'd; and All my Corn is yet safe, and my hay very little damag'd. I have suffer'd most in my Flax-seed. But that I am less concern'd about, than I should be about any thing else. Varley is abroad, too early I think. But He would not stay within any longer.

I am sorry for your Swivel.[1] Go to Mr Holmes, and see whether the damage can be repair'd – I have now given you all the time I can spare. So My Dear Girl Adieu.

yours &c.
Edw: Elphin

If John does not send down every thing that I have wrote for quickly I shall be much distress'd. Tell Mrs Jourdan that Peter is very well, and will, I believe, prove a good Coach-man.

You'll find gilt paper in the middle drawer of the second tier – I shew'd it you there, Madam giddy, before I left you.

The Bishop &c. are come. Madam is as brisk as usual. They all enquir'd very affectionately for you all.

[Free Edw:Elphin]

1. Swivel: a turning metal ring on a watch.

110

Elphin. Aug. 18, 1750

If my Dear Girl is as much pleas'd with the Change of her pens and manner of writing, as I am, She will not grudge any pains it may have cost her. Persist in it, My Dearest, and in a little time, you'll write better and with more ease than your ugly diffidence of your Self has hitherto suffer'd you to hope. But guard against false spellings. You have wrote goutty. There ought to be but one t.

The Weather has indeed been very bad, and uncomfortable. But one way or other I have contriv'd to get my morning rides, except on three or four days in which the rain was continu'd. A Showr now and then I matter not. A good Coat, and my oyl'd hood effectually Secure me. Yesterday was fair only that We had one Severe Showr. But the Men wrought all the afternoon at the Hay with good effect.[1] This day has been hitherto fine. It is now near twelve. I have some fears about the afternoon. If it holds fair, I hope to have all my Wheat in stack; and every thing else, except my Flax-seed which is gone past retrieve, in very good order.

I can add nothing to what I wrote in my last, in relation to the Dome-stick affair. For the sake of two good Servants, I would bear with a little gout. But much will render the Man an Useless burthen. You probably know before this all that Miss Leigh can say as to this. If that gives you room to hope, I see not why you may not send for the Woman and speak plain to her, or get Miss Leigh to do it. You'll then be able to judge how prudent it may be to venture, and should you find this malady more griev-

ous on trial, than their account of it, there will be less difficulty in dismissing them. I really know not what to resolve on. On the one hand I am
strongly tempted by the prospect of two good Servants so much wanting.
On the other I am much afraid of engaging with them lest, I should be
oblig'd soon to dismiss them. Think for me, you and Mrs Jourdan; and do
what you judge best on the whole. Whatever it be, I promise you, I'll not
find fault.

The poor Boy is by this time on his way to Town. His name is McCormuck. I bid Shannon write by him to Will, who knows him. He'll go with
him to the Doctor.

I believe Sullivane visits the Cellar oftner than there is occasion. But I
dare not say any thing to him on this head, lest, if any accident happens,
He may throw the blame on me. His account to me has been, that the
Wine was on an high frett.² If so, I know it must be watch'd. Mrs Jourdan
must be content and bear his officious impertinence. If the Wine proves
Episcopal, It will make her some amends.

I believe it will be right to buy me some shirts. My way of old was to
have a few bought every year, so as to keep up a good Stock. By Shannon's
account I have a great many now. Perhaps one piece, and as much of
another as will make the Sleeves may be a Convenient addition. But do as
you please; and buy them and the Sheets from Tom King.

You say nothing of the grand affair. The account here is That the
young dame went on Sunday in Mr Ormsby's coach to Coll. Brown's³
house. As that is very near Artane, you may perhaps be embarrass'd.
Manage with as much dexterity as you can, so as neither to offend, nor
appear an Approver, and so make me pass for one. Perhaps it may be your
best way to discontinue dining, on account of bad roads, and shorter days.
I hint this only, without directing it. But No visit to the young Dame.

The Bishop &c. seem very easy here, and they are so to me. They love
early hours as well as I do. They all desire Compliments. You, Jeny, and
Mrs Jourdan must take them as if properly made. For my Self I say God
bless you all and so Adieu.

yours &c.
Edw: Elphin

Now privilege is on the brink of out you must have recourse to your
Franks. I'll procure you a Supply from the Speaker.⁴ The whole day fine,
and much good work done. But I am in pain for to morrow.

[Free Edw:Elphin]

1. Charles Varley recommended that hay should be cut in rainy weather, 'because
the odds are above twenty to one that it will not rain above two or three days together,

without an intermission of a dry day or two.' *A New System of Husbandry* p.184.

2. High frett: undergoing secondary fermentation.

3. Colonel William Brown was first commissioned captain in Lord Tyrawley's Regiment of Horse on 14 May 1715; major 10 May 1738. He commanded the 1st Regiment of Foot in the 1740s. Nehemiah Donnellan IV enlisted in Col Brown's regiment in 1744. PRO, WO64/11, f.13; *A List of the Colonels* (London 1740), p.63.

4. Henry Boyle (1682-1764), Speaker of the House of Commons 1733-56. In 1753 he opposed the appropriation of the Irish exchequer surplus. In 1756 he became 1st earl of Shannon. He lived at 11 Henrietta Street. Burke (1916), p.1829. O'Donovan, passim; *Georgian Society Records*, Vol.2, p.21.

111

Elphin. Aug. 21, 1750

My Dear Girl

Now privilege is out, I must take the large paper, and you must have the trouble of conveying orders to John and others.

Bid him go to Smith,[1] and order him immediatly to prepare six Scutching boards, six Scutching Handles, 6 foot hatchils; and three Breaks[2] – He must take care to make these more perfect than He did the last.

Tell John I have his letter enclosing the three papers. When the things come He shall know in what Condition. When next He sees Sullivane, desire him to let him know, that I have his letter, but do not chuse to put him to the expense of a groat to tell him so, or thank him for his present. He must tell him also that I shall want 3. or 4. Gross more of bottles at least, when a supply of them comes in, He may send so many down, without further orders.

You see by my last that I expected you would have such an Adventure as you have had. If you meet agen there, to which I have no objection, you need not any of you behave with Shyness. But Avoid all intercourse any where else. I see nothing likely to pinch you, unless your friend Kitty should take notice of your behaviour. If she does, e'en tell her the true reason, but do it under a promise of her keeping your Secret; and tell her further, that I bid you open your Self to her only.

Nancy French's affair has been slightly mention'd here by some of my Visitants. Her Father told me of it last Winter. But I am quite silent. I don't know yet, whether it will come to any thing. My wishes are the same with yours.

I have been much surpriz'd at your long Silence about Mrs Silver, and intended often to have question'd you about it, but as often forgot to do it. Pray Give her my best respects, and Tell her that, Old as I am, I am always pleas'd, when Ladys please themselves.

I believe Miss Leigh will find out the truth for you in relation to gout &c. You have spelt the word, pump'd, wrong. You write it with an o.

Our Weather has been very passable since Saturday noon; and We have made the best use of it. All my Corn is stack'd; and what Hay is cut will be safe if it holds up till night. I am not sure that it will. – It has.

All letters came free yesterday. That deliver'd by the Woman, was not a petition, but one forgot at the post. You might have seen the Post-mark on it. Keep Lennox's receit safe.

In one of your letters you wrote of Pat Hurly, with the indignation, which his villany deserv'd.[3] What would you have said, if after conviction and sentence He had escap'd that Death which was design'd for him? You would certainly have been in pain for me and the whole Country. And yet if He had not, as the rabble say, been born to be hang'd, He would certainly have escap'd. Some way or other He got a Collar, and harness so artfully contriv'd, and nicely put on, that after hanging an hour and five minutes, He was as much alive, as I am now. Till He had hung half an hour and five minutes, there was not the least suspicion. A slight motion of one of his Legs at that time gave the first; and It was heighten'd by observing His hands Preserv'd the natural Colour. The block head had two pair of white Gloves in his pocket, given by friends, that He might make a good figure. On these appearances the Wise Sheriff Ignat. Kelly[4] waited half an hour, before He directed a further examination. But at last the Contrivance was discover'd; and the Gent. was hang'd in Earnest; and so the Country is freed from a very Artfull and determin'd rogue. Now will I lay two pence, that Mrs Jourdan and you will have for a minute or two some Workings of your good nature, and think it was a pity, that He had not one chance more given him of being honest. Confess: am I right or not – and So Adieu.

 yours &c.
 Edw: Elphin

Mrs Whetcombe is very well, and gay. The Bishop graver than usual. The young ones, such as you know them to be every where else. No changelings. They'll be soon in town, and from thence to Bath.

1. Smith: the blacksmith.
2. Scutchers were implements to prepare flax by beating; hatchils or hackles were to comb out the fibres of flax; brakes were toothed instruments for breaking or crushing flax.
3. Patrick Hurly was a burglar who stole silver from Luke Dowell of Mantua. 'Last Wednesday evening one Patrick Hurly was detected in selling Part of the Plate adver-

tised about a year ago to have been stolen from Luke Dowell, Esq. He was apprehended by Mr Williamson, Silversmith in Castle Street, where he came to sell part of the Plate, who suspecting it to be stolen, kept him in Discourse, 'till he sent for a Constable, who carried him before the Right Hon the Lord Mayor by whom he was committed to New-gate. On examining his Chest where he lodged there were found upward of 100 ounces of Plate, the Property of said Mr Dowell, which tho' broke in Pieces, were discoverable by the Crests and Arms. The Prisoner has since confessed the Fact and informed on two of his Accomplices.' *Dublin Courant*, 9-12 June 1750.

4. Ignatius Kelly, son of Edward Kelly of Castle Ruby, Co. Roscommon, was admitted to the Middle Temple in 1725. MacGeagh, p.297.

112

Elphin. Aug. 24, 1750

My Dear Girl

I take my sheet, tho' I have not much to say and am straiten'd in time.

My letters came free on Monday. But I was sous'd yesterday. Yet all my own. I am tir'd with answering some and am forc'd to post-pone others to next post.

Your writing does not this time appear as well as it would, if you had air'd your paper. Do it for the future. If you do not improve by your stopping Exercises, It is not because you are a Dunce; But because you are giddy. You'll amend of this fault sooner than you could of the other.

I am glad you have resolv'd to take leave at Artane. By a letter from Mr D. yesterday, I find He judges of Mr N. much as Miss Leigh does.[1] For his, the father's, sake I wish things may take a good turn. But I am very little concern'd about the young ones; and, Fall what will, I never would have your intercourse with the young Adventuress, go further than Cold Civility. *Entre nous*, It is on the whole, a bad affair; I fear not one is perfectly blameless.

The disguise of gout, gives me a bad opinion of the admir'd Couple. But I'll wait for the account you promise of your interview with the Woman and then give you my Opinion.

I might have told you in my last that All the Carriage was come safe. But I am not sure that I did. They came after I had wrote, but before I seal'd my letter. Carbery has thriven well in the Hospital. He is as fat as a Puffen. He is yet here; and shall continue, if his head continues Well. The Lee, It ought to be wrote, Lye,[2] shall be us'd to it.

Tell John that He has mistaken me quite as to the Lantherns. I wanted a hand one, to carry a Candle in from office to office; and such a one He must send. One will do. Those that are come will be usefull. I never saw any of the kind before.

I believe John blunders about bottles. By a letter from Sullivane rec'd on Monday last two Gross were bought and at no high price, only twenty four shill[ings] the Gross. If these were sent down, I could wait for more till they fell to the usual Value. So that if John has hurry'd Sullivane to provide more immediatly, Either I have mistaken in sending, or He in reading, my orders. But it is no great matter. I must, as John says, have bottles at any rate.

I am much better pleas'd at your being fond of Mrs Hamilton, than I should be, if you were so of the other Dame. Now and then, you may go there to amuse your Self, and make honey. Often I hope you'll not chuse, and when you don't chuse, you may contrive to escape. For instance, To her second invitation for this day se'night, the present answer might have been: you would if you could, or you were not sure that you could. By Thursday next, you might have contriv'd something to bring you off. I own this is a sort of shifting. But she is not deceiv'd. She knows what I think of her Routs &c. and will impute your Excusing your Self, to the true Cause. I shall not be sorry if she ascribes part of the Demerit to your own Sweet Self.

I understand the paper, which you enclos'd, very well, and know the Jessop³ who gave it to John, but cannot imagine for what reason He gave it, or desir'd it should be sent me. The Man is certainly crack'd. I think I have heard that He was. I have not seen him a long time. He was, when I knew him, a low muddling Attorney, and much inclin'd to fish in troubled Waters. Sure He has no conceit in his head about that part of my Estate, to which I am entitled by the Deed of which He has sent a right Abstract.

The Bishop &c. left me yesterday morning, very well pleas'd with their Entertainment. They'll I believe, be in town, the middle of next Month.

I had yesterday a letter from your Uncle, in which He says that poor Betty is in the same pitiable way. I am in great pain about them, and begin to wish they were in town.

Our Weather yesterday and to day has been Worse than for some days before. But as there has been but little rain, All Harvest-affairs go on very well. My Corn is coming home: and I hope, the Hay will soon follow, all that is cut. But I am mowing now. Upon the best enquiry I can make, the Country has not yet suffer'd much. But As the Weather is tending to Worse, I am in some pain. The Wind is very high now. I dread it's ending in rain. But in this, and every thing else, God's Will be done. Adieu.

yours &c.
Edw: Elphin

Ask John when He intends to set about dunging his Meadows.

1. Obscure: relates to the Donnellan marriage.
2. Lye: a strong alkaline solution made from water with vegetable ashes.
3. Jessop: not known.

113

Elphin. Aug. 28, 1750

My Dear Girl

Your quarrel at the Chan[cello]r made me laugh. You may better bear his Exactness, since the Speaker is so complaisant. But He treats you as He does every one else; and besides, the Franks are design'd for me. If you desir'd any for your other Correspondence, Probably He would not refuse. But what do you mean by saying 'He has a mighty giddy opinion of me'? Is his opinion giddy? You know how you ought to have wrote and I know what you mean. But your Expression is not Exact; and is some proof that you are, in this instance at least, what you suspect He fancys you to be.

You have given another in this letter. Tho' you say you will not tell your story by halves in relation to the Wilkinsons, you don't say which demands the £20.–:– and which the 12 Guineas. My guess is, that the Woman values her Self highest.

I really am somewhat at a loss what to resolve in relation to these people. I cannot think they would be such fools, as to deny so steadily what a little time must prove upon them, and imagine therefore that the Alderman was either misinform'd, or mistaken. You told me before, that the Woman was old but hale. By the History of his Gout, the Man must be old too. Is his appearance hale? If not, it will be wrong to meddle with them. It is at best a sort of Adventure; and yet it is one that I am inclin'd to run, if Mrs Jourdan and you approve of it. Don't be nice now either of you, and decline giving your Opinion. You who have seen and talk'd to them can judge much better than I can; and I have told you already, what I now repeat. That Let what will fall, I will not blame you for any thing but Shyness in speaking your minds. If what you've been told be true; the Woman is most to be valu'd. But the Man will do well enough, if He keeps up to what He says of himself; and, if He be thoroughly honest and trusty, He must be low indeed, if He be not better than poor Stupid Shannon.

That Silly block-head has vex'd me this morning. As, from your accounts I thought it not impossible but that We might hire these people, I told him that I had such a thing under Consideration, and what my intentions were with respect to him. His first Speech was, that He hop'd whoever I took would serve me, as well as He had done. He was going on to praise himself, but I stopp'd him, and desir'd He would speak to the point and say whether He would stay on the Terms I propos'd to him. The Gent then ask'd whether his appointments were to be lessen'd. I said, no; on which He mutter'd, that He should be sorry to leave me, and would stay. But He said this in so silly and absurd a Manner, that I thought it necessary to have a more steady and Explicite answer. The result was that after a good deal of non-sense, and commendation of himself He said that It was hard, after living with me, and serving me faithfully, for above six years, He should be degraded instead of being advanc'd. I have neither time nor inclination to trouble you with all the Conversation between us. But when I desir'd his answer, He very impertinently ask'd whether I would not be content with one, when We return'd to Dublin. Provok'd at this, I told him, that He must give his answer then; and that if He did not, I would at once put an End to all matters between us. He continu'd silent; and so I told him that He should go. I have so much pity for this simple fellow and his Family, as to be sorry for this Egregious folly; and if you and Mrs Jourdan, can, by talking to his Wife, whom probably you see sometimes, convince her, and by her him, of it, so as that He may apply to me to keep him, I even yet will. But two things I am now fix'd in: One is, that If He stays at all, It shall be in that station; Whether you think it adviseable to hire these people or not, I will get some person or other assoon as I possibly can, to be a House-steward, and Governour of my Family. Let not therefore any thought about Shannon's continuing such, influence your resolutions concerning them. He positively shall not, if I can find another above ground. The other point in which I am fix'd is that I will not make the least advance to the Silly fellow, nor even consent to his staying, but upon the most earnest intreaty. If therefore you speak to his Wife, which you may do or not, as you please, apprize her of our parting as a thing absolutely fix'd [*damaged ms*]on; and Give her not the least hint, that you imagine I will, now on [*damaged ms*] Terms, keep him. If she talks of applying, Don't discourage her. If she does not, do not move her to it. I must break my chains, for indeed they gall me every day more and more. Upon this scheme, I might hope for more ease and comfort, if Wilkinson, or any other fill'd well the office of a Steward &c. in Dublin. But Shannon shall, no longer than I can provide another, continue to plague me in it. Here He will be of less consequence to me than ever: For I have lately hir'd a very orderly sensible Man to be my House and Land-steward. His Character is extremely well vouch'd, and All I yet see of him answers. Thus I have told you a long story, and given you all the hints and advice I can. Do now as you judge best. If you still doubt what to do, I am sure you may have time to communicate your doubts, and have my opinion upon them. But as well as I can judge, you already know as much as you can hope to know before trial and Therefore in my Opinion the best way will be to be off or on, without more ado. I believe £30 a year to the two will do. You may therefore, if you judge it proper to go so far, offer this; and in case they adhere to their demand, desire time to write to the person for whom They are design'd, and have his answer. This will give you an Opportunity of saying any thing more you have to say, and me of considering it; and Difference about wages may furnish a good reason for being off, tho' the true one should be somewhat else. I confess I shall be better pleas'd that there be none. But if you think of speaking at all to Shannon's Wife, you need not wait for this. For with respect to him, I am absolutely determin'd.

Now I am upon these affairs, It comes into my mind to tell you, that Robinson must dispose of himself some way or other at my going to town. I resolve to carry Brewster up with me. By Carleboe's and Mrs Heap's account, He promises to make a much better Cook than the other.

Bid John go to Sullivane and tell him that I was within an inch of loosing the Aulm of Hock,[1] by Mr Tighe's[2] neglect. I order'd him to put four Iron Hoops on it; and He put but two. Some of the Wooden ones are flown. But it is yet Staunch; and I'll bottle it to morrow. I am in pain about the Claret hogsheads, tho' All is yet in appearance very well. Assoon as I get bottles, I'll bottle them off.

John must also speak to Woodward, and desire him to buy as much coarse stout Broad-cloth of some dark colour as will make what they call an Hunts-man's Coat, for a young Man rather tall, and Slender. The Coat I mean is to be a sort of Close Coat, but to have two rows of buttons on the breast and a cape. He sent down green Cloth for such a one last year, and if I forget not, the Quantity was three yards. Whatever it was, the same will do for this. But the Cloth must be of a dark colour, and about six shill[ings] the yard. He must also send lining, and whatever else is necessary for making it up. The Buttons had best be mettal, the same as are for my liverys. The young Man must also have a Waste-coat either one or two; and Let Woodward determine thus: If two stripp'd flannel waste-Coats will cost less than one of cloth, computing the making and all, Let him provide two such, and send them down to be made here. If one Cloth will cost about the same, Let him send Cloth for that as well as the Coat, and lining and trimmings with it. These Clothes are design'd for a [*damaged ms*] Lad, whom I have taken on trial. I would have them stout and Warm. But there need be no great niceity about them. For fear of mistakes you had better send for Woodward and give him directions your Self.

I am most heartily griev'd at little Jeny Curtis's[3] ilness – God send she may recover, and be a Comfort to poor Ned and his Wife, as you are, and I hope always will be to

your most affectionate Father

Edw: Elphin

If you talk to those people agen, you must strongly inculcate great regularity and great quietness. The Man shall have proper Authority over the servants, i.e. footmen &c. But Carleboe, John, and the Stupid fool, if He stays shall have no master but me. It will be right to let them know, on what foot these servants are with me, that there may be no vying nor endeavour to supplant.

When you see Woodward, Ask if he has secur'd Cloth for the Servants clothes.

Let John tell Sullivane, that I wish it fell in his way to get me some of the light Green bottles. He promis'd last winter that He would. I should be glad of a doz. unless they be dear. If they be, I'll have none of them. The two Gross which are bought must be sent down instantly without waiting for more. I shall be greatly distress'd if I have them not next Week – I unseal'd my letter to write this.

1. Aulm of hock: an auln was a forty-gallon container used for Rhenish wine.
2. Mr Tighe: a cooper.
3. Jane Curtis: daughter of Edward Curtis.

114

My Dear Girl will have little for her groat this bout, more than what I know she'll think worth two, and that is, that, I bless God, I am very well.

The Salt-Cellers (so you should write I think, but am not certain) will do very well. Tho' not exactly the same with what I had, they are like them.

My Compliments to Mrs Silver; and tell her that [*damaged ms*]she is mistaken. I will not insult. I hope [*damaged ms*] from hence, that I am not quite so conceited as [*damaged ms*] I was. But what will she say to me when you [*damaged ms*] further, that I don't imagine she then spoke as [*damaged ms*] Oh! The Vain creature, she'll say. No! I am not [*damaged ms*] I know her to be polite; and Ironical abuse is the [*damaged ms*] Compliment.

I am afraid our friends are much blam'd by others, because they blame themselves. They cannot do this more than they deserve. I wish Father and Mother may be thought innocent.

Tell John I am very glad, He has sent off the Bottles. I think I wrote lately for a Gross of pints. If I did I retract that order. But two Gross more of Quarts must come some time within a month.

Whichever of you writes to Roscrea, I desire, would let your Uncle know, with my love to all, that I rec'd his, but don't write because I have nothing to say but what He knows already: and Let Molly be told, that the Bargain is made; and that she is from hence-forth my head Dairy-maid.

Yesterday was hazy, and dropping. The Evening, night, and this morning a Vast deal of rain fell, which, after very fine Weather on Wedensday, struck us all of a heap. But the day has taken up, and is now very fine. God grant it may continue. The Country will otherwise be undone. Adieu – God bless you all

yours &c.
Edw: Elphin

[*damaged ms*] He must desire Sullivane to provide six [*damaged ms*] the best kind. And next time He comes to teaze with [*damaged ms*] a Visit to the Cellar, I desire she or you would [*damaged ms*] that if He approves, I would have the hogshead of Wine [*damaged ms*] from him, and now lyes in the Cellar with you, bottled [*damaged ms*] Cooper must do it, and a day must be fix'd when [*damaged ms*] attend. I suppose I have bottles enough for that, [*damaged ms*] by this time. The Wine Cooper must see that they are perfectly well wash'd. The Bin I design for it is that out of which you've had your Wine this summer. I suppose it is by this time near Empty. What remains may be carefully remov'd, and put in the Gang-way of the innermost part of the Cellar.

115

Elphin. September 4, 1750

My Dear Girl

Some Company here, and more expected; you must agen be content, with what you can get. I write in the morning, before my Judges are stirring. A great fog keeps me within. But it promises a fine day.

Most of your giddinesses have been in trifles. This in relation to the Woman Wilkinson, has been the only one of consequence. If you had told me earlier of her imperfections, you had sav'd me and your Self some trouble. I think it not prudent to engage with a deaf wizen'd old Woman and a gouty Old Man. So you must look out for an House-keeper, and I for a Steward. As to the former I leave you absolutely to your Selves, and will not be troubled with giving any Opinion about one. If you won't judge and chuse for your Selves, Let it alone.

You are much disturb'd, I see, at what I wrote about your being influenc'd by too much pity for simple Shannon, and you have express'd your

Self with less Caution on that subject than you should have done. *You scorn to do any thing underhand, are mightily vex'd that I should suspect you of it, Something so mean* &c. Read what I wrote agen, My Dear, and I believe you'll find there is not much reason for Speeches of this strong kind; and consider that by them you in your turn accuse me, of what I am as little guilty, as you are of what you fancy I impute to you. I am very sure you did not mean this. But indeed, My Dear Girl, you have wrote too unguardedly here. Avoid it for the future. When you have liv'd longer in the World, and made more observations on your Self and others, you'll find that People are often influenc'd without being conscious to themselves that they are so; and to suspect that you, whom I know to be very good natur'd, might possibly be thus influenc'd, is not much to your disadvantage.

I am sorry for the loss of my fruit. But Are you sure and certain, the thieves came over the Wall? If All the upper garden was rifled, that part of it which is next the Church-yard,[1] and must have oblig'd them to have gone cross Gannon's house, as well as that next the waste-ground, Gannon must have slept very sound.

Bid John go to Sullivane, and tell him that I did not, till yesterday taste his Champaign, and that I think it good, and therefore desire He would keep an Hamper of it for me. If He has Burgundy, that He can be sure is as good, as what I had from him before, I desire He would keep an Hamper of that also for me. The Terms I'll leave to himself. Let him tell him further, that the Bottles of his Champaign will answer the use for which I wanted the green ones, and that therefore He need not trouble himself further about getting any.

Bid John also get me half a dozen Mouse traps, half of the Cage-kind, and half of those with Holes. My granarys, notwithstanding all my Care, are infested with Mice, and I fear some of them are got into the House. Let him also get me ten or a dozen sheets of Tin, such as may be fit to nail on the bottoms of doors, to keep such vermin out. If He be at a loss about these, Let him consult Mr Nicholson, who will direct him to the kind, and where they may be had. I have time for no more.

yours &c.
Edw: Elphin

The day has not answer'd as I expected. But the little rain we had did not hinder my guests from a fine ride.

Don't be uneasy at what I have wrote. When you say, or do, or write any thing that you ought not, I must take notice of it, to guard you against mistakes of the same kind with respect to others. I am pretty sure, that I wrote nothing, which gave you just occasion for so much Emotion. But if I had, consider that there should be a decency in your manner of shewing resentment, suited to the person who has given the offence. If you ever fail of this, I had rather you did to me, than to any one else; and It is not on mine own account but yours, and what may happen with respect to others, that I have taken so much notice of it.

Pray How are your Grapes? I am glad you have had so much good fruit of other kinds.

L[or]d Chan[cello]r and his son[2] are just come at two from Mullingar. 10. at night

On further trial of the Champaign I do not like it as well as I did the first bottle. Let not John therefore say any thing to Sullivane either about that or Burgundy. But He may speak to him not to trouble himself about the Green Bottles. I unseal'd my letter to write this. So that if there be any bungling about the Wax, you are not to mind it.

While the Chanc[ello]r is abroad, use the Speaker's Franks.

[To Miss Synge Cavan Street Dublin Free Newport][3]

1. The wall of St Kevin's churchyard ran along Synge's eastern boundary.

2. Robert Jocelyn (1731-97): only son of Lord Newport, the Lord Chancellor. MP for Old Leighlin 1745-55; Auditor-General of Ireland 1750. He became 1st earl of Roden in 1771. Burke (1916), p.1726.

3. Franked by Lord Newport, the Lord Chancellor.

116

Elphin. September 7, 1750

You are very right, My Dear Girl, you must expect no longer letters till I clear out. The Judges went off this morning. The Chan[cello]r stays till Monday. Judge York[1] will either carry or send to you my Box with the hinge broken. See him to be sure, if you be at home. He talk'd of his Wife[2] waiting on you &c. If she does, I need not desire you to make the proper return.

I'll deduct a groat or 8d out of your allowance. When you had so many franks, could you not have afforded me one? Or, if you thought that too much, you might have enclos'd to the Chan[cello]r here – you see I save your money when I can.

I have already set you right about the Pint-bottles – I want none. But the Quarts and 6 Gross of best Corks must come.

Send the Enclos'd to poor Mrs Armstrong.[3] I am still in pain about little Jeny. Tell Ned she may have all the Sack in the Cellar.

yours &c.

Edw: Elphin

1. William York (1700-76): Justice of the Common Pleas in Ireland 1743. Educated Charterhouse and Cambridge. He bought Rathmines Castle in 1746. In 1753 he became Chief Justice of the Common Pleas after Henry Singleton. Died in Brentford, London, of accidental poisoning. He lived in William Street and Rathmines Castle. Ball, Vol. 2, p.207.

2. Charity Singleton: niece of Lord Chief Justice Singleton, married William York in 1744. In later life she lived in Hanover Square, London, and her will was proved in 1779. Ball, Vol. 2, p.207; Vicars, p.502.

3. Mrs Armstrong: not known.

117

Elphin. September 11, 1750

I had no letter from you yesterday, My Dear Girl. If I said, that this gives me no uneasiness, you would not be pleas'd, and I should not write strict truth. But this I am sure of, that I am not the hund'redth part so uneasy, as you would be on missing one from me. If any thing had been amiss, I should one way or other have heard it. As I know nothing of you at all, I comfort my Self with the hope, that all is well, and that your letter has miscarry'd as you know some of mine did last Spring. But if this be the case, I will certainly do, what I did not do then, complain to Sr Marm.[1] Whomever you sent your letter by, examine strictly as to the time and manner of delivering it. Unless I can make clear proof of this, I can't support my complaint.

The Chan[cello]r left me yesterday morning very early, intending to take a late dinner at Garbally, and pass the night there. As this is a great journey, He sent his post-Chaise and Horses to Roscommon the night before; and my Coach carry'd him thither by nine. But unluckily his Chaise broke on the Way to Roscommon, and was not refitted till half an hour past one. This I learn'd on the return of the Coach; and am sure He must have been in the night. [*sic*] I am sorry for it, but pleas'd; that no cross accident happen'd him in my Carriage, by me or mine, or, any way else. He seem'd to like every thing, house and Entertainment, and was as idle and Vacant as the best of us. So was L[or]d Ch[ief] Justice. We pass'd our time merrily; and Carleboe &c. did their parts mighty well; and now Lawson and I are alone. The Variety pleases.

Send the letter you receive with this to Mr Sullivane; and tell John that I find three Gross of quart bottles will answer my occasions. Let him therefore send no more. Bid him also speak to Turner to have ready five hundred of half flat Iron, two hundred of Flat, and three hundred of Square of the kind He us'd to send. The Sooner He gets Carrs for the Bottles and these the better; and bid him send with them such an Hand Lanthern as He sent before. I find two will be necessary.

Tho' I have not yet fix'd any time even in mine own thoughts for going to town, yet I think it will be right to send to the Brewer to lay in some Ale. I hope He has us'd you well. If He has not, I'll quit him. But if He has serv'd you as He ought, or as well as you can hope another will, Send for him, and try to prevail on him to brew some Ale on purpose, such as you know I like, pale, soft, smooth, and not too bitter, and lay in some, three or four half Barrels, assoon as brew'd and continue afterwards to lay in one every week to be ready to succeed them. Give like orders about Small Beer. As there is no fear now of hot weather, Both Ale and small beer will take some time to ripen. Adieu. With all my coolness I shall long for the next post.

yours &c.
Edw: Elphin

Let not the six Gross of Corks be forgotten.

1. Possibly Mr Martin at the post office. See Letter 119.

118

Elphin. September 15, 1750

Well, My Dear Girl. Your last letter came safe; and whatever uneasiness, I had is quite remov'd. Do you from this incident, learn a lesson, which some time or other you may have occasion for. All may be well, tho' you have no letter. If you have not done it already. I desire that you would give notice at the Post-office of the miscarriage of your last. It will put them upon enquiring what is become of it. When next you see Mrs Hamilton tell her of it, and add, with my Service, that She'll oblige me by giving George Buchanan[1] an hearty chiding about this neglect. I know not whether He be the guilty person. But whoever is, will know his fault, if He does. I wish We may recover the letter. For want of it, I do not throughly understand some parts of your last, that particularly which relates to your poor Aunt.

It is easy to see that your's was wrote in some hurry. But there are false-spellings in it, for which I won't allow hurry to be an excuse. The true spelling is, house-Wife. This shews the reason of the name. You omit the o and e.. I wonder more at your mispelling Ireland. So it ought to be. You have left out the e. If you had put in the Asterisk thus Ir'land, this had been allowable. But the other is the best way; and you were certainly very absent when you wrote a Word wrong, that you have seen ten thousand times.

The formal ill-written Card must probably have been a foot-man's. The Judge writes a fair hand. It is possible it might have been his Dame's. I know nothing of her more than you do. But when He mention'd in the Cant polite terms, her having the honour of waiting on you, I could not say no. You may keep the Box by you till I to to town. I have got one from Carleboe, that does very well.

I am sorry you are so servantless. But such things will happen; and It is not amiss sometimes to be put to your shifts. You don't know what may happen to you in the Course of your life. But Take this as a piece of advice, which is of more importance than it may seem. Do as many things your Self about your Self as you can. Remember I tell you, that tho' you should be as well attended the remainder of your days, as you have hitherto been, which by the by is more than will probably happen, you'll find great comfort in it.

I am much rejoic'd at your account of little Jeny Curtis and her Father. It will give me very great pleasure, to know that Both, and the good Woman are perfectly well.

Send the Enclos'd to Mrs Armstrong. I chuse to pay for it, rather than she should. I believe she is poor enough indeed, and know her to be extremely unfortunate, tho' not by her own fault. But your manner of speaking of her makes me apprehend some new distress. Pray explain your Self. Adieu. God bless you all

yours &c.
Edw: Elphin

Bid John order Smith to provide two more Looms and when they are ready, to let me know it.

1. George Buchanan: a postal official. See Letter 8.

119

Elphin. September 18, 1750

I have yours, My Dear Girl, and one from Mrs Jourdan, the only one, I ever had from her, which I wish she had not wrote. But you, Miss Scruple, not she, are to blame. And what will you get by it? Not much. For All I shall

say on the Subject is; that As to one, I am much surpriz'd to find her propos'd and her Character descanted on, against whom, or rather her Husband, you made an objection which is indeed *sans replique*,[1] and which you
seem'd to think so, by saying so that affair's over. Have you a mind to
resume it? If not, why was she mention'd? If you have, Do as you please.
As to the other, If you or Mrs Jourdan hesitate about her, you may for me.
For I positively will give no opinion, and you ought not to have urg'd me
thus to it. When I leave a thing to your own prudence, you ought to act as
you would do, if I were no way concern'd; and Not to do it, is a childish
Weakness, of which you ought to cure your Self as fast as you can.

Assoon as you get this, Send Will back to the post-office; bid him
enquire for Mr Martin, and tell him that He goes to him by my order to
give the History of the Estray-letter. Let him give it with strict regard to
truth. For I am determin'd to pursue my Complaint, which I have this day
made in strong terms, to the Utmost.

Send for Woodward, and tell him that his question shews how little He
minds my business. I told him several times before I left town, that I
should want livery Cloths, and big Coats also for my Servants. If He had
forgot this, He ought to have ask'd long since, that He might have had a
piece made on purpose, which cannot, I believe, be now done. But if I am
disappointed by him now, I'll never depend on him more. Tell him further, that not only my Servants Cloths, but mine own have been this year
so ill made, and the linings, buttons, and every thing so unusually bad, as
to give me very great offence. Unless He retrieves himself, We shall quarrel outright. For my breeches, and Waste-coats, are now in raggs, which
us'd to last me the whole Winter, after the Summer's Wearing.

Tell John that He must get Carrs immediatly. For I want iron, Bottles,
every thing I have wrote for, in great haste. He certainly is not as Active in
this matter, this Season, as He us'd to be, when He had much more of this
kind of business on his hands. Desire him to let me know the state of his
After-grass. I propose to send forty or fifty sheep up to him from Balnasloe fair;[2] and intend that He should in proper time buy in a few Cows
at Smithfield to fatten better on it, and give us beef at my return.

By yours and Mrs Jourdan's account I have the comfort to know that
your hoarsness is slight. I am sorry however that you have it, because it will
confine you. I expect that it will as usual turn to a slight Cough, for which
staying within is the best, tho' no very agreable, remedy. I am concern'd for
my friend Jane's ruffle, which according to custom, has, I find, been pretty
violent. But I hope it is by this time over. God bless and preserve you all.

yours &c.
Edw: Elphin

Fine Weather. Hay coming home. Every thing pleasant. Mr Palmer came hither yesterday. He looks very well, and says He is so. His wife has been ill, but by his account is now much better than of late years she has been.

I am sorry for poor Lucy. I think you would do well to make her a morning visit. By enquiring for her only, you may, if you will, shew that you think the Mistress of the House has neglected you. But in my judgment 'tis better overlook it; especially as I am not sure that according to the Rules of nice breeding you have right on your side.

Suppose now I were inclin'd to give an Opinion, which you so urge me to, Consider a little, What could I say. If Miss Parnel,[3] who is not young or giddy tells truth, the Case is as plain as that two and two make four. And How can I possibly judge whether she does or not? Indeed indeed, Ally, you are very Simple in this affair. Caution is right in all things of importance. Over caution is folly. But I have known many people in my life time, who never could prevail on themselves to do right, for fear of doing wrong.

1. Unanswerable.
2. In 1750 Ballinasloe Fair was held for four days from Monday 24 September. Watson (1750), p.89.
3. Miss Parnel: not known.

120

Elphin. September 21, 1750

I am sure My Dear Girl was neither in fret nor fuss, when she wrote her's now before me – It is wrote as I wish all yours to be. If you were throughly sensible of the difference between this, and some which not very long since I have had, It would determine you still more to keep your good resolutions. I really can see nothing amiss in it, but a few mistakes in stopping – you must still continue the exercise design'd to remedy that defect. But if you persevere and succeed in what you tell me is your present Study, this will be an universal remedy for all your defects. I am so pleas'd with it, that I must give you back your own Words in form of a document, as usefull as any I ever gave you. 'Let: your wish and Study be to gain such calmness as to be able to turn your Self to different sorts of real business after one another, without jumble or hurry.' Thus I or rather you your Self preach. Do but practice and I'll answer for every thing else.

What Mrs Jourdan and you write about Miss P and the house-keeper is surprizing enough. I can account for it but one way, in which I am unwilling to account for it. I must keep their Secrets, who are in possession of mine – I think you were in the wrong to trouble your self to write to the Sister, and as to letting the grave well spoken Dame know, that she is discover'd, tell Mrs Jourdan that, if she goes on that Errand, she must resolve to give her an hearty scolding. Is she sure that she'll be a match for her? – But see now, My Dear Girl, of how little use it is to teaze me on subjects of this sort, on which if I determine at all I must determine on your accounts. You must, you ought in common sense to judge for your selves; and by what had happen'd of late, I am sure you are convinc'd that you cannot be too exact in previous Enquirys. As to Fanny, you long since know my sentiments. But I believe it will be best, whatever you really intend, not to make her establish'd House-keeper. She'll be more carefull to discharge the office well, while she thinks her continuance in it depends on good behaviour.

I forgot last post to answer a most important question of Mrs J's – But I hope I am time enough now. When your Bin is empty, go to that behind the cellar-door. I suppose the hogshead which I order'd to be, is before this, bottled. But Neither you nor John have told me so. I take it for granted, that when it was going, you tasted it. Let me know Mrs J's opinion of it.

John has been guilty of a very great omission, for which He deserves a check, because He has neglected my positive orders. Either He has not agreed with the Carr-man for his carriage: Or if He has, He has neglected to tell me what He has agreed for: So that when the things come I shall be at a loss what to pay. Tell him that what He intends about the Hay is right. Let him do it as fast as He can. I suppose this year's Hay is still in the field. He must loose no time in getting it home. I am afraid it is too late to think of removing his Dunghil, if He has not already begun. He must wait for frost in winter to do it. Nothing must be done that will spoil the After-grass.

I can't allow Boyer to be good authority for English, who is not admitted as such for his Mother Tongue. I believe however that the word is spelt as you and He spell it, tho' oft'ner the other way by Correct Writers. Mine is certainly the right Spelling, and thus the Word gives the Idea of the thing. For this reason I preferr it.

I am glad your Cold is better. I hope it is by this time well. By your and Mrs Jourdan's account, I have the pleasure to find it is a slight one, as I guessed.

The Widow Wynne has been for some days at Charles-town. Mr King rode over hither on Wedensday morning and gave me an account of it. I made a morning visit there yesterday; and to morrow they all dine with me. Both she and Mrs King enquir'd for you, with much politeness: So did your good friend Mrs Mahon, who din'd here two days ago. Little Nancy was with her, who gave us a laugh. Lawson told her she must chuse him or me for a husband. She declar'd at once in my favour, and sticks to it. If she be as constant as little Jane, she'll always do so. I never see her, but she demands a letter from Jacky Synge. So she calls Ned, and retains the fondness she shew'd for him when here. She is a very fine Girl.

My blessing to Jane. I am much rejoic'd that she has so soon, and so effectually got the better of her ugly brush. I hope she'll have no more of them. Service to Mrs J – Tell her I desire she would give mine to Miss P – when she goes to let her know she is discover'd. I am

yours &c.
Edw: Elphin

Tell Ned Curtis that I rejoice much at his Jeny's recovery. I wish most heartily that his may be as complete.

121

Elphin. September 25, 1750

Letters of business and a very fine day conspire to shorten my Dear Girl's entertainment by this post. But the standing dish it is in my power to give. I bless God I am very well, and much rejoic'd that you've got out after your late confinement. If you had not had that just excuse for declining Mrs F's[1] invitation you ought to have gone there. You must submit sometimes to innocent things that you do not like rather than offend.

Press'd as I am in time I must desire you to make Ned Curtis or some body get for you the Daily Courant of Saturday the 15th of this Month. I can't omit directing you to a letter printed there, which will entertain you, and afford some usefull instruction, which I hope however you do not much want. Mrs J will perhaps not like it, because it contains a severe Satire on the Ladys of a Country, which she sometimes takes it in her head to think hers.[2] When in this way, She puts me in mind of a French officer in the D[uke] of Marlborough's army, who join'd heartily in drubbing the French, and then sat down and cry'd that they were beaten. Tell her, with my Service, that I thank her for her letter, but desire that she won't seal the next in the same ingenious manner. The account she gives of your Aunt will leave me in great suspense till I see what comes of it. That of Bab delights me.

I am sorry Will has been ill. Philip has been so here. But He is now well. I hope your Valet is so too. I was surpriz'd to see his Brother with Palmer.

Lawson was yesterday somewhat distress'd with a Sore throat. But He is this day much better. Adieu.

yours &c.
Edw: Elphin

How differently is this last letter wrote from the former one? Tell John his Carriage is come.

1. Mrs F: probably Mrs Fitzmaurice.
2. The *Dublin Courant* had published a letter about a duel and a French lady: 'A satirical Piece, having been published at Paris with great Applause, intitled, A Letter to a young Lady newly married, we shall give our Readers the following Extract from it. She is an English Lady, but married to a French nobleman.' 11-15 September 1750.

122

(undated) October 1750

My Dear Girl

Before the post comes I write two or three Words, which hurry prevented my writing in my last.

I have caught you at a terrible false-spelling. I give it that hard name, because it tallys with a bad pronunciation, which is down-right Irish. If you are at all guilty, Take care and break your Self of it. You have omitted the first e in believe. And thus, not Brogadeers only, but most people pronounce. Poor Butler[1] was remarkable for it.

Tell Woodward I will not have any Cloth bespoke at this Season of the year for Great-Coats. When I go to town, I'll do as well as I can. He is very good at speeches and professions. But He grows worse in Work.

Ask John whether he has provided Hogs. If He obey'd my orders, He has done this long since. Let him tell me how the Market for oats, is, and is like to be. He should now call at Smithfield Market, and watch his opportunity of buying in four or five Cows cheap, and very good – Mr Wallace[2] will assist him. They must be such as will weigh 500. He knows what his after-grass will do. Let him buy accordingly, and either two or more at a time as He judges most convenient. He'll soon, I hope, have 50 sheep sent him up from Mr Palmer.

Yours is come, by which I have the great pleasure to find, that you are well, tho' you do not say so. I collect it from your being abroad in the Evening.

But I am sorry to find you don't keep up to your Standard in writing.

Neither this nor your last are at all comparable to that I commended – of the two this is least bad. There are marks of hurry in it, beside the writing. Speaking of the Dean's tedious visit, you write *which would not have insupportable.* I need not tell you that this is non-sense, which is the more remarkable as you made two interlineations to cobble up your first hasty writing – I suppose your uneasiness at the visit return'd on you, when you were giving an account of it.

Your friend and you made your selves a great deal more business, than you needed, about the house keeper. To what purpose to write to Mrs Parnel,[3] when you resolv'd to depend on the other accounts you had rec'd of her? You were indeed right in this. But why ask a Character of one against whom you were on good grounds determin'd? I can see no reason, unless Mrs J had hopes of materials for the interview she then intended. But this did not answer. The Lady's letter, as well as the Damsels account, is in the palliating way. I won't call you Dunce for the same reason that you don't call your Self so. But I am a little surpriz'd that you were both so puzzled. Is any thing more Common than to speak or write in the first person what is meant in the third? Sure it could not enter into either of your heads that Miss P— the House-keeper had any Secrets of mine in their keeping. It was not impossible that the latter had some of the former's.

I had an account of the clock from Mr Lennox; so that your forget was of no other consequence than to afford an additional proof that you are not quite cur'd of your Giddiness. If I have no future ones, you'll be well off.

Desire John to let Mr Sullivane know that I have rec'd his; and that as soon as I get to town, I'll fix with him about the Rouen-ware. I hope so short a delay will not be inconvenient to him.

Let Woodward know to comfort him, that I like the Cloth He has sent down very well.

Tell Ned Curtis that He may give Avy Prowde her Legacy when He pleases. I am not sure whether He has any of the discharges I got from Cudmore or George Prowde in his power.[4] If He has not, He must take a bond both from Husband and Wife as a Security, till I return to you. I am sorry you don't give a better account of him.

You needed not have mention'd Mrs J reading your letter, For I see Corrections of her pen. I don't care to mortify you, My Dear But upon my honest word this Epistle of your's carrys more marks of carelesness, than most I have ever rec'd from you. Prithee never tire your Self with writing to me. You might have spar'd a good deal of what you have written, and Less well wrote would please me better.

your very affectionate &c.
Edw: Elphin

There is one passage in your letter, by which you seem to mean something, but I am at a loss what. Mentioning the coming of the Clock, you say you think It was *a propos*. By the by you here spell *think* wrong with an e at the end. But How *a propos*? Did you hang it by your side in the place of your Watch? Or is the House-clock out of order? Explain, Mistress, Explain – and whenever you aim at a turn, Take care there be sense in it

1. Mr Butler: not known.
2. George or James Wallace: salemasters, Smithfield. Watson (1760), p.44.
3. Mrs Parnel: not known.
4. Edward Synge, archbishop of Tuam, left £20 in his will to Nicholas Prowde, a clerk, probably his brother-in-law. Avy and George Prowde were Nicholas Proud's children. In his turn, Edward Synge the younger paid the Proud children an annuity during his lifetime and in his will urged Alicia to continue to do so. Jane Cudmore, the wife of the bookbinder, was born a Miss Proud. Welply, Vol.12, p.6; will, f.254.

123

Elphin. October 2, 1750

My Dear Girl.

You already know my thoughts of the writing of your two last letters. This now before me, which you suspect, tho' not equal to the one I approv'd of, is rather better than them. But I see you are not always dispos'd to do, as well, as sometimes you can; and this may happen without your fault. I know by experience that there is an inequality in performances at different times. What is well done at one, with great ease, It costs much pains to do indifferently at another. As this is an imperfection you must strive to cure it; and there is one great one in most of your letters, which whatever pains it cost, you must cure. I mean, Omissions of Words. They are frequent in every letter, and I see them sometimes supply'd in Mrs Jourdan's hand. This arises from hurry. Sedateness will cure it.

I am sorry for Betty Donnelan. If her situation be unhappy, I believe it will be found, that she has contributed much her self to make it so. You know my thoughts of her already.[1]

Give my service to Mrs Jourdan, and tell her she does me too much honour. I really knew nothing of the letter, till I saw it in the News-paper, but I agree in opinion with her, that it is not the Work of a French-man, tho' if Travellers speak truth, there are in that polite nation many polite Ladys, who are proper subjects of that Satire. I fear numbers may be found else where. Perhaps some of the strokes may hit, tho' they were not calculated for, you. But pray make your Confession, and Tell me which. I am at present so blind to your faults, that I can see but one which glances at you. But in writing on this, you have committed a gross one in spelling Duels. Is it so spelt in the paper?

Next time you see the Doctor, Enquire about the boy that went from hence to his Hospital. I have another here, the son of a favorite Labourer, who I wish, were with him. But perhaps He may give me some directions, that may help him here. His Malady is a pain in his thigh, midway between hip and knee. There is no swelling, nor is the flesh discolour'd; and it is not sore to the touch. It is worse when he rises, than after He has been for a little time in motion. But it is so bad as to disable him from work, and if he happens to strike his toe or heel against any thing, the pain is Exquis-ite. He has been affected with this disorder these nine months, but in Summer He was able to work. Now He is not. His account of the first affec-tion is imperfect. As well as I can judge by it, He got it in the field, where He was at work, early last Spring. Not knowing what to do, and our Apothecary being unwilling to meddle with him, I order'd him to chafe the part well with Spirit of Opodeldock.[2] He is a stout lusty young fellow, and his looks betoken health. I can't find that He has any other com-plaint. I wish the Doctor may upon this description be able to order some-thing that may relieve him. If He be not reliev'd, He must be a Beggar.

Why would you bottle the Ale without consulting me? I did not intend it should have been bottled these two months. But if it were perfectly fine, It may for ought I know be as well now. If it was not, I shall abuse both you and your friend.

Whatever Gannon may say, I believe his scheme is to go to some other service. Some steps were taken last spring towards his going to General Richbell.[3] But when I spoke to him about it, He denied his knowing any thing of the matter. Take no notice to him nor any one of this suspicion: But tell him that since He chuses to go, He may for me; and bid John to look out for another Gardiner. I would fain have a good one, if such a one can be got. I know no person so likely to direct him to one, as Mr Boyle's gardiner at Rathfarnam. But Let him speak to Magahan, Hawker and every body. When it is known that I want, enough will offer themselves. The difficulty will be to get one skilfull and honest.

As your Aunt has of late been rather better, I wish that this very fine Weather had tempted your Uncle to stay some Weeks longer in the Coun-try. I advis'd him to do so. But He is usually fix'd in his purposes, and I can't say, but that in this He may be right. I shall long impatiently for an account of their being safe in town. Blessing to Jane. I am

your very affectionate &c.
Edw: Elphin

As Fires are now in fashion, it will be an easy matter for you to air your
paper before you sit down to write. I believe this would prevent your ink
sinking as it does in some places.

[In another hand To the Right Reverend]

1. Obscure.
2. Spirits of Opodeldoc: a solution of soap in alcohol with camphor and oils of ori-
ganum and rosemary.
3. Edward Richbell became a captain in Col Ponsonby's Regiment of Foot on 24
March 1708; a major 3 June 1720 and lieutenant colonel 18 May 1722. He was made
colonel brigadier general on 14 June 1743. PRO WO64/10, f.120; WO64/11, f.323.

124

Elphin. October 5, 1750

My Dear Girl.

My remarks on your writing, and your Apologys and resolutions take
up half our letters. It is best to have done with them – I am fully satisfy'd
that you do and will endeavour to correct every thing I find fault with; and
if at last you do not succeed, I shall not blame you, tho' I shall be very
sorry. I have said every thing I could to inform you; and It is very unlucky,
that when for two or three letters you write as if you were well inform'd,
you return to the Old way. That is the Case at present. Yours now before
me, is wrote exactly like some the beginning of Summer. It looks as if your
hand shook, or your fingers were benumm'd with Cold. The Capital fault
is that you do not bear enough on your paper. That would give firmness
and grace to your letters. But the Contrary habit is strong in you. I fear
you'll never break it.

Your words about the Clock are these. *I think it was a propos My watch
after &c. went mad.* What other sense will these bear, than what I put on
them? My Dear Dear It is a matter of more importance what you write
than how. Guard therefore against the frequent Omissions of words and
disjointedness in sense. There is some of this in your Explanation. But I
won't teaze you with finding fault.

Mr Cunningham mistook. I gave him no charge to see you. Lawson is
still here. He leaves me on Wedensday. Dic. Doherty will come and stay

with me till I go to town, which I propose God willing to do, at the very End of the month. But I have yet fix'd nothing.

The fine season has made the Country unusually pleasant, and I have a vast deal to do.

I have no objection to your visiting Mrs Dawson. Mrs Hamilton's character is enough to make me think well of her.[1] I have seen her at your Uncle's and like her behaviour.

My friends of Wills-grove came hither yesterday. Godfrey is employ'd abroad, and I must go to him. So Adieu.

yours &c.
Edw:Elphin

1. Mrs Dawson is not known. Mrs Hamilton was a Miss Dawson before her marriage to Henry Hamilton.

125

Elphin. October 9, 1750

My Dear Girl.

Lawson leaves me to morrow. I wish his business would have suffer'd him to stay till mine would have suffer'd me to go. But As that cannot be, I'll do as well as I can; and if the Want of him makes me go somewhat earlier to town, I believe you will not be sorry. My scheme now is to set out on Thursday the 25th. But should the Weather then be bad, I'll stay to the Monday following, or longer.

I thank you for the particular account you have given me of your poor Aunt &c.[1] I am glad they are safe in town; but am much distress'd at the melancholy condition in which you describe her, whom I so much love and admire. Observe her, my Dear, with attention. Her admirable behaviour under such a load of misery may afford many usefull lessons. But God forbid that you should ever have occasion to practice them.

My blessing to Jane, and thanks for her letter, which pleases me much. But tho' Her writing be very well, Tell her it would be still better, if she made it a little blacker. Like you, she just touches the paper.

Service to Mrs Jourdan. I must not call her paper a letter, for she says a third would have been burthensome. Is not this a refinement? She is right about the Ale, and I submit. But that she may not insult too much, Tell her this short story. A fortune-hunter persisting in his addresses to a very rich Widow Lady; She, after repeated Civil denials, told him that if he came to her agen, She would order her foot-men to kick him down stairs. He came notwithstanding; and just as He was to undergo the threaten'd discipline, He look'd cooly at one of the fellows, and said Kick softly, you rascal. It will be my turn to kick soon. So it was. In a fortnight He marry'd the Lady. I hope my Story does not want Application.

No hopes from Jane's Dairy. Orr's *Sermons*[2] were not forgot. Carpeting, and some coarse Linnen are just going off. So are Candles and Bacon. Enquiry shall be made for Honey. But in the Opinion of this Author, it is better buy it in town. Carriage will more than ballance difference of price. Solomon says, that it is too late. I imitate your friend's manner and conciseness.

I am pleas'd that you've made an experiment of the Mushroom seed; and hope it will succeed. As scarce any of the Hyacinths were good, I less regret the loss of them. As to Tulips &c. Let John or Gannon consult Magahan. You know that He was here; He then promis'd me that He would see them planted himself. The latter end of this month, the Weather fair, is, the proper Season for Tulips. Somewhat later for Ranunculus, and Anemonys. But follow Magahan's directions.

You are mistaken, Madam; I am too attentive to every thing that relates to you to forget any of your imperfections; So that I ask'd, not for information, but for trial; and chiefly with a view to one, which I only suspect and you have not confess'd. Perhaps you are not guilty. A liking to DUELS. If you have that foible, stiffle it in embryo. As to the other, I knew you guilty. Remember you have promis'd to amend it. – Tho' I forbear all remarks of another kind on your writing yet false spellings must never escape, and I have found a very bad one. *This Summur's Visitants.* Giddy, Giddy! When will you be cur'd?

I have just now a letter from Will. French in which He tells me that All things are setled for Nancy. Assoon as a proper setlement can be drawn, she'll be marry'd; I hope and believe, happily.

Mr Wills &c. are still with me. He is still busy, and I must attend him. So Adieu.

yours &c.
Edw: Elphin

There is a passage in yours, Mistress, which if Mrs Jourdan has notic'd, I am sure she has rally'd you upon. *There are many other things in the letter, that I wish to make a good use of.*

I am glad Betty Donnelan is recover'd. Blair, who is now here, tells me that Kitty, her husband and Company are well at Tubber-vaddy.

Our heavy Baggage went off this day. Jac. Egan[3] will carry to John Miller a Bill of particulars.

1750

1. Jane Synge, wife of Nicholas Synge.

2. John Orr, *Fourteen sermons upon the following subjects. The natural advantages of men ... The spiritual and moral liberty of men.* (London 1739) or *Sermons upon the following subjects. The natural difference between moral good and evil ... The love of our country, explained, illustrated, and inforced* (London 1749).

3. Jac. Egan: not known.

126

Elphin. October 12, 1750

My Dear Girl.

These Garden Robberys are very teazing and vexatious. Every thing must be done to discover and prevent them. With the latter view, Let John order the labourers to watch by turns if there be any thing left worth watching. To make this easier to the poor fellows, Let a bed of straw and a Caddow[1] be provided in the Garden house for them to sleep on the beginning of the night, and a Gun put into their hands. Gannon may and must help by watching some part of the time – When it is known that there is a Watch, No attempt will be made. I am sorry I did not think of this, till the Steed was stolen. To discover the past thefts Let John get the following Advertisement put into Falkner.

The Bishop of Elphin's Gardens near Kevin-street having been twice robbed this Season, once on or about Aug. 29 – and a second time October 7. Whoever within two months from the date hereof discovers any person or persons concern'd in either of these robberys, so as that He or they may be convicted, shall have five pounds reward, and be forgiven, if an Accomplice.

October 12, 1750. Edw: Elphin[2]

I put in, the time of the first robbery at a venture. You can among you recollect the true one. Insert it just in the same manner. Let John carry money with him to pay for the first Advertising and continuing it in three subsequent Papers. About half a Guinea will do; and bid him give my Service to Mr Falkner,[3] and tell him He'll oblige me by printing it with some mark that may catch the Eye of his Readers. On second thoughts you had better get Lawson to charge himself with this. Perhaps Mr Falkner may be scrupulous, if apply'd to only by a Servant, as He knows I am not in town. Excuse thus your troubling the Doctor with such an Affair.

Give my Service to your Doctor and tell him I despair of getting him proper answers to his very proper Questions, and when I leave this, there is no creature on whom I could depend for following his directions. As He

261

approves of the Opodelduc, I'll continue it. If it has not good effects I'll order the poor Lad up, if He'll give me leave. As you say nothing of little John, I hope he is well of his late disorder. You were right not to trouble Palmer with an answer, as I shall see him so soon.

I am and shall be in great suspense about your poor Aunt. The Operations on her must have great effects, of what kind, I can't judge. God grant they be good ones. In her deplorable Condition It is a good deal, if they contribute to greater present Ease.

I know nothing of Mr Adderley's bundle, and should be sorry it were Cloth. If it be, it is intended as a present, which will distress me either to accept or refuse. By one of the letters you enclos'd I have some chance for it's being papers. You seem to wonder that my Correspondents direct to me in Dublin – I desire my constant ones to do so, and I wish all did – Don't you see, Mistress, that thus half-postage is sav'd. But it is too early for you to think of such things, and yet a little proper attention, to avoid unnecessary expense even in small things, is not amiss – A saying of Old Judge Daly's[4] is in every one's Mouth. Take care of the pence, the pounds will take care of themselves. What think you? Is there sense in this? Judge by your own expenses in trifles.

Instead of wanting Company, I shall probably have too much, to allow sufficient time for business. Mr Sandford will be here next Week. Rachel[5] at Cary's, where are Mr and Mrs Lushington.[6] I expect also Will. French, and his intended Son in Law,[7] beside some of my Clergy, whom I want to see. I hope however to setle all affairs by the time I mention'd in my last. As that draws nigh, I shall be more impatient to see you all. God send us an happy meeting. I am My Dear Girl's

> most affect &c.
> Edw: Elphin

Two false spellings. One faulty. Offer'd to *Seal*. It should be *sale*. The other, is in Mr Daunt's name. Thus he writes it.

By your account of Weather you had more rain that We. Here there has been little till yesterday, and then none heavy. But I do not wonder, that the Cold with wet has confin'd you, when without it, it prevented my riding from Saturday to yesterday. But, I bless God, I am very well, and have been so all along.

After all, the shortest and best way will be to order John to carry the Advertisement as on the other side, to Falkner, and pay him.[8] He knows my hand. I would have it, if possible, in next Tuesday's paper. If it produces any thing, Let John carry the Accuser to Mr Vipond, and desire him to prosecute him to the Utmost.

If Molly Fagan says true, I have a great accusation against you, Madam,

She says you did not tell her She was to come down hither to stay; and I once thought that I must have brought her back agen. But when I spoke to her my Self, I found her more reasonable than Silly Shannon represented her.

1. Caddow: a rough woollen covering.

2. This advertisement appeared in *Faulkner's Dublin Journal* 13-16 October 1750.

3. George Faulkner (?1699-1775): bookseller and publisher of *Faulkner's Dublin Journal. DNB.*

4. Denis Daly (*c.*1643-1721): eldest son of James Daly of Laragh, Co. Galway. Called to the Bar, Middle Temple 1673; admitted to the King's Inns 1678; Justice of Common Pleas 1686; member of the privy council. In 1689 he compared James II's House of Commons with Masaniello's assembly, and was threatened with impeachment. Resident in Galway 1691, and assisted in ensuring submission to William and Mary. Married Mary Power of Park, Co. Limerick. Ball, Vol.1, p.362.

5. Rachel Sandford, Mrs Lushington's sister, was a Miss Southwell before marriage.

6. William Lushington married Jane Southwell in June 1748. See Biographical Register. A witness of Edward Nicholson's will. His own will was proved in 1786. *St Peter and St Kevin*, p.326; Eustace, Vol. 2, p.612, 301; Vicars, p.294.

7. The Rev. Holt Waring who married Arabella French. Burke (1916), p.610.

8. Part of the facing paper has been cut away.

127

Elphin. October 16, 1750

My Dear Girl.

I am glad I told you my Suspicion, not only because, being unjust, you have remov'd it, but because I have given you an opportunity of opening your Self on the Subject in a manner which has greatly pleas'd me. What an odd mixture of a girl are you! On some occasions you shew sense and reflexion beyond your years, on others giddiness, and trifling below them. But the latter will wear off, I hope, the former improve. There is a mixture of clay in us all. If it were possible, I would have you all gold. The way to come near this perfection is to rate every kind of thing according to it's real value, and early to accustom your Self to do so; Nor must you consider things so much with a view to making a figure, as for their intrinsick Worth; tho' by preferring the one, I would not exclude the other. Your thoughts and Ambition taking this train, Ornaments of the Person, especially expensive ones will have a low place. I did indeed fear you valu'd those of the kind I mention'd; and I'll tell you why. Your friend and Cosen have sometimes spoken favorably of them; and you, tho' silent, seem'd to look approbation. See Huzzy, how you are watch'd. But I have caught you here at a little bit of false English. There *is* not many Girls. It should be *are*.

You do well to be often with your poor Aunt. But I see no occasion for dining there so constantly. Do not offend. It will not, I hope, be long, before this will cease. I believe I long as much for our meeting as you can do. God send us an happy one. My suspense about that good Woman does, and must continue. You are not particular enough in your account. You should have told me what effect the discharge has had on her bulk. I don't like that on her Spirits – I think I see here a false Spelling. good Sted you write. Perhaps this may be supported. But the Common was [*sic*] is Stead. Would you write insted?

Service to Mrs Jourdan. I thank her much for her rebuke to Mrs Heap. She is in possession of her paper. Molly Byrne as well as she is to blame, and I have an hundred times spoken to both on the Subject, and had the fullest assurance that the most Exact care was taken. But pray what is now to be done? Will it not be best to have all the Feathers taken out and air'd, when I go off? Signify your pleasure among you, you shall be obey'd, if I can.

I see in the Papers an Advertisement of some of Shakespear's plays. Any of them that you &c. chuse, see in time if you can get Mrs Nicholson to go with you to.[1] You or your friend or both may probably say No! not till my L[or]d comes. But possibly the one you chuse may not be acted till after, and yet if you do not speak in time, you may not get places you like – If you wish for more than one. I have no objection.

Tell John that I sent no Carr-man of the name of Hanly, or any other to him.[2] One Harly carry'd up our goods, which I hope are before this safe with you. I am glad He likes the Sheep. I shall soon send him ten more of the same parcel. They are too many here; and He complain'd last Season that He had too few.

Mr Wills and Family left me yesterday morning. My Coach carry'd them to Rathcroghan, where their own rec'd them. On it's return Poor Rachel Sandford pick'd it up. She was on horseback coming on a visit to Mrs Cary, and her Sister Lushington, and miserable with her head-ach. The Coach from Shankil was a seasonable relief. I expect the Coll. here this day at diner – I don't remember that I have mention'd that Mrs L[ushington] to you. I do not like her as well as I do her Sister.

I told you already that if the Weather was bad when I intended setting out, I would wait for good. Another Accident may stop me. If the Archbishop of Tuam and I should meet at Palmer's, We should all be distress'd. I must avoid this, and have with that view desir'd Palmer to advize me of his motions – I hope they will not interfare with mine. But as I am subject to these contingencys, I may perhaps not keep my time. And you must not be uneasy. Adieu.

yours &c.
Edw: Elphin

Yours is dated the 12th. I suppose this a mistake. Shall I agen say
Giddy?

1. 'At the Theatre Royal in Smock Alley, the six following Tragedies will speedily be
represented at the Theatre Royal in which the Manager will perform the chief characters at two each week, viz Richard the III, Hamlet, Othello, Macbeth, Julius Caesar and
Romeo and Juliet.' *Dublin Courant*, 9-13 August 1750.
2. Edward Synge wrote 'Hanly' in his letter of 1 July 1750.

128

Elphin. October 20, 1750

Three lines, My Dear Girl, to tell you that I hold my resolution. If the
Weather holds, my journey, barr accidents will be pleasant. But at all
Events, the roads can hardly be so much hurt between this and Thursday
as to distress travellers. My design is to dine with you this day se'night. If
you order some fish, and a roasted fowl, the rest of a little dinner may be
as you chuse.

If the Bishop of Clonfert be still wind-bound, let him know that I have
both his letters, and do not write because the Wind may change the next
minute. Say further that I wish him and his Dame a good voyage and safe
return. Desire him to enquire before He goes, whether the Declarations
are not filed. Mr Costello told me some time ago that they were.

Tell Lawson I hope soon to thank him in person for his letter, and to
abuse him for his swelling word. Magnificently I don't like. Hospitably is
enough. I accept his notice.

In return to this, direct as usuall on the same Occasion, to Glanmore.
Adieu My Dearest. God send us an happy meeting.

yours &c.
Edw: Elphin

Let John get the plate home on Saturday, the receit is in it's old place.
Let him get a bag of flower. Transcribe the Bishop's paragraph and send
it to him.

129

Elphin. October 24, 1750

Well, My Dearest, on Thursday, God willing, I set out, unless snow or other violent change of Weather make it impracticable or hazardous. We have at present an hard frost much harder than you can be sensible of, and it seems setled. But what may happen I know not. Should I not get to you as I propose, and hope I shall; be assur'd that Weather must be the Cause and that only. For All is ready, and I am impatient, and I bless God as well as I have been these seven years. – You'll find me disorder'd only in mine hair; and to remedy that, pray order Will or some one to secure Hamilton to be with me on Sunday morning to cut it.

Thus far yesterday. I went to bed last night persuaded that I should find thick snow on the ground this morning. But there is none. I hope there wo'n't or any other change of Weather to stop me – I long to be with you.

yours &c.
Edw:Elphin

1751

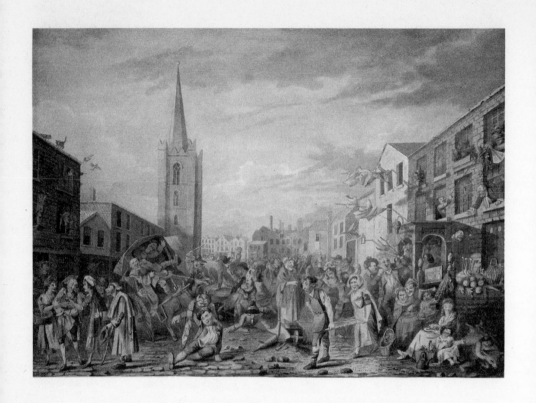

'... the rabble amongst whom you do, and I must live' (Letter 138):
'The Surroundings of St Patrick's Cathedral, Dublin' (watercolour
by John Nixon [c.1750-1818], courtesy Agnew's of London).

130

Glanmore. May 15, 1751

Here I am, my Dear Girl, safe and sound, I bless God, and without the least cross Accident on the road. I have the pleasure to find Palmer and his wife with better looks, than we saw them. She was much out of order on her return home, but says she is now better than before she went abroad. Cary is just come in, whose looks bespeak health and peace of mind. He says his Wife and Willy are well.

You were under some uneasiness about my dinner &c. yesterday. I far'd extremely well. Carleboe laid hold of a little loin of Mutton at the new Inn, which was as good as any of Kevin-street, and at night my Land-lady sent me up the finest little boil'd chicken I ever saw. Thus with mine own bread and wine I liv'd like an Epicure. The account makes me hungry now; and I am every minute in Expectation of Dinner. So My Dear Dear Girl Adieu – I shall be impatient for Monday, that I may have a full account of you all. God send me a good one.

Your &c.
Edw:Elphin

Let me have an account of Charlotte.[1]

1. Charlotte Jourdan.

131

Elphin. May 17, 1751

This goes to let my Dear Girl know that I got safe and well hither yester-day between one and two. It was fair when I left Mr Palmer's But rain came on soon, and continued till I got home, sometimes heavy. In this, my usual good fortune left me. But it was to me no sort of inconvenience, nor a great one to Servants or Horses. The road between Lanesborough and Strokes-town was in many places broken so as to give Peter a good oppor-tunity of shewing his skill in driving, and He brought me through very well, nor had I occasion even once to alight. As I am now well past it, I am glad I found it in such a Condition, because this will give me more foun-dation to teaze my friend Mr Mahon to have it effectually repair'd.[1] I sent

Philip yesterday as I pass'd, to enquire about him &c. All well. But I have yet seen none of them.

At my coming hither I met with a mortification, tho' I hope it will be only a little one. Carleboe was not well on the road, and complain'd so much at Lanesborough, that Shannon gave him his place in the post-chaise, and rode himself. The Consequence was, He was wet to the Skin; which, considering the bad cold He had at leaving town, I fear'd would lay him up. But it has not. He says he is very well, and I believe He is for Stafford says so too. If He had had the Wit to have staid at Lanesborough till I came up, I could have brought him on in the Coach. You'd have laugh'd, had you seen his look, when I said this. He seem'd surpriz'd that He had not thought of it. I should have been much surpriz'd if he had. Stafford hopes Carleboe's disorder will go off easily. But you know I am in no distress by it. Mrs Heap is very well.

Talking to her yesterday evening about house hold matters, I happen'd to mention your distress for a house-keeper, and a maid. She said in a very modest manner, that She wish'd her niece who is here, were qualify'd to wait on you.[2] My answer was, that She could tell as well as any one, whether she was or not. She reply'd, that she work'd well at her needle, and could wash, but not clear starch, but she hop'd she could easily learn. I ask'd, if she had instructed her in any of her branches of knowledge. Cookery &c. No! She had no opportunity in Winter. I told her she had enough in Summer, and that for her sake she ought to have done it. She had not, she said. To my questions about her temper and [*damaged ms*], Her answer was that she was sedate, modest, and meek. I told her I fear'd she was too meek, and said in plain terms that I suspected she was Simple. She assur'd me she was not, but had sense enough. I never exchang'd a word with her in my life, but according to my skill in Physiognomy I suspect her rather deficient than abounding. If upon this account you and Mrs Jourdan think it worth while to deliberate about her, I'll inform my Self about this, and every thing else relative to her as fully as I can. She is going seventeen, I thought her older. Her *figure* (Let Jane know I use that word) is well enough. Her manner was rather awkard. I have not seen her since I came. Her Aunt says, she writes prettily. But when I ask'd if she understood Arithmetick, Her answer made me smile; She seemed not to understand the Word, but much ado I got out of her, that She had done some Summs.

I think it right to tell you this, and yet I do it with some reluctance, lest I should influence more than I mean. But I beg and insist upon it, that neither you nor Mrs Jourdan consider what I write other wise than a meer matter of Fact told you by one, on whose Veracity you may depend. As to the Expediency of medling with such a Girl, whom you certainly must be at the trouble of forming in some respects, Judge, I not only allow but require you to judge for your Selves. All that I shall say, and it is all that I think, is, that If she can be taught soon, and easily, this is in her favour, that being well descended and soberly educated, She is probably free and may be kept free from those vices, and bad qualitys, with which practic'd Servants are, ten to one, infected. Whether you venture on her or not My opinion is, that you get some one to wait on you all. I am absolutely against Lady Frances's[3] ever being retain'd about you in that Station, which I never thought her fit for. The truth is I never thought well of her at all, and rather suffer'd than approv'd of her continuing in any shape in my family, and Assoon as you [can *damaged ms*] get a good House-keeper, and a proper person to wait on you My vote shall be for dismissing her. But even in this, I will not prescribe. Look out for such Servants as will make you easy. Then I shall be so.

Tell John Miller, that He must redouble his diligence in Enquiring after a good House and Land Steward. Short a time as I have been here, I have found the present one to be even more inept and silly than I before thought him, tho' I had a very indifferent opinion of him before. His mule and horses perform'd very well. I intend to send them off to morrow. And by them 6 Muskets, which He must get put into order by a Gun-smith. I believe I shall send him up some Flax too. But if I do, I'll write to him about it.

I rec'd yours at Glanmore and made your Compliments. On further observation Mrs Palmer did not appear to me as well as I thought her when I wrote to you. Your little adopted, has, it seems, got a scald head,[4] for which a pitch'd cap is apply'd by Mrs Jourdan's direction, as the Mother says. She is really a fine Girl.

I din'd yesterday at Cary's. He and she are very well, and remember you all with great affection.

That you may be in no pain about my living, know that I have good Beef, mutton, Veal, Lamb, big Turkys, Ducks, Chickens, and better bread than you have or can get. About liquors you have no doubt; So that if I spend my Summer with usual health, and have the great comfort of knowing that you do the same, I have no doubt of spending it with as much satisfaction as I can have divided from you. I am My Dearest

Your most affec &c.
Edw: Elphin

1. In his will, Edward Synge bequeathed his debentures in the Lanesborough turnpike to William Cary, Oliver Cary's son. 'I gave him these some years since but his father treating them with contempt I gave him in lieu thereof one hundred and fifty pounds which I valued them at in consideration of which he assigned them to Godfrey

Wills Esquire as this was in trust for me I desire Mr Wills may reassign them to him with all interest due upon them.' Will, f.254.

2. Mrs Heap's niece was Nancy Poor or Power, who became Alicia Synge's maid.

3. Fanny, Alicia's maid in 1750.

4. Scald head: affected with the 'scall', scabby.

132

Elphin. May 21, 1751

Just as I was sitting down to write to my Dear Girl, in came Blair, and soon after him Godfrey Wills. So you must be content with a very short letter. I bless God I am very well, and rejoice much that you are so. I hope poor Jane will find more sensible benefit from her Medicine in some time. Much cannot yet be expected. Your account of poor Charlotte pleases me much. I long, for her own, and all our sakes, to have her quite well. What I propos'd to you the morning I left town, I am persuaded will be a means to it. I desire and insist that it be done. There are twenty reasons for it, which I have not now time to give and not one against it.

When next you see Miss Leigh, I wish you or Mrs Jourdan would take an occasion of speaking about the Setting Dog; and I care not how much you aggravate my disappointment. But not a Word or hint as if you spoke by direction from me. Mr L. has play'd with me now a Second year in a way I cannot like, nay! which I really take very ill. I wish He knew it and from her He may.

Shannon affirms positively that there were five pints of Hoc', so it is spelt, in the Bin. The Want of two is no great matter; and yet it amuses me much. Let the saw-dust be carefully examin'd. You know where to go, when they are spent.

Bid John tell Williamson[1] that Mr. Reeves's[2] horse will not do for me at all. I wish he were fairly back agen and so for this time Adieu.

Your &c.
Edw: Elphin

Lennox will soon send you a receit for £55:16:10. Lay it by in the little drawer, in which you saw me lay by papers of that sort. Or keep it safe some where else. Do you know any thing of Matty's affair?

Carleboe and Every body are well.

1. Williamson: a farrier.

2. Mr Reeves: not known.

133

Elphin. May 24, 1751

My Dear Girl.

I am so much pleas'd with your manner of pleading, that I will make no observations on the matter, but leave you at full liberty to follow your own good natur'd intentions. In this one point I have a mind to interpose, or rather that you should. I order'd her to be paid the last quarter's Wages at the rate of £6:-:- a year as an Encouragement for her doing what I expected she would, and still think she might have done. Will it be right to continue that on the present scheme. In my opinion, It ought to be reduc'd to five; and you ought your self to reduce it; and tell her the reasons when you put her on her new footing, which should be when you hire the House-keeper. I am glad you have so good a prospect of one to your mind. If she answers on further Enquiry, Engage her without more ado. I will not be consulted. After you have fix'd things you may say what you please. Her living so long with Lady Limerick,[1] and leaving her on such an occasion with so good a discharge are very good Omens. The Lady is a very prudent discreet Woman.

But one thing, Madam, I must take you a little to task for – *You should have said, what you've now wrote, before I left town, had you known I thought of having two maids!* If by *two maids* you mean, as I think you do, a House-keeper and a Maid, Could I have express'd my intentions more fully than I did, both in our Sunday's Conference and that shorter one on Tuesday morning?

As to Ally Late's affair,[2] I wish that instead of sending me the letter you had sent to the Writer to give you a more perfect account of the subject of it. Do this immediatly, and send a note to Mr Vipond to desire him to come to you some Morning, the Sooner the better. Lay the matter before him, and Enjoin him from me and from your Self, to do whatever is proper with the utmost care and dispatch. He'll promise you to do it, and very Sincerely. But do not depend absolutely on this. Send John now and then to put him in mind, and to learn from him what is done. Let him also ask about the other affair, which I gave him in charge before I left town.[3]

I am sorry you miss'd Lady Kildare. According to my notions of politeness and respect, you ought to attempt seeing her soon agen. But Do as your friend Harriet advises.[4] The Lady's Card seems to me skilfull. But I think you should act as if you believ'd it, and leave your ticket at her door, if she be not gone. For you will not be let in. You probably had been glad they had serv'd you so at Lady B's.[5] – Always, be sure, My Compliments to Mrs Silver. I write this once for all, till my return.

Pray tell me, Ladys all, Have you not been as negligent of Mrs Carter,[6] as that same Wealthy Lady had been of you, till her card brought her about. I protest I think you have. Retrieve it immediately. She has been very good in going near you.

I am as well provided hitherto of Company as of provisions. G. Wills, Blair, Barton and Dean Sandford[7] are here. To morrow will make a clear Stage. One body or other comes in almost every day. I have din'd but once alone. I had the big Table full yesterday. Lord Kingsborough among others.

But I'll tell you a piece of news of my Self. I have not a coat to my back in which it is fit to appear. Very idly I neglected looking at my Habit till it was too late to get a new one. I found it shabbyer than I thought But I comforted myself with having others that would do. All bad. I must get a new one. Send for Woodward, and bid him get as much dark Raven Grey Cloth English, as will make me a Coat, not like my morning Coats, but of the same kind with my Habit, and all proper Trimmings, and Lining. I'll have it made here. I order English Cloth, because of that Colour which approaches to black, I never saw any but English good; and Charge him to get the darkest, the stoutest and firmest He can, with buttons and Every thing else to make it up. Let him also get as much green Cloth as will make a Hunts-man's Coat for poor Young, my Fowler, the same person whom He got one for this time two year, with Mettal Buttons, Lining and Trimming. These two parcels may be made up in one Box to be sent down by the first carefull Carrier that can be got.

Desire John to go to Mr Turner, and chuse the Scythes, and have them and two Stones for each, made up, ready to be sent off at the same time. I shall want them soon. One of my Meadows is fit to cut now. I must cut it in a fortnight or Three Weeks, while He complains, that His at Finglas grow very Slow. When He has bounc'd at this, Tell him my Meadow is rey-grass, and the richest I ever saw. The Money that He gave you, Charge your Self with in your account. He says it was £3:2:6. Bid him see about having my Flax sold. If He can't soon get a better Market for it, Let him apply to Mr Ewing,[8] who I suppose will take it as He did the former parcel. Charge him to take great care of the Box, in which the Cloth is to be pack'd up. That drunken beast George Stephens made the Case so ill, that some rain got in But luckily no great Damage. The Damas Linnen escap'd.

I am sorry for Essex-bridge. They who desire a new one, will be much pleas'd with this Event. I hope I need not caution you against venturing over it.[9]

Jane's complaints trouble me much. I know not what to make of this new one. Give my Service to the Doctor and Ned, both whom you frequently see. And let me know how the one's John, and the others Jane do. Tell them, that the Weather being too hot for broth, and Tea not agreeing with me, I have for these two or three mornings, breakfasted on a Lunch of Bread and Butter-milk. This Liquor is very agreable, and I fancy it is wholesome. If they'll let me, I intend to continue it. Even Ned need not fear it's being too Cool, if Wine enough at dinner will ballance it. I believe I take rather more of this, than our Doctor would prescribe. I bless God I am very well, much better than when I left town. And So Adieu.

Your &c.
Edw: Elphin

How does Brewster perform? We are getting a successor for him here. When you see Woodward, tell him that notwithstanding all his boasts and promises of carefull making my breeches and Waistcoats, There was a breach in the former which I wore about a fortnight before I left town, in two days after I came hither for want of staying; and It must be repair'd by a better, at least a more carefull, Taylor here. I am very angry at this, and will find some way to help my Self.

If I could have you all here and back agen with a Wish, I should wish for this among a thousand other reasons, just at this time, that you might view the glory of those rascally Tulips which came down two years ago. It would astonish you. They are singly as bad, as bad can be, but are so strong in their stems, The Cups so large, and the Colours so lively, that Altogether they make a very fine glare. Every body views them with pleasure and Surprize. I really think you should send down some of your fine sickly ones to recover themselves by this Air and Soil. I'll tell you a little Story of that Extraordinary person Saunders. As I was viewing them with him, and he diverted me with his pretending to know what He was entirely ignorant of, We came to a fine red and yellow one of which I ask'd him the Name. He did not know. I'll tell you then quoth I. It is Saunders's Coat. He bow'd with great complacency and seeming satisfaction, thinking I had paid him a great Compliment. [*damaged ms*] when in two minutes I told him the right name, He was [*damaged ms* de]jected, as He had been Exalted before, and more so, when I told Madam Jenette[10] the passage before him, who laugh'd heartily at him. [*damaged ms*]

I am glad 'Terence'[11] pleases you. When the mourning Livery [*damaged ms*] rusty, as mine here are already by the journey, Let your folks appear [*damaged ms*] Blue ones.[12] Manage this, so as that they may wear the latter for [*damaged ms*] and wear the other when there is no Company, or in their Work. I am glad poor Jac. Davies is better. Let John Miller or some one enquire of him now and then, that He may not apprehend himself neglected.

Just return'd from Stroaks'town. All there very well and much your humble Servants.

How have the Apple-trees escap'd in the Garden? And how says John, is the Orchard at Finglas? Let him take care of the Coals. [*damaged ms*]

1. Henrietta: daughter of William Bentinck, 1st earl of Portland and Jane, daughter of Sir John Temple. She married James Hamilton, viscount Limerick and baron Clandeboye in 1728, and died at Templeogue, Dublin in 1792. Cokayne, Vol. 3, p.212.

2. Ally Late or Leight. See Letter 95.

3. Her 'affair' is not known.

4. Harriet Nicholson: niece of the dowager Lady Kildare.

5. Lady B: not known.

6. Mary Carter, wife of Thomas Carter (d.1763), the Master of the Rolls. She was daughter and co-heiress with her sister of Thomas Claxton of Dublin. Thomas Carter built 9 Henrietta Street. Ball, Vol.2, p.202; *Georgian Society Records* Vol.2, p.16.

7. The Rev. George Sandford (?-1757): dean of Armagh. His will was proved in 1758. *Gentleman's Magazine* (1757), p.436; Vicars, p.414.

8. Ewing: flax buyer. Not known.

9. In 1750 Essex Bridge (now Capel Street or Grattan Bridge) was the most easterly bridge on the Liffey. The Custom House lay between it and the sea. The site of the old city was just west of the bridge including the castle, cathedrals, law courts, Tholsel and merchants' exchange. The fashionable world went to this part of Dublin for a *levée* or the theatre, but they increasingly lived in the newly built eastern part of Dublin, both north and south of the river. In 1749 a parliamentary committee investigated the traffic congestion on Essex Bridge which was caused by the lack of a bridge to serve the new developments in the city. However, a new bridge east of Essex Bridge would have cut off access by tall ships to the Custom House, and opposition on this score succeeded in preventing its construction. In 1751 Essex Bridge became unsafe, and a meeting at the Guildhall on 3 June 1751 called for plans to rebuild it. On 20 June it was resolved to have a temporary wooden bridge while the new bridge was being built. 'It may not be improper to inform the Publick, that the Pillars which support some of the Arches of Essex Bridge have so far given Way, that all Carriages are prevented from passing that way, and the Pavement of the Bridge has separated so as to render it dangerous even to Foot Passengers.' Edward McParland, 'Strategy in the Planning of Dublin 1750-1800', in P. Butel and L.M. Cullen, *Cities and Merchants* (1986), pp.97-9; *Dublin Courant*, 18-21 August 1751.

10. Jennet: the still-room maid.

11. Terence: a horse.

12. Frederick, Prince of Wales, died on 20 March and was buried on 13 April 1751. Prominent families, particularly those connected with the crown, church and parliament, put their household servants into mourning. Lou Taylor, *Mourning Dress: A Costume and Social History* (London 1983), p.104.

134

My Dear Girl.

I forgot Mat. and his breeches in my last. Order John to get him a new pair. What they call Ram's-skin will be the best. Shannon says, He knows the Man who works for me. 'Tis too much niceity in you, to consult me about these Common things, which sometimes do not admit of delay. And besides I do not care for the trouble of writing about them.

Your's this minute come in, brings very unexpected tidings. As I have no doubt, but that Fellow and his Gang, intended to rob the House, I am far from being sorry that He met his Fate.[1] God be thanked you are all well, and escap'd being frighten'd. I believe No one will attempt you agen. However, Do Every thing you can think of to secure yourselves. Let Barrs be got for the Window (Mrs Jourdan calls it Door) facing the Back stairs, and longer Bolts for the other Windows, tho' I don't see the Use of them. But better do too much than too little. I must repeat with more force, the check I just now gave about Mat.'s breeches. It is very idle, in such a Case as this, to wait for orders from me. It will be right to have two men to watch. John must seek out, for such as may be depended on, for honesty and Courage. Poor Morgan[2] is a Cypher. I wish He could get two or three Galaghers.[3] I am much pleas'd with that poor Fellow. Tell him I am; and Bid him be under no concern. No harm can or shall come to him, and for this instance of his faithfulness and resolution, I'll take care of him, as long as I live. John was indiscreet in his Search. Had he been quiet, The affair would have pass'd over in Silence. Now there must be some fiddle faddle. But it will signify nothing. I'll write to Mr Vipond particularly about it. You did very right in sending for him. But I wonder you did it, without orders from me. He has wrote as He promis'd He would. Tho' John has got his Muskets, I shall not chuse, you should trust to them; even when in order. Robinson's Arms are more to be depended on.[4] Let him know, that I am much oblig'd to him for them; and desire He would allow me the use of them, for some time longer, till I can provide some as good for my Self. I think it will be prudent that None of the Servants speak of this thing, much less name the person who shot. The only thing to be guarded against is, Any malicious Examination, which may subject the poor Fellow to confinement, before He can be try'd. I am much pleas'd to find by Mrs Jourdan's, as well as your own account, that you were not in a great flutter. I hope you'll every day acquire more and more calm resolution. It is the best support in the various accidents of life. Let no fright remain in your mind. You are ten times more secure now, than before; yet Charge John to be always on his guard. This is the way to be safe at all Events.

Now for the House keeper. Here agen I must repeat my check. Suppose she be engaged, before you hear from me; What will you say? Recollect what I wrote to you on this subject last Summer, what I said to you the Sunday before I left town; and then say, whether this behaviour of yours be right. I order you positively to do a thing without more ado, and you will not. Upon my Word, Ally, I am far from being pleas'd at this. It shews an Obstinacy in your own purposes, which I had rather you had not. To shew your regards for me, and unwillingness to do any thing without consulting me, you disobey my positive commands. But I hope my last peremptory declaration, that I would not be consulted, has got the better of your restiveness, and that I shall have an account in your next, that the Woman is hir'd. If I have not, I shall be more displeas'd, than I am now; and I promise you, that is not a little.

You mention your Company on Sunday, they were all welcome but one, whom I desire never to see nor hear nam'd.[5] I can't forgive her, her mean insidious application to poor Mrs Jourdan, her urging piety to her Parents, to free her self from some additional trouble, which she was asham'd not to take, during poor Charlotte's ilness and absence; and For which, Had she thought cooly, She must have seen that this could have been, but a Temporary Expedient; and that the Fatigue which certainly had hurt the one Sister, would soon have demolished the other. All this I say, without any regard either to you or me, whose distress, had she prevail'd, she could not but see, and ought, I think, a little to have consider'd. It should have occurr'd also to her, how far, driving poor Mrs J. to such an extremity, might have affected her in several important respects. But she was less easy her self, and therefore consider'd no body else. I can't think of her with patience; and To say the truth I am as little pleas'd with Mrs Rothwell.[6] Suppose her affairs had, as probably they would have, suffer'd, by some absence, Was she not a daughter as well as Mrs J? And Were not her Mrs J's Engagements as important at least? Might not she have been more hurt by breaking them? I give my self freer vent upon this subject, because some broken dark speeches of poor Mrs J. which her distraction, heighten'd by these two Worthy persons canting and interested letters, dictated; and of which I then knew not the Cause, made a great and disadvantageous impression on my mind. Had she been, as she ought to have been, more open, and told me her distress, and the Causes of it, and freed me from the anxious uncertainty I was in, about her own intentions and purposes, which secretly gnaw'd upon my Vitals, this could not have happen'd. But it is now entirely remov'd; and I have a better Opinion both of her prudence and honour, even than I had before, and there is nothing in my power, which may make the good old people, poor Charlotte, and my friend Katty,[7] whom I honour as much as I despise the other two, easy, that I shall not be ready to do. One thing only, I fear, I must continue to blame her for, which I have done from my first knowledge of her, Her too great, and on some occasions, appearingly Sullen reserve. How much uneasiness at different times would she have sav'd both her self and me, if she had taken my Advice by breaking it? How much may she save, if she can even yet be prevail'd on to break it? It is almost the only thing in her, which I wish otherwise than it is.

She has given me a particular history of the Setting Dog. If you had given that rascal a Guinea instead of half a Crown, the Dog had not been taken away. I don't blame you for not doing it, because you know nothing of such things. But I desire you would tell Miss Leigh, that I told you, you ought to have done it; and so there's an end of it. I'll give my self no more trouble. You may find an opportunity of saying the same thing to young Leigh. You should not neglect his Wife and in a visit to her, you may excuse the smalness of your gratuity to that rogue by owning your ignorance what ought to have been done; and free me from the imputation of under-valuing Mr Leigh's present. I ask'd Shannon about 'the Fawn's' Collar. He says, He never had it; that He dy'd when He was in the Country. It is possible the Dog may be sent back, or another instead of him. If either of these happens, Make John provide a right Dog Collar, which is of Buff or some soft thick leather (Let it be of the best kind) and keep him safe ty'd, till I send for him.

I bless God I am very well. God be thanked you are so. I am

Your &c.
Edw: Elphin

Your delaying to get Barrs and bolts, till you get orders from me, brings to my mind the story of Mrs Walls, and the Bishop of Clogher's leaky hogshead.[8] Oh! What folly, monstrous folly. It will be best that Gallagher keeps quietly in my house and Garden. When He does not Watch, He may sleep in the Hall on a straw-bed such, poor fellow, as He is us'd to; and Order him Victuals. I don't know whether He has a Family. If He has Let his usual Wages be given for their Support. As to Every thing else relating to him Let Mr Vipond's directions be follow'd.

You write of Lord Tullamoore's man Barry[9] as of a person whom I ought to know. Who is he and in what capacity there? I would have you take rather more notice than usual of Jeny Trench,[10] while She continues in town, that she may see that her Father's simple behaviour has made no change in us with respect to the rest of the Family.

My Service to the Doctor. Tell him, I have sent him up a Patient for his Hospital, the lame Lad about whom I consulted him last summer. He is to go to you. Send Will. with him to the Doctors.

1. William Jackson, a butcher from Kevin Street, was shot when he and his brother attempted to burgle the house. *Dublin Courant*, 12-15 May 1751.

2. Morgan: not known.

3. James Gallagher: watchman at Kevin Street.

4. Possibly Anthony Robinson. See Letter 87.

5. The person 'whom I desire never to see nor hear nam'd.': not known.

6. Mary Jourdan: Mrs Jourdan's sister, was born at Dunshaughlin on 25 April 1702, a daughter of John and Blandine Jourdan. She married Thomas Rothwell of Berford, Co. Meath, in April 1741. Bouhéreau, 3 May 1702; Burke (1912), p.608.

7. Cathérine Jourdan.

8. Mrs Walls was the wife of Thomas Walls (1672-?), archdeacon of Achonry. Born in England, he was admitted to TCD in 1692 and took BA 1697; MA 1700; DD 1747. He was schoolmaster of St Patrick's 1698-1710; incumbent of Castleknock, Co. Dublin. The bishop of Clogher was probably St George Ashe. *Alumni*, p.852; Thompson, pp.xlii-xliii.

9. Barry: not known.

10. Jane Trench: daughter of Frederick Trench II and Elizabeth Warburton. Cooke-Trench, Table 11, p.26.

135

Elphin. May 31, 1751

My Dear Girl.

I was not as much surpriz'd at your Second adventure, as I was at your first.[1] For I expected it. It is happily over, God be thanked. I hope and believe you'll now have no more. However Be still on your guard. I am much pleas'd with your Courageous behaviour, of which Mrs Jourdan gives the same account that you do your Self. L[or]d Chan[cello]r does honour to her and Jane as well as to you. He stiles you in his letter the three Heroines. He has indeed been very kind. You need not doubt but that I have thank'd him heartily for it. Very probably He'll continue his Visits. You'll always be ready to receive them. I wish you had accepted his offer of Arms. Probably He may make it agen, or you may draw him to make it, by speaking of your Muskets, which I would not have you depend on. I fancy He has some to spare. His offer of either of his houses was mighty kind. But you did well in declining it. In short you have all conducted your Selves as well as I could have wish'd, and some of you, as to Courage, better than I expected. I write a Second time to Mr Vipond to

desire him to pursue the discovery, which I hope the Securing the two ruf-
fians, may enable him to make, and Bid trusty John to continue his
Enquirys with the greatest care. Let him consult your good friends and
mine the Robinsons. I write my thanks to them my self. I don't know Hall
the Marshal.[2] He seems to have acted with great zeal and honesty for your
Service. Let John thank him from me; and if money be proper, Let him
give it. Bid him consult the Robinsons. Let him also give my thanks to Mr
Classon.[3] Let him also wait on Mr Drury[4] with particular thanks from me.
In general Let acknowledgments be made to every one who appear'd to
assist you in any Shape, *from me*, and Money be given where proper. If John
can find out the Officer, who came with the twelve Men, He must wait on
him with a Compliment from me, and Let him try to find out all the Cen-
tinels, who reliev'd your Guard, and give them a Crown to drink. Let every
thing in every shape that may either shew your gratitude, or contribute to
your future Security be properly done, rather too much, than too little. As
for the Civilitys of your friends, You know how to return them. But pray
give my particular thanks to your kind friend Mrs Silver. I desire she would
let Mr Dean[5] know how much oblig'd I am to him.

Gallagher is here. But He came not till three hours after your letter
by post. The greatest mark of fear, I won't call it, but hurry, which you
have shewn in your letters is your not computing the time well that was
necessary to bring him hither on foot. But you thought perhaps that He
was as nimble a foot-man as Mark. He has told me some passages which I
knew not before, which confirm me in the Opinion of his prudence and
resolution. Mathew Smith[6] too deserves great praise. His shutting the gate
was as much an Act of a General, as your sending for the guard. In short
you've all done very well; and Depend upon it I am as easy as you could
wish me to be. I have from the first been much more so, than you thought
I was. I remember the Text of Scripture Madam, as well as you. Tho' at
this distance I could give you no Succour, yet I reflected with Comfort on
those you had in your power. God be thanked they have answer'd my
hopes. Order John to give Gallagher's Wife his usual wages every Week. If
Mrs J. had not tapp'd the Ale I should have abus'd her. I hope it was all
Drank. On such occasions spare neither money nor drink. Give her my
Service, and thanks for her two letters. Love to Jane I am glad she is well.

A Word now about Butter-milk. I drank it but two mornings and it
agreed perfectly well with me. But partly because the Weather grew
cooler, and partly because I had a mind to know the Opinion of those
Gents. I have since intermitted it. I'll for the future obey their orders, tho'
I am not fully satisfy'd that it would be a bad thing for me. Boer[7] have
often prescribed it, particularly for Weak Bowels. Runnet whey[8] I have
try'd formerly. It never agreed with me. I'll shift with Broth and Tea.

Will French has been here these three days. He is very well. He commends your Courage as others do. By the by, It had best be known publickly that Gallagher is gone from you, tho' not, whither. He shall be ready at a Call.

One of the finest young Women of her time, Great Aunt to young Beecher, when about your Age, a Maiden, defended her Father's Castel of Sherky against robberys, and not only plaid the Gent. well, but her self fir'd the great Guns and beat them off. I would have you like her in Courage, tho' I don't wish it may ever be so try'd.[9] You can't excell her in gentleness.

You'll be surpriz'd when you see part of this Page vacant, if vacant it be, which I am not yet sure of, and the two following ones full; and you'll be more surpriz'd when you read them. I need not tell you they were wrote before yours yesterday arrived. But you may see by them that I was in no violent agitation about your Safety, when I could employ my self so long in a dissertation on such a Subject. Once more I expect no answer to it. But I expect that you'll think or act like a Woman of Sense as well as Courage. Oh! My Dear Girl, if you were as perfect as I wish you, you'd be a Paragon. But if you'll do your part towards being as perfect as you may be, I'll be content. You'll then be the pride of your fond Father and your friend. Don't be vain, Huzzy, at my saying that you are so already, perhaps somewhat more than you deserve. And So God bless and protect you, her, and Jane.

> I am Yours &c
> Edw: Elphin

Give me a particular Account of what they write from Roscrea upon your Adventures. I dare say your Uncle was more alarmed, than I have been.

Billy Beaty is down agen. Another Pleurisy, got I believe by playing Ball. He has a worse chance now, as not having the same Assistance. He is very ill.

Honest John Miller is entitled to very particular thanks. Yet I had almost forgot to give them. But there is nothing right or clever, or trusty that I do not expect from him. Let him deliver the enclosed, as directed.

Wedensday

I have had a loss, my Dear Girl, since I came hither; and what do you think it is? Of the ramaining tooth in mine upper Jaw. I was right glad to be rid of it. It plagu'd me both in Speaking and Eating.

Desire John to speak to Mr Eaton, and get him to provide an 8. or 10. Gallon Cask of Lyn Seed Oil. Let the Cask be got immediatly but not filled with Oyl, till He has an Opportunity of sending it off. The most Exact care must be taken to have it Staunch and to keep it so. He must send it off with the Scythes &c. or by the first safe Carrier He can get. Let it be paid for immediatly.

Tell him also that the Chains to the Haims of the new Carr-tackle are too short. I try'd them to day. I must add a link to each. He has been mistaken, and Wilkinson has not us'd me Well.

You know Mrs Southwell[10] was expected here. She came on Monday excessively fatigu'd and out of order. By Cary's account she is, has been for many years, and always will be out of order, and this misery she owes to one most egregious piece of folly. A Severe cold, got at a critical time, and conceal'd by the false Modesty, which ruins Multitudes, laid the foundation of grievous irremediable disorders, which affect both body and mind, and make her a burthen to her Self every day of her life. This is in it's nature a Secret, and must not therefore transpire to any one but her to whom you have no reserve.

You see my End in telling it you. My Dear Dear Child, answer it; and if this instance be not sufficient, Recollect your poor Aunt's Case, whose long misery, and untimely death were owing to a piece of folly of the same kind. Your good Mother lost her health the same way: And probably to this it is owing, that for so many years, I have mourn'd, and shall mourn to the end of life. Oh! Ah *Dieu ne plaise*,[11] that ever I should deplore the loss of you on this or any other account. If so baneful an event could admit of height'ning, It would be arising from such a Cause.

I have often resolv'd to speak to you of this. But I spar'd your Confusion. I left town, determin'd to write, and should have done it, before this apt occasion offer'd, if I had had time.

My Dear Dear Girl. Consider. You are a Female, I won't say Woman. Every thing therefore that belongs to Females, belongs to you. Your Frame and Nature is what the great God of Nature has given you. Can any thing then that is natural, be matter of reproach, or be conceal'd as a shamefull Imperfection? It is not one. To want it, would be. I knew one Lady who had this Want. She was a Woman of Condition, and in her youth had every good quality, that could be wish'd for. This imperfection, and the constant agitation of her mind on account of it, made her a Monster, tho' her husband never reproach'd her with barreness. I learn'd from him, the true cause of what astonish'd me and all her friends. They were a miserable pair. Her death at last eas'd both.

Modesty, My Dear, is the great Ornament of your Sex. I see with pleasure in how great a degree you possess it. I'll go further with you. Shame facedness in young persons if an imperfection, is a beautifull one; and great regard is always to be had to what Decency requires. And this varys in different Countrys. The same thing, perfectly innocent, may be indecent in one Country, not so in another. In France A Lady will speak with more ease of *ses Ordinaires,*[12] than I now write the Word. I could scarce write it in English. Such is the force of Custom. But their decency is more Sensible than ours; yet Every one ought, they must observe the Decencys of their Country. Far it be it from me, to move you to transgress this Law. It must be obey'd, tho' not always approv'd of.

You probably remember to have heard me tell a Story, of a French Dame who traveling with Men in a Stage-Coach, cry'd out *Helas! Cocher. Arrettez; il faut que je pisse.*[13] If this be French breeding, I blame it. *C'est quelque chose de grossière.*[14] But even this is better, than the Decency among us, which often submits you Ladys to difficultys. However as the Law is so, you must, in the Common course of life, submit and manage as well as you can.

But suppose a Lady had a Suppression of Urine, Would it be immodest in her to speak of this to her Physician? No! Certainly. Suppose it were necessary, for him to ask her, *Vous êtes vous presentée Madame?*[15] Would it be incumbent on her to receive this question with a blush and frown, or resent it from the person advis'd with about her health? And what is there in the other Case more than this?

You may guess by my writing to you on this delicate subject, that I know the State of your late disorder, which struck me at first with so much terror, and would have shock'd me more, but that the Doctor inform'd me, of what He rightly judg'd to be the Cause of it. I know too the difficultys He was under in the Course of it, from want of information. I remember particularly one night, that on asking a question from Mrs J. who was to do for you what you would not do for your self, He chang'd his directions. Slight as this change may have appear'd, For ought I know your life depended on it – Your then situation was extremely delicate. So it must always be in like Circumstances. The most innocent thing at another time, may then be Fatal. Sr. Tho' Molyneux[16] either not enquiring, or ill inform'd, some years since kill'd a Sister of L[or]d C[hief Justice] Reynolds's[17] by a prescription, at another time right, as effectually, as if He had shot her, as James did Jackson. He was blam'd. Most probably the Lady's folly was the true cause of her death. Physicians are under great difficultys on this account. Every one, whom I have employ'd, have lamented them to me, and own'd that they have been some times so embarrass'd by them as that they knew not what to do, and I have no doubt but multitudes of Women are every year thus destroy'd. How can it be otherwise? If they have health, they are once a month in the same Circumstances. If single Women are not, some thing is wrong; and this, too, frequently happens. But there is such a false delicacy forsooth in speaking or being spoken to even by a Physician, That they neither know how to manage on the approach, or, while it is on them, nor can they receive directions, because they will not give information. No! 'Tis an affront to speak to them even in the most distant, and best couch'd terms on the Subject.

You have hitherto thrown all this on Mrs J. – or rather she has taken it very kindly upon her. But why should she? Princes have whipping boys, who are corrected when they offend. Must you have one to be indecent for you? But, besides that you may not always have her with you, tho' I hope you long will, Consider that No information from her, can be as Exact as from your Self. She may not know the proper Questions to ask, or you may frump at her asking them.

I shall say no more. I think I have said enough to convince you of the monstrous folly of this *fausse delicatesse*. Yet I don't expect you'll immediatly get rid of it. But I require and conjure you, by your regards for me and your Self, as you value your own health and life, and the remains of mine, which depend upon it. As you would avoid the imputation of Weakness, from one whom you most esteem, and the hazard of bringing your Self to misery or untimely death, and my grey-heirs with Sorrow to the grave,[18] That you attempt to break through this ridiculous, tho' common, niceness; That you suffer the Doctor and Ned to speak to you about these matters, as about any thing else; that you consent Mrs J. should encourage them to do it. If it costs you a few blushes at first, What signifys it? They'll soon be over, and you and I both easy. I shall not be so, till I know this letter has had it's proper effect and yet I do not expect a Word of answer.

1. On the Monday following the manslaughter of William Jackson a mob, led by Jackson's father and brother, entered Edward Synge's grounds in Kevin Street and attempted to seize James Gallagher. The *Dublin Courant* believed that if they had had the chance 'they would have given him Gallows Paul's fate'. (Gallows Paul was Paul Farrell, a police informer who two years earlier had been torn apart by a crowd.) *Dublin Courant*, 31 May 1751; Connolly, p.213.

2. Charles Hall: marshal of the Seneschal of St Sepulchre's. Watson (1751), p.50.

3. A James Classon signed the Declaration of the Inhabitants of St Patrick's 1733-4. Swift, *Miscellanies and Autobiographical Pieces*, p.342.

4. Possibly Isaac Drury, son of the Rev. Dr Edward Drury of Dublin. Admitted to Lincoln's Inn 1750. *Records of the Honorable Society of Lincoln's Inn*, Vol. 1, Admissions, p.438.

5. Mr Dean: not known.

6. Mathew Smith: a servant.

7. Hermann Boerhaave (1668-1738): a Dutch physician, professor of botany, medicine and chemistry at Leyden. He was thought to be the first to show that smallpox was contagious. Boerhaave wrote *Institutiones Medicae* (1728). In his *Aphorisms* (1715) he prescribed milk-whey for inflammation of the guts. Buttermilk was part of the diet prescribed for scurvy. Hermann Boerhaave, *Aphorisms concerning the Knowledge and cure of Diseases* Translated from the last Edition printed at Leyden 1715 (London 1715),

pp.253, 320. Kiple, p.1114.

8. Runnet whey: junket. Made with rennet, curdled milk taken from a calf's stomach.

9. The woman whose bravery was commended would have been a member of the Becher family of Aughadown, Co. Cork. Sherkin Island is in Baltimore Bay. In the early years of the eighteenth century there was a garrison on Barrack Point commanded by Thomas Beecher, MP for Baltimore, who had been a strong supporter of William III. Burke (1979), p.100; James M. Burke, 'Sherkin Island', *Journal of the Cork Archaeological and Historical Society* Vol 11 (1905), 65, p.67.

10. Mrs Southwell: possibly Oliver Cary's mother-in-law. Frances Cary was a Miss Southwell before marriage.

11. God forbid.

12. *Ses ordinaires*: menstruation. A. Spiers, *Dictionnaire Générale Français-Anglais* (Paris 1854).

13. 'Stop; I want to pee.'

14. 'This is vulgar.'

15. 'Have you opened your bowels today, Madame?'

16. Sir Thomas Molyneux (1661-1733): physician. Brother of William Molyneux, the philosopher. He was admitted to TCD in 1676 and took MD Leyden and Dublin 1687. He became president of the King's and Queen's College of Physicians 1702 and professor of medicine in the university of Dublin. He was appointed State Physician in 1725. MP for Ratoath and trustee of Steevens' Hospital. He was a member of the Dublin Philosophical Society and a Fellow of the Royal Society and contributed to their Philosophical Transactions. Created baronet 1730. Wrote articles on forts and round towers in Ireland. He lived in Peter Street. J.B. Lyons, *Brief Lives of Irish Doctors* (Dublin 1978), pp.38-40; *Georgian Society Records*, Vol.2, p.5.

17. Sir James Reynolds (1684-1747): Chief Justice of Common Pleas in Ireland. He was educated at Eton and Cambridge and admitted to Lincoln's Inn in 1710 and called to the Bar in 1712. Reynolds was made Chief Justice of the Common Pleas in Ireland in 1727. According to Ball, in 1732 he lost a sister who lived with him in York Street. In 1740 he returned to England to be a baron of the Exchequer. Ball, Vol. 2, pp.200-1.

18. 'And he said, My son shall not go down with you, for his brother is dead, and he is left alone: if mischief befall him by the way in the which you go, then shall you bring down my grey hairs with sorrow to the grave.' Genesis 42:38.

136

Elphin. June 4, 1751

My Dear Girl.

In the first place I rejoice that you are well, and have been quite quiet since Monday. I doubt not but that you'll continue so. But Let John continue his Watch, and all prudent precautions.

The *Courant* vexes me as much as it does you.[1] I know not whether it be worth while to oblige him publickly to retract it. I'll write to Vipond upon it, and desire him to advise with you, whether any thing of this kind, shall be, if it can be, done. He is very much vex'd at Gallagher whose shewing himself occasion'd the Second and greater bustle; and so am I. But there is now no help for it; and, God be thanked, no bad consequence of any kind.

If I lov'd you less, I should be less mov'd at any thing I think wrong in your Conduct; and indeed, My Dear, you have acted very wrong in this affair of the House-keeper. You probably have my last year's letters by you. Look over them, and see how I wrote then on the same subject. If you say, you forgot them, My answer is that I had wrote enough to you on the Occasion of this, to refresh your Memory, or, if not that, to shew you what I expected. *I will not be consulted,* are some of my Words. How then could you imagine that what you did was all I would expect? The principle that governs you, is a right one. But you push it too far. Can any thing be idler than to shew your observance of your Father, by disobeying his positive Commands – what can I call it but obstinacy? Yes, My Dearest, I may call it Weakness, Weakness, that you ought to be, and, I hope, are asham'd of. How ridiculously could I paint the other instance you have given of the same kind? An attempt is made on my house, and when a view is taken of Weak places, in order to secure it against a Second, My daughter, tho' expos'd to fright and hazard, will not suffer a few Barrs and Bolts to be provided for a full Week, till her Father is consulted! This is the plain fact. It is capable of great embellishments, but it wants them not. It is as high as Mr Walls's, nay! higher, as much as your Safety is of more consequence than an hogshead of Wine. Among the lessons I have given you from this place, I am sure you had one on Scrupulousness, which has some connexion with the matter in hand. It would not be amiss, if you now and then employ'd a leisure hour in reading over my letters of that kind. I design'd them to be instructions for life. Don't be disturb'd at this, My Dear. I write with the Utmost coolness. Anger, where you are the object, can never remain long. Passions of a tenderer kind succeed. As I told you in my last, I wish you to be all perfection. But indeed this is an imperfection of an Ugly kind. You may, you must get rid of it.

I am pleas'd you have din'd with your good friend. Pray make her my Compliments. I would have you for some time chuse to be abroad, as much as conveniently you can. This will be the best way to confute the *Courant.*

Tell Woodward that I like both his patterns well enough. One seems firmer than the other, and is rather a shade lighter. This I like best. Let him send one or other off with the Hunts-man's Coat for the fowler.

I am sorry your Ranunculuss blew so poorly. They must be earlier, and better planted next year. Take them the Double Anemonys and the Tulips up in the proper Season as last year. Before that Season comes, you'll probably see Mr. Hawker or I may give more particular directions, if you ask for them. I hope the Tulips are all mark'd, which ought to be.

Tell John I have his, and have full dependance on his honesty and Courage. I suppose the Coals are by this laid in.

Kitty Ormsby, her husband, Mrs Stuart and her Major[2] and Captain Ormsby are here. They came yesterday Evening. Yyour friend Kitty is very well. She, and the rest who know you express great satisfaction in hearing that you are so. Do you never see or hear from your Artaine friends?

Adieu, My Dearest.
Yours &c
Edw: Elphin

Kitty Mahon is to be marry'd next Week. They say, to young Ormsby of Grange. His Mother is one of the Lloyd's, possibly you remember her.

Will. Smith the Bookseller in Dame-street[3] is a great acquaintance of Ned Curtis's. Insist on Ned's speaking to him about the Impertinent lye of the *Courant.* He is interested in that paper.

1. When the Dublin crowd attacked the house in Kevin Street, the newspaper reported that 'His Lordship's Daughter was so frighted that she has been in successive fits since.' *Dublin Courant,* 28 May-1 June 1751.
2. Major and Mrs Stuart: not known.
3. William Smith: bookseller at the Duchess's Head. Watson (1760), p.40.

137

Elphin. June 7, 1751

My Dear Girl.

I am, and have been full as easy, as I said I was, from the first account of your routs. At the same time I hope I need not tell you, that Nothing could have affected me so much, as your being in hazard or distress. But in both Cases, the same letters which brought the disagreeable accounts, gave me full satisfaction as to your safety; and health. I had the additional pleasure of knowing also, that you had behav'd your Self with as much Resolution as I could have wish'd, and somewhat more than I hop'd; and I comforted my self with the hope that All was over, and that there would be no more disturbance. To my great joy, I find I judg'd right; and I now think you more Secure, than if nothing had happen'd. However let Honest John be still on his guard. You can say nothing higher of him than

He deserves. Desire him to see Mr Nelson[1] agen, and give him in writing the Depth of the other Well. 'Tis twenty three feet six inches to the level of the Pavement. When He has given this account to Mr Nelson, Let him desire from him instructions for the Pump-maker; and bid him – ply him close himself to get the pumps finish'd with all Expedition. I want them greatly, and if they can be got ready by Midsummer, He may have choice of Carriers by whom to send them down, after Mullingar Fair.[2] He must be active and bestir himself in this affair. For poor Nelson is not what He was; and I apply to him now, that the Honest Man, who has been so usefull to me, may not feel the pain of being pass'd by. But the real business must be done by John with the pump-maker. He must know from him whether He has seen my letter to Mr Nelson, and get him to send down in writing the most particular instructions for setting the Pumps. It just comes into my head, that our friend Anthony Robinson, with whom the late Bustles have made John more intimate, was bred a Pump-maker, tho' He does not follow it. Advise John to consult him as from himself, and to get him to view and Examine what is doing or done. It will be of the last consequence to me to have them very complete. Tell John that I am in great want of the Scythes, the Keg of Oyl, and the Cloth for mine own Coat, and Young's. He must send them off immediately; and that He may have somewhat worth while for a Carrier, Let him order Smith immediatly to make up Creels as usual, of wheels as far as 120 – to be sent off with these little parcels, the first instant He can get Carrs to his Mind. One reel to every ten wheels will be enough. Bid him also to send down one Loom. Write a note for these things to Smith your Self, and on the back of it Let John give receits for what He delivers. This will be his Voucher, when I settle with him. Desire John to let me know particularly what quantity of Parsnip-seed He sent down hither this Spring. I order'd a pound for Hogs, besides the Usual allowance. Saunders says it never came. He tells so many lyes that I never believe him in any thing of this Sort – So much for Commissions – Now for other matters.

You conclude your letter thus. My *two friends* present their Duty &c and I see by your letter that at the time of writing you were much frump'd with one of them; and from some Expressions I suspect that you have great, and no sudden, disgust at her, and the whole Family. Whether you are right or wrong, I can't say, till you open your Self more fully. But since the Fact is so, I commend you for having said so much, as puts me upon enquiring further, and I desire you would write to me fully and frankly, and say every thing that is in your heart as to the Commencement, progress, heighth and causes of this disgust. I observe a great tartness in some of your Expressions, which somewhat surprises me. But till I know more, I can say nothing to it. Your Postcript wants a little Explanation too.

If no letters come to Jane but from Bab, or Madge, I shall not wonder at the Composedness of them about your routs. This may be the effect of giddiness. If your Uncle has wrote, I shall see the thing in another light. You see I am in some Suspense. Relieve me asoon and as fully as you can.

What you said to Captain Pomeroy,[3] I can't deny to have been deserv'd by his Sister.[4] But upon my Word, Mistress, this as well as what you've wrote on the other subject, shews that you can conceive deep resentment, and express yourself with great Smartness. I don't absolutely condemn this Spirit – But I recommend it to you to moderate it. Never be offended beyond the Cause, nor aggravate appearing or real neglects, especially if there be room to suppose a general good disposition towards you in the person, whom you think to have neglected or offended you in a particular instance. And As to Miss P. when she comes, I recommend it to you, that you shew no resentment further than a little Expostulation mix'd with pleasantry *'fear'd she had forgot you glad you were mistaken'* and live with her, just as if no such thing had happen'd. I have not time to go on with Documents. See Prov. 16.32 and C. 19.11.[5]

But see, My bold-face, My Gastril in petticoats. (That you mayn't stare at this, I must tell you that in one of B. Johnston's plays, There is a person call'd Gastril the Angry boy)[6] See, My Dear Girl, how you'll defend your Self against an accusation of the same kind, with that you bring against Miss P. Your friend Kitty complains that you've wrote to her much seldomer than she wish'd, and looks as who should say, seldomer than she had reason to Expect. She does this indeed with great sweetness, and speaks of you with much affection. She and Mrs Stuart desire their Compliments to you all. Their Husbands have left them. But I believe Lewis will return before I seal this. Kitty's looks and cheerfulness betoken health, more than she had, a good deal, especially considering her Condition. The other is Stout as in her Maiden-state. By the by I think you would do well to wait on her mother[7] who enquir'd after you with so much friendship in your distress, and return her thanks. She's a very good old Woman.

I see the Puppy *Courant*[8] has attempted to make you reparation, and has shewn as much awkwardness in that, as he did impertinence, in the lying intelligence which obliged him to a retractation. He is not worth minding. God be thanked you are well. May you long long be so to the joy and Comfort of

Your &c
Edw: Elphin

I wish you had thought of Lissy's affair[9] when Mr Vipond made you the long visit. When next you see, speak to him about it, and the other. Whatever they be, they ought to be follow'd. If neglected, Occasions may be lost, which will not return. Another Commission for John, which I had like to have forgot, and if I had should have been undone. Tell him that Mr Ryves's[10] Bay Horse will be deliver'd to him by a Man of Mr Palmer's on Wedensday Evening. He must keep him that night, and provide for him in the best manner, and have him well dress'd and clean'd in the morning. Then He must make Will or some one lead him to Mr Ryves's, and go with him himself, and deliver him with my Service, and bring back with him the Black-horse, whom Williamson and He view'd, whom He is to deliver to Mr Palmer's Man the same day, Thursday, to bring down hither. [*damaged ms*] has a great mind I should try him, and therefore I will. Williamson has been quite mistaken in his judgment of one Horse. Who knows but He may be so as to the other? Tell John in his ear, that I have within these two days learn'd that fellow's true Character from one of Legionier's Officers, who has known him for many years. He says He is an excellent Farrier, but a very great Rogue. Let him make his best of his skill of one kind, and silently guard against his skill of the other. Charge him to take no notice to any one of what I have written. My information is from Major Stuart, who came hither with his Wife. She rose luckily, Let Mrs J. explain this, When she got him.

Beaty is recovering. I really think little Huy[11] is a good Doctor. He has treated him just as Doctor A[nderson] did.

1. Mr Nelson: not known.

2. In 1751 Mullingar Fair was on Tuesday 24 June. Watson (1751), p.97.

3. John Pomeroy: son of the Ven. John Pomeroy archdeacon of Cork. The brother of Arthur Pomeroy, he was unmarried. He was commissioned captain in the 8th regiment of Dragoons in July 1749 and became lieutenant general and colonel-in-chief of the 64th Foot. His will was proved in 1790. *List*; Burke (1916), p.985; Vicars, p.380.

4. Captain Pomeroy's sister: not known.

5. Proverbs 16.32, 'He that is slow to anger, is better than the mighty; and he that ruleth his spirit than he that taketh a city'; Proverbs 19.11, 'The discretion of a man deferreth his anger; and it is his glory to pass over a transgression.'

6. Kastril, the Angry Boy, is a bumpkin who attempts to learn the language of quarrelling in Ben Jonson, *The Alchemist* (1612).

7. Mrs Stuart's mother: not known.

8. 'That part of a paragraph in our last which mentioned the Bishop of Elphin's daughter being thrown into four or five fits on the Occasion of the Attempt made on his Lordship's house, was owing to wrong Information as we are well assured that Lady has never been afflicted with such disorders.' *Dublin Courant* 1-4 June 1751.

9. Lissy: not known.

10. Mr Ryves: not known. He may be the same as Mr Reeves in Letter 132.

11. Hugh Stafford.

138

Elphin. June 11, 1751

My Dear Girl.

All I shall say of Mrs Fany, is – I am glad she is gone. One time or other, you and your friend will come to say, as Hamlet does, I'll take the Ghost's word for a thousand pounds.[1] Excess of good nature often misleads you both, and makes you think me severe in my censures and purposes, till the Event proves me right. You must guard against this, which, with an appearance lovely enough, is a great, a dangerous imperfection; and oftner betrays into wrong Conduct, than the Contrary Extreme. More people, Women particularly, have been undone, by thinking too well of others, than ever suffer'd by the Contrary extreme. Moroseness I blame. A Suspicious temper is not easy to one's self or to any one else. But some degree of suspicion deserves a better name. It is prudence. We all affect to appear better than We are, and the Mode is over-flowing Courtesy. If this passes upon you for friendship, esteem &c. you are deceiv'd, and will be, till undeceiv'd to your Cost. Suspect therefore, so as to be on your guard; and let not self-love, and that Vanity which we all have more or less of, betray you into the Snare, of fancying all that is said to you sincere, because you deserve it. The longer you live, the more you'll see, that Mankind are not what they appear; and tho' it be somewhat dishonorable to Humane nature to say, yet the Honest truth is, Rochefaucault's Maxims[2] are generally just. Let him be so far your Master, as to make you extremly cautious of entring into friendships and intimacys; however free and easy you may be in your general deportment towards all with whom you converse. While nothing wrong appears in them, Justice requires you to think, that they *may be* what they desire to appear. But it will be prudent to consider at the same time, that they *may not.* A proper reserve therefore should govern your Conduct to all, except a very very few, try'd and found Sterling – your worthy maid is not the subject of these hints, tho' she has given occasion to them. But you know my manner is to lay hold sometimes of a slight occasion of giving you documents, which I think may be usefull; and the same turn of mind, which dispos'd you to think of a worthless servant so much better than she deserv'd, may have the same effect in the Case of an Artfull, designing acquaintance. I have no particular person in view; tho' I am not equally clear as to the Merits of all, whom you converse freely with. Keep a good look out, and Remember this lesson. Better it is to *confide* too little than too much.

Poor Maca! I hope you've been in no real pain about her.[3] If you have, You have thought me more severe than I am. As she has no part in her daughter's follys, It would be cruel to make her suffer for them. She is safe for my life, and yours. God preserve you, My dearest.

Before I received your answer to my first letter about Nancy Poor, I had made the fullest enquiry I could about her. I consulted Mrs Cary particularly, who speaks well of her, and thinks her likely to do. Her Aunt[4] is very modest in her account. She'll certainly want a good deal of instruction. But I hope you'll find her docile. I suspect her to be rather indolent. If you find any thing of that, you must keep her up, and not suffer it to grow on her. She's a clean well looking Girl enough and seems a fitter Bed-fellow for Jeny, than Fany was. But leave that to her choice. You've judg'd very right in resolving to write to Mrs Heap. Write plainly and fully. Tell every thing she is to do, constantly or occasionally; and Tell her, that if she behaves her self well, you'll have her taught whatever may make her more usefull to you, or to her Self. Mention her Wages – £5 – I think enough to begin with, especially as you must pay for her instruction in some things. When she deserves more She shall have it. I ask'd her Aunt the Question this day. Her answer was what you pleas'd. I compute that she may be with you by Saturday se'night. I'll send a Man and Horse with her to Mullingar. From thence the Stage may convey her to you.[5] I hope she'll answer to your satisfaction.

I am glad you have begun your Airings in the Chair. But unless you be out very early, You can't continue them this Weather. It is very fine, and makes the Country delicious. Tell John I have nine Mowers at work to day. I hope his Finglas meadows are now in a good way. All mine are better much than they have been these three years. – Your Horses I presume are Stout. I hope they'll continue so. All mine are in Carrs, laying out great Dunghils on 15 Acres for Turnips – Be sure tell Mr D[onnellan] this when you see him. I am glad she said nothing of your going to A[rtane]. Do not go there for some time. I had rather that intercourse dropp'd. Kitty left me yesterday morning. She seems well for her, and cheerfull and easy enough. But I suspect some things are wrong among them. Nothing between her and Lewis. His fondness is the same, and will, I believe, always be so. But He is not fond of the Old Gentlewoman.[6] He said somewhat of this to me, and would have said more, had I encourag'd it. I am afraid, if they come into the Country, there will be some *coup d'eclat*.[7]

Tell John if He does not send down the Scythes soon, He may keep them. I am satisfy'd, Carrs may be got now every day; and He has loading enough to invite them. He may send 40, 80 or 120 Wheels as best suits the number of Carrs, and if this be not enough, He must at all events send half a Tunn of Iron. The kinds I'll learn from Cary, before I seal this. But positively, if these things are not sent soon, I shall be peevish, and have great reason to be so – What I wrote in my last about Williamson, will, I suppose, make him a little more cautious, than He was, in trusting him particularly as to buying Horses. Mullingar fair will now be soon. Let him not send him there, nor am I fond of his sending him any where else. But if He knows the Man from whom Sympson bought the last three Horses, I really think He would do well to speak to him in time, and let him know, that if He'll bring a Couple of choice ones, He'll deal for them. If He says this at all, He should say it before the Fair. As my set is full, and all well, He may be nice, and not meddle with any but what are tip-top. Such only I would chuse, and tho' I would rather have them four past, I would buy very fine ones, at three. But care must be taken that I pay not for more Age than I have. If none offer perfectly to his mind, We can wait for the later fairs, or longer. I have nine now, beside your two immortal ones. I am glad their late driver is better. But what says the Doctor? Will He be able to drive agen?

I am sorry you miss'd the Chan[cello]r. I don't understand *his ticket*. Did He come in the Evening agen? You and your Man Jac. were each in a hurry, as on a former Occasion. I wish you were both cur'd of it. It's odd it makes you deaf. As L[or]d C[hancello]r has put in for Melons, Furnish him plentifully. They can't be better bestow'd. When you have plenty, A fine one or two to L[or]d Ch[ief] J[ustice] Singleton *from me*, will not be wrong. But lay in for the Seed. For they are all new kinds, and very fine, I hope. The rest dispose of as you please. I doubt not but Mrs Silver, Mrs Nicholson, and Mrs Hamilton will have share. I see in the News, an account of the death of Sr M. Deane.[8] If that be true, Mrs Silver won't cry, nor you neither. You commend your habit. I am glad it pleases. This brings to my mind Second mourning.[9] Furnish your Self with what is handsome. You appear more in Summer than Winter. And Don't be afraid of an empty purse in Vanity-Season. Consult Harriet.[10] You may, if you will, give her my Service.

I have no letter from Sullivane. I am sorry for it. Pray send for him and ask him for the list I gave him of what Rouen Ware I wanted. If He has it, Get him to open the Chest, and See, you and your friend, whether it contains, what I desir'd might be wrote for. If it does, All, or the most part, Get him to pack up immediately so much, and Let John send them off with all Expedition. My Complaint to what I have, you know to be this. The Dishes are all margen'd blue. The plates with other Colours. What I desir'd was, dishes like the Plates. I hope He has the pattern one. I am sure you saw and 'tis probable you remember it. But I added more dishes, some round, and some Tirrenes, and other things. Let my list speak for it self, and Let your Eye or memory determine for you, whether what is come, be like what I wrote for. If you think it So, Let it be sent off as quick as may be. For my shew day, is July 3.[11] It would please me much to have them here for that Occasion. Probably He may be for sending all. I should not chuse that, if there be many things not in my list. But if He persists, yield, [*damaged ms*] telling him that He must do it at his own hazard. Say this from your Self. As to the [*damaged ms*] Champaign, I shall say nothing till He writes. But pray Are He and his Cooper frequent in their Visits to the Cellar? And what say they about it? Make him write to me, and send his letter to you.

As to Flowers, Get Will to bring Hawker to you, some morning that may be convenient. He can and will tell you every thing I intend or that ought to be done, better than I can; and will attend you when the Season comes for taking up. There is another later acquaintance, His name, Walsh, The Gardiner knows him. I desir'd him to visit the Garden some-times. Direct Roberts[12] to let you know when He is there, and See him. You may have the Assistance of those two if you please in every step, and you can't have better. I think all the Tulips should be taken up. Best- Midling, and Breeders, Each put by themselves. The Borders must follow; from all I expect a large-heap of refuse to adorn Elphin. Anemonies and Ranun-culus' must be taken up. The Single Anemonies also. I doubt about Joun-quilles. Let those two determine the point.

You know already that I had seen the *Courant*'s Second paragraph before you sent it. It's best not trouble your head more about him. In his paper, which came hither yesterday, i.e. last Saturday's, is one of the pret-tiest letters I have read . Get it. Adieu. God bless you all.

Your &c
Edw: Elphin

You say nothing of Charlotte or Dunshaghlin. No reverse there, I hope. It would please me much to know that A proper person were pro-vided, according to my directions. Tell John He need not trouble himself any more about Officer or Soldiers.

If Mr Vipond applys to you to propose or consent to any measures, for letting those two persons in Confinement, the Father and Brother, drop easily, My opinion is that you should agree to and promote them. I do not think it right, that you or I should be objects of the resentment of the rabble among whom you do, and I must live whether deserv'd or not, and if by leaning to mercy, you can conciliate them, and make your self lov'd rather than fear'd, You'll be for the future more Easy and Secure. This to your Self &c – But speak to John. Advise him against swaggering and bois'trousness. He may be calm: nay! shew concern for what has hap-pen'd, and be at the same time stout and fearless.

Once more the pumps. Let them be expedited. Dic Doherty is here, very well. Mr Vipond writes that you desir'd the *Courant*'s last Paragraph might be re-published with the word *false* instead of *wrong*. It had been better let alone.[13]

When you see Miss Leigh, Enquire as from your Self about the setting Dog, and the rogue that robb'd you of him, and lament my loss. I care not how often you do this. For 'tis indeed a great one: And I suspect her Brother is very indifferent about it. He would otherwise do himself right against a h-l who has abuz'd him by ill treating me. He ought to think thus. I am not sure that He does.

1. Hamlet: 'O good Horatio, I'll take the ghost's word for a thousand pound. Didst perceive?'
Horatio: 'Very well, my lord.' *Hamlet* Act III, Scene 2.
2. François La Rochefoucault, *Réflexions ou sentences et maximes morales.* First published 1665. Rochefoucault believed that men and women are ruled by their passions rather than by their belief in higher conduct and moral obligation.
3. Maca: not known.
4. Mrs Heap.
5. A coach travelled from Smithfield, Dublin to Mullingar, on Mondays and Fridays, leaving at seven and returned on Wednesday and Saturday at six in the evening. The fare from Dublin to Mullingar was 8.11d. Watson (1747), p.6.
6. Old Gentlewoman: not known.
7. *Coup d'éclat.* Trouble.
8. Sir Matthew Deane, 4th bart (?-1751): MP for city of Cork. *Pue's Occurrences*, 11-15 June 1751; Burke, (1900), p.1104.
9. Full or deep mourning was followed by second mourning which was followed by stages of half-mourning. When George II died on 25 October 1760, full mourning lasted until 25 January 1761. Full mourning required dress (usually black in the eighteenth century) in matt or dull materials. During second mourning, slightly less austere dress was allowed. Taylor, pp.102, 103 and 108.
10. Mrs Nicholson.
11. His Visitation day.
12. Roberts: a servant.
13. The newspaper repeated the apology in the edition of 8-11 June 1751.

139

Elphin. June 14, 1751

My Dear Girl.

By comparing yours now before me, with the letter of yesterday se'night, I see plainly that you were a little chafed when you wrote the one, and cool at writing the other. This is not the only proof you have given of having your Father's quickness. Moderate it, My Dear, in time. Like the Spirit of a generous horse, It is of great use, under perfect command. But if it prompts him to seize the Bit in his Teeth, and run away with his rider stupid Dulness is preferable. By long experience I know how dangerous a quality this is, how difficult to manage right, tho' rightly manag'd, how usefull. I have felt the effects of both, and to this day feel them. I would have the good only fall to your share, and the way is to keep a Watch on yourself, and to call in the cool aid of reason and reflexion, to temper the Sallys of a Warm and active tho' generous temper.

You do not like, *disgusted,* nor *frump'd.* Well then! I'll try if I can please you with a Word. The high-bred Irish Ladys say on such occasions, to their intimates, or those they wish to consider as such, *I have a great jealousy of you.* You, my Dear, shew in both your letters, a great jealousy of your Cosens. *An almost defac'd Memorandum that I was daughter to her Uncle. An alien from their Family* &c. I could transcribe half a score more sentences which shew you wrote in a ferment; and even in your last I see that it has not quite subsided. Some swell remains, tho' you are calm.

I believe you'll allow me to be at least an equal judge between you. Be assur'd that whatever partiality I have, is not against you; and yet I can't help saying, that Either Ned told his Sisters or his Mistress more than He had Authority for, or He could say nothing, which was worth making a Confidence of with you; and I heartily wish that Jane had been silent to this minute.

If I do not forget, We had some Conference on this subject, when Matters run high between your Uncle and Ned.[1] I am not sure whether We had or not, or oft'ner than once. But this I know, that I thought, the less you knew of it, the better; to prevent your being embarrass'd, as I perceive you have been, by questions to which it was not in my power to furnish you with proper Answers. Nor did I chuse that you should be in a situation, which would lay you under a necessity of shewing a dislike, to what may possibly be; or expressing your Self in favour of what I could not, as to the Manner at least, by any means approve of.

Your uncle knew of this some Weeks, suspected it much longer, before He gave the least hint of it to me. But when he open'd himself, I found him so highly, and with so great reason, provok'd at his son, that I was in great pain for both, for the one, lest a continu'd ferment might have the Worst effects on his health, for the other, lest He should be driven to Extremitys, and ruin'd whether He persisted or not. He appear'd to me on the brink of it. I thought it therefore became me to moderate between them; and when with much difficulty I had prevail'd on your Uncle to consider this as what might one day be yielded to, if it could not be prevented; I upon that and that only foundation, took Ned in hand; and after having in very strong terms laid before him the egregious folly, and wickedness, and ingratitude of his Conduct, I represented to him the destructive consequences of his pursuing what He was upon *at that time*, advis'd him to go on with the scheme of entring into orders, which both His father and He assur'd me He had long resolv'd on, and so to put himself on some footing in the World, and not to suffer his mind to be embarrass'd with his silly love-affair, so as to continue, in the state in which He then was, less capable of attending any thing else. I shew'd him He could at that time have no expectations from his Father, and assur'd him He had no ground for present ones from me. I told him that if the Damsel knew his true Situation she probably would, or if she were as silly as He, Her friends would certainly influence her, to change her Measures and suppos'd intentions; and that if He chose to speak plainly and apprize her of all, what I thought as an honest Man He ought to do, unless as I wish'd He would give all up, He might not improbably find that Her part was not so disinterested, as He fondly imagin'd. This was the Substance of a three hours Conference one Sunday morning, in which, beside some account I gave of my future intentions towards him, the only favorable thing I said, which indeed govern'd my whole Conduct both to his Father and him, was this, that I was taught to think very well of the young Lady. Upon this foundation I went, to convince the one, that this ought at last to be submitted to, if the other persisted; and I gave it as my only reason for thinking in the same way my self. I said to both, that if she were worthless, I thought it would be rather better to stand the chance of his being undone, by traversing his inclinations, than to consent to his certain ruin by yielding to them. Our Conference ended, Ned left me more satisfy'd than He came, and I found, that or the next day, that He had open'd himself to his Father, and that they were on very good Terms. I suppose they continue so, and I can't say but your Uncle may have gone from the Extreme of too determin'd an aversion, to the other of too quick Compliance. Whether He has or not, I can't tell. For after this setling, such as it was, I don't recollect We had any conference about the business, more than now and then a casual mention of her name. I one day indeed saw her Brother at the Green, and He was presented to me. But I on purpose gave him a cold, very cold, reception. About a fortnight before they went to Roscrea, Lawson, who told me of the thing before your Uncle did, spoke to me at Ned's instance and intimated Miss's expectation of Overtures &c. This I, for my part, positively refus'd, saying It was an affair of their own, they might conduct it as they pleas'd, but that I would not, at that time, make any further step in it.

Thus My Dear Girl, I have given you a full account of every thing material in this affair, which has pass'd within my knowlege. And now answer me honestly a question or two: Had Ned sufficient Authority from this to say, that I (Let your Uncle answer for himself) had no objection, as I had heard a very good character of her? Is there any thing properly on foot with my full Approbation? And Were not you better in your state of ignorance, than you are or will be, now that you are fully and truly inform'd? I well remember your meeting her one Evening at Mrs Maxwel's,[2] and As I know Miss's friendship for her, so I had no doubt of the reason of her being there. But I pleas'd my self with the thought, that your ignorance freed you from Embarrasment, on that interview. Your Cards will be now more difficult to play. But if you conform yourself, as I am sure you will, to my advice, You'll neither make nor receive advances to further acquaintance; You'll avoid speaking of this affair as much as you [*sic*]; and when constrain'd to it, You'll speak of her, as I believe she deserves, with great regard, own, if you please, your Cosen's liking, but say that you apprehend it yet to be an affair of his own; that you don't know that His Father or yours have taken any step in it; and that you are uncertain as to their intentions. You may indeed well be of mine, because I am so this minute my self. Let Mrs J. advise Jane to the same sort of conduct and discourse. As to her *defac'd Memorandum* &c. I think she ought to have told you what her Brother told her sooner, since she told it at all. But I wish she had held her tongue to this minute. And now after all this writing on the only subject of *jealousy* which you have mention'd a short word on Confidences in general, which you seem to think the Test of friendship. I don't wonder at it. Nothing young people are fonder of. But trust me and my grey Hairs, My Dear Dear Child; Nothing that is not wicked young people ought more carefully to avoid. They are oft'ner the bane, than the Cement of friendship. They must be mutual and they are oftner betray'd than kept. On a slight quarrel Every thing comes out; and thus they hate one another for life, who had they trusted each other less might have continu'd friends to mutual Satisfaction. There is but one person in the World, beside my Self, to whom I recommend it to you to have no reserve. If you can't guess her, You may let it alone. This reserve should be more or less, as you find the person on trial to deserve more or less confidence. But some there ought in prudence to be to every one, except the bosom friend. It is consistent not only with ease and freedom of behaviour but with esteem and real friendship. A latin maxim has great good sense in it. I'll translate it for you. Love, as if you may come to hate; Hate as if you may come to love.[3]

But who do you think is here? Poor Lucy[4] on her way to Swanling-bar.[5] Her instructions were to pass me by, and on that scheme she baited, and din'd most wretchedly at Tulsk, and drove thro' the Town. But A letter from the Coll.[6] was deliver'd by his Servant time enough for me to send for her back. Her stage was to have been Carrick.[7] She goes thither this Evening. Poor Girl! She was so tir'd that a day's rest was very convenient to her. Longer she will not be prevail'd on to stay. She travels in a Chariot, with a Man to attend her. So far Well. But they have sent with her the Errantest Irish trull you ever saw. It vex'd me to have her put in one of my pretty beds. But it was right she should be near her. Her looks, and Spirits are just as in Dublin. She has two patches on her Nose. Beside rest, and good sleep and living for a day, she will, I hope, have a further advantage by my stopping her. Mrs Sherman, the Captain's Lady[8] who call'd you Witch, is at Swanling-bar. Mrs Southwell has very obligingly promis'd, at my request, to write to her, and recommend Lucy to her protection. She is to know nothing of this, till she finds it by the Effects. If Jeny writes to Garbally Let her mention this carelessly; and say further, that I send a little provision with her for to morrow, when Her journey will be thro' a Country desolate enough. I would fain have them See and feel that Friends esteem that poor neglected daughter as she deserves.[9]

I had, you know, a letter yesterday from Sullivane. My answer will bring him to you, about the Rouen Ware. If Mrs J. and you think it will suit my plates, or please better, Do not oppose his Sending, but rather encourage. I make a motley figure with blue Dishes, and other Colour'd plates.

Pray Tell John that I know He may get Carrs for this, and Every thing else, if He pleases, So that if they don't come Speedily I shall blame him. Desire him also to tell Turner, that the Bad Iron which I complain'd of before I left town, Necessity drove them to use here, before the last parcel came down, but that that is for the most part as bad as it. I therefore will try elsewhere. The fault is too great brittleness. He may say this at his leisure. But Let him go instantly to Mr Constable, the Tenant in High-street,[10] and Tell him I desire He would furnish him with half a Tonn of right good Tough Iron, fit for Horse-shoes, Carrs, and Farm affairs. If He sends right good, and at a reasonable rate, It will encourage me to deal more with him. Let the price be fix'd; and Let John enquire else-where so as to guard against imposition. As for the Flax-money, there is no haste. When privilege is in, I'll draw a Bill on Mr Ewing for it.

John writes that Mr Drury has bail'd the two Jackson's by Mr Vipond's orders. You see by my last that I inclin'd that way. I am very sure, that the Unhappy person, who was shot, was upon a very ill design; and yet I am truly sorry that such a misfortune happen'd. Besides I can't help feeling for these two, one of whom lost a Son, the other a Brother. I would therefore have them treated with as much gentleness as there is room for, more than they deserve; and I recommend it to you to shew a forwardness to this. I had rather have you the object of Love than of fear, among your low neighbours; and They seldom distinguish between Justice and Cruelty. Nothing conciliates them so much as Compassion deserv'd or not.

Tell Jane I thank her for her letter, but should have been more pleas'd, if she had told me, that the Salt-water does her good. I hope it does. God bless you

Your &c
Edw: Elphin

Long as this is, I must take notice of a false Spelling or two, and remember, Madam, they are not the first, tho' to do justice they have been very few. But you have wrote *rearly* for rarely, and Ladies, as I guess, for Lady's. Your next will explain.

Tell John that one hundred of the Iron must be small square Barr. The other nine half flat. Desire him to ask Mr. Constable, whether He deals in Socks for Plows,[11] and knows the best kinds. Let him get his Answer in writing. I shall want some soon, but will not order any, till I am better inform'd.

Lucy is gone, much reviv'd. She seems to have much more strength than in Dublin. She walk'd all over the house, from top to Bottom, visited every yard out-house, Barn &c. Not a hole or corner Escap'd her. Mr Doherty squir'd her. But she wanted no help for up and down stairs, and seem'd not at all fatigu'd. She eats her dinner well, and went off in very good Spirits.

I must retract what I said about Irish Trull. The person with her is a Protestant, of an English Family, and a very creditable one, tho' now low in Condition. But she is an house-keeper, near Galway, and attended Lucy with great care and affection last year at the Salt Water. By her account She could not have a better person about her; and yet her appearance is just as I describ'd it.

1. This passage refers to a family quarrel between bishop Nicholas Synge and his son about young Edward Synge's relationship with a woman. Edward Synge married Sophia Hutchinson on 15 February 1752. *St Andrew, St Anne, St Audoen and St Bride*, p.52.

2. Mrs Maxwell: not known.

3. Love as if you may come to hate/Hate as if you may come to love. Diogenes Laertius (*fl*.211-35) *Chilon.*

4. Lucy Caulfield.

5. Swanlinbar, Co. Cavan. Between Enniskillen and Ballinamore. 'A chalybeate spa ... long drew to the town considerable numbers of invalids and *ennuyées* in quest of health.' *Gazetteer*, p.294.

6. Probably Frederick Trench II, Lucy Caulfield's brother

7. Carrick on Shannon, Co. Leitrim, eight miles north-east of Elphin.

8. Mrs Sherman: not known.

9. Lucy Caulfield's situation is mysterious. Her family apparently neglects her and there are no references to her husband or to their three children.

10. Edward and Thomas Constable were ironmongers in Bride Street and High Street. William Constable, ironmonger, leased land in High Street, Dublin from

Edward Synge. Watson (1752), p.8; R.D. Curtis and others, 42 493 27154, 29 October 1724; Synge and others 195 121 129 275, 5 August 1758.

11. Socks for ploughs: ploughshares.

140

Elphin. June 18, 1751. Your Uncle's Birth day

I have yours, My Dear, with the enclos'd letters, but no Memorandum for Shannon. Giddy-boots.

I read yours to Mrs Heap. It is a very proper one. Nancy will go off, on Friday, and be with you on Saturday. You would do well to send Will. to where the Stage sets up, to receive and bring her home. For she knows not the town. It must cost you six pence for a Coach for her, and her Cloak-bag. She goes to Mullingar in a chair, and I'll give her a Guinea for her Stage and charges. I hope she'll answer.

But I have little hope of your Licy.[1] You might well call her late exploit, a *coup d'Eclat*. The boldness and treachery of it startle me. So enterprising a spirit will be too hard for you. But I am not against your trying. Only this in my opinion you should insist on; that All which is done, be undone. If her friends will not trust her affairs to your management, why should you be troubled with her? And unless her Guardian be well chosen, she may suffer as much as by Cunningham. I apprehend she is not yet of Age to choose a Guardian. But if the one appointed be a good one, and will deposite whatever she is intitl'd to in your hands, there will be no need to change. What that is, I know not, having had no letter from Mr Vipond. Follow his advice in whatever you do. You'll then not want any from me. This alone I recommend in general Either have the intire direction, or Send her to those who are to manage her Affairs. Why should you take yourself, or give Mr Vipond, fruitless trouble?

A few days hence, It is probable that Coun[illor] Anthony Foster[2] will send you Mr Lennox's receit for £226:7:7¾ which He owes me. If He does, send him a receit for it. That you may not blunder in the first step you take as a Woman of business, I'll give you the form.

Recd from Anthony Foster Esqr Mr Lennox's accountable receit for £226:7:7¾

Dublin June 1751   For the use of my Father the Bishop of Elphin.
        A. Synge

If he does not send, trouble not your Self to enquire.

I see in Faulkner an Advertisement of a Pamphlet with this Title. *A Brief Narrative of the late Campaigns in Germany and Flanders* &c.[3] I heard of it, before I left town, and such an account was given, as makes me fear some imposition. I intend writing to Lawson this day about it, and if He sends you one, or desires you to get it, Enclose it to me in your next Cover. The Letter I took notice of in the *Courant,* appear'd the following post in the Gazette, which you always take in. It was a Letter from an Aunt to her niece, on Occasion of the death of Mr Dalton.[4] If it has escap'd all your notice, you are either giddy or Stupid. Take your choice. I have some charges of the first kind against you, which will come out by degrees. One Take now. You never mention'd the poor Lad McCormick[5] whom I sent up to the Doctor.

Send immediatly to Sullivane, and Tell him I will not on any account have him send down the Chest of Rouen Ware hither. By your description It is odds, I shall not like them; and I'll shift with what I have. Desire him to take them home. But if He chuses to let them remain where they are till my return, consent. Only Tell him it is his own Act. I believe his Correspondent is to blame, not He. You say the colours are more glaring than Mrs Card's. If they be more strong and lively, I may possibly like them. For the faintness of those disgusted me most. But I can determine nothing till I see them; and I won't run the risque my Self nor expose S. to that of double Carriage.

I had a letter from John; as you'll see by my return. You must be troubled with my Commissions to him, till privilege comes in. Tell him I am much surpriz'd at his account of his Meadows; For mine, as I think I have said already, are better than they have been these two years. But since so it is, He must be content with late mowing and wish for rain. We had a good deal here on Saturday, some flying show'rs since. We wish for more, but are in no distress for want of it. Some things will be better without it. He has never mention'd the Bullocks and Dry Cow. I suppose they are at Coolblow. Tell him that As He has so bad a prospect of Hay, I think He had better sell them, if fat, in case He can get a good price for them. I mean Bullocks only. For the Cow must be kept over, and He may bring his fine Heifer, and miserable Calf from Finglas to be company for her. None of them must go under £5:-:- a piece. As much over, as He can get. If the Pumps be ready, when the Maker promises, It will be the best time, the whole Season for Carriage. But Let him take the most exact care, that every thing be complete before He sends them. I want them much. Let him know that Mr Ryves's horse came safe here yesterday morning. He should have told me, whether the other got safe to town. I hope He did. I suppose He has shorn his sheep at Finglas. I make him a present of the Wool.

I have said nothing to you of your writing. It is, as usual, unequal. But it would appear much better if you air'd your paper. It sinks, tho' of the best kind. This is easily done. Your interlineations are fewer, tho' yet too many; and now and then they are fewer than they ought to be. In yours now before me, some Words are omitted. Your stopping is not yet perfect, tho' better; and you err more in kind than Number, or place. Try, My Dear Girl, to guard against these inaccuracys. The way to be perfect, is to endeavour to be so. You write *coup declat* – You forgot the Asterisk, and write *declat*, as one Word. You spell guardien. It should be guardian. But in this you follow the French. I can't make the same excuse for the next. Occassion. A double s. Fye upon it. You write lutestring[7] as Grogan[8] would. But it is wrong. Lustring is the Word. Here end Criticisms.

I am much pleas'd with your account of poor Charlotte. I hope she'll recover strength in the Country. A Vacant mind, and freedom from fatigue will be great Means. On both accounts I should be glad to know that you had among you got the Servant I directed. And so God bless you all. I am

Your &c
Edw: Elphin

Bid Jane let them know at Roscrea that I do not forget it.

Poor Mrs Gunning is dead.[9] She went to dye at her Father's. Kitty Mahon, they say, is marry'd.[10] If she be not, she is near it.

You see I have turn'd my Paper up side down. It is no great matter.

1. Licy: not known.

2. Anthony Foster (1705-79): lawyer. He was admitted to TCD in 1721 and took BA 1726. A King's Counsel, he practised in King Street, St Stephen's Green. He became chief baron of the Exchequer. *Alumni*, p.302; Ball, Vol. 2, pp.213-14.

3. [George, Marquis Townshend], *A brief narrative of the late campaigns in Germany and Flanders. In a letter to a member of Parliament* (London 1751). An attack on the mismanagement of the campaign in the Low Countries between 1743 and 1747.

4. Mr Dalton of Hill Street, Berkeley Square, London, died as the result of an argument about a young lady. *Dublin Courant*, 1-4 June 1751.

5. Donald McCormick. See Letter 107.

6. Possibly the wife of Samuel Card of Dublin, who leased land from Edward Synge in Cork. Bishop of Elphin and others to Wills and another, RD 160 108 106640, 9 February 1753.

7. Lutestring: a glossy silk fabric.

8. Overstreet Grogan, mercer, Dame Street. Watson (1752), p.13.

9. Mrs Gunning: the wife of Alexander Gunning, the schoolmaster at Bishop Hodson's School, Elphin. They married in 1747. See Letter 25.

10. Catherine Mahon married Gilbert Ormsby of Grange, Co. Roscommon. Burke (1912), p.542.

141

Elphin. June 20, 1751

My Dear Girl.

I can't let Nancy Power go off, without writing a line to tell you that I bless God I am well. You'll get this two days before that which I shall write to morrow.

The enclos'd came here to day. The Contents surprize me. Let me know the truth. I hope you'll get this, before your Saturday letter is seal'd. If John has neglected to pay Gallagher's Wife, He has been much to blame. Charge him to take better care, and Let him order the Woman to write no more letters. For her husband has no money to pay for them. Bid him stop a groat of the Week's wages, which Shannon paid for this. But Let this be his own act. It will oblige her to do what I order. God bless you all.

Your &c
Edw: Elphin

Send the enclose to Ned. You never mention him, Rachel, or Jeny.

[To Miss Synge]

142

Elphin. June 21, 1751

My Dear Dear Girl.

The turn of mind which you have shewn, in your late letters particularly, gives me infinite satisfaction. God continue and improve it. So will you be a lasting Comfort to your fond Father, and worthy of your most Excellent Mother. She exceeded me as far in every thing good and Valuable, as I wish you to exceed us both.

I know no way in which I can so much contribute to this, as by admonishing you of your failings, and I see none, which it is not in your power to remedy.

You ascribe many of your *beveues*[1] to giddiness. So do I. But you must not extend the Sense or province of giddiness too far. The real cause of many of your mistakes, which you impute to this, is not giddiness, but Hurry, which is a very different thing. The former implys Levity and Want of thought. The Latter, thinking and consequently acting too fast. Your thoughts jostle, and leap over one Another's backs, and, in this tumult, you may attempt to do every thing but do nothing well. The remedy is Sedateness. Bring your self to follow De Wit the famous States-man's[2] Maxim, by which He went thro' an infinite load of business (I think I have mention'd it before) Do one thing at once. Thus you'll have time for every thing, and do every thing well.

Tho' I know your letters to me are your principal and most pleasing business, Yet I see hurry in them frequently. Even in that now before me, which pleases so much, there are traces of it. You should be very sorry, you say, to give room *for* that many ey'd, and more than argus, many tongu'd Monster to say &c your *for* ought to be to. But what I would remark is, that this looks as if you thought Argus had many tongues; I know only of his Eyes.[3] Now here, Fancy run away with you in your hurry. Sedateness would have taught you, to put it right, tho' 'tis a little hard to do it. The best way I can think of is thus; *That, more than Argus, many-ey'd, and many-tongu'd Monster* &c. But more Sedateness would have taught you to lay aside the image as too Swelling. I have caution'd you against this way of writing, and must on this Occasion, do it agen. I know it is apt to please young people; and your Cosen at Inane,[4] whom you justly esteem, uses it much. But it is not right. In letters particularly, All should be simple easy, and natural, nothing Poetick, no flights of any kind. Madam Sevigny is the best pattern I know; For she follows nature. Lawson sent down hither a new Edition of her letters in 6 Vol. which afford me much agreable entertainment.[5]

Desire him to get a set for you. If you won't pay them I will. But upon my Word, Ladys, I was and am serious about your Watches. It will teach you to take more Care of them. If I owe any thing at Holmes's, Clear me, when you clear your Selves. I thought you had Rochefaulcaut among your french Books. I am sure it is in my study, or here. Till I find it, borrow from Lawson. Half a page after breakfast is enough at once. It will teach you Wisdom and Caution tho' I expect to hear you'll all be very angry at him for thinking so ill of mankind. Just room before I turn over to abuse you for a false Spelling. *Spake* for *Speak*. Huzzy!

I believe you have answer'd my questions *honestly*. But the answer to the second gives occasion to another question, which will pinch you more. Why were you uneasy? Ought you to have been so? You certainly might not, and for a reason which you'll at once admit to be *sans replique*. Because if things had been really in the State in which you believ'd them, previous to, or at the recalling the defac'd Memorandum, My behaviour to you would not have been right, any more than your Cousin's. By the by I know not which Cosen (That's the correct Spelling, tho' the other is us'd) you mean; Jane or Ned, by whose directions you say she spoke. Tell me? You ought therefore to have argu'd thus. If things had been so far advanc'd, My Father would have given me some hint of it, before he left town. There must therefore be some mistake. I will not be uneasy, but trust him, whatever I may do others. Methinks now I see my Dear Girl redden with Confusion. But Away with it. I blame you not in the least. However make this use of it. Guard against hurry and quickness and Take it as a general Rule of the utmost importance. Never *presume* a slight. Be absolutely certain before you *resent* even in thought. As you were so uneasy in your state of ignorance, I am glad you are out of it. But I still think, You might, nay! ought to have been easy in that state, for which reason alone I chose to leave you in it; and that in other respects your province had been less difficult, than now it must be. Manage with as much prudence as you can; and Let this govern your Conduct. It is very likely the thing will be, whether I or your Uncle fully approve or not. Conduct your self therefore, so as that if it be, you may come into it with the best grace. I give you the rule, which I follow my self. I agree it is better to say nothing to Jane, till Occasions arise, for the reason you give. If any do, I think, between you you'll be able to influence her to act as you do your selves.

I write to Mr Vipond about the Jacksons. He'll see you; follow his Advice. But this one Word to your Self. If you see them at all, Resolve to forgive them. Settle this with him before hand. But Do it, as from your Self. For the rest, I referr you to mine to him. I pity the Wretches from my heart. If they behave themselves with Candor You may, beside forgiveness, assure them of favour and Countenance, such as may be proper for you to shew. For the rest I referr you to mine to him. I am likely to have a heavy hand with Gallagher. Poor fellow! He was in high Vapours, before He received the letter which I sent you by Nancy. That increas'd them. I long for your answer to relieve him.

You may make up Mr A.'s linnen for yourselves when you please. I thought you had done it long ago. I am not in haste about the Hamborough Linnen.[6] What you wrote about the letter from Garbally concerning your fright &c. made me think Jeny corresponded there. No writing on purpose; and I've learn'd since by J. Mara[7] that Mrs Sherman was not there. But Coll. Wynne was, and poor Lucy very well setled. I wish she may receive benefit by the Waters. I am sorry Jane receives none by hers. I hope she will. I thank you for *Harriet Stuart.*[8] I see advertis'd another call'd *Constantia.*[9] Ask Lawson about it. If it be good, send it down, not otherwise. Shannon says, He never had the Key of that Oak Chest and I believe him. If you can't find the Key your selves, Get Turner's Man, to open it. John will fancy I mistake, because I order'd him to buy half a Tonn of Iron from Constable. But I do not. I do not intend to break with Turner, tho' in the Article of Iron He has not us'd me well.

Tell John I think him right about the Pumps. Let him send them down by mine own Horses. If I had the Scythes here, I could wait to have every thing else come by them. But they press. I hope therefore that He'll find Carrs to send the other things, with them, off. Next Week will be his time for variety and Cheapness of carriage. Have you had no rain? We had a very heavy show'r on Wedensday, and the sky lowr'd yesterday. But it now looks setled Fair. And So – God bless you all. I am, My Dearest

    Your &c
    Edw: Elphin

When next you see, Mr Vipond, read to him, what I wrote in a late letter, about Licy and her *Coup d'Eclat.*

1. *Bevues*: errors due to lack of attention.
2. Johan de Witte (1625-72) Dutch statesman. Grand pensionary of Holland and leader of the United Provinces in the First and Second Anglo-Dutch wars. He rebuilt the Dutch navy, improved the country's finances and exploited the East Indies trade. He was murdered.
3. Argus, in the Greek fable, had a hundred eyes.
4. Inane, Co. Tipperary. Possibly Molly Curtis.
5. Mme de Sévigné, *Recueil des Lettres de Madame la Marquise de Sévigné à Madame la Comtesse de Grignan, sa fille* [Edited by D.M. de Penin] 6 vols (Paris 1734-7 or Leide, 1736-9).
6. 'Germany narrow' linens were imported through Hamburg, a major centre for the export of linen from Silesia, Saxony and Brunswick. Gill, pp.14, 178n.
7. J. Mara: not known.
8. [C. Lennox] *The Life of Harriot Stuart, written by herself,* 2 vols. (London 1751).
9. *Constantia: or, a true picture of human life, represented in fifteen evening conversations, after the manner of Boccace ... To which is prefixed, a short discourse on novel writing* (Dublin 1751). Advertised in the *Dublin Courant,* 8-11 June 1751.

143

Elphin. June 25, 1751

My Dear Girl.

Tho' I take my sheet as usual, I believe I shan't write a great deal this bout. I have other letters on my hands, and Mr Sandford[1] is here, Rachel at Mr Cary's. They are both very well, and express great pleasure at your being so. L[or]d C[hancello]r did not send the Pamphlet. So Between two stools &c. But it is no great matter. Lawson gives but an indifferent Character of it. So do not send it. It would have been easy for you, when L[or]d C[hancello]r ask'd, to have said I'll look in my L[or]d's letter; and

I wish you had done it. But you were *hurry'd*.

I hope you'll come to a steady good hand. It will help, if you leave off all Turns to your letters. m. This is wrong m. right. So of every one. Your stopping will yet require a good deal of care. You are almost as much afraid of full stops, as of Colons, or Semi's. Most of your Sentences conclude with plain Commas. Till you reform this, You'll not be even in the Way of stopping right.

I am very sorry that good Mr Jourdan is out of order. I hope next post will bring a better account. I don't wonder that Every thing is out of tune at Dunshaghlin, if He be.

I am glad Nancy is safe with you. I hope she'll do. She went hence with the strongest resolution to do all in her power. I have but one Word of Advice to give you about her. Keep or make her Active. She seems to me to want a Spur, rather than a Rein. I judge from her looks and motion. For I am not sure that I ever Spoke to her.

You did right to stop Sullivane's sending down Dish or Plate. For the rest, Let him take his own Way.

John is somewhat in the right about Gallagher's Wife. Let him reduce her allowance to three shillings a Week; and Let that be punctually paid. But bid him make it his own Act. By Mr Vipond's letters It is probable the Man may stay here a great while. But I have yet given him nothing except his victuals and lodging, and two Shirts and Cloths. The remaining eighteen pence shall ballance this, and be something for that poor Fellow himself. He is better of his Vapours.

Tell John that All his Carriage came safe. But He ought to have wrote by the Carr-men themselves. For they were here on Sunday; and I was forc'd to maintain them and their Horses, till yours arriv'd yesterday. He did right about the Iron. I have your Book. I can yet say nothing about it. Did you read it?

In his last He talk'd of sending the pumps by mine own Carrs. In this He says He's looking for Carrs. I care not which way they come, so they come safe. If by mine own Carrs, Mrs Heap is preparing for you a present of a Cask of flower, which, if it goes safe, will please. I really think my bread now outdoes it's usual out-doings. Do you know that this is one of Mr Cibber's flights?[2] I am to account to you for using it. Adieu. God bless you all.

Your &c
Edw: Elphin

Bid John tell Mr Constable that his account of Socks is imperfect. He tells only the price, but says not which are thought best, or whether He deals in them.

1. Henry Sandford of Castlerea, Co. Roscommon.
2. Colley Cibber (1671-1757): playwright. Noted for his concern for theatrical effect at the expense of literary merit.

144

Elphin. June 28, 1751

My Dear Girl.

I am glad the Jackson's affair is finish'd. I don't wonder you were mov'd. If you had not, I should have blam'd you, as I did the fine dame, who sat with dry Eyes at the E[arl] of Essex[1] – I would have you carry your Compassion further; and give the Man five pounds at such time and in such manner, as Mr Vipond shall direct. To make this more your own Act, give it out of your own purse, if you have it, and Let it be known that you do. You may trust me. Tho' I advise and desire this, I am far from being satisfy'd that the Miserable Man has been ingenuous.

You promise you'll set your whole mind to leave off hurrys. I hope you'll perform. Believe me you'll find your account in it. But remember, My Dear that *Hurry*, in my Sense of the Word, takes in a great deal, even such incidents as that of which you give me an account, at which I see plainly you were a little hurry'd. And As things of this kind will probably often occurr, So, according to Custom I take occasion from this to give you a little advice.

If you converse with that innocent freedom among your friends, which I not only allow but recommend, and If sometimes you appear in publick places, you must expect to meet young Gents., and an Accidental meeting or two either way, may by some casual Conversation commence a Sort of acquaintance, as far as a Bow or a How-do-you. As the World goes, very little is sufficient for this; and the Young and gay of one Sex will thus take notice, of the young and not disagreable of the other. Where there is nothing mean in their rank, nor Exceptionable in their Manners, or Character, this ought not to give offence to the nicest; And Here 'tis in their power to stop, and with the Common run they ought to do so. But there are some who are entitled to be treated with somewhat less reserve. Good sense and prudence will easily make the distinction between the persons, and thus determine the behaviour, which may, which ought indeed to be free and Easy to such, without becoming familiar. A decent reserve without prudery is the Top behaviour for a young Lady. But shyness is as bad as forwardness, and oft'ner put on. Where it is, it aims at the same End with the other; *Incense*. A little of this Every one of you are pleas'd with.

But It is great, most egregious folly, to seek it, or take great Gulps, when offer'd. Yet this is, not seldom, as much the Secret aim, of the shy Lady, who retires into a Corner of the room, and from thence Watches, whose Eyes are in quest of her, as of her, who is fond of getting all the young fellows about her, and laughing with one, and giving another a Tap with her Fan. There is indeed a Shyness of a more innocent kind. Tis what Swift calls the Demure and Coy,[2] and may be more or less observ'd in all young persons of ingenuous minds in their first advances into the World. You have had a good deal and still have some of it, which I think you may part with, without any danger of running into the Contrary Extreme. And the Way is, Avoid hurry every where, in all Cases. Be sedate, collected within your Self, so as never to be surpriz'd or disconcerted, at any little incident in Company. Thus you'll be easy, courteous affable, decently free without levity, and compos'd without gloom or Superciliousness. Thus you'll preserve enough of the *stand off*, to free you from all impertinence, and arrive at that true dignity of behaviour which will procure you the Esteem of those, whose Esteem is worth desiring.

These, My Dear Girl, are my general Documents. Now to apply them, to the incident, which I have already told you, I think, hurry'd you a little. It appears to me a trifling one; which you might and should have view'd with absolute indifference.

You say *you could not put it in yr head that He would be so strange* &c. I transcribe your Words, to put you in mind, That your Sentence is not *bien tournée*.[3] But I know what you mean; and think your two friends were wiser than you. I don't judge from the Event. Probability was on their side before, nay! I believe your friend, who sent the present design'd it so. That He did is certain, because He came For which I think him neither very wise nor very polite. But He thought, to be sure, that your accidental meeting at breakfast, gave him sufficient foundation to go without an introducer. I think it did not. Perhaps the mode is against me. As the World goes, the least intercourse is consider'd as an Acquaintance – But if such a person thus sought an Occasion of seeing you, Was there any great matter in it? I see nothing that ought to have given you a moment's uneasyness, or have influenc'd you to take any measures to avoid it. If indeed his and your friend gave you any hint of his intention, You were absolutely right. Otherwise not. You should have left things *courir leur train*.[4]1 If you were at home, So. If not, So. A quarter of an hour had put an End to the Visit, without giving the least Occasion for more. I think therefore that your Sollicitude to avoid it, shew'd a little bit of Shyness, very innocent Shyness indeed, and rather on the whole to be approv'd; but yet such, as if by degrees you get the better of it, You'll come nearer that perfection of behaviour, to which I would have you aspire. You say, you've 'scap'd an Acquaintance. I tell you, you have not, unless you avoid the Lady now on her journey; which on Such an Account would be extremely simple; and What objection to such an Acquaintance? I care not if you had twenty such. You must expect some Worse, unless you shut your Self out from the intercourse of the World. Any thing further is indeed of a more serious nature, and you cannot be too much on your guard. But never presume design, nor, whatever you suspect, Act as if you did, till 'tis avow'd. Many a female has thus made herself ridiculous. I could rally you a little severely on what glances that way in your account of this incident. But it would be too cruel. I see the *naiveté* of your heart in every Word you have written, and am greatly pleas'd with it, and tho' I have thus criticis'd your Conduct, am far from disapproving it. Too much Caution in such Cases is vastly better than too little. But the Golden mean in all things is best, if you can hit it. To that All my hints and advices tend; and to make them more usefull, I descend to the Smallest things. A Painter must note the Smallest blemishes in a picture which He would have a *chef d'oeuvre.* Oh! My Dear Dear Girl, May you be so. I hope you will, in Religion and Virtue, in Sense and prudence, in modesty and good nature, in an amiable behaviour equally remov'd from levity and Starch'dness, in humility, innocence and truth. I shall never have done; in every thing praise-worthy and commendable, which may rejoice your Father's heart, and gain you universal Esteem; and May you be as happy as such good Qualitys deserve. And now, to put an End to this long dissertation I'll tell you my opinion of this Visit, which has a little perplex'd you. I verily believe it to have been the Effect at most of a little Curiosity, excited by partial accounts of your two Common friends. If I had the least Suspicion of any thing more, tho' I should have thought as I do, Yet I would not have laid hold on the Occasion, to write as I have done. I think I have wrote in much the same manner before. But No matter. There is no harm in a repetition of usefull advice.

Your Confession in the other affair is so ingenuous, that I'll say no more of it but this, that I wonder you could satisfy your Self as you did. What all the Town knew, as you said, before the recall'd Memorandum, you judg'd I kept a Secret from you, because they did not chuse to trust you. A Groupe of improbabilitys! If I suspected you of Art, I should think you practic'd some here. But I do not, and hope I never shall. Be to me always without disguize.

I am glad the Pumps are on the way. I am quite ready for them. John's account of Meadows and Garden is very bad. No remedy but patience. By the return of the Carrs Mrs Heap will send the flower, and what linnen she can Spare. It is not much.

Next time Sullivane calls at your Cellar, tell him it will be time enough to answer his when privilege comes in. I am sure, fall what can fall, that I can hold out here longer than to that. He is very good at Commending his things. Let him be ask'd, whether He has any of that Wine which He so highly commends in hogsheads. I'll not meddle with any in bottles either for Dublin or here.

Mr Sandford and Rachel left me this morning. So I have leisure for this long Epistle. I can't say I am tir'd with it, But it is time to have done. God bless you all.

Your &c
Edw: Elphin

You say nothing about Mr Jourdan. Don't you remember that in your last, You told me He was not well, and Charlotte but So So. Why would you leave me in Suspense?

This Postcript will surprize you, as yours did me which I saw but this instant. Yours concluding so fully at the bottom of the page, I look'd no further. I wonder it so long escap'd me. But I saw it time enough to retract my charge.

I am sorry poor Jeny Curtis has been so ill. The kind of ilness is to be expected. I hope she'll weather it, and that Ned don't get a Second Cold. He is too careless of himself. The poor Woman has a sad time of it between them. Have they any country-house but at the Green? I was pleas'd with what you wrote to Mrs Heap about Tea, but was pretty sure you'd find matters as you do. I have no objection to what you propose. But if Mrs Barry[5] be a Tea drinker, It may give her umbrage. As I believe she is, you may as well tell Nancy, that if she will drink Tea, she must find it for her self as her Aunt does, and that you expect she'll not waste time at it. It will be impossible to keep her from it.

How does your Fole? Have you ever seen it? I have one of mine own, a Mule, which I visit often. A Crown boot between it, and it's Dam, and a Mare of the same kind bought formerly with such another Fole, purchas'd it.[6]

Have you ever thought of speaking to Miss Leigh about the Setting Dog? I wish you would find or make an Occasion of asking, Whether her Brother ever took any notice of the Adventure and whether the fellow who us'd us both so ill was ever punish'd for it. You may speak of the disappointment to me in as strong terms as you please, if you take care not to hint my making any complaint. It [*damaged ms*] great one; and if Mr Leigh has received it, as I apprehend he has, It looks as if the Sending the Dog was Grimace, and the taking him away no offence, perhaps concerted. I think they should at least return you your half Crown.

1. Possibly a reference to the execution of Robert Devereux, earl of Essex in 1601. The context is obscure; it may have been a play.

2. Demure and coy. Not traced.

3. *Bien tournée*: well phrased.

4. *Courir leur train*: to run their course.

5. Mrs Barry: a servant.

6. Edward Synge had trouble with his mules. When Arthur Young visited Synge's son-in-law Joshua Cooper in 1776, he was told that the late bishop of Elphin had lost all his mules because he fed them wheat straw cut into chaff. A.W. Hutton (ed.), *Arthur Young's Tour in Ireland (1776-1779)*, 2 vols (London 1892), Vol. 1, p.240.

145

Elphin. July 2, 1751

No letter from you, My Dear Girl, by yesterday's post. But I suppose it miscarry'd as one did last year, and in that hope am Easy. In my favorite M. Sevigny's letters, I often meet great Complaints of the miscarriage or delay of those of her Daughter, and she comforts her self, as I do. But I can't write on that or any other Subject with such life, and prettyness as she does. If I had ever so much to say to you, I have no time to say it now. For to morrow is my Visitation. God bless you all. I am

Your most affectionate &c
Edw. Elphin

Tell John his Mule is better. He shall certainly have her agen, when well.

146

Thursday. [July 5, 1751]

I hope, My Dear Girl, I shall have a letter from you to day with All well. In that Confidence I sit down to write before the post comes in.

My Visitation, and the Clutter, which is the worst part of it, are happily over. Carleboe did very well as usual. So did Shannon unusually. I am sure you and your friend have often thought I blam'd him for follys &c. not in his power. His behaviour since He came here, has shewn I was right. Now and then there has been a Shannonism. But in the main, you'd be surpriz'd to see him. He was remarkably clever yesterday. I wanted no Supple, nor a better in his place.

If your Weather has been like ours, John can no longer complain of want of rain for his meadows. We have had a great deal; Yesterday particularly two most heavy Showr's. They have done no hurt. More will here, I fear, For it has threaten'd all day.

Tell him his Mule is better; and that I have contriv'd a method of his having her back, when well, that will answer some Convenience.

I am fitting up a Forge; and He must provide bellows for it. Let him consult my Smith and whom else He pleases, and get me a pair Completely made. The Smith here speaks of one on Astons-Quaye as the best Maker of them in Dublin.[1] He has forgot his name. The bulk of my Work is Horse-Shoes, and Spokes for Carrs. Let the size and kind be such as will best answer those kinds of Work. Let them not be unnecessarily large: But in all respects as clever as He can get them, these with an Anvil, and Sledge, and a Hammer or two, which He must also provide, as my Smith, or who else He pleases, advise, will be loading for a Carr down. Mathew may come with it, and return with his favorite. Let him get these things ready assoon as He can, but not send them till He has notice from me. He shall have it, when the Mule is throughly well. Care must be taken to secure the Bellows from Accidents of Carriage.

If this be not loading enough, as I believe it will not, He may make it up with another thing, which I very much want, and must have some way or other – Iron hoops. I am greatly plagu'd with wooden ones. They either get bad ones, or the best won't stand the Closeness of my Cellars. Shannon lost the other day the best part of an hogshead of Ale. By good luck it was not the best We had. Now, the only remedy I can think of, is to hoop all with Iron; and As I resolve to try that scheme, so I must have an hundred Iron-hoops Where He can get them best, and at the best hard, I can't tell. Sullivane can, and, I believe, will. I had rather He ask'd him than his Wine-Cooper who may be interested in my buying them dear. But I would have him ask Turner and Constable also, and follow his own discretion in buying. I wish him to buy, if He can from one of those two. And of the two I had rather Turner. I would not appear to quit him; and probably, He finding I can quit him in one Article, may hope to bring me back, by using me well in another. As many of these, as He can send with Bellows &c to make up a full load will be welcome; and Let him get from Mr Tighe full instructions in writing for rivetting, and putting them on. Country Coopers are strangers to them.

Give my best respects to Mrs Silver, and tell her that I was this morning agreably surpriz'd. One of my clergy who wants a curate nam'd Mr Bradish[2] to me. I remembr'd what She had on several Occasions said of that Gent., and at once consented. If he'll venture on this side the Shannon, I wish him to make haste down. His family may follow, when He has provided a place for them: Or He return for them.

Give my Service to the Doctor and Tell him that a poor young Man a Protestant has lately apply'd to me for help which I know not how to give him. His disorder is beyond us, and yet I am satisfy'd He could cure it. I wish him in the Hospital, but will not send him without his leave; and Let him not give it, if it be against Rules, or inconvenient. He is able to work, consequently to travel, and from his own account and H. Stafford's judgment there seems to me something very Singular in his Case. How does McCormick?

Both your letters come together. I am pleas'd on many accounts, on this among the rest, that I see your prattle, and no body else. I was vex'd at one of your letters being irrecoverably lost last year. As this may happen agen, It may be proper on some occasions to write only the initial Letter of names, when by it I may know whom you mean. I see you were in a stew about my letter this day se'night. If it happens so agen, think as I do on the occasion. I have so us'd my self to write every post, that I shall certainly continue it. But as there is so much carelessness in the office, you may expect some to go astray. No gloomy apprehensions on that account. Depend on it; that when you hear nothing all is well. I bless God I am as well, as I have been these seven years.

Fright and hurry are nearly ally'd. One produces the other. The Cure of both is the same. Use will help. One would think you had seen that great Man often enough to be us'd to him. But perhaps the Big Wig, and long train keep up your awe. L[or]d Halifax's[3] rule is All I have written, in few Words. I am glad it is so grav'd on your mind. I doubt not of the good Effects.

You know why Lawson does not come hither. He can't early, if he would: and I have advis'd him against coming late. Be under no concern. I shall not want Company; and, if the Weather be good I can dispense very well with being some times alone. You may send the Pamphlet, and trouble not your Self about *Constantia*. Your censure of *Harriet Stuart* is just.

I am much griev'd at your account of Jeny Curtis. But I still have hopes she'll do. Children bear a great deal. If she drop, My Concern will be for Ned and Rachel. I am glad He is well. Tell him, that in desiring him to lodge the money with Mr Baily,[4] I follow'd Mr Forrister's[5] directions. He may find some opportunity of saying this to Mr Baily. I should not be sorry if he waited agen on Mr Forrister with my Compliments, and told him that I apprehended by his letter to Mr Cary, that He had a mind the money should be lodg'd, that I am greatly oblig'd by his kindness in promising to discharge that Man, and shall wait his time for the doing it. That the Money shall be ready whenever He pleases. Unless something of this kind be said, He'll think me importunate, tho' I really have done just as He directed.

You were very lucky in taking up your Tulips. I doubt not but that you keep each sort by themselves. I am glad there has been so great an increase of breeders. When they are dry, I would have the Off-sets seperated from the grown roots to be sent down hither. Enough will remain with you. When the Weather setles, make Roberts take up all of every kind in the two borders, and dress them. Let him be carefull particularly of the Anemonies. When these borders are fully planted, All the refuse must travel hither. Next time you see Hawker Ask about the proper time of taking up the Ranunculus's and Anemonies single and double. If you do not see him soon, Send Will. for him. I think they ought to be taken up, if the grass be wither'd.

If I recollect right, What I intended to write to Eaton about was the carelessness of his Painter, and his raising his rate. But I had rather you spoke than put him to the Expense of a groat. Direct John Miller to desire him to come to you. If He'll engage that Mr Moore will do his Work well, and upon the terms, He first wrought, order it to be gone about assoon as you please, or He advises. It is time enough. But the Weather must be attended to. Eaton knows what kind is best. Be sure ask him for his son, but know first, if He be alive. Say I bid you.

I am glad you have good hopes of Nancy. But what think you of your house-keeper? You can by this time form some judgment. If the B[isho]p of Clonfert and his Dame be in town, Give them my Service, and tell them I am glad they are so well. He might have spar'd his letter from Bath, which came Enclos'd in yours. But I expect He'll write when He gets to Clonfert.

Mr Constable's answer is come in good time. But Let John inform himself whether I am likely to get better Socks from him or Turner, and if there be any modern improvements to them. I fancy there are, and I would willingly have them most perfect.

I did not even in my thoughts charge you with art. But what you said so long since to your friend, frees you from Suspicion. At the same time it fixes on you another charge of Simple refinement. How have you perplex'd yourself with Supposing things to be, which were not, which you had strong plain reasons to be sure were not, and then accounting for them? I am sure I have caution'd you against this turn before, and desir'd you to ask Dr Lawson, what the meaning of *Nodum in Scirpo*[8] was. If you have forgot ask agen. I had like to have forgot taking you to task, Madam for a false Spelling, in L[o]rd H[alifax]'s golden rule. You write *forbiding*. There ought to be two ds. When you see the Pomeroys give them my Service.

I want three or four bottles either of stone, or black glaiz'd Crockery Ware, I care not which, Let the price determine, which will hold from three to four Gallons. Less size will do, if so large are not to be got, or you think them unweildy, but you must then increase the Number. I want them to keep Whisky in for Labourers, Fish-men &c. and if they be sent soon, I may impregnate it with black Cherrys, a dram of which pleases often more than Six pence.[7] Get them you and your friend, and Make John send them off. With these you must get one or two glaiz'd Crocks for infusing Hops according to Mrs Silver's directions. Consult her about the figure of them. I imagine that they ought to be deep, and narrow, especially at the mouth. The last Winter and Spring, My Wise ones here infus'd them very carelesly, so that the greater part of my drink is bad, some sow'r; while a few Vessels with the same quantity of Malt and Hops are as good as ever was tasted. This proves the difference to arise only from management. As Mrs Silver's practice is new here, they have, as to all new things, a great aversion to it. But I am determin'd not to quit it, and must therefore provide the properest conveniences. They have hitherto infus'd in broad shallow Milk pans, which they could not cover close. I imagine that Crocks much deeper, and with narrow mouths will do infinitely better. Let our good friend, who advis'd the manner, direct the Vessels. To provide such as she advises; and Whatever you provide, Get proper boxes for them, I fancy they ought to be close luted down.[8] She'll tell you. Corks for the stone, or Glaiz'd bottles must also be sent. Five pound of hops is the most I have occasion to infuse at a time. One or two vessels so are equal.

I hope poor Jane will find benefit by the Cheltenham Waters. You write *My Cosen Jeny* has begun &c. This may have been by Chance. But it is the language of coolness.

Dic. Doherty is here. I find He expects his Mother to come down to live with him. It seems she has already quitted Mrs Sterling, and lodges at Miss Ince's in George's lane,[9] where her Gran'daughter boards.[10] I desire you would see her there, or get her to you, and Tell her, with my most affect Service, that I cannot by any means approve of this Scheme, either on her own account, her son's, or the little Girl's. Her own part will be the heaviest. She will not desire or suffer him to stay constantly at home. He can't do it without neglecting his duty, and loosing the many friends He has in so short a time made; and yet unless He does, She must pass her time in Solitude. No Company there at hand as in Dublin. Nor can she go often abroad to seek them, that may be had. I question whether she can ride, and I fear Dic is not rich enough to keep a chair. Besides she'll want a thousand little Conveniences, which her Age and infirmitys require, and no Expense can procure in his Situation. She may be oblig'd to send twelve Miles for a Medicine and as far for a quarter of Mutton in Spring;

and if she wants a Physician she may send twenty, and not get him. In short Her being there must be both extremely uncomfortable, and Extremely hazardous. As to Dic himself, she may on a little reflexion see the consequences. With pleasure I see in him so much Filial piety, that I know he'll devote himself entirely to make the remainder of her life easy, regardless of every thing else, and I applaud him greatly for this. But I really think she ought not to lay him under the difficultys, which upon this Scheme He must be laid under; especially as she must really hurt her Self as well as him by doing it. Then what will become of the poor little Girl of whom She is so fond? Her father will marry, Who can blame him? But if He does, tho' his affection continues, It may depend on the will of another, how far He shall shew it. Can she bear the thought of that poor Child's being left destitute of the Care of any Parent? If she continues with her, she'll take effectual care of her in all points. This strikes so strong, that more Words are unnecessary. You may enforce what I have written in what manner you please. I hope it will convince. But you may tell her if you see Occasion, that So many Evils will in my judgment follow to her, her Son, and Grandchild on her pursuing this scheme, that I do, I must, absolutely declare against it. To be sure she'll wish sometimes to see her Son, and So she may. He may get his Church supply'd for a Sunday or two, and make her a Visit. And As to Expense, I am satisfy'd that He may, at less, supply her with whatever she wants in Dublin, than He can provide much worse for her here. I am sure he will with the utmost cheerfulness supply her, as far as his little enables him to do it. This thing is much on my mind. Loose no time in communicating my thoughts; and Assure her they are absolutely mine own. I write even without Dic's knowlege.

I rejoice that good Mr Jourdan is well, and Charlotte better.

1. 'I have received but three of those delightful letters which so affect my heart. One is yet wanting. Was I not so fond of them, and that I am loth to lose any thing that you send me, I should not think I had lost much; for nothing can be wished for beyond what I find in those I have already received ...' Mme de Sevigné to the Comtesse de Grignan 11 February 1671. *Letters from the Marchioness de Sevigné to her daughter the Countess de Grignan* (London 1927), p.38

2. The Rev. William Bradish was a minister at St Kevin's church, Dublin. *St Peter and St Kevin*, pp.326, 327.

3. Probably Charles Montagu, 1st earl of Halifax (1661-1715), politician. The reference is obscure. *DNB.*

4. John and Thomas Bayly were Agents to the widows of officers, Treasury Office, Dublin. Watson (1751), p.57.

5. Mr Forrister: not known.

6. See Letter 50.

7. Whiskey was a valuable social commodity for treating at marriages, funerals and fairs, where there were 'no dry bargains'. One must assume that Edward Synge's

whiskey was Parliament whiskey, on which duty had been paid, as opposed to illicit poteen. Connell, p.49.

8. To lute was to stop up an opening with strong clay or cement.

9. Miss Ince: not known.

10. Possibly a daughter of Richard Doherty.

147

Elphin. July 9, 1751

My Dear Girl

I have little time to write in, and by good luck not much to say – Company hinders. And who do you think? Mrs Jourdan's and your friend Sir Richard Gethin.[1] He is now here for the Second time this Summer? Don't you pity me? You need not. He is here on business, and his Visits are short.

I am glad the setting Dog is got. I hope you won't loose him agen. I intend to send Young, Jemy's Father, who is to be his Master, for him, with orders to remain with you, for a Week or longer, till He makes the Dog very fond of him. John must provide a Collar of the best kind and a Chain to lead him by. Since Money is to be return'd, if He be not a perfect good one, I'll take care that a true-report be made of him. Otherwise it would be as wrong to find fault with a Gift-dog, as to look a Gift Horse in the Mouth.

To make John amends for his Tears, Tell him his Mule is quite well and that it will be his own fault, if He has her not Soon. Assoon as the Bellows &c. are ready, Let him send Mathew off without further orders. He need not even wait for the Hoops, if they cannot be soon provided. I am impatient till she's gone. I fear she'll suffer in her health by full feeding and laziness. I don't care that any of my fellows should work her.

I am glad your flour pleases. I can't tell whether Carlboe will pick up Jennet's art. If He does not, I am sure No one else here will. And yet it may be learn'd. Mrs Cary's maid has learn'd from her, so as that there is as good bread there, as I have. But pray try what you can do with Brewster your Selves. Sure in this Season of more leisure, you may get your Baker to instruct him. Get John to try what He can do, by his Means or any one's else. It will mortify me much, to have as indifferent bread this Winter coming, as We had the last. Pray Has your house-keeper no skill of this kind? L[ad]y Limerick liv'd in the Country.

Mrs Jourdan is right. As you describe your friend Matty's behaviour. It would please me greatly. But it is such as I expected from her. Tell her I wish her as much happiness, as she can Wish her Self.[2] Let her lay aside her fears. I know she was sincere. I thought so at the time, but wond'red a little at her ignorance.

I am very sorry for Mrs Doherty's ilness. Had I know it a few days ago, I had sav'd a long dissertation, about what this has put an end to.

I can't tell by the B[isho]p of Clonfert's Memorandum whether He has sent you all the Books I wrote to him for or not. I desir'd Kay's Abridgment of English Statutes, and the Acts of the last Session in England, before that just concluded. These may all pass under the general name of, English Acts of Parliament. But send for Cudmore to Examine them. If the Abridgment be there, Let him bind it in full binding. It is 2 Vol. Fol. the Acts of the last Session He must bind, as the others in my Study are bound. He bound them in Parchment Covers – The *Treatise on Clandestine Marriages*[4] may remain as it is.

I was yesterday at Strokes-town. All well there, and remember you with great kindness. Should not you, when Privilege comes in, write to your good friend Mrs Mahon? I hope and believe that Kitty Mahon is well marry'd. Adieu. God bless you all.

Your &c.
Edw: Elphin

What has been the matter with Ned and Molly?

Since I wrote this letter, I consulted a great Sports-man about the Dog. He says there is no occasion for the Man's staying in town to be acquainted with him, For That in traveling ten Miles the Dog will contract such a fondness for him, as to stick close by him. He advises a Dog-chain with a Leather Collar to lead him by. But He advises me to provide also a Brass Collar, with a lock to it, and my Name or Title (Bishop of Elphin) engrav'd on it, that He may wear when here. The best place, He says, for providing such a one is one Ogle's[5] in Hell. Let one be provided of the best kind. John must take care to get one Easy to the Dog's neck, neither too Strait, nor Wide. Young may put it in his pocket, and you may keep him one two or three days in town, till all is got ready. I would have John ride with him four or five Miles out of town for fear of Accidents.

I had like to have forgot in my hurry your Empty purse. Replenish it with £5 – or more if you want it.

1. Sir Richard Gethin married the Hon. Mary St Lawrence, daughter of William, 26th baron of Howth in August 1750. Burke (1916), p.877.

2. Martha Lennox was engaged to marry George French.

3. Kay's edition of the Abridgement of English Statutes does not appear in the *Eighteenth Century Short-Title Catalogue* (CD-Rom 1994). A similar work would have been *An abstract of all the acts passed in the fourth session of the Tenth Parliament of Great Britain, and in the twenty fourth year of the reign of our most gracious sovereign Lord King George the Second*

(London: printed by Thomas Baskett 1751).

4. *A critical and impartial narrative of the proceedings in a cause of clandestine marriage between J—— B——, of C——, and the Rev Mr D——, for the information of strangers* (Dublin, printed for John Wilson [1750]). In the copy in TCD, the blanks have been filled in to read 'J—— Brown of Cork, and the Rev Mr Dallas'.

5. Mary Ogle: toyseller, Hell. Watson (1749), p.16.

148

Elphin. July 12, 1751

Hurry'd agen, My Dear Girl. You must be content with a short letter, and Mrs Jourdan must wait, till privilege comes in. But Tell her in the mean time, that Her account of N.[1] made me laugh. Yet I fear it is more than *naiveté – J'ai peur qu'elle est sotte.*[2] You'll soon find whether she be or not, and If you must say so, and not attempt impossibilitys. If you could mould her, and your little pupil together, two better than either might come out.

I see some marks of carelessness in yours, Madam, tho' well written. Did you read it over, before you seal'd it? I always do, and thus correct many mistakes. One of yours is an Omission of a Word. *None of letters, my* or *your,* wanting. Either will do. The next is an Odd Spelling. A Compound of French and English but, like L[or]d Taafe's language, neither Correct.[3] *Estomach.* The E. French., The h English. One should be away. Rather the E. To write English *à la française,* looks like affectation, tho' I charge you not with it. Another false Spelling, which I don't charge as a fault. Lodanum. It should be Laudanum.[4] But in the next line, *Vomitting* you are to answer for. There should be but one t. I am griev'd at the unlucky accident, that has happen'd to the A[rch]B[isho]p.[5] It must hasten him. Mr W. was more to blame than Button, tho' He is not to be excus'd.

Thanks to the Doctor for his Ticket. It's best have the Man on the Spot. I'll send him off in a day or two. Let the Doctor see him, assoon as He gets to you, and Support him, till a Bed is empty. John may make him work.

A Word now for John. He knows already that his Mule waits for Mathew. I suppose therefore that He'll hasten the Bellows. When they are ready, Let him send them, and the Crockery Ware, and not wait for Sledge and Hammers. But I did or ought to have mention'd an Anvill. He must send one. Let him choose two doz. Iron-hoops for Barrels; the rest for hogsheads. And So My Dear Dear Girl for this time Adieu.

Your &c.
Edw: Elphin

Our Weather from Sunday has been fine. To day very wet. I am in pain for my fine Wheat. Bid John not mow, till All is setled. I fancy his grass is in a growing state. The Pamphlet is a very bad one.

1. N.: not known.
2. I fear she is stupid.
3. Lord Taafe's language would have been a mixture of French and English because of his birth and subsequent career. A Catholic, Nicholas, 6th viscount Taafe (1677-1769), was educated in Lorraine, his family having followed James II into exile. He himself was allowed to keep his estates at Ballymote, Co. Sligo, because of his service in the army of the Holy Roman Emperor, an ally of William III. He became field marshal in the service of the German Empire and fought in battles against the Turks in 1738. *DNB*; Simms, p.154.
4. A tincture of opium made by mixing opium with distilled water and alcohol.
5. Josiah Hort, archbishop of Tuam, who died on 14 December 1751.

149

Elphin. July 14, 1751

My Dear Child.

The Bearer is the young Man I wrote about. Send the enclos'd with him to the Doctor. Till He can take him in, you must support him. A little will do. He is sometimes able to work. When He is John may employ him in the Garden at 6d. a day, unless the Doctor forbids it. But He must neither eat nor sleep in the House. God bless you all. I am very well

Your &c
Edw: Elphin

150

Elphin. July 16, 1751

My Dear Girl.

I spent yesterday quite alone; and It was one of the pleasantest days, I have had since I came hither. The morning was fine. I was on horse-back before six, and view'd all my Works. Every thing was going on, as it ought to be. I saw my Corn which had been ruffled by bad Weather, all erect, and as well as if it had never yielded to rain: and had eleven Mowers cutting as rich Meadow as ever I had at Elphin, as gay and cheerful in the midst of hard labour, as the best of us, and happier far than multitudes, who were at that hour sleeping on Beds of Down, or endeavouring to sleep. These delighted me much. When it grew warm, I came in, and after a Dish of Tea, amus'd my self in my study, till the Post brought yours which gave my Spirits a new filip. It always does when you tell me, you are well, or I see by your letter that you are. O! May I ever have that great comfort. A short dinner. A little time serves to eat. But I ate heartily, and *sans ennui.* I preferr'd my solitude to any Company I could then think of but yours, and that I durst not wish for. I must always preferr your Security and advantage to mine own satisfaction. No! I do not. For those are to me the greatest satisfaction. At five, To Horse again. All my Works view'd over and over. More jokes from my jolly mowers. Fresh pleasure from the improv'd state of my Corn; which led me on to imagine it reap'd, safe in the haggard, and bread and drink from it in abundance. I flatter'd my self that All ruffle from Weather were over, and that there was a certainty of a joyfull and plentifull harvest.

With these pleasing thoughts, Having taken a bit of bread, and two or three glasses of wine, and recommended you and my self to God's protection, I went to bed about ten, and slept well. How was I surpriz'd, when Philip coming to me this morning before six, brought the dolefull tidings of much rain in the night, and a sky that threaten'd more. On rising I found it so. But in the intervals of very heavy show'rs, I ventur'd out to view the Scene. How chang'd from the night before! Corn bent, and bending, Mowers struck off. Cut grass poss'd[1] in wet, the ground all sloppy, and Men, Horses, and Mules, where they could at all work, labouring and suffering by return of violent rain. One of these drove me in, and I have not been out since, nor will I, till the sky is again Serene. I pray God it may soon be so. For tho' No mischief be yet done, the Continuance of this Ugly Weather must do infinite.[2]

But why all this to you? I hope you see already. Whether you do or no, I'll tell you. What happens in the Farm and Harvest, happens in all other affairs, in all Circumstances, every Condition of life. Nothing is certain, but uncertainty. We indulge fond hopes. It is our turn, *penchant,* to do so; and in a certain degree it is an innocent nay! an usefull one. To torture our Selves with constant apprehensions of Evils which may not happen, would be to live a life of constant gloom and uneasiness. On the other hand, An innocent enjoyment of the present, and temperate indulgence of pleasing hopes, cheer the heart, and make it glad; and Thus much is not only innocent but our duty. Thus We make a right use of the blessings God bestows, and shew our gratitude for his bestowing them. But if We say in our Hearts, We shall never be mov'd &c. The least reverse sinks us. It come upon us unprepar'd. We are not able to bear it. Learn hence, My

Dearest, these two important lessons. Accustom your self to consider all things in this World as uncertain, and Let it be ever in your thoughts that God's mercy is over all his Works. You, I, the Universe and All that is in it are under the direction of his All-wise providence. He appoints what is best on the whole. Our lot, as far as is consistent with that, will be according to our deserts. To love and fear him, is the sure way, either to be secure from Evils, or to have strength to support our selves under them. But whatever happens here, They who are steadily and uniformly virtuous in this life, will be finally happy in that which is to come.

John's folly did not vex, but made me Smile. I will not however suffer R[igh]t. R[everen]d. on the Collar. If I can't get it defac'd, He must provide another. Pray tell him that I thought He had more respect for Rt. Rd. than to put it about a Dog's neck.[3]

As I am not sure, that this will go free, I send a short Commission to John From hence forth you shall be eas'd. Tell him then that the Fowler mistook – The Coal which the Smith commonly uses is of the same kind with your Sea-Coal. Now and then when by his own negligence He is unprovided of that He is driven to use Stone Coal.[4] I'll take care that that shall not happen in my forge. However it is best to have bellows fitted for either. Tell him further that He need not hurry. For his Mule is better taken care of than ever she was in her life. She grew so fat and Wanton that I was afraid she would do or suffer mischief. I therefore resolv'd to put her to work, and she works very kindly with the Coach-horses, so that she is under Peter's care in working, and Jemy's for the rest. He may therefore leave her here as long as He pleases. But I desire him only to wait till He get full loading for the Carr. It would be idle not to do it.

When the Captain of a ship comes, Tell him I know no such person. The letter you sent is subscrib'd Eleanor Brady.[5] She writes as if she had left my house improperly twelve years ago, a Girl; and mentions you and your Brothers. For my life I cannot recollect her. Next post I'll send you the letter, if I do not forget it.

I had a conference this morning with Jane about Bread &c. She says, the main thing is the Barm, and Her doctrine and practice about Barm is thus. The Best Barm is that which works out of the Vessels of Ale when drink is tunn'd, the first twenty four hours. She uses no other when she can help it. What she gets of this, she keeps in a Vessel by it self unmix'd with any thing. From whence she takes every day such quantity as she wants. About a quart does for Ordinary days. More on great occasions. This she mixes with Cold Water, and having stirr'd it very well, she leaves to pitch. All dirt, and dross thus falls to the bottom, from whence she pours it off clean into another Vessel, and if any dirt remains, she strains it. But for this there is seldom occasion. For fear of writing wrong or imperfectly I stopp'd here, and sent for Jane. My caution was not amiss. I now find that the straining must be, when the Barm and Water are first mix'd. To take things in order, the whole proces is thus. All Barm that works out of the Bung, whether the first or second day, whether from Ale or Small Beer, she holds equally good. This in a Vessel by it self, will keep good a Week or ten days. What she uses one day, she prepares constantly the day before; and she prepares it thus. Her quantity is in proportion to the Bread intended; and she mixes that with three or four times the quantity of Cold Water, and strains it immediatly to get clear of Hop-Seeds &c. Then she lets it pitch for a quarter of an hour or thereabouts, not longer. This is time enough for dross and dirt to sink to the bottom, while the clean Barm continues in a floating state. Longer time would occasion it's falling again to the bottom, and mixing with the dirt. This blended liquor she pours very carefully off into another Clean Vessel, so as to leave all dross behind; and here she leaves it till next morning, when she finds the clean Barm at the bottom, from which she pours the Water off. With this thus purify'd, she makes her Bread; and she says that tho' She got Barm but the day she mix'd it, what is purify'd, is as white as Starch. This is all the bleaching she uses, or approves of. When she pours off the liquor first from the dross, it looks as if there were little or no Barm in it. But a quart of foul usually gives the next day a pint purify'd, and subsided to the Bottom from the Water. A little more or less makes no difference in the Bread. The Vessels she uses are Glaz'd Pans and Crocks, such as she has for her dairy. Her Vessel into which she strains her Barm and water that the Dirt may pitch, is a shallow pan, of size proportion'd to the Liquor. The same will do for the second pitching of the clean Barm from the Water. In pouring off the first, Assoon as she sees any dross rise, she stops, and leaves what remains to settle more, then pours again. Sometimes she puts more Water to the dross, when she thinks any good Barm is among it, and stirs agen, and after a quarter of an hour pours agen. I suppose this is when Barm is scarce. To the liquor pour'd off she usually puts more Water. No niceity as to Quantity. She likes a good deal, and says that next morning she finds at the bottom, Barm as white and as tough as Starch. To this she chiefly ascribes the goodness of her Bread. How that may be I know not. But certainly her Bread is Excellent, and almost constantly so. Her worst is better than the best We had last Winter; and, unless you can get Brewster to follow her method, I fear I may say, than We shall have the next. For Carleboe despises all this, as Jane tells me. I can't help it. She affirms that she instructed Brewster in the whole last Summer. If she did, It is plain He minded it not. Nor will He unless you force him. You must inspect it your self and give it in charge to the House-keeper. And Tell the Gent., that unless He retrieves himself with me, by learning to do completely now, what I enjoined him to learn when here, I shall never trouble my head about him. A long story. But if it answers, I shall not repent having written so minutely.

My Company staid but one day longer than was necessary. It was no great matter. I contriv'd to provide other Company and Cards.

Your News about E.T. does not surprize.[6] I have all along thought it would be so. By a letter from Mr. Lennox, I find your friend Matty's affair is near a conclusion, I hope and believe, a happy one. By all means Write to your Uncle. Adieu.

Your &c
Edw: Elphin

I have caught you, Mistress, at a bit of giddiness properly so call'd. You had wrote thus *I write to Mrs Mahon very soon*. Afterwards you interlin'd a Word, which was necessary. And what word think you? Why, *will*, to be sure, you'll say. No such matter. You have wrote *write* agen. How will you get off of this Madam?

Tell Ned Curtis, He's a fool. He'll want more Grey-beards[7] for Whisky. You say nothing of Jeny, you ought to have done it. I have been in pain about the Brat, for the sake of her Parents. By your account poor Mrs Doherty's misery will not continue long. Tell Dic, when you see him, that I will not stress him about his stay. I am sure it will not be longer than is necessary. Let him get Mr Tisdal to attend for him other Sundays, as He did, the first of his absence.

How have Strawberrys been with you? We have had here a multitude of fine ones. You say nothing of Melons. Sure you have had some ripe before this.

[Free Edw:Elphin]

1. Poss'd: beaten flat.
2. July 1751 saw 'frequent and plentiful rains'. Rutty, p.163.
3. Inscribing the name of its owner on a dog's collar was customary. Lord Lanesborough advertised for a cream-coloured greyhound which had been stolen or had strayed from his house in St Stephen's Green. It had 'a brass collar round his neck with these words on it:– "I belong to the Rt. Hon. the Lord Viscount Lanesborough."' *Faulkner's Dublin Journal*, 1-9 1751.
4. Sea coal: coal brought by sea. Stone coal (cannel): a type of coal that burnt to a stone rather than ash.
5. Eleanor Brady: not known.
6. E.T. was Emilia Trench, daughter of Frederick Trench II, who married Richard Eyre in June 1752. See Letter 191. T. Cooke-Trench, Table 11, p.26.
7. Greybeards: crude vessel for holding liquors. L.A. Clarkson and E.M. Crawford, *Ways to Wealth: The Cust family of eighteenth-century Armagh* (Belfast 1985), p.83.

151

My Dear Girl.

I have just finish'd a long Epistle to your friend. A short one must therefore do for you. For I care not to repeat. I had once a mind not to write at all; You may expect that I'll play you this trick, if it be one, hereafter; and I write chiefly now, to desire you would send to Mrs Armstrong, and deliver the Enclos'd to her. I would not have her Mother know any thing of it.

Now for gleanings. I can easily conceive that the Laudanum or rather the Vomit &c. may have been of use to the A[rch]B[isho]p. But what He says himself is next to impossible. I suspect his judgment is a little unhing'd. I thought so, when I saw him. Too high Spirits are as sure, indeed a Surer, indication of this, than too low.

Your account of Young reliev'd me from some Uneasiness about my Dog. If He has not left town, when you get this, which possibly may be the Case, Make John get him a pair of Second hand Boots, big enough, that will stand Boggs &c. and Let them be given as a Present from you. I won't increase his demands upon me. He is a harmless silly Creature, but has two or three the finest little boys I ever saw, in raggs.[1] Yet His Wife a very orderly Woman, He sober, and His income good for such a family – Without management nothing right any where. This brings to my mind, your friend's account of your attention to your house-Affairs. I am much pleas'd with it. So I am with what you say of N. – I hope you are not mistaken. In mine to Mrs J. you'll see what I thought about her. But my Suspicions were grounded entirely on her humorous description of her. If she has sense, the other Qualitys you mention will make her worth your pains. As for the other, I despair. But try your hand with her, as long as you please. It will be an Exercise to your Wits, if she does not vex you too much.

You have been hasty about the off-sets. But that's Hawker's fault not yours. If they be perfectly dry put up, they'll come safe. But I have great doubts about so early planting. Tell him so when you see him. My ground here is a stiff clay, which holds the Water. If the Tulips I have were to remain one year in it, Three fourths would rot; and I know no way to guard against it, but by planting them in Turf mold.

I am sorry you miss'd L[or]d K and L[ad]y A.[2] But that misfortune may be easily retriev'd. At another Visit, you may try to fix them for Tea and a Walk in the Garden some fine Evening; and get leave to send when the Weather is good. If this be comply'd with So! If not, No great harm done. I had a mind you should shew respect to the Children of one, who always shew'd so much to me.

Our Weather is broken and unpleasant, but no mischief is yet done, nor will be unless it grows Worse. I long to have it setled chiefly on account of my hay, which must be cut. I have eleven Mowers at Work. And So my Dear Girl, God bless you

Yours &c

E E.

Send for Woodward, and Ask him whether I can depend on having some right English Raven-grey Drab to make me a Coat or two. If not, he may give a hint to some Draper to write for one. I would have it to keep me Warm in Winter, and dry in my Summer rides, if I live, next Season.

[Free Edw:Elphin]

1. In 1749, Andrew Young, Edward Synge's fowler, had two children under fourteen and one child over fourteen. Census, f.2.

2. Lord K and Lady A are probably Francis Thomas Petty Fitzmaurice, 3rd earl of Kerry (?-1818), who succeeded his father in 1747, and his sister Lady Anna Fitzmaurice, who married Maurice Fitzgerald, Knight of Kerry. Burke (1916), p.1206.

152

Elphin. July 23, 1751

Be Under no concern, My Dear Girl, about my being alone. I have company enough, sometimes more than enough. But I have, and shall have that which is agreable always in my power. Mr Cary, his Wife &c. come as often as I desire and when I desire them. So do Mr. Conroy and his Wife. I pass my time with them very agreably. The Variety of being alone sometimes, pleases. Mr Wills &c. have been engag'd at home. They'll come when they can.

Our Weather has been bad since Friday night, when I thought it more likely to setle into Fair, than at any time this month. Another instance of Uncertainty But bad as it has been, I took my usual ride Saturday and Sunday without being Wet. Yesterday was too bad, and this so threat'ning, that I have not yet ventur'd. Probably I shall. Don't now imagine that I expose my Self too much. Depend on it, I do not; and if I get a little Wet, I change my Coat, the minute I Come on. My oyl'd hoods keep me absolutely dry about head and Neck. They are the most convenient things that ever were invented. But the fellow who makes them is a Rogue. I have a Crow to Pluck with him. But I'll wait till I get to town.

You are in great pain for my Corn. It is yet safe. All the distress I am in is about Hay. But I hope the Weather will mend, and that be safe, too. To continue my instructions from my hay-yard, so you should write it, a proper reliance on Providence will always keep us from Security on the one hand, and from desponding on the other. By the by, My Dear, in this part of your letter, by attempting to mend a Sentence, you have made it worse. How beautifull are your instructions drawn from your hay-yard. Thus you wrote at first; and afterwards interlin'd *to me*. The Sentence was better before. Too much precision, especially in familiar letters, is a fault as well as too little. Clearness with ease is the point. The Sentence hobbles more with this addition, and there was no want of the Words to make it intelligible. I think I observe a little fondness in you for the Word beautifull, the same in your friend. I don't say it is improper. But it is strong, and savours of Poetick. Use it therefore seldom. In general the frequent use of any strong Word should be avoided. You'll be known by it, as Ladys sometimes are by one fine Coat. My Dear Child, God give you grace to pursue your good resolutions; and May steady uniform virtue make you happy here, You know it will here after.

I perfectly recollect Nora[1] and the manner in which she left my house. I have sent her letter, whatever answer you think hers to me requires, Give it your Self, and Let the poor Wretch know that I sent the Enclos'd to her Father. I sent it to Palmer, who, you know, is near Longford.

You have done mighty right in excusing your self from going to M.L's wedding.[2] I believe the invitation was design'd by the Father and Mother, as a Mark of distinguish'd respect to me, as well as by the Girl her self, as a token of the Cordial friendship between you. But I am sure, the former are better pleas'd you have declin'd it. It would have embarrass'd them with regard to others, who might have taken offence at not being ask'd.

What you write of E.T. shocks me.[3] Parents may, they ought indeed to, controle their Children's imprudent inclinations. But To abuse or force them to compliance, against so setled Aversion, is cruel, is Wicked, and to do this for the chance of an Estate, distant and uncertain, is Madness. I can't think of them with patience.

I had an account from H. Sandford of his two Boys,[4] but He writes, that they are both well. I was going to have told him in return, that About the same time one of my Cows brought forth two fine Bull Calves. But I fear'd I might offend the Lady, and dropp'd my joke. The Fact however is true, and, what is more surprising, one of them lay unnotic'd in the field since Friday, neither Dam nor any other Cow near, and was found this morning as brisk as a Bee, and so wild that three Men had enough to do to catch him. Jennet is much delighted at this Adventure, and will, I am sure, take thorough pains to make these Twins as good as any Calves I have. She has seven Pea-chicks nursing, and hopes for more. Those wild Creatures make their nests in such odd places, that Many of their Eggs, and young have been lost. But she is mighty diligent in her Searches, and carefull of what she gets. So she is of every thing, that she thinks will please you. If I have a mind to make her particularly Watchfull about any thing, I cannot take a more effectual method than by telling her you desire or will like it. If, when you have nothing else to do you wrote her a bit of a letter of thanks and directions if you can find any, She'll be at the Top of the house. I have made her very happy already, by giving her thanks from you and Mrs J for her instructions about Barm. I have just had another conference with her on the Subject, and she confirms what I had before written to Mrs. J. – Indeed, My Lord, says she, I get Barm sometimes as red as a Fox, sometimes black, full of Hop-leaves, Bog-bane, Wormwood, Artichoak leaves, and a long &c. of other like ingredients. By straining I get rid of all these; and the first Sheering, so she calls pouring, after the liquor has stood about a quarter of an hour, frees it from the great dross, which remains in the bottom, red like brick-dust, or darker; the Second, after standing a night, gives me barm as white and as tough as Starch. With this, My Lord, I make all your bread, and Many a hard shift I make to get it. Thus she run on, till I was tir'd. Either she says true, or the goodness of Bread depends less on Barm than We imagine. For better never was, than I have almost constantly: So that my niceity on my return, instead of less'ning will be greater. Continue therefore your Experiments, till you unravel this great mistery. I'll send you by John's Mule a Couple of Barrels of Wheat, which John is to sell. With the money you may buy more flowr for more trials. A little at a time will be best, tho' you pay more for it. A Bag will be too much. You should send back Mrs Heap's Vessel in which the late cargo of flow'r went up. Such things are Scarce here.

You do not ask about the D[onnellans] – All I know of them is this. He before he left town, express'd great impatience to be here, and said that Assoon as He got to T[ubbervaddy] and had enjoy'd his K[itty Ormsby] a little, He would write for the Post-chaise. Assoon as I knew He was there, I wrote to tell him the Chaise should be ready, whenever He pleas'd; and I expected a summons for it for last Monday se'night. Instead of this, A letter the post before, owning his intentions, but making an Apology. The Women had arrested him; and here things rest. I have not renewed my instances to him to make an Excursion by himself, nor will I. But Assoon as the Weather takes up, I intend to invite them all hither. I can't tell whether they'll come. I fear Matters are not in the most comfortable Way in that quarter.

I am sorry you have been so ill off with Straw-berrys. If you do not succeed better next Season, I shall impute it to the Soil. Lest that should be the case, Desire John to plant some at Finglas. Next month will be a very good time. If He doubts, Tell him I say so, and desire He would try. I ask'd him about Wall-fruit there. He has given me no Answer. We have been very unlucky as to Apples. All the Orchards hereabouts have hit better than usual.

I thank you for *Constantia.* It amus'd me. The design is good. The Execution moderate. Some of the storys are pretty enough. The Poetry is the Worst part. I judge from a Taste. It did not invite me to more, so I Skipp'd it.

I see by Mrs J.s letter, that Lawson's right shoulder suffer'd. I had rather it has been the left. But I hope that will soon be a matter indifferent. You have been uneasy at his not coming down here. See now how things fall out. This was his usual time of coming. Suppose this accident had happen'd here. What a Condition had I been in? To see him in the hands of Dr Crofton, or Dr Conry?[5] It would have griev'd me and you too. You would have wish'd him in town. There He is. All things happen for the best.

Mr and Mrs Mahon, Nelly, Nan, the two boys and Luke have just left me. This morning I had not a prospect of so agreable Company. There are sudden changes for the better as well as the Worse. I must tell you a speech of her's, like one of her Pats to Lawson. Luke is building an house for himself at Strokes-town, and I said that it was in order to a Wife.[*sic*][6] Oh! my L[or]d. says He there is but one room in it. After a little pause, She said with great gentleness, then it seems you and your Wife can't live in the same room. The few things of this sort, that now and then drop from her, are so just, that I am satisfy'd she might say more, if she pleas'd. Appearing but now and then, they set her off more, than if she were on the Watch for occasions of shewing.

Mathew is arriv'd. All things safe, But He not well. He is just blouded. If He does not return assoon as John expects, this is the reason. Mule and loading are ready.

Three Pea-chicks more come in to day. I hope Jennet will rear them all. Adieu. I have almost fill'd my paper, and scribbled mine Eyes out. God bless you all.

Your &c
Edw: Elphin

Tell Mrs Jourdan, that her brown Crock is the fittest for the purpose that can be.

By letters from polite people, I see it is time for you to leave off your black Wax. I'll use my stick out. But take notice, Madam, Black Wax, with gilt paper is a blunder. How could you be guilty of it?

Young is just return'd from trying 'Caesar', on Grouse. His report is, that He will not set at all. I have given Mr Leigh an account of it, as He desir'd. But perhaps on future trials, He may behave himself better.

This Afternoon has been fine, and my Hay is in a much better condition, than when I begun to write this morning. But I fear the Weather is not yet setled.

1. Nora: not known but probably a servant.

2. Martha Lennox's marriage to George French. 'Last Saturday night, George French, son of Arthur French Esq. Member of Parliament for the Borough of Boyle, was married to Miss Martha Lennox, Daughter of William Lennox Esq. a very eminent Banker, a young Lady of great Beauty and all the accomplishments that can make the married State happy, with a very large Fortune.' *Faulkner's Dublin Journal*, 27 June-3 July 1751; Burke (1912), p.624.

3. Emilia Trench. See Letter 150 and 191.

4. Henry Sandford's two boys: not known.

5. Dr Conry: not known.

6. Luke Mahon does not appear to have married.

153

Elphin. July 26, 1751

My Dear Girl.

This, hitherto, has been the best day We have had for some time and I hope will continue so, tho' I have laid a Wager with Cary, that it will rain. I have been abroad all the morning, and intend going again, assoon as I have done this. As it happens I have not much to say to you this bout.

Give my best Service to Mrs Silver; and tell her I have seen Mr Bradish, who appears to me very worthy of her regards. He has declined the acceptance of the Cure; and easily convinc'd me that He was very right in doing so. I had the pleasure of seeing him only one day. He came to Mr Cary's the day before; But I knew nothing of him till next morning. And I could not prevail on him to stay another. I was thus unluckily depriv'd, of an Opportunity of shewing even a little Civility, to one whom your good friend and mine so much and so justly esteems.

Your Expression is not wrong. The Word *Task*, by it self, is inoffensive. But the Epithet, *pleasing*, determines it to an Agreable sense, to something that demands attention, yet exercises the mind in a pleasing manner.

Desire Mr Eaton to order the House &c. to be painted on such Terms, as He thinks reasonable. If He takes care of it, It will be carefully done. Try if you can Squeeze in the pannels and carving of your dressing room into the £6:-:- But get them done, whether you compass this or not. It's a trifle.

I leave Licy to you. I sent N's letter to her Aunt.[1] I see by the Superscription that she does not write well. Try if you can improve her – you'll thus improve your Self, tho' you do very well. Your letter before me is well written. I hope, that to your Uncle, was at least equal.

If ever I suspect you or your friend of being too mercifull to poor John, I am mistaken. But upon my Word, you have been in this case so cruel, that I am almost tempted to call you ill-natur'd. You ought to have undeceiv'd him, before bed time. I had a bouncing paragraph from him; and in return have try'd a little to set him on your backs. His Mule is very safe and Mathew well. They shall set out to morrow, if it be a good day. So No letter by him.

Mr Hawker has been very simple. The flower roots were not dry enough I fear they have suffer'd in the Carriage. I'll do all I can to retrieve them. Have you taken up your Anemonies? And what stock of single ones? Any for me here? Be very carefull, in leasure drying of them. They are apt to mould.

Tell Mrs J. I desire she would write a note to Mr French, and make all your Complaints she justly can, of the bad bottles; His name is Arthur. I believe he'll immediatly go to you, and offer to change them. If He does, Let him; and setle it with him, to lay by whatever more you find faulty. I desire this may be done both in justice to my self; and to shew him that As much care is not taken in his Cellar as ought to be. I have spoken gravely to him on this point two or three times. If He does not mend, It will hurt him. Tell him your whole sufferings, tho' some of them do not appear. Adieu.

Your &c
Edw: Elphin

[Free Edw:Elphin]

1. Nancy Poor or Power: Alicia's maid and niece of Mrs Heap.

154

Elphin. July 29, 1751

A word or two, My Dear Girl, before the post comes, of what might otherwise slip out of my mind.

A Faithfull servant is disabled. My close Box-comb, like it's master, has lost some Teeth. I have another, not quite so good, but it does well. Look out for a Supply. I have heard you and your friend complain, that those things are scarce. To lazy folks that would be an excuse for not seeking. But you are not lazy, or, if you are a bit, You must not be so. The thing is wanting, Get it then. Remember Saunders and the High-lands. That kind of peremptoryness rightly conducted, is of great use. Many things are not done, because not attempted. I have said this to you often before. A trifle occasions my saying it now. But the Lesson is usefull.

As you are almost always in my thoughts, I sometimes think of your reading. Part of it has been of the usefull, the most usefull kind; such as was proper to form *vos moeurs, et manières*.[1] Those French Words are very expressive. Do you perfectly understand the force of, and difference between them? The rest has been chiefly meer amusement. Now where would be the hurt, if continuing always some of the first kind, and what you like of the Second, you accustom'd your self to a third kind, compounded of both, that has a mixture of use and Amusement. History answers the description. You seem'd to point at something of this kind before I left you; and I nam'd Clarendon,[2] and if I mistake not, Rapin.[3] Have you tasted Either? I fancy not, because you've never mention'd them. Now I wish you would take some book of this sort into your hands. Read as much and when you like. If a play or Novel, or other meerly amusing book falls in your Way Neglect, if you will, your standing dish for a day, or a Week. You'll come again with more relish to it. But I think it not so right that your reading should continue, as it has been for the most, of the quite grave, or quite idle kind. I am far from advising against the last kind. If I did, my practice would rise up against me. But too much of this rather hurts, and enfeebles the mind. There are many instances among the Ladys and All grave on the other hand is apt to disgust. Books which please and instruct both are those for which if you have not, you should acquire a Taste. The more Girls know the better, if they have prudence to avoid Ostentation in shewing their knowlege. I never knew any one in this point equal or near equal to your good Mother. Oh! how often have I seen her sit silent in a Conversation, where she could have appear'd better than any, as I afterwards found by her Observations, when We were by our Selves. She carry'd this backwardness too far. It was however the most pardonable extreme. But she had more, and more usefull knowlege than any Woman I ever knew. Part of this was the effect of a Cause, which I can't wish may operate on you. The disagreableness of her situation, with very fond parents, threw her into books, and retirement. She sometimes read trifling ones, but never over-valu'd them. Her taste was for more solid food. In the first and happiest years of our Marriage, She has often surpriz'd and delighted me, with the fruits of her maiden studys. One Book particularly she was a much better Master of, than I was. Prideaux's *Con-*

nection.⁴ It is in my Study. I had thoughts of giving it you sometime or other and telling you this. It comes out now to chance. How easily am I drawn in to prattle to my Dear Girl. When I took up my pen, I did not intend to write above six lines. No more now, till yours comes.

It is come, and Mrs J's ticket, with the most welcome tidings. May I always have them. But, Mistress, you wrote this letter in haste. Confess, Did you not? The writing is not so good as the last, and you are returning to flourishes.

I am much disturb'd at honest John's ilness, tho' you and Mrs J. tell me He is better. Pray Let him be watch'd narrowly, till He is quite well; and give him Claret as long and as much as the Doctor pleases. His negligence of himself makes more care of him necessary.

He'll some time or other dye by his own Tricks. But Has it never come across either of you, that the Ferment you put him in, may have contributed to his disorder. Without a joke, I am far from sure that it did not, tho' I don't believe that alone produc'd it. I hope he is by this time well, and has his Favorite safe with him. Looking over your letter, I see one horrible blunder in stopping, which I can't help abusing you for. *We had had an invitation* &c and you have put a, between the two hads. You might as well have put one between Substantive and Adjective. This must have been haste. It is the only excuse I can find for it.

Mr Hawker has been very simple about the Tulip-roots. They have suffer'd more by their journey, pack'd up before quite dry, than they would have done if kept out of ground till February. Some I hope will recover. Those that do, I'll manage mine own Way. I thank you for your intention of sending Myrtles. But they wo'n't do here; and I am not so fond of them as you are. I went from writing to look at the Tulips. That you may not be uneasy about them, I tell you that Most of them appear unhurt. Some are certainly lost.

If I had known your inclinations to see and hear your Dear friend pronounce the irrevocable Words, I should have indulg'd them. I told you my chief reason against it. Had I thought the distress had been from your not going, You should, for me, have gone. But it is no great matter. You'll see your friend when she comes to town and continue your intercourse with her. It will now be more easy than formerly. Mrs F.⁵ tho' a little formal, will be no hindrance; and you'll find your friend's name-sake a good Sort of Girl. Let your self down to her. But Fail not, the first opportunity, to acknowlege properly both to Mrs L[ennox] and Matty the intended Compliment. It was a very particular one.

Half a bag of Flour! Why Do you know how much that is? Above an hundred weight. But He that can procure half, will procure a quarter. The fresher, the better. Yet you can't be sure of greater freshness by your having it at any certain time, especially if it be English. Guard against lumps, or the least Sowrness. Flower with either is good for nothing. I am glad Brewster is so meek. But if He has not already made good Bread, I shall fear that Jennet's instructions, and my pains in conveying them are thrown away.

I can say no more about 'Caesar', till He is try'd at Partridge, for which the Season is not yet come in. But the Sports-men here say, that He may set these very well, tho' He will not set Grouse. I hope He will.

We have had the better of you in point of Weather. I recollect no rain on Friday Evening, or night. But Saturday was a very fine day, in which We made up abundance of Hay. There were two smart show'rs in the Afternoon, but so short as not to stop the Work. The Evening was fine. So was Sunday. So was yesterday. A great deal more Hay sav'd. Some little rain in the Afternoon, but so complaisant as not to stop them. This day is gloomy, and We have had a show'r or two. But, now at twelve, It promises a good afternoon. I have been very fortunate in this. For there have been great rains near us. I saw the Showers at a distance. But they went off, and did not touch us.

Pray did Mrs J. lay hold of the favorable opportunity, when she and S[ullivane] were drinking together in the Cellar, to ask for French Snuff? I fancy not. Else she would have reported his polite answer, as she did his pompous manner of commending his own Wine. But thus it is, When Ladys get leave to do a thing. They grow indifferent about it. I hope there's no further occasion for stopping John's packets. That of the last was right, but unlucky. It will be still more so, if a return has made it necessary to stop that which went by last post. Should any such occasion happen agen, Open my letters to him, that if there be any thing in them which requires haste you may get it done some way.

Who do you think is just come in? Lancaster. See how Company comes Unexpected. He says All is well at Garbally; and gives a very pleasing account of poor Lucy. She is greatly mended, and writes that she hopes to return quite well and sound. I know this will please you. Adieu. God bless you all. I am

Your &c
Edw: Elphin

Send the enclos'd, as directed. By Lancaster's account E.T.'s match is not so much *contre gré*.[6]

[Free Edw:Elphin]

1. Your taste and your manners.

2. Edward Hyde, earl of Clarendon, *The history of the rebellion and civil wars in England, begun in the year 1641* ... Written by the Right Honourable Edward Earl of Clarendon, ... (Dublin 1719).

3. *The history of England, as well ecclesiastical as civil. By Mr Rapin de Thoyras.* ... Done into English from the French, with large and useful notes ... by N. Tindal, ... (Dublin 1726-1732); or *The history of England, by Mr Rapin de Thoyras. Contained from the revolution to the accession of King George II.* By N. Tindal ... Adorned with the heads of the kings and queens. ... (Dublin 1747).

4. [Humphrey Prideaux], *Dr Prideaux's connection of the Old and New Testament compleated: or, the sacred history of the Jewish and Christian church,* ... The whole carefully revised, greatly corrected, and much improved, by William Whiston, ... Containing, a proposal for a new and cheap edition of all the primitive writers. ... (London 1741?).

5. Edward Synge is referring to George French's mother, Jane. She was a Miss Percival, and married Arthur French in 1722. Burke (1916), p.610.

6. *Contre gré*: against fashion or taste.

155

Elphin. August 2, 1751

My Dear Girl.

I hope I have found out the Secret of Jennet's bread. It came out by chance. But she had no intention to conceal it. As I was manging my Crust yesterday morning on horse-back, I found the disagreable toughness of Kevin-street bread. This being very new here, I immediatly complain'd of it to Jennet. Her plea was that, just as she was going to make the bread, the day before, she was seiz'd with a Violent fit of Cholick, and was forc'd to leave the Bread to Mrs Heap, *who wet it too much.* What, said I. Is that the cause of this Weight and toughness? Yes, says she, it is; and you shall see it shan't be so to day. It is needless to tell all my Questions, and her Answers. The sum is the less you moisten your flower, so as that you can knead it, the lighter, shorter, and better in all respects your Bread will be. Oblige Brewster to try this with the utmost Exactness. He must be watch'd, because the less Wet, the more labour, a thing, which I believe He is not over fond of. If this does not do, I must e'en despair. Every thing about Barm you know already. To be sure a good deal depends on that. But something more is necessary. If it be not this, I know not what it is. It will give me great pleasure if you succeed, for two reasons; One, because We shall have good bread; the other, because you know I always said Carleboe spoil'd his bread by wetting too much. Nothing We are fonder of, than to find our Selves in the right. Contentions about it occasion half the little angry disputes in the World.

Yours come in, with the usual good tidings of you and your friends. God continue [*damaged ms*]. But I am much mortify'd at the account of John's new disorder, and should have been more so, but for the Doctor's letter. I hope He is, by this, in a way of being reliev'd. I know He's a most unruly patient. But the Doctor must bully, and you must lock him up. Let him not set his foot out of Doors without the Doctor's free Consent.

Tho' I can't blame your Caution about my letters to him, Yet the delay occasion'd by it, has been very unlucky. I wish it had come into your heads to open them your Selves, to see if you could not execute some of the Commissions without him. You could not sure imagine there were any Secrets in them. Pray Do this instantly, if you have not done it already. One of my Commissions was ¼ Ounce of Colly-flower Seed, and the same quantity of brown Lettuce. The Delay in this trifle has been very inconvenient. If Saunders be blam'd next Summer for wanting these things early, He'll plead this in Excuse right or wrong. Send them by the return of the Post. If John can't go himself, send Jac to Mr Bruce in Corn-market,[1] with a Note signifying who they are for, and desiring him to send good. John may write the Note himself. And Be sure, send the pacquets enclos'd in some letters to Dr Roberts. I wonder the size of one did not strike you, that there was something in it, which might want Expedition, especially if you knew that I had by John convey'd a former letter to the same person. You have thought by halves about this matter. I suppose Mathew is before this arriv'd.

I wish Mrs Silver may succeed in her Search. She will, if any one. I am afraid of trying Mrs D[onnellan]. He'll be here next Week by himself, unless the Wind changes. If I have a fair Occasion, I'll try him.

I was much pleas'd with your account of Sandford's basket. But I don't understand. *Heathen.* His own children us'd to be baptiz'd before they were sent off. If the boy lives, He'll be a favorite. The Lieutenant was a good guesser.

Assoon as the Weather setles into dry, Let Roberts dress the borders, and new plant them. A row of Crocus's as usual, next the Box on one side, and on the out-edge on the other. Let all the rest be *stuffed,* chiefly with Tulips. Some narcissus, single, and double, more of the latter than of the former. A good many Tags,[2] and Single Anemonies, and some Flower de luce[3] if you have them. But Let them not be planted in rows, but mix'd in a little kind of confusion, which in flow'ring time will, you'll see, have a very agreable Effect. Let him plant very thick, and the Tulips be predominant. A Good many single Anemonies will contribute much to beauty as they flower earliest. This done, what remains, and the refuse of all lay by dry, till an opportunity offers of sending them hither. Your leavings will adorn us Country folks, as Fine Ladys clothes do their Abigails.[4] By the by, what is become of your fine Lady Fany.[5]

I was surpriz'd at Mrs J.'s account of your Aunt's and consequently Mrs A.'s distress.[6] You did very well to relieve it. But it was very simple in them to sleep in Dr Delany's aversion, when they could have avoided it.[7]

Tell your friend that I take very ill her sending me a Copy of her letter to Mrs F.[8] Does she think I doubt of her Abilitys to write a fit letter on such an Occasion? Paltry diffidence. Imitate it not. But if she doubts, she shall. For I will not say whether I think it a proper one or not. Whatever amends the Gent. offers, Take it to the full Extent of your damage, either by Wine you did not drink, or bad that you did. He deserves to smart for his negligence, and He shall, more ways than one. Such careleness [*sic*] may ruin him with Customers more indifferent to him than I am. I wish Mrs J.'s friend S[ullivane] did not know this. But I'll warrant He does already.

I heard a day or two ago that Mrs Crofton was in town. See her be sure, and ask them to dine, honest Jac. boys and all.[9] Treat her with strong Beer. The mention of this brings to my mind, that you'd do well some day e're long to send for Mr Preston,[10] and desire him to think in time of laying in Ale, so as to be fit to drink the middle of October, and put him in mind of the promise He made me before I left town, that He'd provide finer, and lighter than formerly.

Our Weather is grown Worse. Tuesday and Wedensday were very fine. Yesterday the same, till just before dinner. I took my *beautifull* ride, See I use your Word, with Lancaster. The Afternoon We had showrs, some heavy. The same to-day. A very Severe one is just over; and the Sun shines agen. This is less agreable, but no damage yet. There was none at ten this morning. All my Hay that is cut is in Cock, so as to be tolerably safe.[11] I wish however for setled fair, yet more for my Harvest than my Self. For I get my ride almost constantly and am I bless God very well. Adieu

Your &c
Edw: Elphin

Jane was as good as her Word. The Bread was yesterday as good as it us'd to be. The fault therefore was what she assign'd Too much Wetting, or some thing that She does not know, tho' She cures it.

I intend to have the Laurus-tinus,[12] so it should be spelt, planted between the Elms on the upper Walk. Make Roberts clear places for them. Two between each Tree, I fancy, will be enough. But if you judge three will do better, order it so. Let the intervals between each of them and the trees be Equal. We have no Wall-flowers, I think, here. I am not sure. For I seldom visit the Garden. The Fields are pleasanter. But Slips won't carry. Let Roberts make a little nursery of them. When rooted, they may be transported hither. I should be much fonder of honey-suckles, the

Common kind. I have a scheme for perfuming all my ditches, and fields with them. This will require a Million. The way to get them at last, is to begin, and get what We can. You have some in the Garden. Towards the end of the month, or the beginning of the next, make Roberts cut the Vines, and subdivide them into Sets about half a foot long, and plant them close in a Nursery. Hit or miss – Every joint will grow. When they get roots, I'll bring them hither for a beginning. When John is well Make him order the ditches about Finglas to be search'd, and a large Nursery made of them there. I am on the same scheme here, but have few materials.

I find by the Doctor that John Davies has quitted the Hospital. Let notice therefore be sent him immediately that He must take care of himself. When He is able to return to his Service, He may, if He pleases. But I will not humour such Gents in their whims, nor be at the Expense of supporting him in his own way, who declines a Comfortable support in mine. I desire you to treat him accordingly.

[Free Edw:Elphin]

1. George Bruce, seedsman, Cornmarket. He imported seed from England & Holland. Watson (1752) p.6. Advertisement *Dublin Courant* 31 March-3 April 1750.

2. Tags: wild daffodils, *narcissus pseudonarcissus*.

3. Flower de luce: irises.

4. Abigail. A lady's maid. The word is derived from Abigail who described herself as David's handmaid. Samuel 25:24-28.

5. Lady Fany: Alicia's dismissed servant.

6. Obscure.

7. Dr Patrick Delany (1685?-1768): dean of Down. Archbishop King's Lecturer 1722; professor of Oratory and History 1724. A popular preacher and tutor and an intimate of Swift. Married first, Margaret Tenison, a rich widow who died in 1741. He then married Mary Pendarves. He never received further promotion, probably because he was thought to be politically unreliable, and his reputation is overshadowed by that of Mary Delany. *Alumni*, p.222; *DNB*.

8. Mrs F.: not known.

9. John Crofton (?-1764), a magistrate of Lissadoorn, parish of Aghrim, Co. Roscommon, was a son of George and Elizabeth Crofton. He married Catherine, daughter of Col John French of Frenchpark. They had six children and a household of five Catholic and five Protestant servants. Crofton, p.186; Census, f.28.

10. Mr Preston: not known.

11. In order to dry cut hay quickly, Varley recommended that haycocks should be constructed 'by way of a foot' to allow air to circulate around them. *A New System of Husbandry* pp.184-6.

12. *Viburnum tinus*.

156

Elphin. August 6, 1751

My Dear Girl

Mrs. J told me in a late letter that you were grown an Active stirring body in the House-affairs. In that Character, which pleases me much, I put you in mind of the Hogs. Between Mrs. B and Brewster, see that they be fatted as well as offal of Garden and Kitchen can fat them, ready for Carleboe's feeding: nay! I don't care if you advance-em so as to be more ready for the knife. But they must be tip top, or you are among you bad Hog-Masters. Recollect how long they have been in the yard. I think Mrs J. very knowing in this *metier*.[1] Let her shew her skill.

A lame horse occasions great expense of Vinegar. The next opportunity, send a small Keg as a supply.

Mr Wills, Major Stuart and his Brother are here. So that I shan't be able to write much.

'Tis with others as with you. I have often taken pains at one time to do worse, than I have done at another without any. So it is with you in writing. But do not in striving to do better return to that labour'd stifness, which is as disagreable in this as in behaviour. You fall into it about this time every year. When will you write in a manner as *degagée*[2] as Mrs J. and I do? Aim at it. The Excuse of bad Pens I never will admit. Make better. You do some times. But Does a bad pen make you spell wrong, Mistress? *Spaking* for speaking. Fye!

Don't distract your self with too many books at a time. The one I mention'd may be in reserve, or perhaps do better a year or two hence. Your good Mother had some kinds of knowlege which I never intended you should have. Such as you can get, will be Ornamental and usefull. Better read to some purpose, than none, or next to none.

I thank you for your Magazine. The Bill of fare shock'd me. But it is curious.

I am glad you were at Rathfarnam.[3] Go there as often as you are inclin'd, if desir'd. Their account of my friend delights me. But I fear He will not take care. Lawson tells me himself He is in a very good way and his Letter is as well wrote as usual. A good Sign.

Mr D[onnellan] had fix'd this day for coming hither. But yesterday He sent an Excuse. His Mother's death.[4] Take care of the full decency of mourning for her.

Tell Jeny and Mrs J. that I thank them for their letters, but have no

time to write. Assure the latter that I am a Conjurer. For I read every word
of her letter with great ease. Thank the Doctor for his. Adieu.

Your &c
Edw: Elphin

[Free Edw:Elphin]

1. Trade.
2. Freely.
3. Rathfarnham Castle, Rathfarnham, Co. Dublin. The sixteenth-century castle was
altered and refaced in the eighteenth century. Bence-Jones, p.239.
4. Martha Percival (1677-1751): a daughter of Sir William Ussher and Elizabeth Par-
sons. She married, first Chief Baron Nehemiah Donnellan (1649-1705), and secondly
in 1712 the Hon. Philip Percival (1686-1748), the younger brother of Lord Percival,
later first earl of Egmont. Edward Synge shared an interest in music with Philip Percival who was the president of a musical academy in Dublin. Martha Percival was the
mother of Nehemiah Donnellan II of Artane Castle and Anne Donnellan. Burke
(1912), p.717; Edward Synge to Jonathan Swift, 18 September 1738 in *Correspondence*,
Vol. 5, p.124.

157

Elphin. August 6, 1751

My Dear Girl.

On opening yours yesterday, the first appearance was like a Stain from
Claret. What, thought I, Has Ally been carrowzing? On turning the leaf, I
found it was honest ink. I am sure it put you into a great flutter. But you
should never be so for a meer mischance.

When I reprimand or Expostulate, the Task is ungratefull. Yet I must
do it, when necessary. As the boy beat his Mother for her good. On the
contrary, to approve or commend always give me pleasure. God be
thanked. More of the latter has hitherto fallen to my share, with respect
to you, than of the former. I hope that will always be the Case. It will, if
you please, madam.

Your letter is well stopp'd. There are some mistakes scarce worth
notice. Two only are considerable, in which, as the Man said of the V.
Mary, you have shewn, you can't be good, but you must be too good. Your
fault has been, putting shorter stops instead of long ones. Now, it is the
reverse. I'll transcribe both the passages. *His great readiness, to give me
encouragement, when in the least degree I deserve it, would amply make up for it.*
You have put a ; at it, It ought to be a , *Readiness* is the Nominative Case,
to *would.* – The other is this. *Your approbation of my letter, of this day se'night,*

had a much greater share in it; than your intended present. tho' that gave me as much pleasure as a new gown could. You have put a . at present. It ought to be a : The Sense is not complete, till you come to *could*; where you have rightly put a . : tho' the next Sentence begins with For. These are indeed niceities. But a little time with care, will make you mistress of them. I am glad you like my present. Provide it as you please.

I take notice of a little *bevue* in your Sense here, Madam. *It is then Mr B. had he seen me, would have said, I look'd saucy: but that would quite spoil all. That!* What! Would looking saucy, or Mr B's saying so, spoil all? I know what you mean. But you have not express'd your Self right. Another Criticism. You repeat the same Words too often. *I suppose,* twice in three lines. The same often, of, *I am sure, I must own* and such like. Expressions of this kind should be vary'd; and seldomer us'd. Another little criticism yet. *How highly yours yesterdays.* This is not right. It should be either *yours of yesterday* or *your yesterday's.* The former is best. A remark in my last will explain this. You and Mrs J. should take all proper occasions of letting Mrs S. know my gratefull Sense of her kindness to you, which is indeed very great. You'd be much to blame, if you did not take care to please her. Tell her that I could, with great pleasure, take share of such a dinner, as she gave you, for the sake of her Company. But I am sure, my Potatoes are better than Hers. I never saw so good, as I have this Season, in my life. In dressing these, or any thing else, No one can rival her. But Carleboe does them, so as to please and Surprize the Wills's, who sup on them every night; except when Oysters seduce Mrs Wills and my grandmother.[1] The other two never meddle with them. They are still here. They intended going away to morrow. But I have prevail'd on them to stay, I hope, another Week. They have enabled me to pass very bad Weather with comfort. Never two more shocking days, than yesterday, and the day before. It has been fair all to day; and I got a good ride. But the Sky seems not setled. A return of rain will ruin the Country. I have suffer'd yet but a little. My neighbours are in a much worse condition.

H. Sandford had told me your story. He believes it. Sir Marm's part pleas'd me much. Mrs S's behaviour is easy, but not quite natural. You know how much every degree of Affectation disgusts me.

Tell Mr Woodward that I knew as well as He did, that there was no Cloth provided last Season for great Coats. But the Gentleman has forgot, that He put me in mind of this just before I left town, and offer'd to provide it this Summer. Assure him I shall call him to a severe account for having neglected it. If He does not immediatly get it, of a perfect good kind, I'll absolutely break with him. He grows worse and worse every day. Send for, and read this to, him.

Give my Service to your friend, and say, that She has told her Story in the most polite terms. Were she here, she might learn, she must hear, grosser, such as I believe she heard from John. Desire her to tell him, That the intrigue, if real, is of no great Consequence. All the matter is, the Lady doom'd to dye, must dye earlier, for her transgression of Orders. She paints extremely well. I see John with all his Emotion and eagerness, while I read. – If she hates short sheets of paper, why does she take them? – I am sorry you've had so much Employment for Doctors &c. But God be thanked, It has not been for your Selves.

I am very sorry a right person cannot be found for Dunshaghlin. If she thinks poor J. Curtis's Nurse, will be of use, Let her agree with and Send her there directly. I am pleas'd with her news, about disconsolate Rachy. God send her well thro' her *grossesse*.[2] It will be the likeliest cure for the heavy affliction of both. Yet at best it will bring great anxiety with it. It was very lucky, that poor Charlotte so soon discover'd her Man's roguery. I am sorry she has any Complaints, but pleas'd that she is so chearfull under them. And so Adieu.

Your &c
Edw: Elphin

Two or three times Mrs J has criticiz'd on my Spelling. In revenge, I examine hers very minutely, to no purpose often: But now I have caught her tripping. She writes *poultess'd*. It ought to be strictly, *pultice*. But use has made it *poultice*.

[Free Edw:Elphin]

1. Obscure.
2. *Grossesse*: pregnancy.

158

Elphin. August 9, 1751

My Dear Girl.

Our Weather has been very bad since my last. I bless God, it has had no effect on my health, nor on my Spirits, other than that I cannot help some gloomy reflexions on the misery in prospect, if it continues. I hear of a Vast deal of Corn lodg'd, particularly Oats. I have none. But A scarcity will affect me. I use above 700 Barrels a year. The Flax too has suffer'd in many places. Some is safe. All the Bear[1] is; and if Wheat in other places stands, the Buffet as well as mine, the loss hitherto will not be great. But I see no prospect of dry or Sun-shine. And without a good deal of both, No

corn can ripen. Before this time last year, All wheat was in Stack. A fortnight's very hot Sunny Weather would not ripen it this year. God's will be
done.

Your letter is very well wrote this bout. Only a few interlineations
deface it. But Tell me honestly, Did you air your Paper before you sat
down to write? I fancy not, and to this impute the sinking in some places.
There's another thing, which if you'd attend to, it would make your Writing appear better. Leave the Spaces between your Words a little and but a
little, larger Those between Sentences, should be a little larger than them.
Your Words are so close that there is scarce any distinction between them.
But I have caught you again, Mistress, at a great blunder in stopping. Your
words are *I could not have any thing to say against her taking her.* Is not this all
one Sentence? Yet you have put a . at *say.* Place it there in my Transcript,
and see what a figure it will make.

This same stopping, I see, perplexes you. You do not improve in it. I'll
therefore try once more if I can help you, by a plainer and fuller repetition of Documents formerly given.

Stops in writing answer to pauses in Speaking, or reading. In speaking
We make these pauses without adverting to it. Common Sense determines
us. But unless We made them, We should speak absurdly, often unintelli-
gibly. The same in reading. Where Books are well stopp'd, Notice is thus
given of all pauses. But Few are, as I have before told you; and unless the
defect be supply'd by the good sense of the reader, A well wrote book may
in reading appear to hearers jargon and Non-sense. This last defect is frequent in Ladys with voluble tongues and inclin'd to sillyness. They run on
without fear or wit, till their breath fails, thus run Sentences into one
Another, and stop panting in the middle. If ever you heard one read thus,
Say was it not disagreable, ridiculous? As pauses and Stops are necessary,
So is it necessary that they should be made and put in right places, and be
of different lengths; And these different lengths are, in writing or printing, distinguish'd by different signs. The longest pause in speaking, is at
the end of an entire sentence. The Mark of this pause is . which should
always be put at the end of Each complete Sentence and *no where else.* But
every sentence of any length consists of parts, which are really each a short
Sentence, but have a relation, and Connexion in a long one. Sometimes
they consist of two principal parts, each subdivided into smaller ones. And
Here is the place for the other stops, which are marks of different pauses.
The : is the mark of the next longest pause to the . This therefore is to be
put, where one principal part of a Sentence ends, and the other begins.
Often each principal part consists of entire Sentences, connected each to
other, and parts of the whole, and these are to be marked with ; which
denotes a pause shorter than the : and then each of these small sentences

has parts, in which there should be some, tho' very short, pauses, the mark of which is the , This is the most exact and plain description I can give you of the nature and reason of the Several Stops, which correspond to pauses in reading or Speaking. And, to try you, Mistress, whether you understand me, and will buckle your self in Earnest to this nice affair, which hitherto has foil'd you; I enclose a pretty long Sentence, without any stop at all, but in which there are places for every kind. Let me see now how you'll stop it. You may let Jeny try her hand at it if you please. But I forbid all help or hint from Mrs J., and if you give it to Jane, see not her Copy, nor shew yours but send them both to me. It is indeed a very difficult one to stop right, and I contriv'd it so on purpose. I therefore expect many faults. But in correcting these I may find occasion to convey all the directions I can give to help you to do what you have hitherto fail'd more in, than in any thing else which I have recommended. The best general Rule I can give you is this. Mark your pauses in Speaking, where and of what length. Like these be your stops in writing. This well observ'd, will seldom fail. If you attend to this matter Seriously, You'll see, that these pauses, tho' seldom observ'd (noted I mean) give grace, and clearness to all Speaking. Without them All would be hurry and Confusion; and, if made at wrong places, Non-Sense. Take a short Sentence. *I am very sorry you do not improve more in your Stopping.* Stop here now, and repeat this Sentence two or three times in an easy natural way. Then write it down, and, where you made, pauses, put Stops. Having done this, read on. See, I agen write the same sentence, and stop it wrong on purpose. I am very, sorry you, do not improve, more in your, stopping. Read it now with pauses, where my stops are. Observe the ridiculous figure. Just such a one is a letter ill stopp'd. I hope, my Dear Girl, that I have in some measure explain'd to you the Mystery of Stopping. If I have not, it must for me continue so. Yet Attention and practice will do, if you'll persevere.

You should not call your self dull, but stupid, that's the fashionable word, about the seeds. But they are come time enough. I am sorry John is not yet well. By the Doctor's account I hope He soon will be. I thought of your fine day at Merion, and enjoy'd it more, on that account. I can't believe that the C[hancello]r has any thought of coming hither this Summer.

You already know from me that Mrs Percival is dead, ay! absolutely dead, as you emphatically write. Mr D[onnellan] gets by this £800 a year, but some way I know not how, as to part, embarrass'd. You know he excus'd his coming hither on that account. When I see, I'll speak to him about Honey-Suckles. But when John is well, He'll find enough in the Hedges. Take notice the Best slips or Sets are those of Wood a year old.
Adieu

Your &c
Edw: Elphin

I forgot to desire in my last that if any of poor Charlotte's Bottles be faulty, Mrs J. may insist on amends from Mr F. It must be so. I care not how much He suffers for his Negligence. I am very sorry that poor Girl is not as well as I wish.

If Ned Curtis fails you, You may get flour enough in Francis Street.[2] I hope care is taken of the wheat. If it got any Wet on the road, it should be open'd and air'd.

Don't hurry your self in stopping your paragraph. I'll give you a Week to do it in. Longer you can't want.

[Free Edw:Elphin]

[On a separate sheet, pinned to the letter]:

As, all young Ladys, who desire to Excell, must take pains; As, they must attend carefully to instruction, and imprint every document, they receive from their Parents, or Tutors, on their minds; so as to have them ready, when Occasions offer, of putting them in practice: So, they who will persevere in taking these pains, without forgetting Documents formerly given, or satisfying themselves, with little Excuses, of hurry, want of time, &c. when they frequently transgress them; If Nature has been at all kind to such young Ladys; If they have even moderate endowments, and a reasonable portion of Sense; they will not fail of complete success, to their own honour, and the Unspeakable joy, of their Parents and Instructors.

1. Bear: barley.
2. Possibly Thomas Kelly or Dennis and William Tool, grocers, Francis Street. Watson (1752), p.25.

159

Elphin. Aug 13, 1751

My Dear Girl.

This is a time of hurry. To morrow is the ABp's Visitation. I expect Mr Hort every minute.

Settle the matter with Mrs Barry as you please, but let it be by an addition of Wages. If this be a pretence, she'll soon shew it. If reall; It would be idle to loose a good Servant for the difference of twenty or thirty shillings a year. See now what a way you had been in, if you had given N. her bowl of Tea, as you propos'd.

You did well to send an account of what Robinson told you, to Mr Vipond. It may be of use to free Galagher. He is very well.

Since you've begun Prideaux, go on with it as you like. Your and Mrs Jourdan's account of poor John shew that that poor fellow has been in an Ugly way. I am glad He is in some measure reliev'd; and hope he'll soon be well. In the meantime what becomes of Finglas? Enquire now and then from Mathew about the Hay particularly. That I am most anxious about. I should be glad also that the Bullocks at Cool-blow were sold, according to the directions in own of mine to John. But say nothing to him of this or any thing else, till you see him in a Condition fit to think and direct without hurt to himself. When next you see Mathew, Enquire about the Mule, and give me an account of her. It is my turn now to be anxious. Mr Lloyd told me yesterday, that He met her going into town very lame. If she be not quite well, See that Williamson attends her, as carefully as He would the best horse I have in the World.

Tell Mrs Jourdan, that I see no occasion for any other than the Common Small beer. If clear and well tasted I preferr it to stronger. So do most people. Good Ale is the thing I wish.

I am glad you met Lady Kildare. Her manner and Countenance are Majestick; and for that I like them. I did not think her look severe. By the by, you spell *majestically* wrong. But I do not blame you for it, as it is a Word you have probably not us'd before, and yours is the true Gramatical Spelling. But use has dropp'd the k. I am very well. God be thanked you are so. Adieu.

Your &c
Edw:Elphin

Bad news about your Pea-chicks. Jennet told me just now she fear'd they would all dye. She imputes this to the bad Weather.

Send the enclos'd, as directed.

[Free Edw:Elphin]

160

Elphin. Aug 16, 1751

My Dear Girl.

Your letter now before me is one of the best written, I ever received from you. No despair therefore of establishing yourself in a good usefull hand. Some of your words are yet too close together; and you have wrote *depair.* An s. forgotten. This to be sure is a slip of pen. But that I'll never take as an Excuse; nor your saying you are asham'd, as about the letters. By good luck the delay of them was not material. But, My Dear Girl, Attention is to be acquir'd by habit. So are a great many other things about which I have given you documents. Till you acquire them Must not I say, or think at least, that my Documents are so far without effect?

I have observ'd minutely your stopping in this letter, and think you in an hopefull way. But you have sometimes put a : where there ought to be a . and in one place at least, a longer stop, instead of a shorter. I'll transcribe the Sentence, that I may explain my remark. *Any of the documents, he has been at the pains to bestow on his daughter, have been without effect.* See I have put a , after daughter; You a ; which is wrong. It is one Sentence, you can't subdivide it into two. However with this and a few other mistakes, I see plainly, that you have *attended* more, to your stopping this letter, than ever you did before. One, which I can scarce call a mistake furnishes Occasion for a rule, which escap'd me before. There are some Sentences, which may go well enough without an intermediate stop, but if you put one, you must put two. You write thus. *but I hope it is by this, considerably mended.* and so you have stopp'd it. Now, as the sentence is very short, it might go very well without any, at *this:* yet it is rather more Exact to put a , But if you put one at this, you ought to put one also at is. Put it there and you'll see the reason. The two words, *by this,* interrupt the Connexion between *is,* and *considerably mended.* They are therefore a less kind of Parenthesis, and ought, in nice stopping, to be included within two. However, as I said before, It may go very well without one. Attend now to this document. You'll have frequent Occasion for it.

You are writing here of the Weather. Ours has been like yours. I fear yours is now like ours. After four very fine days, We had last night excessive rain with a sort of Storm; and To day, since I sat down here to write, two very severe show'rs of hail which beat so against the Window, that I expected it would crack the glass. If such Weather continues, the Country is undone.

I never will think you conceited for desiring to be very clean both in your person and Apartment. Finicalness Avaunt. I think it is right to have the breakfast room painted.

I am glad you have got flour, tho' the price is very high. Get Ned Curtis to ask his friend Mr Weld[1] what he now *sells* his English for. I ask not to point that out to you, but for other reasons. I hope your bread experiments answer. It will make us very happy, if they do. You don't say what your Ticket from Mr White was. The Lavender Water may have been a present from Bradock, if good for any thing. Keep it, unless you find the Owner. I have handkerchiefs enough. It is well your Pea-Family is increasing at Finglas. It is much lessen'd here. Ten, out of Eleven young, are dead.

1 have no letter from the Doctor about John; nor was any necessary. Mrs Jourdan's is full and exact. All her accounts are so. Learn this among other things from her. She'll see by this advice that I approve, tho' I sometimes rally her upon it. Give my service, and tell her that I laugh'd as much at her Serious justification, as I did at her Sending a copy of her letter to Mr French; and as for her Swaggering *en passant* because she remembered the Hogs, I should be mighty glad to have my note chang'd into Every thing is thought of. This is a hopefull Specimen. All I can say about poor John is, that it is well it is no worse. We must wait with patience; and beg the Doctor not to let him think himself well too soon. He may give directions about hay &c. at Finglas to Mathew. Every thing else may wait, till He is abroad. The Occasions of some of my Commissions are over. My Coach horse particularly is well. You ask'd me about feeing Daunt. I am not sure that I answer'd you. I therefore do it now. There is no Occasion.

If Sullivane Speaks again about fining &c. Desire Mrs J. to tell him, that she knows I have committed the Wine absolutely to his Management, and that He may do what He pleases. His formal exactness is sometimes teazing. But No news of Tobacco. I have time for no more.

Your &c
Edw: Elphin

I expect Mr Donnelan every minute. The Post chaise went for him this morning.

Poor Shannon has got a Whittle on his great Toe, which lames him. This is teazing. But I must make the best of it. He hops about to do, what only He can do.

Very heavy rain all this Evening and night. There will be more, before morning.

[Free Edw:Elphin]

1. Matthew Weld, merchant, and Thomas Weld, merchant, both of Pill Lane. Watson (1752), p.26.

161

Elphin. August 20, 1751

My Dear Girl.

For my censure of your and Jeny's performances, I referr you to mine to Mrs J. You'll see by it, that I leave you to give judgment your Selves. But

Take notice, Mistress That whenever I catch you hereafter at wrong stopping, as catch you I shall, I will not admit the Plea of ignorance. It will however be necessary now and then to give you cautions against mistakes, which will arise from your not perfectly understanding my Rules, plain as they are. Yours now before me gives great Occasion for one. In one respect it is very exactly stopp'd, i.e. there are stops in all right places, except one, but they are not the right kind. You have very often put a ; or : where there ought to be a . And as well as I can collect from the Sense of the places, in which you have made this kind of mistake, It arises from an opinion, that Where the Sense runs, or is connected, It is all one Sentence. Now this is not so. There may be, there are very commonly, entire complete Sentences, between which there is such Connexion; Yet each of them should be clos'd by a . . I'll give you an instance or two from many, with which your letter abounds *M. French &c. is setled at Coll. French's; We went to see her* &c. Where you have put a ; there ought to be a . The reason of your mistake I guess to be, that, *her* you thought, connected what follows with what went before. So it does as to Sense. But a new Sentence begins at *We.* The former one therefore should be clos'd with a . . The same thing agen, and for the same reason – *John is now so well, that He begins to fret about Finglas; He sent us word* &c. At Finglas should be a . . One more, which is stronger against you, than either of the former. *He will bring the heifer to her for company; My Lord Chancellor enquir'd for the heifer.* Here because *heifer* is mention'd in the latter part, You have put a ; at *Company.* It ought to be a . You will, I hope, by these instances, be able to apply my Caution in others. See that you do it. By the by, I see an error in your English, which I don't much blame, because there's a little niceity in the phrase. *She could not dispense her self.* So you have wrote. It ought to be *dispense with.* Your whole letter is very well written, and, which pleases me much, one whole page is without interlineation, and only two in the Second. But, what difference there is, your former one is better written than this. I'll hold a penny, that your pen, with which you wrote this last, was harder nibb'd than the one you us'd in the former. It wants some of the beauty and ease which arises from a proper yielding of the pen.

Our Weather has kept pace with yours. Yesterday was for the most part dry, and windy. This is fine, but the sky seems not setled. However I have 50 Men reaping my Wheat. It has suffer'd very little. My Hay too is very well, all things consider'd. A Few good days would set me up, and the Country too. But the Waters are more out, than I remember them. The view from my Windows, is by this means more beautifull. But I had rather want it, than the Country should suffer.

Your account of matters at Finglas is much better than I expected, and that of poor John pleases much. It will be hard to keep him from fretting.

But Tell the Doctor I beg he would not suffer him out, till He is more than quite well. He must allow me to thank him by you for his letters. For I really have not time to write. Desire him to dismiss McCormick whenever He pleases.

I understood you as you meant, an addition of Wages to Mrs B. I hope you have setled with her. I am glad you've got the better of N., and that you like her so well. If she has Sense, you may mould her as you please.

I have had no letter from my little Lord, tho' He promis'd to write. But I had the favour of one from Ned Curtis last post. Thank him.

In your last paragraph I see mistakes in stopping, and of another kind. The shortest way to shew them to you is, to transcribe it, as you have wrote, and then as it ought to be. *I enclose your Paragraph, with the third Edition of Stops; I fear it will shew, I had no help, but hope it is not worse than you expect.* Thus you. Thus it should be. I'll enclose your paragraph, with the third Edition of stops. I fear it will shew, I had no help; but &c.

God bless you, My Dearest, and all of you. I am
Your &c
Edw: Elphin

Compliments to be sure to Mrs S.

Looking again over your letter, I see a Sentence which affords more Criticism. As you point it, 'Tis thus. *The poor Coll. was wheezing frightfully, it appear'd to us, they call'd it, a slight fit, He was joking in the midst of it; I sent them a fine melon.* Here are many faults. You'll see them, by my writing the sentence agen, and stopping it right.

The poor Coll. was wheezing; frightfully, it appear'd to us: They call'd it a slight fit. He was joking in the midst of it. I sent them a fine melon.

You see here that in one place where you have put a , I have put a : in another a . and the same in a third, where you have put a ;. These depend on what I have already explain'd. But there remains a fourth Variation, which will require a little comment. I have put a stop between wheezing and frightfully, a ; Consider the sense, and you'll see the reason. The Sentence fill'd up would be thus. *The Coll was wheezing; It appear'd to us, that He was wheezing frightfully.* This you express in short very properly. But don't you now perceive, that *frightfully* is connected with *it appear'd to us?* and that therefore, if you were to speak these Words, you ought to make a pause at *wheezing*, and not of the shortest kind? These may appear little things. But, depend on it, My Dearest, that they must be closely attended to, if you desire to speak, or read or write with exact propriety. Read now deliberately the Sentence according to your own stopping. Then read according to mine. Judge your Self which conveys your true meaning with proper Emphasis. Read as you have stopp'd it is flat, and approaching to

Non-Sense.

You and your friend will probably have great Curiosity (For Females are always curious) to know what the three and four pence from Mr Roberts means. I'll tell you. He sent me a pacquet above Weight, which cost me so much. I am resolv'd He shall pay for it. I censure or punish giddiness, wherever I meet it.

Mr Lennox will send you a receit for £65.4. Lay it by carefully.

[Free Edw:Elphin]

162

Elphin. August 23, 1751

My Dear Girl.

Mr Donnelan is still here. He leaves me to morrow. Mr Waller came on Wedensday. I hope He'll stay longer. While they are here, I don't care to be much from them. So that you must be satisfy'd with a short letter; and luckily I have not much to say. For your bold push, as you call it, will soon be dispatch'd. You've made it so late, that there cannot be time for Executing it this Season, and before another. We shall have time to talk about it. Think not by this Answer that I am in the least displeas'd with your proposal, tho' it goes somewhat beyond my meaning, in what you have laid hold of as an Apt occasion, of making it. But, as I have often told you, You have at all times full liberty to make any proposal to me; and tho' I say less, I am as fully dispos'd to gratify you, as you are to please.

Your &c.

Edw: Elphin

You ask'd about Carleboe's and Shannon's performance, and I omitted to answer. The former's was as usual, very well. But the latter play'd me one of the truest Shannon tricks, that He ever plaid in his life. The wine wanted racking, and I order'd him to rack two or three doz in the morning. This He did carelesly and some into musty bottles. I was much confounded, but could not then help my self. He has ever since been lame of a Sore Toe, but is now pretty well.

[Free Edw:Elphin]

163

Elphin. August 27, 1751

My Dear Girl.

I am greatly griev'd at the death of little Jeny Curtis, not on her own account, but that of her poor parents. I have so contemptible a notion of the World, that I cannot be uneasy at Such young Creatures being remov'd out of it. Their loss is gain to them. My concern is for the Survivors, who having indulg'd to the full their fond affections, are miserable when they loose the Object of them. How great that misery, I know by sad Experience. Were I to begin the World agen, I would endeavour not to give such a loose to them as I have done. I wish poor Ned and Rachy had not done it. But when tender parents have once taken this bent, Advice is to no purpose, they cannot follow it. If young persons would benefit by the experience of those who have gone before them, there is scarce any lesson more usefull to be thus learn'd, than this. Not to be over fond of any person or thing in this World. I grant that by restraining these most pleasing Affections, We lessen our joy. But We are thus better prepar'd against the melancholy contingencys to which We, and All that is dear to us, are Every hour subjects; and the true state of the Account is this, somewhat less joy: A great deal less sorrow, for a loss, or anxiety without one. Ah *Dieu ne plaise* that the former should ever be my hard fate for you the Dear remaining object of all my fondness. But the latter I do and must always feel more than I wish either for your Sake or mine own. As I eagerly desire you should be perfect in all respects, so I often feel, and give you uneasiness on matters, which, were I less fond, might well enough pass without any observation at all. I am going to do it this instant, and cannot help it. I am mortify'd at yours now before me. It is as ill stopp'd, as almost any one I have received from you, ever since I first mention'd stopping to you. How many times, think you, have you offended against one of my plainest rules? I have counted them and in no less than 17 places have you put shorter stops, instead of a . There are a good many mistakes of other kinds, which I have neither time nor inclination to point out. In one place only, you have put a . where it ought not to be. I cannot admit the plea of ignorance for these numerous mistakes. For tho' your paragraph was not exactly stopp'd, the Errors were comparatively few; and the whole was much better than I expected. After this Specimen and your letter next before this I can impute your failure only to want of care and attention; and this failure is more mortifying on account of the many promises you have made. My Dear Dear child, With respect to this, and *many other matters,* Either promise less, or do more. See here one effect of my overflowing fondness. I am uneasy and make you so, about things which were I more indifferent, would pass without notice. An unlucky effect, you'll say, of a good Cause. But I cannot help it; and you must allow me once for all to say, that Many of my documents do not make so *lasting* an impression as you promise and I wish. I hope they will in time, if you revive them sometimes in your thoughts, and remember that Every thing of this kind proceeds from a Solicitude for your Welfare in all respects, which is the strongest passion I have or shall have during my life.

Harry Sandford and his Wife came hither yesterday evening; Night, I should say, For it was almost nine when they arriv'd. She bore a long journey from Mullingar very well. Her behaviour during the very short time she has been here, has been much more engaging that I thought it in town. I believe I shall grow to like her much. Poor Lucy came in the morning. She does not boast much of the good effects of the Waters, but has still great hopes. She carrys an horse-load of the Water to drink for a Month to come. Thus far she is visibly better. She has no patch on her nose, and only a little redness remains. But what she tells me is a drawback on this, that It has been so, two or three times and broke out agen. She is cheerfull and agreable as usual, and desires to be remembred to you all with great affection. But what do you think? She knew nothing of the intended marriage, till I told her of it. So much do they neglect the poor Girl, as not to inform her of the Occurrences in their own Family. Yet her Mother sometimes wrote to her.

Poor Ned Curtis's letter to me has prov'd more grievous to him, than He knew, when He regretted his having wrote it. My answer, was very chearfull. It must have shock'd him. I am in great pain about the effects of this most unfortunate accident on his health.

I less apprehended 'Jolly's' failing than your other Horse's. But thus it is with Brutes as well as men. The strongest in appearance often sink soonest. I am glad you could make so good a Shift. If He does not recover, and you want, I'll send you horses from hence. As both your horses are old, I have thought it for a long time likely they would be disabled or dye; and with a view to this, on leaving town, directed John to look out for young ones. He declin'd doing it my way, and took one of his own, which has not succeeded. I desire that you or Mrs J. would, when you see it convenient, ask him from me, whether He has seen the Man from whom I bought the last horses; and whether He has any hopes from him of getting a pair of right ones? If not, they must be look'd out for. But As the Horses I bought from him have prov'd very good, I am much inclin'd to deal with him agen, if John has no Objection. I would rather have a pair four years old, but would buy choice ones of three. I chuse to write this to you rather than to him, tho' I write to him this post, but not about business. Ask him, or rather Mathew what Quantity of Hay Finglas will afford this year. I am sure it is before this all made up. If there be any to Spare there, I have thoughts of lending some to your Uncle, as they tell me the price of Hay will this Season be Excessive. Learn from John what instructions He has from him about buying; and if Mathew's report be good, Without discovering my intention, Advise him to delay, or to buy but a little for present use. Send the enclos'd to Jones the Coach-maker. It is to order a new Set of harness. My old ones are failing.

All my harvest affairs are now in a very fine way. My wheat in Stack, Hay will to night be finish'd in large Cock, only one Meadow, which I am now cutting a Second time. There seems to be a good prospect still of Weather. If it holds for a Week or fortnight longer, the distress of the Country will be perfectly reliev'd.

The Difference between the price of Mr Weld's flower, and the Master's is so great, that you ought, if you can, to get some of the former. Poor Ned is the person, who, if any one can, can get you such a quantity as will answer your Occasions. Employ him, to chuse at this time. It will be usefull to him.

In that view, Tell him I desire He would go immediatly, and lodge the £5 English with Mr Baily for the Soldier's discharge according to the instructions formerly given. He'll now receive it. I wish this to be done, the day you receive this, or at furthest next morning; therefore if you do not see, write to him about it.

I can now pronounce positively, that 'Caesar' is not worth two pence. Young Cooper is here, who, tho' a very hard student is a Sports-man. He went yesterday to try him, and says roundly He's good for nothing. I'll bring him up with me, and re-deliver him. I shall not want this Season. Mr Conroy has a very good one.

The delay of the letter has this time been inconvenient, tho' not much so. But with what coolness, Mistress, do you write of a new Species of giddiness, who have, this Summer, and before, made me so many strong promises, to avoid every kind of it. I hope you will in time. But you must learn to attend more than you do, to my documents, and your own promises. Be not mortify'd at what I have written; but consider it as the Admonition of

Your over-fond Father
Edw: Elphin

Send the Enclos'd to Dr Roberts.
Send for Woodward and order him to set about making the Liverys

and Frocks, and Big Coats for the Servants. Shannon says you have the key of the chest where the Cloth is. Whether he shall make any for Lawrence or not will depend on you. You have never said any thing to me of his behaviour.

It will be time now to order Roberts to plant his borders, according to the directions formerly given. You'll then know what refuse you'll have to send me. It is rather too early for planting the choice ones.

Tell Mrs J. that the Bristow water has been wrote for this month. When will she give as good an account of Tobacco?

We have had some rain this Evening. But the night promises well.

Don't stop John about Hay for my Brother. Learn only what directions He has.

[Free Edw:Elphin]

164

Elphin. August 30, 1751

My Dear Girl.

My last, was, part of it, very grave; and, I believe, made you so. I need not tell you, that I have as little pleasure, in writing such letters, as you can have in reading them. But what can I do? You'd be sorry, if I resolv'd to pass such things by in silence. Yet this, or telling you of your faults is all my choice. 'Tis only in your power to make both your self and me easy, by performing your promises. As I never recommend any thing, but what I know to be for your good, so I never blame you for omissions or neglects but when I am sure they are the effect of negligence and inattention. Wilfulness I do not charge you with. I am fully satisfy'd of your general good disposition to observe all my injunctions. But to some you find a reluctance, and you postpone doing any thing towards observing them, till, it may be, the Opportunity is lost. Have a care that I do not find this to be the Case with regard to one given you early this Summer. I will not press you further on the delicate subject. But remember, my Dearest, that the Advice went from the fondest Father that ever was, and was supported by reasons, which I defy you, and all the nice Females in the World to answer. Consider them sometimes cooly. They'll gradually make impression. I know this must be the work of time. But if you never begin, you never can advance. I should not even hint at this agen, but that I think it may be of the last consequence even to your life. Oh! Had your good Mother been in time advis'd in the same manner, I had not, probably, for so many years deplor'd her loss.

I think I do you no more than justice in believing, That this is the single point in which, if in this, I have put you to any severe trial. For I have with infinite pleasure observ'd your ready compliance to all my Admonitions, so far as to promise to observe them; and As I have not the least doubt but that you have always been sincere and honest in making such promises, so I have had the satisfaction to see great effects from them. But, Huzzy, you sometimes fail. Certain things call'd, Hurry and giddiness, against which you've made so many resolutions, still shew, on some Occasions, that they are not yet overcome; and where you don't own this your self, you furnish me with arguments to prove it upon you. Thus, in what occasion'd my writing last post with some spice of sow'rness, I have now before me the strongest proof of the justice of my charge. Your letter is not only ten times better wrote than the last, but accurately stopp'd. I have examin'd it over and over, and find no mistake in it worth notice, but one, and that of the kind, of which in the former there were 17; but so small a one of that kind, that had I not a mind to inculcate more fully a rule which I have found you so apt to mistake I should not observe it at all. *Our horse is almost well; They say, he may* safely be work'd in a few days. There ought to be a . at *well,* tho there be a connection of sense with the following sentence. Try this by the fundamental rule of right stopping. *Stops in writing answer pauses in speaking.* With this single inconsiderable mistake, your letter is as well stopp'd, as Dr. Swift could have stopp'd it. Now what says the Proverb Mistress? A Bird that can sing &c.[1] To carry on the Metaphor, You are caught in your own net. Since you have shewn that you can do well, you must always do as well as you can.

H. Sandford and Wife left me yesterday morning. The day was very fine. This is the most shocking one We have had this Season. A violent storm of Wind and rain, and no sign of it's falling. I am in so good a way, as that I shall be scarce at all hurt by it. But it will do infinite damage to the Country.[2]

I am glad you pass'd a day with Mrs N[icholson]. You need not have told me that it was an agreable one. Tho' I like her Sister-in-law better than I did, she will not rival her in my regards.[3]

I have for some time had it in my thoughts to make you a Present, Madam, and what do you think it is? A Suit of Black Velvet. I imagin'd at first that it might be proper at the End of the publick mourning; but in that I find I am mistaken. However it will be right to have it for slight mournings, which happen often; and It is a dress I am very fond of. Provide your self of the best of the very best kind that can be had. If the Town affords not a perfect one, I suppose your friend Grogan will import one. Probably you and your friend will consult Mrs N., perhaps Mrs S. This last loves to be employ'd, and is a notable Hunter. I suppose she has not succeeded in her hunt for China.

Mrs J.'s account of poor Ned Curtis's shewing her my letter, has added to my affliction for him, and his Wife. You see I was aware of the heightning this would be to their distress. God almighty comfort them. You or she may take proper Occasions of letting both know how much I feel for them I cannot write.

I don't know whether I told you in my last, that the Wills-grove folks were all here. They came on Tuesday; which was a day of more hurry, by accident, than I have had since I knew Elphin. They, H. Sandford and Wife, Lucy, and young Cooper in the house: the Carys and Conrys to dine by invitation; and Just before dinner in came, Mr Crofton, Lt Donnelan, Mr Dowel, and Mr Lowther the Old Captain's son.[4] But We got through all very well. Mr Crofton's Coach with his Lady, Mr D's and others, pass'd by three minutes before the Men came to the door. I did not desire the Husbands to bring them back. Mentioning this Crofton brings to my mind the other. Have you ever had Kate,[5] and poor Jac. to dine? I think I desir'd it. I am sure I desir'd you would write to Jennet, and you promis'd you would. I am glad you did not. For she is in great disgrace. By mis-management She was the Cause of the death of the ten Pea-chicks, which I mention'd before; and in this day has suffer'd a fine one which W. Cary rear'd and sent to her last night, as past danger, to stray and perish in the Storm. God bless you all. I am

Your &c
Edw: Elphin

Send the enclos'd.

Mr Lennox will send you a receit for £523:10:-. Lay it carefully up.

You sometimes put your stops a little too low. The tops of them ought always to be in a line with the bottom of your letters. You are driven to this by not leaving space enough always between Words, and Sentences.

[Free Edw:Elphin]

1. See Letter 25, fn.30.
2. August 1751 was wet and September was 'A wet month, few fair days a great glut of rain the twentieth, twenty first, twenty second and great floods.' Rutty, p.163.
3. Poss. Rachel Sandford, Henry Sandford's wife. Mrs Nicholson was a Miss Sandford.
4. Mr Lowther: not known.
5. Catherine: daughter of John and Catherine Crofton of Lissadoorn, Co. Roscommon. She married John Yeadon Lloyd of Anneville, Co. Roscommon. Crofton, p.204.

165

Elphin. September 4, 1751

My Dear Girl.

My last makes it unnecessary to say much to the former part of your letter. I am pleas'd with the manner of your writing your Apology; – But somewhat surpriz'd that you have more than once committed the same fault in stopping, which was the immediate occasion, tho' not the only cause of my grave Expostulation. I hope what I added in my last, as a further Explanation of my Rule, will complete your Cure. But that I may, if possible, guard you yet further, I'll transcribe another of your Sentences, where you've made this mistake. 'Tis the first in your letter. *I must own, tho' I am sorry to do it, that your touching reproach is in appearance just; For my mistakes,* &c. You have put a ; at *just.* It ought to be a . The Sentence is there Complete. *For* begins a new one. I can't make the thing plainer: So I must leave it to your giddiness or Attention to do for the future, what the Governing inclination dictates. But pray, Mistress, How long do you intend to keep up your pretensions to the Character of *giddy Girl?* 'Tis one you would not like from others, any more than you would rebukes from any, except Mrs J. and me. You have had allowances on that score, But your title to them lessens every day.

Some time ago I took notice of your sealing gilt paper with black Wax. Now, for a penny, Have you observ'd, that I in my last made the same blunder? As Tutors ought carefully to avoid doing things, against which they caution their pupils, I think it right to account for this. I have scarce any but black Wax. I must reserve the little red left for letters, which should go with Exact decorum.

You've mention'd 'Terence' sometimes, but never gave any account of his behaviour. I am glad it has pleas'd. Order Cloaths to be made for him. I am pleas'd your 'Jolly' is recover'd. I believe his distemper was what the Work-Horses here have frequently. Jemy cures them in a day. What comes of Jac. Davies? I can't but be concern'd for the poor fellow, tho' His Egregious folly much disgusted me. Ask the Doctor about the last patient sent from hence. McCormick is come home in Excellent plight. I hope He'll be able to work, tho' with caution.

Poor Lucy got home safe, the day before the Family set out for the Assizes. I had this account from the Man whom I sent home with her. For the Servant who came with her, fell ill, and continues so, here, of a Pleurisie. He has been in great danger. They tell me, He is somewhat better to day. It was much more lucky for the poor Fellow to have that dangerous distemper here, than at Garbally.

When next you see Mrs S. Give her my service, And Tell her that the Experiment has been try'd here of feeding Pigs with Parsnips, and has answer'd fully as to Pork. I never ate better. Mrs Heap and Carleboe think they'll do as well for Bacon. Mrs. J may try, if she pleases, by ordering Roberts to thin the Parsnips in the Garden. It will be of use to her Hogs, perhaps to that of 'Pharaoh's' breed. Those which remain will grow larger.

Mr Baily's receit might as well have remain'd in town. But you were in the right to send it, since Ned Curtis bid you. Poor Man! I am glad He is so well, and bears his great affliction better than you Expected. I wish however, that this be not appearance. You do very well to comfort him, and the good Woman as much as you can.

I know not what to resolve about Hay for your Uncle, till I know this year's strength at Finglas. You may learn it from Mathew. In the mean time Advise John against buying any new Hay for him, till He can go abroad.

I suppose the planting of the Borders is by this time finished. I am glad you have so large an Over-plus. The trash with you, they'll embellish here. But send only half the Single Anemonies, and Make Roberts plant the other half immediatly in a bed in the Flower Ground for a reserve. When John is enlarg'd, Let him get a Cask that will hold all the Roots, and send them down the first Opportunity. See that they be perfectly dry; and do not put them up, till the Carr be ready to take them off. I shall be glad to have them here, before I leave it. You may send a few Orange Lillys, and a few white, if you can spare them. I fear it is rather late For if I mistake not, they both begin to Spring about this Season. If so, they must be let alone, till next year.

I am glad you've had the Croftons with you. The pleasure the good little Woman shews, will, I am sure, dispose you to continue some little Civilitys to her. As for your friend Matty [Lennox], I have no doubt but that her behaviour will always entitle her to your love and Esteem. Pray How has her sister B.[1] behav'd herself on this trying occasion? I should be glad she gave you reason to alter your Opinion of her for a better.

Our Weather has been to the full as bad as yours. Yesterday was one of the most shocking days I ever saw; Cold as December. Several Severe show'rs of Hail, and Wind N. West, little short of a Storm. In the midst of all, I was cutting my Barley, for fear of it's shedding. This day is somewhat milder, but very severe. Yet on both I got my ride, and am, I bless God, very well. We have fires as well as you, and comfort our Selves with them, and good meat and drink, so as to feel no inconvenience, but from reflexions on the misery to the Country, in prospect; unless it pleases God to send us better Weather. If such comes in any time, All will be yet well.

The Cork papers diverted me. They are well enough calculated for the Rabble. I'll thank Dr Lawson for the Pamphlet. Adieu. I am, My Dearest

Your &c
Edw:Elphin

Mrs Cary has been confin'd these two days. I believe she's breeding, but ask no Questions. Have you seen her Sister,[2] since her going to town? In point of form, you ought to go first. She is a very good kind of Woman. But you may do or let it alone as you please.

We are in great distress for want of Duck-shot. Ned Curtis provided none, and Wise Shannon, according to custom, never told me this, till now that the time is come for using it. Desire him to get a parcel. I am no judge of the Quantity; but as it is not a very dear Commodity, I had rather have it too large than too small. It may come with the Cask of Flow'r-roots and As I want it much, I wish that, on that Account, the Sending of them may be hasten'd. Send Will to hunt for a Carr-man. Let him apply particularly to Mr Dominick French in Abby-street, who may be very likely to help him. He knows him. If He fails there, Let him go to Mr Tew's on Ussher's Quaye,[3] or to Mr Hudson's Grocer in Castel-street. Those two often send goods to this place.

I take notice of a little mistake in your writing, which is not a fault now, but will be, if you make it agen. You write *no one else's*. You should have wrote *no one's else*. You see the reason. The Sentence at length would be, *The approbation of no one else*. The 's is an abbreviation put for *of*. It ought therefore to be join'd as the *of* is to no one, which really is one Word.

[Free Edw:Elphin]

1. B. Lennox; not known.
2. Mrs Cary's sister would have been another daughter of Col William Southwell.
3. John Tew, high sheriff of the City of Dublin, merchant, Usher's Quay. Watson (1752), p.24.

166

Elphin. September 10, 1751

I see, My Dear Girl, that you are the V. Mary still. Longer stops, instead of shorter, is now the Mode; and, which surprizes me most, All palpable offences against the plain Rule, I have over and over inculcated, that punctums should be put only, where the Sense is Complete. I shall transcribe two or three.

The Condition of the Country, in consequence of it. as well as what We feel here. So you have stopp'd. Is the Sense complete at *it?* Again. *Of which perhaps she was too sensible. and it may be it occasion'd her odd behaviour.* Does the Sense end at *sensible?*

Again. *She came here the other evening in a chair. So loaden* &c. This is, if possible, more glaring than either of the former. The sense is so far from being complete at Chair, that the next Words are necessarily connected with *She came.*

One more. Thursday night was concluded *with bone fires and other demonstrations of joy. on account* &c. I need not repeat my remark. You'll see the thing at once. These are proofs, with more which this letter furnishes, that my Dear giddy Girl has not yet learn'd Attention. Pray learn it as fast as you can. I'll neither chide nor remark more on this head; but leave you to the repeated admonitions I have given. I cannot give fuller or plainer.

I observe one false spelling. The trees look pretty *bear.* It should be *bare.*

You had the advantage of us last Friday. It was mild here, but there were some heavy show'rs, which hind'red Harvest Work. We were unlucky. For it was quite fair three or four Miles off. Saturday, too, was quite fair, An high Wind, excessively cold, dry'd much; but, at night, rain return'd; and Sunday was an Excessive bad day: Rain, not continu'd, but heavy showrs: One particularly as We came from Church. The beating on the head of the Coach, was so violent, that it was, in Sound, like hail. We came with both glasses up. Yesterday was a dead day; a good deal of rain, but soft. No Harvest work possible. This day is hitherto fair. I write at one. But lo'wring clouds, the Wind in the same point, and with it's horrid Whistle, that has tormented me so long and often this summer. These are Symptoms of a return of rain. However I had a fine ride this morning; and am making the best use of Sunshine, while it lasts. If my poorer neighbours could do the same, they would be better, than they are. The Country has suffer'd much, particularly in Oats. All the Bear, and Most of the Wheat is safe in the field. But not a sheaf any where drawn home; nor Hay. All mine is abroad. God's will be done. The account Mrs J had from her Brother[1] heightens the distress. If things were well in England, We should have help from them. Coll Trench's servant is recovering.

Will must search for Carrs, till He finds one. As your loading is very little, It would be better, if He got some one of the Persons, nam'd in my last, to take charge of it. If it be not sent off, before this reaches you, Let Two dozen of ridge-Tiles be sent with it. As John is confin'd, Write a note to Mr Nelson for them. He knows where they are to be had, and will order them to be properly pack'd up. I don't chuse to have more than half the grown Anemonies come, till I know, whether my ground will agree with, or Saunders can manage, them. He is as strange a fellow as ever.

Mr Wills &c. are still here. He confesses the Fact which Mr Lennox told you: But by his account, which I believe is true, there's nothing in it. The flies were troublesome, and so both He and Cromie[2] dismounted. A fresh instance of your Virgin-Mary ship here offers it Self. I can't pass it by. *He got on horse-back, for the first time, since He went to the Country. when Mr Cromie was with him.* Is the Sense clos'd at Country? Yet you have put a . there. This by the by. But I am my self a Witness, that this was not the first time of his getting on Horse-back, since He came to the Country; For He had rode hither before. However by their Confessions, and what I observe here, I am sure they lead a very indolent life. This affects not her. She is ditto. But I think his state of health very indifferent. I have said all I could, to alarm him. He has, beside his usual head-aches, what He calls, a Rheumatism, in his head; and I believe He calls it right. He had some in other parts so violently, that He could not put on his clothes. Physick reliev'd him. He promis'd two or three times since He came hither, to take more. But being somewhat reliev'd, He would not. He lives with great guard, but is not as apprehensive of bad effects as He ought to be. When We get him in town, We must try to make him do what He ought. They talk'd of passing the Winter at Wills-grove. But either they were not quite in earnest; or I have prevail'd on them to change their purpose. They resolve now to be in town before Xtmas.

Mrs Cary told me yesterday, that Mrs Nicholson is at Castelrea.[3] By a letter from him, I knew that He would be. But He said nothing of her. If you knew of this Sally of hers, Why did you not tell me?

I grieve for Lady Kildare. A Father and Mother lost in so short a time. As they were a shining pattern of Conjugal Fidelity, and happiness, very rare among Dukes and Dutchesses.[4] I wish a Monument was erected to them, and on it, these Lines. I think they are, B. Johnsons?

He first departed, she without him tryd
a while to live, but lik'd it not, and dy'd.[5]

Mrs J's accounts of her Dialogues with John, entertain me greatly. Yet I long for an End of them by his being well and abroad. He is not to wait for orders from me. I referr him to the Doctor. I am glad to find that my Brother has any old Hay. She may easily get out of John, what quantity He has orders to buy; and How many horses He thinks he'll keep in house. I would fain save him the buying too dear. But I must first know mine own strength and his Wants. I glean'd a false Spelling or two out of Mrs J's. last. This affords a fuller harvest. She'll excuse them with *griffonage*.[6] However she shall have them; and this must not stop her Writing. You ought to take it as a Compliment, Madam, that I convey them by you. Two or three years ago, I would not have put it in your way, to know, that she had even so slight a defect. I'll put them down on the next page: and So Adieu

Your &c
Edw: Elphin

Mrs J	E.E.
swaring	swearing
teribly	terribly
Barril	Barrel
Linster	Leinster. This last not a fault; or at most, but half a one.

If you should be driven to the necessity of loading a whole Carr, to get what I want down, which will weigh very little, Let such a Quantity of Iron be got from Mr Constable, as will load one. John may write for it. If not, you may. Let the kind be half flat. Mr C. will understand you. He must be charg'd to send very good.

Fair all day: But I much fear rain before morning.

[Free Edw:Elphin]

1. Either Henry Jourdan, born 9 April 1700 or Aldebert/Albert born 22 June 1711. Bouhéreau, 20 April 1700; 22 June 1711.

2. Possibly Michael or John Crommie. See Letter 52.

3. Henry Sandford's house.

4. Charles Lennox, 2nd duke of Richmond, died on 8 August 1750. His wife Sarah, a daughter of earl Cadogan died in 1751. '[The] Duke and Duchess of Richmond, both handsome enough to have been tempted to every inconstancy but too handsome to have ever found what they would have lost by the exchange.' Burke (1916), p.1708; Stella Tillyard, *Aristocrats* (London 1994), pp.10-11; Horace Walpole to Lord Lincoln n.d., W.S. Lewis (ed.), *Horace Walpole's Correspondence* (London 1937), 43 vols, Vol. 30, p.46.

5. 'He first deceas'd, she for a little try'd/To live without him, lik'd it not, and di'd.' Sir Henry Wotton (1568-1639) 'Death of Sir Albertus Morton's Wife'.

6. *Griffonage*: scribbling.

167

Elphin. September 13, 1751

My Dear Girl.

Yesterday was fair, tho' the whistling Wind and lowring clouds continu'd. To day is just the same; and I have ventur'd to begin drawing my hay. Attendance on this, and the pleasure of being abroad have made me sit down very late to write. You know the consequence.

I read your account to the Wills's. He look'd silly, She archly. The Girls laugh'd and seem'd to assent. The description is in the main true, but somewhat *outrée.*[1] In one Article it certainly is. She goes every Sunday to Church. But the Man is certainly very lazy, and He makes the rest so. I wish He do not suffer by it. I made him a present of a pretty Poem, which I found here by Chance; the *Castle of Indolence.*[2] This, my raillery and Scolding, and your letter, occasion'd their making an effort to day to prove they were falsly accus'd. And what do you think it was? They went in my Coach as far as Shanhill to see the little House Mr Conry is building, and – return'd.[3]

According to Custom, I was told yesterday that Brown Sugar was wanting. If you have not sent off the other things, Send a stone or two for the uses of the House. I apprehend, that for Bacon is of a Worse kind. It will be time enough to send it with other ingredients, two months hence. The Pears you shall have; All: Carleboe shall use none here; and yet we have none other. Saunders says there are a good many. Mrs Heap has no carpeting. She shall make you some this Winter. I order'd her to try about Diaper.[4] She has none, nor am I sure, She can get any made.

Tell Mrs Silver with my service, that Nothing shall be done with my Consent in my house which she thinks a shame. So the parsnips shall be reserv'd for Bacon, and I'll be content with worse Pork.

The false Spelling you accus'd your self of, escap'd me. But it is as you say. You see I am not so exact as you think me. I am

Your &c.
Edw: Elphin

Give the enclos'd to Williamson.

Next time you see poor Ned Curtis, Ask him if I have any chance for the Hock from Aldm Dunne.[5]

If Mr Nelson sends for the Carr, to bring home a Vessel of Tar, order it. If He sends it by a Porter, take it in, and Let it be plac'd in the Cellar under the Stairs.

Tell John, that I see in the News-papers accounts of the cheapness of Cattel in Smithfield Market. He knows that this would be our time of buying for the house next Winter, if he were well. As He is not, I must take my chance; unless He can employ some friend to buy as He us'd to do himself. If He'll let me, I'll send or speak to Mr Wallace. I believe I shall see him here next Week.

[Free Edw:Elphin]

1. Exaggerated.
2. James Thomson, *The Castle of Indolence*: an allegorical poem. Written in imitation of Spenser (Dublin 1748).

3. According to Edward Conroy, the land at Shankhill 'was held of Elphin, granted by the See of Tuam to John Conry as a "Bishop's Lease": that is, a lease renewable on a fine for ever. The Bishop of Elphin was then a Dr Synge, a great friend of Johnny Conroy, through whom John Conry obtained from Dr Hort, Archbp of Tuam, a lease of Shankhill about year 1747. He built a lodge upon it, and called it Bettyfield in honor of his wife Elizabeth Foulke and they resided there many years before they went to live in Dublin.' The house was destroyed by fire in the nineteenth century. Conroy Papers Item 13d.

4. Diaper: a floor covering made of a linen and wool mixture; a kind of drugget.

5. James Dunne, alderman and merchant, Lower Ormond Quay, Watson (1752), p.10.

168

Elphin. September 17, 1751

My Dear Girl

Mr Palmer came hither yesterday; and He and I have been sauntering so long this very fine day, that I shall scarce have time to clean my self before dinner. Again I say, you know the Consequence. But luckily I have not much to say, nor is there much in yours that calls for a return.

Mrs S. is certainly what you think her. The instance you give, is a strong proof of it. Your criticism on your self is unjust. There's nothing improper, in what you've wrote. Your *this* referrs very naturally to the whole relation you had before given, not to the Curtis's being pretty well. If you be thus exact in remarking on your Self, I shall no longer have room to accuse you of want of attention.

Since your friend trusted you with her intended Expedition, as a Secret, You did well to keep it. But she has bilk'd me. Her Father is the Cause. He won't suffer her to quit him, till she is oblig'd to go directly to Dublin.[1]

Tell your friend Matty that I rejoice much at her happiness, and hope it will continue, as far as a Change of Circumstances will admit. But the happiest marriage brings Cares &c. It was a saying of your Grandmother's,[2] when a young Damsel was gay and cheerfull. The Black Ox has not yet trod on her foot. An homely image of Matrimony, but too too often a just one. I have a very pleasant long letter from Mrs J. What answer I have time to give, She must take here.

Does she mean me the person who don't cross T's or mark i. She has put I – Who ever wrote that with a pip?

By her History, the transactions in the Cellar are all right; and she was

368

serv'd no worse than I should have been. My guess has been always, Whites of Eggs.[3] I am glad to find it was a good one. Let her Enter the number of hoops in her Memorandum paper. I shall forget it.

Her account of John is diverting as former ones. I hope she rebukes him for swearing. She may tell him seriously that I am much offended at it. By her account I fear I must quit my scheme of aiding my Brother as to Hay. I suspect that I have less even of last year's than I hop'd. A Question or two to John will determine the point. You or she ask him, Whether any remains of the Old But of the year before last, which I left in the yard? And Whether He has cut that of last year to fill my loft? If He has, How much He has put in of it? And what remains of the Reek?[4] These Questions will, I know, make him bounce. But I beg his answers with all his bouncing. Tell him He must pay Mr Stopford[5] whatever He insists on. As He has not been able to deliver mine to Mr Ewing[6] all this time, Let him not deliver it at all.

Since the blackness of my Cieling disgusts her so much, Let her e'en get it whiten'd. The reason of my orders against it was, Propriety, That the room might be all of a piece. How happy is she now, Her curiosity reliev'd and her wishes comply'd with! But my comfort is, My Candles will quickly blacken it agen. Mentioning Candles puts me in mind to ask whether you may not as well lay in your Stock of Wax ones now, when you are less hurry'd? You may possibly get them better, as having the whole Stock to chuse out of. You should provide more than last year, I think. But I leave it to you.

Your &c
Edw: Elphin

Ask John how many Cows or Bullocks his after-grass will support cleverly. Now is the time for buying in Smithfield; and since He can't go thither himself, I have it in my thoughts to get Mr Palmer to procure them.

[Free Edw:Elphin]

1. This passage is obscure. The 'Mrs S.' may be either Mrs Silver or possibly Mrs Southwell.
2. Probably Edward Synge's mother, Jane Proud, daughter of the Rev. Nicholas Proud of Cork. She died in 1723.
3. Whites of eggs were used for fining wine drawn off from casks, prior to bottling. Hartley, p.537.
4. Reek: a stack of hay or corn.
5. Mr Stopford: not known.
6. Mr Ewing: possibly Ewing who bought flax from Edward Synge. See Letter 133.

169

Elphin. September 20, 1751

And so, Madam, You comforted your self with the thought that you had no more faults than I discover'd and charg'd you with. You see you are mistaken. What happen'd with regard to a false Spelling, may have happen'd with regard to other matters. Great affection of one kind blinds. You remember Waller's pretty verses 'You have no faults, &c.'[1] But that of a Parent is often the reverse. Where they have sense, They are rather too exact and quick-sighted. This, I believe, is my case; and yet, Don't be sawcy, Madam. You may have other faults, which I have not yet noted, any more than I did that same false spelling. Find them out in your self, if you can, and Correct them. The more severe you are on your self, the less room you'll give others to be so. Did you ever read a little paper of your Grandfather's, call'd, *The Rule of Self-Examination.*[2] It is an excellent one for the purpose for which it is design'd. But some of the Advice may be usefull in the lesser matters of Conduct and behaviour. As you learn attention, You must learn to turn it upon your self; and not only observe your Actions, but the true Springs and motives of them. With respect to these We every day deceive the World, often our Selves.

We have had a week good Weather; from Sunday, very fine. But yesterday Evening it broke, and there was a good deal of rain last night. There has been some to day, not continu'd, nor so violent as to keep me within. But there's a full stop to drawing home Hay or Corn. My reek is but half made and one of my great Wheat-stacks is unfinish'd: Both in some measure Expos'd, till Sun-shine returns; but so secur'd as that they won't receive much damage. So that with regard to mine own affairs, I am easy: I am much more so than I was with respect to the Country in general. The last Week has made a vast change for the better. Unless there be a return of as bad Weather, as We have had, the Harvest will be tolerably well sav'd, and if it be, the year will be plentifull. God send.

On Wedensday I had my house full. The Judges came hither from Carrick, din'd, slept, and away next morning to Roscommon. Eyre Trench came with them. There were beside, Nicholson, Palmer, Blair, Dean Sandford and one or two more of my Clergy. All now gone, several ways. But Palmer will return this Evening from the Fair of Boyle.[3] Tell John that I'll get him to write to Wallace to buy for me. I am indeed greatly pleas'd, that that poor fellow is so near being quite well. It will be happy, if his long Confinement teaches him wit, and makes him more carefull of himself for the future. He should be possess'd with an Opinion, that A Relapse may be apprehended, and would be fatal.

I think I told you in my last, that the Wills's left me on Saturday. I had an account from him yesterday, that they got home well, and are so. He has taken some Physick, and is much better for it. Your Lines are very properly apply'd to them. Your letter did afford us great diversion.

No news of the Carr yet. But I know the Man to be a loiterer. I believe all is safe.

It is very well, that Trusty John took notice of the bad state of the roof, so early in the Season. The Slater is much to blame for not doing it himself.

Williamson's paper is nothing to the purpose. He either does not, or affects not to, understand mine. So I'll take my own way, and turn the Horse out.

The letter you sent was from Cork. It was only a Cover enclosing some Election Wit, very Simple. Don't be surpriz'd that my Correspondents direct as they do. I desire them always to do it. Unless you forget, Mistress, My letters come thus more securely to me, than if they were directed hither. Adieu. God bless you all. I am

Your &c
Edw: Elphin

I think you live with Mrs Silver.

In your late letters you scarce ever mention your Uncle &c.

Some Gentlemen who saw Mr Leigh's fine Setter here the other day, said positively He was a dog of a bad kind, not through bred, whom therefore no discipline would make good. This mortifys me more than the rest. Either Mr Leigh must have been very indifferent what sort of Dog He gave me, or much abus'd by that Fellow. I hope the latter was the Case. You may speak of this last discovery to Madam Judy, if a Natural occasion falls in your way.

Nicholson left me on Thursday morning for Castelrea. I believe they'll be in town before this is.

As I am writing, the Carriage is come in.

You mention'd Barton for some flower-roots. He shall have some next Season. But I'll plant all here, lest I give what I would choose to keep. By the Wills's account That poor Man is very unhappy in his marriage. And indeed the Appearances are much so. She is peevish and uneasy beyond measure; and has of late violent Hystericks into the bargain. The effects of both shew'd themselves lately. He was here when the Wills's were. He came on Monday, and propos'd staying till Saturday. But on Wedensday morning came a Messenger with a letter from the Doctor of that quarter, to let him know, that she was extremely ill; and to desire him to return instantly, and, if he could, to bring your friend Dignan, with him: Off he went poor Man before diner in one of our Worst days. His speech to them at parting, was Ah! I hop'd to have spent one pleasant Week. When He got home, only a strong hysterick fit, worse from some Physick before taken, on which they rally'd poor Barton, as if He expected a riddance and was disappointed. But she was in no dangerous way. Luckily Dignan was not in the Way. So He sav'd that expense, tho' He lost his diner, and was wet. I find by Mrs Wills, that this is a trick of hers. They are very fond of him at Wills-grove; and He has more comfort there, than any where else. Very Seldom He goes there except to dine. If He propose staying three or four days, A Messenger usually come the second with an Alarm of ilness &c. This is very bad. I am sorry for it. So will you. Mr W. is greatly provok'd at her. He does not speak of her with patience.

The day after you receive this, Lennox and French will send you their receit for £70. Lay it up with the rest.

Saunders tells me that most of the roots are Narcissus and Crocus: Very few Tulips. This is a baulk. But you could send only such as you had. It seems We had both White and Orange Lillys before. You told me, I think, that you had sent twelve of the latter. There came but ten.

Desire John to let Mr Wallace know what number of Beasts He can provide well for on his after-grass.

[Free Edw:Elphin]

1. Edmund Waller (1606-87). The verses have not been traced.
2. Edward Synge, *The Rule of Self-examination; or The only way of banishing doubts and scruples* (London 1715).
3. Boyle Fair was on Friday 20 September 1751. Watson (1751), p.101.

170

Elphin. September 24, 1751

My Dear Girl.

If your description be not too strong: our Weather on Friday and Saturday last was better than yours. The morning of Friday was wet, but not so as to hinder any Work, but drawing hay and corn. Saturday was a tolerable day. Sunday morning very fine. But rain came on, tho' not much. Yesterday was fair. All that remain'd abroad of my Corn was brought home, and is safe made up. This has been a moist day hitherto; a drop now and then of rain, but not enough to stop drawing home hay. I choose to draw at some hazard, and a little loss in dirt, rather than let it lye longer abroad, it may be, for worse Weather.

This is a fine traveling day for your Uncle &c. I long to hear of their being safe in their Winter Quarters. Faulkner's mistake was natural. He is however too careless in such matters.[1] The Bishop of Kilalla has been ill, but was better. So said my intelligence last week.[2] It was by chance I had any. For He is at a great distance,[3] and I never enquire about him. Upon the arrival of a Lord Lieutenant two or three Bishops must be kill'd at least in news-papers.[4] You spell Kilalla wrong. The last should be a double l.

I must repeat what I said in my last. I think you live with Mrs Silver. Her friendship to you is remarkably great. But Tell her with my best respects, that it is very hard she will not suffer persons so much oblig'd to make even Acknowlegment.

I am sorry your little Sailor does not like his trade. It is the fittest that could have been chosen for him. I hope He'll relish it in time.[5]

I believe business brings Mrs Pomeroy's sister over. If I mistake not, they are on a division of the Estate.[6]

You have done very right with the Laurus-tinus; So it should be spelt. What remain will stop gaps, if any dye. When All is safe there, I may perhaps bring a few down here. As for your Myrtles, if you can teach them to bear the Winter, they may be pretty. But I fear you won't.

You have interlin'd a Word toward the Close of your letter, for which there was no occasion. At first you had wrote thus. *Your whole family here are pleas'd,* and afterwards you interlin'd *all.* This was quite unnecessary, and borders on Tautology.

When Palmer was here the other day He gave me an account of Miss Gore's marriage with Mr Harman, and the Consequences.[7] Nothing extraordinary except the behaviour to Mrs Watson.[8] Mr H. made her a present of £50. took his Wife in a Week to his Mother's, and left her with the Judge,[9] who it is thought will get rid of her on his going to town. If I thought that your indignation would not rise very high on this account of such unworthy treatment of a Gentlewoman, who had behav'd her self so very well, in so important a trust, I should have a Worse opinion of you than I have. Say nothing of this abroad. They deserve infamy; and will have it, but not from you. God bless you all. I am

Your &c
Edw: Elphin

The night seems to be set for rain: Send Will. to Smith the Wheelwright to know, whether six Looms long since bespoke for Mr Wills be ready. I thought I had wrote to you about them before.

[Free Edw:Elphin]

1. 'By private Letters from the Country we hear, that the Right Reverend the Lord Bishop of Killaloe, and the Right Reverend the Lord Bishop of Limerick are dangerously ill.' In the same issue of *Faulkner's*, the arrival of the duke of Dorset and his entourage is reported. False reports on the deaths of bishops were indeed common. In 1725, Primate Boulter wrote of the Bishop of Cork that 'there have been reports, though false, that he was dead.' *Faulkner's Dublin Journal* 17-21 September 1751; Boulter to the duke of Newcastle 10 January 1728/9 *Letters*, p.278.

2. Mordecai Cary died on 2 October 1751. *NHI*, Vol. 9, p.437.

3. Killala, Co. Mayo, is on the far side of the Slieve Gamph mountains and over fifty miles from Elphin.

4. The Duke of Dorset was sworn in as Lord Lieutenant on 19 September 1751. Lionel Sackville (1688-1765) first duke of Dorset succeeded his father as earl of Dorset in 1706 and was created duke of Dorset in 1720. He was first appointed Lord Lieutenant of Ireland in 1730 and remained until 1737. In 1750 he was reappointed. During his second viceroyalty, he was said to have been in the hands of two men: his son, Lord George Sackville, who acted as his first secretary and the Primate, Archbishop Stone. Their dominance led to the creation of an opposition in the Irish parliament and the money bill crisis of late 1751, which was renewed in 1753. In 1755 Dorset was told that he was to be removed from Ireland; Horace Walpole said that 'he bore the notification ill'. *DNB*.

5. Obscure.

6. Mrs Pomeroy was a daughter of Edmond Donnellan and grand-daughter of Mrs Percival, who had died in August. She and her sister – who may have lived in England – would have had an interest in her estate.

7. The Very Rev. Cutts Harman (*c.*1706-84): dean of Waterford, married Bridget, daughter of George Gore of Tenelick, Co. Longford. *Dublin Courant*, 23-27 July 1751; Burke (1912), p.297.

8. Mrs Watson: not known.

9. George Gore, son of Sir Arthur Gore of Newtown, Co. Mayo and Eleanor St George of Carrickdrumrusk, Co. Leitrim. He attended Shrewsbury School and matriculated from Dublin University in 1691. Admitted to the Middle Temple in 1693, he was called to the Irish Bar in 1700. He married Bridget Sankey of Terelick, Co. Longford, in 1703 and became MP for Co. Longford in 1709. He was attorney general in 1714 and Justice of the Common Pleas in 1720. He lived in Oxmantown. Ball, Vol.2, pp.194-5.

171

Elphin. September 27, 1751

My Dear Girl.

You already know that our thoughts were, last Tuesday, employ'd on the same Object, but in a different way. If your Uncle had our Weather, He had no reason to complain nor you to be sorry. But All that is now over, I hope, and He and his Caravan safe and well at the Green.

Whatever advantage, We have of late had over you in point of

Weather, I am sure you could not have worse than We have had this afternoon. The morning promis'd well, held up till after twelve. From thence heavy rain. One consequence of it has been, Capt King's[1] being detain'd here, who came to dine. Will. French came too: his first Visit since his return from the North. Swell'd gums have kept him from me. These two interrupted me just as I was going to write in the morning. I have but a minute now at night to write in.

Your news shocks me. The young Man's folly in persisting is great. But I can't find terms strong enough to express my detestation of the behaviour of the parents to sacrifice a Child to Convenience and County interests.[2]

I don't wonder that Severe discipline and long confinement have alter'd poor John. Recommend him strongly to the Doctor's care, to guard, as well as you can, against his own rashness.

Your letter is wrote with Care, tho' you have made some interlineations. By more calmness and attention, I hope you'll learn entirely to avoid them. I see in your first page but one material mistake in stopping a . instead of a :. *I am sensible the advice you give me, of being severe on my self, is excellent. but shall still trust &c.* Remember my rule. Does the sense end at *excellent?* So far otherwise that the I which begins the Sentence is the Nominative case to *shall.*

I wrote agen last post about Mr Wills's Looms. I thought you had forgot them. Perhaps I miscomputed the time when I wrote before. I fancy'd I might have had an Answer before yesterday. I am glad they are ready. I have time for no more. God bless you all.

Your &c
Edw: Elphin

It's hard if you can't find room for a few Turn-Crowns.[3] If you wish'd them here, Why did you not send them? Trouble your self no more about the Dog, unless a fair occasion falls in your way.

[Free Edw:Elphin]

1. Captain King may have been John King, brother of Gilbert King of Charlestown.
2. Edward Synge shared Francis Hutcheson's distaste for marriages openly engaged in for money and position. Hutcheson, on his marriage to Mary Wilson in Dublin, showed 'the same liberal and generous principles in this transaction, which appeared in all the other steps of his life. He had an abhorrence of that spirit of traffic which often mingles so deeply in forming this alliance: he was determined solely by the good sense, lovely dispositions and virtuous accomplishments of the lady.' Preface *A System of Moral Philosophy*, pp.xlii-xliii.
3. Turn-crowns: not known.

172

Elphin. October 1, 1751

My Dear Girl.

I am very glad your Uncle &c. are safe in town. His swell'd face will, I hope, be soon over. Your grand disappointment was easily made up, since Will's grave forbidding, did not prevent your being together. You'll have a greater this minute, or I am mistaken; and yet if a worse never happen to you, You'll be happy beyond the usual fate of Mortals.

Your Uncle writes, that D. Lawson told him, I propos'd, either to leave this, or be in town the 18th. I suppose He has told you the same. If He has, I know you too well, to doubt of your being much mortify'd at my informing you; that the Gent. had no authority from me for this, and that my present intention is to remain here ten days longer at least. You know I never fix absolutely, till near the time. But my present scheme is to leave this on Monday the 28th and dine with you on the birth-day:[1] So that when other Damsels are shewing themselves and finery at Court, You'll be otherwise employ'd, more, I really believe, to your Satisfaction. Tom. Mahon says he'll go with me. He is a little uncertain always in his motions. I hope he will; tho' traveling alone is not to me disagreable. Mrs Mahon is in a way I do not like. She has had an Ugly cold on her these six Weeks. It's near a month since I saw her. She then said it was better. But by accounts since, it sticks still, and a letter from him yesterday, describes it as heavy. This, and it's long continuance make me fear consequences to one of her delicate frame. I hope no bad ones will follow. For she is indeed a very good Woman.

The mention of Birth-day finery brings your friend Grogan to my mind. Is he arriv'd? I suppose not, because you say nothing of your Velvet. If He comes not soon, He'll be too late for Vanity-fair.[2] I count there will be great scrambling for first choice at his Arrival; and As I suppose you, and Jeny intend, I think indeed you ought, to enlarge your Ward-robe, so, since I purpose to stay so long here, I would have you chuse for your selves, and not wait for my fancy. You, I know, are fond of it. But it's better follow your own, assisted by your friends on the Spot, than take up with Culls. I speak in the Stile of a Farmer. Culls are what remain of Sheep or Cattel, the best taken out. You know my taste. Cloths not gawdy, and rather Elegant than rich. Yet if a Sprig of Gold or Silver be the mode, I limit you not. I would have you singular in nothing but goodness. Get your money both of you from Ned Curtis whenever you please. He'll furnish mine to pay for your Velvet.

Our weather, I see, differs from yours. But the quantity of bad is nearly Equal. The days which, you say, were tolerable with you, were bad here. Rain began about one on Friday, and there fell much more that afternoon and night, than in Equal time this whole Season. Saturday too was wet, but not so as to hinder some Works. Sunday was fair, Yesterday a better day, and last night so fine, that I began to hope We should have setled good Weather. But the Sun rose red this morning,[3] and the Wind high. Tho' fair now at noon I fear rain. However I comfort my self with the prospect of better. If the Proverb be right, Long foul, Long fair. There will be a fine October; and I, unless my usual good luck fails, shall have good Weather for my journey. But you know that I am well provided against bad. Therefore be in no pain about me. I bless God, I am very well.

You and Mrs Jourdan write so about John, that I know not what judgment to make even of his present Condition, further than this that He is not yet well. Tell the Doctor he'll oblige me much, if when He has leisure, He'll give me an account of it. I have no distinct conception of his danger, or the prospect there is of a perfect cure. I beg he may be kept under all necessary restrictions, as long as there is the least occasion for them. You tell me my letter afflicted him. What am I to do then? Will he, by his fretting, deprive me of the benefit I might have from his directing, till He is able to execute? You must among you argue him out of this folly. I shall have many things to give orders about before I leave this.

Mrs Nicholson's staying in the Country, I knew not of, till yours mention'd it. Nor am I, from any intelligence here certain, whether she be still at Castelrea or not. Mrs Cary knows as little as I. She has accounts both ways. If she be there, or staid after her husband, It is not owing to the Cause you mention, but to the breaking of her Chariot, presently after her setting out. That she and He were overturn'd, is certain, no hurt to her, little to him: and One Man from Castelrea said that He left her behind to go up with Mrs Preston:[4] Another that the Chariot being mended, they both went off together. What wonder if there be false accounts of things at a great distance, when We can't depend on what We hear about a person just under our Noses. With respect to Mrs W. about whom too you have so different accounts, I wish Mrs C's may be true but believe the other is. Mr P. is not apt to say things lightly. He added, that He believ'd Mrs W. would soon dye. She was breaking her heart. The neglect and ingratitude are ascrib'd to the pupil. You are a little mistaken about the Old Man. He has odditys enough. But stinginess in the Common Sense of the Word is not his Vice. He spends all his income, and a very large one it is; and therefore cares not to Spare any part of it where He ought. This is an immoral cast. But the proper name of it is Selfishness.[5]

Your letter is well stopp'd for the most part. Some less errors I pass by. There are two which deserve notice. *I wrote a neat bill of fare: next, came the market bill.* So you stop. There ought to be a . at fare. The Sense concludes there. The other is this. *As he is sometimes, rather glad, of an Excuse* &c. Thus you. It ought to be thus. *As he is sometimes, rather glad of, an Excuse* &c. There are two faults here, which I at first call'd one, and both very gross ones. If my rules had been present to your mind, you could not have been guilty of them. You might have wrote as far as *of* without any stop at all, But as you put one after *sometimes* there ought to have been one before it. I am sure I pointed out to you this particular case. So I did the other, the , between *glad* and *of* is as absurd, as if you had put one between *My* and *Father*. No necessity for one after *of*.

Enclos'd is a Memorandum of Mrs Heap's. I send it thus early, to discharge my self of further care about it. Let it be yours to have all things ready in due time for the Carrs which are to come for luggage. She complains most heavily of the Brown Sugar that came down for the Bacon last Season: More than half, she affirms, was perfect dirt, great Lumps as big as her fist. Sican[6] ought to know this, and Care must be taken for the future. Coarse Sugar is good enough for that purpose, But it ought to be clean. You remember the receit you got from Will. French for Hams: Canton Hams[7] he call'd them. Find it, and send with these a small parcel of what other ingredients you find are requir'd to make them. Let Jac. also copy the receit and send it down. I'll have three or four made this Season.

You talk of fine Veal. I wish I could send you a quarter. I have seldom tasted such as the last kill'd. Indeed All I have had this Summer has been excellent. Such are the effects of proper Conveniencys, and Cleanliness. I have two still for the time I have to stay; so that you must find something else to treat me with. I expect not so good in town. You know by this time, whether I am to expect as good bread. I doubt not.

Tell John that Mr Palmer could not get any Sheep for him at B-nasloe.[8] He hopes to pick up proper ones at some of the later fairs. He shall have notice in time. Ask him how 'Darraci' the Coach-horse is?

No room left on the other side to tell you that I am

Your &c
Edw: Elphin

I had like to have forgot. Let the Lees be given to Tighe. He or Sullivane supply me with what I want.

I must brag a little more. I have as fine fowl here, as ever I saw in Dublin.

As I fear'd, a Wet afternoon.

[Free Edw:Elphin]

1. George II was born on 30 October 1683.

2. Vanity-fair: the Dublin winter season began in November and lasted until March, when it was followed by a short 'afterseason' in late April and May. Tighearnan Mooney and Fiona White, 'The Gentry's Winter Season' in David Dickson (ed.), *The Gorgeous Mask: Dublin 1700-1850* (Dublin 1987), pp.1-2.

3. 'Red sky in the morning, shepherd's warning.' An augury of bad weather.

4. Mrs Preston: not known.

5. Obscure.

6. John Sican, grocer, Essex Street. Watson (1752), p.23.

7. The recipe for 'Canton hams' may have been from Switzerland.

8. Ballinasloe Fair was held from Tuesday 24 to Friday 28 September 1751. Watson (1751), p.101.

173

Elphin. October 4, 1751

My Dear Girl.

I take large paper too, tho' at setting out I have not much in view to fill it.

Tho' yours be not so well written as some of your late ones, Yet it is far from deserving the hard censure you give it. But your Excuse about ink is very bad. Had Ned Curtis none? Or Don't you, at this time of day, know that a little Water thins ink without less'ning it's blackness?

I am glad Jac. Davies is mending. But part of his Excuse for his folly is a lye; Or the Apothecary of the Hospital lyes.[1] For the Doctor's account to me was that the Apothecary had appriz'd of him of this Countermand, and He refus'd to obey. This made me so angry; and still, for Example's sake, I am unwilling to order him any support. You may give him some. Perhaps I may pay you. If He recovers, I'll take him in, in some shape or other, or recommend him.

When next you go that way, call at Lamprey's,[2] and tell him I never knew that He dealt constantly in Lisbon wine,[3] but thought He had only a parcel once occasionally. Desire him to lay by a choice hogshead for me. If I like it on tasting I'll have it. But say, that It is too much to raise the price of that, as well as of his Candles I paid for the last but £13.

I find by Mrs J's that you counted on my being in town, next Saturday. I am sorry you did, because it's a baulk. But your hopes were in appearance founded, because these two or three last times, I have gone to town just before the opening of the Parliament. But upon recollection you'll find that was not always my Custom; and I have as little reason now to make haste as ever.[4] Except the great pleasure of seeing you all, and a few private friends, I have no joy at all in the thought of returning to town.

All that I shall say to Mrs J. about her pets the hogs, is, that Provided they be the finest that ever were seen, I shall not *jouer*[5] at the expense of feeding. If Parsnips will make and keep them so, till I get to you, I should chuse them both for the Experiment, and for cheapness.

Take care among you that John does not plague me or himself with long Explanations and Apologys about Hay. The single point in which I desire exact information is what Quantity of Old and New I have left, that I may take my measures accordingly. In one point He is certainly mistaken. I order'd but five Load for Mr D[onnellan] and did not know certainly that He had six, till now. It's true he ask'd for that Number; and so I told you. But positively I order'd but five. Don't add to John's affliction by telling him this.

I am sorry Ned Curtis has teaz'd his friend about the Hoc. He told me before I left you that He made difficultys. But I understood that He had got the better of them. Since he has not, I desire He would urge him no more.

I believe Mrs J's account of Mrs Cary's condition is true. But I know nothing. I once ask'd him. His answer was mysterious. So I leave them to their own way. How matters will go with *le bel esprit*[6] I know not. But He is in a right way. His Father has given him a Farm stock'd; and He seems to take very kindly to it, goes to Fairs &c. as diligently as the best.

My fears about Mrs Mahon had some foundation. I had an account from her yesterday, that She had been blooded, and taken Physick, and was better. He too has not been well, but says He is.

Mention was made here the other day by some one, Who I can't recollect, of one Williams a famous Operator for Teeth. The account given of his method appear'd to me very reasonable. He's against brushes, and the Use of any thing hard or gritty; recommends a spunge, and a linctus which cleans with a kind of lather, without fretting gums.[7] It may be worth while to get Ned Curtis to enquire about him.

Weather still unpleasant, tho' not down-right bad. Last night and that before very fine. The mornings cloudy and threat'ning. Yesterday was soft and pleasant. This windy. But every day almost, I get my ride, and am I bless God very well. The long evenings do not lye on my hands. The Carys and Conrys furnish a little party at Whist, when I please, and some one or other is usually with me. Blair is at present, and will be next Week. Will French has promis'd too. Did I tell you the misfortune that befel him in his way home? He had a violent Tooth ach, and sent for a famous Operator to draw. Unluckily there are two of that profession in the same town. One skilfull, the other a Botch; and this last his Servant by mistake, or not well directed, apply'd to, much to his master's hurt. For the fellow first pull'd out a sound tooth instead of the diseas'd one; and then in attempting to pull this out too, tore his jaw from his cheek. The Consequence was great pain and swelling not yet perfectly remov'd. He came hither this day se'night, was caught in bad Weather, and oblig'd to return in the same on Saturday. But by an account from him since, He escap'd without new cold. Mrs French is purely; and Nancy ready to tumble, not well recover'd from a Fever.

Considering how I set out, I think I have done pretty well. Adieu. God bless you all.

Your &c
Edw: Elphin

Make Jac. superscribe the Enclos'd to Dr Lawson and send it in the morning to the College. You are amus'd probably at my enclosing so many to Dr K – to you – I had no mind that our correspondence should be observ'd. The same reason now.[8] Desire John to bespeak from Bagshaw half a stone, or a Stone of Plow-line. It is like Sash Cord. The use is for reins for the horses in the little plows, when one Man holds and drives.

[Free Edw:Elphin]

1. Edward Croker was the apothecary at Mercer's Hospital. Watson (1755), p.68.

2. Arthur Lamprey, wax-chandler and wine merchant, Big-Ship Street. Watson (1752), p.16.

3. Lisbon wine was probably port, which was imported in large quantities to Britain in the eighteenth century after the signing of the Treaty of Methuen with Portugal in 1703.

4. Parliament resumed in 1751 on 8 October. *NHI*, Vol. 9, p.606.

5. *Jouer*: Mock at.

6. *Le bel esprit*: the young spark. Possibly referring to young William Cary, Oliver Cary's son.

7. Toothbrushes made of horsehair and linen, were in use in the early eighteenth century. Pierre Fauchard, in *Le Chirurgien Dentiste ou Traité des Dents* (Paris 1733), recommended the use of a sponge wetted with water, fortified with a drop of aqua vitae. He also prescribed a paste made from sarsaparilla, aristolochia rotunda, orange and lemon rinds, cloves and mustard and wild rocket seeds, mixed with sugar, honey and spirits of wine, cooked in a retort and combined with various gums. Fauchard believed that lack of care in cleaning teeth was the usual cause of decay. Vincenzo Guerini, *A History of Dentistry* (Philadelphia 1909), pp.266-7.

8. Obscure.

174

Elphin. October 8, 1751

You already know, my Dear Girl, that I accounted for your baulk in the manner you do you Self. If I had thought of it in time, I would have prevented it, by letting you know my intentions.

I hold my purpose of setting out at the time mention'd in my former letter; and have this day wrote to John full directions about sending down the Carrs. See that He goes quietly about observing them. You'll send down by them Mrs Heap's things, and whatever else has been wrote for; and Send beside 2 Bottles of Sallad-Oyl. It need not be nice tho' of that kind. It is for Oyling Chairs and tables. Send ingredients for no more than two Canton Hams. They'll be enough to make an Experiment; and Carleboe shall try his hand too with one of Mrs J.'s pets.

As for you, and your friend Grogan, since you have a mind that things should lye till I get to you, Be it so. He is obliging indeed, if he reserves the silks you've laid by. But I doubt he will not, if others fancy them. I believe however you'll have choice enough left.

I am glad you've seen Mrs Ormsby, and that she looks so well. I intended last post to have told you she was gone to town, but forgot it. I find there has been great harmony among them all this Summer. It pleases me much.

I am sorry you have any reverse in Bread. See and retrieve it, if you can. For I have no better hopes of Carleboe than last year; and I am grown fonder of bread than ever. A piece is always my Supper when alone.

I had a letter yesterday from your Uncle, in which He expresses his apprehensions of the hurry of this day. I hope he'll get no hurt by it. I am clear, and hugg my Self at being so. My joy would be higher if the Weather were better. But for some time past that has been rather disagreable than bad. I never miss my ride. If the day be as good with you as here, the D[uke of Dorset] is well off for his shew.[1]

Poor Shannon is in great distress. His wife has wrote, it seems, that Bob and the little Girl are very ill; and that the Doctor said the latter would not live. I hope things are not so bad, as you mention them not. I discover'd by his countenance that something was amiss. I fancy you have left out a not in one Sentence. You say; *Shannon knows He did buy the brown Sugar from Sican last year.* I spoke to him about it, but He remembers nothing distinctly.

Send to Woodward to know whether the Servants Cloaths be ready and give him only a Week's time to get them so, if not already made. I shall want them the minute I get to you: For all my tribe here are ragged enough.

Since the Cold Weather came in, I suspect a tendency in one or two fingers towards, chopping,² as you remember some did last winter. It is yet but a trifle. I would willingly keep it so. Ask the learn'd what I shall do. I wear thin wash-leather gloves constantly. Warmth, I fancy, is good for them. I was advis'd to bath in warm Brandy and milk. But I love not tampering; and indeed there is scarce any thing to tamper with. But I would prevent, and have a remedy ready, if there should be occasion. In every other respect, I bless God, I am as well as ever, and hope to be so at our meeting, and to have the great pleasure to find you, My Dearest, and the rest of you so. According to custom. Now I have fix'd my time I shall grow impatient. Adieu. God bless you all. I am

Your &c
Edw: Elphin

[Free Edw:Elphin]

1. The duke of Dorset was sworn in at Dublin Castle as Lord Lieutenant of Ireland on 8 October 1751.
2. A chop. A fissure or crack in the skin.

175

Elphin. October 11, 1751

Nearer meeting, my Dear Girl. Shorter letters. However I begin on a sheet. I can't tell what may happen.

Your letter shews it was wrote in a hurry. I therefore remark not on the faults in stopping, which are pretty numerous. I am sorry you were disappointed; and so I am sure was the D[uke of Dorset]. But it will be repair'd to you both the next shew day. Your curiosity was extremely natural. Why should you not indulge it?

The account you give of Jac. Davies lessens his fault somewhat, but does not remove it. I'll determine about him when I get to town. You see, it was not my fault that I was mistaken.

You know me to be strict and Severe with regard to the Conduct of Servants. This is not the effect of temper, but prudence. Harshness, irksome to my self, I find necessary to keep them in order. Oft'ner, even this won't do. As little will gentle admonitions. I have try'd both with Beaty,[1] I fear, to little purpose. He is at present in great disgrace; and I have told him I'll dismiss him. I am not so resolv'd on this, but that I'll admit of your intercession, if he applys for it. But stop the making his Clothes, if it be not too late. I would have no hope left him in appearance.

I am very sorry for the ilness of Shannon's Children. I hope next post will bring a better account. The distress of the poor fellow moves me greatly.

It is impossible for me to recollect the Wine; and the odds is that it was of a parcel all drank out. But if it has caught hold of poor Rachy's[2] imagination, She must not be told that it is. On the Contrary, It will be a bit of innocent fraud, to tell her, as I desire you would from me, that the Wine you give her is the very Wine she wishes for; and there is some chance that it is so. Take out of the furthest Bin inward of the left hand, and give her as much as she pleases. But let it be rack'd nicely at the Bin-head. If the bottle be not quite full, Let her know the reason. Better this than spoil a Second to fill up. If she thirsts for Gallons, Let her have them. Unless it be chang'd since I left town, It is the best in my Cellar, or, I believe, any where else. If this does not hit, Give her from the Bin next the door on the left hand. These with what you drink are the only kinds of Claret I had.

I believe Mrs P. advises you very right about your Teeth. The difficulty will be to find a safe and skilfull person. I have no opinion of Steel,[3] but hope you'll have a good account of Williams. Him or any one else more approv'd of you may employ. But let nothing be done that the Doctor and Ned do not consent to. I know by sad experience of what consequence it is to preserve Teeth, and without some such method be taken, I fear yours will decay as your good Mothers did and mine have done.

I am much rejoic'd at your friend Kitty's escape. The mention of her brings to my thoughts Nancy Donnelan.[4] If she be at Delville,[5] I think it would be right in you to make her a morning visit. Will it not be right too to Mrs D[elany]?

Our Weather has been good since Tuesday. This is a very fine day. Please God it continues, the distress of the Country will be greatly reliev'd. I shall enjoy my self while I stay, and have a pleasant journey. Be in no pain about my wanting company. I have and shall have enough. God send us an happy meeting. I am, My Dear Girl,

Your &c
Edw: Elphin

Your account of the Archbishop of Tuam[6] does not surprize. It is what I expected.

I thank you for the Speech.[7] But the Clerk sent one. I had a third from the C[hancello]r. The Paper you enclos'd is not Burlesque, but Grub-street.

[Free Edw:Elphin]

1. Billy Beaty.

2. Rachel Curtis.

3. Samuel Steel: a dentist. 'Samuel Steel Surgeon and Operator for the teeth, living on Ormonde Key opposite the Custom House Dublin, whose experience in drawing teeth is very well known.' *Dublin Weekly Journal,* 12 March 1726, quoted Fagan (1986), p.97.

4. Anne Donnellan (*c.*1700-62): daughter of Chief Baron Nehemiah Donnellan and Martha Ussher. She was a close friend of Mary Delany and is an important figure in her letters. Her beautiful singing voice gave her the nickname 'Philomel' or 'Phill'.

5. Delville, Glasnevin, Co. Dublin. The seat of Dr Patrick Delany, dean of Down. He and his wife, Mary Delany, landscaped the garden and she decorated a grotto and temple. Built in the early eighteenth century, the house was demolished in the 1950s. Bence-Jones, p.101.

6. Dr Josiah Hort.

7. Possibly the speech from the throne on the opening of parliament at the beginning of October.

176

Elphin. October 15, 1751

My Dear Girl

I believe impatience is the fashion with the fine folks of both sexes; some for the day; Others possibly for the arrival of their Clothes, if any they expect. This was the D's case on his shew-day. If any should, like him, be disappointed, Would not you laugh?

Mrs Cary read me yesterday a letter from her Sister giving an account of the profusion of finery. It has made me nauseate, Gold, Silver, *Point d'Espagne* &c more than I did. By her account the richest dress'd Lady there will not be the handsomest. This Palm she gives to Miss F. What folly to pay so much for making ugliness conspicuous! The day that they are all displaying their charms and finery, I hope to be happy my self and make you so. God send us an happy meeting. Tell Jane I thank her for her letter, and will answer it in person.

Mr Mahon still says he'll go with me. I doubt, both on account of his own uncertainty of temper in such things; and which troubles me more, good Mrs Mahon's being not yet well. He was here on Saturday, and said she was better. But she had been bled a Second time and continu'd hoarse. This does not well agree with his account. I intend to see her to morrow, if the Weather stands, but will return before diner. If He travels with me, I must ask him to dine. I believe He will but had rather He did not that day, that We may prattle by our Selves. No rout about him. Some fish, if the pomp of that day leaves any for poor folks, and mutton, is all I desire. Make John kill one of his, the Friday before; and Eat what you please of it your Selves. Tell him I fear a letter to Mr Palmer to send fewer sheep, will be too late; so that He must e'en take his hazard, with the Number that goes. The morning that I propose being in town, you had best send for the plate to Mr Lennox's. The day before would be better, as free from hurry; and you need not now fear robbers. But if this should give any of you the least uneasiness; and that be at all inconvenient, Let it alone, till I get to you. The receit for my Chest is in the Scriptoire. That should be sent. I mention these things now, as they come into my head, and I have leisure. Next post I may probably be hurry'd.

The mention of Robbers brings poor Gallagher to my thoughts. Here he is and, for ought I see, here like to remain. I dare not carry him to town, nor encourage him to go. Have you ever seen his Wife? What sort of a creature is she? If good for any thing, or like the Man, harmless, I think the best way would be to setle them here. I shall do nothing till We meet. But give me your thoughts of the Woman. For I must say something to the poor fellow at parting. I am pleas'd with your card to Dr Pullein.[2]

The poor Archbiship of T. is in such a Condition, that I really think it would be better for his Family as well as himself, that it pleas'd God to release him from his misery. No hope of recovery; and the dutifull affectionate Care of his daughters, tho' it puts them in an amiable light, will affect their health.

I am very glad that Shannon's Children are better. It was very wrong in his Wife, to give a worse account of them, than she had Authority for. The distress of the poor fellow mov'd me much. He is now very happy.

Thank the Doctor for his letter. Part of his prescriptions, Bran and Water, and Warmth, I had us'd, before I got it, and found benefit. My Fingers are much better. Indeed they were never bad. No Crack, but a little swoln, one of them. It is now almost well. Perhaps the Tar-Water[3] will make it quite so. By the part of it relating to John, I see that I had a right notion of his Case. But your and Mrs J's speaking of him as having been in danger puzzled me.

If the Carrs are not gone, when you get this, Desire John to stay them till Saturday, if by that time He can get a Keg of Coarse Colours fit for painting field-Gates and such things, to send by them. I believe and hope Mr Eaton, if apply'd to, will presently provide them. I care not about

Colour or fineness. He knows what is fit. Let him send a midling Kegg. But let not the Carrs wait longer for it than Saturday. If they are clear of town, that night, they'll be here time Enough. Mr Lennox sent the receit by my order. I forgot to mention it to you.

Your petition is granted, Madam. But have a care that a larger Table, does not crowd the place, tho' it may shew your plate to more advantage. I fear it will. But do as you please. I am

My Dear Girl
Your &c
Edw: Elphin

Mr Mead[4] will keep till I get to town. Mr Heap has set about spinning, to make coarse linnen for here and there.

If your Servants are so ragged, you may give them their new Frocks, and Waistcoats in honour of the Birth-day, and my return.

[Free Edw:Elphin]

1. *Point d'espagne*: a form of lace.
2. Dr Pullein is possibly Samuel Pullein, son of Rev. William Pullein, the treasurer of Dromore. Born in Dromore, Samuel Pullein was admitted to TCD in 1729/30 and took BA in 1734; MA 1738. He was rector of Castleblakeney 1765-84 and rector of St Catherine's Dublin 1769-84. Leslie, Elphin p.119; *Alumni*, p.685.
3. Tar water was extremely popular as a specific for many ills.
4. Probably Thomas Mead, the linen draper. See Letter 39.

177

Elphin. October 18, 1751

This day, My Dear Girl, your beloved Father is sixty complete. I will not say with Jacob 'Few and Evil &c.'[1] No! My days have been many, and prosperous: prosperous in all points, except the grievous domestick afflictions, with which it pleas'd God to visit me. These have imbitter'd my other comforts, which without them had been such as fall to few Mens share in this World. But I have endeavour'd to make a right use of them; Time and reflexion have in some measure blunted their Edge: and, thanks be to God, I have you, my Dear, to gladden my Eyes and heart, and to be the staff of my declining years. Continue in the way, in which with exquisite pleasure I have seen you hitherto walk, and you'll be to me in the place of many sons. I cannot go higher. The loss of your good Mother nothing can compensate. But God's name be blessed in all things. I have the highest reason to bless him with thankfulness of heart, for his goodness from my youth up until now; nay! even for those afflictions, which I hope have been fatherly corrections, have taught me early to have a right sense of my self, and the frail condition of mortal men in this world; and brought me at last to a state of tranquillity, which I believe to be the happiest in this World. Every thing in it, but you, sits loose enough upon me; and while I enjoy the Comforts of life, I have a proper indifference about the Continuance of it. If I know my Self, I could part with it to morrow, without uneasiness, except for that, which you, and a few others would feel. I hope however that God will spare me for a few years; and the Appearances are fair enough. My health is as good as it has been these seven years; nor do I find the decay of my senses or facultys increase, as much as a few years ago I fear'd they would, or my relish for the innocent comforts and amusements in my power, one jot abated. In these Circumstances, and free, God be thanked, from any painfull distemper, I have a prospect of passing the remainder of life, whatever it be, with tolerable ease and satisfaction. But this must not hinder me from reflecting constantly, That 'The days of our years; are threescore years and ten' &c.[2] You, my Dear, ought to think of this too. I know your fondness for me. I cannot say, I wish it less. But I would have it such, as that you may think with as much ease of my leaving the World, as I do myself. I will not go on. I see the tears gush into your Eyes. Wipe them away; and Let this be your comfort and stay. God's mercy is over all his Works: You I and every thing in this World are under his over-ruling providence; and He has hitherto been to me so good and gracious; that Few persons of my age, have had more blessings, or are this day in a happier state both of mind and body, than I am. If you have any doubt of this, I hope to convince you next Wedensday se'night. God send us an happy meeting. The return to this is the last I shall, this Season, receive from you here. But write to me to Mr Palmer's. I have time for no more; and scarce any thing to say, if I had time.

Your &c
Edw: Elphin
Young's little boy will answer for himself. I bring him with me.

[Free Edw:Elphin]

1. And Jacob said unto Pharoah The days of the years of my pilgrimage are an hundred and thirty years: few and evil have the days of the years of my life been and have not attained unto the days of the years of my fathers, in the days of their pilgrimage. Genesis, 47:9.

2. The days of our age are threescore years and ten; and though men be so strong that they come to fourscore years: yet is their strength then but labour and sorrow; so soon passeth it away, and we are gone. Psalm 90:10.

178

Elphin. October 22, 1751

Well, My Dear Girl, in less than a Week now, I shall, God willing set out towards you. The time, as usual, will be long; yet I shall be fully employ'd.

I have a little Employment for you too, Madam. I find warmth a better remedy for my fingers than any other. So that I am come to wear Gloves. But the best kind I have not. See and get me a pair or two of knit Woolen ones. The Sailors use them much. You may hear of them in their quarter of the Town. Yarn I fancy are better than worsted. The softest and warmest are best. It comes into my mind, that Beaver gloves will be still better. Get a pair some where. They may be had at Berangers.[1]

I believe Mr Mahon will not go with me. As I suspected it from the beginning, it will be no baulk. Besides, tho' I like his Company well here, and at Strokes-town, I had rather be alone on my road. I love to be at entire liberty there. His excuse will be Mrs Mahon's cold, which continues.

If Miss C.[2] has such a mind to be acquainted with you, Why should you decline it? It is surprizing, that, Her manner being so perfectly the same with her Sister's, Your friend should like the one and not the other. You I suppose with more consistency will like both.

Our Weather stands. But I fear a change. It begins to drop, while I am writing. I hope it will not be much. But at worst I have been and shall be a gainer by the fine days We have had, not only as to the Enjoyment here, but as the roads will be good, tho' there should be a good deal of Wet, before I set out. Nothing but Snow can hurt. I hope there is no danger of it. That would stop me, and retard our mutual joy.

Blessing to Jane, and Service to Mrs J. with thanks for her letter. Tell her I'll answer it in person. But I must give her a Pat, for a false i.e. a careless, spelling. *Cloas.* Your Apology for writing this bout I'll take. But if I had time, I could give you a long list of false Stopping. Commas instead of . in half a Score places. But, so near meeting, I'll not complain of that or any thing else. I know you are in a flutter, till you see

Your &c
Edw: Elphin

A Cask of flow'r will be sent you by the Carrs, to begin the World with. If they come before us, See, that it be taken out, and air'd, so as to lye light. The same management with the Pears.

I enclose W. French's receit. You may have it ready for Carleboe. I made Shannon copy it.

I hope Mrs J.'s pleasant draft has had full effect every way.

[Free Edw:Elphin]

1. David Beranger had a coffee-house and shop on the west side of St Stephen's Green, where he sold snuff, wines, Hungary, Lavender and Orange flower water and 'Beaver Stockings caps and Gloves for Gentlemen and Ladies, and milled caps for Gentlemen.' *Georgian Society Records* Vol.2, p.103; *Faulkner's Dublin Journal* 14-17 September 1751.

2. Miss C.: not known.

1752

Edward Synge's house and garden, Kevin Street (detail from John Rocque's 'An exact survey of the city and suburbs of Dublin', 1756; the area is denoted in bold).

179

Glanmore. [May 19, 1752]

It is wrong, they say, to give a good child a bad use. But when once this is done, there's no drawing back, or changing: and indeed I am never dispos'd to omit any thing that may give my Dear, must I say, good? child, pleasure. I am sure it will to know if I am, God be praised, safe and well here: No accident on the road. I fear'd indeed this morning, if I should have had a very wet journey hither – But after waiting till half an hour past eight to no purpose for fair Weather, I told Will. French I would go and look for it, I did and found it in less than half an hour and kept it the whole way. My good fortune, you see, has not yet deserted me. Yesterday there was something amusing in the road. Till we came near Kilcock all finely wetted. From thence to near Clonarde,[1] All dust. Not a drop of rain the day before. As We advanced, the road very wet and for that reason very pleasant. When we came to Kinnegad we found it had rain'd hard the afternoon, but not a drop fell on us.

Mrs Palmer is in her Chair. Both she and her husband affirm she is as well as she can be. But she looks pale and languid. – I am in pain lest I incommode her, I have time for no more. God bless you, my Dearest, and you two Comrogues.

Wedensday past 3 very hungry,

Yours &c
Edw. Elphin

1. Clonard, Co. Meath.

180

Elphin. May 22, 1752

Here I am, my Dear girl, safe and well, I bless God. I got hither about two yesterday. We had rain on the road, but not enough to hurt either man or beast; nor had I the least accident on the road. The only disaster that befel any of us was that Philip was immoderately gall'd; and having now a large plaister of Diaculum[1] to his posteriors, he stradles, as if, to speak in Falstaffe's stile, He had Gyves on.[2] Every body else is well, and I hope will continue so.

I found all things here as usual; not much better or worse. I long now for fair Summer Weather. But tho' this day has been rough and showry, I have been on Horseback, and taken a view of almost every thing without doors. Tell your Uncle this, and that I expect he'll follow my Example. Otherwise I shall grudge him the black Horse. But bid Ned send for him when He gets to Roscrea.

Mrs Heap looks better than ever I saw her. Molly Fagan at least as well as last year. Jennet too is improv'd. But she is at this time very miserable. Some mischievous people of the Town have within these few days kill'd three of her Pea-hens, and yesterday a Pea-cock, whose tail she describes so magnificently as to make me think slightly of those at Finglas. I am vex'd at this, but know not how to help my self. There is but one way. Not to trouble my head more about them.

You know already that I was at Glanmore – I found it would have been great distress if I had passed them by; and I believe the pleasure of my going there was heighten'd by my offering my self for Godfather. All the Children were at home and All well. But the Eldest son is in my opinion the flower of the flock. I never saw a boy with a more ingenuous Countenance. I preferr him much to the Governour, tho' I would not venture to say so to Mrs Palmer. Nan is a fine girl, but her Eyes are still tender. There I got your letter, which is the rarest scrawl I ever got ever from you, but in other respects such as I shall be pleased to find all your letters. It brought to my mind that your Grandfather us'd often to say of me, that when I did things quickest I did them best. However, it is good to revise a little, and it is never good to hurry. Remember your Mistress. I join heartily in your prayer that We may pass the Summer happily, and meet in health at the end of it. God bless you and your friends. Love and Service at the Green.

Yours &c
Edw. Elphin

If Mr Sweetenham a Wine-Cooper[3] calls to look at the hogshead of Claret which I bought from Mr Newburgh,[4] Desire Mrs Jourdan to give him admittance. It is the inmost on the left hand. I think the only one. Those on the right are Sullivane's. His Cooper, I suppose, will call to examine them now and then. I would not have him touch Newburgh's, nor Newburgh's Cooper meddle with his. A very bad account of Bradley.[5] I resolve to pack him off. But what to do for a Man in his place, I know not. Bid John Enquire every where, and if he hears of any one, to carry him to Mr Vipond. I dare not trust his judgment.

1. This may be *diacodion*, a medicine or poultice prepared from the juice of poppies, *papaver somniferum.*

2. Falstaff: 'I'll not march through Coventry with them, that's flat: nay, and the villains march wide betwixt the legs, as if they had gyves on.' Henry IV, Part I, Act IV, Scene 2. Gyves are shackles.

3. Kilner Swettenham, wine cooper, Big Strand Street. Watson (1752), p.24.

4. Arthur Newburgh was Clerk to the Trustees of the Linen Manufacture. Watson (1752), p.53.

5. Mr Bradley: not known.

181

May 25, 1752

My Dear Girl,

You'll receive this from a poor Lad, the son of one of my labourers. As he was a sort of favourite you possibly remember him, Mathew Murtogh.[1] He has a strange swelling in his breast which Stafford says is dangerous. Commit him to the Care of our good friend the Doctor. I write this just to introduce him. You'll probably have more particulars in mine by post. I am

Your affectionate father
Edw:Elphin

1. Matthew Murtogh: labourer, lived in Elphin with his mother, wife and four children, one under fourteen and three over fourteen. Census, f.1.

182

Elphin. May 26, 1752 Monday morning

The day is bad, My dear Girl. Writing to you will be a relief from the gloom of it.[1] I bless God I am very well, but not so happy, as if the Sun shone. But I live in hopes. Better wet now than a fortnight hence when mowing will begin here. I feel the wet weather now more on my Brother's account than mine own. If it continues, It will be prudent in him to deferr setting out. I hope the hint I gave Mrs Jourdan last post will divert him or Ned from their thoughts of the black Horse. Circumstanced as I am it will be very inconvenient to me to part with him. If I do, I shall stand a fair chance of being on foot myself.

Mrs Cary is much out of order. The Cause, a cold got at a critical time. I tremble when I think of the incorrigible folly of Women in that point,

Oh! May I never suffer for yours. Let good sense be your guide in that as in every thing else, Her cold affects her Eyes principally, and, by her Husband's account, in a very unusual manner, much inflam'd and painful beyond measure. Bleeding and Physick have not reliev'd her. She intends to blister to night. Neither He nor she seem alarm'd. I am. Say nothing of this.

I am angry with Cudmore.[2] If Shannon tells truth I have reason, and I believe He does. Six weeks ago He bespoke from him a little account book, such as we use for the Marketing. He promised it from time to time, but never made it up. It might have been made as well in two days as in two hundred and Wise Shannon, because He got it not from him, came without one, tho' such are to be sold in every stationer's shop in Town – But We can do well enough without it. And this is the only forget I have yet discover'd. So that on the whole I am well off.

The day I came hither I was much surpris'd to find Mr Nicholson at Cary's. He din'd and went off but promise'd to return to morrow and stay Wedensday. The mention of him brings his wife to my Mind. I think I have observ'd of late a less disposition in you than formerly to keep up an intimacy with her; as I remember I once spoke to you about it. Is this so? and If, what does it proceed from? If from any suspicion of a change in her, All I have to say is, that Suspicions of this sort ought not to be easily indul'd. If you think her gay turn is rather increas'd; and that frequent intercourse between you is therefore less agreable on either side, I can't tell but you may be right; and sure I am that I would not have you in this conform your manners to hers. However, My Dear, coldness and indifference succeeding suddenly to intimacy and fondness without apparent reason argues fickleness which is no perfection. Avoid the imputation, and if you are to be less intimate, Let the change be gradual, and arise from her. Furnish no occasion for it – Perhaps there is no sort of occasion for my writing thus. Whether there be or not, It matters not much. You see by it how attentive I am to all your motions; and I have also an opportunity of repeating a most important rule of conduct formerly given. Be Civil and Courteous to all, But Avoid particular intimacys. It is often inconvenient to continue, or to drop them.

I have no doubt but that Mrs Jourdan did her part about the Wine. I hope it pleas'd at the Chancellor's. You may know from Bradock; and pray get from her the empty bottles.

Ned Curtis gave me so little of his company the day before I left town that I had not time to speak to him about Mr Oughton's[3] Wine; and other things drove it out of my head, so as that I said nothing to you or Mrs Jourdan – Pray Tell him, or rather his Wife, that I desire 5 dozen or a quarter of a hogshead. But I think it ought in this way to come cheaper than by the galon. Twenty shillings a doz. I really think enough. But if it must be more, so be it. Get it in pint Bottles; and let them be boil'd well, before they are put to rence in cold water, I suppose Simple Jac. knows how Shannon did it. They must be laid in the Boiler, and cold water pour'd on them. No more now till yours comes in.

Tuesday

Well, my Dear Girl, you see you had as good tidings on Monday as on Friday. I send the same now. All well, but the Weather. Yet, that does not keep me within nor has it yet done any damage, except a little to two of my Reygrass fields. If it does not take up soon, I shall, without a joke, suffer greatly in them. What little mischief is yet done, I may bear for the pleasure of boasting that May 25 my meadows were lodg'd. Who about Dublin can make the same complaint?

The greatest pain I feel from the Weather is on my Brother's account. I doubt whether He has resolution to face it. I rather hope He has not, lest He or the Girls should suffer by wet or cold. Yesterday Evening, the rain was excessive hard and continu'd for many hours in the night. There has been a little this morning. It is now fair about noon, but threatens. This stay will be convenient to you, but I don't wish it on that account. You must shift as well as you can, till Brewster recovers, as I hope He will. If not, you must hire the best you can get in his place for the Summer.

Since you had a thief in the house the discovery of her is lucky. Take care to get an honest one in her place. I think you have a full right to charge her with every thing that has been lost during her time. As to your own things, Ladys, do as you please: what belongs to me, she or some one must answer for. The small copper-pot particularly about which Mrs J. enquires. Philip's account is that He kept it for a particular use, to heat Water to steep my razors in Winter, that a day or two before We left town, He saw it with her, and desir'd her not to meddle with it. Her answer was that it was in Mrs Barry's account. She certainly has made it away and must answer for it. Very little wages are due to her. The whole Family was paid to and for March 25. I am sure therefore she is entitled to nothing; and when you give a discharge insert in it the reason, *the strongest suspicion of dishonesty:* If you can warrant, *certainly* say it. Think not this severity. It is prudence. The least indulgence to such a Creature may encourage others to offend.

This is the usual effect of indulgence for lesser offences; and for that reason I am extending my strictness to Mr Gautier.[4] I was to pay him so much upon a condition, which He did not perform. What right then has he to a shill.? And if I pay him for nothing when I covenanted to pay for something. Is not this to encourage him to use you, if you should hereafter employ him, as ill as He has done already? Believe me, my Dear, this is folly, and if you discover an inclination to act thus in every case, you'll be liable in every case to be impos'd on. His saying that He had given a good deal of attendance without any gratuity is a downright fallacy. I suppose He means that He attended sometimes since He was last paid, or since the time to which He computes the payments; and this I believe is true. But How many neglects had the Gent been guilty of during the time that He was paid to? More I am sure than ballance his few attendances after; so that upon the whole He rec'd more than he earn'd, I have said all this to you before, and wish therefore that I had not been put to the trouble of writing it. It is owing to the gentleness of your nature, which I am far from blaming: But you must not indulge it too far. If you do, you'll in the course of your life be liable to a thousand impositions. To use every person as they deserve, with a proper biass to the good-natur'd and equitable side, This is prudence. To go further is Weakness. But pray let me know what this Gent's demand is? I'll lay a penny, He charges as much after the Spinnet went home as before; and indeed in one respect He is in the right of it. For his business was Equal, i.e. almost none at all. You say nothing of Mr Walsh.[5] As you seem'd inclin'd to learn from him, I expect'd that before this you would have made some step towards getting him. If you learn you'll want one to tune your harpsicord more frequently; and you may if you please make a new bargain with Mr Gautier, tho' I fancy you might get some one else to serve you better. But whoever you Employ, Be explicit with him. His pay shall depend on his performance. I said this over and over to the Gent, which makes his present demand more unreasonable.

You see I had not forgot Mr Oulton's (I thought his name was Oughton) wine. Jeny's is No. 16. Shannon says that the consumption of Small Beer was seven Barrels in a Kalender month, rather less than more. But your best way with Wise Jac. will be to suit the allowance to the number of persons in the family and peremptorily to insist on his not exceeding it. Great exactness will be necessary to make any thing of the Spark. I doubt whether even that will do.

I am glad you have got the account book, and hope to receive it from Mr Conry. If Cudmore's speech was just what you write, He has been guilty of unfairness. Shannon affirms what I wrote before, and adds now, that He spoke three or four times to Mrs Cudmore[6] about it, and that once she sent her maid for the Book, but her husband was not at home. If He has pass'd this upon you, as sent for on the sudden, and only brought an hour too late, see how He has attempted to deceive. I must remark such things to you, wherever I meet them. You'll hereafter see the importance of being early arm'd against every little Art of which the World is full, more than you can possibly now.

I expect Mr Mahon to day at diner. By a note rec'd on Sunday, He left Mrs Mahon as well as she had been. His turn is Sanguine. I hope however that the Expedition to Bristol will answer. Most heartily I wish it may. It would have pleas'd me much to have had Dr B's advice confirmed by Dr A. But there's no forcing people in such cases.

I am griev'd for poor Mrs Cook.[7] Most heartily I wish that her child may recover.

As you've made your first visit to Miss H.[8] and she has returned it, I think you'll do right to enter by degrees into a freer intercourse with her. If she be, as she's represented, she'll be a valuable acquaintance. Next winter probably will convert her into a near relation.

Mrs Cary is better this day. What relief she has had has been owing to a second bleeding. No blister yet. I hope there will not be occasion for any.

After so long a letter, you'll bear an abrupt conclusion. Adieu. God bless you all.

Yours &c.
Edw: Elphin

I have not time for remarks on your writing or stopping; nor do I observe much occasion for them. But in your former one I observ'd one thing, which ought not to pass un-notic'd *my respect, affection, and duty to my Dear Dada every day increases,* It ought to be increase, Two or more Nominatives *Singular,* the Verb ought to be plural. This is a *grammar* rule. I blame my self, that you were not taught it early. We must try, as well as we can, to supply that defect.

The Chocolate bought from Mr Meredith[9] was not paid for, There were, you know, six pounds. Send John Miller with the money. It is somewhat under Five shillings the pound, Whatever he says, Let John give.

I had almost forgot my Lad by whom I wrote yesterday. He'll probably be with you as early as this. Till the Doctor can take him into the Hospital, support him. Tell him that Stafford suspects somewhat of the Evil. He says it is in the Family.

Tell John that I find the Elms as Sir Maurice Crosbie[10] reported them. He has been greatly impos'd on. All the amends He can now make me is to search during Summer among the Nursery-men if he may know where to find right English ones in the Winter.

Bid John tell Mr Constable that He has us'd me extremely ill. He has impos'd a Malt-miln on me for a Wheat one and mine own his bungling Work-man has absolutely ruin'd. Mr Nicholson examin'd both yesterday. I'll send up the poor ruin miln the first opportunity. The other I must make shift with till I can get a right one. But I will not for that trust a Man who has thus impos'd on me.

1. May 1752 was 'a moist dropping month'. Rutty, pp.166-7.

2. Daniel Cudmore: the bookbinder. See Letter 84.

3. This was probably Charles Oulton, merchant of Dame Steet. Charles Oulton (1712-67) lived in Spring Gardens, and later in Cow Lane, Dublin. He married Anne, daughter of Walter Peter of Eyre's Court, Drumcondra. L. Oulton 'Concerning the Oulton Family' (n.d.); Watson (1752), p.20.

4. Mr Gautier: tuner of musical instruments.

5. George Walsh: music teacher. See Letter 84.

6. Mrs Cudmore: formerly Jane Proud. She married Daniel Cudmore on 6 April 1743. *St Andrew, St Anne, St Audeon and St Bride* p.146.

7. Mrs Cook: not known.

8. Miss H.: not known.

9. Mr Meredith: not known.

10. Sir Maurice Crosbie (1690-1762) of Ardfert, Co. Kerry, Jane Mahon's father. Admitted to TCD in 1706, he became MP for Co. Kerry 1713. Maurice Crosbie was elevated to the peerage as Lord Brandon in 1758. He married Lady Anne Fitzmaurice, daughter of the 1st earl of Kerry. *Alumni*, p.196; Burke(1916), p.1206.

183

Elphin. May 29, 1752

As Mrs J. has taken John for her pupil, she must be content to have commissions to him, convey'd by her. I shall set them down, as they come into my head.

Let him speak to Mr Constable for 12 iron-Shovels. He must take care to chuse right good ones, and fix the price. He knows what I us'd to give. Let him ask about the Turnip-Hoes. I much fear I shall be disappointed in them. Another – To speak to Smith[1] to have 120 right good wheels and one Loom ready for my call. The time to get these things down will be by the return-Carrs after the fair of Mullingar.[2] I will not for the future take from his Guardian, the answer I often get from him, that None were to be had. She therefore must not take it but make use of my Expedient, The High-lands.

Yours just now come in, makes me as happy, as you, Madam. I hope in God every post will afford the same mutual happiness.

I am sorry for your domestick distresses, but by your account there is a near prospect of a good ending.

Poor Shannon is in great distress. I pity him heartily. But what mean you by the bad humours with which his child was devour'd? Were they of body or mind?

You were certainly right not to give Dr James's powders[3] without consulting the Doctor. Did He give any? You say you got him a *paquet* of the powder. You spell that word wrong.

Yesterday was very fine. This almost as fine. My Brother has been much favour'd by weather in his journey; and may ride, if he pleases, not withstanding his resolutions. I hope He will. I am sure he'll suffer if he does not. I wish I could spare him the black Horse. But I really cannot. I have rode no other since Sunday: Indeed I had no other to ride. He carrys me as well as I can desire.

I believe the Bishop of Down[4] has left Mrs W behind him. Tell her therefore that I forgot to look out Sir William Petty's maps,[5] which I own I promis'd. I wish you could find them in the study. They are in the Outer one.

I can account for the Coll.'s visit, but not for the Man's which Crowns.[6] It is no great matter.

Your news of poor Jac. Davis's good fortune was a pleasing surprise. I am very glad the poor fellow is so well provided for.

The Adventure of the Carrs, and John's Wrath of which Mrs Jourdan gives an account made me laugh heartily, I have it too from himself, As I must write an answer, the Guardian will be eas'd of a Commission or two.

But there is one, which she must Execute with some address, John abuses the Oats that went last from hence most horribly, and I believe, deservedly. But I want mightily to have a more particular account of them, and I dare not ask him, because I have no mind He should know the reason of my curiosity. It is this. By Bradley's idleness, drunkeness, and I fear, dishonesty into the Bargain, bad Oats were receiv'd in, and for want of being turn'd and air'd, heated and began to rot. Mr Cary either knew not the Extent of the Evil, or had no mind I should know it. I suspect indeed something of both for the great mischief was done while He was in town and in one of his first letters after his return He mentioned it rather as what was near happening that as what had happened; and so I was easy about it, and should have continued so, but that Mrs Heap frankly and honestly told me all. Upon this I spoke to Mr C who then allow'd something amiss, but not near so much as Mrs Heap represented. John's account being a new Evidence, I shew'd it him yesterday. He was much surprized, but is still for palliating and cannot conceive that the Oats should deserve the Character John gives. In short He is conscious that whatever I have suffer'd is the consequence of his long stay in town, and Willy's indolence, and has therefore a mind to lessen the Evil. I must therefore beg the Guardian to lead the Pupil into talk about them, to ask all the questions which occur and to write his answers so as that I may shew the letter to Mr Cary. Let her write them in their full strength as He gives them. I hope He'll abuse them plentifully. For I am sure they deserve it. Let her ask particularly what difference between this and the former parcels sent from hence? If she acquits her self well of this Commission, she shall have more of my Custom. But I shall expect thanks for employing her. For I fancy the Conference will be a pleasant one. Advise him, one of you, at least to take them to Finglas to feed the Work-horses; and the Pea-cocks as a means to keep them out of the Garden.

You mistook if you thought I intended you should feed your family solely on Mutton. Kill a sheep now and then when 'tis convenient or pleasant to yourselves, and what you don't chuse to eat yourselves, Give the family. So less Beef will do. I have a few and but a few sheep at Finglas which will be better thus dispos'd of than kept. The stock is rather too heavy for the grass.

You know you are a very indifferent writer, you say. A very cool speech Mistress. My answer is, Learn then to be a better. You have opportunitys enough: and remember my old Aphorism. Many things are not done, because thought not possible to be done. If I thought you incapable of improvement, I would not exhort you to fruitless attempts. God bless you, and your Companions. I am My Dear Girl –

Yours &c
 Edw: Elphin

Mrs Cary mends slowly.

No news yet of Mrs Conroy.

Mr Mahon propos'd setting out this morning. He lent me *Jac. Connor.*[7] By the little I have read of it, it seems to me a pretty book, and worth not reading only, but buying.

John must buy a pound of la Lucerne seed; and you must among you send it down to me in little paquets three or four each post. Take care they be all within weight.

I have this minute made a whimsical discovery. As it had rain'd this afternoon, I chose to stay within, tho' it became fair; and going into the closet of one of the rooms to see what was doing abroad, I saw a letter or two half written in a Scrole hand, and by them one or two old ones, in a fine one. I could not resist the curiosity of looking at them, and found the old letters to be two of Molly Curtis's to you; and part of one of them was wrote in the Scrole hand with some variation. I fancy Molly was the Writer. For she came in, I believe, to finish, and so I went off. The letter was to *My Dearest Betty*. But who Betty is I know not. I have further reason to think the writing hers, by an affectionate mention of a Mother. But see how odly your giddiness is discovered. If thus you keep your letters, I must take care what I write. Upon my Word you are much to blame for this, Be more careful here after.

Tell Mrs Jourdan that I left the Study-Window open on purpose; for some days before I went out of town. As the Weather was fair I deferr'd shutting it several times when I passed to and fro; and at last forgot it.

Be sure compliment Mrs S[hannon] from me on Boby's[8] recovery, which I hope to have an account of soon. But take care not to do it, till I may have your account and make a return.

Mr and Mrs Conroy just come.

What a pretty figure this letter would make if it fell into Molly Byrne's hands?

[Free Edw:Elphin]

1. John Smith: blacksmith. See Letter 1.

2. Mullingar Fair was held on 23 June in 1752. Watson (1752), p.97.

3. Dr James's Powders were a popular patent medicine originally prepared by Dr Robert James (1703-76). Used to reduce fevers, it was a mixture of antimony and phosphate of lime.

4. John Whitcombe, bishop of Down. See Biographical Register.

5. Sir William Petty (1623-87): he came to Ireland as Physician General in the army and in 1654 undertook the first cartography of Ireland, the Down Survey, which was used to deal with all conflicts over land grants. One of the first political economists, he wrote *The Political Anatomy of Ireland* (1691). The Down Survey maps used by Edward Synge in 1752 were used again by Alicia Synge's grandson, Richard Wordsworth Cooper, in 1847 to survey land at Athnid and Kilcloony, Co. Tipperary, which had been leased by Edward Synge in 1748 for ninety-nine years. *DNB*; NLI ms 2102, f.21-2; Tipperary Estate accounts, May 1847, Cooper papers, in private possession.

6. Obscure.

7. [William Chaigneau], *The history of Jack Connor in two volumes* (Dublin 1752). *Jack Connor* is a picaresque novel which satirizes the condition of Ireland.

8. Boby: a Shannon child.

184

Elphin. June 2, 1752

My Dear Girl

I am pleas'd with your letter. That's all I can now say to it. For I am hurry'd with Company and fatigu'd with a dozen letters, and the minute I can command to write to you in, must be otherwise employed.

I had yesterday a letter from Mr Vipond giving me an account of a Servant. It seems He liv'd with Sir Tho. Maude,[1] in the Station in which I want one; and He has from him a good account of him. But young Men are not, in such a case, the best judges. What I desire is that you would, assoon as you can after you receive this, go, or get Mrs J. to go to Mrs Silver with my Compliments, and beg that she would inform her Self minutely of him from Lady Maude.[2] I think she is still in Dublin. You know how to ask all proper questions; So will Mrs Silver without being prompted. All I shall say to you is, that I want an house-Steward and Farmer in the same person; but that Honesty, Care, and Strict Sobriety are the prime qualitys. With these, Moderate skill in farming will do, if there be a disposition to learn and follow directions. Let me know the result of your Enquirys, assoon as you can. If Mr Vipond sends to you, Let him know it also, but not unless He sends. I have directed him to apply to you for information, if He wants it. The Man's name is Cowgell,[3] from Yorkshire. He has a Wife; I should be glad to know, what sort a one?

Bad Weather makes the Country less pleasant. I contrive however to get out every day; and have had Company to relieve the solitude of Confinement. My Archbishop[4] came hither on Saturday, and left me this morning. Godfrey Wills, Palmer, Barton, Blair and Mr Hort[5] are here now. I bless God, I am very well, and happy since you are so.

My hearty service to your Uncle and Aunt, and blessing to the Girls. I am pleas'd with your account of them, but very sorry I cannot see them my self. God bless you and your friends. I am My Dear Girl

Yours &c
Edw: Elphin

[Free Edw:Elphin]

1. Sir Thomas Maude (d. 1777): son of Sir Robert and Lady Maude, became baron de Montalt in 1766. Burke (1916), p.1014.
2. Sir Thomas Maude dsp and Burke is not clear whether he was married. Lady Maude may be Sir Thomas's wife or his mother. Burke (1916), p.1014.
3. Edward Synge says that Cowgell is a relation of Lady Tullamore, whose maiden name was Coghill. Cowgell was still in Edward Synge's household in 1760. Edward Synge to Godfrey Wills, RCB, 426/1-15.
4. Dr Josiah Hort: archbishop of Tuam.
5. Either Josiah (1732-86) or John (?-1807) Hort: sons of Josiah Hort. Burke (1916), p.1078.

185

Elphin June 5, 1752 Thursday

Still bad Weather, my dearest. Tuesday night and yesterday morning a rank Storm with some heavy Show'rs. The Evening fine, but at fall of night it set in for rain and about bed-time pour'd. So it did early this morning. Since Seven it has been sun-shine and rain alternate. On the whole disagreable enough.[1] Yet I have got out Every day; and No damage is done even to the Rey-grass, tho' it is in danger from a Continuance.

I am much pleas'd with your prattle about the same Rey-grass. Indulge yourself in such Sallys as much as you please. It will be always agreable to see and hear your thoughts and reflexions of every kind. But Tell me, Huzzy, had not you one Ally Synge in your thoughts while you were writing? And if you had are not you somewhat a Sawcy Girl? But I'll forgive that, if you make the Application. It does indeed stand you upon to make it. For, how deservedly it matters not, you have attracted not my attention only, but the World's; and a high standard of merit is set for you. Aspire to, and Go beyond it. You may, if you please.

It is possible you may judge right about Mrs N[icholson]. But I rather think there is, in your opinion, a Mixture, at least, of your own diffidence with a little of the *mauvaise honte*[2] which still remains in you. This you ought certainly to get clear of in your intercourse with her and every one else; and thus you may come to be certain one way or other. If ever you were a burthen to her, It was when going with you to publick places interfer'd with her other Amusements. But As she gave up these amusements, in part at least, or strove to make them consistent with her going with you, this is in her favour. And since Nothing of the same kind can happen now, I see not how you can be a burthen, unless she has taken some disgust, so as to dislike your Company. I am certain she has not. But you may quickly know whether she has or not, by keeping up with her your former freedom. If you change your morning into evening Visits and of these, Book-keeper Jane takes an account, debtor and cr[editor], there may soon be a real Coolness between you, with as little inclination on Her side as there is on yours; and She may have directly the same suspicions of you, that you have of her. And the behaviour you describe may confirm them. If you look foolish, are afraid to speak, and are on thorns in her Company, she'll see it; and, if innocent her self, will think you faulty, and with reason think you so. But why should you behave so to her or any one else? Why should you fancy you are disagreable or a burthen when you are not conscious to your Self of having done any thing to make you so? Her turn and amusements were the same in the heighth of your intimacy that they are now. Are you chang'd, and for the Worse? I think not. But you've observ'd more narrowly and perhaps indulg'd Suspicions further than you ought; and on these suspicions have alter'd your behaviour, so as to occasion some in her. This is an untoward kind of situation with respect to one to whom you are, and think your self oblig'd. Take your Self out of it. The way is easy. See her in the old way. Seek occasions of seeing her, and let your behaviour be with the assuredness of innocence. By her returns, your suspicions will either be remov'd or confirm'd; and as you find matters you may drop gradually, or continue. Don't imagine now, by my dwelling on this point, that I have any remarkable fondness for your keeping up or recovering this intimacy. Whatever may have been the case in your greener years, I think, that now 'tis as desirable to her as to you; and my pride forbids the least thought of obtruding you on any one. But As I wish to have you act properly on every occasion; and as many like this may in the Course of your life occurr; So, according to custom, I lay hold of one occasion, to give you documents that may be of use upon every one of like kind. Shall I tell you now what I think the truth of the case? You are not of a turn for many intimates and you have one, besides Mrs J., who is more suited to you than Mrs N. that same Mrs P.[3] whom you mention for the first time. I am far from blaming your choice. But why should she engross you?

I am glad you've begun with Mr Walsh; and hope you'll find amusement by returning to your harpsicord. But if his visits be as short as usual, you'll improve little. In my opinion you ought not to suffer this; and if you insist on his staying longer, He will. If you do not, I shall call you Sheep; and tell you that you are, as I really think you are, very deficient in firmness, and proper resolution. As for Mr Gautier, His stale and, I think, unreasonable demand shall lye over till my return. Are you sure that He computes right? I agree that it will be best not to engage with any one till you see how you go on with the Harpsicord; and if you do employ any one, I had as lief, it were another as He. In that, do as you please. But make your bargain explicite both as to price and times of attendance, and suffer not your Self to be impos'd on. I never paid more than a Guinea a year except to Mr G. and was better attended than ever He attended you. I don't think He or any one else deserves more, as your Harpsicord stands the best in tune of any I ever knew.

By your account of the interview between you, and your negligent Correspondent[4] I fancy you were too serious and shew'd that you took her not writing, as I know you did, too much to heart. In this you were mistaken. Omissions of this kind between friends and relations are a fitter subject for a little raillery, than for grave looks, or words, the calmness of which shews resentment. I presume that before this, she has made her excuse; and probably the true one was, that French letters cost her too much pains. You, Mistress, would have wrote seldomer if you had labour'd to write as Correctly as she did. I was sorry that Correspondence dropp'd, because it tended to improve you. I hope it will be resum'd, when she returns to the Country; tho' while I am here, Letters to me will find you Employment. I should be glad to see some without blots, or interlineations, and right stopp'd. In this last point, I see you as deficient, as last year. But As I have given all the rules I can, I shall let your defects of this kind pass without animadversion. False spellings I shall take notice of; and I meet two in yours now before me. You write *exagerate*. The g. should be doubled. The other is worse, because it shews giddiness. You might have learn'd from mine how to spell Rey-grass. You spell Rye-grass.

You believ'd I wonder'd at your not mentioning Mrs P–. Honestly I did not. For tho' I esteem her greatly she is not quite so much in my thoughts as in yours. But I did and do wonder that you never mentioned the little Pet.[5] What is become of it? I heard last Sunday of honest Lucy the donor.[6] She is very well. I intend to see her soon. But no stirring from home this Weather.

All this before yours came in. See what you get by bad Weather. Your's now come will not, I think, furnish occasion for lengthening much. God be thanked you are all well. So says Mrs J. But among you, I have no news. How comes that?

Your letter is better wrote, and better stopp'd than your former ones. But still room to improve; and if you do not improve, you will not prove your Self an intolerable dunce, but an incorrigible something else.

You have setled very properly with Mr Walsh. See that you keep him to his Terms. As for Gautier, I don't think Mr Walsh an unexceptionable witness. These Folks, of professions that depend on each other, have favorites, and play into each others hands. There may be other Tuners as much to be depended on as He; and I am sure there was one when I took him, more in vogue. But it's all one to me whether you employ him or any one else. It's better perhaps chuse him, as Walsh wo'n't be easy with another. I don't like either of the methods He proposes for paying him. If you pay him so much for so many visits, He may make three in a week; and the same thing will happen, if you go by the times of tuning, and leave him to judge; nay! Whether you do or no, He'll tune imperfectly that he may be called soon agen. Your best way will be to agree by the year or quarter, and fix the times of his coming, as before, and for every time He misses, to deduct so much. If this be done and *stuck to*, you'll be either well attended or not pay, as I have done, for nothing. Two Guineas is too much, Nor is attendance six times a quarter necessary. Once a month, ordinarily, is enough, and for that a Guinea. As I have told you above, I never paid more, tho' attended oft'ner. But it is on the face of it absurd, that the Gent. should have as much for attending an Harpsicord solely, as He had for that and a Spinnet. And Now, make your bargain as you can. I should not have wrote so much about it, but that I love to teach you in trifles that Exactness, which may be of real use in affairs of more importance.

I thank you for your Wishes about the Pine-apple. I am full as well pleas'd you have it. You should invite your benefactor to partake of it. I am sure you won't eat it by your Selves. I hope you have eaten it already.

You need not trouble your Self further about Sir W. P.'s maps, unless the Bishop on his return to town asks agen for them. I am not fond of letting them out of my hands. *Jac. Connor* does not answer throughout. There is a great deal indifferent, with some very good.[7]

You say you were always carefull of my letters, tho' not near so much as you ought. Pray explain your Self Madam. Do you mean, keeping them, or following my advice. For once 'twould please me better, that you avow the former, rather than the letter. Scarce any of mine are fit for the view of any one but your self, and your prime intimate. Give her my thanks, and tell her I'll acknowledge her favours, more properly assoon as I can get time. But I am oppress'd with letters, and yet see what a long one I write to you. It is time to put an end to it. God bless you all.

Yours &c
Edw: Elphin

I had almost forgot the Lucerne. It was so ill made up, that it broke in the Bagg, and all that could be gather'd up was short of 7 oz. Let another pound be bought on the same Terms, and sent in thicker paper, or in small parcels as I directed before. This had been the better way.

I am glad to find you've so good Stomachs. A Mutton in two days is a large allowance. But provide properly for all, and make as much of your Selves as you will. Only have a Care of Waste. Miss Conry was marry'd on Sunday to one Mr Kelly,[8] a Gent of good fortune, and fair Character. He was a Widower; whether with Children I know not; not old, but rather too great a disproportion in their years. All Circumstances cannot be as one wishes.

I return Maria's letter, but have not time to write a Word to Mrs J. about that or any thing else.

Mr Wills, Barton, and Blair here still. More have been this week, who are gone. Enough remain to make me happy as I can be such Weather.

If Mrs J.'s pupil made up the Lucerne who deserves to be chid? He, or she who trusted her Minor?

On conference with Saunders I retract the order of sending more Lucerne. I need not desire you to take proper notice of Nelly Mahon[9] and the little ones. Her going up with them just at this time looks as if good Mrs Mahon had gloomy apprehensions, and desir'd to take a last leave. I hope it will not be so.

1. The weather in June 1752 was 'Cloudy, wet, cool and winter like.' Rutty, p.167.
2. *Mauvaise honte*: false pride.
3. Mrs P. Not known.

4. Molly Curtis.

5. A mouse. See Letter 187.

6. Lucy Caulfield.

7. In *Jack Connor*, William Chaigneau lampoons a dissolute Roman Catholic priest, Father Kelly, who kisses a woman's breast, but he also guys a Church of Ireland bishop, a subject to which Edward Synge may well have taken objection. *Jack Connor*, Vol. 1, p.20; Vol. 2, pp.5-6.

8. 'Last week Edmond Kelly of Churchborough Esq was married to Miss Molly Condry, Daughter of John Condry of Cloonhee Esq; a beautiful young Lady, possessed of every good Qualification and six thousand pounds Fortune.' Mary Conry's parents were John Conry, a magistrate, and his wife Margaret. *Faulkner's Dublin Journal*, 6-9 June 1752; Census, f.45.

9. Either Eleanor, daughter of Nicholas Mahon or Eleanor, one of Thomas and Jane Mahon's daughters.

186

Elphin. June 9, 1752.

The Guardian must order the pupil to provide half a hundred of ridge tiles, to send down by the next Carrs, and put him in mind of the small cord He bespoke for the bells here.

She or you must tell Ned Curtis, That I want some coarse strong Cannon powder for blasting rocks. What He sent down is too good for such uses. The other is cheaper. Desire him to get a Keg or large bottle of it ready to come with the other things. Tell him also that He forgot to enquire about Mitchel;[1] or if He did, to tell me the result. He'll know what I mean.

You told me in a late letter of your carrying Nancy[2] to Dunlary.[3] Her surprise was natural,[4] and you describe it well, I am far from blaming you for thus pleasing her or your self. But I had rather you had told me of your having set her to learn to wash &c. Upon my word, Mistress, if you don't get this done completely this summer I'll chide. So much before hand.

Now for yours, which shews you are well, tho' you don't say so. God be thanked. I too am well, but peevish at the Weather. Nine mowers at work yesterday and to day. Both afternoons wet. But better it is to venture to cut than let the grass rot uncut. I am in pain for it.

Mr Wills run away from me this morning, while I was abroad. I am now alone and not displeased at being so. There are charms in variety.

From your description I can easily imagine what figure poor Nancy makes. Reflect, My Dear as often as you see her, that had you been neglected as she has been, you might have been as she is: Bless God for the advantages you have had and have, and Make a right use, and improvement of them. Her awkard and savage air may easily be corrected enough for all valuable purposes in one of her rank; unless that large grain of obstinacy stand in the way which, as you justly observe, is the bane of all improvements. But while you observe and censure this in her, Turn your Eyes inward, and see whether you have not a little spice of it your self. I sometimes fancy you have. You are apt to take your bent suddenly, and are not easily wrought on to like doing the same thing, another way; and tho' you comply, you shew by a significant look, or some other way, an impatience even in compliance. I have often observ'd this with concern, and sometimes taken notice of it to you. Now this, my Dearest, is a little bit of obstinacy, however disguis'd. You do not shew it like a savage, because you are not a savage. But what signifys this? The Common people vent their hatred or anger in reproachfull Words. The polite are as angry and vindictive as they, and yet observe decencys. Where is the real difference in their moral Characters? The Temper in both is the same – their manners vary the Expression of it – As I am writing, the Bishop of Killala[5] comes in. I am forc'd to break off. God bless you and make you perfect in every thing that is good. I am

Yours &c
Edw: Elphin

[Free Edw:Elphin]

1. Possibly Hugh Mitchel, merchant, Capel Street .Watson (1752), p.19.
2. Nancy Poor or Power: Alicia's maid.
3. Dunlary: Dun Laoghaire, Co. Dublin.
4. Her surprise was probably at seeing the sea for the first time.
5. Richard Robinson was nominated bishop of Killala on 31 October 1751. He was translated to Ferns on 19 April 1759; translated from Ferns to Kildare on 26 March 1761 and from Kildare to Armagh 8 February 1765. He remained archbishop of Armagh until his death on 10 October 1794. He was created baron Rokeby on 26 February 1777. His Dublin house was in St Stephen's Green. *NHI*, Vol. 9, pp.437, 428, 394; *Georgian Society Records*, Vol.2, p.63.

187

Elphin. June 12, 1752

I have more joy in My Dear Girl's letter than I am able to express. With such Sentiments, and the Conduct which they must inspire, there is no doubt but that, by God's blessing, you'll come up to the Standard of merit fix'd for you; and a high one it is.

You have endeavour'd, dextrously enough, to free your self from the charge of sauciness and Vanity, and you have done it effectually, but not in the way you imagine. It is true the Attention of the World is more turn'd to you, because you are my daughter. The child of a more obscure person would not have been so much in the way of notice, and more has been taken even of you, because you are visibly the Object of all my care. But if you had, notwithstanding all mine and Mrs J's endeavours, shew'd your self, hitherto, a dolt, a Savage, or of a crooked perverse disposition, the World would have pitied us, and set no standard of merit for you. As, God be thanked, you have hitherto shew'd yourself a Soil not ungrateful to the tiller's care, Fruits of the best kind are expected from you. This you see, and I rejoice that you see it. But then, huzzy, you must see your Self as you are, and know that you are or may be good for something; and if you do not over-rate your good qualitys, if a consciousness of them animates you, to improve such as you have, and to perfect your self, by acquiring such as you are yet deficient in, the better opinion you have of your self, the more likely you'll be to answer fully my fondest hopes. As your letter shews, that your thoughts take this turn, and As I think you perfectly honest and without guile in what you write, So I acquit you absolutely of the Charge of sauciness or Vanity, which indeed I never seriously brought against you. I hope you are free from those hateful vices, and will always continue so. You will, if you carefully observe these rules. Never ascribe to your Self any perfection to which you have but a doubtfull title: Over-rate not those to which you have a clear one; and Avoid all invidious comparisons with others, as much as possible, in your Secret thoughts. Let me exemplify my rules in the lowest kind of perfections, on which yet We are apt, in the beginning of life at least, to set the greatest value, those of the Body. You are tall, strait, and of no ungracefull figure. It is not Vanity to think your Self so, and even to aim at acquiring more grace, and elegance in your air and behaviour. When you go further, you'll be vain, you'll ascribe to your Self what you have not. If, on account of what you have of this kind, you think your Self entitled to more esteem and regard from others, this also is Vanity. You value your Self on what is not really valuable. But if on account of any, even real, Excellence of this end, you despise and look down on others who want it, and detract from their, to enhance your own merit, you then are, God forbid you ever should be, vain in the most hateful sense of the Word. What I have said of bodily perfections, you'll easily apply to those superior ones of the mind, which are alone truly valuable. I shall only add, that Vanity is as much the bane of improvement, as Obstinacy and that the surest Test of your being perfectly free from it, is to shew on every occasion a disposition to allow every other person as much merit of every kind as they have any sort of claim to. Censoriousness and vanity are inseperable. I hope you are, and will always be free from them both. But you may think as well of your Self, as with the least justice you can, as long as these thoughts inspire you with a noble Emulation of excelling others in every thing praise-worthy and Commendable.

I have no objection to your having a freer and more frequent intercourse with those young Ladys. You know the friendship there is between me and their Father; the total neglect of such obliging overtures, as you say have been made, is more delicate on that account. And what if you like only one Sister? Is there any thing in the other so forbidding, as to determine you, on that account, to avoid both? I hope not, for her, and her Father's sake. But do as you please. If you live you must expect to have many acquaintances, whom you do not quite like. But there is a great difference between even free acquaintance, and intimacy. To this last, few should be admitted, none but by degrees, and upon full trial of their temper and dispositions.

I had your news the post before. Had not the Bishop of Killalla come in upon me, I should have wrote it to you, to shew how much earlier intelligence I have from other correspondents than from you. But I blame you not for coming late to the knowlege of such Events. The raptures of the Ladys about the Speaker's behaviour,[1] might as well have been spar'd. A spiteful person may say, that it pleas'd so much, from a secret Wish, that their parents, on the same trying occasion, might behave in the same manner. As I know him to be a wise man, so I really believe the true motive of this behaviour to be, that he thinks, this, tho' a very improvident, Marriage, gives him some choice for reformation in a Wild, I had almost said an abandon'd, young Man. But whatever I may think of him, I can't think with patience of the admir'd Lady, who behaves so prettily to him. To make such a use of the intimacy to which she was admitted in that Family; To captivate a giddy unthinking young Man with her charms, nay! To consent to his being caught in Nets, which she did not design to lay, and steal her Self thus into an Alliance, which she had no reason to think would be agreable! It is abominable. She has a fair chance for being unhappy, tho' the beginnings are so fair. I shall not pity her, if she be. True honour would have prompted her to another kind of conduct; to have discourag'd his addresses; if He persisted, to have disclos'd them to her own Father, and, by him, to his. The consequence might, I really believe, would, have been, that the S[peaker], charm'd with such generous behaviour, would with joy have admitted her into his Son's bosom, and his own, and thought her a Treasure more valuable than many thousands. But whether this had happen'd or not, she had been justly the object of Universal Esteem; and that, with her other perfections, would have open'd the most honorable way to some match as advantageous, as that into which she has thus stolen her self. The young Man's Tears please me much. There seems to be sense in them. For his Father's sake and his own I hope he'll reform. As for the fair Enchantress, I matter not what comes of her. And yet perhaps she is not so much to blame, as Her Education. Few young persons have the advantage which you, My dearest, have had, of an early opening their minds, and turning them to make just reflexions on the proper Conduct on such critical occasions. If dress, gayety, and Diversions have engross'd their attention, If their chief point all their lives has been to please, No wonder, that when they find they do please, they resolve at once to make the most of it. The sin is not so much theirs, as their parents. I have none of that kind to answer for, and I have the fullest confidence in you that you won't. God direct you, my Dearest, in all your ways.

I am sorry you receiv'd no more light from Lady Maud about Cowgel. I expect him or another this day or to morrow. Vipond chuses. If Cowgel comes, I'll get an account of him from Davis,[2] whom Mrs J. mentions. Try therefore to learn somewhat more of that same Mr Davis from Mrs Silver.

My service to the Guardian, and tell her, if she gives her Self the trouble of so large Apologys for trifles, I'll discharge her. Almost a Folio page about the Lucerne. Hers us'd to be more agreably fill'd. But As she has said so much about it, It will please her to know, that I have suffer'd very little by the Pupil's and Wheel-wright's Contrivance. The Second paper came entire last post, and the four Small pacquets, this.

I have now a Commission for her, which I hope she'll attend, in part her self. We want Bottles; and Shannon says he left a Multitude behind him in the long garret. He advises the bringing them down, and I think He is right. Her best way will be to send to the Complaisant Sullivane, who will be proud of obeying her Commands, and get him to provide Hampers, and a Man to pack. The pupil can count as well as the best; and thus they may be made up ready to come with the return Carrs after Mullingar fair. If the Pupil does not secure a Number sufficient for this and every other purpose, I desire she would take no excuse. He cannot make a good one.

I had an answer to my letter from Mr Mahon. He was my intelligencer. But I was very sorry to find, He thought good Mrs Mahon worse. This from him was a great deal. He was always before sanguine in his hopes and account. As Nelly is so near you, I hope you'll see her, and the Girls often. I think you'll be pleas'd with the younger. Pray take all the friendly notice you can of Mrs Warren.[3] I have not seen her since her marriage. But I am not surpriz'd at the change you perceive in her. It is almost the Constant fate of beauty, to decay; and earlier as it is greater. Some comfort to those who have it not, tho', if folks were wise, there would be no occasion for any.

I am glad 'Mousy' is alive and well, and in favour. Mrs J. did give me an account of the hunt. I wish you had more of them, that that paltry fear of so harmless an Animal, may be completely remov'd. God bless you all. I am, My Dear Girl's

> most affectionate &c
> Edw: Elphin

Yesterday and this day hitherto fine. But I live in fear of rain every minute so make the most of those which are fair. Most of my hay that is cut, will, this night, be tolerably well secur'd. Such a quantity as I have on one field, I never saw before on the same quantity of Land. Night come. No rain. Hay safe.

I have a heavy Charge against you or some one. Some of my Shirts have ragged wrists. They certainly came down so. For Shannon tells me I have not yet worn one wash'd here. It's no great matter.

Desire Ned Curtis to ask his friend Mr Weld[4] what is become of my Hock; and Tell him that the powder for blasting must be of the Strongest kind. Cheapness without this signifies nothing. I had better use what I have. What is like to become of my Lad at the Hospital?

1. Henry Boyle: speaker of the Irish House of Commons. See Letter 112.
2. Mr Davis/Davies: not known.
3. Mrs Warren: not known.
4. Matthew Weld: merchant. See Letter 160.

188

Elphin, June 16, 1752

My Dear Girl,

I don't remember I told you, that Cudmore lyes in saying that Shannon never spoke to him about the account book. He affirms He did, and affirms it with such Circumstances, as incline me to believe him. As He was standing at Doyle the Plummer's shop,[1] talking to Lizzy's Cosen, Cudmore pass'd by. He then and there spoke to him, for the Book. C[udmore] ask'd would He have it rul'd? Yes! A Common Market book was the answer. I'll send it immediatly was the Reply. His other applications He admits were to the Wife. This affair is of no Consequence in it self. But it is of consequence to let a Liar know that He does not deceive. I wish you would chide C[udmore] or his Wife heartily for this.

I see advertis'd in the *Gazette* An Address to the D of Dorset by James Digges La touche. price 3d.² Ask Ned Curtis about it. If it be good for any thing, or will give me a laugh, send it. I hear since it is good for nothing. Mind it not.

I got yours by Cowgil on Sunday afternoon. This Man may, for ought I know, be a relation of Lady Tullamoore's.³ Her family is Yorkshire from whence He came, and the prountiation [*sic*] is the same, tho' the spelling different, of the name. This signifys nothing. Her Ladyship perhaps would not like the remark. But such hauteur is folly. There was one Synge, a hatter at Drogheda,⁴ who was my relation and I acknowledg'd him as freely as if his rank had been equal to mine own, and supported his son, till I found him worthless. I then dismiss'd, and know not what is become of him. This is the right temper with respect to poor relations. I observe with pleasure that you have it.

Your letter by him was very welcome. I should be glad to hear from you every day. As your welfare is the greatest concern I have in and of this World, so the account of it cannot be too frequent, when We are divided.

I fear your Exultations in Summer Weather, like mine, have been of short continuance. Thursday and Friday were fine, but All the morning on Saturday was very wet. With you I find it was otherwise. But I fancy the ballance was made in the Afternoon. You say nothing of it. But the Guardian writes, Heavy rain since three. Our afternoon was very fine and I rode out. Sunday too was very fine. But yesterday between nine and ten rain came on, which lasted thick and heavy the whole day, and, for ought I know, the night. For the morning is now very wet, and threatens continuance. This is disagreable, and unless it pleases God soon to send a change, will prove very hurtful to the Country. I have yet suffer'd no real damage, but the stoppage of my Works. For my hay is all in Cock. Afternoon fair.

It will vex you to find that I am already embarrass'd about this same Yorkshire Man. He appears indeed a plain sensible man, and by his answers to a multitude of questions, shews sufficient knowlege in the affairs, in which [he] is to be employ'd. What embarrasses me is, He has brought down his Wife big with Child. This is worse, as He told Vipond He would leave her for some Months in town, and actually got a Guinea from him to leave with her. His account for this, and He gives it with appearing *naiveté*, is that That was really his Scheme. But that the Woman was very unwilling to be left behind, and He yielded to her importunity, after He had left Mr Vipond. When I told him that He ought to have appriz'd Mr V. of the change, and got new directions, He confess'd it, but said He thought it a matter of perfect indifference, whether She was here, or any where else, imagining that He might get fitting accommodation for her here, on very easy terms. It seems the people at the 'Cock and Bull' gave him high notions of the plentifulness of this place. He said they spoke from my servants. But He does not own to his having talk'd to any of them on the Subject. Enquire and let me know. As He finds himself in this miserably mistaken, He seems as much embarrass'd as I am. And I am embarrass'd, because tho' I see what is done, I can't certainly discover the true motives. If this rash step has been the effect of fondness for his Wife, I can't entirely blame it, If of cunning and management, It would justly give me a bad impression of him. I'll try to come at the truth, and accordingly resolve. But I see already, that I must either keep both or send both back. The Woman is at present at Jac. Brian's,[5] a place which He seems to like as little as I do. I can't consent that My Manager should have such a pretence as this to resort every hour to a Dram-shop. If He be now sober, He'll soon become otherwise. Yet there is no other place. I must bring her hither, or pack both off. Don't now be vex'd at this. You'd be surpriz'd to see how little I am mov'd at it. At worst I can jogg on with Collins,[6] till I can provide a good Manager. Not knowing whether this one be so or not, This incident sits lighter upon me.

Your picture of the gaming table is indeed a shocking one. I wish it appear'd as much so to her who drew it, as it does to you. I fear it does not. Tell me honestly your thoughts. If, tho' she refrains from one game, and is almost *exempted*, you should have said, *excluded* from another, she shews a liking or approbation of such wicked and hateful licence in others, and would take it her self, if her Husband and circumstances allow'd it. This shews a perverted mind, which indeed I should be sorry to find in her, but, if so it be, I shall no longer wish much less recommend your keeping up any intercourse, but what meer decency requires. Tho' I think my self very sure of you, Yet I care not to have you in the way of infection; nor shall I think an intimacy with an Approver of such persons and their Conduct, for your honour. Let me have yours and Mrs J.'s thoughts on this very delicate point without reserve. Your reflexions on this and other points give me the greatest pleasure. May that God, who has put it into your heart, to think and write in such a manner, give you his Grace to observe a suitable Conduct in the Course of a long, happy, and, in this way, a truly glorious life.

You are so ingenuous in owning your faults, that I need say no more about them. I bless God I see none in you, but what may, and therefore, I doubt not, will be easily corrected. That which I call'd, perhaps by too hard a name, Obstinacy, is owing to impetuosity. But want of Attention is not the only cause of that. It is in part owing to temper, which you must master by degrees; and The Sooner you begin The Easier your Work will be. Let me tell you, Mistress, you have not now much time to loose.

Remember, Huzzy, you are almost out of your teens.[7] But take notice you may be obstinate in many cases, without being wrong in your judgment. Your way may be really the best, and yet your Contending for, and adhering to it faulty. In things that may be done this or that way, It is sense, It is prudence to yield to the opinion of others of those Especially who have a right to advise, and this should always be done at once, and with the best grace. Nothing is more Engaging than a proper Complaisance in such matters; and Thus you'll get a mastery of your temper that may fit you for severer trials. I hope none will fall to your share. But, 'tis odds that they do; and often great disputes and quarrels arise from want of this sort of winning behaviour in smaller matters. Remember your Uncle's story of Blackbirds and thrushes. I was going on when Company came in upon me, and They have left me so late that I have neither time nor light to add more. I am My Dear Dear Girl

Your most affectionate &c
Edw: Elphin

l think I know your Ladys. But who is Mr C. Write the names of this Hero, and of all your detestable Heroines at length.

I was very near forgetting to take notice of your Caution about Mr Oulton's Wine, tho' it made me laugh when I read the passage in your letter by the English-man. This looks as if you would act like Old Walls with the Bishop of Clogher's Wine, who would not stop a leak, till He received directions from him at Clogher.

Prithee, My Dear put the Wine into any Bin that is empty. As to the price I think as I did, but for such a trifle it signifys not. I shall not deal deeper with one who talks so in general Terms. It is the Cant of the business. He paid a great deal for it. So do All the Wine Merchants for Claret the lowest priz'd in France and known to be so.

You spell *promises* wrong – So it should be. You write *promisses*. I tell you you ought to have wrote *excluded* instead of *exempted*. The reason is this. The latter is always us'd of *burthens*. The former of privilege or Favour. Exempted from taxes, is right. Excluded from mercy or favour. In one passage, you commit a small fault by attempting to avoid one. *The reflexions you bid me make, I have always* done. You should have wrote *made*. The repetition of the same Word in this and like Cases, is so far from being faulty, that it is proper and Elegant.

Wedensday morning.
Wet and Windy. The Post waits.

1. Thomas Doyle: plumber, shot caster and merchant, Cook Street. Watson (1760), p.4.

2. [James Digges La Touche] *Mr La Touche's address to His Grace the Duke of Dorset* (Dublin 1752).

3. See Letter 50.

4. Edward Synge: hatter of Drogheda, had land transactions in the 1760s. Synge and Knight, 6 October 1760, RD 205 462 136927.

5. Jack Brian: may be John O'Brien, shopkeeper, Elphin, a Catholic with three Catholic servants. Census, f.1.

6. Tom Collins: a land steward.

7. Alicia Synge was to be nineteen years old in December 1752.

189

Elphin. June 19, 1752

Well! My Dear Girl. If praise does not make you vain, It is just you should have, whenever you deserve, it: and I really think you deserve great praise for your late letters. I have the pleasure to see by them, that my part will for the future be easy. I need only give hints. You'll improve them by proper reflexions your Self.

But while I thus commend the matter of your letters I must express my concern at your manner of writing. I see by it, that Every letter takes up much time and costs you great pains, and yet you do not mend in the way you are in. Let me then recommend it to you to try another, or rather to return to that which I formerly recommended, and you try'd usually towards the latter end of Summer. Begin upon it now, and See what you can make of it. Since writing in a Set hand, and taking what care you can to cut every letter Exactly, does not answer, Let your pen run more freely; and as fast as your thoughts flow in upon you, Scrawl away, as in your billets to Bab.[1] Only write legibly, and Let your lines, and Words be at a proper distance. Take notice, I say, *Words*: For in all your letters, they are always too close, which, be the hand what it will, is a great fault, makes your letters less intelligible at first view, and prevents your Stops, even when rightly plac'd, from appearing as they ought to do. I have great hopes, that by some practice in this way, you'll come to write with ease to your Self, and well enough to answer all valuable purposes. Whereas if you persist in the way in which you are, the drudgery of committing your thoughts to paper may indispose you to the doing it at all: Or if you do write, you'll have little time to any thing else. When you have more business on your hands than now, this will be more disagreable, and inconvenient. I am sure it is even now greatly So. Be not discourag'd by any apprehensions, that I shall not like. Depend on it, I will, nay! I really believe I shall like them and I have great hopes that in this way you'll acquire an easy, plain manner of writing, which will do very well, tho' it be not so fine as Molly Curtis's. To encourage you to make the Experiment, I tell you this was your good Mother's way. Your Grandfather us'd to call her Pengallop. The matter of her letters was Excellent, but her Writing was a Sort of Scrawl, tho' a very legible one. I heartily regret my having burn'd a multitude of them.

Your observation on the advantage you have from my absence in Summer is just; and the account you give of your Emotion on my reprimands when present is in part so. But Depend on it, My Dear Girl, there is in this a mixture of Temper. Yours is naturally quick and sudden, and I know whence you derive it. But you must by degrees acquire more mastery of it, than I have done.

Another thing about your letters, which that now before me give occasion to remark. You don't divide them sufficiently into Paragraphs. *The admir'd Lady* ought to have begun a new one. By the by, the Farther Excuse made for her is a bad one. All the Commands of Parents ought to be lawfull and decorous. Where they are not, Children are not bound to obey, nay! they are bound not to obey. I question much the genuiness of the Sister's anger.

I had a very cheerfull letter yesterday from Mr Mahon from Chester, which gives the same account that you had from Nelly, rather a better. Most heartily I wish that the Success may answer these beginnings.

I am pleas'd that you were pleas'd with your jaunt to Finglas, and with what Mrs J. writes, that you had the Mahons with you. I have no objection to your dining there. Take care only to chuse your days well. But how or where do you propose to get your diner dress'd? Or Is your Scheme Cold Meat? I have no objection if the Doctor has not. If you meet any more grass-mice I hope you'll join in the hunt, with as little fear as you saw the late one. Depend upon it, while you pursue, the little animal will never attempt to climb your petty-coats.

I gave you in my last a full account of Cowgil and his Wife. She now sleeps and eats here, and shall do so, till I determine upon them. I am at present inclin'd to keep them. The Trunk of which Mrs J. gives an account, confirms me in my Opinion, that the hasty bringing her down, was more the effect of Simplicity than Art without hopes and intention of setling here, they would not have been in such haste to bring down their things. Let John send down the Trunk with my things, and Tell the Guardian that I write this day to the Pupil for half an hundred of Boards. George Stephens[2] and He are to chuse. She'll admonish him not to neglect.

Shannon's account of Cowgil's Wife made me laugh. What sort of Woman is she? Why, My Lord, She's a Short, Coarse, English bred,

Woman, and speaks mighty broad. You can't imagine with what a face of Contempt He utter'd these Words. But, as it usually happens, this depretiating Character turn'd to her advantage. It is true, She speaks broad, and is no beauty. But she is neither short nor Coarse. Her figure is not unlike Old Miss, the great Man's Sister,[3] who goes every where under the protection of a Matron. But she appears on the whole like a tight Servant and her answers to my questions shew'd innocence without folly. I find they are no straglers. He has a copy-hold Estate in York-shire of £15. a year, but much incumb'red, and they have left it to clear it Self, and came hither in hopes of getting Land for nothing. Disappointed in this, they chuse to go to Service. How they'll prove, I know not. The Man is certainly sensible and knowing. I'll therefore try him. I am sure I can't be worse than I was, with him or any one else. About the Woman I can determine nothing but just to give her food and a bed, till she has lain in. By Mrs J.'s letter, It looks as if she had not known of the Man's coming off. She seems surpriz'd at finding his Trunk in the parlor on Sunday, and yours by him is dated the Thursday before. You'll probably think from what I've writ that I design the Woman shall lye in in the house. I do not.

You mention two poor boys at the infirmary. I know of but one, about whom I wrote to you. I fancy the Doctor has been impos'd on. Give him my Service, and Tell him I desire He would not mind any who apply to him in my Name, without proper Credentials. I'll always write either to him or you on such Occasions, and they shall be as few as I possibly can.

I return N. Watts's[4] letter. It is certainly a begging one, and artfully enough wrote. One part I don't like: Her saying that N. Curtis witheld from her some things which I order'd for her. I don't, can't, believe it. I think you would do well to enquire into her real Character and Circumstances, before you determine any thing about her.

I am glad your Peacocks are in a way of multiplying. I have given up all care about mine. Here they are, Sometimes making an hideous noise, sometimes strutting before the door, but with disfigur'd tails. They say they have nests. If any young appear, they'll perhaps rear them better themselves, than We have done with all our Care.

Tell Mrs J. that in her Conferences with the most complaisant Man alive, I hope she will not forget to give a gentle hint about French Roll.[5] As to Bottles, if the number at home will not fill the three Hampers, She must desire him to furnish a few to fill them. Corks I have a multitude.

Mrs J. tells me your sheets are in rags. I write this day to Mr Newburgh who promis'd to supply me if He could. Send Mrs Barry to him some morning to know if He can, and if He can, to tell your Wants, and not your particular ones only, but those of the House in general. If Mr N. engages,

He'll supply them all better than you can any way else. Buy more or less as you find the Market. His house is at the Linnen-Hall.[6] If He can't help you, you must help your Selves as well as you can. I can't find the Complaint Mrs J. says there is of our Linnen from England in this day's paper. I wish she would direct me to it, or, if it be in another paper, send it. I believe she means the Advertisement of ten pieces fraudulently lapp'd.[7] That signifys nothing to our purpose.

She complains that you do not get your letters in the morning. To be sure, this is very inconvenient. I write to the Post-office about it. Let Will call there constantly at twelve on Post-days.

I am very sorry for the death of poor *En passant's* youngest Son.[8] Mrs J. writes of Mrs Warren's being well in a way that makes me suspect she has been otherwise. See her in a familiar way, and get her, Mrs G. and Miss Holt[9] to pass an Evening with you some times.

A Letter goes to the Pupil with some Commissions, which Mrs J. will call for. Very bad Weather, and likely to continue. This makes me less happy. But I bless God I am very well, and have hitherto contriv'd to ride every day. God bless you all.

Your &c
Edw: Elphin

You never mention N. Curtis's daughter, nor have you, that I remember, once said a Word of Dunshaglin. These are Omissions Mistress.
Do you continue to kill any sheep? You may if you find it convenient.

1. Barbara Synge. See Letter 21.
2. George Stephens: a carpenter. See Letter 7.
3. Not known.
4. N. Watts: not known.
5. French Roll. Snuff.
6. The construction of the Linen Hall off Bolton Street was begun by the Trustees of the Linen Board in Dublin in 1722, when the import and export of linen to Ireland was increasing and when it was thought that a central market hall would be advantageous. Built with grants from the government, the models for the Dublin hall were the Cloth Hall in Hamburg and the Drapers Hall in London. The interior of the Hall had a large exchange and warehouses and a council room for the Trustees was added later in the century. In its final form, it covered 2½ Irish acres, was three storeys high and had 550 rooms. In 1874 it was converted to a barracks. Gill, pp.79-81, 297-8, 310.
7. 'Whereas ten Pieces of Linen Cloth, returned from England for being fraudulently lapp'd by John M'Carter of the County of Donegal, were this day laid before the Linen Board, and it appearing that they were all deficient in measure, and Several of them faulty in other Respects, the said John M'Carter was fined 40 shillings for each Piece, and is hereby discharged, of which all Dealers in Linen are desired to take

Notice. Arthur Newburgh Dublin Castle 15 May 1752.' *Faulkner's Dublin Journal* 6-9 June 1752.

8. '*En passant*': not known.

9. Mrs G and Miss Holt: not known.

190

Elphin. June 23, 1752

My Dear Girl must be content with a very short letter to day. Mine to Jeny will tell you the reasons.

Your account of your friend is very Candid, and, I fear, very true. I am sorry for it. Let your Conduct to her be in a Medium between your own former intentions, and my Advice. Your judgment was certainly right, but rather rigidly so. A reputable acquaintance and friend she may always be; But no intimacy without Similitude of manners found or made. God forbid that yours should ever be like hers in that blameable respect. Nor would I have you initiated in what is so bewitching, even by frequent Conversation on the Subject.

Last Saturday I sent off my Miln, which you know was spoil'd. It will probably be with you before this is. Whoever leaves it, pay him nothing. He is either paid already, or will be another way. This Caution probably goes too late. But I could not send it earlier. Let it not go into any hands till Mr Nicholson sees it. I believe He'll send to let you know when He'll call for that purpose. If He does, order John Miller to be sure to have Mr Constable there. Every thing further Mr N. will order as He pleases.

My Service to the Guardian. Tell her she must take another pupil. For I forgot Coals as well as her Mignon.[1] Desire her to order him to seek out Spedan, and make what other enquirys He can about them. Adieu. God bless you all. I am

Your &c
Edw: Elphin

I have set you a pattern of a Scrole. I was greatly hurry'd, when I wrote.

[Free Edw:Elphin]

1. Mignon: may be a form of lace.

191

And Was my Dear Girl's now before me wrote in the manner I advis'd? Upon my Word, if it was, you need be in no apprehensions of a Scrawl, but may, if you persist, come, at a jerk, to write both well and quick. I really think your letter on the whole, the best wrote, I have had from you this year; and It is certainly freest from blots or interlineations of any. There are none, of either worth notice. In one thing only it is otherwise than I wish. Your stopping, Huzzy, is abominable, commas frequently, where there ought to be punctums, Sometimes the reverse. You ought to attend to this more carefully, as Want of right stopping, will bring you under a Suspicion of not understanding, what you right. Recollect my old rule. It is indeed universally true. The Sense points out the Stops. When I write in a hurry I omit many Stops. If I read my letter over, I supply them. Take this way. Better no stops than wrong ones. You have mended, in some degree, the too great closeness of your Words, but not perfectly. You will by degrees. I have observ'd two mottos on coaches, Each a single Word, which furnish excellent rules, not for the present purpose only, but for the whole Conduct of life. Try. Persevere.[1] I think I have mention'd them to you before. No Matter. They cannot be too much imprinted on your mind.

You may pursue your Finglas scheme which way you will. If you like, and the Doctor thinks cold meat as wholesome as Hot, I have no objection to it. You may go to Chappel-izod to see Miss H. The Gardens will please you. Your rule with regard to that Damsel, ought to be, an easy familiar intercourse, without intimacy or fondness. I am glad you were at Rathfarnam. When you go next there, Make my Compliments, and be sure make them always to your Uncle and Aunt Curtis. As for Mrs Heaton,[2] Tell her once for all that I have no doubt of her regards, and hope she has none of mine.

From your Aunt's account of Mrs Watts, I think she does not deserve your notice. Prithee Tell me the boy's name who was in the Hospital, before I left town.

I am much mistaken if I did not leave directions with Ned Curtis about the Hoc when it arriv'd. Desire him to get it instantly remov'd, or plac'd in the hogshead Cellar, on the left side. There is but one hogshead there. As it is so superlatively good, He must get his and my friend Mat Weld, to have four Iron hoops put upon each Aulm. I count upon two, before it is stirr'd, for fear of accidents, and Let the Wooden hoops be effectually secur'd or supply'd with new ones Assoon as it is plac'd in it's station, I desire He would pay for it. I shall not be satisfy'd, till I know that is done.

Ask him with what view He bid you tell me of the lottery?[3] If, that I may subscribe, With all my heart, as far as ten Tickets, tho' my only Motive is to encourage the Bridge. But they must be taken in some feign'd or obscure name. The thing is right in it self, therefore I do it. The letter, tho' not the intention of the Law, is against it, therefore I do not care to appear in it.[4] Tell him the account you give of his Girl delights me.

Not so that of Dunshaglin. I am particularly sorry for the good Old Man's swimming in his head.[5] I fear it is a prelude to what must happen, but I wish may be long deferr'd. God's Will be done in us all.

You already know that poor Lucy[6] is gone. I was much affected with the Sight of her, and cannot but regret her death, tho' it has put an end to a life made miserable by ill health, and more so by underserv'd neglect. The news reach'd G[arbally] about the time of their Arrival. I know not whether it pall'd their joy in the other Event.[7] I doubt much whether it prove a joyous one.

I am seldom without company, tho' I do not always mention them. Blair and Doherty are now here. Will French left me yesterday. He'll return next week, and the following one. I shall have company enough. My Visitation is July 8. In good Weather I matter company less. Ours this Week was not quite so fine as yours. Tuesday was the only very fine day. Sunday morning was very Wet. Wednesday so much so, that I was forc'd to strike off all Work. Yesterday some flying show'rs in the Morning, but a very high and drying wind the remainder of the day. This morning was fair, but there have been some showrs. One drove me in a while ago to write. Very bad all this for Midsummer. But I bless God I am very well, and live in hopes of better.

You may continue to kill a sheep a Week as long as you like it. I regard that more than what you call convenience. But I would willingly have as many reserv'd, as will serve us next Winter. Consult the pupil on this, and let him reserve the Smallest.

Your account of the C.B. made me laugh. He's an Old Fop. Is not He?[8]

Pray, Mistress How could you say so positively, that you'd be before hand with *Faulkner*? Do you count on my reading yours before I read my News-papers? and, if you do, Are not you a Sawcy girl? You are however in the right. Your letter is always first open'd; and when I see in it or by it, that you are well, I rejoice in the agreable tidings. May I always have them

Your &c
Edw: Elphin

Desire the Guardian to ask the Pupil about Hogs which I order'd him to provide six months ago, and He has not done it that I know of. I chuse not to mention them to him, because I really am weary of chiding. I order'd three midling ones. If there be a good prospect of parsnips, I wish they were provided, otherwise not.

If Mr Mitchel the Woolen-draper of whom you sent an account from Ned Curtis, calls to see the Liverys and Frocks, Direct that they be shewn him. I intend to deal with him.

Carleboe desires some Crockery for potting Venison &c. I fear I write too late. If the things are not sent off, Get a few and let them come with them. I should be glad also of a few little handled cups of the White Stone Ware, such as the one which us'd to stand on the Table in my Bed-chamber.

From tea this morning to now eleven at night, the Worst Weather I've seen since I came hither, and no sign of mending.

[Free Edw:Elphin]

1. 'Try' is the motto of the Gethin family of Gethinstown, Co. Cork; 'Persevere' is the motto of the Congreve family of Mount Congreve, Co. Waterford.

2. Probably Elizabeth Heaton. See Letter 21.

3. A lottery was announced to raise £13,700 to rebuild Essex Bridge and for other 'public and charitable uses'. 100,000 tickets were to be issued at a guinea each. *Gentleman's Magazine*, Vol. 22 (1752), p.381.

4. Edward Synge was right: the proposed lottery was illegal. It foundered because it was held to contravene the act of 12 George II *c*.26 'An Act for the more effectual preventing of excessive and deceitful Gaming', aimed to stamp out the fraudulent sale of lottery tickets to 'Children and Servants of several Gentlemen, Traders and Merchants ... to the utter Ruin and Impoverishment of many Families.' Punitive fines and sentences of imprisonment were proposed, both for those who sold the tickets and those who bought them. In August 1752 the Lords Justices suppressed the Essex Bridge lottery. *Gentleman's Magazine*, Vol. 22 (1752), p.431.

5. The Rev. John Jourdan.

6. Lucy Caulfield.

7. Emilia Trench (see Letter 150) had married Richard Eyre earlier in the month. 'Last Sunday evening was married in Cuff Street Capt. Richard Eyre, of Eyre Court Esq, to Miss Emilia Trench, younger daughter of Col French [*sic*] Knight of the Shire for the County of Galway, a young Lady of very good Fortune with the most amiable Qualities and Accomplishments and early next Morning they set out for Garbally the seat of Col Trench.' *Faulkner's Dublin Journal* 20-23 June 1752.

8. 'The C.B.' is almost certainly John Bowes (1691-1767) the Chief Baron. Called to the Irish Bar in 1725, he was MP for Taghmon in 1731 and was Chief Baron from 1741 to 1757. He was created Baron Bowes of Clonlyon, Co. Meath, in 1758. He was unmarried. Ball's entry for Bowes includes a poem with a verse: 'There's Bowes, a great beau,/That here makes a show/And thinks all about him are fools, Sir;/He winks and he speaks/His brief and fee takes/And quotes for it English rules, Sir.' *King's Inns*, p.47; Ball, Vol. 2, p.111.

192

Elphin. June 30, 1752

I don't know at setting out, but that My Dear Girl must take up with almost as short a letter this post, as she had this day se'night. However I can give you the same Satisfaction I did then. I bless God, I am very well; tho' down about the Weather. I was in hopes of a change at the Change of the Moon, because others were. For I am far from being sure that the Moon has any influence on the Weather. But it was new Moon this morning between 7 and 8 and We have had since heavy showr's, one very heavy one – God's will be done. But indeed the prospect is alarming.

You appear so affected with your little friend's death, that I am pleas'd at my not having told it to Jeny at once. But that was the effect of chance more than Caution. I had no account of Lucy's death, when I wrote my letter tho' I was sure it would soon happen. Late at night I received the news, and was going to have added it. But on recollection I thought it was better to write to Ned. He was a Simpleton for not telling it you on Monday. Your reflexions on her &c. are too well founded. Keep them to your Self.

If my friend Katty[1] be still in town, Tell her, her poor fellow gives his service to her, and is very sorry He is out of town when she is there. I hope you have had her often with you and done every thing in your power to make her short excursion agreable.

I am glad Mrs Warren was with you. Prithee be upon an easy footing with her, if she likes, and you have no Objection. Why mayn't you when next you see her, in a merry free way propose her Spending a day with you three Girls? You may easily shift off the Captain[2] saying you are not in a way of asking persons to dine, but hope you may make free with her. As I think her very good, I wish you were free with her, and I am sure her good Father and Mother[3] count upon it. He was here yesterday when I got yours, and on my telling him that Nancy had spent two hours with you, He shew'd joy in his Countenance and said that Kevin-street was a great Article in her Dublin satisfactions.

When next you see Madam Pomeroy, Give her my service, and Tell her I now insist on her never practicing with Dr James's powder on her Self or any one else. An officer at Derry has lately lost his life by it, as certainly as if He had been shot. The account of his death you had in the news-papers. He was a Major; His name Tho. Ashe Lee.[4] He was seiz'd with a fever, from which for a Couple of days He seem'd in some hazard. But the fourth day it subsided, and He was so well, that the Physicians who attended, pronounc'd positively all to be over, and the Army-Doctor, who was one, congratulated his poor Wife on his being out of danger, and went off some where to attend another patient. That night about twelve the Major found a return of some heat, which alarm'd him, and He sent for his Physician in town, who over and over assur'd him that the heat was nothing more than what was usual at nights in such cases, when the disorder was going off, and that He was in no sort of danger. Unluckily for him, his Coll. Coll. Murray, who had great faith in the powder, offer'd some, when his fever was at worst, but the Physicians would not administer it. The Major at that time press'd for it most eagerly, and told the Physician in a reproachful way, that He would let him slip thro' his fingers, and that He should loose his life, because He would not give him the powder. Stung with these reproaches the Doctor very simply yielded, tho' he persisted in his disapprobation. The powder was given about one, and at five the Patient was dead. It set him a Vomiting. From that He fell into convulsions, violent at first, but gradually less'ning, till he expir'd. I am thus Circumstantial in my account as I had it from the Bishop of Clonfert, who call'd here in his way from Derry to Clonfert, and left me this morning. He was at Derry, when the thing happen'd, was well acquainted with the Gent. and inform'd him self minutely of his fate and the Cause of it; and after giving me this account twice, He said as I did just now, That He was kill'd by that powder, as surely as if He had been shot thro' the head.

My Service to the Guardian; and Tell her that she must, if she pleases, do something more about Coals, than she does or need do, about some other things. When Capt Spedan arrives, I wish her to have an interview with him; and Let her try what she can make of him. He is not near so complaisant as Mr S. Two points are to be manag'd. The kind of Coals and the price. The former of more importance than the latter. I doubt much that our last Season were not White-haven,[5] they burn'd too quick for them; and I think 15 shillings a Tonn high. But the Coals must be laid in; and she may order the pupil to make enquirys as to both points before the interview. I wish she could get N. Curtis to make some. For the honest truth is the pupil has lost his credit with me, as to every thing, but downright honesty. As I know her niceity, so I chuse to add; Let her do what she thinks right. I desire to know nothing further, but that the Coals are laid in; and As to that let her take her own time. I wish I had 20 Tonn here. Turf is the greatest distress in prospect; and Some there will be, tho' the Weather should take up from this hour.

I see Mrs Silver takes every opportunity of obliging. You will not fail to make proper returns. I hope you frequently give her my *respects*.

Methinks this is a tolerably long letter considering that at setting out I promis'd or threaten'd a short one. God bless you all.

Your &c
Edw: Elphin

It just comes into my head to tell you that as Midsummer is past, you and Jane are entitled to call for your allowances, if you want, as very likely you do. Ned Curtis will answer your Calls.

It will please you to know that I have a very good account of Cowgil and his Wife from Mr Davies. I wrote to him directly, promising Secrecy, if occasion. He knows more of the Man than of her, and therefore says more, but very well of her. This to your Self and your second self.

You should sometimes send your Compliments to Mrs Cary. She always enquires after you, as does Mrs Conry.

1. Cathérine Jourdan. See Letter 99.
2. Captain Warren: not known.
3. Mrs Warren's parents: not known.
4. Death of Major Thomas Ashe Lee: 'Saturday Se'nnight died of a malignant fever, after four Day's Illness at London Derry, Major Thomas Alli [*sic*] Lee of the Hon. Col Thomas Murray's Regiment of Foot.' *Faulkner's Dublin Journal* 20-23 June 1752.
5. Coal was imported into Ireland from Whitehaven, Cumberland.

193

Elphin. July 3, 1752

Never fear, My Dear Girl. Do as you resolve, Persevere and you'll write as well as you need desire. But I would advise you to get better paper. That which We both use, is not of the best kind, tho' gilt round the edges. So Ladies with fair outsides are not always the most valuable. The ink sinks too much into it, and that makes your writing look worse. Try some of the plain in the lower drawer of the Scriptoire. If that has the same imperfection, Speak to Ned Curtis to get you a quire of the very best that is to be had. What they call Pro patria is most esteem'd, and I think deservedly. Your censure of your letter before this, is just; but you have accounted for it. This now before me is written a trifle as well as the first in this way. Go on, my dear. No danger, but you'll succeed.

I believe they take your friend's death quietly enough. I had this minute a letter from the Coll.[1] the only one since that happen'd, in which He makes great acknowledgments of my goodness to her, and says of her,

'She is happier than We could otherways make her, and her death can be no surprize to any of her friends'. I think him the least faulty among them with respect to her. He gives a very good account of himself, and says that He and Mrs Trench will make me a visit soon if I'll give them leave. I intend to tell him presently, that I shall be glad to see them, if he'll promise to be well. I find He intends going first to Roscrea. He mentions not the other affair, nor will I.

I remember well the boy whom you describe, tho' I can't recollect his name. He is now the good Doctor's patient, not mine. I wish for both their sakes, He may be able to cure so inveterate and rooted an evil. He is not the son of a favorite mower. That Lad is now mowing stoutly himself. But Oh! my poor hay. All lately cut lyes under the rain. Yesterday was fine. But at the close of day rain came on, and fell very heavily in the night. There has been a good deal, not continu'd, this day; and I see no good prospect of to morrow. It is very bad. But, God's will be done. Thanks to him, I am very well.

I believe your Uncle will not let the Girls go to Mrs Whetcombe. I think He would do right to let Bab and Madge² make such an Excursion. The other two are better at home.

Do what you please about Sheep. I know that these Hogs were bought long since. But I order'd three more, two months before I left town, and John from time to time promis'd to provide them on the strength of Parsnips I had a mind to have good pork as well as good Bacon next winter.

Let Mr Newburgh be paid immediately; and As the linnen He has got you is not very good, tho' the best He could get, I think it would not be amiss if you desir'd him, when any very good falls in his way, to buy you some more, of the same kinds or finer, such as I use, or may be wanting here. You know better than I how soon a supply of these last will be wanting.

I am much pleas'd that Mr Jourdan is very well agen. May He be long so. Your account of poor Katy is very affecting. What pity it is, that one so amiable should have such infirmitys. But Who can tell? Perhaps those very infirmitys have brought her to that temper of mind. If so, they are not so much to be deplor'd. They certainly are more grievous to her friends than to her. I believe they are so particularly to Mrs J. I know she always esteem'd her in a particular manner, and remember well, that when some years since she thought her self dying, she was for recommending you to her care. But, thank God, she has liv'd, and I hope will live long to take care of you her self. You in return will take the best care of her.

Next week I hold my Visitation, so shall have company enough. The following one I expect Kitty and her husband, and for ought I know Mr

and Mrs Wills and the girls. Before they go off, Lawson will be here, and
then No danger of Solitude. But that, the little that has fallen to my share,
has not been near so grievous as the Weather. Yet I support my self bravely
under both, and contrive to ride constantly. I have miss'd but one day,
since I came hither, last Sunday. The Morning was wet, and the Bishop of
Clonfert hind'red me in the Evening, tho' it was not so fine here as you
describe it. It is late. God bless you all.

> Your &c
> Edw: Elphin

There has been some misunderstanding between the Coll. and Dic.[3] I
am afraid it still continues. I did what I could to compose it. With what
effect, I do not yet know. I think the son more to blame than the Father,
tho' He is not quite free. But Fany and her Father[4] have been more in
fault than either Father or Son. The young Councillor[5] too has his share.
Interest sets private familys as well as kingdoms together by the ears. The
Coll. promises in his letter to take my Advice; If He does, I am in great
hopes their differences will soon be compos'd.

Send the enclos'd to the post-office. Mr Mahon's account of his Wife
is a very good one; the pain in her breast gone, her Cough easier and less,
and the Waters agree with her. But probably you know all this already.

[Free Edw: Elphin]

1. 'The Coll.': Frederick Trench II.
2. Madge: Margery Synge. See Letter 53.
3. Richard Trench (1710-?), son of Frederick Trench II, was admitted to TCD in
1725. Cooke-Trench, Table 11, p.26; *Alumni*, p.823.
4. Richard Trench married Frances, daughter of David Power. Cooke-Trench, Table
11, p.26.
5. Frederick Trench: son of Frederick Trench II, was admitted to Lincoln's Inn in
1745 and became MP for Banagher. *Lincoln's Inn*, Vol. I, Admissions, p.430.

194

Elphin. July 7, 1752

My being in a hurry, when I received your letter, My Dear Girl, was no
reason for your writing on a Small sheet. I must be hurry'd indeed when
I can't find time to read your prattle. I am hurry'd now, tho' not yet with
Visitation affairs. Shocking rain yesterday has so distress'd my Hay-affairs,
that I have been all this morning busy in aiding Cowgil to retrieve them.[1]

He is not yet setled in his geers. His own part He does extremely well. But He has not got his troops under Command. He will in a short time. If this day holds, We shall be well enough. I write at past two; and 'tis yet fair, and looks as if it would continue so, with a brisk wind, which is very usefull to the Hay, and to my Wheat also, which was much bent yesterday, but now raises it's head. I believe our Weather has been rather worse than yours. But Thursday last was a very fine day here, and Friday and Saturday at least as good as you describe. Sunday too was fine; and We were so dry that Will. French and I had a fine Walk in the fields. With night, rain came on. It was less in the morning, so that I rode before breakfast. About ten it set in heavy, and continu'd till night.

I am engag'd at present in building a Poultry-house for breeding and rearing. Two yards are design'd to keep different kinds distinct; and one of them I devote in my mind to the little Bantams. Mrs Whetcombe has many of them. Write to her, and put in your Claim. I think she promis'd us some. No matter whether she did or not. She'll give, if she has them. Write to her either Saturday or Tuesday. By that time I believe she'll be returned: Or if she be not, she'll get your letter when she does. Best be early, because every thing of that sort will be given away, and you may lay in for any other fowl, that are pretty and uncommon. I'll get them hither.

I sometimes please my Self with the thought of seeing you and your Companions diverting your Selves here in those yards. and a Rabbit-yard which is to be next them, for which I shall soon put you upon providing; tho' how, I can't yet tell. To have you here would give me vast pleasure. Care of your health, hitherto determines against it. Perhaps it may always. I can't tell. But this part of the World is not proper to be sick in. There is a Melancholy proof of this now in my neighbourhood. Young St George, the General's son,[2] is in a most miserable Condition with gout; and there is something in his case beyond meer pain, which seems to me alarming. His Lady is come down to him, as well instructed as she could be by Dr Weld:[3] and yet it is odds but they are at a loss for want of a skilfull person on the Spot.

Writing thus brings to my mind poor Lucy, and of consequence. The lost mouse, which she, with so much good Sense and good nature, procur'd for you. I am seriously concern'd at it's escape, both on her account and your own; tho' if you have, by it, got rid of that simple fear which yet I could not blame; there will be no Occasion for such a memorial of the deserving neglected little creature, now at rest. I am sure you will not easily forget her. I heard from Mr Lawder[4] on Sunday, that there had been great mirth at Garbally but I enquir'd no further.

Your account of the price of the Hoc. surprizes me. If it be superlatively good, I am sure it is superlatively cheap. I knew not how to spell

Aum, till you instructed me; and you have done it with great politeness. Your guess at the Author of *Jac. Connor*, was an unlucky one. But He has no reason, on the whole, to be proud of his performance. It begins much better than it proceeds. I had read but a short way, when I commended it. You don't Spell the Author's name right. It is Chaigneau. Is He not a Clergy-man?[5] But what mean you by saying, like the Gossip in the Song &c? I am sure, you don't mean to publish him.

I must take you to task for your Stopping, Mistress, tho' I said I would not, and I'll do it by transcribing a Sentence stopp'd as you have done it. *I believe all people may be kept at a distance by a proper manner, to hit. That is the skill, and a very great one it is.* Sure never was good sense so murder'd by pointing. From a stranger I should imagine it, an Aphorism, transcrib'd from a book, by a person, who did not understand, what she wrote. But the Sense is your own, and very good sense it is. The Stopping too is your own. Are not you asham'd of it? There are many other mistakes in this single paragraph; a multitude in the latter; and in every one I have from you. But this is so glaring, that I could not pass it by. As the ink has sunk just in that place Lest you should be at a loss, I tell you that you've put a , after *manner* where there ought to have been a . and a . after hit, where there ought to have been no stop at all. Strange! that All I can say, cannot beat that single rule into my Dear giddy girl's pate. The Sense is to determine stopping. In this single letter, there are 20 transgressions of that rule. Commas where there ought to be full stops; and sometimes, where your stops are right, they are so small and so close to the Word, that with difficulty I can discover them. Prithee observe how they are in printed books, or even in my careless writing.

I gave you the account of Major Lee, just as I had it from the Bishop and Dr Henry.[6] I am sure it is the true one. I think your friend and her husband ought to have depended on it. They may enquire further if they please, and believe what they like. Pleasing lies pass better than disagreable truths.

Make proper returns to your Uncle's &c. kind remembrances. Adieu.

Your &c
Edw: Elphin

Do you get your letters in time now?
Jane has four fine pea chicks. What's come of your broods?

[Free Edw:Elphin]

1. The weather in July 1752 was 'Excessively wet ... very few days quite free from rain.' Rutty, p.168.
2. General Richard St George had no legitimate issue. His son Richard and young

Mrs St George do not, therefore, appear in the St George pedigree. Richard St George was made colonel of a regiment of Dragoons in the militia in September 1747. Lady St George, wife of Col Richard St George, had a son in June 1748. The St George family lived at 9 Henrietta Street. [Anon]: Pedigree of the family of St George; *Georgian Society Records*, Vol.2, p.17.

3. Dr Richard Weld (?-1755): studied medicine at Leyden in 1725. Licentiate King's and Queen's College of Physicians 1728. Died in Bath. Kirkpatrick.

4. James Lawder of Lowfield, parish of Kilmore, near Carrick on Shannon, married Jane Contarine, Oliver Goldsmith's cousin. James Lawder was murdered by his servants in 1776. He had two Protestant and three Catholic servants. Ginger, p.78, footnote; Census, f.38.

5. William Chaigneau (1709-81): born in Dublin, where he became army agent at Dublin Castle. The Chaigneaus, who came to Ireland before 1685, were 'one of the most pervasive and widely scattered of all the Huguenot families in Ireland ...'. A.M. Brady and B. Cleeve, *A Biographical Dictionary of Irish Writers* (Mullingar 1985); Hylton, p.165.

6. William Henry (?-1768): Henry took MA at TCD in 1748 and BD and DD in 1750. He became chaplain to the archbishop of Dublin and rector of Killesher, Co. Fermanagh, and rector of Urney, Co. Derry. He became dean of Killaloe in 1761. William Henry was a popular preacher and observer of natural phenonema; he was elected FRS in 1755. He advocated religious liberty and wrote a number of pamphlets advocating temperance. *Alumni*, p.390; *DNB*.

195

Elphin. July 10, 1752

I have advis'd my Dear Girl to change her paper; and tho' I see the good effects in her writing yet I stick to the old myself. Nothing more common than for folks to give advice, which they do not take. But I'll tell you my reason. I have a mind to try what a change in my ink will do. Hitherto it Succeeds. If it goes on, It will recommend it self to you, tho' I would have you stick to your new paper. But if you have not cotton in your ink-glass, put some, and stir from the bottom whenever you pour fresh ink. The thinness of that occasions sinking. I think you have done more than tolerably this bout. But still I see by the Cut of your letters, that your fingers are stiff; and do not move with the freedom they ought. Try, give them their way; and suppose you write a little Worse, Write fast. When you've got a Confirm'd habit of this, you may draw up, and come to write fast and well too. But Have a care of false Spellings. I meet a very bad one in your well wrote letter. desided. It should be decided. It is french as well as English. This makes the matter worse.

I am very much griev'd at the account you give of Dr D[elany]'s cause, not so much for the loss, as for the Evil report &c.[1] I know a good deal of that matter, and hope and believe that He is more innocent than He is thought to be.

I am glad the Tulips are so improv'd. I think you had e'en as good stick to what flowers you have, and not trouble Ned or his friends. Ten to one if you get good, whatever they may cost. I never succeeded but once, and then the person who sent was very nice himself. Probably none of Ned's friends have a Correspondent of this kind: and He is not likely to make such a matter the object of much attention. I can give you no account of the Tulips here, further than that there are a multitude. But their bloom was almost over when I came. To my great Surprize there were as few Tags here, as at Kevin-street.

You say, John promises to get three more Hogs. But did He confess that I had order'd them four months ago? If the Guardian has not chid him soundly for this, I'll chide her – if I can.

Three fine days, since Monday, which was here very bad; and This is a tolerable one. A show'r or two, but no interruption to Works, except Hay, which is in a very good Condition, and in great abundance. I have time for no more. God bless you all.

Your &c
Edw: Elphin

I see this paper won't do well. If I have any of the same kind with yours I'll use it for the future; and keep this for Envelopes, for which I have no great Occasion. It is fit for nothing else.

The letter you sent was an English one. Mr Bristow[2] brought, and I suppose, forgot it. It was dated June 3. Enclos'd is the Answer which send to the Post-office.

I think I forgot the Cap that Mr Dexter left, in my last. I had like to have forgot it in this. You may send it, if you find a very Convenient opportunity. But 'tis no matter whether you send it or not.

[Free Edw:Elphin]

1. Dr Delany's first wife, Margaret Tenison, died in 1741. Delany was sued by her family, the Tenisons, about her estate. He had unwisely destroyed his copy of their marriage settlement, and the Tenison family demanded an account of the estate, charging Delany with impropriety. In 1752 Delany was sued in the Irish Court of Chancery and lost. But on the advice of Edward Synge among others, in 1758 he appealed to the English House of Lords, where the decision was reversed. Mrs Delany said of Edward Synge's interest in her husband's cause 'He is a good man.' Delany, Vol. 3, p.71 *passim* and p.490.
2. Mr Bristow: not known.

196

Elphin. July 14, 1752

House full; So My Dear Girl is likely to have but a short letter. Kitty, her husband, and his Sister – Mr Sandford, here; Rachel[1] at Cary's. I expect Mr Wills every minute; and half a doz. more at diner. I am told too that Mr Cooper[2] will be here this Week. I am not, you see, likely to be dull for want of Company; and before they are gone, I expect Lawson.

I am a good deal uneasy about poor Mrs Heap. A very unfortunate accident has lately befallen her. About a fortnight ago, as she was washing one of the black glaiz'd pickling pots, A Splinter of the glaizing stuck in her thumb. She thinks she took it out. It became an Ugly Sore, which for two or three days she doctor'd her Self. Stafford was then call'd in who on Saturday senight pronounc'd the Case a bad one, and advis'd the Sending for a Surgeon. She dally'd about it till last Sunday, when Conry was sent for, who at once pronounc'd the bone Carious, and the most expeditious and certain way of cure to be, cutting off. Stafford agrees, and I verily believe they are right, and the Man by all accounts is Equal to the Operation. She poor Woman! is very averse to loosing part of her thumb, tho' it is the left; and I am in a great strait what to do. I'll tell you my present purpose. Whether I shall execute it, I can't yet say. But I must advise you now of my intention, or else, should I execute, it would be too late to give you notice. I have thoughts of sending her to Dublin, if she persists in her Aversion to amputation. To morrow is to decide concerning the necessity of it; and I shall have a very convenient opportunity by Mr Wills's Coach, which is to go Saturday or Sunday next to Mullingar for Mr and Mrs Card.[3] That may take her up at Lanesborough, and the Stage will convey her to Dublin. Let Shannon's room be got ready for her. If she goes at all, she'll be with you on Monday or Tuesday. Shannon must be house-keeper in her absence, with the assistance of Mollys Fagan, and Byrne. I'll make any shift rather than the poor Woman should suffer, or even fancy she suffers by being detain'd here. She really deserves my care.

I don't know but that your Expedient about Stopping may be a good one. It will help you yet more, if after having wrote, you read over your letter as if you were Speaking. There is no doubt but you make the proper pauses in Speaking or reading. Stop according to these; and all will be right. Your chief fault is shorter stops instead of longer. I see several , where there ought to be . even in this, which is not on the whole so ill stopp'd as that for which I abus'd you. But there's a fault of another kind, which I must not let pass. When you would say *They did eat,* or *They have eaten* you should write *They ate.* You say of the Gold-fish They eat before us. That's wrong, tho' Common.

I am not surpriz'd at Mrs M's[4] ilness tho' much so at her holding out under so frequent returns. I see you have no great stomach to Visits there and indeed I agree with you that just what decency requires is enough. Your other jaunt was I find more pleasing. You may repeat that whenever you are inclin'd. I suppose the Damsel will not fail in making proper returns. Those must govern you.

Weather still bad. Much rain yesterday till twelve; All the night before wet, very wet. It begun about four in the afternoon, just as I was set out on a Visit to Coll St George, whose life, I believe, Dignan has sav'd. It turn'd me back, when I had pass'd Lisdurne. This day is gusty, some showers, but not heavy, nor do they stop any Work, but Hay. Friday and Saturday last We had the advantage of you. The former was a very fine day. The latter a good one, only a flying showr or two in the morning. But the afternoon fine, and much hay made up. I have time for no more.

Your &c
Edw: Elphin

Tell Jeny her letter pleases me. That's all I can now say to it. I hope the Guardian has order'd the Coals to be immediatly laid in.

Kitty desires her Compliments &c to you all.

[Free Edw:Elphin]

1. Rachel Sandford: Henry Sandford's wife.
2. Joshua Cooper: Alicia's future husband. See Biographical Register.
3. Samuel Card: the only son of Ralph Card of Dublin, merchant, was admitted to the Middle Temple in 1722-3. He was named in a lease of entailed lands in Cork which Edward Synge had inherited from Samuel Synge. MacGeagh, Vol. 1, p.293; bishop of Elphin and others to Wills and another, 9 February 1753. RD 160 108 106640.
4. Mrs M: not known.

197

Elphin. July 17, 1752

My Dear Girl.

By my last you'll expect Mrs Heap. She does not go. Her thumb is better, tho' Mr Conry still says it ought to be cut off, because the best that can happen is that after a tedious cure, the remains of it be useless. She won't without necessity part with her thumb; and fancys that He talks thus to enhance the merit of the Cure. I can't say but that she may be in the right of it.

The Marriage[1] vexes me; The Manner more than the thing. On long Experience I find that it is impossible to guard people of that rank against doing such things. One end of punishment is therefore lost upon them. They cannot be set up as an Example to deter others. So that by turning them out, We should chiefly punish our Selves, by the loss of two good Servants. I observe you are not inclin'd to this; Nor, to say the truth, am I. your best way therefore, I think, will be this. On it's being notify'd, shew great but calm resentment, mix'd with concern for the *necessity* of parting. Let Mrs J. afterwards expostulate seperately, and at last be prevail'd on to mediate with you. Do you then talk to the Lady, and be prevail'd on to mediate with me. If she be in great woe &c. she'll give all the satisfaction she can as to future behaviour. I'll take my cue from you – and So I leave it with you.

Your writing is really very well; and no part of the merit can so early be ascrib'd to your Cotton. Ink must be sometime on it, before it contracts that superior blackness, which is afterwards communicated to new put in, if you stir up from the bottom. I always use Cotton, and am not plagu'd with hairs. But I often neglect to stir. Of late I have taken care to do it; and I think I perceive a difference. You can judge.

In your present way of quick-writing, Have a care of Errors. There are some in this well-wrote letter. You have wrote *I can say* – where you certainly mean *can't*. *I can say I expect much,* are your Words. In another place you write *lawers* for *lawyers,* Prideux for *Prideaux.*

But there is a Worse carelessness, or, *what shall I call it?* than this. Speaking of Molly Curtis, you say she bid me not let on *that she told me of him.*

I know what you mean, but see how lamely you've express'd your Self; and which heightens it, an interlineation of *me* shews that this sentence was review'd. I wonder how you could let it pass thus. Stopping still the same. Commas for . perpetually. It's astonishing that you do not understand me: For to that alone, I am willing to impute, your not doing, what I have so often recommended. To give you a Specimen, and, if possible, explain my self further, I'll transcribe a Sentence. *The other part I try to day for the first time, I can say I expect much from it, as it is apt to be very troublesome in filling the pen with hairs, However it shall have a fair trial.* Thus you stop. Now there ought to be a . at time, a ; at *from it* and a . at *hairs* – If this won't explain my meaning to you, I despair. There are twenty mistakes of a like kind in this letter.

Kitty and her husband left me this morning. She spoke often of you with great affection, and desir'd me to tell you that she's gone to Sligo, to bath. You must direct thither, if you write. I suppose you will.

Your Uncle is positive, when He takes a thing once in his head. I can't approve of his management about the French letters. If you resume your Correspondence, Continue to write in French. That may give you an opportunity of doing, what you wish, and so do I too, that you had done. As Molly has confess'd, She won't take it amiss that you Extort returns from her in the same language. I say She won't, because I am sure she ought not. But don't teaze her.

Yesterday was very fine; and last night Every one else exulted on the prospect of setled Weather. I croak'd; and unhappily was right. The morning has been wet. But it is now fair. I have some hopes, tho' faint ones. But I make use of every fair hour, so that my hay is in a good Condition.

A Sad misfortune has happen'd to us. Don't be alarm'd. It is only about Pea-chicks. The night before last, A dog destroy'd two of our four. But, which was worse to me, Jennet laid hold of me the next morning, and pour'd forth such a torrent of shrill tragical Eloquence, as downright o'er-whelm'd me. In vain I endeavour'd to cut her short by asking the only question I thought material, Whether All were killed? She would not be put out of her way, but went on with a very long vehement and pompous description of every minute accident, even to a feather and at last releas'd me by telling all I wanted to know, that two had Escap'd.

More Bad news! Mrs L[ushington] is coming or come hither. I can't help it. But I hear her Husband comes too whom I like. However she'll do sometimes. There is a pleasure in Variety. Such you have in Spending a day sometimes alone. You'll fancy perhaps that I would by this insinuate a Suspicion that you don't much affect that way of Spending time. But be easy, I do not suspect you and should be very sorry I had reason. Next to downright vices, I scarce know any thing worse in man or Woman, than that impotency of mind and idleness of disposition which disqualify them from passing days, weeks agreably alone. This is always either the Cause or the Effect of Want of reflexion, folly, or levity, and betrays folks into a thousand inconveniences.

I had a letter this post from Mr Newburgh, in which He in a very genteel modest manner expresses his desire that you would in your Airings to Finglas, call at his house which lyes on that road, nearer town than the bridge. It is on the left hand as you go, a new house. You probably know it already. If not, John can tell you. I wish you would call there the first time you go that way. Or if you went on purpose, no great matter. It will be a little airing. The afternoon will be the likeliest time to meet him. Should He not be at home, You may ask for his Wife, and introduce your Self. You may tell her that I directed you. What she is I know not. He is as good a kind of man as I ever knew. As He has desir'd this, He would be apt to think it heighth, if his Civility were declin'd. You may speak to him about more linnen, if you please.

I have order'd John to send down his Carrs with boards and Iron. You may take the opportunity of them to send down the little things I wrote for some-time since. If you send the Cap, you must get a little tight box made for it, and commit it in a particular manner to Mathew's Care.

Mr Sandford is gone to day to Mr King's to see a Bull which cost 50 Guineas.² I doubt not but if he can he'll buy him at 70. His passion that way is next to madness. I left Rachel &c. to themselves and Mr Wills and I have pass'd this day very agreably by our Selves, only that W. French made a third at diner.

Adieu. You &c
Edw: Elphin

[Free Edw:Elphin]

1. The marriage of two of his servants. One of them was Peter, probably Peter Healy his coachman; the other is not known. See Letter 202.
2. Gilbert King sold a quantity of stock in 1751. 'To be sold at Publick Cant at the town of Elphin on Wednesday 16th day of October next, the Property of Gilbert King of Charles-town, some good Cows, with Bull calves and Heifer Calves at their Feet, some choice two year old Heifers, some choice yearling Heifers, 3 yearling Bulls, 1 two years old Bull, all of the best kind.' *Faulkner's Dublin Journal* 14-17 September 1751.

198

Elphin. July 21, 1752

A word or two, My Dear Girl, before your letter comes in. The Father of the poor boy whom I sent this Season to the Hospital, is in the Utmost grief. Some have told him that His Son is Extremely ill; Others that He is dead. Pray Ask the Doctor and let me have a particular account of him.

I have got some Wild-ducks on my Canal, which were rear'd last year. They are pinion'd so that they cannot fly; but they ramble so about the fields there, and hide so in the grass and Corn, that I can never get a sight of them when I go there. Nor can Simple Young¹ gather them to feed. I fancy that We may train them to the Whistle. Get two Common ones of the same tone, and shirlness;[*sic*] one I'll give to Young, the other I'll keep my Self. I hope they'll be brought to answer this Call, when they find it signifys Oats.

On Sunday afternoon I went to visit Mr and Mrs St George. I found him very ill. He had, it seems, relaps'd; and this was imputed to cold got walking out the Evening before. I can't tell but that might have been the cause. But He appear'd to me so wasted, and worn down that I can scarce think He was so well, as they represented him to have been the Thursday before. If He be set up at all, It must be the Work of long time. Mr Sandford who went with me thinks worse of him than I do. His opinion is, that He can't be set up at all. She is much to be pitied. Her distress for her husband's ilness, heighten'd by his being at such a distance from the best help, and so weak that it is impossible to carry him to it; and by want of proper accommodation for her self and him, in a Cabin fit only for health and summer; and which makes all this Worse, she has not one Female friend with or near her, but is expos'd to too much company of another kind, some not very pleasing. He has, it seems, encourag'd low people in the neighbourhood to be about him, and they stick to the meat and drink notwithstanding the ilness. At past five I found five or six, two thirds of this kind, at their bottle, He lain down. As she had no choice, she brought the Coll. and me into the room, where We staid till He crawl'd out. Our visit was very short. But I really felt for the poor Lady. She seem'd asham'd of part of her Company, and, as far as I could judge, had reason, only that they were her husband's. I had heard much good of her, but never saw her before. She comes up to every thing I had heard. Her person and behaviour are both engaging.

I forgot to take notice in my last of what you write about Walsh. I am glad you agree so well. If you don't grow idle by his missing; whatever be the cause, the effect will be no damage to you. Understand his lessons when present, and practice during his absence, You'll thus get more for less money. Now for yours.

You already know that the Stop of Mr Wills's Coach has been no disappointment to Mrs Heap. I am sorry for Mrs Card's ilness. I propos'd great pleasure in seeing her, and her fat laughing husband here. I fear now I shall not have it this Summer.

I can't say I am sorry for the Archbishop of Cashel's death, tho' I lov'd and esteem'd Him.[2] But after his stroke, I think 'twas a happiness both to himself and his friends that his fate was so quickly determin'd. My wishes for the Bishop of Down are the same with yours. I am very sorry for Mrs Paliser. She is at a time of life, that may struggle with her disorder and in some degree get the better of it. I sincerely hope she will. The Account of good Mrs Mahon is by no means pleasing. While the spitting of bloud remains, I shall make little account of any other Signs of Amendment.

Your meeting Lord Kerry, occasion'd, I suppose your Visit to Lady Anne. Or Did you refrain on account of her ilness? You should not drop her. The same reason that induc'd you to begin, still continues. Treat her and the sweet little Lord as you did last Summer.

This brings the Garden to my mind. How goes fruit there? In what way are melons? But a bad one, I suspect, because you have not mention'd them. If you have any fine, dispense them as usual; and don't forget the Chan[cello]r. He is entitled as on other accounts, so for his haunch, which came so opportunely. How go grapes?

Lady Dean's³ mistake was a laughable one. But in high politeness you ought not to have taken notice of it, especially if much Company were by. Between her and you there was no great matter in it; and It was hard to contain. But let it always be a rule with you, never to say any thing that may put a person you esteem into Confusion. I know as well as if I had been by, how all came about. At her mistake you blush'd, and were in some Confusion your Self. To cover which you with a hearty laugh took notice of it, not adverting to the indelicacy of doing it. Perhaps there was a little bit of revenge in it too. For by what you say of being asham'd to wear the gloves, I see it touch'd you to have the redness of your fists mistaken for lining of that Colour. Why should it? They are a sign of health, which is better than beauty.

Mr Sandford is still here. He was going off on Saturday: but I press'd him to stay some days longer. I wish'd him to do this on mine own account. But I had a great mind that poor Rachel should enjoy her friends for a Week more. So he comply'd, went home on Saturday to order his affairs, and return'd at night. I believe he'll stay till He has the same call home the next. Rachel and the two Sisters⁴ are gone to day to dine with Mrs St George. He is, it seems, better. But from the way in which I saw him on Sunday, of which you have an account here wrote yesterday, I think it Scarce possible that He can be in a Condition fit to receive Company. However they were ask'd and had a mind to go. So I have my Coll to my self.

Our Weather from Friday afternoon has been very fine. But a falling glass puts me in a fright for a Change. However I am prepar'd for it. All my hay is up, except what has been cut yesterday and to day.

I have a fine story for the Guardian of her pupil. At the beginning of this month I ask'd him how many *Horses* he had at Finglas, and ask'd in such Words as distinguish'd them from his Mule. His answer I send in his own Words. *I have five carr-horses, there are but four a going. For Leister the Water-horse took up a Channel nail in his for foot and is lame.*

Would not any one think by this, that He not only knew the number of his horses, but was very attentive about them? Yet yesterday's letter informs me thus. *I have but 4 Carr-horses, and the Mule: for Palmer the Carr-horse was taken from me. Mr French's Servant rode him down when your Lordship went to Elphin; it was by your Lordship's orders.* This is the very cool easy account which the Pupil gives; and I'll lay a penny, that when you speak to him about it he'll gravely plead my orders about the Horse call'd 'Palmer', as an excuse for his not knowing for two months the number of his horses, which He ought to have seen Every day; and that you'll find it hard to convince him He has been to blame. I am more griev'd than angry at this. For after such gross stupid negligence, I shall be afraid to depend on him for any thing; and yet I am unwilling to dismiss him. Here's matter for more lesson, tho' I really think they are all thrown away upon him. By the by, Mistress, when you speak in yours the post before this, of lessons to him from Mrs J. and you, you have wrote a little bit of false English. *has got many lessons from Mrs J. and I.* It should be me. Ask him for the letter which he'll receive when you do this.

I made your Compliments to Mrs Cary and Conry. They return them. I have never seen your God-daughter. But they say she is a fine Child. Mrs Conry says she promis'd you some Fox-tails. She'll get them if she can. Mrs L. speaks of Mrs Cooke's child in a most desponding way. She thinks it impossible it can live. I am sorry for it. Adieu.

> Your &c
> E:E

What stock of Tea sent you down with me? I remember your resolving to wait for part of your Annual provision, but am not sure whether you sent with me the usual Compliment. If you did, I believe there's no occasion for more. If you did not, you may send a recruit conveniently by Mr Read,[5] whom I have directed J. Miller to charge with the Tarr. Dr Lawson is come.

[Free Edw:Elphin]

1. Andrew Young: Edward Synge's fowler. See Letter 53.
2. Dr Arthur Price (?-1752): Arthur Price was nominated bishop of Clonfert on 19 March 1724; translated to Ferns 26 May 1730; translated to Meath 2 February 1734, and translated to Cashel on 7 May 1744. He was archbishop of Cashel until his death on 17 July 1752; 'Yesterday Morning died at his house in Queen Street Dr Price, Archbishop of Cashel, vice-Chancellor of the University of Dublin and Governor of the Dundalk Company. He was much esteemed when living for his many good qualities, and his death is greatly lamented by all his friends.' *Faulkner's Dublin Journal,* 14-18 July 1752. *NHI* Vol. 9, p.434, 426, 407, 411.
3. Lady Dean: Salisbury, daughter of Robert Davis of Manley Hall, Co. Chester. She died in 1755. Burke (1900), p.1104.
4. Mrs Lushington and Mrs Cary.
5. William Read, grocer, Cow Lane. Watson (1752), p.21.

199

Elphin. July 24, 1752

My Dear Girl is so severe on her Self for her great and very giddy forget, that I will not say any thing to aggravate it. It will lessen your Concern to know that the delay is of no Consequence. Mr Bristow has fully excus'd himself for his. I wrote to him upon it.

Your letter is better stopp'd, than some late ones. Yet still there are mistakes of that kind, which I have so often admonish'd you of. As I take this to be owing to your not yet fully understanding the grand rule which I have so often inculcated, I'll transcribe three or four passages in which these mistakes are made. One offers at the beginning of yours.

In yr last letter my Dear Father, you mention several marks of giddiness you have lately observ'd in my letters; I am sorry for them, &c.

There ought to be a , after *letter,* Another after *giddiness* This by the by. What I would principally observe is: that at *letters,* where you put ; there ought to be . Recollect, my Dear, that I have told you over and over, that where the Sentence ends fully, there ought to be a . tho' the Sense runs into the next. The not attending to this, is the Cause of most of your Errors. So Again.

Mrs Paliser is much better, We sent there yesterday, and heard &c. There ought to be a . at better.

Again. *He is vastly recover'd, I never saw* &c. There should be a . at recover'd.

I ought here to have begun a line above. There's another mistake. *We saw yr poor Hospital boy on Sunday and talk'd a great deal to him:* He is &c. your : at him ought to be a . There's another in the following line. *We were much pleas'd with him,* He has &c. The , at him ought to be a . .

One more out of many of a like kind. *Lady Anne came yesterday evening, We were just going out* &c. There ought to be a . at Evening.

You see these Errors are all of a kind and proceed from the Same Cause. I must add one more, because you have err'd in the very Sentence, in which you tell me, You never took so much pains about Stopping. Your next Words are, *as I have done in this letter: I hope you will find an Amendment.* There should be a . at *letter.* Your stop of interrogation you make so small, that I can't always discover whether it be it or no. Make it boldly ? So much for stopping. The writing of your letter pleases me much. It is fair, your lines and words at proper distances, and if I mistake not, your fingers have learn'd to move more glibly than I did.

Mr Sandford did not buy the Bull. He offer'd money for him and some heifers which Mr King would not take. He is fully intitled to the word you let slip; and which adds to his folly, He is as injudicious in his management, as Extravagant in his prices. He has lost many Calves this year, by not feeding these fine Cows sufficiently. Mr Wills says so positively, and I believe He is right. We reason'd with him upon the point, but to no purpose. In your Sentence here, there are two Omissions of Stops, not so faulty as the others, but which are yet faulty ones. *O my! What a Word I have let Slip?* I stop as it ought to be. You have put none at all.

I am very sorry for Mrs Slack's[1] misfortune. Such a sum she can ill bear the loss of. But the account seems improbable. A shop, to the street, and in a street so frequented as Church-street, to be robb'd, in the open day, in Church time? It must be from within. I have known people rob themselves. Count Barret[2] here is suspected to have done so. He has sworn the other day to his being robb'd of about £60. What sort of man is her Husband? Possibly He has robb'd her. Enquire into the matter carefully; and if she has been really robb'd, without hope of reprizal; Send her five pounds by Ned Curtis. Send it as from your Self. I'll repay it to you.

You know already that Mrs L[ushington] is here; and ditto. Dr Lawson made me laugh with a Scene between her and Dignan yesterday Evening at Cary's. He, in commending Mrs St George for her easy natural unaffected behaviour, whipp'd her notably for her affectations. He vex'd her visibly. One of his Speeches, I remember. She has fine eyes, but does not wink with them.

However Lady K. may desire to conceal her Sore Eyes, Her friends do not. Mrs L. gave me a full account of the disorder, and that She is in Cuningham the Surgeon's hands, who has perform'd, and is to perform some operations, which I think dangerous. Get Ned Curtis to enquire about them, and the Success. He may know all from his friend Dr Weld, thro' whom Cunningham was recommended there, and who is himself consulted as Physician to the exclusion of the Ordinary one Dr Nisbitt.[3] I have great Curiosity about this, and am in some pain for the poor Lady.

Our weather continu'd fine till last night. There has since fallen a good deal of rain with an high Wind. But it looks now about ten as if it would take up. It has been very unfortunate, particularly for the Turf. But I have yet received no damage.

Mr Sandford left me on Wedensday. Lawson, young Cooper, and I have since liv'd by our Selves very happily. I bless God continue very well. I am,

My Dear Girl
Your &c

Edw: Elphin

Your account of Mathew Murtogh has reliev'd the poor Father from great distress. I have taken notice of the boy as having a promising appearance, but on some trials made of him about the House, I found him like the rest. To make any good of such Creatures, they must be taken earlier from their parents. It is well, if even that does. Assoon as He is *quite* well, send him home.

Mrs Jourdan gives me a very pleasing account of your progress on the Harpsicord, but laments as you do Walsh's ill-health, which disables him from regular attendance, and says that you are tir'd of playing the same over and over. This is very natural. But I assure you, my Dear, that nothing can be of more use to you. As I consider this only as an Amusement, I wish you to have it in the most pleasing way. But if you desire to play well, Be assur'd that the only way for you to arrive at any thing like perfection, is to dwell upon the same Tunes, till you play them as completely as your Master does. When once you can do this with those you have, you'll find the learning new ones, infinitely easier than you can imagine. She tells me also that you apply your Selves to Speaking and reading French. I commend you much for it. Persist, and you'll hereafter find the advantage of it.

Dignan's words, as I have since learn'd more exactly, were these. She's a beauty, but none of your Winkers.

[Free Edw:Elphin]

1. Benjamin Slack was a goldsmith in Fishamble Street, Dublin. Watson (1752), p.23.
2. Count Barret: not known.
3. Dr Ezekiel Nesbitt (*c.*1709-*c.*79): took BA at TCD in 1732, and MD in 1740. He became a fellow of the King's and Queen's College of Physicians in 1745/6, and was president in 1753 and 1763. He was Physician to the Rotunda Hospital, 1759-74. He married the widow of Sir Edward Crofton in 1747. He lived in St Stephen's Green. Kirkpatrick; *Georgian Society Records*, Vol.2, p.74.

200

Elphin. July 28, 1752

My Dear Girl.

I see with great pleasure that your new manner of writing answers better and better every post. I never would desire to see any thing from you better wrote than the first page, of your letter now before me. The whole is very well, but that remarkably so. But there are still Errors, and negligences in stopping. If the directions in my last do not cure them, I must leave your improvement to time practice and attention. But one thing I expect you'll take care to amend immediatly. I have mention'd it before; but you do not yet take heed to it. Whatever stops you put, make them distinct, and at a proper distance from the Word. They should be in the middle of the Space between that, and the following one. You'll see them thus in all printed books. One little document yours gives occasion for, which I have not given before. Be sparing in the use of Capitals in the middle of a Sentence; and never use them there in particles. For instance, Writing of wise John, you say, *He did not make the excuse you thought He would, nor, I think, any other; But assur'd me* &c. Now your B. ought to be b. But is a particle, and it stands here in the middle of a sentence. Every sentence ought to begin with a Capital, and some Words, such as *I am* or do, ought always to be so. But the fewer otherwise there are in the Sentence, the better. To do you justice, you do not often offend against this rule. As to John, He made the Excuse to me, which He did not make to you. If you had seen my letter to him, you had thought it a bad one. But I'll not trouble my self or you further about him. He was always a little puzzle-pated, but is of late grown much more so. I fear it will be hard to reform him.

Mr St George has mended so much since my last account of him, that He and his Lady ventur'd to come here yesterday to diner. I don't yet know whether He has suffer'd by it. I fear He has. For indeed He is still very weak, and the distance between us is at least five miles. I go it in my post chaise within the hour; but He was more than two coming; and propos'd to be as long on his return. He can't bear the least quickness of motion in the Chariot. I therefore drove them out of my house as early as I could, to prevent his being in the night air. You ask what sort of man he is? Nothing extraordinary any way; well behav'd enough, and neither very wise nor very foolish. But He has set out here with a view of making himself popular; and this has expos'd him to such Company; with whom He has drank too much, and thus has brought himself into the miserable Condition in which He now is. I question whether He'll ever perfectly get clear of it. They talk of going to town assoon as He is able to travel and from thence to Bath, which, if any thing, will relieve him.[1] But I find his habit of hard-drinking is too much confirm'd, to hope for a total reformation. His wife is indeed to be pity'd on this account. Her behaviour yesterday has not lessen'd my good opinion of her. She seems to have good sense, and has not the least scrap of affectation. I was in some perplexity at her coming hither just before three. She quite a stranger, and not a Woman here to receive her, or shew the house, or – In this Exigence I dispatch'd Will French to Mrs Cary, who came not, because she was not, I believe, dress'd. But Mrs L. did with great good nature, and behav'd her self with more ease and propriety, than I had ever seen her before. She pleas'd me much, and Mrs C. came to Tea. So that I was well enough off. But I believe the poor Lady suffer'd for want of retiring before diner. The Doctor was of the Company, who diverted us, as usual.

If you do not already know it, you'll be surpriz'd at my telling you, that Mr and Mrs Conry are in Dublin. They left this on the sudden on Saturday. I knew nothing of their intention, till they were gone, nor of the Occasion of their going till C. told it me yesterday. It seems the Old fool her Mother is about committing matrimony with an Old Man of Seventy; and they are gone to prevent it, if they can.[2] As they said nothing to me of their Expedition, So I think you had better take no notice of them. If she goes to you, you'll receive her as usual.

l lost no time, after I got your former letter, in removing the Anxiety of the Hospital-boy's father. The Man seem'd pleas'd, but shew'd no Emotion. I have observ'd the same thing in others of his sort on many other Occasions; and I believe it is owing to their Condition, in which there is no variety, little highly pleasing, and of consequence less distress. They are not agitated with so strong passions as We are, or rather are in such a state, as that there is less room for shewing them. On the death of child, husband, or Wife, there's a great deal of clamorous grief, which is more outside, than from the heart. All is soon over, and they return to their usual Employment. Their necessitys oblige them to it; and As they have not leisure to grieve, the impression soon goes off. If they have less pleasure than We, I verily believe they have less pains.

l am glad I mistook you about the Glove affair. I should be sorry to have you the least uneasy about the Colour of your fists. I am pleas'd at it, as it is an indication of health. But I think you had better not wear gloves that must shew them. Those which Mrs P. recommended were of another kind; and I believe she advis'd them, not to hide your hands, but a little to mend their hue. I think she was right.

Your account of fruit &c is bad enough. No remedy. If every thing else falls out right, We may bear this loss. But I really believe that Roberts has been negligent, and that his apology for the loss of his first Crop of Melons is, in plain English, a lying Excuse; Or, if it be true, what can He say for his suffering his frames to be in such a Condition? I am much mistaken, if they were not all repair'd this Spring, in such manner as He directed. Pray examine this matter, and, if there be occasion, Send for Mr Eaton, and tell him what the Gardiner has said, and Let the Saddle be put upon the right horse. That fellow, tho' in other respects not a bad Servant, abounds with lying Excuses beyond any I have met with. Pray speak to him and to John too, about Winter and Spring Crops. If I be not better supply'd than last year, He shall certainly pack off. Enquire particularly about Brocoli. Remember how good it was last year. Take some Occasion of putting N. Curtis in mind, that We never got the Seed, which Mr Weld promis'd to write for, and which He, more than once, told me was actually coming. He may easily provide some for us for next Season.

I told Mrs J. that Cowgil's Wife was brought to bed. On considering the matter, I think it is best not to take her into my family. So she is to get some place in the town. By Mrs Heap's account She is too high for any Station, I could put her into; and as all is easy now in her quarter, I care not to bring in a person, that may give me, and her disturbance. It will please you to know that her thumb is likely to do very well.

I am not easy at Jeny's Complaints, and shall be very glad to know that they are quite remov'd. God bless you all.

Your &c
Edw: Elphin

Mrs Card's little ilness has been unlucky. It has not only depriv'd me of her Company, but of Mr Wills's also. They stay at home now to receive her. They would otherwise have been here now.

The Bride St George is in another Country.³ We know nothing of her, or their feasting on her account. I had not known she was married, till the News proclaim'd it, but that Lawson saw them on the road.

Your God-daughter is not well. I hope it is only teeth. Since my last, our Weather has been fair. I fear rain to night. Tell John the Carrs are come. They arriv'd about three. All safe.

1. '[Tuesday last] the Hon. Richard St. George Esq who for some Time hath lain dangerously ill at his House in Carrick on Shannon, arrived in Town.' *Pue's Occurences* 4-8 August 1752.

2. Mrs Conroy was a Miss Fowke before her marriage to John Conroy. Her mother was the widow of Robert Fowke of Mallow, Co. Cork. It is not known if she married again.

3. The 'Bride St. George' was Elizabeth Dominick, daughter of Christopher Dominick, who married St George Usher. She had a fortune of £30,000. *Faulkner's Dublin Journal* 21-25 July 1752.

201

Elphin. July 31, 1752

I have time but for three lines, My Dear Girl. A heap of letters has tir'd me, and I expect the diner-bell every minute. But I won't quit my pen, till

I have told you, that in Examining yours from one End to the other, I do not find one mistake in stopping of the kind, which I have so much complain'd of. I see that you now understand me perfectly in that point. If you transgress agen, you cannot plead ignorance.

If your progress on the Harpsicord be trifling, it is your own fault. You may play well, if you please. But I don't desire you should drudge without inclination. Three Weeks is indeed a long time to drum over the same tune. But have you no more in your book? Or Are you perfect in all except that you began last to learn? I fancy not. If now and then, you began, and plaid them all over carefully, It would contribute greatly to your improvement.

Your writing in this, is not quite so good, as the last. Two months ago, It would have deserv'd Commendation. You impute the difference to your fingers moving too glibly. I had rather it were the effect of their moving too Slow. But of that you are the best judge. I have the pleasure to see that you are now in a fair way both of writing and stopping well. Adieu. God bless you all. I am

Your &c
Edw: Elphin

[Free Edw:Elphin]

202

Elphin. August 4, 1752

I believe, I have told my Dear girl before, the Answer that one of my masters, when a boy, gave my Father. Master Nedy does well, but he ought do more. He was a Scots-man. This I may apply to you, but not perfectly in the Same Sense. My not doing more was owing to meer idleness, and love of play. I can't with honesty accuse you of this. I have seen with joy and Comfort your gradual improvements, and, for your age, a commendable attention to all Mrs Jourdan's and my documents. But Old as you are, the time of improvement of every kind is not over with you. You may be better and better every day, and with that strong desire which you tell me you have, I am sure you will be so. Make a right use of the advantages of various kinds which God has given you, and you'll be, if you are not already, every thing that your fond father wishes.

I am sorry you have had even a slight indisposition, but much rejoic'd that it was so slight, at a time when sore throats have been pretty frequent, and some dangerous. I hope yours is before this over. Have proper care of your Self, my Dearest. I am sure you will. The Doctor and Mrs J. will give the proper directions; and I have no doubt but that you'll conform to them. The Weather is now very fine. I hope you are at liberty to enjoy it abroad.

Your news surpriz'd me greatly. The Lady is very right. She and Peter have us'd us extremely ill. I leave her to you: For, As you are grown up, I shall give my Self no sort of trouble about the female part of my family. Manage it as you please. About the Gentleman I can determine nothing till I go to town. They have plaid the fool Egregiously, and deserve to smart for it. I blame not your good nature in interceding. Have a care that it does not carry you too far. I have had no great reason to boast of the gratitude of Servants. They are very ready at confession, and begging pardon, while they have hope of forgiveness; but seldom shew a just sense of it when obtain'd.

I hope you'll have it in your power to see Mrs Donnelan, before she leaves Ireland. If you do, Be sure make her my Compliments, and tell her I sincerely wish her all happiness. I have taken notice of the change in the Artane-folks. Mind it not. He and the young ones are I believe the same they always were. *Madame est quelque-fois bizarre. N'importe.*[1]

Return any thing like Civility that comes thence; and Prithee when your heels are at liberty, call at Mr Newburgh's. Your disorder is now your Excuse; tho' I think you might have gone thither before that came on you.

If your accounts be Exact, We have still the advantage of you in point of Weather. The rain on Friday began here about the same time, but was much more moderate, and by the appearance next morning was not so violent nor lasted so long in the night. It has done me no damage. Saturday was fine. Sunday about night-fall, I fear'd We should have very great rain. Some there was, but it ceas'd before bed time. Yesterday was a good day. This hitherto is the most a Summer's day I have seen this Season; and likely to continue so. All hands at hay, and a little bit of reaping. I can stay no longer from them. God bless you all.

Your &c
Edw: Elphin

Send the Enclos'd to the Post-office. Mr Mahon gives a very cheerfull account. But by what He writes, I believe you have before this one from her your Self.

See I have found gilt paper that bears the ink as well as the other. It is Pro patria. Perhaps some of yours may be so, but for writing to me it is no matter. Stick to what you have us'd of late.

I note a false Spelling, Madam. *omitt.* There ought to be but one t. In *omitted*, the t, you see is doubled.

I was greatly surpriz'd at the Sudden death of Sir Peter Warren.[2] Few incidents in my time furnish a more proper Occasion for grave reflexions on the Vanity of this world. Young as you are I believe you have made them. Make them on every Occasion that presents it Self; and Let it be a principle strongly ingrafted in your Mind. That the World and all that is therein is not worth an anxious thought. Fear God and keep his Commandments. For every thing else a noble indifference. This is true Wisdom. This the Way to happiness here, and hereafter.

[Free Edw:Elphin]

1. Madame is sometimes very odd. It matters not.
2. Sir Peter Warren (1703-52): MP for Westminster. Vice admiral of the Red, who captured Louisburg in 1745. 'All the Bells in this City have Rung muffled every Day since Sir PETER WARREN died.' *DNB*; *Pue's Occurrences* 28 July-1 August 1752.

203

Elphin. August 7, 1752

My Dear Girl.

I take large paper too, tho' I have as little prospect as you had of filling it. The day is so fine, that I have not much time to spare; and luckily, like you, I have not much to write.

It is very true. Your news was the most pleasing you could send. But I don't see the Sauciness of your thinking so. A puppy b—ch soon discovers who is fond of her. I dare not write the word at length for fear of Mrs J. But 'tis quite another affair, to think that you are good for something. That however I'll allow you to do, as long as you think you may improve, and endeavour to do so.

You are really a childish Creature, you say. I am glad o'n't. The more things you have a turn to receive innocent pleasure from, the better. I wish Jeny were in these things as childish as your Ladyship. If any of her grave indifference were put on, I should be apt to abuse her for it. But I fear her late disorder made her grave. Let her know that I have great pleasure in the hope, that it is by this time entirely remov'd. I envy you the pleasure you had in Nancy's astonishment. I'm glad the poor Girl is well.

Your paper, you tell me, is the same. Yet your ink has sunk more than usual. How comes this? I suppose you did not air it. That you should always do. You'll see here the same effect from the same cause. But you must not imitate me in carelessness.

You have made a blot in your first page, and I can't tell certainly, whether it was to write false English, or to correct it. *She is not to have any company but We, and Miss Borough.*[1] You have manag'd so, as that I can't discover certainly whether you intended *We* should stand, or Us. The latter is the right. There is another little inaccuracy. The *franchises was* &c. it should be *were.* Franchises is the plural number. You are indeed a good deal mended in your stopping, but in a place or two, like the V.M., you are too good. *One of her mistresses accompany'd her. at least, in the last.* So you have stopp'd. The . at *her* is wrong. It is all one Sentence. Leave out the words, *at least,* and you'll see it.

I had heard your news.[2] Such marriages shock me, however frequent. The Parents, in such cases, seem to have no view, but to get their Children off their hands, regardless of what is to happen to them afterwards. Such nursery-Girls are very fit to be Mothers, and Mistresses of Familys, or to make Men of Sense happy. But those who chuse thus, are usually as great Babys as those whom they do chuse: Or they marry for interest and conveniency. Hence so many miserable pairs. If this marriage takes effect, Some of you should send Madge a Willow.[3] If I mistake not, the Gent. is he with whom We us'd to teaze her.

You have not of late mention'd Roscrea in your letters. I hope they are all well.

Give Mrs J. my thanks for hers. Instead of writing, I free one from Lawson, which I presume will give her more entertainment than I could. He seems very well, and is very gay. Adieu. God bless you all. I am

Your &c
Edw: Elphin

[Free Edw:Elphin]

1. Miss Borough: not known.
2. The projected marriage here is not known.
3. 'Madge' may be Nicholas Synge's daughter Margery. Willow is a symbol of a lost love.

204

Elphin. August 11, 1752

I am sorry my Dear girl has had even a slight Complaint of another kind. But God be thanked it is so slight. I hope your next will give me the great pleasure of knowing that it is entirely remov'd.

Yours follow'd me yesterday to Clonfree,[1] where I din'd for the first time this summer. I spent the whole day in a very pleasing manner. The Doctor and I sally'd forth in the post-chaise about eight in the morning, and breakfasted with the Major and Luke at Strokes-town. That over, We took our horses, and rode thro' the park to the Mountain.[2] The day was fine, and the ride delightfull. It ended at Kilglass Church,[3] which I am now about to rebuild. Barth.[4] and Luke were with us. The Major you know never rides. But He din'd with us. Our ride in and out was about four hours, and the mountain-Air sharpen'd our Stomachs, so that We devour'd a piece of mutton as good as Strokes-town. We and the brothers with Garret were all the Company; So that We din'd without hurry, and I had the pleasure of all the Children about me. They diverted me much. They are a fine little flock, three boys, two Girls.[5] The younger of the two is one of the handsomest Children I have seen. The post-chaise brought us home at our ease in good time; and We are very well after it this morning. The Doctor has begun his Spa to day. I hope it will agree with him. But neither of us are to be as happy to day as We were yesterday. We are to dine at Cary's with Ignatius Kelly[6] and his Wife. We had much rather have been excus'd.

Yesterday I began to draw home hay. I am at the same work to day, tho' not so fine. A flying show'r or two have frighten'd us a little. But they blow off, and We go on. I can stay no longer from that pleasing work. Adieu therefore. God bless and preserve you all.

Yours &c
Edw: Elphin

I had a letter from your Uncle yesterday. All well. When I was at Clonfree Mrs Mahon receiv'd a letter from her Sister,[7] which did not tally with the pleasing account I had from him. The Spitting of bloud continues at intervals. Till that is quite remov'd, I shall have no opinion of other Symptoms of recovery.

Just as I had finish'd this in the morning, and was going to my hay, in came Mr Wills, and soon after, she and the Girls. They are very well, and enquir'd with great affection after you all. I think the Grandmother is grown.[8] Bess as she was.

[Free Edw:Elphin]

1. Clonfree, Co. Roscommon, south-east of Strokestown, the home of Bartholomew Mahon.

2. Possibly the river Mountain, which runs into lake Kilglass north-west of Strokestown.

3. Kilglass, Co. Roscommon, five miles north-east of Strokestown.

4. Bartholomew Mahon: son of Nicholas Mahon and Magdalen French. Burke

(1979), p.773.

5. In 1749 Bartholomew Mahon and his wife had four children under fourteen. Census, f.106.

6. Sheriff Ignatius Kelly. See Letter 111.

7. Bartholomew Mahon married Anne Crosbie, daughter of Sir Maurice Crosbie of Ardfert, and Jane Mahon's sister. *Irish Builder*, Vol. 27 (1895), p.40.

8. Grandmother: obscure.

205

Elphin. August 14, 1752

My Dear Girl's words, in the letter to which she referrs, are, 'You know I have improv'd in sauciness this Summer'. Now, I say you have not *improv'd*; but shew'd most in your first step which brought on you that charge. So some Authors first performances are best. The Rey-grass letter gave the first occasion for that raillery. You attempted, dextrously enough, to avoid the charge, but I prov'd it upon you. Your later claims I do not allow. What great merit is it in you, that you see my fondness. But I confess it is some, that I am fond. I should not be so but that I think you are, and will continue good. Go on, my Dear, and try what will rise highest, your merit, or my fondness. While I have hopes of the one, I freely indulge my self in the other, and at present. No news can be so pleasing, as that you are very well. God keep you so.

By your and Mrs J's account We have had the advantage of you in Weather. Sunday was very fine, no thunder; A very little rain between six and seven, soon over. I rode till night. Monday and Tuesday you have already an account of. Wedensday, there was heavy rain at Strokes-town, and Tulsk. Else where the same, I believe; But here We had only the tails of two or three show'rs.[1] Hay drawing home without interruption or damage. Yesterday indeed there was a good deal of heavy rain, which stopp'd all Works, but within doors. But evening and night fair; and this day there's a show'r now and then, but the Sun has it's turn, and the Wind is very high. Were the Corn in a shedding way, I should be in pain for it. But I have been all round, and see no damage done or likely. However the day is not pleasant. If yours be no better, you have not yet got abroad.

You suspect your Writing. I have indeed seen better of late; but some time ago should have thought it extremely well; and whatever defect there is in it, is not owing to Mrs J's exhortations, but to other Causes. I'll lay a peny you did not write this as briskly as sometimes, and, if I guess right, you could not. The nib of your pen, like that with which I now write, was too small. I see it by the Cut of your letters. You make your own pens, you say. Nib them a little broader, and gallop away. There will then appear more firmness, and a better form in your hand. Whenever stooping is or is thought inconvenient, Write short. Tho' I love your prattle, I don't desire it at the least inconvenience to your Self. I observe you write thank-God. That mark of Connection is wrong. They should stand as two Words.

Between Lawson and me there has been a forget. I am most to blame, tho' He is not free. He brought two letters, to be freed, while I was shaving. I bid the Gent. leave them in my study. He did, but not in the right place. They went out of my head, and were not in my view at night, which is always my time of making up my dispatches, and He did not remind me. They go by this post. One of them is for Mrs J.

Your reflexions on the premature marriage are just. The more such you make to Mrs J. or me, the more pleasure you'll give us. To others, as you rightly remark, They are not proper, at least, They should be made with less bluntness of Expression. But I should be sorry, if you had not a most hearty contempt of such parents.

Your stopping is generally right. There are some omissions, which I shall teach you, more easily, to supply properly, when We are together. But in this part of your letter, I observe a mistake, which I do not blame, but ought to set you right in, because you are led into it, by that very rule, which I have so often inculcated. I'll transcribe your Words, that you may the better understand me. *I have great pity for her, that is to be thrown into the World before it is possible she can know how to conduct her self in it. A World that will be ready* &c. The repetition of the word *World* here, is not only proper, but elegant. But, consider Mistress, That repetition not only continues the Sense, but the Sentence. There ought not therefore to have been a . at *it*, but a : There ought also to have been a , at the first *World*. These are the kind of omissions, which I often observe. They are not faults, but defects. I hope to teach you to supply them.

I told you in my last, that the Wills's were come. They are all, just as they us'd to be, easy and agreable. I see no change in Bess. Matty is grown a little. But tho' I see no change in them, I think I see some in their Caps, or their putting them on. Their hair is puff'd, so as that nothing else appears at the Crown, to the ribbon. I am awkard in descriptions of dress. But I fancy, that if I saw your Cap and hair thus adjusted, it would to me give you an air of boldness. But it is as good be out of the World, as out of the fashion. Is this a town, or a Country one? I imagine that their neighbour Mrs. Kelly,[2] just arriv'd from Dublin, has imported it.

You dispos'd mighty well of your haunch. I hope you do not neglect the Lady from whose husband it came. I wonder not that you are all in love with little Jeny. But if you saw Miss Bell of Clonfree,[3] you would, I am sure, give the prize of beauty to her. Mrs. L[ushington]'s Critique upon it made me smile. *She has, I don't know how, too much fierceness in her Eyes.* These were her Words. I could not help telling her, that Females always found or fancied some defect in every face that deserv'd and had praise. She has chosen unluckily. For, to me, the Girl's Eyes are remarkably fine. I can prattle no more. God bless you all. I am

> Your &c
> Edw: Elphin

John will give you some money. Lay it by. I think the sum is £13.15.1. For Wheat. Shan't I grow rich by farming? Mr and Mrs Conroy are come. They have left the Old Woman behind. I am glad of it with all my heart. She would have been a great incumbrance.

[Free Edw:Elphin]

1. The weather in August 1752 was 'Cloudy and wet'. Rutty (1752), p.168.
2. A member of the Kelly family of Castle Ruby, Co. Roscommon.
3. Miss Bell of Clonfree: not known.

206

Elphin. August 19, 1752

My Dear Girl.

I must repeat what I wrote some time ago. I am sorry that you have even a slight complaint; but since you have any, am right glad that it is but a slight one. I hope next post will bring me the account you wish to give, and I to have, that All is over. If I do not forget, you have had a disorder of this kind these two or three Summers, except the last; and they have been usually after the drinking the Spa. The Doctor can tell better than I, whether they are in any degree the Effect of it. I believe not. Give him my service, and thanks for his letter, which gives more satisfaction than either yours or Mrs J.'s. For tho' you both write of your disorder as slight, yet you betray an anxiety, which would make me fear it were not so, if I had not had an account from him. However I am in some suspense. I can't help being so, when, you, My Dearest, are in the Case; and therefore wait with a little impatience for Thursday. God send you as well as I wish.

Sunday Evening We had very heavy rain, and All, except Lawson, and the Females were caught in it. It came on at once unexpected. Cary and his Son got a Sound wetting. They rode out Secure without Coats. I was more cautious. My foul-weather coat,[1] by good luck, was on, which, with my hood, kept me perfectly dry, tho' the rain was heaviest at first, and came on when I was at a great distance. Mr Wills on his walk was nearer home and escap'd only with a Sprinkling. But We were all much down about harvest. As far as appears, little or no damage has been done. Yesterday was very fine, so fine that the Ladies walk'd about the fields, and enjoy'd the sweetest Evening that has been this Season. Mrs Conry was with them. We admit her every day, the others only on high days. One Sister gives the Exclusion to the other. We none of us like, tho' We sometimes bear, the affectation, the winking, to speak in your friend the Doctor's stile of Mrs. L. I divert my Self with it. She often makes me laugh in my Sleeve. I have some malt drink here, which she likes much. It is about the strength of Mr Preston's. At the beginning of diner she calls for Cyder. I say, Drink a glass of beer. Oh! it is too strong, I am afraid of it. However she's prevail'd on, and when once enter'd, she calls for three or four without hesitation. She never indeed exceeds, but the doo that she makes, occasions her drinking that manly liquor to be more notic'd. Her way, she says, is to eat but of one thing; and she does it heartily, but if more that she likes come in her way, She can be persuaded. She is particularly fond of Grouse, which We have had in plenty since the first of the month. On Sunday I offer'd her some. No! she had eaten too much Beef. So far was true; She had ate very heartily of it. But she consented to a little bit. On my offering a Wing, I said, it may be she had rather have the Breast. Yes! for there is less on it. There was twice as much, and she pick'd the bones. She is passionately fond of Cards, and fairly owns it. They say she makes W. Cary play with her morning and night. Bragg,[2] you have heard, is her game. But as she can't get that here, she is content to take up with our Six-penny Whist, and she plays very ill. Rare sport to me, when Cary and she are partners. I seldom fail to breed a quarrel between them about her mistakes; and then He becomes the principal figure. His explanations she does not always understand, and is as little dispos'd, as other people, to be convinc'd she is wrong. It affords great mirth to see his warmth kept in by high respect for his thick-blouded Sister, and ever and anon breaking out in the Contention for what He thinks to be, and generally is, right. I blow the Coals, siding one while with the one, presently with the other. The other Evening Matters rose so high, that she told him, He should never be her partner more. She has not kept her Word; and they have had more disputes, and will have to the End of the Chapter. Is not this somewhat like Scandal, you'll say? It is, but it is to you, My Dearest, and Mrs J. and I must sometimes draw pictures of what I dislike for you, as well as of what I approve of. You'll make a right use of both. Affectation of every kind is hatefull. I see none in you yet. I hope I never shall. The Contrast between the Sisters heightens these Scenes. You know the other's manner. It does not quite please. She is not indeed affected, but reserv'd. An imperfection this, as well, tho' not as bad, as the other. But she has good sense enough to see the ridicule of her Sister's behaviour, and shews that she does, generally in a pretty manner enough. I wish the other were at quarters, that I might see her with more freedom. Variety makes these follys sometimes tolerable. Always they would be irksome. Which is it Lady Plyant, or Lady Froth in the play,[3] that makes such a rout with her child whom she had not seen in two hours? Much the same rout is made with an Emily here. I sent the little thing a card in form the other day to invite her to diner. It made the Dame as happy as a Princess. It was the first she had ever received and she must send it enclos'd to her husband. It would give him great pleasure. But enough and more than enough of this grey coquette.

What I wrote just now about Beer, brings to my mind the barrel in Kevin-street Cellar. Tell Mrs J., I fancy it is time to try, and, if it be right good, to bottle it. I'll submit entirely to her taste, since I can't have Mrs L's. If she does not fully approve Let the pupil go to the Brewer and desire him to take it back. Have you an Empty bin in the Wine Cellar? If you have, you must keep it for a hogshead of Wine, which I shall soon give orders for bottling. What then shall be done with the Beer if good? Shift for that as you may. A place in the Cellar under the Stairs is fittest for it.

I had a letter yesterday from Palmer, the first, since their return from the North. He tells me his Wife has not been so healthy these four years. But they have bury'd my little Godson of the Small pox.[4] I am sorry for it. We are not lucky people there.

You owe this long prattle chiefly to a doubtfull day. It has threaten'd since morning, so that having taken my first ride before breakfast, I was not in haste for a Second after. It still holds up and seems more likely to be fair now, than it was three hours ago. A great deal of hay is come, and coming home. I must give it a look before diner. God bless and preserve you, My Dearest Dear to

Your most affectionate &c
Edw: Elphin

Have you ventur'd on fruit of any kind this Season? I know you do not, unless it be allow'd. But As the Weather has been, I fancy it can't be good for you or any one, and must be apt to produce gripes which I take to have been a part of your disorder, tho' you do not say so. My remedy in any affection of that kind is Broth in abundance.

Let the pupil have orders to bespeak immediately from Savage at Kilmainham two Sledges, each of 18 pound Weight, the form to be flat at one end, and a blunt point at the other. They are known by the name of Scabling Sledges.⁵ They must be got ready immediatly, that they may come down the next time the Carrs do. Tell him I suppose He has forgot the looms I wrote for near two months ago.

Desire Ned Curtis to provide another parcel of blasting powder, what was sent is almost spent.

An Ugly night. I fear much rain.

[Free Edw:Elphin]

1. Edward Synge's foul-weather coat was probably a great coat or surtout, made of oiled cloth. Cunnington, p.78.
2. Brag is a game of cards for two or more people. The rules are essentially the same as those of poker. Swift played basset, ombre, piquet and whist for money with other clergymen. He lost 4s.6d. at ombre to the bishop of Clogher in 1703. Thompson, p.2.
3. 'Lady Froth and Lady Plyant in the play.' Characters in William Congreve, *The Double Dealer* (1694). Lady Froth, 'A great coquette, pretender to poetry, wit and learning'; Lady Plyant, 'Insolent to her husband and easy to any pretender'.
4. See Letter 180.
5. Scabling sledges: sledgehammers for rough-dressing stone.

207

Elphin. August 21, 1752

My Dear Girl.

Mrs J. hopes that after having read her pacquet, I shall have no anxiety &c. Tell her, that is too much. I can't avoid some anxiety, while you, my Dearest, are the least out of order. But I assure you honestly, that what I had is considerably abated, and that I now have a comfortable hope, that next post will quite remove it. Yesterday I received as good tidings as I expected. Had they been such as in your former letter you wish'd to be able to give, I should have been most agreably disappointed; nay! I'll tell you further, that had I not made large allowances for the turn which I know you both have, when any thing ails *you*, Your letters, design'd to lessen my anxiety, would have rais'd it much higher than it was. Your affected caution in always calling your complaint *slight*, made me Suspect that it was not slight; and Mrs J.'s account of good sleep, good pulse, good every thing, tho' you were not quite well, contributed to perplex me. Even the Doctor's letter, which you did very well in desiring him to write, was not quite satisfactory, because not quite plain. His manner, you know, is *une peu sêche*,¹ and He told me facts without giving any opinion either of the nature or causes of your Complaints. This way in him is partly from temper, partly from his profession. Upon the whole I saw something was wrong, and that the Seat of the disorder was Stomach and bowels. But by your account the Vomit shew'd you had a clean stomach, and the Doctor says only that you threw up some tough phlegm, not much. It's having purg'd you, Mrs J. said, had been of great use. For what, thought I? How are my Dear Girl's bowels affected? There is a latent disorder which does not yet fully shew it self; and the longer it is in shewing it self, the worse it may prove. You'll say perhaps, that I was a little ingenius in tormenting my self, and I confess it. But among you, you furnish'd the materials to work upon. I blame you not; and as I told you just now, knowing your turn I was less mov'd than otherwise I should have been. When I have the pleasure of knowing that your complaint is quite remov'd, I shall probably rally you upon all this, and describe you to your Selves. All I shall say at present is, that you are too apt to frighten one another. Then your thoughts are turn'd immediately on me. My Dada, My Lord will be uneasy. You put me in mind of the Story of Ama and Poetus.² I think you know it. You love me, as that fond Wife did her husband; and are, I believe really more concern'd about my uneasiness, than about your own disorder. Tho' I would not for the World but you lov'd me well, Yet I had much rather your love did not take that turn; especially as by it, you undesignedly do the very thing you intend to avoid. You aggravate your own disorder, and consequently my pain. *Courage! ma chère*. Behave your self on this and every such future occasion, like a Woman. You are now almost one. Be not alarm'd your Self, nor alarm me unwittingly, further than there is reason. You must not, nor can I expect that you should be exempt from the common lot of Mortals. God be thanked, that your health has been for some years past vastly better, than once I fear'd it ever would have been; and I trust in him that this disorder when over, will yet further establish it. While there are any remains of it, Continue to do, as, I am sure, you have done. Follow directions; and be easy and compos'd both with respect to your self and me. As I have an absolute dependance on your truth, You must have the same on mine, when I assure you that I am now vastly easier than I was, and have a most comfortable hope that this ruffle will soon be, if it be not already, happily over. I could call 15 Witnesses to prove this, if there were occasion. So many I had yesterday at diner. By the by I told none of them but Lawson, that any thing ail'd you, nor had I told him, but to procure you some diversion. But I can appeal to him, I could to them all, whether any alteration appear'd in my usual behaviour. Oh! My Dear Child, had I been alarm'd about you, I could not have contain'd. I trust in God, I have no reason.

Who were these 15 you'll say? I'll tell you. Cary's folks and mine own, Will French, Barton, two younger Lloyds, one He with the blemish on his

Eye, and young Ned Kelly,[3] who is a near neighbour and intimate of Mr
Wills's, and chose I suppose, to make his visit to me, while He was here. I
made him stay all night, and here he is Weather bound with a dirty shirt.
By what appears yet, He'll not be able to get away, For the day is shocking,
a rank storm of Wind and rain.

At diner things pass'd as usual. The Grey coquette ate and drank her
beer heartily, and the farce of grouse was agen aired, with this height'n-
ing that she refus'd longer and devour'd more. Her sister smil'd, and said
in a Whisper to Mrs Conroy, Lord! see how Jeny eats. She does indeed
most stoutly, and is grown fat as a puffen.

Diner over, and Day-Customers gone, Tea and Cards. My point was to
steer clear of my coquette; and As We had enough for two Tables, I set her
with those, whom for other reasons I did not chuse to play with, W. French,
Barton, &c. There she squabbled and lost, plaid and left off, and plaid agen.
She seem'd not quite pleas'd, but I minded her not. She must take every
thing here as she can get it, and she will. After all, her follys are rather
diverting, than troublesome. I pitied her on Wedensday. The day was very
bad, tho' not near so bad as this, and they were engag'd to dine at Charles-
town.[4] Seven miles in Wind and rain! But they escap'd without cold or disaster on the way. See what a fine town Lady can do, when she is put to it.

As I am sure laughing is good for you, I'll tell you a passage which will
give you a laugh, if you have one in the World. Ten days ago I saw an
Advertisement in *Faulkner* which I suspected to be Mr Donnelan's. As 'tis
short, I'll transcribe it. 'A person is wanted to take care of a Farm of about
100 Acres. 20 Miles from Dublin in the County of Kildare. Good recom-
mendations and Dublin Security for the honest discharge of his duty, will
be expected, and that He understands the best modern methods of
tillage, the even and true sowing of Corn, grass-seeds, and Turnips, and
the buying and selling of fat and store Cattel and sheep.'[5] Sure that He was
the person wanting, I gravely recommended Tom Collins. I think that
worthy Wight was in Employment when you were here. If so, I need not
tell you, that He is a great fool, and never can be otherwise, consequently,
as little fit for D's purpose, as I to command a fleet; and as He had seen
him often here, and was often witness to his blunders and my chidings
and complaints, I had no doubt but that He knew him to be a complete
fool as well as I did. I was indeed so strongly possess'd of this, that while I
was writing, I thought I deserv'd to have my head broke for my joke. I ventur'd on it, partly for a little mirth, and partly to shew him my opinion of
his scheme, which I think by no means a prudent one; and what do you
think? In a letter from him yesterday, He says He does not know whether
I was serious about Collins, and if I were, He could hang himself for
having engag'd. I was greatly surpriz'd and burst into a loud fit of laugh-

ter, tho' alone. Must not I, think you, have wrote very dextrously to leave him thus at a loss, and to make him think so favorably of one, whom He knew to be a Dolt? And yet I assure you, I said not one Word of my friend Tom, that was not strictly true, nor that I suspected would change the opinion I was sure He had of him. I resolve to leave him in his Suspense, and hope to have rare Sport with it next Winter.

And now having told my Story, I bid my dearest for this time adieu; After repeating the assurances I have given already, that I am as easy on your score, as you can desire I should be; nor shall I be cast down, tho' your next account should not be quite as good as yet I wish or hope they will be. The judgment I have made upon the whole of your disorder is, that it proceeds, in part at least, from a delicate fibre. That's a term of art, which Ned Curtis often uses, and therefore I leave to him to explain. I had rather you had it not but am not surpriz'd that you have it. You have an hereditary right to it both by Father and Mother. If my Conjecture be right, instead of being surpriz'd at your present Complaints, I ought to rejoice that they are not more frequent; and I know by experience that they are rather tearing, and troublesome than dangerous; and Regimen will set you up, and by God's blessing keep you so. Under the direction of his good providence, I leave you in the hands of the good Doctor and your Carefull, tender, but rather too sollicitous, friend. I think it is impossible you can be in better. God bless their Endeavours, and preserve you, My Dearest dear to

Your most affectionate father
Edw: Elphin

As I know your niceity about truth, Mistress, so I must guard against your misunderstanding an Expression at the beginning of this letter. When I take notice of *your affected caution* &c. I do not mean, to intimate that you wrote of your disorder otherwise than you thought it to be, and I hope it will prove. But I did and do suspect that in writing so, you attended more to the encouraging expressions of the Doctor and the friend, than to your own feelings, and having their Authority wrote of your Complaint in the manner in which you had a mind I should think of them. If there was a little bit of fraud in this, It was a pious one. But you see I am sharp-sighted, where you are concern'd. I lament this shocking Weather, as on every other account, so on this, that it makes it impossible for you to stir out to take the Air.

I am very glad you had so fair an occasion of letting Mr Newburgh know your intentions, and that you laid hold of it; Mrs J.'s informs me. This pleases me better even than the very good Sheeting, which yet I am pleas'd at.

1. *Une peu sêche*: a bit dry.

2. Ama and Poetus: not traced.

3. Edward Kelly was probably a relation of Ignatius Kelly of Castle Ruby, Co. Roscommon. MacGeagh, Vol. 1, p.297.

4. Charlestown: the seat of Gilbert King.

5. The advertisement appeared in *Faulkner's Dublin Journal* 11-15 August 1752.

208

Elphin. August 25, 1752

God be thanked, My Dear Girl is well, and I am happy. As matters fall out, I have time to say little more this bout.

By a letter yesterday from Garbally, it is likely that the Coll and Lady are by this time in town. If they are, or Assoon as they are, you or Jeny give my Service to him, and tell him that I received his, that it gave me great pleasure, and that I would have wrote, but that his made me uncertain where a letter would find him.

You have been severe on your Self for bad writing of late. Considering the Circumstances, in which you wrote, you had no reason. But you have mended in this as in your health. Still however I say, You write with pens too fine nibb'd.

On Friday last I thought all my Corn was ruin'd. It is now safe. I hope my neighbours have had as good luck. After all our fears, there is a fair prospect of a plentifull harvest. But nothing yet like setled Weather. Sunday evening, and the first of the night excessive bad. More wind than rain. For an hour or two a meer Hurricane. I can't learn that much corn was shed. Yesterday fine. To day hitherto so.

The Wills's still here. Poor Betty plagu'd with tooth-ach. My Dearest Dear God bless and preserve you to

Your &c
Edw: Elphin

How did you manage with your friend Mrs Silver, while you were out of order? The Bantams and Guinea-fowl are come safe. Coll. Trench sent them, and I have wrote to him; so you need say nothing.

[Free Edw:Elphin]

209

Elphin. August 29, 1752

I am heartily vex' d that my Dear Girl should be teaz'd with the tooth-ach immediatly after her late Complaints. But my concern for the one is of a different kind from what I had for the other. I hope too that it is, by this time, over. The great swelling of your gum is a good prognostick of Ease. Would it had broke, before you clos'd yours, that I might have had the pleasure of knowing, that you were sure of an Easy night, and of satisfying your craving appetite the next day. I can't judge by your account whether a Single Tooth or many are affected. The swelling of your Gum inclines me to think the latter, but if it be the former, and the tooth it Self decay'd, I am apt to think the best way will be to have it out. But in this I leave you to your friend, your Doctor and trusty Ned. If it be resolv'd on, I am sure all possible care will be taken to find out the best Operator, Skilfull and not rash. I think less caution is necessary about an upper tooth than an Under. I have been much plague'd with this sort of pain, tho' I don't fancy I ever had it in the most exquisite degree. Want of teeth secures me now. My remedys were, toasted figs,[1] to the Swell'd Gums, and Syrrup of Onions in the Ear. The former never fail'd to break the Swelling, nor the latter to lessen the pain. I told you in my last, I think, that Betty Wills was plagu'd with the same disorder here. She left me yesterday with it on her, but lessen'd. She had recourse to pultices, brandy, and Tobacco.[2] The two latter are not very decorous things for a young damsel's use. I take neither to be good, particularly the former. I believe Laudanum was us'd. Mrs Wills brought some from Stafford's. I hope my Dear Girl has not had occasion for such remedys.

I have had more opportunity, this visit, than before, of observing those Girls. Betty supports her Character, of great Sweetness of temper, with sense neither Shining nor deficient. But I think my friend Matty's smartness does not increase with her years. She does not so well support or return, the raillery or badinage of the Doctor. There has been a great deal of it, and Blair has had his part. One while the one was in favour, then the other, Sometimes both out. But she did not play her part so well as some years ago; i.e. I expected more. That same pretty Poem, or some other of the Doctors to K. street afforded a great deal of Sport. I know nothing of these dispatches, but that I usually free them. But one post the pacquet went to Mr Wills, who frees as well as I do.[3] This rais'd Martha's curiosity, and to heighten it, the Doctor let her see at a distance, that the paper contain'd Verses, but with great affected caution conceal'd the Address. This set her upon the tenters.[4] She teaz'd and importun'd to know more. He told her at last, that the letter was address'd to a Milaner in Capel-street.[5] But she was only a Conveyance. The real person was a Secret not to be disclosed, and He insisted on it, that she should not tell me a Word of what He told her. It was pleasant to see this working for several days. After supper was the principal time, She giving distant broken hints of what she knew, He still insisting that she should not betray a Secret with which He had trusted her. She stood it a great while, but at last I work'd her up to such a pitch, that out it came, when I, cruelly enough, join'd him against her, said she had told me nothing; that she had really been trusted with nothing; and that the effect of her discovery was nothing more than to shew, that she could not keep a Secret. She bore our teazing well, but look'd simply enough.

As uncertain as the Weather, is justly a Proverb. Never a stronger instance of it, than just now. Sunday night I told you of. From that, the Weather was very fine, and yesterday morning We all agreed that it seem'd more setled than it had been this whole Summer. Riding about twelve, I observ'd the Wind change, and pronounc'd that the Weather would. So it did, but not till night was just coming on. It disturb'd a little the last turn of my hay. There been some rain in the night, and a little this morning, not violent. All works but hay and Corn are going on, and the former is all at home, good part of my wheat in Stack in the field, the rest safe. I am in no pain about any thing but Turf; and that is now drawing home. We were before so reduc'd, as scarce to have enough to dress diner. Thanks to Cary.

Every thing else in this world in some degree uncertain as well as Weather. I don't know when I had more calm serene joy than yesterday morning as I rode about my fields. You, my most important care, well, and the Weather fine. The distress of the Country reliev'd, and all my Works going on around me with spirit and cheerfulness. I promis'd my Self a Continuance of my joy. On the sudden the wind chang'd, which foreboded what has happen'd, and in came the post with an account that my Dear Girl tho' not sick was in pain. I was less happy on both accounts, tho' not much. The day, tho' dropping, is now sowr, and will I hope take up and I comfort my self with the Expectation, that next post, by my knowing that you are easy, I shall be so too. God bless and preserve you, my Dearest, to

Your most affectionate &c
Edw: Elphin

You mention the Hospital-boy, but not a Word of Galagher's Wife. It will probably be news to you, that she has been here this fortnight. John ought to have known this. I will say nothing to him, because you tell me he is very weak. The strength of the Expression alarms me about him. But pray Enquire, to whom He has paid the three shillings a Week, and Stop payment.

You say you have had no complaint in your bowels, till lately these four Summers. So says Mrs J. It is upon my mind, that Each of the two Summers preceding the last, you had a *slight* complaint of this sort, after you had left off your Spa.

[Free Edw:Elphin]

1. The use of figs, *ficus carica*, for poultices has a long history. The first fig poultice was said to have been prescribed for King Hezekiah. They were often used for swollen glands. Wheelwright, p.62.
2. Tobacco, *nicotiana tabacum*, was thought to have a soothing effect.
3. Godfrey Wills was lieutenant colonel of the Roscommon Militia and became high sheriff of Roscommon in 1755. These posts may have entitled him to frank post for his friends.
4. On the tenters: to be in a state of strain or uneasiness.
5. Capel Street, Dublin.

210

[Undated]

My poor Mumper

Right sorry I am that you have been so: I won't say *are*, because I hope that you are, by this, effectually reliev'd. It pleases me that the only certain way of being so, has been resolv'd on; and I comfort my Self with the thought that it has before this been happily executed. Mrs J. writes, that she made an attempt on Daunt. I am glad she fail'd. The best Surgeons are not therefore the best Tooth-drawers. There is a nack in it, to be acquir'd only by practice. The best tooth-drawer of his Age was not Surgeon enough to dress a green wound. He was the best bleeder also. Daunt is reputed an Excellent one. Eminent Surgeons are not always. I was bled once by Proby,[1] with more pain than ever in my life. Had Mr D. his fee for lancing? If not, Let Ned give it him. It ought not to be less than ½ a Guinea. More, if He thinks proper, but more is Extravagant. Let it however be done. Those things must grow when deferr'd.

Mrs J.'s account of my Dear girl's eyes filling, when her Ugly tooth would not suffer her to eat, tho' hungry, made me smile; and brought to my mind your lamentation here, when Dignan was for starving you. But I have real pleasure in what she writes of your resolution and patience. Considering the accidents, maladys and distresses to which all Mortals are subject, Patience and fortitude are most usefull as well as laudable virtues. They make the pain or distress, whatever it be, more tolerable to the persons, who suffer, and at the same time set them in the most amiable light to their friends. If it be possible, Mrs J. loves you better than she did. Indeed she writes as if she did. I hope you know by this time, that the pain of drawing, is comparatively small to what you have born. I find your pain coming on the heels of your former Complaints, has confin'd you to your own apartment. I shall long to have you enlarg'd; and wish that Assoon as the Doctor and Mrs J. think you may safely do it, you would take the liberty of the whole floor, before you go down. Fires to air the rooms will be necessary. I find you have them already; and, as your Weather has been, It was better have them, tho' you had had no ailment. Our Weather has been better. Every day, but Friday, good last Week. Sunday fine. This day, Monday, a sort of smur, as Cary calls it. No more. The day very good for all Works but about corn and Hay. I fear however that before I seal this, I shall give you an account of Worse. The sky lowr's. The Wind whistles and the glass is fall'n. But all my farm affairs are in a way secure enough. Nothing but a long continuance of very bad Weather can hurt them.

The teasing you have had about Cashel was natural enough.[2] But you that bear pain so heroically, why should you call that even a little plague? Methinks it should have diverted you. Your answers were right; and they were better given as your opinion, than if you had said, as I think you might have done, that you *knew*, because thus you shew'd your own sense, as well as mine, of those trifles on which so high a value is commonly set. Grace! There never was a time in my life, in which I would have given two pence for the pompous title. But from my coming hither, and knowing my whole Situation, my resolutions were fix'd, never to quit it. Indeed in an ilness of Dr Bolton's two years before his death, I desir'd the L[or]ds J[ustices] to recommend me, and they agreed to do it. I desir'd on Saturday, and on Monday I retracted, when they were met to perform their Engagement, and before they or I knew that the Archbishop was recovering. From that time, my purpose has been fix'd. I never waver'd even in thought. My income was large enough. Precedence I matter'd not, nor had I ever any fondness for power, that was owing nearly to Station. Whatever has arisen, or may arise from abilitys or Conduct, that alone was or is in my eyes of any value; and sure I was, that my Conduct would be better, by resolving to preserve my independency. He who has views of ambition, can never act freely, seldom virtuously. This has been my plan; I have pursu'd it as well as I could; without making parade of my self-denying intentions. Had I avow'd them, I should have been as little believ'd, as your

Aunt H[eaton] or even the talking familiar Lady believ'd you.[3] (By the by Mistress you have wrote *familier*. But this is not a time to remark on false spellings. Have a care that I catch you not at some, when tooth is out, and gums well). Sow'r grapes! had been the Word. But now, every one sees I might, if I would. If my friend[4] be promoted, I shall dance as well as you; and yet I do in my Conscience think He never will be so happy as He *might have* been at Clonfert. I don't say, was, for He wish'd to change. He did change very disagreably. This remove, if any thing, will please. But by happy Experience I know that the way to be happy, is to be Content; and I believe Fewer in high Stations have this happiness than in low ones. *That Cruel something unpossess'd* &c. You remember Prior.[5] But God be thanked it has fallen to my lot. I trust that He in his infinite goodness will preserve you to me; For all the rest, Nothing that this World can give is worth a thought or a Wish, beyond what is in my power.

I am just now in a pretty kind of way. Diner spoiling in Expectation of a Judge from Carrick. Mr. Whitney[6] sent word, He would dine with me to day, and set off from hence to morrow for Roscommon. Not a word of him yet, and 'tis a good deal past three. I am almost as hungry as you were, when your eyes fill'd. But to this delay you owe the length of this Scribble. It is time now to stop, and look out. Adieu. My Dearest. God bless and preserve you, and your friends.

Your &c
Edw: Elphin

Tuesday

No Judge, nor message. I waited till 5 and then Lawson, Cary and I sat down to a Table of nine and nine. It was vexatious enough. But I thought it was better to laugh. I am still in the dark about the Cause. It will be explain'd by and by. For I expect him and Judge French from Porte to take an earlier diner in their way to Roscommon. All I know yet is, that Whitney was seiz'd on Saturday with your distemper in teeth and Gums, which prevented his coming on Sunday. I suppose it continues. But He might have sent. That He did not requires explanation. What vex'd me most was a lordly Haunch of Venison, which I reserv'd for a shew and Crack. I never saw it's fellow. The largest dish I have, scarce held it. It was as fat as large, and good as either but Alas! not of Roscommon. Leitrim, despis'd Leitrim bred and fed it. It was sent to Ld. K.[7] He sent it to me as a Curiosity. It was indeed a great one. But it ended ignobly. We did not between us eat a pound of it. A violent show'r of hail had driven me in; and scribling to you is more agreable than any thing else. You see I fear'd a Souse of bad Weather yesterday. I was sure of it this morning, and advis'd against medling with Corn. But as the sun shone, Cary was Sanguine, and influenc'd Coghil, himself well inclin'd; so they fell to stacking, and were beaten off, leaving nine or ten of the stacks half-made. I hope they won't suffer, For the Sun shines agen. But the pain for the little I can suffer is balanc'd by the pleasure of having been a true prophet. Poor Lawson has been deceiv'd too, and, what vexes me more than my corn, rode out; Without a Servant too. In that point only He is obstinate. I hope He had a Caban near. For indeed Shelter was necessary. Luckily I was near home when the show'r came on.

Tuesday Evening

Judges come and gone. Whitney could make no good excuse, therefore attempted to joke, but badly. I took it. They went off at three, and I have been since riding in my fields, and have just light enough left to tell you, that the day tho' sowr and unpleasant has not been near so bad as I fear'd in the morning; that my Corn is safe enough, and that the Doctor did not suffer by the hail. He was near home as well as I, and safe in the house in a minute tho' no body could give an account of him. I find you are to have no entertainment from him this post. I abus'd him for it. All the World are gone to the Assizes. So We shall for some days be alone. With all my heart. If next post brings me an account of your having got rid of your ugly tooth, and being in a way of recovering your milk-maid looks, I shall be as happy as I desire to be. Once more, my dearest, God bless and preserve you to your &c. E.E.

My service to Old healthy. Long may she be so for her own sake, yours and mine. I have not time to write to her. Judge French says that Williams is the best Tooth drawer in town. But I hope you are not now to enquire for one.

1. Proby was probably Thomas Proby (1700-?), a surgeon. Wallis, p.901.

2. Dr Price, the archbishop of Cashel, died on 17 July 1752; the reference to Cashel was probably because of Dublin gossip that Edward Synge would succeed him.

3. 'the talking familiar lady': obscure.

4. John Whitcombe, bishop of Clonfert, was translated to Cashel 15 September 1752. *NHI*, Vol. 9, p.411.

5. Matthew Prior (1664-1721). The quotation has not been traced.

6. Judge Whitney does not appear in Ball, *Judges of Ireland*. He is possibly Boleyn Whitney of Newpas, Co. Westmeath. Admitted to the Middle Temple in 1709 and to the King's Inns in 1714. He died in 1758. *King's Inns*, p.511.

7. This may have been James King, 4th baron Kingston (1693-1761), who owned land in Leitrim, Sligo and Roscommon.

211

Elphin. September 16, 1752

Tho' I scribbled a good deal to my Dear Girl last post; yet the hurry of the day infected me, so that I forgot to thank you for yours by the lad from town. I received it on Sunday just rising from Table. It was a pleasing desert. But I was a little disappointed at yours yesterday. I expected to have known by it, that you had got rid of a bad Tenant. Are you acquainted with that saying? If not, ask Mrs J. who will spit, cry Fogh, and tell you. It is a black-guard one, usually apply'd to somewhat less cleanly than a tooth. But in plain English, I hop'd for an account of your having parted with yours. Instead of that, the pain was still before you, and two are condemn'd. I am sorry for it, and that you have so many more bad ones. Perhaps this last may be a sort of reason against drawing any. But you are in hands that can judge about this better than I can. You will I am sure cheerfully submit to whatever they recommend. One thing only I take upon me to advise in. Let this ugly bout, attended probably with the loss of two teeth, dispose you to take better care of what remain. Have you never in your pain thought of Mrs P? I have of late often. I mention'd Williams in my last. Enquire about him. If He be such a man as J. French represents him, He may be useful to you both in drawing the Teeth you must loose, and preserving the rest.

Your Sentiments about the two girls agree with mine. What I wrote about the letter was conjecture. L[awson] certainly made M[atty] believe there was one to some body, and I fancy'd it might have been to you.[1] That added to our Sport. For when I spoke, as if I knew the Secret, It set the Damsel more on the Tenters. But from what you write I am sure there was none to you. Possibly our gay Doctor has other correspondents to entertain sometimes. He is very well, rides constantly, but will ride alone, when He has not a Companion. I cannot prevail on him to take his Servant. I find by Mr Wills that M[atty] has wrote a Ballad on him. It was not own'd, while she was here.

I am not surpriz'd at your account of poor Coll. Trench. When He wrote of his intention to go to Dublin, I counted that He went to dye, tho' He talk'd of returning in a fortnight. Thus apt are we to deceive our Selves, and unwilling to think or see We are mortal. Had not I a good escape? He seem'd very intent on coming hither, and was, I believe, not pleas'd that I did not encourage it. His state and temper have, for a long time past, been such that I doubt whether Mrs Trench will be so much to

470

be pity'd; tho' I am sure it will greatly affect her to loose a husband and bosom-friend of more than 45 years. One thing is very happy. All heart-burnings between him and Dic.² are, I believe, over: I am sure they ought to be. For the Colls. behaviour to him since his coming to the Country has been extremely generous. I have great pleasure in my having been the instrument of this. The day before I left you, He open'd to me his griefs, and I gave advice, which He has follow'd. The Consequence is, that He is easy in his mind, and will leave his family in peace.

I am pleas'd my L[or]d C[hancello]r got in to you. But you write, Huzzy, as if you were almost in love with him. What say you? *Madame la chancelière*, would sound very prettily. But that is the manner only in Mrs J.'s polite Country. I hope the Weather will favour your jaunt; and God forbid you should have any return of disorder of any kind to hinder it. Take care, mistress. No more complaints at your peril. There has been enough of them for one Season already; and for your life, no sore throat at our meeting, as last year. I caution you against this early enough. I long for better weather now on your account as well as the Country's. I wish to have you quite enlarg'd, and as much proof against cold &c. as usual, before a further decline of the Season. This Week has been disagreable enough, tho' not down-right bad. Cold wind, and heavy Show'r's, some Hail. I was out in two bad ones yesterday, but safe with my coat and hood. Works however go on and something is done even at Corn and hay. Hitherto this has been the best day we have had. I write in the morning.

You did mighty well in writing to Mrs Whetcombe. I had a letter yesterday from the Archbishop. His success gives me great joy.

L[or]d Ch[ief]. J[ustice]. S[ingleton]'s letter gave me a laugh, as it did to you. But I have solid pleasure in the good account He gives of himself. He was much out of order, when I left town. His fall would be a publick loss.

I know in general that Mrs N[icholson] intends to pass some days here; but when, or whether here, or at Cary's I know not. It will be much the same either way. I have desir'd Sandford and Rachel to come here too. I know not whether they will.

I am call'd away by the arrival of a very agreable guest, Dr Disney. So my Dear Dear Girl. Adieu.

Your &c
Edw: Elphin

Very odd, that a letter of yours dated September 1 should be so late answer'd. Forgive me this time, and I'll never do so no more. So you, I think, us'd to express your Self when a pratling girl.

I have just superscrib'd a pacquet from the Doctor to Mrs J.

I had a letter from Mr Mahon yesterday in which He speaks very cheerfully of his Wife, yet says of her cough no more than that it is abated, and of her spitting of bloud, that it is very little. They were to go to London for a fortnight, and return immediatly to Ireland. If this resolution be pursu'd, you'll soon hear of them in town.

Rain came on about twelve, not much till about night. From thence till now at Eleven very great and much Wind. I'll go to bed.

[Free Edw:Elphin]

1. Obscure.
2. Richard Trench, his son. See Letter 192.

212

Elphin. September 19, 1752

My Dear Girl

I must repeat what I said in one of my late letters. I can't be quite easy, while any thing ails you. But I am not alarm'd. The Doctor's letter has satisfy'd me fully about the bleeding. I have no doubt but that in proper time you'll find the good effects of it.

You have not with me forfeited your Character for resolution on account of your tears on that occasion. The stoutest cannot guard against surprize. I should blame him for having surpriz'd you, but that I believe you would not have suffer'd him to give his reasons, so that He had nothing left, but to command, and 'twas your business to obey. You did with cheerfulness. So, I am sure, you always will, tho' I care not how few occasions of this sort you have of shewing your truly tractable disposition.

In what relates to you, my dearest, I shall never value Expense. But I really think Mr D[aunt]'s Fee was too high, for doing what an hundred others in Dublin, what Hugh Stafford here can do as well as he. If the Gent. puts himself on that footing, he'll loose instead of gaining. None will send for him. Ned's reason was an idle one. Ten or eleven an Unseasonable hour! But no matter – Be quite well, huzzy and quickly. As to money do what you please. It gives me great pleasure that you are no longer a mumper, but can answer the demands of your good Stomach with ease and pleasure. Do what is thought best about your Teeth. I long to have their fate determin'd one way or other. I need not desire that the person whom the Doctor and Ned chuse be employ'd. I know nothing of Williams but by report; and Nancy Hamilton's account balances the judge's.

Considering the posture in which you wrote, your letter deserves not to be call'd a Scrole. Part of it is wrote, as I would always wish you to write. Your pen seems to have mov'd more freely than when you write more at your Ease. Your thoughts, I am sure, did, and I like the turn of your letter as well as that of any I have received. You have, as you say, told the truth without guarding, and I am much the Easier for it. But I have caught you at a false spelling, Madam. *Partiallity.* There ought to be but one l.

I am prettily serv'd by others as well as my Judge. You know I expected Mrs N[icholson] here; and I think I told you that I had desir'd Mr Sandford and Rachel to meet her. So it was setled, and this to be the day of their meeting. But yesterday's post unhing'd all. It seems Mrs N. was at Packenham's;[1] and He, and his Wife[2] have taken it into their heads to go first to Castelrea with her, and from thence all are to come hither. The Women propose to be all together at Mrs Cary's, and for me they may. But they'll pig finely there. Beside the visiting party, there is Mrs L[ushington] and her husband, who came last Week. However I shall be easier on this footing. We shall be together only in the day, which I shall like very well; and at night none but the Men, one of whom always retires after prayers, and the other shall retire at eleven. This only is vexatious. Carleboe kill'd a very fine Veal yesterday, and I expect a Buck to day for their Entertainment. They'll fare the worse by the delay. But it is their own fault. I care not.

I am very angry with Dr L. and so will you all, when I tell you his Exploit. I had thoughts of dining yesterday at Mantua, but the badness of the Weather made me lay them aside. I thought my self more at liberty, than I really was. For Cary had given Mr D[owell] more reason to expect me, than He ought; and He upon that, had ask'd all his folks; who finding I did not go, would have excus'd themselves also. But Mr D. insisted, and the Scheme was to get L. with them, who was willing enough to be seduc'd. Judge whether He was or not, when the pretence was that Mrs L. wanted some one to bear her Company in the Chaise. Her sister could not go. Something, not much, was amiss with Lucy. In this there was not much amiss. If He chose the Company of the grey Coquette &c. before Disney's and mine, He was at liberty to do so; and We shifted well enough for our Selves. Honest Jac. Crofton made a third at diner, and was entertaining enough. But The Gent. drank Champaign there, return'd in the night past eight, and out of high politeness walk'd thro' the dirt and cold from Cary's hither. He would not suffer Mrs L. to set him down, nor take the Chaise alone. I was very angry and scolded. I hope Mrs J. will abuse him when she writes. I find He either thinks, or would appear to think his late disorder a trifle. I see the Doctor has very different thoughts of it. For this reason I would fain have him take more care of himself than he is inclin'd to do. But I cannot prevail. He is very well this morning, and his looks are much mended since He came hither. *The New stile*[3] will take him and Disney from me eleven days sooner than otherwise they would go. I shall feel this, unless Weather mends, of which I yet see no prospect. It continues very bad, or at best disagreable. This makes me less happy, tho', I bless God, I am very well. But if a bad latter Season brings on Winter earlier than usual, I may perhaps take it into my head to run earlier to my Winter quarters, where, you my Dearest quite well, I shall not be distress'd by bad Weather or any thing else.

I was yesterday reading a french book in which I found a description of what never was nor probably ever will be in it's full proportions. As the day does not invite to a second ride, I have transcrib'd it for you. It will please, I am sure, and may be of use. It shews you, to what you ought to aspire. I don't even wish you to be a *Menoqui*[4] in the graces of the person. But here you see they have, and justly, but the Second place. A great degree of the others you may have, some, to my great joy, you have already. I have no doubt but you'll improve them. The description pleas'd the more as I found it in a grave book of Morals. God bless and preserve you, my Dearest, and make you perfect in every thing that is good.

Your &c.
Edw: Elphin

I am glad you spent the day before your bleeding so pleasantly. But I have particular satisfaction in what you tell me that Mrs P. and her sister[5] are together. Now *Meum* and *tuum* are setled between them, they'll I hope be no longer at a distance but live, and love as sisters ought to do.

My Service to old healthy. Well for you, huzzy, that she has been so some time past. Tell her, that if Mr S[ullivan] chuses to bottle the Wine on any day, when She has not leisure or inclination to attend it, I desire she would commit her part to the care of the pupil. But whether she or He attend, I insist that there be a good fire in the little parlour.

Tell John the looms are come.

Day fair, but rain came on with night, and now at eleven is very heavy.

[Free Edw:Elphin]

1. Pakenham Hall, Castlepollard, Co. Westmeath (now Tullynally Castle). The two-storey eighteenth-century house surrounded by large formal gardens was enlarged in 1780, gothicized by Francis Johnston and enlarged once again by Richard Morrison. Seat of the Pakenham family, now the earls of Longford. Bence-Jones, p.277.

2. Thomas and Elizabeth Pakenham: Thomas Pakenham (1713-66) was created baron of Longford in 1756. Elizabeth, his wife, was the daughter of Michael Cuff and niece of Ambrose Aungier, 2nd earl of Longford. Through her, Thomas Pakenham became baron of Longford, reviving the earldom which had expired in 1704. Burke

(1916), p.1292.

3. An 'Act for regulating the commencement of the year and for correcting the calendar now in use' (24 Geo.II, *c.*23 G.B.), passed in May 1751, brought the Old Style calendar used in the British dominions into conformity with the New Style Gregorian calendar in use on the Continent. It provided that the Julian calendar would cease on 2 September 1752, the following day becoming 14 September.

4. *Menoqui*: the reference is not known and Edward Synge's transcription has not survived.

5. Possibly Elizabeth Pomeroy, who was related to the Donnellan and Ormsby families. See Letter 137.

213

Elphin. September 22, 1752

Tell me honestly, my Dear Miss Brat, when you put me so very gently in mind of the Brewer, did not a secret wish spring up in your mind, that the usual time, for my return to town, or rather to you, were nearer than it is? Were you not inclin'd, if it were convenient and agreable to me, to count by the new Stile? or sometimes, when your uneasiness and yawnings were upon you, to go a little further, and think that if your Dear Father were with you, He might help your cure? I know you've always check'd those thoughts, with this, that it must not be. It would be inconvenient or less agreable to me. You must not therefore expect, you will not wish it. I have upon every occasion found you dispos'd to preferr my pleasure to your own, in the few things in which they have or can interfare and on this account as well as my great fondness for you, I am on my part dispos'd to gratify you to my power. If I were to imitate Madam Sevigny, I should say, I was sorry there were not more difficultys in the way, that I might give you the stronger proof of my Affection by surmounting them. But you want not such proofs, nor do I love high-strain'd Speeches. The honest truth is, That there is in the way no difficulty at all. I have not three peny-worth of real business to do. Shannon has some domestick, which will be setled by him in a very few days; and then I shall be as ready for my March, as I should be at the usual time. To lessen my Complaisance still further, I tell you that mine own reason is on the side of going, without considering you, or your Complaints. The Season has been very bad, and no sign of a good latter one, quite otherwise. In my last I complain'd of the Weather and gave you a hint of what I have since resolv'd. It has been worse since. Yesterday was one of the most shocking days I ever saw in my life: Rank storm and excessive rain. The rain has ceas'd, but the storm continues. It is very uncomfortable, and I feel it rather more than usual, tho' I bless God I am very well. What should I do, when my two agreable friends are run away? I will not stay behind them, and they count by the new Stile, much against their will: So that early next month you may expect me. It is possible I may take it in my head to go earlier. But as to that I am not [*damaged ms*] till I see what time Shannon will want to setle his matters, and have a prospect of better Weather. Don't now imagine, my dearest dear, that this resolution proceeds from my being alarm'd. If I know my self, it would have been the same, tho' your last had told me you were as well as I wish. If I said I were not uneasy, I should lye. I cannot be easy, while I know any thing is amiss with, without being indifferent about, you. Would you have me so? But you remember what I said early to you, that I judg'd your disorders to be teasing rather than dangerous. Your own, Mrs J.'s and the Doctor's accounts confirm me in that opinion. What I think worst, is, that according to my conceptions, It will be some time before they are perfectly remov'd. As good Spirits will expedite your Cure, Keep yours up, till I get to you, and then between us, I'll warrant you, We'll do very well. I believe you were quite at your ease every way when you wrote yours now before me, not only because you say so, but the writing and manner shew that you were. I am greatly pleas'd with both.

I told you that yesterday was a Shocking day. It will please you to know that I narrowly escap'd a good Sousing. It was fair till ten, tho' cloudy, and as the glass had been high the night before and scarce yielded in the morning; My Gent., Lawson, Disney, and with them W. French, were fond of believing what they wish'd, that the day would clear up, and resolv'd to take my favorit ride to Killycloghan; I, tempted by that and their Company, said I would go with them. So I did cross the Demesne; but before I mounted I run to the glass, and finding it fallen, I was more attentive to the Clouds, which soon began to thicken. I then turn'd back, and bid them Good bye. They persisted and got a sound wetting. I rode about the land while it held up, and was hous'd in a minute when the rain came on. They have escap'd without cold. Just before diner in came Nicholson from Castelrea, well sous'd. But that was not enough for him. He went to Boyle after diner, tho' wind and rain continu'd as heavy as ever. He's as hard as Iron. I already gave you an account of the Lady's Scheme. It seems they and the Gent. are to be here to morrow, the former dine with Mrs Cary, the latter with me. They intend lodging in the same way. With all my heart – But *entre nous*, I had as lief have their room as their Company. Their stay will not be long. The worst is, Shannon can do little of what I'd have him, till they are gone.

I have a multitude of letters to answer, else I should prattle more to you: Among the rest one from your Uncle. Desire Jane to give him my thanks for it, I have not time to give them my self. My most cordial love and Service to your faithful friend and Nurse, whom you can never value more than she deserves. God bless and preserve you, my dearest Dear and send us an happy meeting. After the discipline you have undergone, it would be unreasonable in me to expect to see you with the good looks, which you had when I left you. But be well, Huzzy, and those will soon return. My presence shall hasten them.

Your &c.
Edw:Elphin

You may now, Mistress, give what orders you please to Brewer, or any one else: but hurry your self. Mrs Jourdan gives a very bad account of the Ale. I hope it is sent back. Better deferr the botling the Wine, till I get to you.

In your very pretty paragraph about *Madame la Chancelière*, You have made a little mistake. Your a should be *Ah! I fear* &c.

Uneasy as my Dear's disorders are to us both, How much more so would they be if you were here. The distance between us is an Evil, but a necessary one.

Mrs Jourdan writes that your foot is well. I am glad of it, as I am that you are likely to preserve your Teeth. They are at least repriev'd.

Mrs French has secur'd a large parcel of fine feathers. I may have as many or as few as I please. Mrs Heap says 8 or 10 stone will be wanting here. I have a mind to get as many more for town. They are 5 shillings 6d the Stone. But Mrs H. says they must be pick'd. She has a piece of Carpeting, and another of Hucaback[1] for you.

---

1. Huckaback: a rough linen fabric used for towelling.

214

Elphin. September 26, 1752

I need not tell my Dear Sweaty girl that my letters yesterday made me very happy. I had the pleasure to know by them the nature and causes of your Complaints, and to find that they were going off in that way, which on former occasions, the same in kind, tho' less in degree, had been completely successfull. I trust in God they'll be so in this; and that I shall have the joy of meeting her, who is dearer to me than all the World besides, tho' not *bagourah*,[1] yet in a way of being so. It is enough for me that you be well. I care not about looks.

But who was it that thought of your Superscribing Mrs J.'s letter? Whoever it was, upon my Word I am greatly oblig'd to them. For had Shannon come in and told me there was no letter from you, I should have been startled. But seeing your well-known hand, and the Drs next it, I for once gave the preference to his, and by doing so was free from the less degree of surprize, which it would have given me to have seen the letter, superscrib'd by you from Mrs J. You see that by a kind of instinct I obey'd her commands, which were to open the Doctor's letter first. But there was no occasion for the Caution. Hers would have given as much satisfaction as his did. I had the greatest from both.

Now, do you wish or fear that these good tidings will change my purpose of going early to town? I'll tell you what I think. You are divided. I am sure you'll be right glad to see me, and I am as sure, that, according to custom, you would give up even a favorite inclination to mine. I can't on this occasion be even with you. For I assure you upon my Word that in going earlier to town, I follow inclination, and I think I should have done it, tho' you had not had a moment's ilness the whole Summer. Besides the reasons in my former, I have an additional one. Things have not been nor are quite as agreable between C[ary]. and me, as once they were. Her behaviour is perfectly proper; But I do not like the grey Coquette as well as I do her; and the intercourse between us has been, and must be, on this account *un peu gêne.*[2] But his conduct has been absurd beyond measure, and tho' now in appearance less so, is constrain'd. Neither they nor solitude will please in long evenings. I must, for mine own Sake, away to the most pleasing object to me in the World. All the difference that yesterday's good news will make is, that instead of bringing the Wild Doctor, as Mrs J. most justly calls him, with me before his time, My purpose at present is, to go with him at his, which must be the Week after next. I find by him that Disney has thoughts of going earlier. That is to me of no consequence, tho' I like him very well. But one Companion, and He L[awson] will do for me. I deliberate at present about this. Thursday's letters shall determined me. At all Events, as mine own Horses are here, I'll send off my luggage by them. John must not be surpriz'd, if, for that purpose, I detain them two or three days. Tell him, that All things came safe. But Cowgil does not like the Sledges. I must therefore return them. If He has not paid, Forbid him to pay for them.

You expect, to be sure, an account of my numerous Company, and how I do among them; and I want much to give it you. But it is impossible. As the morning was by accident fair, I was forc'd to be abroad with the men, and now I every moment expect the females about my ears; and when once they come, the rest of my time must be given up to them, even from you. Content your self therefore for this bout, my Dear Girl, with my telling you, that Carleboe gives them meat to their mind, Shannon fur-

nishes Cards, and they seem' d to be pleas'd. I was greatly, with the anxiety they shew'd about you, and their joy at yesterday's tidings. Drink, none
of them matter; Only my coquette is constant to her beer, and indeed
stands some smart raillery from the rest about it. Mrs N. will probably tell
you particulars. I like Mrs Packenham much.

Where so many Damsels are together, you'll easily believe that our
wild Doctor is not unengag'd. I told him Mrs J. demanded a pacquet. But
He excuses himself till Saturday. The enclos'd will give you a little enter-
taintment at his Expense. It is Matty's ballad, which I think I mention'd.
All the Comment it wants is, That *Droleen* is the Irish name for a Wren.[3] I
gave him the name by accident, and she was much pleas'd with it. His
Courtship to her was, that Dr Shaw, Minister of Newtown[4] was dying; He
to succeed. She to be his Wife &c. If you want any more, You must wait to
another opportunity. For the Clacks are going. My Dear Dear Girl

God bless and preserve thee to your fond fond Father
Edw: Elphin

Thank your friend, your Nurse, your every thing, from me. I can't
express what I feel on the Occasion. Remember it, I charge you, to her,
your whole life. I am sure you will. Excuse me to the Doctor, the Watch-
fullest and most trusty that ever was; and fail not to bless God for his goodness. I know you wo'n't.

[Free Edw:Elphin]

1. Obscure.
2. *Un peu gêne*: a little awkward.
3. Droleen: *dreólin*, Irish for wren. The ballad may have been the traditional song:
'The wren, the wren, the king of all birds/On St Stephen's night is hid in the furze.'
The wren is considered a treacherous bird in Irish folklore. It was thought to betray
men by flapping its wings and to have betrayed St Stephen.
4. Possibly Robert Shawe (1700-52), born Galway. Admitted to TCD in 1717, he took
BA 1719; MA 1722 and became Fellow 1722; DD 1734. Archbishop King's Lecturer
1730; professor of Oratory and History 1732; Donegal Lecturer 1740; vice-provost.
Rector of Ardstraw. *Alumni*, p.746.

215

Elphin. September 28, 1752

My Dear Girl will receive this from her friend Mrs N. Tho' the *Ordinaire*
went off yesterday, yet since there is an Opportunity to day, there must be
another letter. So you do, and I am pleas'd with it. I ought to do to you,

as I like your doing to me. But all I have to say is, that, I bless God, I am very well, and very happy. I hope my letters to day will make me more so.

The Bishop of Killalla added yesterday to my numerous Company. Assoon as I saw him, I meditated some railling for Rachel. But she unluckily had the head-ach to such a degree, that instead of coming to diner, she was forc'd to go to bed. They are all preparing to go off, and I must away to them. If I stay to write more, I may keep my letter to go by post. God bless and preserve you my dearest to

Your &c.
Edw: Elphin

[To Miss Synge]

1. *Ordinaire*: customary.

216

Elphin. September 29, 1752

I wrote to my Dear Girl yesterday by Mrs Nicholson. This goes by Dr Disney, who told me this minute of his intention of going off, and will put it in Execution in half an hour; so that I have only time to tell you, that I bless God I am very well, and very happy from the good tidings of yesterday. I have told you so already in my letter which will go off by post to morrow. His going off I knew while I was writing to you, and I stopp'd short to write this. You love letters; and I love to gratify you in every thing in my power. God preserve you, my Dearest, and send us an happy meeting. I am

Your most affectionate &c
Edw: Elphin

[To Miss Synge]

217

Elphin. September 29, 1752

My Dear Girl.

Monday's letters, made me, as I told you, very happy. Yesterday's, completely so. The former shew'd me the nature and cause of your teazing complaints, and gave the most comfortable hope that they were in a fine way of being remov'd: the latter has chang'd these hopes into certainty. God be prais'd! I hope, my Dearest, that what has happen'd on this occasion will be of use to you hereafter, and convince you that a free Communication with the good Doctor on a certain nice subject, may be a means of preserving you from any more such flurrys. Recollect a little. The first appearance was a sore throat from Cold got just before a Critical time. Every thing else that has follow'd seems to me to have arisen from the same cause, and Nature at last, aided by the Doctor's judicious care and attention, has forc'd it's way, and you are Well. But I will dwell no longer at this time on the Subject, nor raise your blushes at a distance. Oh! that as to this matter alone, you would lay them aside. Till you do, you will, even in my partial opinion, labour under one very great Weakness at least, which it would become one who thinks and acts so reasonably in other matters, to overcome.

You'll know before you get this, that the females &c. left this place yesterday. They seem'd much pleas'd with their reception and Entertainment. The truth is, they had reason. I have told you already, that I like Mrs P[akenham] much. She is a strong instance, of what I have had twenty in my life, that a Woman may be very agreable without being very handsome. I am much mistaken if she be not a good Wife, and a good Mother. She seems of good sense and a cheerful temper. Her whole behaviour is natural, and unaffected. Nothing to me so pleasing.

I had a very cheerful letter yesterday from Coll. Trench, in which He tells me that Dr Barry has again help'd him. He speaks of this in stronger terms than, I fear, He has reason. But in his case, It is a great deal to be reliev'd for a time. He writes pleasantly about the Sale of his stock, and says that his God-daughter must, to complete her Milesian portion,[1] have another Cow, which He desires me to get some one to chuse out of all and send off hither, from or before the Cant.[2] My answer is, that I think your whole portion already paid, and therefore desire to wave the addition. But if He will make it, It is not your affair, or mine for you, to chuse, but to accept with gratitude what the parent gives. I think it would not be amiss, if you sent him a card or message by Jeny to the same purpose. Thanks for the favor, a modest declining it, but that if so it must be, you leave the choice quite to him, or his direction. Think not, huzzy, that I teach you here to dissemble. I really had rather He had made no such offer. But since He has, We must receive it with proper acknowledgments, and treat it so as not to offend.

It's very odd, and yet it's very true: seeing your Superscription, I was better pleas'd to see the enclos'd even before I read it, Mrs J's than I should have been to have found it yours. I was afraid you would stress your self by that same little letter which you wish'd to write. Do not, my Dearest, attempt any thing of this kind till you are quite well, which I hope will now be soon. It is enough for me to know this from your Doctor, and that same Mrs J. to whose care and attention I am indeed no stranger, and We both are much indebted to. I hope she is as well, as she says she is. I am sure she has had fatigue and anxiety enough to harrass a stronger person. I see by hers, that I judg'd rightly of the state of your mind about my going to town. My last inform'd you fully of my resolutions, which I will not, nor am I inclin'd to, vary. The Week after next, God willing, I'll set out. The time of the Week I have not yet fix'd, nor can I till I have seen Palmer, whom I expect to morrow or Sunday, in order to the fair of Boyle.[3] From thence He'll return, and go to Balnasloe.[4] Till that is over, and He got home, It would not be right for me to move. If I gave him the slip, I should hurt my self by wanting my good quarters. If I mov'd earlier and He knew it, To accommodate me, He would incommode himself. Since it pleases God, that I have it in my power, thus at my ease, to setle my route and time, I'll do it in the way most convenient to every one that I can; and I have the pleasure to tell you, that by Shannon's diligence, I shall leave every thing within doors, as well setled, as if I staid a month longer; if the Weather favours, shall see the same of those without doors. But about them I am less anxious. They are in good hands. Cowgil hitherto shews himself both diligent and skilfull. The Carrs are to go off on Monday with the luggage; but the Feathers can't go by them. Mrs Heap says they must be pick'd. They are not yet come from Porte. My Dear Dear Girl, for this time Adieu. God send us an happy meeting. I am

Your &c.
Edw: Elphin

I apprehend this will cost you a groat. Lawson promises a paquet, which if ready shall go by Disney, if not I'll enclose to the person you so much admire and esteem. But I chuse rather to put you to an Expense than to run a possible hazard of his being any where abroad. If you had not a letter on Monday, what would become of you? Just the same as of me, if in the heighth of your complaints, I had had none from you or your friend – Even the one by Disney, tho' wrote the same day would not content you. Are not We a couple of fools?

I find Lawson's pacquet is ready; and He'll send it by Disney. Should He forget, It shall go as above. You shall not want it. It is gone. You'll have it before you get this. Now for L[or]d C[hancello]rs franks for two or three posts.

[Free Edw:Elphin]

1. Milesian portion: a reference to the mythical division of Ireland into two parts by two of the four surviving sons of Míl, the fictional ancestor of the Irish people, after defeating the Tuatha Dé Danann kings at the battle of Tailtiu.

2. Cant: an Irish term for disposing of stock by auction. An advertisement for the sale of Col Frederick Trench's stock, 'by Publick Cant' on 1 October 1752, appeared in *Faulkner's Dublin Journal* for 11-15 August 1752.

3. Boyle Fair was on Monday 2 October 1752.

4. Ballinasloe Fair was held from 5 October in 1752. Watson (1752), p.102.

218

Elphin. October 1

My Dear Girl

This goes by the Bishop of Killalla's servant. My Couriers and the post doing their duty, you'll have four letters in as many days. If opportunitys of this sort offer'd, I believe We should do little else but write, while asunder. A Couple of Fools! All I have to say is that, I bless God, I am very well. I hope to morrow's letters will bring me an account that you are so.

The Weather is now very fine and seems setled. If it be, in two or three days, All my harvest will be at home and made up. My wheat, the bulkyest part is so already. Turf-drawing must continue longer. That is the heaviest Article not in Expense only but vexation. I'll tell you all when We meet, which I hope We shall at the time appointed; and think not, my Dearest, that the change of Weather will make me even wish to stay a day longer; tho' you must not have the Vanity to place this entirely to your own account. I am

Your &c.
Edw: Elphin

If you receive this by a Porter, pay him.

[To Miss Synge, Kevin-Street]

219

Elphin. October 3, 1752

Oh! how welcome was my Dear Dear Girl's little letter. Nothing in this world could give me so much joy except the Seeing you further advanc'd towards a state of health. I trust in God I shall soon have this happiness. The Doctor's and Mrs Jourdan's accounts of you give me the most pleasing expectation of it. Next Week, please God, I am determin'd to set out. The particular day I cannot yet fix, but believe it must be late; Wedensday or Thursday. I told you in my last that I must either wait a day or two, or give up my quarters at Palmer's. There was indeed a third choice; to incommode him. But that I could not think of. His whole year's profit from his Land might be lost by it. The accounts of and from you being so satisfactory, I am inclin'd a little to consult mine own ease and Convenience tho' the effect be, that I do not see the joy of my heart, by a day or two so soon. I am sure you would have me do it.

Things have fallen out a little unluckily for Palmer, and consequently for me too, this year. He us'd to buy in his stock of Bullocks at Boyle. He has not bought above a fourth part now. By the extravagant demands of the Sellers yesterday, very few Cattel were bought. This will detain him a day or two longer at Balnasloe. He us'd to come off, when the Sheep-fair was over. He has been unlucky in another point. The Fair-day was on Sunday; and for this reason the fair was held on Monday. This shortens the interval between the two fairs, a day, which is extremely inconvenient. He was oblig'd to ride on Sunday from home to Boyle, a long journey. Yesterday evening He came hither tir'd; and this day He must set out, to be tir'd agen.

I have another reason for staying to the middle of the Week, tho' that alone should not influence: Such is my impatience to fold my fond arms about thee. But I am this instant as poor as a Church-Mouse. As this is the Season of paying rents, I hope by the time I set out to be rich. If I am not, you must maintain me out of your privy-purse. A very poor one I know it is! We should both be ill off, if that were our dependance.

But what think you happen'd yesterday? The post did not come in till six in the Evening. The delay was between Athlone and Roscommon. The Cause I know not. Thus you see I waited for my Dear's promised little letter, longer than you thought I should. But the very good accounts of you the post before made me wait without the least uneasiness. Had this accident happen'd that day se'night, it had been a cruel one. But luckily, that day, the letters came in near two hours earlier than usual, and chang'd my state of suspense into a flow of joy, so much the Sooner.

You say, I may guess you are lean and Weak. Considering what has happen'd, I should be sorry you were otherwise. You are in the natural way, in which by your disorder's taking a right turn, you ought to be; and this I am sure is an indication of returning health. Fulness or colour would be a Continuance of disease. Methinks I see my Dear lean girl by this time so far advanc'd as to take a turn across the room, leaning perhaps on her

Dear friend, in every shape her support. You long Gag you! What a figure do you make. In such I expect to see you. But, by God's blessing, That will soon change to the one in which I saw you at parting.

You say very truly that you can never repay that same friend and Nurse. Nor I neither. She has been every thing to you, that I could wish. But no part of her friendly and most affectionate conduct has delighted me more, than her keeping you so absolutely free from Company. I desire she would continue it, at least as long as she or the Doctor think there is the least occasion; nay! longer. Better err on the safe side. She says she won't act like Dr Wall in the affair of the Small-Beer Cellar. I hope she'll act like her self, and have it fix'd in every point completely as it ought to be. Her account of it is shocking. See, My Dear, by this the necessity of Master's or Mistress's [*damaged ms*] into every thing. It escap'd me, I confess. Hearing no complaint, I thought all right; and No one else was charg'd with it, but poor Shannon whom three penny-worth of sense would make a most valuable Servant. He has behav'd himself very well this summer.

The Carrs left this very early on Monday. I wrote to John by them; not to you, because I had wrote that same day to you, by the Bishop of Killalla's servant. He left this on Sunday after Church and a short diner. If I had wrote by the Carrs, I must have wrote that Evening, or have arisen before day. You would not, I am sure, have had me. Yet now, for a peny-Wager, It will be a baulk that you have not a letter by Mathew. If it be, Your friend shall tell, and I'll laugh at, you.

By Mr Moore's price, the Feathers will be a noble bargain. I'll take care that they be brought home, and properly sent up. The hucaback and Carpeting are gone, but you can't get them, till I go to you.

I shall receive the return of this here. But, now I have got the little letter, I had rather you spar'd your Self, and let your friend write. My Dear Dear. God bless and preserve you to

Your most affectionate father
Edw: Elphin

Mr Cary's little one has the measels,[1] hitherto in a kindly way. Let something be said of this in yours or Mrs J.'s.

Tell Mrs J. that Shannon affirms no stilling was broke when He left town: of the troughs &c. He gives so confus'd an account that I do not understand him. She'll soon have it from himself.

When the Bishop of K. came hither, his scheme was to have been in town on Sunday morning. I persuaded him to stay as He did, and said He should preach. He consented but told me I must lend him a Gown; which I did, but was forc'd on that account to stay at home my Self. An old cloth one, which was my refuge, appear'd on Examination not wearable. I tell you this, to prevent a possibility of a moment's uneasiness to my Dearest, in case Mathew should say I was not at Church on Sunday. Be assur'd I am as well this minute as when We parted, nay! better, and happy in the hope of your growing better every hour.

Let the pupil be told that I have just seen one of the Wallace's; and that I find by him, that No application has been made either to him or his brother about Bullocks or Cows for Finglas. This is not as John promis'd.

1. Measles (rubeola) was often confused with smallpox. Highly infectious, it was formerly a major cause of death, the complications of pneumonia and encephalitis following the illness itself. Thomas Sydenham (1629-89) wrote two important treatises on measles in the late seventeenth century and is credited with differentiating it from other rashes. R.J. Kim-Farley, 'Measles' Kiple, pp.872-3.

220

Elphin. October 6, 1752

Well! My Dear lean Gag; Such I expect to find you. No matter, since, blessed be God, I have so well grounded a prospect of finding you in a way of being fatter. This day se'night, I hope to be nearer you than I am at present. I long for it; and assure you upon my Word, that I never left Elphin with so perfect a good Will, as now, since I had you here with me. But don't be vain, Huzzy. This is not all on your account. I have given reasons for part of it in my late letters. It would however not be fair to dissemble, that The pleasure of being with you is the strongest.

To prevent mistakes, you are not to expect me till Saturday. I purpose, God willing, to set out from hence on Thursday. Palmer would fain have had me decamp on Wednesday, and spend a day with him. I ask'd, how He would answer that to you. Well enough, He said, as the difference to you was only my spending a day here or there. But He could not prevail. Business only should detain me; and yet for ought I yet see I may stay to no purpose. Not a peny since my last. But if it comes not while I stay, it must follow me.

The Account of Coll. Trench's death[1] surpriz'd me, tho' I thought his condition hopeless, and believ'd that his death whenever it happen'd would be sudden. Your good grand-father us'd on such incidents to say, God prepare us all. His life and Doctrine shew'd that the best, the only preparation for death was a Christian life.

Mrs J.'s manner of writing added to my Surprize. *Ned Curtis tells you how she was prevented*. Little did I imagine the kind of prevention, till I open'd Ned's letter. Her hint did not even prepare me for it. I have formerly told you, how I thought that event would affect the Survivors. For their sakes, particularly the Widow's, I hope I was right. His last setlement with Dic, tho' in other respects of no effect, will probably keep peace in the family. Poor Lucy is gone. No one will feel the loss so much as Mrs Shawe. You have lost half your portion.[2] No matter. That great loss is balanc'd by my saving the money for another, which I intended to buy. On the whole We are gainers.

Your little God-daughter has been very ill since my last. By the accounts this morning she is rather better.[3] I shall be able to give more certain ones before I seal this. The poor Mother is the Object of my Concern. The next news I expect to hear is, that little L. is down. The Father and Mother say, they expect and even wish it. This incident adds not to the pleasure of staying here, tho' by it I am free from the coquette, and see him. Both please. I do not like her. They all, as well as Mr and Mrs Conroy have express'd great concern for your ilness and joy in your recovery.

Mrs C. tells me, that a match is likely to be between young Dic Townsend,[4] whom you saw last winter, and Miss Fitz-gerald Lady Doneraile's niece. If the character she gives of the young Lady be just, the young Man has chosen well. She has a very good fortune, and a chance for a great one.

Another thing I tell you in a whisper. It is only for you, and your bosom friend. Betty Wills has a Second Spark, Mr Dillon of Clonbrock.[5] Her Father wrote to me about it some time ago. My last account from Wills-grove was All well but Mrs.W. She very ill. I have since heard nothing from him, or of it. This at first gave concern. But it seems the ilness is breeding.

Le bruit court ici,[6] that one Mr Flynn who went some Weeks since to Bristol to be marry'd to a young Damsel, whom by the Laws of Ireland He could not marry, is drown'd and his fair one with him. I don't find any one sorry. They are rather pleas'd that his Children by a former Wife will by this melancholy accident be preserv'd from ruin. I believe indeed that will be the effect, if He be gone to the bottom. Whether He be or not, His exploit has been a most unadvis'd one. A Man of fifty with Several Children, to engage in such an Adventure with a Girl of fifteen. You'll easily believe that She had not much fortune. Wealth alone could be a temptation to her; and of that there was enough. The Man was Brother to him, who was guilty of the Outrage on Miss Dermot, which you remember, made such a noise some years ago. Another Brother was try'd last Assizes at Roscommon for an action which deserv'd hanging, tho' the Law did not make it murder. A happy Family!

I find by Mrs J. that your friend Mrs M[ahon] is arriv'd. As she has not seen her, She can make no judgment of the Effects of her Expedition. Much I fear that they have not been as good as We wish. By the last from him, I learn that their scheme is to come immediatly to Strokes-town; and if it be, I have very ominous apprehensions of the Winter. I wish Mrs J. could prevail to have our good Doctor consulted, before she sets out. I would have her press it, as far, at least, as she thinks decent. Her motive must excuse the importunity. But I doubt her prevailing. He is of a temper to entertain sanguine hopes without foundation: She passive. The End will not be good. I am very sorry, and would do any thing to prevent the Evil.

As I leave this on Thursday, I cannot have a return to this here. But I expect a little letter at Glanmore; and it will do as well from Mrs J. as from you; better indeed, if you should run the least hazard of stressing, or fatiguing your Self by writing. Avoid this, my Dearest, by all means. The true point is, to be well. Do not do the least thing to retard that, by an effort to appear better. Mrs J., who to my great joy writes that she is extremely well, will order the usual preparatives, plate home, Bag of flow'r, mutton kill'd &c. I am indifferent about them. But Take notice, Mistress, that if you make the least change in dress, place or any thing else, more than you would make, if you were not to see me these three months, I'll chide. The Doctor is to determine all. I will not dine in your apartment but in mine own. And I won't have diner, but something to eat; and so My Dear Dear for this time Adieu. My constant wish and prayer is God send us an happy meeting. I shall repeat it in my next.

Your &c
Edw: Elphin

The child is better this Evening.

1. 'Last Tuesday died aged seventy, at his house in Cuff Street, Frederick Trench Knight of the Shire for the County of Galway, whose Death is much lamented by all his Acquaintance. He is succeeded by his son, Frederick Trench Esq Member of Parliament for the Borough of Banagher and his other son, Eyre Trench, Esq hath declared himself candidate for the County and, we hear, that Robert French of Monivea Esq Intends to offer himself a candidate for the said County.' *Faulkner's Dublin Journal* 3-7 October 1752.

2. A cow. See Letter 217.

3. Alicia's god-daughter was probably Oliver and Frances Cary's child, ill with measles. See Letter 219.

4. Richard Townshend (see Letter 53) married Elizabeth Fitzgerald, a daughter of viscount Doneraile. 'Last week was married at the seat of Lord Viscount Doneraile, Richard Townsend Esq, of Castle Townsend in the County of Cork, to Miss Fitzgerald

Daughter to the late Knight of Kerry, sister to the present, and Niece to his Excellency Henry Boyle, a young Lady of great Beauty and a handsome fortune and so polite an Education added to a natural Sweetness of Temper as make her an Ornament to her Sex and must render the marriage State happy.' Burke (1912) p.699; *Faulkner's Dublin Journal,* 17-21 October 1752.

5. One of the Dillon family of Clonbrock, Ahascragh, Co. Galway. Elizabeth Wills married Thomas Mitchell of Castle Strange, Co. Roscommon, in 1753. Burke (1912), p.624.

6. *Le bruit court ici*: The gossip here is.

221

Elphin. October 25, 1752

My Dear Girl.

It falls out as I expected. Mr Mahon does not travel with me. Her cold was the reason assign'd, and a very good one. Yet I hope there is no occasion for being alarm'd about it. I saw her on Wedensday. She thought herself growing better, and by a letter from him yesterday, I had the pleasure to know, that She was still in a better way of being reliev'd. I went thither resolv'd, to divert him from the journey, out of regard to her disorder, and because I knew not of any publick business, that requir'd his going so soon to town. Thus I reliev'd him from the difficulty He was under about me; and, I believe, pleas'd her into the bargain. My opinion about traveling alone, I gave you in my last.

Mathew will leave this to morrow with the luggage. He proposes to be with you on Tuesday. He carrys 460 odd Pears in a Cask, and, a Cask of Flow'r. I told you before, that that should be unpack'd assoon as it arrives. But Mrs Heap said yesterday; that it would be right to have it all sifted, so as to break every the Smallest Lump. I found by her, that Some of what has gone from hence formerly, grew musty. This I never heard of before, nor, I believe, you. So waste happens, even with good Servants, where Master or Mistress do not, or cannot pry minutely into domestick management. But, As, God be thanked, your health is improv'd, So I hope your Activity and Attention to these matters, will be such, as that not even a pound of Flow'r will be sunk without account. I have spoken to Jane about Bread, to gratify your Curiosity. Ten to one, if, taking more pains, she does not make worse; and, It will appear at disadvantage, four days Old. But such as it proves, you shall have it. Mrs Jourdan shall have her toasting cheese too, if I do not forget it. But why may she not as well provide them in Dublin?

I should be very sorry to have the news of the P. of O's death confirm'd.[1] But unless it be a piece of Waggery, I fear. If it be this, It is a pleasant one, tho' not to be justify'd. It has made great fracas among fine folks and Mercers. I differ from the Ladys. As P. of O., they are right. But, in point of Form, the Son-in-law is consider'd as the Son. So it is, you know, with private persons. What ever happens, you are safe, and your Velvet will be more usefull. Adieu, My Dearest, till We meet.

Your &c.
Edw: Elphin

Turn

If your Weather be as ours, Your heart goes pit a pat, lest I should have bad, on my journey. Be under no concern. Dry and Warm in the Coach, the worst can't hurt me much. I shall indeed be in some pain for Servants and Horses. But I'll drive the faster, so as not to be many hours in motion. I think however I have a fair prospect. The Wind stands; and tho' We had a little rain, on Tuesday, Wedensday was as fine as has been these three Weeks. Yesterday was a heavy fogg. It clear'd up about twelve. The Afternoon fine. But the Fogg return'd at night. It went off at Seven this morning. Since, there has been some rain, not much. Men and horses all at Work. I hope it will all fall before I go. It will, if my usual luck attends me. But fall what can fall in this, I am going to you.

How came it to pass, Mistress, that you did not tell me Mrs Lennox[2] had been very ill? Perhaps you knew it. If you did, I hope you sent. By his account yesterday, She is still weak, tho' recovering.

If Dr Bland[3] be come to town, Send the enclos'd instantly to him. If not, Learn when He is expected, and see that He has it assoon as He arrives.

Some bad Stopping in your last. The Old fault! When will you learn to put . where the Sentence closes?

1. The rumour was false. William V (1748-1806) became the Stadtholder and Prince of Orange on the death of his father, William IV, in 1751. His mother was Princess Anne, daughter of George II.

2. Sarah Lennox, Godfrey Wills's sister, married to William Lennox the banker. See Letter 152.

3. Dr Nathaniel Bland. See Letter 10.

To Miss Synge[1]

The days decrease, and Summer wastes away,
Allicia, wherefore this unkind delay?
Returning Springs no more my joys renew,
Springs once so joyful - for they brought me you.
How lovely look our fields, how bright the day!
Haste from the Town, Allicia haste away.

How often have I follow'd where you led,
Play'd round the Coach or Hover'd o'er your head?
How often turn'd away the falling show'r,
And temper'd burning Sunbeams by my power,
Bad fanning breezes cool thy glowing face,
And drove afar the Insects buzzing race:
And when still night has lull'd my tender Fair
Watch'd o'er her slumbers with a Parent's care:
Or studious to instruct her growing age
Mark'd down the moral or well-written page?
Oft have I left for humbler toils my state,
To set thy head-dress, and thy gown to plait,
Then secret-smiling, when well-drest you shone,
Heard Fanny prais'd for labors not her own.

And quit'st thou for the Town's tumultuous scenes,
Thy Friend, her healthful air, her open plains,
To pant in dust and smoke's combining clouds,
Midst hurry, coaches, visits, noises, crowds?
What are the charms a Town like this can boast
To thee, too wise to wish to be a Toast?
That Town, I know not why, alarms my fears –
Ah me that Town a thousand dangers bears;
Pleasures that hurt the health, the beauty waste,
That taint the manners, and pervert the taste:
There grandeur tempts, There dress & flatt'ry please,
Int'rest corrupts, and vanity betrays.
How art thou chang'd, much lov'd, Lamented Jane,

In native ease late sporting o'er my plain!
In vain the Muses wooe whom wealth shall fix
To shine unhappy in her coach and six.
Alas! where Fops and pert Coquettes allure
Can sense, can knowlege gay Fifteen secure?

But hence vain fears – Allicia's Soul I know,
Too high, too virtuous to descend so low,
Quick to discern true worth, and scorning empty show.
Such Harriot was; Like thee she grac'd this wild
Like thine her bloom, Fair, sensible, and mild;
Yet midst an idle world she shines the same,
The sweetest Virgin, and the loveliest Dame:
Such too the Matron, Glory of my plains,
Whom now her Kerry's native clime detains:
Thine be their Fate; In ev'ry age approv'd,
A Matron honor'd, as a Maid belov'd.

Meantime return. Behold, with brighter hue
I cloathe my fields, my skys with purer blue;
Beneath thy passing wheels new flow'rs shall bloom,
Paint the rough heath, the moss-grown cliff perfume:
For thee soft gales shall breath & starting rills
With sudden murmur chear my thirsty hills.
For thee my Friend, to all beside unseen,
I'll lead my dances o'er the circled green.
My mines to deck thee flame with gems and gold;
For thee my shells the lucid pearl infold.
Come gentle Maid; For thee our songs we'll raise,
Ten thousand spirits warbling heavn'ly lays;
Come gentle Maid; a Virgin-Queen invites;
Come gentle Maid, partake our chast delights.

From our Palace under
Racrogan.   MAB the QUEEN.

1. Anon, 1748.

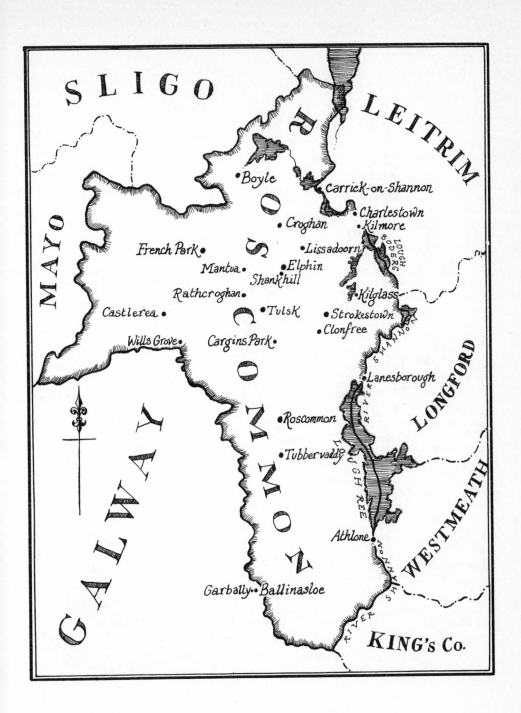

IRELAND
in the
1740s

Sligo
Swanlinbar
Carrick-on-Shannon
Boyle
ELPHIN
Castlerea
Lanesborough
Roscommon
Ballymahon
Dunshaughlin
Dunboyne
Athlone
Mullingar
Clonarde
Finglas
Artane
Kinnegad
Kilcock
DUBLIN
Ballinasloe
Dun
Laoghaire

RIVER SHANNON

Birr

● Route from
Kevin St., Dublin to
Elphin, Co. Roscommon
----- Boundary of
the diocese of
Elphin in the
18th Century

Killaloe
Nenagh
Roscrea
Kilkenny
Cashel

Mallow

Cork
Cloyne

Sherkin Island

©Martin Rawson 1995

Sources and Bibliography

ARCHIVES

BL	British Library, London
IAA	Irish Architectural Archive
Kirkpatrick	Royal College of Physicians of Ireland
NA	National Archives of Ireland
NLI	National Library of Ireland
RCB	Representative Church Body, Dublin
PRO	Public Record Office, London
PRONI	Public Record Office of Northern Ireland
RD	Registry of Deeds
RCSI	Royal College of Surgeons in Ireland
RIBA	Drawings College, Royal Institute of British Architects
TCD	Trinity College, Dublin

MANUSCRIPTS

Ireland

Irish Architectural Archive
  Michael Wills, Cash Book 1731-7.

Marsh's Library, Dublin
  Agreement of the Church Wardens of several Parishes 1725.
  The Diary of Dr Elie Bouhéreau of La Rochelle 1689-1719.
  Roger Kendrick, Maps and Plans of St Patrick's 1741-1825.

National Archives of Ireland
  Census of the diocese of Elphin 1749.

National Library of Ireland
  Beranger, Gabriel, Tour through Connaught in 1779 under the direction of the Rt Hon.
    William Burton.
  Pakenham Mahon Papers.
  Synge Papers.
  Wicklow Papers.

Representative Church Body, Dublin
  St Werburgh's Vestry Book 1720-80.

Royal College of Physicians of Ireland
  Kirkpatrick Archive.

Royal College of Surgeons in Ireland
  Mercer's Hospital Governors' Minute book 1736-72.

Trinity College, Dublin
  Archbishop King Papers.
  Archbishop Edward Synge correspondence with William Wake.

United Kingdom
Balliol College, Oxford
  Conroy Papers.

British Library
  Berkeley Papers.

Public Record Office, London
  War Office Muster Books and Pay Lists.

Public Record Office of Northern Ireland
  Roden Papers.

Royal Institute of British Architects
  Michael Wills, Album of 16 Designs for Private Buildings &c.

PRINTED MATERIAL

A List of the Colonels, Lieutenant Colonels, Majors, Captains, Lieutenants and Ensigns of His Majesty's Forces on the Irish Establishment (London 1740).

E.H. Alton, 'Fragments of College History' Vol. 1, *Hermathena* (1941) pp.57-8.

An Abstract of the Number of Protestant and Popish Families in the Several Counties and Provinces in Ireland (Dublin 1732).

An Excellent New Song, To a Good Old Tune (Dublin 1726).

Andrews, J.H., *Two Maps of 18th Century Dublin and its Surroundings*, (Lympne 1977).

[Anon], 'Pedigree of the family of St George'.

Aström, Sven-Erik, 'English timber imports from northern Europe in the eighteenth century', *Scandinavian Economic History Review* Vol. 18 (1970) pp.12-32.

Aufderheide, Arthur C., 'Lead poisoning' in Kenneth Kiple (ed.), *Cambridge World History of Human Disease* (Cambridge 1993).

Ball, F. Elrington, *The Judges of Ireland 1221-1921* 2 vols (Oxford 1926).

——, *South of Fingall ... a History of the County of Dublin* (Dublin 1920).

Barnard, T.C., 'Crises of identity among Irish protestants 1641-1685', *Past and Present* Vol. 127 (1990) pp.39-83.

——, T.C., 'Gardening, diet and improvement in later seventeenth century Ireland', *Journal of Garden History* Vol. 10, (1990) pp.71-86.

——, T.C., 'The uses of 23 October 1641 and Irish protestant celebrations', *English Historical Review* Vol.106 (October 1991) pp.889-920.

——, 'Improving clergymen' in Alan Ford, James McGuire and Kenneth Milne (eds), *As by Law Established: The Church of Ireland since the Reformation* (Dublin 1995).

——, 'The world of a Galway squire: Robert French of Monivae' in R. Gillespie (ed.), *Galway: History and Society* (forthcoming).

Barrington, Sir Jonah, *The Rise and Fall of the Irish Nation* (Dublin 1868).

Barrow, J., *Dictionarium Medicum Universale* (1749).

Bartlett, Thomas, *The Fall and Rise of the Irish Nation* (Dublin 1992).

Beasley, Jerry C., *Novels of the 1740s* (Athens, Georgia 1982).

Beaufort, D.A., *Memoir of a Map of Ireland* (London 1792).

Benedex, T.G., 'Gout' in Kenneth Kiple (ed.), *Cambridge World History of Human Disease* (Cambridge 1993).

Sources and Bibliography

Berkeley, George, *Sirius: a charm of Philosophical Reflections and Enquiries concerning the Virtues of Tar Water* (1744).

Berman, David, 'Dr Berkly's books', Francis Hutcheson Supplement to *Fortnight* July/August 1992.

Boerhaave, Hermann, *Aphorisms concerning the Knowledge and cure of Diseases* Translated from the last Edition printed at Leyden 1715 (London 1715).

Letters written by His Excellency Hugh Boulter DD Lord Primate of all Ireland 2 vols (1770).

Boydell, Brian, *A Dublin Musical Calendar* (Dublin 1988).

Bradley, Richard, *A General Treatise of Husbandry and Gardening* (London 1724).

Brady, W.M., *The clerical and parochial records of Cork, Cloyne and Ross* (London 1864).

Bric, M.J., 'The tithe system in eighteenth century Ireland', *Proceedings of the Royal Irish Academy* Vol. 86, Sect.C. (1986) pp.271-88.

Brockliss, L.W.B., 'The development of the spa in seventeenth century France' in Roy Porter (ed.), *The Medical History of Waters and Spas* (London 1990).

Burke, James M., 'Sherkin Island', *Journal of the Cork Archaeological and Historical Society* Vol. 11 (1905).

Burtchaell, G.D. and Sadleir, T.U., *Alumni Dubliniensis* (Dublin 1935).

Cadogan, Mary (ed.), Sarah Fielding *The Governess* (1987).

Carroll, W.G., *Succession of Clergy in the parishes of S. Bride, S. Michael le Pole, and S. Stephen, Dublin* (Dublin 1884).

Casey, Christine, '"De Architectura": an Irish eighteenth-century gloss', *Architectural History* Vol. 37 (1994).

——, 'Subscription networks for Irish architectural books 1730-1760', *Long Room*, Vol. 35, (1990).

—— and Rowan, Alistair, *North Leinster* (London 1993).

[Chaigneau, William], *The History of Jack Connor* 2 vols (Dublin 1752).

Clarkson, L.A. and Crawford, E.M., *Ways to Wealth: The Cust Family of Eighteenth-Centuray Armagh* (Belfast 1985).

Connell, K.H., *Irish Peasant Society* (Oxford 1968).

Connolly, Sean, *Religion, Law and Power: the Making of Protestant Ireland 1660-1760* (Oxford 1992).

Cooke-Trench, T., *Memoir of the Trench Family* (1897).

[Sir Richard Cox], *The Case of Edward, Lord Bishop of Elphin in Relation to Money, part of the Rents of the Ranelagh Charity, lodged in a public Bank in Dublin* (Dublin 1760).

Craig, Maurice, *Classic Irish Houses of the Middle Size* (London 1976).

——, *Dublin 1660-1860: A Social and Architectural History* (Dublin 1980).

Crawford, W.H., 'The evolution of the linen trade in Ulster before industrialization', *Irish Economic and Social History* Vol. 15 (1988) pp.132-55.

Crofton, H., *Memoirs of the Crofton Family* (Dublin 1910).

Crosby, A.W., 'Smallpox' in Kenneth Kiple (ed.), *Cambridge World History of Human Disease* (Cambridge 1993).

Cunnington, C. Willett and Cunnington, Phillis, *Handbook of English Costume of the Eighteenth Century* (Buxton 1972).

David, Elizabeth, *English Bread and Yeast Cookery* (London 1977).

——, *French Provincial Cooking* (1960).

Davis, H. (ed.), Jonathan Swift, *Miscellaneous and Autobiographical Pieces, Fragments and Marginalia* (Oxford 1962).

Dickson, David, 'Large-scale developers and the growth of eighteenth century Irish cities' in P. Butel and L.M. Cullen (eds), *Cities and Merchants* (Dublin 1986).

Dunn, F.L., 'Malaria' in Kenneth Kiple (ed.), *Cambridge World History of Human Disease* (Cambridge 1993).

Eustace, P.B., *Registry of Deeds Dublin. Abstracts of Wills* 2 vols (Dublin 1954).

Fagan, Patrick, *Cornelius Nary: Dublin's Turbulent Priest* (Dublin 1991).

——, *The Second City: Portrait of Dublin 1700-1760* (Dublin 1986).

Fitzgerald, Brian (ed.), *Correspondence of Emily, Duchess of Leinster 1731-1814* 3 vols (Dublin 1948-57).

Fleetwood, John, *History of Medicine in Ireland* (Dublin 1951).

Foot, M.R.D. and Matthew, H.C.W. (eds.), *The Gladstone Diaries* 14 vols (1968-94).

French, Roger K., 'Scurvy' in Kenneth Kiple (ed.), *Cambridge World History of Human Disease* (Cambridge 1993).

Galloway, Peter, *The Cathedrals of Ireland* (Belfast 1992).

Georgian Society Records of Eighteenth-Century Domestic Architecture and Decoration in Dublin 5 vols (1909-12).

Gibbs, Graham C., 'Abel Boyer: the making of a British subject', *Proceedings of the Huguenot Society* Vol. 26 (1994) pp.14-44.

Gilbert, J.T., 'The Streets of Dublin - III', *Irish Quarterly Review* Vol. 2, March (1852).

——, *A History of the City of Dublin* 3 vols (facsimile edition, Shannon 1972).

Gill, Conrad, *The Rise of the Irish Linen Industry* (Oxford 1925).

Ginger, John, *The Notable Man: The Life and Times of Oliver Goldsmith* (London 1977).

[Hannah Glasse] A Lady, *The Art of Cookery Made Plain and Easy* (first published 1747, reprinted London 1983).

Glin, the Knight of, *A Directory of the Dublin Furniture Trade 1752-1800* (Dublin 1992).

——, and Malins, Edward, *Lost Demesnes: Irish Landscape Gardening 1660-1845* (London 1976).

——, Griffin, David J. and Robinson, Nicholas K. (eds.), *Vanishing Country Houses of Ireland* (Dublin 1988).

Gray, E.S., 'The Ormsbys of Tobbervaddy', *Irish Genealogist*, Vol. 1 (1941).

Guerini, Vincenzo, *A History of Dentistry* (Philadelphia 1909).

Hamlin, Christopher, 'Chemistry, medicine and the legitimization of English spas 1740-1840' in Roy Porter (ed.), *The Medical History of Waters and Spas* (London 1990).

Harley, David, 'A sword in a madman's hand: professional opposition to popular consumption in the waters literature of southern England and the Midlands 1570-1870' in Roy Porter (ed.), *The Medical History of Waters and Spas* (London 1990).

Hartley, Dorothy, *Food in England* (London 1954).

Hartford, R.R., *Edward Synge, Fellow and Bishop: a Memorial Discourse delivered ... on 2nd June, 1947* (Dublin 1947).

Houghton, Benjamin, *Considerations humbly addressed to the magistrates of the city and county of Dublin: and more particularly to the housekeepers and master-manufacturers thereof* (Dublin 1764).

Hudson, Katherine, *A Royal Conflict* (London 1993).

Hutcheson, Francis, *An Inquiry into the Original of our Ideas of Beauty and Virtue* (second edition, London 1726).

——, *A Short Introduction to Moral Philosophy* (Glasgow 1753).

——, *A System of Moral Philosophy* (London 1755).

James, F.G., 'The Church of Ireland in the early eighteenth century', *Historical Magazine of the Protestant Episcopal Church* Vol. 48 (1979) pp.433-51.

Johnston, E,. 'The diary of Elie Bouhéreau', *Huguenot Society Publications* Vol.15 (1933-4)

Jones, Winston Guthrie, *The Wynnes of Sligo and Leitrim* (Manorhamilton 1994).

Keane, Edward, Phair, P. Beryl and Sadleir, Thomas U. (eds), *King's Inns Admission Papers 1607-1867* (Dublin 1982).

Kelly, James (ed.), *The Letters of Lord Chief Baron Edward Willes to the Earl of Warwick 1757-1762* (Aberystwyth 1990).

Kelly, Patrick, 'Lord Galway and the Penal Laws' in C.E.J. Caldicott, H. Gough and J.P. Pittion (eds), *The Huguenots and Ireland* (Dublin 1987).

Kim-Farley, R.J., 'Measles' in Kenneth Kiple (ed.), *Cambridge World History of Human Disease* (Cambridge 1993).

King, C.S. (ed.), *A Great Archbishop of Dublin: William King DD; 1650-1729* (London 1906).

King, Patrick, *Catalogue 13* (Stony Stratford, Bucks 1987).

Kiple, Kenneth, *Cambridge World History of Human Disease* (Cambridge 1993).

Landa, L., *Swift and the Church of Ireland* (Oxford 1954).

La Touche, J.J. Digges, *The Registers of the French Conformed Churches ...* (Dublin 1893).

Lawlor, H.J., *The Fasti of St Patrick's* (Dublin 1930).

Le Fanu, T.P., 'The Huguenot churches of Dublin and their ministers', *Proceedings of the Huguenot Society of London* Vol. 8 (1905-8).

Le Strange, F., *A History of Herbal Plants* (London 1977).

Lecky, W.E.H., *A History of Ireland in the Eighteenth Century* 5 vols (London 1892).

Leslie, J.B., *Biographical succession list of clergy for the diocese of Killaloe* (1946).

——, *Ferns Clergy and Parishes* (Dublin 1936).

Lewis, W.S. (ed.), *Horace Walpole's Correspondence* 43 vols (London 1937).

Llanover, Lady (ed.), *The Autobiography and Correspondence of Mary Granville, Mrs Delany* 6 vols (London 1861).

Lomax, E., 'Diseases of infancy and early childhood' in Kenneth Kiple (ed.), *Cambridge World History of Human Disease* (Cambridge 1993).

Luckett, Richard, *Handel's Messiah: A Celebration* (London 1992).

Lyons, J.B., *Brief Lives of Irish Doctors* (Dublin 1978).

McBride, Ian, 'The School of Virtue: Francis Hutcheson, Irish Presbyterians and the Scottish Enlightenment' in D. George Boyce, Robert Eccleshall and Vincent Geoghegan (eds), *Political Thought in Ireland since the Seventeenth Century* (London 1993).

McCracken, Eileen, 'Irish nurserymen and seedsmen 1740-1800', *Quarterly Journal of Forestry* Vol. 59, 2 (1965).

MacGeagh, Henry F., *Register of Admissions to the Honourable Society of the Middle Temple* (London 1949).

McParland, Edward, *A Bibliography of Irish Architectural History* reprinted from *Irish Historical Studies* Vol. 26, (1988) 102.

——, 'Strategy in the planning of Dublin 1750-1800' in P. Butel and L.M. Cullen, *Cities and Merchants* (1986).

Malcolmson, Anthony, *The Pursuit of the Heiress: Aristocratic Marriage in Ireland 1750-1820* (Belfast 1982).

Mant, R., *History of the Church of Ireland* 2 vols (London 1849).

Mareschal, M.-A.-A., *Les Faïences anciennes et modernes, Leurs Marques et Décors* (Beauvais 1868).

Mason, W. Monck, *The History of St Patrick's* (Dublin 1820).

Mayo, Janet, *A History of Ecclesiastical Dress* (London 1984).

Moody, T.W. and Vaughan, W.E. (eds), *A New History of Ireland* Vol. 4, *Eighteenth-Century Ireland 1691-1800* (Oxford 1986).

Moody, T.W., Martin, F.X., and Byrne, F.J. (eds), *A New History of Ireland* Vol. 9, *Maps, Genealogies, Lists: A Companion to Irish History* (Oxford 1984).

Mooney, Tighearnan and White, Fiona, 'The Gentry's Winter Season' in David Dickson (ed.), *The Gorgeous Mask: Dublin 1700-1850* (Dublin 1987).

Sources and Bibliography

Munter, R.J., *The History of the Irish Newspaper 1685-1760* (Cambridge 1967).

Murphy, Sean, 'Charles Lucas: a forgotten patriot?', *History Ireland* (autumn 1994) pp.26-9.

Nelson, E.C., 'Some Records (*c.*1690-1830) of greenhouses in Irish gardens', *Moorea*, Vol. 2 (1983).

——, ' "This Garden to adorne with all Varietie": the garden plants of Ireland in the centuries before 1700', *Moorea* Vol. 9 (1990).

Nicholson, Edward, *A Method of Charity-Schools, Recommended, for giving, both a Religious Education, and way of livelihood to the Poor of Ireland* (Dublin 1712).

O'Donovan, Declan, 'The Money Bill Dispute of 1753' in Thomas Bartlett, T. and D.W. Hayton (eds), *Penal Era and Golden Age: Essays in Irish History 1690-1800* (Belfast 1979).

O'Rorke, T., *The History of the Antiquities and Present State of the Parishes of Ballysadare and Kilvarnet* (Dublin 1878).

Orrery, Countess of (ed.), Earl of Orrery, *The Orrery Papers* 2 vols (1903).

O'Sullivan, W. 'Mount Merrion in 1714 – was there a stove-house?', *Moorea* Vol. 3 (1984).

Parish Record Society of Dublin, *Registers of the Parishes of St Andrew, St Anne, St Audoen and St Bride* (Dublin 1913).

——, *The Register of St Patrick's* (Dublin 1907).

——, *The Registers of St Peter and St Kevin* (Dublin 1911).

Patterson, David, 'Meningitis' in Kenneth Kiple (ed.), *Cambridge World History of Human Disease* (Cambridge 1993).

[Pery, Edmund Sexton], *Letters from an Armenian in Ireland to his Friends in Trebisond Translated in the year 1756* (London 1757).

Pilkington, Mrs Laetitia, *Memoirs ... Written by Herself* ed. A.C Elias Jnr (University of Georgia Press forthcoming).

Pim, Sheila, 'The history of gardening in Ireland' in E.C. Nelson and A. Brady (eds), *Irish Gardening and Horticulture* (Dublin 1979).

Pittion, J.-P., 'Religious Conformity and Non-Conformity' in C.E.J. Caldicott, H. Gough and J.-P. Pittion (eds), *The Huguenots and Ireland* (Dublin 1987).

Pollard, M., *Dublin's Trade in Books: 1550-1800* (Oxford 1989).

Porter, Roy (ed.) *The Medical History of Waters and Spas* (London 1990).

Power, Thomas P., *Land, Politics and Society in Eighteenth-Century Tipperary* (Oxford 1993).

Quane, Michael, 'Bishop Hodson's Grammar School, Elphin', *Journal of the Royal Society of Antiquaries of Ireland* Vol. 96 (1966), pp.157-77.

Radcliffe, Stephen, *A Letter to the Rev. Mr. Edward Synge... occasion'd by a Late Sermon* (1725).

Records of the Honorable Society of Lincoln's Inn (London 1896).

Reynolds, Mairead, *A History of the Irish Post Office* (Dublin 1983).

Rutty, John, *A Chronological History of the Weather and Seasons and of the Prevailing Diseases in Dublin* (1770).

Severens, Kenneth, 'A new perspective on Georgian building practice; the rebuilding of St Werburgh's church, Dublin (1754-1759)', *Bulletin of the Irish Georgian Society* Vol. 35 (1992-3) pp.3-11.

Sévigné, Mme de, *Letters from the Marchioness de Sévigné to her daughter the Countess de Grignan* (London 1927).

Simms, J.G., 'County Sligo in the eighteenth century', *Journal of the Royal Society of Antiquaries of Ireland* Vol. 91 (1961).

Simon, André L., *The History of the Wine Trade in England* 3 vols (London 1964).

Smith, C. Sausmarez, *Eighteenth-Century Decoration: Design and the Domestic Interior in England* (London 1993).

Sparkes, Ivan, *An Illustrated History of English Domestic Furniture* (Bourne End 1980).

Sources and Bibliography

[Stephenson, Robert], *Considerations on the Present State of the Linen Manufacture* (Dublin 1754).

——, *Reports and Observations* (Dublin 1762).

Stopford Sackville Mss. Royal Commission on Historical Manuscripts (London 1904) .

Synge, Edward senior, *Sermon against Persecution on account of Religion, Preached ... October the 23. 1721* (Dublin 1721).

Synge, Edward, *The Case of Toleration considered with Respect both to Religion and Civil Government in a Sermon ... preach'd on Saturday 23rd October 1725* (second edition 1726).

——, *A Vindication of a Sermon ... in Answer to the Rev. Mr Radcliffe's Letter* (1726).

——, *Two Affidavits in Relation to the Demands of Tythe Agistment in the Dioces of Leighlin; with an introduction* (Dublin 1736).

[Edward Synge, bishop of Ferns], *A Report from the Lords Committees Appointed to Inspect into the State of the Publick Offices of Record in this Kingdom and in what Manner and Place the Same are now kept* (1740).

Synge, K., *The Family of Synge or Sing* (privately printed 1937).

Taylor, Lou, *Mourning Dress: A Costume and Social History* (London 1983).

Thomas, Keith, *Religion and the Decline of Magic* (London 1973).

Thompson, P.V. and D.J., *The Account Books of Jonathan Swift* (1984).

Tillyard, Stella, *Aristocrats* (London 1994).

Tomalin, Claire, M*rs Jordan's Profession* (London 1994).

Varley, Charles, *A New System of Husbandry* 3 vols (York 1770).

——, *The Floating Ideas of Nature* 2 vols (London 1769).

[Charles Varley], *The Modern Farmer's Guide* by a Real Farmer (Glasgow 1768).

Varlo, Charles [Charles Varley], *Schemes offered for the perusal and Consideration of the Legislature* (London 1775).

Vicars, Arthur, *Index to the Prerogative Wills of Ireland* (1897).

Vigne, Randolph, 'The Good Lord Galway: the Irish and English careers of a Huguenot leader: biographical notes', *Proceedings of the Huguenot Society of London* Vol. 24, pp.532-50.

Ward, R.E., Wrynn, J.F. and Ward, C.C., *Letters of Charles O'Conor of Belanagare* (Ann Arbor, Michigan 1988).

The Works of Sir James Ware, concerning Ireland revised and improved (Dublin 1764).

Wheelwright, E.G., *The Physick Garden* (London 1934).

White, Harry 'Handel in Dublin', *Eighteenth Century Ireland* Vol. 2 (1986).

Williams, H. (ed.), *The Correspondence of Jonathan Swift* 5 vols (Oxford 1965).

Worsley, Giles, 'Strokestown Park', *Country Life* 1 April 1993.

Young, Arthur, *Tour of Ireland* ed. A.W. Hutton 2 vols (London 1892).

NEWSPAPERS AND JOURNALS

The Censor, or Citizen's Journal
Dublin Courant
Faulkner's Dublin Journal
Gentleman's Magazine
Irish Builder
Pue's Occurrences
Universal Advertiser

REFERENCE WORKS

Bailey, N., *An Universal Etymological English Dictionary* (London 1759).

Beale, Paul, (ed.), *A Concise Dictionary of Slang and Unconventional English* (London 1989).

Sources and Bibliography

Bence-Jones, M., *A Guide to Irish Country Houses* (London 1988).

Benezie, E., *Dictionnaire des Peintres, Sculpteurs, Dessinateurs et Graveurs* (1966).

Brady A.M. and Cleeve, B., *A Biographical Dictionary of Irish Writers* (Mullingar 1985).

Burke, *Irish Family Records* (London 1979).

——, *Peerage and Baronetage of Great Britain and Ireland* (1871).

Burke, B., *Dormant, Abeyant, Forfeited and Extinct Peerages* (1883).

Burke, J., *Landed Gentry of Ireland* (1912).

——, *Dictionary of the Peerage and Baronetage of the British Empire* (1916).

Collins-Robert French-English English-French Dictionary (London 1978).

Cokayne, G.E., *The Complete Peerage* 13 vols (London 1949).

Dictionary of National Biography (Oxford 1975).

Eighteenth Century Short-Title Catalogue (CD-Rom 1994).

Imbs, Paul (ed.), *Trésor de la Langue française* (Paris 1978).

Michelin Guide, *Gorges du Tarn* (Paris 1989).

Sadie, Stanley (ed.), *The New Grove Dictionary of Music and Musicians* (London 1980).

Parliamentary Gazetteer of Ireland 1843-44 (Dublin 1844).

Spiers, A., *Dictionnaire Générale Français-Anglais* (Paris 1854).

Robertson, William, *Phraseologia Generalis* (1693).

Shorter Oxford English Dictionary (Oxford 1968).

Wallis, P.J. and R.V., *Eighteenth-Century Medics* (Newcastle-upon-Tyne 1985).

John Watson, *The Dublin Directory for the Year ....* (bound in with *The Gentleman's and Citizen's Almanack*).

THESES AND TYPESCRIPTS

Hylton, Raymond, 'The Hugenot Communities in Dublin 1662-1745' (Ph.D National University of Ireland 1985).

Leslie, J.B., 'Biographical succession list of clergy for the diocese of Elphin' (1934) ts Representative Church Body.

Oulton, L., 'Concerning the Oulton Family' (n.d.) ts in private possession.

Welply, W.H., 'Irish Wills: extracted from wills deposited at the Public Records Office, Dublin' 21 vols (1938) ts in Society of Genealogists, London.

General Index

A., Mrs, 340

Adderley, Thomas, 212, 262

Adlock, Mr; discharged for being dirty, 55

agriculture: after-grass, 250, 252, 254, 369, 372; anvil, 315, 322; barley, harvest *1747*, 77; *1751*, 345, 362, 364; bellows, 314, 322; corn, 164, 345, 454, 463; corn, harvest *1747*, 64, 77; *1750*, 226, 233, 237, 239; *1751*, 323-4, 330; corn, stacking, 469; elms, English, 399; field, levelling and dressing, 16; flax, 271, 345; flax, crop *1747*, 53, 64, 69; flax, harvest *1747*, 77; *1750*, 226; flax, sold, 274; flax, seed harvest (1750), 234; forge, 315; granaries, infested with mice, 245; grass, scarce (1749), 128; harness, bit, 100; harness, bridles, 15; harness, carr-tackle, 283; harness, collars and haims, 17, 139; harness, cruppers, 129; harness, haims chains, 283; harness, mules, 142; harness, ordered, 357; harness, saddle cloths, 361; harness, straddles, 139; harvest *1747*, 46-7; *1751*, 293, 323-4, 357, 362, 364, 370, 372-3; *1752*, 409, 483; hay, at Finglas, 230, 252, 349, 357, 362; hay, harvest *1747*, 46, 50, 53, 54, 77; *1749*, 117, 128, 162; *1750*, 226, 230, 233, 234, 239, 251; *1751*, 330, 337, 340, 357, 364; *1752*, 414, 429, 430, 441, 450, 453, 454, 458; hay stocks, Dublin, 380; hayrick, 369, 370; hoes, turnip, 400; hogs, feeding of, 156, 380; horse shoes, 300, 315; iron, 104, 248, 293, 300, 301, 307, 309, 366, 439; malt-miln, 399; manure, spreading, 239, 293; meadow, ready to cut, 274; meadows, lodged, 397; mowers, 324, 329, 352, 409; oats, bad to feed workhorses and peacock, 402; oats, for hogs, 156; oats, harvest *1747*, 77; *1751*, 345, 364; oats, market, 254; oats, sent to Dublin, 401; oil, linseed, 282, 289; paint, for gates, 386; parsnips, for hogs, 380, 425, 429; pickaxes, 115; plough socks, 309, 317; ploughs, 115, 301, 309, 317, 381; poultry house, 431; pumps, 296, 303, 307, 309, 312; rabbit yard, 431; rakes, iron, 217; rape, 194; ridge tiles, 364, 409; rye-grass, 274, 397, 405; scythes, 274, 283, 289, 293, 308; scythes, stones for sharpening, 274; seed, brown lettuce, 339; seed, cauliflower, 339; seed, flax, 233; seed, from Dublin, 347; seed, grass, 205, 206; seed, lucerne, 402, 408, 413; seed, parsnip, 289; seed, rape, 295; seed, turnip, 142; shovels, 103, 400; sledgehammers, 115, 315; sledgehammers, scabling, 458-9, 478; soil at Elphin, xviii; spades, 30, 169; tar, 367, 442; tin, 245; turnips, 293; wheat, harvest *1747*, 10, 47, 53, 54, 69, 71, 77; *1749*, 154; *1750*, 230, 234; *1751*, 323, 352; wheat, sold in Dublin, 331; wheat, stacks, 370, 465; wheat-miln, 399, 422; wheel barrows, 216

Allen, Lady [Margaret] (?-1798), 61

Ama & Poetus, story of, ES cites, 460

Anderson, Dr John (*c.*1708-62), 9, 33, 62

animals: bantams, 431, 463; blackbird, 150; bull, 439, 444; bullocks, 14, 22, 303, 349, 369, 484, 486; calves, 330, 444; canary, 184, 219; cat, 140; cattle, 303, 367, 486; cow, 9, 303; cow, 'Alicia', 196; cow, Alicia's, 216; cow, Frederick Trench's, 481; cows, 11, 216, 254, 303, 369, 486; cows, purchased for fattening, 250; dog, 'Caesar', 272, 279, 313, 320, 321, 328, 333, 337, 357, 371, 375; dog, chain, 141, 320, 321; dog, collar, 141, 320, described, 321, inscription unsuitable, 325; dog, 'Fawn', 279; dog, greyhound, 'Hector', 139, 141; dog, 'Rover', mad, 98; ducks, wild, 439: fowl, ornamental, 431; goldfish, 436; grouse, setting, 337; grouse, since 1st August, 457; guinea-fowl, 463; heifer, 303, 444; hogs, 254, 380, 382, 425,

503

Letters' Index